NATIVE NATIONS OF NORTH AMERICA
AN INDIGENOUS PERSPECTIVE

Steve Talbot
Oregon State University

PEARSON

Boston   Columbus   Indianapolis   New York   San Francisco   Upper Saddle River
Amsterdam   Cape Town   Dubai   London   Madrid   Milan   Munich   Paris   Montréal   Toronto
Delhi   Mexico City   São Paulo   Sydney   Hong Kong   Seoul   Singapore   Taipei   Tokyo

Editor in Chief: Ashley Dodge
Publisher: Nancy Roberts
Editorial Assistant: Molly White
Marketing Coordinator: Jessica Warren
Managing Editor: Denise Forlow
Program Manager: Mayda Bosco
Project Manager: Nitin Agarwal/Aptara®, Inc.
Senior Operations Supervisor: Mary Fischer
Operations Specialist: Eileen Corallo
Art Director: Jayne Conte
Cover Designer: Suzanne Behnke

Cover Artwork: Gerald Dawavendewa/Fourth World Design
Director of Digital Media: Brian Hyland
Digital Media Project Management: Learning Mate
Solutions, Ltd./Lynn Cohen
Digital Media Project Manager: Tina Gagliostro
Full-Service Project Management and Composition:
Nitin Agarwal/Aptara®, Inc.
Printer/Binder: Courier Corp.
Cover Printer: Courier Corp.
Text Font: Palatino LT Std

On the cover: A sacred eagle feather carries a circle representing the four directions with clouds holding life-giving rain. Behind the feather are symbols of corn, birds, water and rain, dragonfly, land and culture. It is a representation that all Native cultures are interconnected with the world and must be treated with respect and dignity.

Credits and acknowledgments borrowed from other sources and reproduced, with permission, in this textbook appear on page 391.

Library of Congress Cataloging-in-Publication Data

Talbot, Steve.
    Native nations of North America : an indigenous perspective / Steve Talbot.
        pages cm
    Includes index.
    ISBN-13: 978-0-13-111389-3
    ISBN-10: 0-13-111389-5
1. Indians of North America—History.   2. Indians, Treatment of—North America—History.   3. Indians of North America—Ethnic identity.   4. Indian philosophy—North America.   5. Self-determination, National—North America—History.   I. Title.
    E77.T25   2014
    970.004'97—dc23

                                                                                    2013047761

10 9 8 7 6 5 4 3 2 1

ISBN-13: 978-0-13-111389-3
ISBN-10:   0-13-111389-5

This book is dedicated to the memory of

Jack D. Forbes

1934–2011

Mentor, Colleague, Friend

Photo courtesy of Carolyn Forbes.

CONTENTS

MY FRIEND JACK
REMINISCENCES

Steve Talbot

In February, 2011, Jack Forbes passed to the Spirit World, but his immense academic contribution to Native American and Indigenous Studies will remain an enduring legacy. Several Indian publications were quick to include tributes to him, and undoubtedly there will be more as his academic work is fully noted and evaluated.[1] In reading the initial tributes, however, I was struck by the omission of his early contributions to our paradigm. Jack was a major founder of the field of Native American Studies in California, and an important contributor to the discipline as a whole. The following reminiscences will serve to demonstrate this assertion.

I was Jack's project assistant in the multicultural program at the Far West Laboratory for Educational and Research Development from 1967 to 1969. This government facility was located in the historic Claremont Hotel in Berkeley, California, and Jack was one of its four directors. At the Lab, he wrote ethnic handbooks, including "Native Americans in the Far West" as a pilot project for public schools. Jack's academic training was in history and anthropology, but he took a revisionist approach to these disciplines and employed ethnohistory when it came to the subject of Native peoples. This is demonstrated in his early works, among which are *Apache, Navajo, and Spaniard* (1960), *The Indian in America's Past* (1964), *The Yumas of the Quechan Nation and Their Neighbors* (1965), *Nevada Indians Speak* (1967), and *Native Americans of California and Nevada* (1969).

For a time, the national headquarters of the National Indian Youth Council (NIYC) was also located at the Claremont Hotel. The NIYC was an early Indian protest organization, a forerunner of the 1960s Red Power Movement. Jack's typist was the wife of a NIYC officer. Jack interacted with NIYC Indian leaders whenever they were in town. Indian elders from the San Francisco Bay area urban community also visited Jack at the Lab. I believe that it was about this time that he began working with Dave Risling and the California Indian Education

Association. It was at the Lab where I first met Lehman Brightman, an Indian student at UC Berkeley, who later headed up the United Native Americans (UNA). Jack organized the founding meeting of UNA, and helped Lee, myself, and others to produce the UNA publication *Warpath*.

Jack's daily routine at the Far West Lab often began in the morning at a nearby café where he routinely wrote fifteen to twenty manuscript pages daily for his various academic projects. Remarkably, his manuscript drafts required little if any editing. He displayed a broad knowledge of Indigenous peoples worldwide. One of the tasks he assigned to me was to undertake a comparative survey of the world's Indigenous peoples and national education policy, thereby anticipating the founding of the Native American and Indigenous Studies Association (NAISA) several decades later in 2009.

When I entered the Ph.D. program in anthropology at UC Berkeley in 1968, I continued my association with Jack. On the Berkeley campus he helped the Indian students "liberate" a room where they could meet. One of the organizing meetings for the Indian student occupation of Alcatraz in November, 1969, took place in this room. During the Third World Strike for an ethnic studies college at UC Berkeley, Jack met with student strike leaders to draft courses for the proposed curriculum. He worked with Berkeley Indian students Patty (Silvas) LaPlant, LaNada (Means) Boyer, among others, to found a Native American Studies (NAS) program on the Berkeley campus. Lehman Brightman (Lakota-Creek) became the first program coordinator.

One of Jack's Indian courses was "Native American Liberation," which I taught as a teaching associate in anthropology at UC Berkeley. The Indian students, about one-third of the class, left in the middle of the 1969 Fall term to occupy Alcatraz Island. The course content included Jack's research on Alcatraz concerning the history of persecution and imprisonment of

Indian "freedom fighters" in the past. One of the students in a class report wrote: "We considered many plans, many programs. We felt the only positive way to create self-determination was to do it."

Jack was not directly involved in the Indian occupation of Alcatraz, although he served on the academic support committee, which I headed up for the island's Indians of All Tribes Council. He and Dave Risling (Hupa) were busy leading the Indian and Chicano protest that created D-Q University, a California Indian tribal college, and the founding of a Native American Studies program at UC Davis.

Jack served as a member of my Ph.D. dissertation committee and made helpful suggestions to my dissertation, which was later published as *Roots of Oppression* in 1981. The book received very favorable reviews, including praise from the late Vine Deloria, Jr., who is considered the dean of American Indian academic writing.

It's my understanding that Jack was offered a tenure track position at UC Berkeley but tuned it down for UC Davis instead, where his efforts led to the establishment of the Native American Studies program on that campus. Today, the Native American Studies Department at Davis offers an extensive academic program including a Ph.D.

In the fall of 1971 I joined the NAS program at UC Berkeley as an acting assistant professor, where I taught many of Jack's courses that became the core curricula. They included Indian cultural heritage, tribal government, political movements, contemporary Native Americans, Southwest Indians, and world's Indigenous peoples, among others. One of Jack's publications that became immensely useful as one of the texts for our NAS classes at Berkeley and Davis was his edited volume, *The Indian in America's Past* (1964). Inspired and informed by Jack's research and writing about the Indian heritage of America, I wrote "Why the Native American Heritage Should Be Taught in College," which was published in the *Indian Historian*, vol. 7, no. 1 (Winter 1974).

In 1974 I resigned my faculty position in Native American Studies at Berkeley. Jack offered me a tenure track faculty position in the then developing NAS program at UC Davis, but I turned it down in order to accompany my wife overseas where she had been offered a job with a United Nations-related nongovernmental organization (NGO) based in Finland. I taught Indian courses, which included Jack's research and writing, for Turku and Helsinki Universities, and guest lectured in Denmark, the Netherlands, Germany, and the former Soviet Union. I later joined Jack in England for a Native American Studies symposium at the University of Warrick. Europeans, especially Germans, have always been fascinated by the American Indian story. The New Indian or Red Power Movement of the 1960s–70s and the development of Native American Studies greatly interested them. I believe Jack had several stints of visiting lectureships in Europe.

A decade later, after my return to the United States, Jack recruited me for a visiting lectureship in the Native American Studies department at UC Davis, 1988–90, where I again taught many of Jack's classes and continued to learn from him. In 1990, when funding became problematic for the NAS program, I resigned my position at Davis to accept a tenure track position at San Joaquin Delta Community College. My colleague, Susan Lobo, took over some of my former classes at UC Davis. Inspired by Jack's contribution to the NAS field, and the programs at both UC Berkeley and UC Davis, Dr. Lobo and I submitted a proposal for a "reader" in Native American Studies to HarperCollins, which became Addison Wesley Longman. This was the first edition of *Native American Voices: A Reader*, which came out in 1998. In the most recent, third edition of this popular textbook published by Pearson (as Prentice-Hall), Dr. Lobo and I were joined by coeditor Traci L. Morris (Chickasaw).

These are among the many reasons why the current textbook, *Native Nations of North America: An Indigenous Perspective*, is dedicated to Jack Forbes' memory. The new book is a further examination of the themes presented in the 2010 edition of the *Native American Voices* reader, and is yet another journey on the "good Red Road" that Jack envisioned. His legacy lives on.

NOTE

1. For other tributes to Jack Forbes, see: Tanya Lee, "A Jack of One Trade," *Indian Country Today* 1, no. 22 (June 22, 2011): 32–33; from colleagues: "Tribute to Jack Forbes," *American Indian Culture and Research Journal* 35, no. 33 (2011): viii–xiv; and Steve Crum and Annette Reed, "With Respect: Jack D. Forbes," *News From Native California* 24, no. 4 (2011): 11–13.

FOREWORD
AN INDIGENOUS PARADIGM

Duane Champagne

The points of view and interests of Indigenous peoples are not well acknowledged or fully understood by contemporary government policymakers, academics, and the general public. For many, Indigenous peoples are believed to be doomed for eventual cultural extinguishment, if they have not already vanished, and economic marginalization unless they assimilate into the national culture and its institutions. The story of Indigenous peoples is one of centuries of struggle, resistance, survival, and renewal. When the United Nations General Assembly adopted the Declaration on the Rights of Indigenous Peoples in 2007, the international community acknowledged the continued presence and human rights needs of Indigenous peoples around the world. Yet there is considerable need for greater understanding and recognition of Indigenous perspectives. The best way to achieve better knowledge and understanding of Indigenous nations is through the Indigenous Studies intellectual paradigm or method of study. An Indigenous paradigm should include the history, contemporary and future beliefs, actions, perspectives, and interests of Indigenous nations and their goals in maintaining self-government, cultural autonomy, and territorial integrity. The present book moves toward establishing an Indigenous paradigm through the presentation of a systematic analysis about the history, struggles, and achievements of selected Indigenous peoples of North America.

Much of the present-day intellectual discourse about Indigenous peoples has focused on colonization that sees Indigenous nations as casualties of history with little independent future. Indigenous peoples are externally characterized as marginalized, ethnic, race-based persons or groups whose destiny at best is described by their ultimate assimilation into multicultural nation-states where equal opportunity and civil rights are extended to all genders, sexualities, races, classes, and peoples. Many diplomats at the United Nations see the twenty-first century as a time where onetime monocultural nation-states will evolve toward multicultural nations, where citizens agree to democratic political institutions, while respecting diversity in culture, race, and ethnicity. The conception of multicultural nations is certainly progress and is worthy of wide support, including the support by Indigenous peoples. In many ways the intellectual underpinnings for the future vision of multicultural nations are the contemporary academic perspectives on postmodern, postcolonial, multicultural, gender, cultural studies, and gay rights. All these viewpoints address widespread forms of oppression against various subordinated or discriminated groups and identities. The road to wholeness or full citizenship requires greater understanding, respect, and national inclusion within nation-state legal and normative rules for acceptance, assimilation, and integration, at least at the normative, legal, and political levels. Current activist movements therefore seek expanded definitions of human and civil rights, and greater acknowledgement and inclusion within the protections and values of democratic nation-states.

The vision and work to achieve more inclusive and diversified national communities is important and in many ways a logical extension of the present theory of liberal democratic nation-states to extend full citizenship and civil rights to the diverse range of identities, peoples, and individuals within the larger nation. Political equality, equal opportunity, civil rights, and individual and collective human rights are ideal core values of contemporary democratic nation-states and the movement for international human rights. Groups that struggle for inclusion and equality base their arguments on the view that the inclusion of greater diversity is a core value for democratic nations. Contemporary intellectual and social movements are looking for greater inclusion within and protection by the central political and legal institutions and core values of democratic nation-states.

Indigenous peoples currently are not full participants in the diversity democratic nation-state movement. As citizens of nation-states, most Indigenous persons want equal civil and human rights. However, Indigenous peoples or nations are not primarily interested in assimilation and integration into even a diversified nation-state, let alone a monocultural nation-state which still dominates the nations of the world. For Indigenous nations, a democratic and diversified nation-state is still an external political system that wishes to incorporate them as citizens, while dismantling their own governments and territorial places that are informed by their cultural traditions. For example, the United Nations Declaration on the Rights of Indigenous Peoples, despite many important guarantees, does not have a definition of Indigenous peoples, and does not recognize Indigenous nations and territories outside the policies and laws of the established nation-states. The multicultural or diversified nation-state possibility is premised on acceptance of the legal and political processes of the nation-state. The participants in the diversified nation-state movement want and will accept civil rights and human rights within the nation-state, if the nation-state will uphold their rights to equality and equal opportunity. In the diversified nation-state interpretation, Indigenous peoples are viewed as ethnic groups who are citizens, and who, at least in principle, have the same rights and obligations as other citizens.

A primary goal of Indigenous nations, however, is to preserve their own forms of government, political processes, territories, and cultural orientations that are often closely tied to specific political forms and territorial places. Indigenous people believe that their governments pre-date the formation of contemporary nation-states. Indigenous nations managed their own governments from time immemorial and often from the time of creation within their own traditions.

Indigenous governments have a different form than present-day nation-states. The government of indigenous peoples generally included management of not only internal political, cultural, and social affairs, but also management of relations with other human and nonhuman nations, as well as all the different power beings that formed the cosmic order. In some traditions, every species of plant or animal formed a recognizable nation of power beings, which Indigenous peoples had to honor and respect. Relations with the power beings of the cosmic order such as the sun, moon, and stars had also to be respected and managed to ensure the well-being of the Indigenous nation. Since all forces in the universe or cosmos are interdependent with the people and nations, relations needed to be kept in balance and reciprocity. If relations with other human or nonhuman nations of the cosmos were upset, then specific ceremonies and often negotiations were necessary to restore order and well-being. Government within Indigenous communities usually meant managing relations with all the power beings of the universe.

The original Indigenous governments, laws, social and political groups, and ceremonies are given directly to the people by the creator in the creation as gifts and teachings. The creator made the people, made the land, and gave the ceremonies and rituals, rules of government and social behavior. No other entity is allowed or entitled by the creator to intervene in the national affairs of the people, or to redefine their political order and relations. The government, territory, and the laws given to the people usually are not changed without some spiritual sign or intervention from the creator. The relation between the Indigenous nation and the creator is direct, and no other authority has power to interfere. For example, among many North American Indigenous peoples, political councilors usually smoked a sacred pipe before the beginning of discussions so that the smoke would rise to the sky and inform the creator of the works and thoughts that were exchanged among the people. The mode of Indigenous government, community, and spiritual obligations often is upheld and carried on to the present, in respect for the gifts of the creator, and in thankfulness for the gifts of land, life, and cosmic resources.

Many Indigenous nations believe they have a collective goal and purpose to perform in the cosmic order, otherwise the creator would not have made them. The gifts of consensual politics, respect for the land and cosmic order, spiritual holism, and continuity of ancient wisdom are some of the gifts Indigenous nations believe can benefit all mankind. Indigenous peoples have long-standing beliefs that require them to retain their government, cultures, identities, land, and relations to the cosmic order. Hence, most Indigenous nations have been strongly resistant to colonization and social change. Despite hundreds of years of colonization and domination, many Indigenous nations continue to survive and will do so for the foreseeable future. Indigenous nations believe they have a rightful place among the nations of the world and have been strongly resistant to incorporation and integration into present-day nation-states.

Most nation-states have now granted citizenship to Indigenous peoples, and expect Indigenous peoples to act as citizens and exercise only the rights of citizenship. Some argue that any rights beyond the rights allowed to all other nation-state citizens are special rights that defy the rules of equality. Hence, Indigenous claims to self-government, territory, and cultural autonomy are seen as extra citizenship rights, and therefore counter to nation-state constitutions and national values. Indigenous peoples, on the other hand, generally see themselves as captive nations and captive "citizens," since they often have not consented to nation-state citizenship or to surrendering their rights to self-government. In the United States and Canada, Indigenous peoples are recognized as members or citizens of both Indigenous and nation-state governments. Rather than citizens-plus with special rights, they see themselves as citizens-plural with rights within both the nation-state and rights as members or citizens of Indigenous nations.

The conflict between Indigenous peoples and nation-states cannot be reduced to race, ethnicity, or class. Indigenous nations do not comprise a single race, ethnicity, culture, or nation. In Africa, and in Scandinavia, many Indigenous nations continue to struggle for political, cultural, and territorial autonomy from nation-states, but are from the same racial group. Indigenous peoples exist in many places around the world and have many different forms of political, cultural, and economic organization. Treating Indigenous peoples as racial, ethnic, or class groups enables nation-states to address Indigenous peoples as citizens who are underprivileged and seeking economic and political inclusion. Civil rights approaches at best are a partial solution for Indigenous nations, who continue to seek relations and redress from nation-states that satisfies their own values of self-government, territorial control, and cultural autonomy.

Indigenous nations do not fit well into the visions and current practices of nation-states, and are not well conceptualized by the present-day diversity movement theories and activism that strive for assimilation and integration into nation-state political processes and extension of civil rights. The intellectual tools for indigenous nations, their history, continuity, and futures, are not well understood or analyzed by present-day nation-state policies and critical theories of diversity. The outlier character of Indigenous nations requires its own methods of analysis, and theories of relations to nation-states and the international community, as well as to other Indigenous nations and with the diversity movements and their intellectual infrastructure. Contemporary theories, policies, and human understanding will not be complete until Indigenous nations are conceptualized and understood as participants in the past, present, and future world. Rather than ignored in policy and theory, Indigenous nations need to be recognized on their own terms, and their views and interests included in future intellectual, policy, national, and international fora. The tools for a critical analysis of Indigenous nations will not be measures of the degree of nation-state acceptance and inclusion, but rather by the extent to which Indigenous nations realize their own goals of self-government, cultural organization, and territorial integrity.

An Indigenous paradigm should foster the goals and values of Indigenous nations and communities in the same way that present-day nation-state intellectual institutions and policy foster national goals and interests. An Indigenous paradigm would take the point of view of Indigenous peoples themselves and develop knowledge and understanding that will sustain and empower Indigenous peoples to realize their political, cultural, and economic goals within local, national, and international arenas. Indigenous nations will be around for the indefinite future. Nation-states should move to make democratic and mutually beneficial relations and understandings about the role and place of Indigenous nations within nation-states and the international civil society and community. An Indigenous paradigm should provide an intellectual infrastructure for Indigenous and nation-state negotiations, policies, and actions that enable Indigenous nations to realize their goals of self-government, cultural autonomy, and territorial rights, as well as to develop respectful and mutually beneficial relations with the nation-states of the world on government-to-government bases.

ACKNOWLEDGMENTS

This book is the result of a number of years of research, participant observation, and academic activism in the disciplines of action anthropology and Native American and Indigenous Studies. The various chapters are the product of lectures and published articles and reviews, and my interaction with Indigenous friends and colleagues in the Indian movement, interspersed by periods of research. It was in the early 1970s, when I and my Indian colleagues were endeavoring to implement the new Native American Studies curriculum at the University of California, Berkeley, that Faithkeeper Oren Lyons (Onondaga) addressed one of my large Indian classes, at which he presented an overview of the Native American struggle. After his presentation I told him that it was the best overview of the subject I had ever heard. "I can't believe that you got everything in," I said enthusiastically. Puzzled, he replied: "That wasn't the hard part. The hard part is to know what to leave out." This has been the challenge I have faced in writing the present book. How to tell the story of nine Indigenous nations and their urban relatives within a limited number of pages. I leave it to the reader to judge whether I have succeeded.

There are so many people and institutions to thank for this book that it is difficult to know where to begin. I have dedicated this volume to Jack D. Forbes, to whom I owe a great intellectual debt (see my dedication). My colleague and longtime friend, Susan Lobo, coeditor of the *Native American Voices: A Reader*, must also be thanked at the outset. I owe her an immense debt for many years of academic collaboration. I wish also to acknowledge with great appreciation Nancy Roberts, Pearson editor and publisher, for her continuing support of the Native American and Indigenous Studies paradigm. A special thank you goes to editorial assistant Molly White and copy editor Irene Vartanoff for their infinite patience with me during the production process. I also thank the reviewers of the manuscript for their many helpful comments and suggestions: Tamara Cheshire, Sacramento City College; Vine Deloria, Jr., University of Colorado; Robert Hill, Tulane University; Amanda Paskey, Cosumnes River College; John Phinney, Southern Methodist University; Melissa Rinehart, Miami University; Stephen Saraydar, State University of New York; Joseph Wilson, University of New Haven; and Katharine Woodhouse-Beyer, Rutgers University-New Brunswick. I am especially pleased that Gerald Dawavendewa (Hopi/Cherokee), who did the beautiful book cover and other artwork for the third edition of *Native American Voices: A Reader*, has also agreed to do the cover art for the new book.

I am greatly indebted to Duane Champagne, professor of sociology at the Native Nations Law and Policy Center at the University of California, Los Angeles, who wrote the Foreword to the book, explaining in detail the Native American and Indigenous Studies paradigm. Bruce E. Johansen, professor of Communication and American Indian Studies at the University of Nebraska, Omaha, collaborated with me in writing the chapter on the First Nations of Canada. Professors Champagne and Johansen also reviewed earlier versions of several of the book's chapters and made corrections and helpful comments. Naturally, I hold them blameless for any errors that may have crept into the book, or conclusions with which they may disagree, and for which I take full responsibility. I especially thank my colleague Deanna Kingston Paniatuq (King Island Inupiaq) at Oregon State University for her input into the Alaska chapter. Her untimely death is a loss to Indigenous scholarship.

I also thank the many Indian friends and associates whom I have the great fortune to know and to learn from, although they may be surprised that I count them among my teachers. They include, among others, Deanna Kingston (King Island Yupiaq), Winona LaDuke (Anishinaabeg), Chief Oren Lyons

(Onondaga), Russell Means (Lakota), William A. Means (Lakota) and others in the International Indian Treaty Council, Cipriano Manuel (Tohono O'Odham), Simon J. Ortiz (Acoma Pueblo), David Risling (Hupa), Luana Ross (Salish), David Sohappy, Jr. (Wanapum), Chief Billy Tayac (Piscataway), Haunani-Kay Trask (Hawaiian), and Lanada Boyer Warjack (Bannock-Shoshone). My wife's cousin, the late Jane Monden, and her "ohana" on Maui were very helpful in my gaining an insight into the Hawaiian language and culture.

Among the institutions supporting various stages in the research and writing of the book are the research libraries of the University of Arizona, Stanford University, and the University of California, Berkeley, funded by the Summer Seminar for Teachers of the National Endowment for the Humanities in 1981 and 1986; and a Sabbatical Leave from San Joaquin Delta College in 1996. Earlier, in 1970–71, a Career Fellowship from the National Institute of Mental Health funded much of the historical research detailed in Chapter 10 on Alaska. My tenure on the Desecration Committee of the International Indian Treaty Council (a nongovernmental organization at the United Nations) in the 1980s was an invaluable learning experience. Various preliminary chapters of the book were lectures to my American Indian classes at Oregon State University, and Lane Community College in Florence, Oregon, for which I extend my thanks to those institutions and my students for their indulgence and support.

ABOUT THE AUTHOR

STEVE TALBOT is the author of several books, and many reviews and articles dealing with Native Americans. His books include the acclaimed *Roots of Oppression: The American Indian Question* (1985), *Indianer in den* US (1988), and coeditor of *Native American Voices: A Reader*, now in its third (2010) edition with Pearson (as Prentice-Hall). He received a Masters Degree in anthropology and community development in 1967 from the University of Arizona, and a Ph.D. in anthropology in 1974 from the University of California, Berkeley. His research and publications have focused on government Indian policy, Native American religions and spirituality, the Native struggle and resistance movement, and the academic field of Native American Studies.

Talbot has had extensive experience working in both reservation and Indian urban communities. In the 1950s and 1960s he was a state social worker assigned to the Tohono O'Odahm Reservation in Arizona; a field researcher for the Bureau of Ethnic Research at the University of Arizona; and a fieldworker in Indian community development on the San Carlos Apache Reservation, a project sponsored by the tribe in cooperation with the American Friends Service Committee. In the mid-1960s he moved to the San Francisco Bay Area of California, where he served for two years on the board of the Oakland Intertribal Friendship House. He joined the School of Criminology at the University of California, Berkeley in 1965 as an applied anthropologist, and in 1967 became a research assistant in the multicultural program of the Far West Laboratory in Berkeley, California. Next, as a doctoral student and Teaching Associate in anthropology at the University of California, he was closely associated with the development of the Native American Studies program on that campus, and the 1969 Indian occupation of Alcatraz. From 1969 to 1971 he held a career fellowship from the National Institute of Mental Health in support of research in Alaska on the impact of the oil discovery and impending pipeline construction on Alaska Natives. From 1971 to 1974 he was an acting assistant professor in the Native American Studies program at UC Berkeley. Upon leaving the NAS program he was honored with an eagle feather award for his teaching and advocacy.

In the mid-1970s Talbot lived in Finland where he taught Native American Studies courses at Helsinki University and gave invited lectures in The Netherlands, Demark, Germany, England, and the former Soviet Union. He helped organize, and was a delegate to the historic international Conference on Discrimination Against the Indigenous Populations in the Americas meeting in September, 1977, at the United Nations headquarters in Geneva, Switzerland. This international conference was sponsored by the nongovernmental organizations (NGOs) at the United Nations and was the first world gathering of Indigenous peoples. It was also a precursor to negotiations culminating in the United Nations 2007 Declaration on the Rights of Indigenous Peoples.

From 1977 to 1983 Talbot was chairperson of the sociology and anthropology department at the University of the District of Columbia. In the summers of 1981 and 1986 he was a Visiting Scholar in the Summer Seminar for Teachers sponsored by the National Endowment for the Humanities, first at the University of Arizona and then at Stanford University, where he continued his research of Native American issues, resulting in published articles. Later, in the 1980s he taught courses at Oregon State University and the University of Oregon. In the 1980s he was an active member of the Desecration Committee of the International Indian Treaty Council, the first Indigenous NGO at the United Nations. He has conducted field research in Indian country throughout every Indigenous region of North America covered by the scope of the present book, with the exception of Canada.

From 1988 to 1990 he was a lecturer in Native American Studies at UC Davis before accepting a position with San Joaquin Delta College in California where he taught sociology, anthropology, and Native American Studies. In 1999 he retired from the California community college system but continued to teach courses as an adjunct professor of anthropology at Oregon State University, and as an instructor in sociology and Native American Studies for Lane Community College. He currently resides with his wife in the coastal city of Florence, Oregon.

The author, Steve Talbot, at work. *Photo courtesy of Susan Lobo.*

ABOUT THE ARTIST

GERALD DAWAVENDEWA (Hopi/Cherokee) grew up in the Hopi village of Munqapi, located in northern Arizona. He attended the University of Arizona, receiving a Bachelor's degree in Fine Arts. His work has been shown in museums and galleries throughout the United States.

Dawavendewa has worked with the Arizona State Museum as an exhibit specialist in the development and construction of a ten thousand square foot exhibit entitled "Paths of Life; American Indians of the Southwest." In addition, he was commissioned to create a mural depicting the Hopi world for the exhibit, and the exhibit's logo became the official logo of the Arizona State Museum. Other experience includes an internship with the National Museum of the American Indian, Smithsonian Institution, in Washington, DC.

His artwork includes a piece on deerskin that was sent aboard the Space Shuttle *Endeavor*, launched in 1994. He also designed a mural measuring seven feet by eighty-five feet long that depicts Tucson, Arizona's cultural heritage. The mural was painted by members of the Tucson Artist Group on a building in downtown Tucson. He also authored and illustrated a children's book entitled *The Butterfly Dance*. Other artwork includes a series of forty-nine metal panels containing cutout native imagery that forms the main staircase of the University of Arizona Memorial Student Union Bookstore. One of his latest works is a six-foot-tall sculpture depicting a parrot that illuminates from within. He designed the cover of the third edition of *Native American Voices: A Reader,* published in 2010 by Pearson (as Prentice-Hall).

Through his artwork Gerald hopes to educate the public about the rich heritage of Native cultures and promote a greater understanding of the Indigenous world.

INTRODUCTION
The Indigenous Contribution and Perspective

A Pueblo sun looking at the earth. A Native view of the cosmos as well as a Native perspective of the world. It is a reminder that countless cultures view the cosmos in different ways and each is correct.

As the author of this textbook, I must explain the title, *Native Nations of North America*, at the outset. First, each chapter in the book explores a serious concern or issue experienced by currently existing peoples who are native to North America, or within its political jurisdiction, including those in Alaska, Canada, and Hawai'i. The book also provides an ethnohistorical perspective, because one can only understand the present day through the lens of historical events unique to and from the perspective of the Indigenous people selected.

Second, the Native peoples featured in this book are rightly viewed as *nations* rather than as *tribes*. Therefore, the words *Native* and *Indigenous* are capitalized just as are Caucasian and European in conventional academic works. This book presents an Indigenous perspective, not an anthropological one, because analysis is from the point of view of Native scholarship, i.e., Native American (American Indian) Studies. The word *tribe* employed by cultural anthropologists as a generalized term inadequately defines the variable levels of sociopolitical integration found in North America among Indigenous peoples. The concept of nation, derived from the Latin *natio*, is more than two thousand years old and originally meant the family, language, customs, and beliefs of a people. The term was later extended to the populations of territories, states, individual nationalities, and eventually modern nation-states. It was during the early period of colonial expansion that the invading European powers applied the term *tribes* to American Indian societies to signify the inhabitants of a specific territory who share a common identity, origins, language, and culture. From an Indigenous perspective, if we define Native peoples as nations, it follows that the concept of sovereignty is also included, the right to govern themselves as distinct and independent peoples. This fundamental right was recently underscored when the United Nations General Assembly adopted the Declaration On the Rights of Indigenous Peoples (UNDRIP) on September 13, 2007. There are approximately 375 million Indigenous people in the world, including those in the Americas.

Third, the term *Indigenous* encompasses not only the Native American or Indian peoples of North America, but also Alaska Natives (Indians, Aleuts, and Eskimos), and the First Nations of Canada (Indians, Métis, and Inuit). Native Hawaiians also are included under this rubric. They, along with Native Samoans and the Chamorros of Guam, are today living within the dominating orbit of the United States as semicolonized, Native peoples.

Finally, the term *North America* as used here includes also the Indigenous peoples of Mexico. The common usage of the term to include only the English-speaking part of the continent is clearly Anglocentric and therefore unscientific. The artificial division of the northern part of the Western Hemisphere into English-speaking and Spanish-speaking spheres has occurred only in the last five hundred years and belies the many thousands of years prior to the European conquest during which the region was occupied solely by contiguous Indigenous societies speaking many languages other than English or Spanish, all of which existed without a Mexican border.

This book was conceived as a companion textbook to *Native American Voices: A Reader* (*Reader*) now in its third edition, by Susan Lobo, Steve Talbot, and Traci L. Morris (2010). This text expands on many of the themes detailed in the *Reader*, but in terms of specific Indigenous peoples rather than as thematic categories. For example, Chapter 2, "The Hidden Heritage: the Iroquois and the Evolution of Democracy," presents a longer and more detailed account of the notable Iroquois Confederacy than is described in Part Two of the *Reader*. Similarly, Chapter 3, "Greed and Genocide: California Indians and the Gold Rush," is a fuller treatment of the themes of racism and genocide than is discussed in Part Four of the *Reader*. Chapter 4 in the new book takes up the issue of Native American religious freedom by describing Lakota Sioux spirituality in the context of the 1890 Wounded Knee massacre, and is a case study of "the Sacred" discussed in Part Seven of the *Reader*. The history of the Native Hawaiian struggle for Indigenous sovereignty documented in Chapter 8 of the current book echoes articles in the *Reader* by Poka Lanui (Part Three), Haunani-Kay Trask (Part Eight), and Leanne Hinton (Part Ten). And so on. In addition, each chapter of *Native Nations of North America* includes analytical concepts that can explain the issue under discussion, such as racism, ethnic cleansing, the erosion of tribal sovereignty, subsistence rights, or the abridgement of Indian religious freedom.

The chapters in *Native Nations of North America: An Indigenous Perspective* also present an ethnographic survey of Indigenous North America with issue-oriented essays on the Haudenosaunee Iroquois, California Indians, Lakota Sioux, Navajo and Hopi, Cherokee Nation, the fishing peoples of the Columbia River Basin, Native Hawaiians, and Alaska Natives. Chapter 9 on the Native peoples of Canada includes an Internet survey by Bruce E. Johansen, Professor of Communication at the University of Nebraska at Omaha, of issues facing Canada's First Nations. Chapter 11, "The Trouble with Stereotypes," surveys the phenomenon of Indigenous urbanism, both in its ancient and contemporary manifestations, and is a fuller treatment and analysis of this important but often neglected subject, discussed in Part Nine of the *Reader*.

The selected Native nations also serve as examples for most of the cultural areas common in anthropological usage (see Kehoe 1981), i.e., the Iroquois chapter for the Northeast cultural area, Cherokee for the Southeast, the Lakota Sioux for the Plains, Navajo-Hopi for the Southwest, Alaska and Canada for the Arctic and subarctic, and the California and Northwest chapters for their respective culture areas in addition to Hawai'i. A note to instructors who use this textbook: the chapters do not have to be assigned consecutively. Any one chapter with its themes and its respective bibliography and Study Guide can stand alone.

THE NATIVE AMERICAN CULTURAL HERITAGE

This is a book about the Native Peoples of North America from an Indigenous perspective. First and foremost, this perspective includes a knowledge of and appreciation for the Indian heritage of the Americas. A listing of some of the major elements of this heritage will serve to demonstrate the enormity of the gift.

Population and Language

The importance of producing a textbook on the Native nations of the Americas is seen in the following demographics. Estimates of the number of people Indigenous to the Americas before 1492 range as high as 112 million, about one-fifth of the world's population at the time. By the end of the nineteenth century, due to the subsequent genocide, their numbers reached a low of only a few million. Yet today, the majority population of both Bolivia and Guatemala is Indian, Peru has more than eight million, Mexico at least 10.5 million, and Ecuador about 3.8 million. In the three largest countries, Canada has over one million, the United States several million, and Brazil several hundred thousand American Indians. The Indigenous genetic heritage is clearly the dominant strain in Paraguay, Bolivia, Peru, and Ecuador in South America; in Mexico and most of the countries of Central America; and in Greenland in North America. In Guatemala, Indian people constitute between 70 percent and 80 percent of the total population with at least half speaking one of the many Native languages. Many do not speak Spanish. Indigenous ancestry is one of the important elements in the racially mixed populations of Chile, Columbia, Venezuela, Brazil, and Panama. Native American Indians "survive in every mainland American republic (except in Uruguay where a rural mestizo or mixed-blood population alone survives) and even on a few Caribbean islands" (Forbes 1969, 7).

Linguists estimate fifty-six separate language families for the Native peoples of the Americas, a fact attesting to their long occupancy and complex relationships in the Western Hemisphere. There are as many as 1,700 to 2,000 Indigenous languages many with complex grammars and vocabularies containing up to 20,000 words. In Mexico alone there are thirty-three principal Indian languages still spoken, as little related to each other as are Finnish, Chinese, and Hebrew. It is estimated that there are more than thirty million Indigenous Americans in North, Central, and South America who speak one of the hundreds of still existent Indian languages, while perhaps as many as one hundred million people possess some degree of Indigenous ancestry.

Until recently, it was difficult to estimate the number of persons of Indigenous descent currently residing in the United States because of flawed research methodology by the U.S. Census and failure to enumerate those of mixed racial backgrounds. This changed with the 2000 Census of U.S. population, which found 4.5 million individuals with a significant degree of Indian ancestry, including at least 2.5 million Native Americans who identify primarily as Indian and Alaska Native only. In the 2010 Census, the number of respondents reporting Native American ancestry increased to 5.2 million, with 2.9 million reporting American Indian or Alaska Native alone. One must also consider that most Mexican Americans, and many African Americans, Puerto Ricans, French Canadians, and other population groups possess varying degrees of Indigenous descent. It is obvious that the Indigenous genetic legacy of the Americas is great indeed, especially if one considers the whole of the Americas.

Before the European conquest, the Americas were populated by thousands of different Native communities and nations, organized from the smallest sociopolitical unit, such as the family commune or band, to the largest, such as the urban civilizations of the Aztec, Maya, and Inca, which numbered tens of millions of people. Despite a precipitous decline due principally to the European conquest, a standard estimate for the current American Indian population is ten or more million living in what is now Mexico, another ten million at least in Central America, millions more in Peru, and three million Chibchas in Colombia and Panama.

For years anthropologists estimated that before the European conquest in the fifteenth and sixteenth centuries there were less than one million so-called American Indians living north of the Rio Grande River in the United States and Canada, but recent scientific estimates have pushed that figure up to seven or more million. Demographer Russell Thornton (1998, 19) conservatively estimates that there were "about 5 million people for the coterminous United States and about 2 million for present-day Canada, Alaska, and Greenland combined." In the Andes of South America, twelve million still speak Quechua, the language of the Incas. Many Indians of Mexico still speak Nahuatl, the language of the Aztecs, and there are six million Mayan speakers in Central America. Such is the magnitude of the Indigenous population in Guatemala that were the country to have a completely free election, it could become a modern Mayan republic.

The entry of Europeans into the so-called New World after 1492 led to the rapid collapse and decline of the Indigenous populations. The resultant genocide became the American holocaust. The population decline in Central and South America totaled tens of millions; "the Native American population of the United States, Canada, and Greenland combined reached a nadir of perhaps 375,000 around 1900" (Thornton 1998, 19).

Despite the tragic population collapse, the legacy of Indigenous languages has contributed to our geographical terminology in North America. Twenty-eight (some say twenty-four) states, numerous smaller political units, towns, rivers, lakes, mountain ranges, individual summits, and other landmarks have Native American place names in the United States.

According to the anthropologist Alfred Kroeber (1925), there are 196 place names in California that are derived from Indian languages, and 5,000 place names in New England. In addition, at least 300 other words—names of plants, animals, food, and materials—have contributed to our American English by the various Indigenous languages spoken north of Mexico. (See Keoke and Porterfield 2002).

Food Production and Agriculture

Population was densest in the highlands of Peru and Colombia in South America, and in the Yucatan and the Valley of Mexico. But everywhere "there is every reason to believe that the land was maintaining the maximum population consonant with the state of development of Indian agriculture and industry" (MacLeod 1928, 16). In North America there was no free land in spite of the European view to the contrary. From the European perspective there was plenty of room, "because with European agricultural methods, the Americas, particularly in the temperate zone, could be made to support a greater population" (MacLeod 1928, 17). But every bit of land was utilized by the Indigenous peoples using the methods of horticulture known to them, "and hunting was no haphazard pleasure-jaunting, but a careful and laborious systematic exploitation of the wild animals and wild vegetable products of each region" (MacLeod 1928, 17).

There have been countless economic and cultural contributions made by Indigenous peoples to the contemporary countries of Americas. Two important reference sources are the *Encyclopedia of American Indian Contributions to the World*, by Keoke and Porterfield (2002), and *Native Roots: How the Indians Enriched America*, by Jack Weatherford (1991).

Native Americans over the centuries developed eighteen plants but few draft animals. Corn, cotton, tobacco, potatoes, and peanuts were all gifts of the Native peoples. They also discovered and cultivated sweet potatoes, pumpkins, squash, beans, artichokes, sunflower seeds, and cranberries. Almost one-half of the world's usable food supply came from the Americas. It was in Central America and the Andean region of South America where these basic foods were domesticated and widely cultivated.

Main areas of agriculture in North America were the Mississippi Valley eastward to the Atlantic Coast, from Florida to the 50th parallel, and the Southwest. Maize was so thoroughly domesticated that it will not produce in its wild state. The entire maize complex developed by the Indians was taken over by White settlers. The Euro-American's single contribution was the substitution of the mill for the mortar in the grinding process.

The White settlement of America would have been delayed a century without maize having been available. It is estimated that 60 percent of crops grown in the world today came from the Americas, with corn the most widely grown crop. Want to eat some good Italian food? Guess what? Polenta is made from corn, and tomato sauce is from the American Indian tomato. And all the peppers in the world, except for black pepper, are of American Indian origin.

Although Euro-Americans adopted the new American food crops, they did not always practice the food technology associated with Native crops. Corn, beans, and squash, what the Iroquois call the *three sisters*, were always grown together by Indian horticulturalists. The beans put nitrogen into the soil which corn needs. Corn provides the stalk for beans to climb, and squash needs shade. This form of planting kept out weeds without the use of insecticide.

In aboriginal North America wild foods were especially important as a supplement. A large variety of fruits, nuts, seeds, and roots were gathered. In California there were wild seeds, especially the acorn; in the western Great Lakes area it was wild rice; on the Northwest Plateau roots were a staple, especially the camas, and on the Northwest coast and in south Alaska different kinds of berries augmented a diet of fish and animal foods. Many of these foods are still gathered, prepared, and eaten at traditional Indian ceremonies today and are widely appreciated in the Native American community as an important link to the cultural heritage of Indigenous America.

Medicine

The Native American contribution to medicine is both significant and lasting. More than half of the medicines found in the modern pharmacy, such as aspirin, are from Native American-derived sources. In addition, the Indians cultivated some sixty wild plants for medicinal purposes, including wintergreen, witch hazel, cascara sagrada, chinchona bark, curare, cocaine for the relief of pain, and ephedra, all used in modern medicine (Momaday 1996). Mindful of the harmful side effects of synthetic drugs, many naturopaths, holistic doctors, and clinical ecologists are using natural medicines derived from generic sources as a better alternative for the treatment of the sick.

Indigenous medical knowledge represented the studied accumulation of thousands of years of observation and skilled practice, and the early Europeans widely acknowledged the overall excellent health of Native people. There were treatments for childbirth problems and for fractures and dislocation, and there were surgery techniques. Psychosomatic techniques were also used in curing ceremonies. Many are still

widely in use today and are acknowledged as effective by contemporary psychiatrists. "American Indian physicians used holistic health practices for centuries before the arrival of Europeans" (Keoke and Porterfield 2002, 129)

Other Contributions

Several varieties of Native tobacco were adopted by Europeans. Tobacco circled the world in less than two centuries and was reintroduced by the Russians into Alaska. Originally it was introduced into Europe by Spain in 1558, and then into England in 1586. Tobacco became immensely important to the colonies and was indirectly responsible for the eventual dispossession of the Five Civilized Tribes in Georgia and other southern states. Today, tobacco is one of the most valuable cash crops grown in the United States. Tobacco was used spiritually (and sparingly) in Native religious ceremonies, and in a pure form— not laced with chemicals to make it burn continuously or taste and smell good. As far as can be determined, there were no cancer-related deaths from tobacco used in this manner.

Cotton was known in the Old World, but is also grown in the Americas. Some was originally grown in the Southwest, but mostly it was not grown in North America. Corn and tobacco were at first important to the colonies for two centuries. Cotton, on the other hand, was shipped to England until the late eighteenth century. Invention of the cotton gin in 1793 led to its economic importance in southern United States. The value of Indian lands in the South, and the forced dispossession of the Indians from these lands under the 1830s Indian Removal Acts, was due in large part to the increasing value to Anglo-Americans of cash crops like cotton and tobacco.

Indigenous societies respected the environment by living in harmony with nature. To do otherwise would be to destroy the food sources for societies that were hunters and gatherers or horticulturalists. The land ethic of stewardship was reinforced by Indian spirituality. Supernatural powers governed the natural world and formed a link between mankind and all things both animate and inanimate. "The Indian had a respect bordering on awe for everything he could see, hear or touch: the earth was the mother of life, and each animal, each tree, each living thing was locked into an interrelated web of spiritual existence of which the individual was a small part" (Udall, 1972, 19). This view contrasted to that of land-hungry European immigrants who saw themselves as mastering nature.

Rubber was another Native American contribution. Balls, enema tubes, syringes, water proof clothing all are made from rubber.

Various forms of Native housing influenced early European settlements. These include the adobe pueblo construction, especially in the North American Southwest and California; the bark or thatch covered wigwam (adopted by the first settlers of New England); and the palisaded Indian village. The latter became the defense against attack for eastern forts. The log cabin, on the other hand, was of Scandinavian origin rather than Indian.

The hammock, used by Amazonian Indians, was adopted by the navies of the world. They were infinitely better than fixed bunks when at sea. The parka, the poncho, moccasins, and textile fibers (cotton and sisal) were also borrowed from the American Indians. Tailored clothing made of skins, textiles (cotton), and the use of an outer robe of unshaped animal hide (buffalo, deer, or moose) were all borrowed from Native Americans. One type of Indian clothing used extensively in North America was that of the frontiersman—the deerskin outfit consisting of a shirt, leggings, moccasins, and breechcloth. Taken over by the early settlers or *borderers* of the trans-Allegheny frontier, it became famous as the dress adopted by Daniel Boone. It was admirably adapted to the conditions of wilderness life. George Washington even recommended a modified form of this costume as uniform equipment for the Revolutionary soldier.

The American revolutionists took over the Indian method of fighting from ambush and camouflage. The British generals bitterly complained that the Americans did not fight fair when they hid behind stone fences and trees and fired at the exposed Redcoats marching in ranks along open roads. Most importantly, the example of eastern Indians, particularly the powerful Six Nation Haudenosaunee (Iroquois), to form political confederations was not lost upon the U.S. founding fathers in their efforts to craft a republic. (The Iroquois contribution is discussed in detail in Chapter 2.)

Other Native contributions include jewelry and adornment, and casting by the lost wax method. The Aztec and Incan rulers were richer in terms of gold and silver objects and art works than their counterparts in Europe. Tragically, the beautifully unique gold objects were melted down by the European invaders for gold bullion, and the mines where the Indigenous peoples were enslaved helped finance the birth of the Industrial Revolution in Europe.

Indian weaving is among the finest in the world. Incan weaving, including the sacred textiles of Bolivia, and the much prized blankets of the Navajos are examples. Decorated dress, with shell and bone, porcupine quills and feathers, is not merely a craft, it is an art form. The Mexican art muralists—Diego Rivera, Orosco, Siquieros, Cavarrubias—were heavily influenced by pre-Columbian art. The contemporary Indian art and architecture of the United States has likewise been heavily influenced. Contemporary performing Indian musicians and artists are now making an impact in the United States.

The Native peoples of North America lacked the horse initially for land travel, but the Indian birch bark canoe became essential for Europeans traveling the waterways of the Canadian interior, the Great Lakes region, and the Mississippi Valley. It was especially important for fur traders. The first recorded crossing of the continent by a White man, Alexander Mackenzie, was by canoe in 1793. The early explorers, traders, and settlers made great use of Indian trails and Native geographic knowledge. The forested areas east of the Mississippi River, and especially south of the Great Lakes, were honeycombed with Indian trails, connecting villages, and leading to rock quarries and salt licks. On the North American Plains the trails became wide roads beaten down by the passage of travois poles and large parties. These trails were later used by the Anglo and Spanish missionary, the hunter, the soldier, and the colonist. They evolved from Indian trail to pack trail, to wagon road, and eventually to the modern highway.

Trade was carried on in Native North America widely by barter. Some trade material has been found more than a thousand miles from its nearest possible source or origin. Trade was vital to the Native American economic system, especially for scarce items, including certain foods. Fishing sites on the Columbia River at The Dalles and Celilo Falls in the northwestern United States (now destroyed to make way for modern dams) are but two examples of the great gathering places where Native peoples traded. Standards of value (a sort of money system) included shell beads for both Atlantic and Pacific coast peoples, and animal pelts. The great Indian urban civilizations of Mexico and Central America carried on enormous trade systems, with quetzal feathers among highly prized trade items.

Early Whites utilized Native standards of value and frequently incorporated them as part of their own economies. An obvious example is the fur pelt, such as the beaver, much sought by traders. Beaver pelts remained the standard of value on the North American frontier until the mid-nineteenth century, when the beaver was all but exterminated. In the southeast it was the deer skin; on the Pacific Coast, the sea otter; and on the Plains, the buffalo hide. Weatherford (1988) details many other unknown developments as a result of the European conquest of Native America.

Hidden Heritage

In most conventional historical accounts it is assumed that our modern economic system of capitalism was entirely the product of European ingenuity that ushered in the Industrial Revolution. When the economic system of capitalism arose in England during the eighteenth century, its first form was mercantile or trade capitalism. The English colonies in North America, including the religious pilgrims, were organized as joint stock companies. This stage was followed by industrial capitalism with its factory system of production, and finally in the twentieth century by monopoly capitalism. One may ask why did capitalism arise in Europe and not in some other continent or geographical place? After all, there were a number of civilizations in the world that had pre-capitalist conditions, such as the advanced urban civilizations in Southeast Asia, the Middle East, Africa, and the Americas, where capitalism might have eventually arisen. Europe, after all, was backward both economically and culturally until the Crusades of the twelfth and thirteenth centuries. The Crusades opened up the Silk Road to China and the desire for goods and trade with other precapitalist centers in the world. Two factors that gave Europe the impetus to move ahead on the capitalist path were its sailing ships and navigation ability to sail out of sight of continental coasts across broad oceans to loot the New World. With the gold and silver stolen from the Americas, combined with armies and sailing ships, European nations were then able to dominate and destroy other precapitalist centers around the globe and quickly monopolize world trade. Such an immense amount of gold and silver bullion was looted from Central American and Andean civilizations that the European colonial powers, Spain in the first place, were able to bankrupt other non-European trade centers.

Weatherford (1988, 1–20) argues that the rise of money capitalism is linked to the silver looted from the Andes Mountains of South America. Cerro Rico ("Rich Hill") is a mountain of silver over 2,000 feet high that has been continuously mined since 1545. In

fact, 85 percent of the silver mined in the Andes Mountains of South America came from Cerro Rico. As a consequence, Potosi became the largest city in the New World, with 160,000 inhabitants by 1650. Prior to Columbus's so-called discovery of America, most of Europe's gold came from the Gold Coast of West Africa. After the invasion of the Americas, the Spanish conquistadors did not neglect seizing gold and slaughtering tens of thousands of Native peoples in the process. Spanish conquistador Hernando Cortes demanded gold from the Aztecs, torturing and killing many for it, including the last Aztec leader, Cuauhtemoc. And Francisco Pizarro demanded the greatest ransom ever paid in history from Atahualpa, the Inca emperor, who was then killed. The Inca peoples used gold esthetically, or in a religious sense; there was no gold coin. The Incas decorated the great Temple of the Sun in Cuzco with beaten gold. The emperor had gardens with statues of almost every known animal and plant sculpted in gold and silver. The Spaniards cut up these golden treasures and melted them down into gold bars. The amount of gold looted is estimated at $2.8 billion at contemporary values.

Silver was more suitable than gold for coin to Europeans because of its durability. It became a primary medium of exchange in the developing capitalist world. With so much new money pouring into Europe, the old system mutated into a true money economy. Instead of barter and exchange at European trade fairs under the old feudal system, silver coin became the economic medium of exchange. This hastened the development of a money economy and the ushering in of true capitalism. Soon, the circulation of gold and silver from the Americas trebled in Europe, with the annual output from America ten times the combined output of the rest of the world.

In another chapter Weatherford (1988, 21–38) links the birth of corporations to piracy and slavery. Spain used conquistadors to loot the Americas; the British used pirates and private trading companies. In their quest for gold, the commodity most in demand by the Spaniards soon became slaves. This was because Spain had already killed most of the Indians of the Caribbean and other coastal areas of Spanish America. The British, especially, turned to piracy. Unable to find a Cerro Rico and other mines in North America, they raided Spanish ships carrying gold and silver bullion. In 1562 John Hawkins, with the patronage of Queen Elizabeth I, became the first English slaver. Hawkins' logo on the bow of his ship was a bust of an African slave in chains.

Working for Hawkins was the young Francis Drake, in command of the slave ship *Judith*. Drake assembled a syndicate of investors in 1577 to finance a series of raids on Spanish colonies in South America. He plundered sixteenth century Spanish settlements of present-day Chile, Peru, Central America, and Mexico. It is estimated that his financial backers, who probably included the queen herself, reaped profits as high as 1,000 percent on their investment. The queen gave Drake ten thousand British pounds as his reward and knighted him. Capitalism was born on the twin supports of the African slave trade and the piracy of American silver.

Trade eventually replaced piracy for the British when the flow of gold and silver played out a century later. Fur in North America became a commodity. Hudson's Bay Company, the oldest trading company in the world, was chartered by King Charles II in 1670. Another early trading company was the Northwest Company, founded in 1797 by Scots fleeing the U.S. Revolutionary War. In 1821 it merged with Hudson's Bay and thereafter dominated all of the trading posts in northwestern North America. In these *fur factories*, as they were called, there existed a triple caste system: Scots, French Canadians, and *mixed race* persons who were united through common-law marriage to Indian women.

Other colonizing joint stock companies at the beginning of the seventeenth century (the forerunner of the modern business corporation) included the New France Company, founded in Montreal, the Virginian Company of London, founded in Jamestown, and later, the Dutch West Indies Company, founded in both New Amsterdam and Albany, New York, and the Massachusetts Bay Company. These companies were all founded for profit. As Weatherford explains, eventually these colonizing joint-stock companies founded different kinds of plantations throughout the Caribbean and along the North American coast "to grow sugar cane, tobacco, indigo, rice, maize corn, and some cotton . . . . By 1670 all of the important parts of Anglo North America and the Caribbean had been allotted to one company or another to explore, control, and to exploit" (Weatherford 1988, 33).

It is rarely mentioned in mainstream literature that the thirteen English colonies along the Atlantic seaboard of North America were, in fact, joint stock companies. The Virginia Company first settled Jamestown in the search for gold. The Plymouth Company was a joint stock company in which the merchants and other investors of Plymouth, England,

subsidized the Pilgrims to produce commodities for profit. The Pilgrim Fathers first left England to settle in Holland where they found religious freedom but little in the way of economic opportunity. They consequently decided to emigrate to America in search of the profits that had eluded them in the Netherlands. Their first shipment back to Europe contained furs and lumber to sell. "By the start of the 18th century, the financial institutions of the modern capitalist world operated with well-established joint stock companies, extensive banking networks, and even stock exchanges. The entire economic transformation of the world had taken approximately two centuries from Columbus's discovery of America" (Weatherford 1988, 37).

More than one hundred and fifty years ago, Karl Marx wrote the following assessment of capitalism: "The discovery of gold and silver in America, the extirpation, enslavement and entombment in mines of the aboriginal population, the beginning of the conquest and looting of the East Indies, the turning of Africa into a warren for the commercial hunting of black-skins, signalized the rosy dawn of the era of capitalist production" (quoted in Huberman 1963, 165). In the Americas, capitalist development was marked by the genocide of tens of millions of Indigenous peoples and the destruction of their societies and cultures.

AMERICA'S FIRST ECOLOGISTS?

Generically speaking, ecology is the science devoted to the interrelationships between organisms and their environments. Also included in the definition of ecology is the human activity undertaken to restore or maintain the balance of nature, and an ecologist is an activist in ecological matters. Overwhelming evidence confirms that the nation's first ecologists were the Indigenous peoples. Wilbur R. Jacobs, professor of history at the University of California, Santa Barbara, writes: "Through their burning practices, their patterns of subsistence (by growing, for instance, corn and beans together to preserve the richness of the soil), by creating various hunting preserves for beaver and other animals, and by developing special religious attitudes, Indians preserved a wilderness ecological balance wheel. Even the intensive farming of the Iroquois, without chemical fertilizers and pesticides, protected the ecology of the northern forests" (Jacobs 1980, 49).

In recent decades, Native Americans have been justly concerned about the harmful impact of capitalist development on their remaining reservation lands and resources. Winona LaDuke (Anishinaabeg) is a well-known Native environmental activist. Two-times vice-presidential nominee of the Green Party, she has given many lectures and written many articles and two books on the question of the degradation of the Native American environment. In *All Our Relations: Native Struggles for Land and Life* (1999) she documents the current environmental struggles of nine Native American nations. In a second book, *Recovering the Sacred: The Power of Naming and Claiming* (2005), she examines the Indigenous concept of "the Sacred" that puts into historical context the contemporary struggles of Native American nations to preserve the ecological integrity of their land base and the remains of their ancestors.

Native American concern with the environment is not a new development. In *Ecocide of Native America* (1995), Donald Grinde and Bruce E. Johansen, like historian Jacobs, contend that Native Americans were the country's first ecologists. Like LaDuke, they document the environmental crisis in Native America, but tellingly note in their introductory chapter: "To appreciate the impact of the environmental crisis on Native Americans, it is necessary to understand the earth from a Native American perspective—as a sacred space, as provider for the living, and as shrine for the dead. Ecology and land are intimately connected with Native American spirituality, which entails that land is not regarded merely as real estate, a commodity to be bought, sold, or exploited for financial gain" (Grinde and Johansen 1995, 3–4). In tracing the differences in Indigenous and Euro-American environmental concepts they write that to understand the European concept of the environment one must go back to the Christian Bible with its command to subdue the earth and the idea of progress. The idea of progress, however, is foreign to Native American cultures, which adopt a cyclical view of reality.

Native American religions have sometimes been described as religions of nature. The *Great Mystery* of the Plains Indians becomes an ecological metaphor for their reverence of the land and its creatures, and the remains of their ancestors buried in Mother Earth. "The Native view . . . derives from a belief that all things—human, animal, vegetable, even rocks—share life. There is no such thing as an 'inanimate object'" (Grinde and Johansen 1995, 16). It was Luther Standing Bear who famously said: "We did not think of the great open plains, the beautiful rolling hills, and winding streams with tangled brush, as 'wild.'

Only to the white man was nature 'a wilderness' and only to him was the land 'infested' with 'wild' animals and 'savage' people. To us it was tame. Earth was beautiful, and we are surrounded with the blessings of the Great Mystery" (quoted in Grinde and Johansen 1995, 25). Indians lacked a philosophy of *development* of the earth for profit since their ecological-based economies were not part of the capitalist mode of production. That is not to say, however, that they did not modify their natural resources at times in order to sustain their lives and societies.

Before European conquest, with the exception of the ancient urban-based centers of Cahokia in North America and the Mayan cities of Central America, the Indigenous population density was not great enough to overstress the natural environment. "Instead, early European observers marveled at the natural bounty of America—of Virginia sturgeon six to nine feet long, of Mississippi catfish that weighed more than one hundred pounds, of Massachusetts oysters that grew to nine inches across, as well as lobsters that weighed twenty pounds each . . . at flights of passenger pigeons that sometimes nearly darkened the sky and speculated that a squirrel could travel from Maine to New Orleans without touching the ground [and] bison ranged as far east as Virginia" (Grinde and Johansen 1995, 50–51).

Native American religious rituals reflect the Indigenous reverence for life in part because their lives depended on the bounty of nature. The Sun Dance ceremony of the Plains Indians "is associated with the return of green vegetation in the spring and early summer, as well as the increase in animal populations, especially the buffalo" (Grinde and Johansen 1995, 41). In eastern North America, among the Iroquois and other tribes practicing horticulture, the *three sisters*—corn, beans, and squash—were honored in ceremonies. "Native perspectives on the environment often were virtually the opposite of the views of many early settlers, who sought to 'tame' the 'wilderness.' Many Native peopled endowed all living things with spirit, even objects which Europeans regarded as nonliving, such as rocks. Most Native Americans saw themselves as enmeshed in a web of interdependent and mutually complementary life. As Black Elk said: 'With all beings and all things, we shall be as relatives'" (Grinde and Johansen 1995, 36).

Animals are to be venerated and respected as well as plants and all of creation. Often American Indian spiritual communications are directed through the animal brothers, and the Creator often speaks to American Indian people through visions and stories that involve animals. Through environmentally specific rites, Native Americans hand down to future generations the knowledge of their cultural realities. The environment is a mirror that reflects cultural values. The sweat lodge, the drum, thanksgiving ceremonies, pipe ceremonies, the Sun Dance, and many other rites reinforce the cyclical rhythms of creation and collective connectedness to the immediate environment. (Grinde and Johansen 1995, 263–64)

In the purification sweat lodge, prayers end with "All my relations!"

In April, 1979, Christopher Vecsey and Ruben W. Venables organized a symposium at Hobart and Williams Smith colleges in Geneva, New York, titled "American Indian Environments." The proceedings were then published a year later by Syracuse University Press. The two editors explain at the outset that the "environments" referred to in the publication "are the nonhuman surroundings commonly called 'nature,' or more technically 'ecosystems,' the inhabitable biosphere of earth, air, and water upon which all humans depend for survival. . . . In the Indians' sacred circle of creation, everything—even stone—is equally alive and equally integrated into the balance of life" (Vecsey and Venables 1980, ix). The source of the environmental conflict between the Indigenous nations and the invading Europeans was ideological: the former "saw their environments as the sacred interdependence of the Creator's will," but were confronted with "waves of post Renaissance Europeans who saw in the environment a natural resource ordained by God for their sole benefit" (Vecsey and Venables 1980, x).

Environment is usually defined as the nonhuman world, but the fact that Native peoples also endowed a life force or *mana* into things that non-Indians defined as inanimate, such as stones and Mother Earth itself, broadens the definition from an Indigenous perspective. "In saying that animals, plants, stones, clouds, celestial bodies, and other natural phenomena have life, Indians were declaring that their environment was a world of beings with souls" (Christopher Vecsey 1980, 19). The European scholar Edward Burnett Tyler termed this *animism*.

The early colonists severely altered their natural surroundings as they pushed the American frontier ever westward across the continent and set in motion physical and biological processes that had a negative if not disastrous effect on the Native environment. When Columbus landed on the island in the Bahamas which he called San Salvador, he encountered the Arawak Indians who welcomed him warmly. "They were a peaceful people who made pottery, wove cloth, and carried on a farming-fishing, handicraft lifestyle that held little immediate interest for the admiral because they mined no gold. . . . Within little more than a century . . . San Salvador had experienced an environmental transformation" (Jacobs 1980, 47). The Arawak were gone and were replaced by Spanish cotton plantations worked by African slaves. "By cutting down tropical vegetation and turning fertile land into one-crop agricultural fields, the Spanish planters leached the soil of its nutrients. . . . Eventually the island . . . became a desert . . . the island's fertility and the large Native population of skillful farmers (estimated to have developed the most productive fields in the world—cassava, beans, maize, and other crops) had been destroyed by the 1580s" (Jacobs 1980, 47).

Wild plants were a staple food for many Indian peoples and an important supplement for yet other Indian nations. The Native gatherers were careful not to take all of a plant so that it would continue to grow and provide food for another time. Most plant gathering was done by Indian women who were skillful botanists. "They knew exactly which part of the plant to use, and which time of the year to gather them. Often, each part of the plant would be important for different purposes—roots, stalks, flowers and seeds each had their own use. Plants were not only food sources, they were also used as dyes, teas, medicines, even insect repellents, and for their fibers" (Zucker, Hammel, and Hogfoss 1983, 21). The Native respect for the wild animals they hunted has been widely noted. For example, all the various parts of the bison were used by the Plains Indians so that nothing was wasted. This is in contrast to the White hunters who later nearly eradicated the species in pursuit of buffalo robes, and later just the tongues of these animals which the Indians considered sacred. Native hunters of deer and other creatures killed their prey respectfully, giving a prayer and sometimes making a small offering. Traditional Indians carry on this practice today, "asking permission" before taking wild food needed to feed their families. In Indigenous cultures, "plants and animals had a special meaning beyond the economic . . . humans are privileged to be able to eat natural products and owe thanks to the natural world for this bounty. In ceremonies and religious stories Indians honored the spirits of fish, deer, and plants and passed on traditional knowledge about behavior and habitat" (Zucker, Hammel, and Hogfoss 1983, 15).

"American Progress."

It is true that Native people sometimes modified the land to increase food sources, but they did so without ravaging the environment. In the Willamette Valley of western Oregon, for example, the inland peoples burned forests and prairies to encourage the growth of favored plant species such as berries and camas, the bulb of a wild lily. Later, with the arrival of White settlers, these wild plant resources were destroyed by herds of pioneer livestock.

Contemporary Native Americans still advocate for the environment. In April 2012, a conference was held at Haskell Indian Nation University in Lawrence, Kansas, on "The Rights of Mother Earth: Restoring Indigenous Life Ways of Responsibility and Respect." The Rights of Mother Earth movement "traces its beginning to Evo Morales, Bolivia's first Indigenist president. In April, 2009, a Bolivian delegation successfully proposed the recognition of International Mother Earth Day to the United Nations General Assembly, which subsequently recognized April 22 as International Mother Earth Day" (Pember 2012, 21).

In *God Is Red* (1973), the eminent American Indian scholar Vine Deloria, Jr., examined the current religious crisis in contemporary American life and concluded that Christianity had failed both in its the-ology and in its application to social issues. Rather than maintaining a hold on a religion imported from Europe, he recommended seeking a new religious commitment. He writes that we must seek god here in the North American landscape and among its first inhabitants, the Indians. We must throw out the Judeo-Christian concept of "linear time," from creation to apocalypse through exploitation of people and nature, and think in terms of "space," relating land, community, and religion into an integrated whole, in order to have a proper relationship with other living things. Only by returning to the land can we have an adequate idea of god (Deloria 1973).

THE INDIGENOUS RESEARCH PARADIGM

Given the unique Indigenous cultural heritage described above, it is therefore not surprising that the Indigenous research paradigm differs significantly from that of anthropology, the social sciences, and history.

This book, *Native Nations of North America*, reflects a different research methodology and theoretical approach to Indigenous peoples than that of history and the social sciences, especially anthropology.

In a 2002 journal article appearing in the *American Indian Culture and Research Journal* we described several examples of innovative research by Indigenous scholars that represent the academic paradigm of Native Studies: "American Indian Studies (AIS), or Native American Studies (NAS), arose as a field in the late 1960s and 1970s as part of the 'new Indian' [Red Power] movement and the revitalization of Indian culture and identity. . . . Although multidisciplinary in nature, and drawing from the humanities, history and the social sciences, AIS/NAS is informed by its own paradigm." (Talbot 2002, 67). The Indigenous paradigm (research model) has its own theoretical premises and methodological approaches as the chapters in this textbook will demonstrate. By theory we mean an explanation for which there is evidence that illuminates the question, problem, or topic addressed. By methodology we mean a theory and analysis of how research does or should proceed, while a research method is simply a technique for gathering data or evidence, ethnohistory for example.

The topical chapters in this book explore some of the Indigenous research and conceptual thinking by Native scholars and elaborate what was presented in the 2002 journal article. Following this line of reasoning of thinking outside the box, we have included in this book theoretical constructs and concepts for analysis that could explain the chapter issue under discussion.

Two groundbreaking publications exemplify the new Native American and Indigenous studies paradigm. They are *Natives and Academics: Researching and Writing About American Indians*, edited by Devon A. Mihesuah (1998); and the volume by Linda Tuhiwai Smith, *Decolonizing Methodologies: Research and Indigenous Peoples* (2001).

The basis for *Natives and Academics* was a Winter 1996 special issue of *American Indian Quarterly*, of which historian Mihesuah was the editor. In her introduction Mihesuah recommends using "the Indian voice" in historical research. She writes that "the problem with many books and articles about Indians is not which is included but with what is omitted," and also notes that many non-Indian scholars write as if they have a monopoly on the truth. Among the contributions to the Mihesuah volume are articles and critiques by Duane Champagne (Chippewa), Vine Deloria, Jr. (Standing Rock Sioux), Donald L. Fixico (Shawnee, Sac and Fox; Seminole and Moscogee), and Elizabeth Cook Lynn (Crow Creek Sioux).

"In *Decolonizing Methodologies*, Tuhiwai Smith urges research that utilizes the Indigenous paradigm, which is defined as utilizing culturally appropriate research protocols and methodologies, and an Indigenous research agenda . . . She critically examines the historical and philosophical basis for Western mainstream research. She critiques the rise of social scientific research of Indigenous peoples that has historically occurred under the aegis of Western imperialism and colonialism" (Talbot 2002, 68).

Several years after the Mihesuah and Smith books, Clara Sue Kidwell and Alan Velie published a slim but comprehensive volume entitled simply *Native American Studies* (2005). In it the authors describe the canon or intellectual premises of the new field in terms of five topical components: land and identity, historical contact and conflict, tribal sovereignty, language, and Indian aesthetics (literature and art).

In Chapter One on "land and identity," they contend that despite the fact that most Native peoples in the United States today live in urban areas, and many are Christianized, Indigenous identity remains tied to reservation communities and a land-based spirituality: "We argue, therefore, that knowledge and understanding of the association of one's ancestors with a particular homeland is an essential part of a Native American Studies curriculum" (Kidwell and Velie 2005, 22).

The political importance of the land ethic is reflected in the history of Native American treaty rights and tribal sovereignty, which is the subject of Chapters Three and Four in the Kidwell and Velie volume. The authors contend that ethnohistory is an important part of the Indigenous methodology: "Indian ways of telling the past are essentially different from European ways of writing history, Indian voices must be heard, and their understandings of their interactions with Europeans must be part of historical accounts" (Kidwell and Velie 2005, 43). They give a useful historical summary of the U.S. legal decisions and governmental policies regarding Indian treaty sovereignty, which initially was recognized, but then underwent a steady legislative and judicial process of erosion. Thus, history courses dealing with this subject must include an Indigenous viewpoint on the diminishing of sovereignty (the *Indian voice*). Sovereignty is an important part of the Native American Studies curriculum. The authors also propose a new methodology when it comes to history, because Indian history is cyclical and oral rather than linear as in the Western historical tradition. "The challenge to Native American/American Indian Studies, then, is to bring to the fore the perspectives of Native people, to establish the legitimacy of their way of telling their own histories" (Kidwell and Velie 2005, 55).

The importance of Indigenous languages is examined in Chapter Five of *Native American Studies*: "The fourth premise of Native American/American Indian Studies is that language is key to understanding Native World views. Accordingly most programs teach one or more Native language" (Kidwell and Vellie 2005, 83).

Finally, in Chapters Six and Seven, the authors contend that Indian literature, art and expressive culture also define the new field. Again, the importance of Native languages is underscored.

The Kidwell and Velie volume is a useful guide to the course content for Native American/American Indian Studies programs and academic departments. A fuller discussion of Indigenous research methodology appears in an article by Métis scholar Adam J. P. Gaudry in the *Wicazo Sa Review*, titled "Insurgent Research" (2011). Writing in the tradition of Mihesuah and Tuhiwai Smith, Gaudry criticizes research by the mainstream disciplines on Indigenous peoples as being *extractive* rather than *insurgent*. "Rarely are the people who participate in the research process as participants or 'informants' considered to be the primary audience when it comes time to disseminate the research. This type of research functions on an *extraction methodology*. Lost in this extraction process are the *context, values,* and *on-the-ground struggles* of the peoples and communities that provide information and insight to the researcher. . . . Research on Indigenous peoples tend to reproduce tired colonial narratives that justify occupation and oppression" (Gaudry 2011, 113–14).

Gaudry proposes to replace extraction methodology with an insurgent research paradigm. This is accomplished by refocusing research methodology dealing with Native peoples in four ways: (1) employing Indigenous worldviews, (2) "orienting knowledge creation towards Indigenous peoples and their communities," (3) "by seeing our responsibility as researchers as directed almost exclusively towards the [Indigenous] community and participants," and (4) "promoting community-based action that targets the demise of colonial interference within our lives and communities" (2011, 114).

Native Studies Departments and Programs

A subject of concern to Indigenous scholars is the current status of the Native American/American Indian Studies academic programs and departments in the United States and Canada. This subject was addressed in the introduction to Part One of *Native American Voices: A Reader*, and with a listing of current programs in an appendix (Lobo, Talbot, and Morris 2010, 2, 501–2):

Native American Studies (NAS), also known as American Indian Studies (AIS), arose as an academic field of study in the late 1960s during the "new Indian" movement. . . . As part of this development, 46 undergraduate programs in NAS were founded, 19 programs on college and university campuses in California alone. A 1999 survey by the Association of the Study of American Literatures found 13 programs and departments offering graduate degrees in NAS, at least 4 with Ph.D. programs, and more than 350 professors in more than 100 colleges and universities were identifying themselves as Native American or Alaska Native. The 2008 revised *A Guide to Native American Studies in the United States and Canada* found 130 institutions of higher learning with NAS programs, 26 offering related graduate degrees, 46 with majors, 81 offering minors, and 23 offering concentrations.

Kidwell and Velie (2005, 131–41) also devote a chapter in their book to the history and current status of Native American Studies. They point to the new field's activist origins when Native students challenged university administrators about the lack of *the Native voice* in standard college courses, and the lack of an Indigenous curriculum. The first institutions of higher learning to offer a Master's degree in Native Studies were the University of California at Los Angeles in 1982 and the University of Arizona in 1983. Earlier, in 1976, the University of California at Berkeley offered a Ph.D. in Ethnic Studies that included Native American Studies as one of its components. Other noteworthy developments followed.

In 1996 the University of Arizona established the first American Indian Studies Ph.D. program in the nation. In 1995 the University of Oklahoma, in a state that is currently home to thirty-nine federally recognized tribes, established an interdisciplinary bachelor's degree program in Native Studies, and in 2003 the Native American Studies program gained approval for a Master's degree. Montana State University established a new graduate program focused on education in 1997, and the University of California at Davis established Master's and doctoral degree programs in 2000. (Kidwell and Velie 2005, 132)

Unfortunately, this promising development experienced a decline during the 1990s, with the number of college and university NA/AI Studies programs shrinking, due principally to funding problems and lack of administrative support. Duane Champagne (Turtle Mountain Chippewa) examined this question in an article titled "The Rise and Fall of Native American Studies in the United States" that appeared in an edited volume, *American Indian Nations* (Horse Capture, Champagne, and Jackson, 2007, 129–47), and is reprinted in Part One of *Native American Voices: A Reader*. Despite the decline, which Champagne documents, he remains optimistic that "there is great promise for American Indian Studies in the twenty-first century as a new and substantial paradigm" (Champagne 2007, 129).

Like Kidwell and Velie, Champagne chronicles the activist origins of Native American Studies. "The programs reflected the social movement and social change trends of the 1960s and 1970s by efforts to bring more inclusion to members of historically excluded and disadvantaged groups," such as African American, Asian American, Chicano/Latino, as well as American Indian (Champagne 2007, 131). He also notes the development of ethnohistory—"a synthesis of historical documentary and anthropological ethnographic approaches"—which became an important tool of the NAS/AIS paradigm.

Champagne contends that main cause for the decline of Native American Studies programs is structural. "The great majority of the programs have not formed departments but are organized as interdisciplinary programs. American Indian Studies departments are rare; most notable are the University of California, Davis, and the University of Minnesota, Minneapolis, which both have departments, and some of the Canadian universities have departments. . . . The interdepartmental model, where the faculty have different home departments . . . is the most common form of organization" (Champagne 2007, 138).

A second model, therefore, is the academic department. Departmental status means tenured faculty with a good measure of administrative and academic protection. "A few universities have adopted departments, and often many Indian faculty see the department as an ideal arrangement for Indian Studies. Departments can hire a core of committed faculty. . . . A third model might be called a mixed model, which is a combination

of department and associated core faculty. . . . [It] works best when it can explore the strengths of the departmental and interdisciplinary models" (Champagne 2007, 139). Champagne cites as an example the American Indian Studies program at the University of Arizona as one of the most successful examples of the mixed model approach. It has about a dozen core faculty, "and another ten faculty who have other disciplinary departments but are committed to teaching and participation in the Indian Studies Department" (Champagne 2007, 140). There is also a core curriculum in these arrangements, such as introductory courses in Native Studies, with other related courses cross-listed from those taught by the participating, noncore faculty from traditional departments, such as history, sociology, anthropology, and literature.

To summarize Champagne's assessment: "While I have great faith that an internationally recognized paradigm will be worked out and gain broad acceptance, the university bureaucratic environment, weak resource support, the emphasis on race and ethnic paradigms, and the relegation of Indian Studies to serve general diversity interests for the university will continue to constrain, and often will prevent, full development of Indigenous Studies departments and programs at many universities" (Champagne 2007, 142).

A notable exception to the numerical decline in Native American Studies programs has been the rapid growth of tribally controlled Indian community colleges. At last count, there were thirty-eight tribal colleges and universities in the United States, including Alaska and Canada. (See the map on page 299 of *Native American Voices: A Reader*, and the listing of the tribal colleges in Appendix C.) "Because the colleges operate under tribal charters but are governed by independent boards, they have largely been able to protect their academic freedom while still responding to community needs" (Kidwell and Velie 2005, 135). "Reservation-based colleges are unique institutions that meet the needs of their own particular communities. Most offer some curriculum that addresses the specific language(s) and culture(s) of the reservation" (Champagne 2007, 134).

Despite the decline in Native Studies programs, Champagne believes there have been promising developments. He observes, for example, the establishment of creditable NAS/AIS journals, including the *American Indian Quarterly, American Indian Culture and Research Journal, Wicazo Sa Review, Red Ink,* and the *Journal of American Indian Education.* And more recently, the field has seen the creation of NAISA, the Native American and Indigenous Studies Association, with over five hundred members. An organizing meeting of Native American Studies took place at the University of Oklahoma, Norman, in May of 2007, followed by a second founding meeting by the Institute of Native American Studies at the University of Georgia in April 2008. NAISA was then incorporated in May 2009, with the first annual meeting of the association held in the same year at the University of Minnesota. Current plans of the Association include an academic journal, *NAIS*, to be published by the University of Minnesota Press twice a year.

Champagne ends his somewhat bleak assessment of the current state of Native American Studies in the United States on an optimistic note in the belief that the future of the discipline in North America is inevitably tied to the world's several hundred million Indigenous peoples (see Fagan 1998):

> They do not share a common culture, race, or ethnicity, but they share common features, such as culturally holistic, institutionally non-differentiated, self-governing societies engaged in negotiations for preserving land, self-government and cultural integrity with a surrounding nation state. . . . Races, classes, ethnicities, especially in the United States, do not aspire to the territorial, political, and cultural claims that are at the forefront for American Indian communities. . . . The search for Native American Studies is a search for an Indigenous paradigm. (Champagne 2007, 143)

CHAPTER REVIEW

DISCUSSION QUESTIONS

1. What is meant by the Native American cultural heritage to America? Give some examples.
2. What is meant by the hidden cultural heritage? Give an example.
3. Why can Native Americans be considered America's first ecologists?
4. Explain the relationship or link between Indian spirituality (religion) and their respect and concern for the environment.
5. Explain the Indigenous (NAS/AIS) research paradigm.
6. What are the three models or types of Native American/American Indian Studies programs? Which one, according to Duane Champagne, has been the most successful?
7. Why has there been a decline in NAS/AIS programs in recent years? What has been the exception? Why is Champagne nevertheless optimistic about the future of the field?

SUGGESTED READINGS

CHAMPAGNE, DUANE, ed., 2001. *The Native North American Almanac* [reference]. 2nd ed. Farmington Hills, MI: Gale Group.

DELORIA, VINE, JR. 1995. *Red Earth, White Lies: Native Americans and the Myth of Scientific Fact.* New York: Scribner.

FORBES, JACK, ed. 1964. *The Indian in America's Past.* Englewood Cliffs, NJ: Prentice Hall.

GRINDE, DONALD A., and BRUCE E. JOHANSEN, eds. 1995. *Ecocide in Native America.* Santa Fe, NM: Clear Light.

HORSE CAPTURE, GEORGE, DUANE CHAMPAGNE, and CHANDLER C. JACKSON eds. 2007. *American Indian Nations: Yesterday, Today, and Tomorrow.* AltaMira Press.

KIDWELL, CLARA SUE, and ALAN VELIE. 2005. *Native American Studies.* Lincoln: University of Nebraska.

ORTIZ, SIMONE J. 1992. *Woven Stone* [poetry]. Tucson: University of Arizona Press.

VECSEY, CHRISTOPHER, and ROBERT W. VENABLES, eds. 1980. *American Indian Environments.* Syracuse, NY: Syracuse University Press.

WEATHERFORD, JACK. 1988. *Indian Givers: How the Indians of America Transformed the World.* New York: Fawcett Books.

———. 1991. *Native Roots: How the Indians Enriched America.* New York: Fawcett Books.

REFERENCES

CHAMPAGNE, DUANE. 2007. "The Rise and Fall of Native American Studies in the United States." In *American Indian Nations: Yesterday, Today, and Tomorrow*, edited by George Horse Capture, Duane Champagne, and Chandler C. Jackson, 129–47. Lanham, MD: AltaMira Press. Reprinted in Lobo, Susan, Steve Talbot, and Traci L. Morris, eds., 2010. *Native American Voices: A Reader*, 16–25. Upper Saddle River, NJ: Pearson/Prentice Hall.

DELORIA, VINE, JR. 1973. *God Is Red.* New York: Grosset & Dunlap.

FAGAN, BRIAN M. 1998. *Clash of Cultures.* 2nd ed. Walnut Creek, CA: AltaMira Press.

FORBES, JACK D. 1969. *Native Americans of the Far West: A Handbook.* Berkeley, CA: Far West Laboratory for Research and Educational Development.

GAUDRY, ADAM J. P. 2011. "Insurgent Research." *Wicazo Sa Review*, 26 (1): 113–36.

GRINDE, DONALD A., and BRUCE E. JOHANSEN. *Ecocide of Native America: Environmental Destruction of Native Lands and Peoples.* Santa Fe: Clear Light.

HORSE CAPTURE, GEORGE, DUANE CHAMPAGNE, and CHANDLER C. JACKSON, eds. 2007. *American Indian Nations: Yesterday, Today, and Tomorrow.* Lanham, MD: AltaMira Press.

HUBERMAN, LEO. 1963. *Man's Worldly Goods: The Story of the Wealth of Nations.* New York: Monthly Review Press.

JACOBS, WILBUR R. 1980. "Indians as Ecologists and Other Environmental Themes in American Frontier History." In *American Indian Environments*, edited by Christopher Vecsey and Robert W. Venables, 46–64. Syracuse, NY: Syracuse University Press.

KEHOE, ALICE R. 1981. *North American Indians: A Comprehensive Account.* Englewood Cliffs, NJ: Prentice-Hall.

KEOKE, EMORY DEAN, and KAY MARIE PORTERFIELD. 2002. *Encyclopedia of American Indian Contributions to the World.* New York: Facts On File.

KIDWELL, CLARA SUE, and ALAN VELIE. 2005. *Native American Studies.* Lincoln: University of Nebraska Press.

KROEBER, ALFRED L. 1925. *Handbook of the Indians of California, Bureau of American Ethnology Bulletin No. 78.* Washington, DC: U.S. Government Printing Office.

LADUKE, WINONA. 1999. *All Our Relations: Native Struggles for Land and Life.* Cambridge, MA: South End Press.

———. 2005. *Recovering the Sacred: The Power of Naming and Claiming.* Cambridge, MA: South End Press.

LOBO, SUSAN, STEVE TALBOT, and TRACI L. MORRIS. 2010. *Native American Voices: A Reader.* Upper Saddle River, NJ: Pearson Education/Prentice Hall.

MacLEOD, WILLIAM CHRISTIE. 1928. *The American Indian Frontier.* New York: Alfred A. Knopf.

MIHESUAH, DEVON A. 1998. *Natives and Academics: Research and Writing About American Indians.* Lincoln: University of Nebraska Press.

MOMADAY, N. SCOTT. 1996. *More Than Bows and Arrows.* Camera One Productions. Videocassette (VHS), 60 min.

PEMBER, MARY ANNETTE. 2012. "Advocating for the Planet: Conference Addresses the Rights of Mother Earth." *Indian Country Today* 2 (May): 21.

SMITH, LINDA TUHIWAI. 2001. *Decolonizing Methodologies: Research and Indigenous Peoples.* London, UK and Dunedin, NZ: Zed Books and University of Otago Press.

TALBOT, STEVE. 2002. "Academic Indianismo: Social Scientific Research in American Indian Studies." *American Indian Culture and Research Journal* 26 (4): 67–96.

THORNTON, RUSSELL. 1998. "The Demography of Colonialism and 'Old' and 'New' Native Americans." In *Studying Native America: Problems and Prospects*, edited by Russell Thornton, 17–39. Madison: University of Wisconsin Press.

UDALL, STEWART E. 1972. Quoted in *Look to the Mountain Top*, edited by Charles Jones. New York: American Airlines Indian Book.

VECSEY, CHRISTOPHER. 1980. "American Indian Environmental Religions." In *American Indian Environments*, edited by Christopher Vecsey and Robert W. Venables, 1–37. Syracuse, NY: Syracuse University Press.

———, and RUBEN W. VENABLES, eds. 1980. *American Indian Environments.* Syracuse, NY: Syracuse University Press.

WEATHERFORD, JACK. 1988. *Indian Givers: How the Indians of the Americas Transformed the World.* Columbine, NY: Fawcett.

———. 1991. *Native Roots: How the Indians Enriched America.* Columbine, NY: Fawcett.

ZUCKER, JEFF, KAY HUMMEL, and BOB HOGFOSS. 1983. *Oregon Indians: Culture, History and Current Affairs.* Portland, OR: Oregon Historical Society, Western Imprints.

HIDDEN HERITAGE

THE IROQUOIS AND THE EVOLUTION OF DEMOCRACY

Iroquois Confederation's sacred Tree of Peace. The Tree of Peace is an Eastern white pine, which has a bundle of five needles representing the first five nations to join under "The Great Law of Peace."

Iroquois chiefs were among the hundreds of delegates who attended an international gathering of Indigenous Peoples of the Americas at the United Nations headquarters in Geneva, Switzerland, in the spring of 1977. This was the NGO-sponsored Conference on Discrimination against Indigenous Populations in the Americas. NGO refers to the nongovernmental organizational structure in which international organizations can serve in a consultative status to U.N. bodies. The 1977 conference was the largest of its kind ever held at the United Nations under the auspices of the NGO structure, and the first international conference on Indigenous rights. It was sponsored by the NGOs' Subcommittee on Racism, Racial Discrimination, Apartheid and Decolonization in cooperation with the International Indian Treaty Council (IITC), a new Indigenous NGO based primarily in the United States. The conference documented stark evidence concerning the genocide, human rights violations, and massive land expropriation taking place throughout the Americas against the Native peoples. It received extensive coverage in the European media, although not in the United States. "The Indian delegates represented 96 different Indian peoples from countries throughout the Americas, including the Iroquois delegation. It was also attended by 46 national and international organizations and observers from 27 different national governments represented at the United Nations" (Mohawk 1989, 16).

A second international Indigenous conference was held in 1981, again at the United Nations European headquarters in Geneva under the same auspices. This time the focus was on the land question. In both conferences, the U.S.-based International Indian Treaty Council (IITC), an affiliate of the American Indian Movement (AIM), played a key organizational role. In 1975 the IITC received official

Indian Delegates at the 1977 conference held at the United Nations in Geneva, Switzerland.

status in the Economic and Social Council of the United Nations as a NGO in Category II with the privilege of participating in major U.N. functions and giving testimony before U.N. bodies. It then began the difficult task of organizing world public opinion in support of the 31.5 million Indigenous peoples of the Western Hemisphere (Maybury-Lewis 1997, 10). Following IITC's initiative, the World Council of Indigenous Peoples, a Canadian-based organization, and the Center for Indian Law, representing the Haudenosaunee (Iroquois) at Akwesasne, also obtained NGO status. In their own language the Iroquois call themselves *Haudenosaunee*, translated as "People of the Longhouse."

In both the 1977 and 1981 United Nations gatherings the Iroquois chiefs and other traditional Indian leaders provided key spiritual and ideological guidance. For the 1977 conference, the NGOs at the United Nations had called for position papers that would describe the conditions of oppression suffered by the Native peoples of the Americas. "The Haudenosaunee, the traditional Six Nations council at Onondaga, sent forth three papers which constitute an abbreviated analysis of Western history, and which called for a consciousness of the Sacred Web of Life in the Universe" (Mohawk 1977, iv).

The year 1977 was not the first time that Iroquois traditional leaders had traveled abroad in the struggle for decolonization and Indigenous rights. In 1923, Deskaheh, a Cayuga traditional chief of the Six Nations Iroquois in Canada, attended the League of Nations in Geneva to press for Iroquois sovereignty, but his words were never heeded by the world leaders. He and the other Iroquois delegates traveled on Six Nations passports, which Switzerland accepted. "Deskaheh and his American lawyer . . . had prepared a sophisticated brief: *The Redman's Appeal for Justice: The Position of the Six Nations That They Constitute an Independent State.* The document included treaty texts illustrating that the Six Nations had long been regarded as a sovereign people. . . . Deskaheh got a sympathetic hearing from the delegates of Persia, Ireland, Estonia, and Panama, whose nations knew the taste of violated sovereignty," but his appeal in the end was never formally heard due to the opposition of the Canadian delegation (Wright 1992, 322–23). In 1949 a delegation of the Iroquois attended the founding ceremony for the United Nations building in New York City, and in 1974 they journeyed to Sweden to take part in an international conference on the environment and ecology.

The Haudenosaunee message of peace and harmony among peoples harks back to the founding of their unique confederacy under the Great Law of Peace. Recent research indicates August 31, 1142, as the probable date when the five then "warring Iroquoian nations—Mohawk, Oneida, Onondaga, Cayuga, and Seneca—lay down their weapons of war and established the Great Law of Peace" (Mann and Fields 1997, 105). They were later joined by the Tuscarora about 1720 to form the Six Nations Confederacy. It is believed that the confederacy thus formed became the world's first successful example of a "united nations."

CHAPTER OVERVIEW

There are several parts or themes to this chapter on the Haudenosaunee. First, we present the analytical and theoretical concepts that seem relevant to our subject. These include the concept of cultural revitalization and the theory of social differentiation. Then we recount the story of the origin of the Iroquois Confederacy and how this Indigenous "United Nations" with its Great Law of Peace came to be formed. Third, we present a political sketch of the Iroquois, the part the Confederacy played in seventeenth and eighteenth century colonial affairs, and its ultimate collapse at the outset of the American Revolution.

The story of the founding, structure, and function of the Confederacy and its Great Law of Peace is well worth telling. It is highly relevant to the issues of war and peace that confront all of us living today in the contemporary world, and it is also important because American history does not commence with Columbus and the so-called discovery of America in 1492. In point of fact, American history begins thousands of years earlier with the Indigenous peoples of the Americas, their origins, migrations, accomplishments, and in the Iroquois case, their intellectual contributions to American democracy.

We continue our story of the Iroquois by summarizing the current debate on what is termed the *Iroquois influence theory*. Based on the contemporary research by professors Donald Grinde, Jr. (Yamasee) and Bruce E. Johansen, it is now believed that many of the precepts of American democracy and the U.S. Constitution are heavily indebted to Iroquois political thought and their confederation model of government. It is argued that the American idea for a federation of states, a bicameral legislature, and a balance of powers among the executive, judicial, and legislative branches of government are influenced by the Iroquois example. Yet there are some anthropologists and ethnohistorians who categorically reject this thesis despite the evidence supplied by Grinde and Johansen. This is an important issue, because if the Iroquois were instrumental in helping to shape the structure of American democracy, we should acknowledge it as an important facet of U.S. history, and teach the Iroquois heritage in colleges and universities. At the very least, it is obvious that Iroquois democratic traditions antedate those of the United States by several hundred years.

The influence debate also illustrates how power relationships enter into the telling of history. Heretofore, Indigenous peoples like the Iroquois have not been permitted to tell their own histories. Instead, the mainstream version of Iroquois history produced by a largely White academe became the doctrinaire version.

After considering the scholarly debate on the influence theory, we present a detailed discussion of Iroquois society and culture. By society we mean the Iroquois people and how they organize themselves in their communities. Culture, on the other hand, is the way of life of a people, their values, customary practices, traditions, and ideas. A familiarity with Iroquois society and culture will also enable the reader to bett understand the sociocultural changes that took place in Iroquois communities in the early part of the nineteenth century, when they experienced a revival of their culture and traditions under the Code of Handsome Lake.

At the end of the chapter we consider the Iroquois as they exist today, living mainly on small state reservations in the northeastern United States and Canada. The revitalization and protection of their old cultural traditions and system of self-government continue to be important themes of contemporary life and struggle. The *origin*, *death*, and *rebirth* of the Six Nations Iroquois is the subject of this chapter. It is an amazing story.

ANALYTICAL AND THEORETICAL CONCEPTS

In *The Death and Rebirth of the Seneca*, Anthony F. C. Wallace (1969) presents an in-depth description of the sociocultural collapse and then revitalization of the Seneca movement led by the prophet Handsome Lake. American Indian societies made different responses to European colonization and political hegemony in eighteenth century North America. Some resisted militarily for as long as they could; others adapted by giving up traditional culture, converting to Christianity, learning English, and taking up Western technology. Others like the Cherokee responded by evolving into full-scale Indian republics; and still others, as in the case of the traditional Iroquois Confederacy, simply collapsed before the European onslaught and ceased to function as a viable political and ethnic entity.

The American revolt against the British monarchy at the end of the eighteenth century presented the Iroquois Confederacy with a major political dilemma: whether to side with their former English ally or to join the American rebels. When the Iroquois nations divided on this issue, the Confederacy collapsed, and the collective punishment and oppressive conditions imposed upon them under the new U.S. government caused the rapid disintegration of Iroquois culture and society. It was then that the prophet Handsome Lake began to teach a religiously inspired message or *code* that enabled the dispirited Iroquois to adapt to the new conditions of conquest, but at the same time bring back much of their old culture and traditions. This is what is meant by the *rebirth* of the Iroquois, and this is the story that Wallace describes in his classic study.

Description is not explanation, however. Wallace provides an excellent overview of the Seneca Iroquois death and rebirth, but in social science we need also to explain the phenomenon under investigation, in this instance, the religious revitalization that took place among the Iroquois. Why did the powerful and highly integrated Iroquois Confederacy that had endured for hundreds of years suddenly collapse at the end of the eighteenth century? Why did their culture and society shatter under American hegemony, and the people go into severe social and psychological depression? And why did the rebirth of the Haudenosaunee then take the form of a religious movement led by a prophet? We will examine the topic of Indian revitalization movements in more detail at the end of this chapter, but to fully address the questions we have raised above, to answer the "why question," we need a theoretical explanation. The organization theory suggested by sociologist Duane Champagne (Turtle Mountain Chippewa) is the logical explanation.

In a series of articles and monographs, Champagne has reviewed the histories of a number of American Indian societies in order to understand their different responses in the eighteenth and nineteenth centuries to Euro-American hegemony (see Talbot 2002). To comprehend these variable responses, Champagne applies social organization (or social differentiation) theory to the responses made by these Indian societies. Social differentiation refers to the extent to which the various functions of society—familial, political, economic, religious, defense and the like—have become institutionalized and distinct from one another. In other words, in some societies the various social functions have become institutionalized so that one may speak of the economy, political system, religion, education and the like as more or less distinct from one another. This is especially true for Western industrialized societies. Among many Indigenous societies, on the other hand, many of these functions were not yet developed as separate parts of the society. With many American Indian societies, for example, the political and religious leaders are one and the same, so that one cannot differentiate between these functions as separate institutions. The latter are what Champagne terms *non-differentiated* societies.

Some traditional Indian societies, such as the Iroquois, were non-differentiated, while others, such as the Cherokee (whom we feature in Chapter 6), were differentiated. The Iroquois combined the various functions mentioned above into a kinship-based confederacy. This made them powerful among their Native adversaries, but when confronted with Anglo-American hegemony (political domination), their inflexible social system collapsed. In other words, differential social organization in Champagne's theory is the independent variable that can explain the different Indian change responses. We will return to his theoretical formulation in our conclusions at the end of the chapter.

WHO ARE THE IROQUOIS?

In 1988 a Congressional Resolution passed by the U.S. House and Senate concurrently read:

> Whereas the original framers of the Constitution, including most notably, George Washington and Benjamin Franklin, are known to have greatly admired the concepts of the Six Nations of the Iroquois Confederacy;
>
> Whereas the confederation of the original Thirteen Colonies into one republic was influenced by the political system developed by the Iroquois Confederacy as were many of the democratic principles which were incorporated into the Constitution itself;
>
> Be it resolved by the Senate (the House of Representatives concurring), that the Congress, on the occasion of the two hundredth anniversary of the signing of the United States Constitution, acknowledges the historical debt which the Republic of the United States of America owes to the Iroquois Confederacy and other Indian nations for their demonstration of enlightened, democratic principles of government and the example of independent Indian nations.

The Iroquois Woodland League of Nations, as it has been termed by some writers, held a powerful and pivotal position between the French and English during the colonial period of North America. During the first half of the eighteenth century, the Iroquois were England's allies in its imperial wars against the French for the American possessions. Without the political role that the League played in this early colonial history, the United States today might have become a French-speaking, Franco-American nation instead of an Anglo-American one.

The word *Iroquois* is derived from an Algonkian word translated as "real adder," with a French suffix. In their own language, Haudenosaunee means People of the Extended Lodge (or Longhouse). The English referred to them as the Six Nations. The Iroquois language is of the Macro-Siouan phylum and the Iroquoian language family. The various Iroquois dialects are representative of the six nations of the Confederacy.

The original homeland of the Six Nations Iroquois, or People of the Longhouse, lay in what today is upper New York State. From east to west they were originally the Mohawk, Oneida, Onondaga, Cayuga, and Seneca nations. These nations were situated along the Finger Lakes "where the Creator had raked his glacial nails through the world." (Wright 1992, 115). In 1713 they were joined by the Tuscarora who fled incursions by the North Carolina colonists and the Cherokees, making them six nations. Wright (1992, 123) estimates that the Iroquois might have numbered several hundred thousand people before the great disease pandemic of the 1520s, and that they were reduced in numbers to no more than seventy-five thousand a century later. In colonial times their twenty villages comprised some fifty lineages of prominent families who represented eight or so clans. Today, their current population in the United States and Canada taken together is estimated as being more than sixty thousand. The 2000 U.S. Census found over forty-five thousand persons claiming "Iroquois only" as their "race," and almost eighty thousand claiming part-Iroquois. They are currently found mainly on six state reservations in upstate New York and on the Six Nations Reserve in Canada. Members of these Iroquois nations can also be found living and working throughout North America. The men excel as ironworkers and are famous for their construction work in "high steel" on bridges and skyscrapers. They are also statesmen, teachers, and artists. Iroquois women are known for their dignity and wise counsel, and they hold a high status in contemporary Iroquois society as clan mothers and in advising the men.

ORIGIN OF THE CONFEDERACY AND THE GREAT LAW OF PEACE

For centuries the Six Nations Iroquois inhabited the area where we find many of them today, in upstate New York around the southern border of Lake Ontario, and along the St. Lawrence River. Iroquois oral history, however, speaks of an original migration from the mouth of the Mississippi River (see Akweks 1972). For some unknown reason the early Iroquois peoples started migrating up the Ohio River toward the Great Lakes in the distant past. Various bands split off and eventually became the Huron, Tobacco, Erie, and Neuter nations of the Great Lakes. Others settled along the Susquehana River and the Upper Ohio. The main Iroquois speaking band continued down the St. Lawrence River until they met the Bark Eaters, or Adirondack People. These early Iroquois were defeated in battle by the more numerous Adirondacks and had to submit to their dominance. Eventually they escaped and were able to settle near the mouth of the Oswego River. In time, they prospered and multiplied until different bands split off to seek better hunting regions.

> From their homeland along the Oswego River, their trails led south, east, and west. The Flint People, who are called by others the Mohawks, settled along the Mohawk River. Around Oneida Lake, the Standing Stone People, or Oneidas, built their villages. The People of the Hills, or Onondagas, settled along Onondaga Creek. To the west, along Cayuga Lake, the Great Pipe People, or Cayugas, built their towns. Along Canadaigua Lake settled the People of the Great Mountain, the Senecas. Another band, the Akotaskarore, or Tuscaroras, travelled far to the south to what later became known as the Carolinas. Now they, the one band, had become six separate bands. (Akweks 1972, 23–25)

Oral tradition tells of internecine warfare among the Iroquois tribes in ancient times. The killing and blood feuds became so intense that something had to be done. Thus the Confederacy, or League, was formed as a result of a great need for peace and union among the warring tribes of linguistically and culturally similar peoples. In addition to ending internecine strife, confederation also offered common defense against enemy nations that threaten the general peace.

The formation of the League of the Iroquois and its Great Law of Peace was the work of two gifted men, Deganawidah and Aiionwatha (Hiawatha), who saw a need for peace and union among the separate Iroquois nations. Deganawidah, a linguistically related Huron who was adopted into the Mohawk Nation, envisioned the idea of "right thinking" and peaceful relations. He taught that all human beings possess the power of rational thought and in this fact is found the power to create peaceful relations. Logic is the major tool, and this is the first principle. "Unless we believe that all human beings possess rational thought, we are powerless to act in any way that will bring peace short of the absolute destruction of the other. . . . We must believe they are not suicidal or homicidal by nature, that we can reason with them. Thus the first principle that will bring us the power to act is the confidence in the belief that all people are rational human beings and that we can take measures to reach accord with them" (Mohawk 1986, 17).

Deganawidah taught a second principle that with a judicious application of rationality, "a society could be created in which human beings can create governments dedicated to the proposition that no human being should abuse another" (Mohawk 1986). He promised the Iroquois power, not military power, but the power of righteousness.

Deganawidah, known also as "the Peacemaker," was instructed in a vision from the Creator to give the Great Law of Peace to the feuding Iroquois nations. The Great Law is a set of rules and procedures for working out differences and settling disputes and hostilities between nations. He then traveled among the respective Iroquois nations to spread the message of peace, but was unable to persuade the Iroquois to adopt his plan for confederation because of his Huron birth and, it is said, also because of a speech impediment. Most Iroquois rejected his message until he recruited Hiawatha. An Onondaga Indian by birth, but like Deganawidah a Mohawk by adoption, Hiawatha was the person whose eloquence won converts to Deganawidah's vision. Hiawatha, the statesman, presented Deganawidah's plans to the clan chiefs of the warring Iroquois nations. Most agreed, but an "evil chief" of the Onondaga, Thadodaho, was at first reluctant and became the last holdout. Nevertheless, Hiawatha was a persuasive orator. After he suffered many personal tribulations during a long period of negotiations, the clan leaders of the various nations agreed to maintain peace through an oral constitution, the Great Binding Law, or Great Law of Peace.

Deganawidah not only brought a plan of harmony and peace to the five warring Iroquois nations, but also a means to settle their disputes peacefully at annual gatherings of the Confederate Council meeting at the Onondaga nation. The Great Binding Law (or Constitution) outlawed the blood feuds that had contributed to so much violent behavior and replaced them with the condolence (funeral) ceremony, where kin of the deceased were condoled and compensated. It also offered the Iroquois nations the security of union while at the same time maintaining the sovereignty of each constituent Iroquois nation. "Out of this reformation came a confederacy that called for the establishment of a hereditary council of fifty confederate clan chiefs, *sachems*, from the five tribes appointed by clan matrons, a decision-making process based on consensus, and a political and ceremonial protocol rooted in the kinship structure and worldview of the people" (Starna, Campisi, and Hauptman 1996, 279).

Gayanashagona, the Great Binding Law

There are four sections to the League's Great Binding Law (Murphy, n.d.). The first section recounts the legend of Deganawidah, the Great Law Giver. The second section is the Great Binding Law itself, or *Gayanashagona*. It includes the federal structure of the Confederation; the rights, duties, and qualifications for sachems; the election of the Pine Tree (secular) chiefs; the names, duties, and rights of war chiefs; the rules of the clans; the official symbolism; the laws of adoption; the laws of emigration; the rights of foreign nations; the rights and powers of war; the terms for treason or the succession of a nation; the religious ceremonies; the protection of the households; and the funeral addresses. The third section is the traditional narrative of the origin of the Confederation of the Five Nations. The last section is the Hiawatha tradition, a long narrative telling of the trials and tribulations of Hiawatha in his efforts to bring the various nations into the confederacy, and of his personal struggle with Thadodaho.

There are 117 *wampum* or articles to the Iroquois constitution. The first two articles in a preamble read in part: "I am Deganawidah and with the Five Nations' confederate lords I plant the Tree of the Great Peace. . . . Roots have spread out from the Tree of the Great Peace . . . and the name of these roots is the Great White Roots of Peace. If any man or any nation outside of the Five Nations shall show a desire to obey the laws of the Great Peace . . . they may trace the roots to their source . . . and they shall be welcomed to take shelter beneath the Tree. . . . I, Deganawidah, and the confederate lords now uproot

the tallest pine tree and into the cavity thereby made we cast all weapons of strife. We bury them from sight forever and plant again the tree. Thus shall a Great Peace be established and hostilities shall no longer be known between the Five Nations but only peace to a united people" (Murphy, n.d., 1). Compare this with the Preamble to the Constitution of the United Nations when it was founded in San Francisco in 1945: "We, the peoples of the United Nations, determined to save succeeding generations from the scourge of war . . . and to reaffirm faith in fundamental human rights . . . and to establish conditions under which justice and respect for law can be maintained . . . do hereby establish an international organization to be known as the United Nations." Yet, the Iroquois Confederacy and its Great Law of Peace pre-date by hundreds of years our modern United Nations and in this sense is the world's oldest United Nations.

The metaphor of the White Roots of Peace (the *pax Iroquois*) is a strong theme of the Deganawidah oral history and tradition. The initial purpose of the League was to implement peaceful coexistence between and among the warring Iroquois nations. Soon, however, Native philosophers extended this idea of the White Roots of Peace to all humankind; "the white roots of the Great Tree of Peace will continue to grow," the founders taught. Should any nation reject the Iroquois offer after three invitations to come under the Great Tree, then the Confederacy was obliged to use force. During the turbulent years of the eighteenth century when the Iroquois Confederacy became embroiled in the imperial wars of the European colonizing nations, the force part of the *pax Iroquois*, exacerbated by competition in the fur trade, resulted in a crescendo of violence and a destabilizing influence on the Confederacy.

The Great Binding Law was transmitted orally from one generation to another by certain sachems known for their powers of memorization. It was preserved by a sacred collection of wampum belts and strings, comprised of purple and white sea shells, each serving to recall a law or regulation, including treaties with the United States and foreign powers in the colonial and early postcolonial periods of North American history. It was Hiawatha who introduced the idea of offering wampum as part of the condolence and other official ceremonies. Its special functions in Haudenosaunee public affairs include official communications, ritualistic, and fiduciary transactions. Wampum ratified treaties, opened government deliberations, confirmed leaders into office, registered the history of the Iroquois constitution, memorialized the dead, confessed the penitent, and aided prayer. "This belt preserves my words" is the frequent closing remark of Iroquois speeches. It served much the same function as the affixing of a signature, or notarizing a document in contemporary United States, and as a means of written communication.

In the Iroquois political system as crafted by its founders, the Onondaga Nation became the wampum keepers, the keepers of the archives, and one of their chiefs the Keeper of the Wampum for the Confederacy. Although not regarded as money by the Indians, in colonial times wampum came to have value for White people who "used it as a form of currency much as they used Spanish, Portuguese, French, and Dutch coins in addition to English ones" (Tooker 1978, 422). The Indians, on the other hand, used wampum as gifts in condolence ceremonies to prevent hostilities between the nations when a man of one nation killed another from a different nation. Ten strings of wampum were given for the life of a man and twenty strings for that of a woman. "Thus, if a man killed a woman, 30 strings were given—20 for the life of the murdered woman and 10 for the life of the murderer that had been forfeited by his act" (Tooker 1978, 423).

The Great Law of Peace also offered a dynamic body of diplomatic law and protocol that played an important part in Iroquoian and non-Indian relationships during the colonial period in U.S. history.

Iroquois traditional leaders and a growing number of scholars now believe that U.S. democratic institutions and structures of government were shaped by the example of the Iroquois Confederacy and its Great Binding Law. The evidence for this proposition is examined later in this chapter in the section on the Iroquois influence debate.

IROQUOIS POLITICAL HISTORY

When first contacted by Europeans in the early 1500s, the Iroquoian peoples were living along the St. Lawrence River in what is present-day upper New York State, along the lower Great Lakes, and in the Susquehanna River Valley in present-day Pennsylvania. (See Figure 2.1.)

They were strategically based geographically, which enabled them to play an important role in colonial history. They held the Mohawk Valley, one of two gateways through the mountains and an important route for access to the fur trade. Their villages were protected by mountains to the south, and the Susquehanna, Delaware, and Ohio rivers afforded convenient routes to the beaver grounds to the south and west. To the north lay Lake Ontario, sometimes called the Lake of the Iroquois.

Sometime between the years 1000 and 1350 AD (possibly in 1142), five Iroquois nations formed the great confederacy comprised of clan chiefs drawn

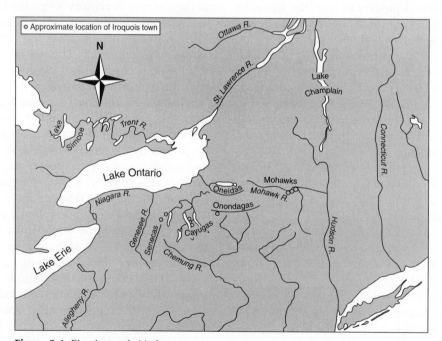

Figure 2.1 Five Iroquois Nations.

from forty-nine noble families. Deganawidah, the Law Giver, and his spokesman, Hiawatha, planted a Great Tree of Peace at the Onondaga Nation near present-day Syracuse, NY, to resolve the blood feuds that had been dividing the Haudenosaunee people.

Later, when the European colonizers entered northeastern North America, the Confederacy had to decide whether to ally itself with the Dutch, French, British, or to remain neutral. Early relations with these colonizing powers centered on the fur trade, principally for beaver, because it provided the Iroquois with desired goods such as firearms. As it turned out, the Iroquois Confederacy lay in a pivotal position to frustrate French trading interests, and the Confederacy soon became a military force with which to contend. In fact, the Iroquois Confederacy played a major role during the next two centuries in the geopolitics of the region.

The French, under the explorer Jacques Cartier, entered the St. Lawrence River system as early as 1534. Then in 1609, Samuel de Champlain allied himself with the Algonkians in his explorations against the Iroquois. It was Champlain who introduced firearms to the Native nations of the region. After a major military defeat by Champlain, the Iroquois began raiding French and Indian settlements along the St. Lawrence River. This led to the Beaver Wars of the 1600s. Beaver furs were in great demand in Europe where they were shaped into a variety of hats. When the Iroquois received guns as a principal trade item from the New Netherlands Dutch traders, and then from the English when the latter took over Dutch New York in 1664, having these weapons placed the Iroquois at a considerable advantage over their French-backed Algonkian and Huron enemies in the beaver trade. Iroquois warfare thus "challenged the increasing French and Indian allies' domination of the Great Lakes country fur trade and the French penetration of the Mississippi Valley" (Smith 1988, 53).

As a result of the Iroquois War against the French in 1664, the Iroquois were able to subdue their enemies and dominate the fur trade. By 1649 they had eliminated a related Iroquoian people, the Hurons, who occupied the upper St. Lawrence Valley, from the trade with the French. This was followed by war on the Neuters and the Eries, whom they also eliminated as nations in battle, but then absorbed as refugees into the Iroquois Confederation through adoption. By 1670 the Iroquois controlled all the territory from the Hudson to the Ohio River—territory of the Miamis, Potawatomis, and Kickapoos. By 1680

they dominated the Delawares, Nanticokes, and smaller groups of Algonkians.

The Imperial Wars

Between 1689 and 1763, four wars were fought among the competing European powers in which the Indian nations became involved. These were King William's War (1689–97), Queen Anne's War (1702–13), King George's War (1739–48), and the French and Indian, or Seven Years' War (1754–63). During these imperial wars, the Iroquois Confederacy occupied a pivotal role between France and England. (See Gibson 1980; MacLeod 1928; and Weeks 1988.)

What is known as the Iroquois War became part of King William's War between the French and the English. King William's War was fought largely in the St. Lawrence Valley and lower Canada. It broke out because the British threatened the French fur trade with better quality goods at lower prices. Because of the Confederacy's territorial and military position, the Iroquois became involved in protecting English settlements in the Lower Hudson Valley.

Queen Anne's War broke out as a result of French reaction to British commercial and territorial expansion in the trans-Appalachian West. The Iroquois, except for some Mohawk, remained neutral. The French in the South, however, tried to draw in the Creek, Cherokee, Choctaw, and Chickasaw nations. The war ended in 1713 with the consolidation of English control over much of North America under the Treaty of Utrecht. The English then unilaterally declared the Iroquois subjects of the British Crown.

King George's War saw the continuation of French and British rivalry. Despite their neutrality, the Iroquois, fearful of the French, encouraged the British to build forts for common protection. "In the 1770s, British traders expanded into Ohio under the protection of their Iroquois allies. These traders continued moving westward from 1740 to 1748 during King George's War. . . . At that time the Iroquois attempted to remain neutral, although some Mohawk fought the French" (Oswalt and Neeley 1999, 409). In the South, the Cherokee remained allied with the British and warred against the French, Choctaw, and Creek factions.

France strove to consolidate the region around lakes Erie and Ontario and establish closer ties with the Cayuga, Onondaga, and Seneca by building a religious mission. As tensions grew between the two colonial powers, a new war broke out in 1756. On the continent it was known as the Seven Years' War, and in North America, the French and Indian War.

The two colonial powers fought over the trans-Appalachian West, i.e., the region at the forks of the Ohio River. The English were at first soundly defeated, but in the end they prevailed and France had to relinquish Quebec. Although the Iroquois Confederacy again declared a policy of neutrality, some Mohawk supported the English whereas the Seneca sided with the French. "With an English victory the political power of the Iroquois diminished because the English no longer needed them as a buffer against the French. As a result, English colonists now became able to settle Indian lands to the west without serious Iroquois intervention" (Oswalt and Neeley 1999, 410).

During Pontiac's Rebellion in 1763, the Seneca joined several Algonkian Indian nations to rise up against the British, which had just secured the Ohio Territory from the French. Later, the Seneca returned to the Six Nations Confederacy. In the wake of Pontiac's War, the British declared the Royal Proclamation of 1763, forbidding British settlement west of the Appalachian Mountains. The American colonists, however, ignored the English proclamation and streamed westward over the mountains into Indian territory. This threatened the British fur trade and the Indians who had become dependent upon it.

The importance of the fur trade for the Iroquois and other northeastern Indians cannot be discounted as a compelling factor in White-Indian relations. "Pelts were the gold of the woods. With them a man could buy guns, powder, lead, knives, hatchets, axes, needles and awls, scissors, kettles, traps, cloth, ready-made shirts, blankets, paint (for cosmetic purposes), and various notions; steel springs to pluck out disfiguring beard, scalp, and body hair; silver bracelets and armbands and tubes for coiling hair; rings to hang from nose and ears; mirrors; tinkling bells" (Wallace 1969, 14–15).

The motives of the European colonial powers for involving Indians in their imperial wars were: (1) the use of Indian auxiliaries and scouts, and (2) the use of Indian nations like the Iroquois as buffers against rival European powers (Gibson 1980, chapter 10). For the Indian nations, there were several reasons for their involvement in the imperial wars. The first was self-interest, to maintain sovereignty and play one European power against another. The Indians also were prodded by European military officers to participate as the duty of a proprietary (trading) Indian nation to its colonial patron. Third, Indians desired bounty, regular pay, rations, blankets, ammunition, and firearms. There was also the motive to "replace" deceased family members and those killed in battle—the mourned-for dead—with enemy scalps or prisoners. The unintended consequence was that at times during the seventeenth century when war casualties were heavy, "as many as two-thirds of the population of the Oneida Nation were adoptees, and the other nations . . . similarly depended heavily on adopted manpower" (Wallace 1969, 103).

The Iroquois Confederacy became much stronger militarily towards the end of the seventeenth century. The Beaver Wars, in which the Iroquois competed with the French and their Indian allies for the beaver pelts as a valuable trade commodity, greatly strengthened the power of Iroquois war leaders. "The post-1700 Iroquois Confederacy emerged as a political organization that made military, political, and trade policy, looked after the general welfare of the confederacy, and continued to manage internal disputes between the five [later six] nations" (Champagne 1983, 756). During the late eighteenth century, when guns were introduced and the wars by the colonial powers were being fought for economic and political supremacy, the power of the Iroquois warriors became paramount. The fur trade created competition among eastern Indian nations, and the European powers sought Indian mercenaries in their imperial struggles for domination. As a consequence, "small guerrilla bands under rising leaders replaced large expeditions led by distinguished chiefs and shamans. Individual initiative supplanted policy and group action" (Fenton 1978, 315). These unintended consequences meant that the power of the hereditary sachems of the Confederacy was eclipsed by the power of the war chiefs. In the end, this hastened the decline of the Confederacy. Then, with the collapse of the fur trade, the Iroquois no longer had the means to carry on trade for guns, metal tools, and textiles that had become necessities for them.

The American Revolution

The outbreak of the Revolutionary War fragmented the Iroquois Confederacy and led to its rapid decline. "The council fire of the Confederacy was extinguished in 1777, when the five tribes could not agree on which side to support in the American Revolution" (Starna, Campisi, and Hauptman 1996, 279). The Mohawk, Onondaga, Cayuga, and Seneca were sympathetic to the British, who had tried to preserve Indian lands from the colonists to protect their fur trade interests. The Oneida and Tuscarora sided with the American rebels. At first the Confederacy tried to remain neutral between the two belligerents, the British and the Americans. "The Six Nations had no wish to be drawn, yet again, into fighting foreigners' wars. They declared themselves neutral, but warned that the first side to molest them would become their foe. At this critical time small pox attacked the Onondagas. . . . The losses, requiring condolence rites and new election, crippled the Six Nations parliament" (Wright 1992, 138). Mohawk leader Joseph Brandt then talked four of the Six Nations into supporting the British cause, while the Christianized Oneidas and the Tuscaroras took the American side. The Confederacy was effectively split in two.

Political forces unleashed by the American Revolution thus shattered the solidary Iroquois as a non-differentiated society. The confederacy had been carefully constructed upon the principle of kinship as understood in the Iroquois longhouse. Once this political system was ruptured, then the entire society began to unravel.

Joseph Brant (Thayendanegea) was a Mohawk tribal leader (not a clan chief) who became a British army officer. He also was a devout Episcopalian. His sister, Molly, married Sir William Johnson, who was superintendent for Northern Indian Affairs under Great Britain. Brandt became a translator and diplomat who helped the English negotiate with the Iroquois nations. When the American Revolution broke out, Brandt aligned himself with the Loyalist cause and traveled to England where he was commissioned a colonel in the British army. Upon his return, he continued to organize and lead Loyalist Iroquois against the American settlements in the Ohio Valley.

Following the Revolutionary War, George Washington ordered Iroquois settlements destroyed because of their supposed Tory sentiments. "In 1779, General John Sullivan cut down orchards and crops, burning 500 houses and nearly a million bushels of corn" (Wright 1992, 139). The Treaty of Paris of 1783 contained no provisions for Indian nations who fought on the British side. Indian allies of the British felt betrayed, but they had no choice but to flee the expanding American colonies and move to British Canada. About 1,600 Mohawks and other Iroquois under Joseph Brandt emigrated to Canada in 1784, eventually settling on the Six Nations Reserve near Brantford, Ontario, where they established a confederacy council. "Most of those who remained in New York moved to the Buffalo Creek Reservation, founding a second confederacy council that today sits at Onondaga" (Starna, Campisi, and Hauptman 1996, 279). This started the political division between Canadian and American Iroquois that became permanent following the War of 1812.

After the American Revolution, those Iroquois who remained in the new United States were under intense pressure to acculturate. "During the 1780s and 1790s the New York Iroquois ceded most of their territory to American and foreign land companies" (Champagne 1983, 756). The political pressure for the Indians to sell their lands lay in the fact that "both the states and the Continental Congress had come out of the war with heavy debts and poor credit; the troops had been paid, when funds were available, in a rapidly depreciating currency, and many had not been paid in full or at all, and the new government was faced with further outlays that demanded both public credit and a reasonably stable currency" (Wallace 1969, 150). The solution to these problems lay in the public lands, which of course meant Indian lands. In 1797, at the Treaty of Big Tree, the Seneca sold their lands. "With the exception of a few reservations, all of the Iroquois territory in New York east of the Genesee River had already been sold" (Wallace 1969, 179).

In addition, great pressure was brought to bear on Iroquois men to take up individualized farming (a role reversal since the women traditionally were the horticulturalists) and to become Christian. At the same time, land alienation rapidly increased. The remnant Indian communities became "slums in the wilderness" (Wallace 1969, 184). Beginning with the American Revolution and ending with the Treaty of Big Tree in 1797, the Iroquois population was cut in half. Casualties had been severe during the fighting; epidemics of dysentery and smallpox further decimated the population. By 1794 there were only about 4,000 Iroquois remaining, some 3,500 in New York and about 500 in Canada As a result, "many sought escape from this dilemma in drink. Violence born of despair and alcohol became endemic. . . . Women aborted their babies rather than bring them into a ruined world," and suicides became frequent (Wright 1992, 233). "The loss of morale and disintegrating conditions on the reservations resulted in idleness, chronic drunkenness, gossip, violent disputes, and family instability" (Graymont 1988, 99). Many of the most distinguished men among the Six Nations became notorious drunkards. Under these deteriorating social conditions, people grew suspicious of one another and charges of witchcraft increased sharply, further dividing families and communities. It was at this time, during the annual Strawberry Festival, that an Iroquois Turtle clan chief, Ganiodaiyo, or Handsome Lake, brought the *Gawiio*, or Good Word, to the despairing Iroquois people, which will be discussed later.

Due to the persecution they suffered from the Americans following the Revolutionary War, and also the betrayal by the British at the Treaty of Paris in 1783, Mohawk loyalists under Brandt fled to Canada to settle on the Grand River Reserve at the west end of the Niagara peninsula. A number of the immigrants to Canada were baptized Christians, and many, like Brandt, spoke English. Another group of Mohawk loyalists settled near modern Kingston on the Bay of Quinte, just north of the St. Lawrence River.

When the council fire of the Confederacy was extinguished in 1777 it was left for each Iroquois nation to seek its own course. Later that year when the Mohawks were attacked, many fled the valley. Two years later, many Senecas were forced to abandon their villages as well. Since the 1783 Treaty of Paris negotiated by England and the new United States made no provision for the Indians, each Iroquois community had to make its own decisions. The Lower Mohawks settled at the Bay of Quinte in Canada, and the Upper Mohawks, who had been living at Niagara, resettled on land along the Grand River in Ontario. "With the Upper Mohawks went a number of Cayugas, some Onondagas, and a few Senecas. Other Cayugas and Onondagas chose to stay with the Senecas and settled at Buffalo Creek in western New York State, while still others decided to stay in their own homelands: the Cayugas at Cayuga Lake and the Onondagas at Onondaga Creek. Some Senecas determined that they would continue to live in the Genesee Valley" (Tooker 1978, 435). Four of the larger communities eventually became reservations. Today, most of the traditional Iroquois communities are found in upstate New York and consist of a dozen small, scattered state reservations.

Eventually the council fire of the Confederacy was rekindled, but in two separate places: the Six Nations Reserve in Canada, and at Buffalo Creek Reservation in the United States. When Buffalo Creek was sold in the 1840s the council fire was rekindled at Onondaga, which was governed at that time by a council of twenty-seven chiefs, fourteen League chiefs and thirteen assistants. In Canada, for the balance of the nineteenth century, the confederate form of government continued in power on the Six Nations Reserve.

Despite these political developments, which had such a deleterious impact on the Iroquois Confederacy, the Iroquois contribution to the evolution of American democracy was nonetheless considerable. Richard H. Lee, Benjamin Franklin, Thomas Jefferson, and George Washington, among other founders of the United States, were quite familiar with the Iroquois Confederacy as it existed during the colonial period and the formative years of the fledging U.S. republic. Four of the founding fathers were fluent in Indian languages, and colonist William Livingston spent over one year in a Mohawk village (Grinde 1992). One of Franklin's jobs as a journalist was to publish all of the speeches and records of the assemblies and treaty negotiations between the English colonists and the powerful Iroquois Confederacy. Through this work, Franklin became knowledgeable about the political structure of the confederacy. He soon began advocating the Iroquois form of government as a model for the union of the thirteen competing English colonies.

In 1851, the ethnologist Lewis Henry Morgan published the results of his extensive Iroquois research, the *League of the Ho-de-no-sau-nee, or Iroquois* (Morgan 1962). Knowledge of the structure and function of the Confederacy soon disseminated widely and even influenced the theoretical formulations of Karl Marx and Frederic Engels (see Leacock 1972 [1884]). The American founding fathers were significantly influenced by Iroquois democratic precepts when the Constitution and the U.S. political structure were hammered out by the founders. For these reasons alone, a great deal has been known about this remarkable people, their confederate form of government, and their influence on U.S. democratic institutions.

THE IROQUOIS INFLUENCE DEBATE

Why has the Indian story and heritage hitherto been written out of U.S. history? It is a puzzling facet of Eurocentric historiography that American history does not seem to officially commence in North America until the arrival of the White colonists from England. A major history text, for example, adopted in California schools and colleges a few years ago, devoted only a page and a half to America before Columbus. As historian Jack D. Forbes often observed, this reasoning would be the same as saying that English history does not begin until 1066 with the Norman invasion. In point of fact, when Europeans invaded the Americas, they found thriving Indian nations and civilizations, not only in Central America and Andean South America, but also in what is now the eastern United States. The eastern Indian confederacies, especially that of the Iroquois, appear to have had an important influence on the development of the modern concept of democracy and the formation of the political system of government in the United States of America.

Not only have American Indians been written out of North American history generally, but their role in U.S. colonial history is especially ignored by mainstream historians. This changed when the bicentennial of the U.S. Constitution in 1987 began to spark scholarly interest in the question. It was at this time that José Barreiro (Guajiro/Taino), later, editor-in-chief of *Awe:kon Press/Native Americas Journal*, organized an important conference at Cornell University entitled "Cultural Encounter: The Iroquois Great Law of Peace and the U.S. Constitution," that combined traditional Haudenosaunee (Iroquois) speakers and academics. Then, in late 1991, the United States celebrated the two hundredth anniversary of the writing of the Bill of Rights, and finally, a year later, the quincentennial of Christopher Columbus's so-called discovery of America. The highly Eurocentric quincentennial plans of the United States and other Western nations generated broad reaction among the Indigenous peoples of the Americas who viewed 1492 as the beginning of an American holocaust.

In the United States, traditional Indians, Native American scholars, revisionist historians, and activist anthropologists joined forces in their efforts to correct the historical record. An important collective work, *Exiled in the Land of the Free*, edited by Oren Lyons (Onondaga), John Mohawk (Seneca), and others, came out in 1992 (Lyons and Mohawk 1992). Also in the same year, the UCLA American Indian Studies Center sponsored an important conference on the Columbian quincentennary, and the conference papers were later published as *The Unheard Voices* (Gentry and Grinde 1994). Eurocentric history, ethnohistory, anthropology, and demography, all were reexamined through the lens of an Indigenist perspective. There were also many demonstrations throughout the hemisphere by a broad spectrum of Native American peoples and their supporters against the quincentennary celebrations that made the scholarly critiques especially relevant to the Indian experience.

It was in the late 1960s when information began circulating through Indian country about the influence that the Iroquois Confederacy had on the founding fathers and the U.S. constitutional form of government. Much of the credit can be attributed to the White Roots of Peace, an Iroquois traveling college that visited a number of universities and spoke to Indian students and others taking Native American Studies courses. Even so, it had been common knowledge among many traditional Indian leaders and spokespersons who were increasingly interacting

and communicating with one another. It was therefore not entirely surprising when historians Donald Grinde (Yamasee) and Bruce E. Johansen began to document this important facet of the Native American heritage in academic books and articles. What came as a surprise, instead, was the vehement backlash by some mainstream ethnohistorians and anthropologists who sought to discredit what has come to be known as the *Iroquois influence theory*.

The research by Grinde and Johansen convinced them "that it is not a question of *whether* native societies helped shape the evolution of democracy in the colonies and early United States. It is a question of *how* this influence was conveyed and how *pervasive* it was" (Johansen and Grinde 1990, 61). The two scholars had been documenting it for fifteen years before a handful of Iroquoian specialists mounted a backlash attack following the 1987 Cornell University conference. Grinde had already published *The Iroquois and the Founding of the American Nation* in 1977, and Johansen had revised and published his Ph.D. dissertation as a book, *Forgotten Founders: Benjamin Franklin, the Iroquois and the Rationale for the American Revolution* in 1982 (Grinde 1977; Johansen 1982).

Elizabeth Tooker, an anthropology professor at Temple University, initiated the debate by strongly rejecting the influence theory in the journal *Ethnohistory* (Tooker 1987). She categorically stated that "a review of the evidence in the historical and ethnographic documents offers virtually no support for this contention" (Johansen and Grinde 1990, 64). Michael Newman joined the attack in a *New Republic* article by rejecting the idea, as he put it, that the Iroquois ancestors "guided Madison's hand in writing the Constitution" (Newman 1988, 17–18). Both Tooker and Newman limited their anti-influence position to previously published research within the narrow confines of their related disciplines. They oversimplified the problems of American unity and the evolution of the democracy idea that became the foundation of the U.S. Constitution. For example, Johansen and Grinde contended that Tooker "does not . . . address the factual evidence of Iroquois and American interaction, from sending of wampum belts to Iroquois sachems by the Sons of Liberty in 1776 to the lodging of the Iroquois on the second floor of the Pennsylvania State House (Independence Hall) in May and June of 1776" (Johansen and Grinde 1990, 64).

It is generally recognized that the great European political philosophers of the eighteenth century, John Locke and Jean-Jacques Rousseau, were inspired by the free-spirited societies and governments of the

American Indians (Hyams 1990). Locke spent a great deal of time studying aboriginal societies, and through his observations formulated the idea that within a state of nature no man has more power or rights than another; nature's law teaches that people are equal and independent and that no one is to harm another's life, liberty, and possessions. (A key phrase in an early draft of the U.S. Declaration of Independence read "life, liberty, and the pursuit of *property*," but was later substituted with "life, liberty, and the pursuit of *happiness*.") Locke taught that the establishment of government requires a social contract, that a man should not be governed by another without his consent, and government must function under the dictates of the majority. Clearly, Locke's political philosophy bears no resemblance to the monarchial governments of Europe existing in his day, but coincides more closely with the ideas of Deganawidah and the Great Law of Peace. Rousseau was greatly influenced by Locke's ideal democracy concept, although his idea of democracy even more closely mirrored that of the Iroquois. He substituted Locke's direct government idea with one more representative in nature.

Among the many facts in the historical record that support Grinde's and Johansen's influence thesis regarding the Iroquois that were overlooked or ignored by the anti-influence anthropologists and ethnohistorians are the following: In 1744 the Iroquois sachem Canassatego advised the competing English colonies to unite as had the Iroquois nations under their Law of the Great Peace. Canassatego symbolically broke one arrow, then bound a handful to illustrate how difficult it was to break several at a time. He advised the colonists to unite, as the Iroquois nations had done centuries earlier, because in unity there is strength. Today, on the United States' Great Seal and on the back of the dollar bill, the eagle (sacred to the Iroquois and a symbol of their Pine Tree Confederacy) clutches a bundle of thirteen arrows, signifying the original thirteen colonies. Benjamin Franklin, who was quite familiar with the Iroquois League, popularized this image. Indeed, Franklin attended many of the early treaty councils and negotiations, and published the proceedings. "The proceedings of the Lancaster treaty council (and many others) were printed, bound, and sold by Franklin between 1736 and 1762. Franklin used the imagery of 'Join or die' in one of the continent's first editorial cartoons in 1754. Several months earlier, Franklin had attended an Iroquois condolence ceremony (a key ritual in understanding the Iroquois League) at a treaty conference in Carlisle, Pennsylvania" (Johansen and Grinde 1990, 65).

Most important, Franklin was heavily influenced by the Iroquois Confederacy when he proposed the Albany plan of union to the colonists in 1754, at a meeting which the Iroquois attended. "The Albany Plan was an early experiment with a federal system—states within a state. The only practicing examples of such a system at that time were the Iroquois and other Native American confederacies" (Johansen and Grinde 1990, 65). This became the model for the Articles of Confederation, which was authored by Franklin and others. Later, in May and June of 1776, the Iroquois chiefs were lodged on the second floor of the Pennsylvania State House in Philadelphia when the Declaration of Independence was framed. The Iroquois sachems attended the deliberations weekly, while yet other Indians camped on the State House lawn.

The influence of the Six Nations Iroquois Confederacy in the evolution of American democracy is irrefutable. Benjamin Franklin's experience with the Iroquois was woven into his development of revolutionary theory and a federation of free states, or federal union. The Confederacy and its Great Law of Peace or constitution contained many democratic principles we recognize today, but which at the time, especially with respect to the English monarchy and the autocratic kingdoms of Europe, were absent from the world scene. Among these democratic concepts are a bicameral legislature with senators and representatives, women's suffrage, right of popular nomination, right of recall, and the idea for equal representation of political units (nations or states) which differ in population and power.

The separation of powers inherent in the political system of the Confederacy also influenced the thinking of the American founding fathers. The Onondaga, led by Tadadaho the Firekeeper, represented the executive function. The legislative branch was divided into two parts. The Mohawk and Seneca, united as Elder Brothers, formed the upper house similar to the U.S. Senate, while the Oneida and Cayuga comprised the Younger Brothers, similar to the House of Representatives. The noted authority on American Indian law, Felix Cohen, concluded that the League was a model for our own federal system in the United States. "It is out of a

Onondaga Sachem giving John Hancock an Iroquois name at Independence Hall.

rich Indian democratic tradition that the distinctive political ideals of American life emerged. Universal suffrage for women as for men, the pattern of states within a state we call federalism, the habit of treating chiefs as servants of the people instead of their master, the insistence that the community must respect the diversity of men and the diversity of their dreams—all these were part of the American way of life before Columbus landed" (quoted in Johansen 1982, 13).

Other founders besides Franklin who were influenced by the example of the Iroquois confederacy include George Washington, Tom Paine, Thomas Jefferson, John Rutledge, John Adams, and Richard Henry Lee. Paine greatly admired the Iroquois political system, and Jefferson was a serious student of American Indian societies, doing seminal work in both Indian archaeology and linguistics. Rutledge, who chaired the committee for writing the Constitution, like Franklin, was a confirmed "Indian buff." In

fact he "mentioned some American Indian ideas to the Constitutional Convention's drafting committee" (Johansen and Grinde 1990, 70; see also Berkey 1992, and Grinde 1992).

For the colonists, the personal freedom of Indian societies like the Iroquois became a symbol in their protests against British tyranny. This was especially true with the tea tax and explains why the protesters dressed as Mohawk Indians when they dumped English tea into the Boston harbor in the revolutionary Tea Party. To understand the extensive influence of Indian societies on the colonists along the eastern seaboard during the colonial period, Johansen and Grinde suggest that we place ourselves in the colonists' shoes. The colonists were "relatively small groups of immigrants, or sons and daughters of immigrants, on small islands of settlements surrounded, at least for a time, by more widespread American Indian confederacies with whom they traded, socialized, and occasionally made war for almost two centuries before the Constitution was ratified" (Johansen and Grinde 1990, 70).

Nevertheless, by late 1988, in spite of the impressive evidence supporting the Iroquois influence thesis, some of which is described above, the debate continued. The anti-influence academicians leveled their attack on an educational resource guide that was being developed by the Iroquois for the state of New York. On the "influence" side of the argument were Johansen, Grinde, Deloria, Barreiro, and the traditional Haudenosaunee chiefs. On the other side were the "Fentonites," scholars associated with Iroquoianist William Fenton. They included, among others, Jack Campisi, associate professor of anthropology at Wellesley College, Hazel W. Hertzberg, professor of history and education at Columbia University, Laurence Hauptman, professor of history at the State University of New York, William A. Starna, professor and chairman of anthropology at SUNY, College at Oneonta, and James Axtell, professor of history at William and Mary College. The attack and debate is recounted by Grinde and Johansen in the 1990 aforementioned Commentary in the *American Indian Culture and Research Journal*, and more recently in a collaborative work by Johansen, Grinde, and Mann, *Debating Democracy: Native American Legacy of Freedom* (Johansen and Grinde 1990; Johansen, Grinde, and Mann 1998).

The debate was nearly joined later at an annual meeting of the American Society for Ethnohistory. Grinde was originally listed as a discussant on a panel by Axtel in a preliminary program along with Tooker and Fenton, but was removed from the final program. Finally, in May 1989, a real debate took place between the opposing parties at the Kemt Atwater Museum in Philadelphia. At one point, during a face-to-face debate,

> Grinde asked Tooker, the ethnohistorian, . . . whether she was familiar with the historical documents he was citing. For example, he asked, "Have you ever read John Adams's *Defence of the Constitution . . . of the United States*?" Published in 1787, Adams's *Defence* was a lengthy handbook used by delegates to the Constitutional Convention. In the *Defence*, Adams comments on Native American governments as well as those of Europe. He urges American leaders to investigate "the government . . . of modern Indians" because the separation of powers in them "is marked with a precision that excludes all controversy." Adams believed that studying "the legislation of the Indians . . . would be well worth the pains." He observes that "some of the great philosophers . . . of the age" sought to "establish governments

[like] modern Indians." He also commented on "the individual independence of the Mohawks." (Johansen and Grinde 1990, 77–78)

At yet another conference, in October of 1989, feminist historian and biographer, Sally Roesch Wagner, broadened the debate by documenting the influence of Iroquois matrilineality and women-focused society on the suffragettes, as evidenced in the writings of Matilda Josylyn Gage and Elizabeth Cady Stanton. The early feminists' decision to petition for suffrage and assert women's rights resulted from their interaction with the Iroquois, according to Wagner. In 1991, Grinde and Johansen coauthored *Exemplar of Liberty*, in which they restated and enlarged their documentation for the Iroquois influence (Grinde and Johansen 1991). Then, in 1992, Oren Lyons and John Mohawk brought out a definitive collective volume, *Exiled in the Land of the Free*. An annotated bibliography, *Native American Political Systems and the Evolution of Democracy*, which was published by Johansen on the entire affair in 1996, and then also a supplemental bibliography brought out in 1999 (Johansen 1996; 1999).

Although the evidence for the Iroquois contribution to the evolution of American democracy appears to be indisputable, its detractors have not entirely given up their academic turf war. Vine Deloria characterized this state of affairs with the following piece of sarcasm:

> In the last few years there has been a tremendous battle over the degree to which the Six Nations might have influenced the thinking of the Constitution's fathers. Here we have seen the anthros show their true colors. No sooner was the subject raised than a bevy of anthros, lacking even a rudimentary knowledge of the historical papers, charged into the fray spouting a confusing conglomerate of anthropological concepts that made no sense at all. Advocates of the Indian position have found themselves rejected for National Endowment for the Humanities grants, been denied positions at colleges and universities, and seen well-documented books rejected by university presses that feared the wrath of prominent figures in anthropology. (Deloria 1997, 213)

It would be a mistake, however, to view the debate as merely personal, that is, between personalities. Rather, it illustrates the power relationships in academe between the methodology of the older, established disciplines of anthropology and ethnohistory and that of the newer paradigm of Native American Studies. There is also the challenge being made by traditional Indian leaders to non-Indian academicians in telling and interpreting Iroquois history.

Grinde sums up the Iroquois influence theory and debate in the following way: "In denying Iroquois influence upon the American government, academics, and particularly historians, do so despite documentary and oral traditions that clearly indicate a firm connection between Iroquois political theory and American instruments of Government" (Lyons and Mohawk 1992, 228).

IROQUOIS CULTURE AND SOCIETY

Another part of our story concerning the remarkable Iroquois involves the *death* and *rebirth* of their traditional culture and society. As we related earlier in this chapter, by the time of the American Revolution the old Iroquois culture was rapidly disintegrating and the Confederacy ended. It was at this time, or shortly thereafter, that a religious prophet appeared who preached a message of hope and revitalization of the Iroquois world; it became known as the Code of Handsome Lake. Before relating this part of the Iroquois story, however, we are compelled to sketch a brief picture of Iroquois culture and society as it existed before catastrophe struck.

The homeland of the Six Nations Iroquois, with its lakes, mountains, hills, river systems, and valleys became "the Indians' corridors of trade, war, and peace and for Europeans became the avenues of exploration and western expansion. The Iroquois were strategically located to exploit the geopolitics of the region" (Fenton 1978, 297).

Throughout Iroquois country there were deciduous birch, beech, maple, and elm forests, with coniferous pine and hemlock giving way in the north to fir and spruce. Along the Hudson River were found oak, chestnut, and yellow poplar. Elsewhere were huge sycamore, walnut, hickory, sugar maple, American elm, and white pine. Many of the trees or their products were used in Iroquois technology or for food. Elm bark, for example, was important for shelter, containers, and cooking vessels, and birch was used to cover canoes and shingle lodges. Over two hundred plants were used for medicine. Deer, bear, and small mammals inhabited the forests within a day's travel from Iroquois villages, and huge flights of migratory birds, both waterfowl and passenger pigeons, were available food sources. Yet, the Iroquois are best known for their horticulture, especially the *three sisters*, the food staples of corn,

beans, and squash. Women were the cultivators, and they also collected roots, berries, greens, and nuts. Fishing was another important subsistence activity. Hunting, warfare, and attending council meetings were the special province of men. After the fall harvest, hunting parties hunted deer and bear, dried the meat, and packed it home for midwinter.

Before the fur trade decimated the beaver, and to an extent the deer also, the Iroquois showed "respect for the animals they hunted by not throwing their bones to the dogs, by placing skinned carcasses in the crotch of a tree rather than throwing them to the ground, and by sacrificing the first deer to birds of prey" (Fenton 1978, 298). Berry picking, especially the wild strawberries, was another food source, and the annual strawberry festival is an important ceremonial occasion even today. Indian tobacco was grown to a certain extent. Survival foods include the wild onion and the groundnut, or wild potato.

"The typical northern Iroquoian settlement was a cluster of thirty to 150 longhouses surrounded by a palisade, and situated on a height of land accessible to drinking water and not too far removed from a navigable waterway" (Fenton 1978, 306). Family crests of birds, mammals, or reptiles were displayed on the gabled ends of the lodges. The villages of up to 1,500 persons were surrounded by cultivated fields. Women planted, cultivated, and harvested in work parties directed by a senior matron. These important activities were ritually observed in the Green Corn and Harvest festivals.

William Fenton (1978, 300) writes that Iroquois life was marked by "ecological time," "a diurnal round, a yearly round, a duodecennial village movement, and a lifetime of activity." People retired early and were up to meet the dawn; meals were whenever one was hungry. In the 1970s, food was still apportioned at ceremonies according to ritual protocol. "Ecological time is most apparent in the yearly round of activity that synchronized a hunting and gathering cycle with a maize cycle" (Fenton 1978, 300). A lunar calendar was divided into four seasons and marked by a cycle of ceremonies, including a great ceremony at midwinter, and a lesser one in late summer for gathering in the crops. This annual cycle is still followed today.

After taking in the crops, the people took to the forests to hunt and did not return to their villages until the winter solstice. "On the fifth night of the next moon occurred the great midwinter festival held to reveal new dreams and to renew old dreams and fulfill ceremonial obligations so revealed. . . . Two moons from the moon of midwinter, they repaired to the maple groves to tap trees, to gather sap, and to boil it down to syrup and sugar" (Fenton 1978, 300–1). There were also forays for taking passenger pigeons and squabs, and then fish. Then it was time to plant the blessed seed of the "three sisters," corn, beans, and squash.

Iroquois communities apparently varied, in former times as well as now, in the number of ceremonies observed. There are at least six: the Midwinter Ceremony in January or February; Thanks-to-the-Maple in late February or March when the sap started to rise; the Corn Planting Festival in May or June; the Strawberry Festival in June; the Green Corn Ceremony late in August or September; and the Harvest Festival in October.

"The Berry Moon (June) is still remembered for the strawberry, and in the 1970s the strawberry festival in the Seneca Longhouses calls for the preaching of Handsome Lake's message in commemoration of his vision. The Little Water Medicine Society still meets on the fifth night of the new moon to sing over bundles that the holders bring to the meeting and to renew the strength of the 'great good medicine'" (Fenton 1978, 301).

Many different rituals are performed at these festivals. For example, the Iroquois are known for their elaborately carved masks used in the Faces Society to drive out witches and disease, and to cure illness. The Thunder rite invocation is a prayer that asks the Thunders, "our grandfathers," to water the "three sisters." When the corn is ready, the harvesting of the crops is celebrated. "Autumn was the great season for councils. It was also the time when men were free to go on the warpath" (Fenton 1978, 301).

Iroquois society is viewed as a body of relatives ("my people") who are residents of a place or village. They include "grandfathers of old," the founders; chiefs (sachems or lords)"; "women, our mothers, who really count"; as well as the age-grades [i.e., child, youth, young adult, etc.] (Fenton 1978, 315). Kinship is matrilineal and women have a great deal of influence in Iroquois society. This is especially the case for the clan matron or mother. The oldest female in the extended family residence or longhouse occupies a prestigious and dominant position.

Political organization started at the level of village government with a headman and a local council.

The clans had their separate councils; but an *ad hoc* village council of ranking clan chiefs, elders, and wise men made local policy. In a sense, the same thing happened at the national and League levels. Clan chiefs had their offices and titles ascribed in specific maternal families or households, which were segments of clans, and the ranking matrons of that lineage presided over the caucuses that nominated, censured, or recalled them. The holders of these titles were tribal chiefs and they represented their village and nation in the General Council of the League. They enjoyed great prestige but had little power. (Fenton 1978, 314)

There are also civil leaders among whom are war leaders and Pine Tree chiefs. These statuses are achieved in warfare, or for council oratory, and their titles are not hereditary. The positions are honorary and carry no voting power. They include also the Speaker for the Women, and the Speaker for the Warriors.

Even the sachems employed a speaker to announce decisions reached in committee. He was chosen for his ability to grasp principle and fact, for his rhetorical gifts, and for an enormous memory in a society in which all men and women were walking archives. His presence had a powerful effect on history, since the speaker is often identified by colonial recorders when the decision makers are not. . . . To this day Iroquois councils prefer to reach consensus quietly in committee, they reluctantly vote openly in public, and the gifted speaker still exerts influence. Quiet men and women in the background are the real decision makers. (Fenton 1978, 314–15)

The warrior role in Iroquois society was considered an honorable one and was the special province of the young men. Even so, the Iroquois strove to maintain a balance between peace and war. War could be a deliberative decision by the elders and chiefs that was decided in council, or it could be a *little war*, or blood feud vendetta, by which the young men achieved glory in battle without council sanction. The elders and chiefs could only exercise the power of persuasion to keep the young men from a private or little war. Much of the practice of warfare among the Iroquois was ritualistic in nature. An indirect function of warfare was the obligation to replace Iroquois members of one's extended family and kin group by adopting prisoners taken in battle. It is because of internecine warfare, including, it is said, cannibalism and the torture ritual, that Deganawidah, the Law Giver, "brought a message of peace—that all men are brothers, that killing, scalping, and cannibalism should cease, and that the 'great immutable law' should restore civil society" (Fenton 1978, 315).

The influence of Iroquois women in Iroquois society is important to note. The traditional Iroquois are a horticulturally based, matrilineal society. Social scientists have noted the relatively high status of women in this kind of Indigenous society. For the Iroquois, the additional factors of warfare and the absence of men from home are believed to have placed women, especially elder women, in a powerful role. "Women's power was rooted in a predominantly female organization of domestic life and agricultural labor; men spent long periods away from home hunting or warring, and women worked together, controlled the distribution of foodstuffs, decided on marriages, and generally dominated community concerns" (Leacock 1972 [1884], 34: Rosaldo and Lamphere 1974, 37).

Social Organization

The kinship system is the linchpin of Iroquois social organization, and it became the structural basis of the Great Law and confederate government as taught by Deganawidah and Hiawatha. This political system of a council-kin state existed for hundreds of years until its demise at the end of the eighteenth century. Then it was revived through the religious revitalization movement led by Handsome Lake. We may therefore speak of the birth, death, and rebirth of the Six Nations Iroquois Confederacy.

Traditional social organization still largely operates today, although it is missing several of the original clan chiefs. The Akwesasne Mohawks, for example, have a traditional council that does its business in the Mohawk language.

There are two basic principles of Iroquois social organization: social units based on nation or territory, and social units based on kinship; together they form the fabric of Iroquois government. In the time before Europeans, the territorial unit started with the extended lodge or *longhouse*, a physical residential structure. This ancient longhouse or residence of the Iroquois extended family was fifty or sixty yards long, and twelve yards wide, with a passage down the middle. An Iroquois town might have fifty of these structures. In each longhouse a senior woman, or clan mother, would reside with her female kin, their husbands and children, perhaps forty to one hundred people altogether.

At the next level, the individual *village* was comprised of a cluster of longhouses with their extended families. The *nation* (Mohawk, Oneida, Onondaga, etc.) consisted of a number of villages within tribal territory, and with the inhabitants speaking a similar Iroquoian dialect. Finally, the *Grand Council* was a confederacy of villages from each of the constituent nations that met annually in the autumn in the heart of the Onondaga Nation.

Each nation had its own separate territory, located from east to west along the Finger Lakes in what is now upstate New York and along the Canadian border. The Iroquois considered their entire Confederacy territory a great longhouse, and this metaphor along with the appropriate kinship terms and their relationships dominated Confederacy protocol and discourse. The Mohawk were in charge of Confederacy defense as *keepers of the Eastern Door*, the Seneca as *keepers of the Western Door*, with the Onondaga, who were located in the central part of Confederacy territory, as the *firekeepers*.

Cross-cutting these territorially based political units are the matrilineal kinship units in which blood ties are traced through a woman's side of the family. The longhouse was under the authority of the clan mother, usually the oldest female member. Joining the single clan affiliation of the female residents would be the different clan affiliations of the married men. All personal relationships were governed by these kinship statuses. The *hearth* included a mother and her children. Each hearth was part of a wider kin unit called an *otiianer*, and two or more *otiianers* constituted a *clan*. Clans and nations were also grouped into two *moieties* or *sides*. "One or more clans constituted a moiety and acted together as if their memberships were indeed siblings. In an Iroquoian community and tribe there are usually two such moieties. Their functions are mainly ceremonial, since they act reciprocally to condole and bury each other's dead and to perform games and other ritual acts. . . . Frequently, as among the Seneca, there are clans named for birds and the deer grouped on one side, and other mammals and the turtle on the other. . . . At the level of the League two similar moieties of tribes carry out symbolic functions" (Fenton 1978, 310).

Political relationships in the Confederacy are also expressed in kinship terms. For example, the Mohawk, Onondaga, and Seneca comprise the Three Brothers, or Elder Brothers, which is symbolically the Male principle or the Father side. The second moiety originally comprised the Oneida and Cayuga, and later included the Tuscarora and Delaware and other adopted Indian nations. They are now known as the Younger Brothers, or Four Brothers, and represent the Female principle in nature, or the *offspring*. "The two sides [moieties] condole each other's dead chiefs and installing their successors in the Condolence Council" (Fenton 1978, 311).

Each level of Iroquois political organization—the village, tribe or nation, and confederacy—had its special functions. The town or village "decided local issues like the use of nearby hunting lands, the location of houses and cornfields, movement to another site, the acceptance or rejection of visions, and the raising of war parties" (Wallace 1969, 39). It was governed by a village chiefs' council with a chairman or headman and representatives from each of the clans. The council met in the ceremonial longhouse in the presence of the warriors and the women and were guided by consensus. The tribal or national or Grand Council apparently met only occasionally. Its membership included the chiefs of all the village councils, and it dealt with decisions relating to war or peace, and later in history, the sale of lands.

The Grand Council

At the top of the political pyramid was the Grand Council of the Confederacy which met annually in the autumn at Onondaga. The meetings of the council were held in the presence of the assembled people. Every Iroquois could speak, but the council alone decided. The Confederacy clan chiefs discussed "crucial issues affecting the welfare of all the tribes: major wars and peacemakings and alliances; the sale of confederate territory; policy in matters of trade, religion, and relations with the whites; internal disputes that might threaten peace and good order" (Wallace 1969, 40). "The Great League itself was in philosophy and in practice an inward-looking, harmony-maintaining body" (Wallace 1969, 41). In addition to the forty-nine sachems, two Mohawk and Seneca, aided by their assistants, were appointed as war chiefs. They had the duty to protect the Confederacy from its enemies by organizing war parties in the event of a major threat.

The number of the chiefs representing their respective clans varied, depending on the size and importance of the clans, but since consensus rather than majority rule was the principle, this posed no problem. There were originally at least eight clans, although the Mohawk and Oneida had only three of them. The early ethnologist Lewis Henry Morgan and his Seneca interpreter-assistant, Ely S. Parker, recorded the clan representation, termed *sachems*, in the Grand Council of the Confederacy in 1851 as described in Table 2.1 (Morgan n.d. [1877], 132–33; see also Fenton 1978, 313).

Morgan explains that two of the sachemships on the Grand Council have been filled only once in the Confederacy's history. Apparently, these are the titles held by Deganawidah and Hiawatha (Tooker 1978, 424–25). The two Mohawk clan leaders had requested that upon their demise, their positions should remain thereafter vacant. "At all councils for the investiture of sachems their names are still called with the others as a tribute of respect to their memory. The general council, therefore, consisted of but forty-eight members" (Morgan n.d. [1877], 133–34). Elisabeth Tooker, an ethnohistorian, reports that even today in the official Roll Call of Iroquois Chiefs, "since no successor was ever appointed to Deganawida's position, his name does not appear on the list of the 50 chiefs of the League. . . . The second name on this list is Hiawatha, but it remains a position unfilled" (Tooker 1978, 424). Thus, in reality, there are only forty-eight chiefly positions filled.

Political representation was carefully balanced within each Iroquois nation to reflect kinship relations.

Multiple chieftainships are associated with a single town. The Mohawks had three towns, each identified with a clan, but each of these clans had three chieftainships, each belonging to a segment, lineage, or household.

TABLE 2.1 Sachemships of the Iroquois Nations

	Mohawk	Oneida	Onondaga	Cayuga	Seneca	TOTAL
CLANS						
Bear	3	3	3	2	1	12
Wolf	3	3	1	1	1	9
Turtle	3	3	5	2	2	15
Beaver	-	-	1	0	0	1
Deer	-	-	3	1	0	4
Snipe	-	-	1	2	3	6
Heron	-	-	0	2	0	2
Hawk	-	-	0	0	1	1
TOTAL	**9**	**9**	**14**	**10**	**8**	**50**

Moreover, with but a single town Oneida had precisely the same distribution of chieftainships among the same three clans resident within the same palisade. Onondaga, one main town and one satellite, had 14 chieftainships. The ten Cayuga chiefs were distributed among three villages, the eight Seneca chiefs in two great towns and two small ones. Factors other than locality were obviously at work. (Fenton 1978, 309)

Today, in the ritualistic Roll Call of Chiefs for the Confederacy in New York State, the kinship and tribal relationships among the sachems and their assigned functions within Confederacy transactions are clearly defined.

Among both Mohawks and Oneidas, the Turtle and Wolf clans composed one moiety and the Bear clan alone the other moiety. However, they differed in regard to the clan designated as firekeepers. Among the Mohawks the Turtle chiefs served as firekeepers, but among the Oneidas, the Wolf chiefs were the firekeepers of the tribal council.

. . . The names of the three Mohawk Turtle chiefs, the firekeepers, are enumerated first; then the three Wolf chiefs, "siblings" of the Turtle clan as they are in the same moiety; and finally the three Bear chiefs, "cousins" to the Turtle and Bear chiefs of the opposite moiety. Next are listed the chiefs of the Oneidas again beginning with the firekeepers, in this instance the chiefs of the Wolf clan. Next are enumerated the chiefs of the Turtle clan, "siblings" of the Wolf chiefs as they are members of the same moiety. Finally, the three chiefs of the Bear clan, "cousins" of the chiefs of the Wolf and Turtle clans of the opposite moiety. (Tooker 1978, 426)

Morgan reports that the councils of the League in the 1800s were of three kinds: civil, mourning, and religious. "Their civil councils . . . were such as convened to transact business with foreign nations, and to regulate the internal administration of the Confederacy. The mourning councils . . . were those summoned to 'raise up' sachems to fill vacancies . . . and also to ratify the investiture of such chiefs as the nations had raise up in reward of public services. Their religious councils . . . were, as the name imports, devoted to religious observances" (Morgan 1962 [1851], 108–9).

The Iroquois name for the civil councils means *advising together* and is based on the unanimity principle. Each of the Iroquois nations had the power to convene a meeting of the Grand Council.

If the envoy of a foreign people desired to submit a proposition to the sachems of the League, and applied [for example] to the Senecas for that purpose, the sachems of that nation would first determine whether the question was of sufficient importance to authorize a

council. If they arrived at an affirmative conclusion, they immediately sent out runners to the Cayugas, the nation nearest in position, with a belt of wampum. This belt announced that . . . a council of the League would assemble. The Cayugas then notified the Onondagas, they the Oneidas, and these the Mohawks. Each nation, within its own confines spread the information far and wide; and thus, in a space of time astonishingly brief, intelligence of the council was heralded from one extremity of their country to the other. It produced a stir among the people in proportion to the magnitude and importance of the business to be transacted. . . . Sachems, chiefs and warriors, women, and even children, deserted their hunting grounds and woodland seclusions and taking the trail, literally flocked to the place of the council (Morgan 1962 [1851], 109–10).

The fifty *royaneh* (actually forty-eight lords or sachems) of the Grand Council were all clan chiefs who were selected from their respective nations. By tradition they were always men, but they were nominated by the clan mothers and could be removed by them as well. The sachems were required to be of one mind; "[u]nanimity was a fundamental law. The idea of majorities and minorities were entirely unknown." (Morgan 1962 [1851], 111). In their deliberations the sachems represented both their respective clans (bear, turtle, deer, snipe, etc.) and their nations (Mohawk, Oneida, Onondaga, etc.). Unanimity was reached by a series of small caucuses until consensus on an issue was reached.

In a meeting of the Confederacy, the Mohawk sachems would deliberate an issue, reach consensus, and pass their decision to the Seneca who had also undertaken a similar deliberation. Once the two nations reached agreement they would "throw the matter across the fire" to the Younger Brothers, the Oneida and the Cayuga. These two nations had, of course, followed a similar procedure. Once the four nations reached consensus, the Onondaga, Firekeepers, acting as a sort of Supreme Court and Executive, would iron out differences and rule on the issue procedurally, thereby legitimizing the decision of the Confederacy.

We saw in Table 2.1 that sachemships, Confederacy representation by nation and by clan, varied considerably. The Turtle clan had fifteen representatives whereas the Beaver and Hawk had only one each; the Onondaga Nation was represented by fourteen sachems, but the Seneca had only eight. And so on. This was not a problem, however, because deliberation on a given issue was done by a process of reaching consensus. First, the respective clan leaders within each nation debated the issue at hand until a unanimous decision was reached. "No sachem was permitted to express an opinion in council, until he had agreed with the other sachem or sachems of his class [clan]. Thus the eight Seneca sachems, being in four classes [clans], could have but four opinions; the ten Cayuga sachems but four. In this manner each class [clan] was brought to unanimity within itself. A cross-consultation was then held between the four sachems who represented the four classes; and when they had agreed, they appointed one of their number to express their resulting opinion, which was the answer of their nation" (Morgan 1962 [1851], 112). Following a similar protocol, the five (later, six) nations took up the matter. The Younger Brothers, i.e., the Cayugas and Oneidas, debated the matter until agreement was reached. The Elder Brothers, i.e., the Mohawks and the Senecas, did the same. Once unanimity had been reached among these nations, the matter was referred to the Firekeepers, the Onondaga, for ratification. (See Figure 2.2.)

Despite the apparent influence of Iroquois political concepts on the thinking of the founders in their construction of the political system of the United States, there were important differences. The Iroquois emphasis on consensus rather than on majority vote eliminated the inherent conflict in having a disgruntled minority in decision-making. Another important difference was the personalistic, kinship basis of Iroquois government in contrast to the secular, formal nature of the U.S. political system. The Confederacy has aptly been described as a council-kin state. The nature and organization of confederate government was so constructed that an Iroquois child who understood the family and clan relationships in the longhouse at the local level would also have a rudimentary knowledge of the structure and function of Iroquois government at the national (tribal) and confederacy levels of political organization.

In many ways the matrilineal clan is the social glue of the Confederacy despite territorial or national (tribal) differences. Matrilineality means that kinship is determined through women only, rather than bilaterally (through both father's and mother's sides) as with non-Indian Americans. Indian historian Donald Grinde reports that:

All authority sprang from the various clans that comprised the nation. The women who headed these clans appointed the male delegates and deputies who spoke for the clans at tribal meetings. And after consultation with the clan, issues and questions were formulated and subsequently debated in council. Iroquois political philosophy was rooted in the concept that all life is unified spiritually with the natural environment and forces. Furthermore, the Iroquois believed that the spiritual power of one person is limited, but when combined with other individuals in the hearth, *otiianer*, or clan, spiritual power is enhanced. (Grinde 1992, 236).

Because the clan relationship is always through the female line, women have a high position in Iroquoian society. The relatively high status of Iroquois women is also explained in the following way: Men's social roles before White contact were exclusively hunting, warfare, and diplomacy, all of which kept them away from their households for long periods of time. Thus it was left to the women to manage the local economy and politics by themselves during the times that men were absent. In terms of Iroquois traditions, women exercised political power in three main areas of culture: First, it was the senior women who nominated successor clan leaders and chiefs to the Confederacy Council. Second, in the village and tribal town meetings, while the male chiefs did the formal speaking, it was the women who "caucused behind the scenes and lobbied with the spokesmen" (Wallace 1969, 29). And third, it was women who had the power "to demand publicly that a murdered kinsman or kinswoman be replaced by a captive from a non-Iroquois tribe, and her male relatives . . .

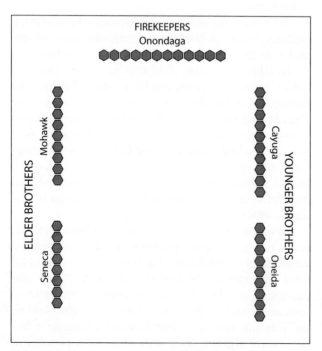

Figure 2.2 The seating pattern of the Grand Council.

were morally obligated to go out in a war party to secure captives. . . . In sum, Iroquois women were entitled formally to select chiefs, to participate in consensual politics, and to start wars" (Wallace 1969, 28–29). Women could also stop wars, adopt, or condemn prisoners.

In terms of social structure, the Iroquois were what sociologist Duane Champagne terms a structurally non-differentiated (segmentary) society, because their economic, political, and major cultural institutions were overshadowed by a strong lineage and clan system (Champagne 1983). This kinship system became the foundation upon which the larger political confederacy was formed. This was the great strength of the Confederacy, but at the same time it became its Achilles heel when it found itself under assault by American political and economic forces following the Revolutionary War.

THE CODE OF HANDSOME LAKE

In 1799, a Seneca prophet emerged by the name of Handsome Lake. He called on the discouraged Iroquois to repent of their sins, return to the old traditions, but at the same time adapt to the new challenges by adopting some Christian beliefs. This was during a time of crisis for the Iroquois. With the collapse of the old Confederacy and serious population decline, the various Iroquois nations had been compelled to sell most of their lands, and the small reservation communities that were left had become "slums in the wilderness" (Wallace 1969, 184). His teaching are called *Gaiwiio*, the Code of Handsome Lake, a kind of New Testament to the old religion. Most of the contemporary members of the hereditary chief councils are today followers of the Code of Handsome Lake.

As a young man and warrior, Handsome Lake had participated in the French and Indian War (1755–59), Pontiac's Rebellion in 1763, and the American Revolutionary War (1775–83). Although a Turtle clan sachem and a well-known medicine man, Handsome Lake is said to have become a drunkard before his spiritual conversion. In May and June of 1799, while deathly ill, he had the first of three visions. In these visions he received instructions from the Creator and was told to preach a new moral code that focused on four evil words: alcohol, witchcraft, black magic, and abortion. These evils were dividing the people and destroying Iroquois society. Wrongdoers who were guilty of these evils should confess and repent of their wickedness. As a result of

Handsome Lake's teaching, many Iroquois communities adopted the new code. Men took up agriculture and constructed family farms, and drunkenness decreased. Many people adopted the new religious teachings, which included traditional practices and beliefs, and returned to a governing council of hereditary chiefs. The oral text of the Code, written down forty years later, takes up more than a hundred printed pages.

Wallace (1969, 239–302), in his study of the Seneca, found that there are two parts to Handsome Lake's Code. The first part is an Apocalyptic Gospel that was the result of three visions. These visions, which took place from 1799 to 1801, emphasize the apocalyptic themes of sin, damnation, and the destruction of the world. Later, and increasingly until his death in 1815, Handsome Lake taught a second, or Social Gospel "which emphasizes the value in daily life of temperance, peace, land retention, acculturation, and domestic morality" (Wallace 1969, 263).

Handsome Lake lay sick and apparently dying when the first vision occurred in June 1799. This was during the time of the annual Strawberry Festival. While deathly ill, he was visited by three beings or angels dressed as Indians in ceremonial clothes. He was told that he would be spared from his sickness, and he was instructed as to the choice of medicine men to effect a cure. He was also told to carry a message to the people from the Creator, and to tell them that the ancient Strawberry Festival should always be held. The Creator's message is summarized in the four evil words mentioned earlier. "People who are guilty of doing these things must admit their wrongdoing, repent, and never sin again" (Wallace 1969, 241). His vision had a deep effect on the dispirited Iroquois.

During a second vision, he was visited by a fourth angel, dressed in sky-blue clothes and carrying a bow and arrow, who took him on a sky journey. The journey was comprised of a series of scenes, upon each of which his guide made a moral commentary. In the course of this journey he met George Washington and Jesus.

Six months later, in a third vision, Handsome Lake was told that the Great Spirit was still troubled by the condition of the Indians, and the prophet was advised to put the message of *Gaiwiiio* into a book so that everyone could remember it. "The children were to be raised in the teachings of *Gaiwiio*. Cornplanter [the brother of Handsome Lake] should visit all the towns of the Six Nations and try to bring unity among the chiefs. The people were to 'keep up their Old form of worship . . . and must never quit it,' particularly the Midwinter Ceremony . . . and the ritual leader known as 'the Minister' must not despair or turn to drink" (Wallace 1969, 248).

The first, or Apocalyptic Gospel contained "three major, interrelated themes: the imminence of world destruction; the definition of sin; and the prescription for salvation" (Wallace 1969, 249). Handsome Lake's message of confession included public communal ritual performed during traditional Iroquois ceremonies. He particularly stressed four of these traditional rituals: the Worship Dance, the Thanksgiving Ceremony, the Great Feather Dance, and the Bowl Game. The custom of having Headmen and Headwomen, and Faithkeepers officiate at these ceremonies was also embraced by the prophet. "Handsome Lake was thus not introducing a radically new religion; he was endorsing and reviving the old. He fully supported the ancient calendar of ceremonies" (Wallace 1969, 251).

In the Social Gospel of Handsome Lake, the first theme, temperance, was the main value stressed. The second tenet addressed the problems of disunity and factionalism in politics and religion. It included also the preservation of good feelings toward Whites. Ending the sale of land holdings for profit, and preserving the Indian land base was yet another theme. A fourth tenet embraced a limited acculturation to White society, especially the importance attending school and learning English. The last tenet was directed towards domestic morality, which included principles such as the duty of sons to obey their fathers, the duty of mothers not to interfere with their daughters' marriages, and the sanctity of the husband-wife relationship.

The rest of the Code contains a number of admonitions such as "a woman should be a good housewife: generous, serving food to visitors and neighbors' children, never a petty thief, always helping the orphaned of the community, and avoiding gossip. A man should 'harvest food for his family,' build a good house, and keep horses and cattle" (Wallace 1969, 284).

Handsome Lake brought a message of hope and right living, and a revival of traditional Iroquois religious practices. As a result of his teachings, a renaissance occurred on the Iroquois reservations in the years between 1799 and 1815 that began to reverse the psychological depression, social pathology, and disunity of the Haudenosaunee people following the American Revolution and the collapse of the Confederacy. In the 1830s, followers of Handsome Lake resurrected the old Confederacy in opposition to the elected chief system that was being imposed on them by White officials. Today, the Iroquois traditional chieftainship system is present on several reservations in New York (Onondaga, Tuscarora, Tonawanda Seneca, and Akwesasne Mohawk). "There, the clan mothers still nominate the chiefs of their clans, and the chiefs are brought into office through an ancient condolence ceremony" (Grinde 1994, 249).

The prophet's message became institutionalized into a church after his death, and the religion today is called the Old Way of Handsome Lake, or simply the Longhouse Religion. It is an example of a syncretic religion, that is, the result of cultural fusion; it draws from Christianity as well as from the old Iroquois religion. The new doctrine was strongly influenced by Quakers (the Religious Society of Friends), who had taken up residence and were regarded favorably by the Iroquois for their temperance, nonviolence, and frugality. "Like the Iroquois, they had no formal temples or priests; they lived frugally and communally; they practiced what they preached. Above all, they had a policy of treating Indians honestly" (Wright 1969, 232). At the same time, "Handsome Lake endorsed the ancient ritual calendar. . . . He sang and passed on the holy songs. The Great Law of the Iroquois Confederacy . . . became in effect an 'Old Testament' reinterpreted in the light of a new [Testament]" (Wright 1992, 236). It gave the dispirited Iroquois a new moral code, and it particularly encouraged Iroquois men to participate in the agricultural economy, remain abstinent, and practice family values.

In his study of the Seneca Indians and the Code of Handsome Lake, Anthony F. C. Wallace (1969) uses the term *revitalization* to signify the attempt by Native people to reconstitute cultural values and social solidarity when faced with cataclysmic changes. Other terms characterizing this phenomenon are resistance, nativistic, or millenarian movements. Among the Native peoples of North America, most of these movements are prophet-based or prophecy oriented (Talbot 1994).

Thus, through a revitalization movement the Iroquois were able to reunite around a common religious ideology that included not only a new moral code to meet the problems of Anglo-American acculturation, but also a resurgence of the Longhouse religion. Revitalization or rebirth also included the reestablishment of longhouse hereditary government, and a period of cultural renaissance that saw the revival of languages, especially Mohawk, and a rise of Iroquois nationalism. Champagne summarizes the situation. "The Iroquois Confederacy continues to be the government of the conservatives [traditionalists], and the Handsome Lake church is now a primary center of Iroquois culture. . . . The reforms of Handsome Lake provided a cultural-normative order and economic reform that enabled many Iroquois to manage the transition from an independent horticultural, hunting, and trade society to a dependent, agricultural reservation community" (Champagne 1989).

Today, the Code is partially recited twice a year on a number of Iroquois reservations in modern constructed longhouses, where the people can assemble to worship the Great Spirit in a thankful or penitent mood, and to discuss politics. At the heart of the Handsome Lake religion is the *Gaiwiio*, or "good word." This gospel is "transmitted by word of mouth from preacher to preacher and memorized so that it can be chanted by a man standing in a longhouse filled with the noise of bustling people, slamming doors, and rattling stove grates, hour after hour, for the mornings of four days" (Wallace 1969, 7). Those who recite the Code have almost a photographic memory; the techniques of verbal memory and "reading" wampum belts harks back hundreds of years in Iroquois traditions. "A Handsome Lake preacher, a 'holder of the *Gaiwiio*,' has no other responsibility than to know the 'good word' and to preach it effectively" (Wallace 1969, 16).

The Code is delivered during the Midwinter Ceremony in January or February, and during the Green Corn Dance in August or September. During these meetings, the *Gaiwiio* is recited in the mornings, the text, confessions, and exhortations in the afternoons, and social dances are held in the evenings. The annual calendar of the Old Way, however, includes also a round of older ceremonies, long antedating Handsome Lake's teachings. Prominent among these ceremonies is the June Strawberry Festival, a first fruits ceremony. A Thanksgiving ceremony is also important, taking place to thank the Creator for the fall harvest.

There are, of course, Iroquois who have converted to Christianity, and on some reservations there are sometimes sharp differences, if not animosities, between the Christian faction and the Handsome Lake followers. Where the latter are strong, the old hereditary chief councils have been restored. The Seneca at Tonawanda, Onondaga, Cayugas, and the Tuscaroras (a nonvoting member) still maintain the system of hereditary chiefs. This system was replaced in 1848 by an elective council at Allegany and Cattaraugas; two Seneca reservations, and the Mohawks, too, at St. Regis (the American side) have an elective system. The hereditary system was reinstituted among the New York Oneidas in the 1980s. Since the 1920s, the Canadian government has tried to replace the hereditary council at the Six Nations Reserve at Grand River with an elective from of government, but for the majority at Grand River, the Confederacy Council of hereditary chiefs remains the true government.

> Today there is less than a full complement of sachems in both confederacies [in Canada and the United States], and there is considerable "borrowing" of chiefs and titles. Neither confederacy is officially recognized by its respective state/province or federal government; nonetheless, they both exert considerable political influence. In New York, an express purpose of the confederacy is to extend its authority over all of the Iroquois communities, replacing the remaining elective systems with hereditary councils. (Starna, Campisi, and Hauptman, 1996, 279)

THEORY AND ANALYSIS

In the search for a theoretical explanation to explain the death and rebirth of the Six Nations Iroquois, we begin by clarifying the nature of revitalization movements.

Our brief sketch of Iroquois political history documented how the American Revolution, and the oppressive conditions that followed it, signaled an end to the Confederacy and initiated the rapid disintegration of Iroquois society and traditions. Beginning in 1799, the revelations and teachings of Handsome Lake facilitated a rebirth of the Iroquois, just as an earlier prophet, Deganawidah, had revitalized Iroquois society in a time of crisis many centuries before.

There were a number of these prophet-led revitalization movements among distressed North American Indian peoples in the seventeenth and eighteenth centuries. They arose in reaction to U.S. colonization of American Indians, and provided "spiritual solutions to the conditions of economic marginalization, political repression, and major losses of territory, as well as the ability to carry on traditional life" (Johnson, Nagel, and Champagne

1997, 10). Examples include the Delaware Prophet, the Shawnee Prophet, and the Winnebago Prophet movements of the late eighteenth and early nineteenth centuries, and the Ghost Dances of 1870 and 1890. Most of these revitalization movements were either suppressed by the U.S. military, or abandoned by their followers when a predicted cataclysmic event failed to take place.

Some revitalization movements among American Indian societies have contained a social component that enabled the new religious transformation to continue into the present, with an established church and religious adherents. The social nature of the new religion in these cases serves "to establish modified forms of community organization designed to better accommodate American-style agriculture, reservation land, and political restrictions" (Johnson, Nagel, and Champagne 1997, 11). This is the case for the Handsome Lake Church that has lasted from 1799 until today. Other revitalization movements of this type include the Delaware Big House Religion lasting from 1760 to 1910; the Kickapoo Prophet movement, 1830 to 1851; the Indian Shaker Church, 1881 to present; and the Native American (Peyote) Church, 1800s to the present (Johnson, Nagel, and Champagne 1997, 12).

In *The Death and Rebirth of the Seneca* (1969), Wallace presents an in-depth description of Handsome Lake's religious revitalization movement on the Seneca reservation. His book chronicles the decline of the Seneca Iroquois and the renaissance that followed under Handsome Lake's Code. Good description is not necessarily explanation, however. So far in this chapter we have been telling the story of the birth, death, and rebirth of the Haudenosaunee, or Six Nations Iroquois, but in social science we need also to explain the events described. Why did the powerful and highly integrated nations of the Iroquois Confederacy fragment politically at the time of the American Revolution and the entire society go into decline? And why was the outcome a religiously oriented revitalization movement instead of a secular response?

In contrast to the Iroquois, the much less solidary and amorphous Indian societies of the Southeast (the Cherokee, Creek, Choctaw, and Chickasaw) successfully survived similar Yankee political pressures, and instead of dissolving, went on to develop state-level political systems and become the much admired Five Civilized Tribes. The Cherokee, whom we feature in Chapter 6, experienced a secular rather than a religious renaissance as a result of American hegemonic pressures. Rather than going into social and cultural decline, Cherokee society responded by becoming more organizationally complex (see Chapter 6). They devised a new political structure and system of government that could better respond to U.S. motives and Indian policies. They methodically crafted an Indian republic, modeled in part on that of the United States, while at the same time preserving much of their traditional culture. These are a few of the questions we need to address.

Duane Champagne, professor of Sociology and American Indian Studies at the University of California at Los Angeles, believes that the answers to these questions may be found in the different kinds of social organization of traditional American Indian societies that gave rise to different outcomes when impacted by Anglo-American pressures. Champagne has reported on his research in a number of published articles (Champagne 1983; 1985a; 1985b; 1987; 1989). In this research he examines the contact history of American Indian societies in order to understand their varied responses to Euro-American hegemony, and he applies social differentiation theory (some critics say functional theory) to explain the different outcomes. Social differentiation refers to the extent to which the various functions of society—familial, political, economic, religious, defense and the like—have become institutionalized and distinct from one another.

The results of an early research endeavor by Champagne along this line of inquiry appeared first in a 1983 article in the *American Sociological Review*. In this article he examines the different social responses made by four Indian societies during the 1795–1860 period of U.S. Indian relations: the Delaware, Iroquois, Cherokee, and Choctaw. He found that the major social, cultural, economic, and political institutions of Cherokee and Choctaw traditional societies were relatively autonomous; they were structurally differentiated. Those of the Delaware and Iroquois had "their major cultural, political, economic and kinship institutions fused within a single institutional framework"; they were structurally non-differentiated societies. Because of the differences in traditional social organization, when confronted with Euro-American political and economic pressures, "the Cherokee and Choctaw developed state political organizations and agrarian class structures, while social change among the Delaware and Iroquois was strongly influenced by revitalization movements" (Champagne 1983, 754).

The traditional Iroquois had a mythically ordained social order, i.e., the Great Law of Peace and a kin-based Confederacy. They were also a structurally non-differentiated (or segmentary) society, because their economic, political, and cultural institutions were subordinated to, or integrated within, the kinship system. We have previously pointed out that the kinship system was the keystone of Iroquois social structure. When pressures became overwhelming during the late eighteenth and early nineteenth centuries, through the imperial wars, the fur trade, depopulation, and land loss, the Iroquois Confederacy collapsed. The Code of Handsome Lake was able to restore the old culture and the hereditary-based confederate form of government by emphasizing Iroquois salvation through a new morality and design for living.

THE IROQUOIS TODAY, CULTURAL RESTORATION

Among the more than forty thousand Iroquois now living on Iroquois reservations in New York State, Quebec, and Ontario today, there are thousands of followers of the Old Way of Handsome Lake. Handsome Lake's message of accommodation to White society, while at the same time maintaining many of the Haudenosaunee traditional ways, saw a revival in the twentieth century on the Caughnawaga and St. Regis Mohawk reservations. Today, the traditional Iroquois political system continues to operate on the Onondaga, Tuscarora, Tonawanda Seneca, and Akwesasne Mohawk Reservations in New York State. Iroquois traditions have survived and the Iroquoian languages are still spoken and are being taught to Indian and non-Indian students alike. At the same time, Iroquois men and women are integrated into the mainstream work world as iron- and steelworkers, teachers, businesspersons, artists, and poets. Yet the Iroquois have managed to preserve the traditional culture in a modern setting.

All important deliberations and rituals still take place among the traditional Iroquois in a modern longhouse building. On the Onondaga Reservation, the meetings are well attended by both reservation and urban Iroquois alike. "The great festivals and thanksgivings continue as part of their lives. They are forging a lifestyle that includes the wisdom of their ancestors and the benefits of modern technology, to create a culture in which they can live comfortably and in peace" (Grinde 1994, 63).

Since the early 1900s, the Iroquois have attempted to travel, many times successfully, under their own passports. The Confederacy opposed the 1924 Indian Citizenship Act, asserting Iroquois citizenship instead. It opposed the 1934 Indian Reorganization Act for much the same reason, and also the Selective Service Act during World War II and after, although it later declared war on the Axis as a sovereign power separate from that of the United States. It also opposed federal efforts to transfer criminal and civil jurisdiction to the state of New York, and opposed the construction of state highways into its territories. In the late 1950s, Wallace "Mad Bear" Anderson, a Tuscarora Indian, helped the Mohawk fend off a New York State income tax on the grounds of Indian sovereignty. Then in 1958, "Mad Bear" Anderson and 150 men, women, and children blocked trucks and personnel from the New York Power Authority from seizing and flooding Tuscarora lands to build a reservoir.

In the 1950s the U.S. Army Corps of Engineers, over the strong objection of the Senecas, proposed building a dam that would flood out "the entire Cornplanter Reservation in Pennsylvania and large sections of the Allegany Reservation in New York" (Graymount 1988, 116). The Kinzua dam would also break the oldest treaty signed by the United States with an Indian nation, the 1794 Treaty of Canandaigua. In spite of an extensive campaign of protest, the dam was built. "The completed dam resulted in the flooding of more than 9,000 acres of Seneca land, necessitating the removal of 130 Seneca families and the relocation of Seneca graves to a safe location" (Graymont 1988, 117). Despite receiving a monetary compensation from the government which they put to good use, the Senecas to this day keenly resent the loss of their traditional lands that were flooded by Kinzua Dam.

During the 1980s, the Confederacy in New York waged a long campaign to get the state to return important wampum belts to the Confederacy. The belts document a record of the past, and "are analogous in importance to U.S. government documents, such as the Declaration of Independence and the United States Constitution" (Grinde 1994, 64). In this struggle the traditional leaders took on anthropologists who lobbied to have the New York State Museum retain the belts instead of returning them to the Iroquois. Finally, in 1989, "the State of New York returned twelve wampum belts to the Onondagas who are holding them in their traditional role as wampum keepers of the Confederacy" (Starna,

Meeting of traditional Iroquois in the longhouse.

Campisi, and Hauptman 1996, 279). Today, as in the past, the tradition-minded Haudenosaunee use the wampum belts as a record of their laws, treaties, and other important events.

Since the 1920s the Iroquois have staged summer border crossing demonstrations into Canada to assert their right under their 1794 Jay Treaty for free and unimpeded passage across the U.S.-Canadian border. In 1968, when Canada tried to restrict the free movement of Mohawk Indians across the international border with the United States, members of the Iroquois Confederacy blocked the Cornwall International Bridge between the two countries. This protest became the subject of a documentary film, "You Are on Indian Land," that helped stimulate an era of militant protest during the New Indian Movement in the 1960s and 1970s. The 1968–69 Cornwall Bridge confrontation also brought about the creation of *Akwesasne Notes,* a national Indian newspaper, that for the next decade became the major media source for Indian Country throughout Canada and the United States. The White Roots of Peace, an Indian traveling college,

was created shortly after the Cornwall Bridge protest. It was committed to the preservation of tradition by bringing back the Great Binding Law through speaking engagements to Indian and non-Indian communities and school audiences throughout North America.

In 1972, the Mohawks who are famous for their "high steel" construction on bridges and skyscrapers reestablished the old Warrior Society. "In 1974 they occupied state land in the New York Adirondacks, proclaiming it Ganienkeh . . . a first step toward repossession of their ancient home" (Wright 1992, 329). In the 1980s, however, a split occurred between the warriors and the more traditional Iroquois over the issue of casinos at Akwesasne. "Bingo and other forms of gambling burgeoned under Warrior 'protection'" (Wright 1992, 329). The issues were complex but included the questionable use of money and guns (see Johansen 1993). Handsome Lake's message to the Iroquois had, after all, emphasized temperance and pacifism: "To profit from others' weaknesses, even in a good cause, was a sin" (Wright 1992, 330).

A long-simmering land dispute at Oka, a French Canadian resort community, broke out again in 1989. It rapidly developed into a major crisis over the issue of Iroquois sovereignty. At one point the Canadian army deployed 2,500 troops within striking distance of Mohawk communities, and tanks and helicopters were thrown against the Mohawk warriors.

In recent years the Iroquois have filed a series of land claims in New York concerning lands that were taken extra-legally in the past; the results have been mixed and the issue remains unresolved. The Iroquois, like traditional Indians throughout the United States, have a strong affinity for the small parcels (reservations) of what remains of their original homeland. "Maintaining and preserving contemporary landholdings is crucial to the continuance of their communities, culture, and identity. The reservation is a place where the Iroquois practice their customs and rituals. Many urban Iroquois return to these homelands to be culturally and spiritually refreshed among their friends and kin. The Iroquois strive to retain their sovereignty, independence, and culture in their reservation communities" (Grinde 1994, 64). Above all, despite the internal disputes that arise from time to time, the traditional Confederacy survives and the Old Religion of Handsome Lake continues to guide the Haudenosaunee in their pursuit of justice and the White Roots of Peace.

CHAPTER REVIEW

DISCUSSION QUESTIONS

1. Explain the significance of the 1977 meeting of American Indians at the European United Nations headquarters in Geneva, Switzerland.
2. What are the names of the Indian nations forming the Haudenosaunee (Iroquois) Confederacy, and where was their original homeland?
3. Explain the Iroquois Great Law of Peace, who was its founder, and why was it instituted?
4. Explain the "Iroquois influence debate." According to Native American Studies scholars Donald Grinde and Bruce Johansen, what were some of the contributions made by the Iroquois to American democracy?
5. Describe some of the features of the organization of the Grand Council of the Iroquois Confederacy.
6. What is the Code of Handsome Lake., and why was it a revitalization movement? According to Duane Champagne, why did it occur among the Iroquois when it did?
7. What is the state of the Iroquois Confederacy and traditional culture today? Give examples.

SUGGESTED READINGS

CHAMPAGNE, DUANE. 1983. "Social Structure, Revitalization Movements and State Building: Social Change in Four Native American Societies." *American Sociological Review*, 48 (December): 754–63.

EWEN, ALEXANDER, ed. 1994. *Voices of Indigenous Peoples: Native People Address the United Nations*. Santa Fe: Clear Light.

GRAYMONT, BARBARA. 1988. *The Iroquois*. New York, Philadelphia: Chelsea House.

GRINDE, DONALD A., JR., and BRUCE E. JOHANSEN. 1991. *Exemplar of Liberty: Native America and the Evolution of Democracy*. Los Angeles: UCLA American Indian Studies Center.

JOHANSEN, BRUCE E. 1998. *Debating Democracy: Native American Legacy of Freedom*. Santa Fe: Clear Light.

LYONS, OREN, JOHN MOHAWK. 1992. *Exiled in the Land of the Free: Democracy, Indian Nations, and the U.S Constitution*. Santa Fe: Clear Light, 1992.

MORGAN, LEWIS HENRY. 1962. [1851]. *League of the Iroquois*. New York: Corinth Books.

REFERENCES

AKWEKS, AREN. 1972. *Migration of the Iroquois.* Illustrations by Kahonhes. 2nd ed. Mohawk Nation at Akwesasne: White Roots of Peace.

BERKEY, CURTIS G. 1992. "United States–Indian Relations: the Constitutional Basis." In *Exiled In the Land of the Free: Democracy, Indian Nations, and the U.S. Constitution,* edited by Oren Lyons, John Mohawk, 189–225. Santa Fe: Clear Light.

CHAMPAGNE, DUANE. 1983. "Social Structure, Revitalization Movements and State Building: Social Change in Four Native American Societies." *American Sociological Review* 48 (December): 754–63.

———. 1985a. "Cherokee Social Movements: A Response to Thornton" *American Sociological Review* 50 (February): 127–30.

———. 1985b. *Strategies and Conditions of Political and Cultural Survival in American Indian Societies.* Occasional Paper 21. Cambridge, MA: Cultural Survival. Monograph.

———. 1987. "From Tribal Society to Democratic State: Political Institution Building Among the Cherokee, Choctaw, Creek and Chickasaw in the 19th Century." Paper presented at the American Sociological Association Convention in Chicago, August 19.

———. 1989. American Indian Societies: Strategies and Conditions of Political and Cultural Survival. Cultural Survival Report 32. Cambridge, MA: Cultural Survival. Monograph.

DELORIA, VINE, JR. 1997. "Conclusions: Anthros, Indians, and Planetary Reality." In *Indians and Anthropologists: Vine Deloria, Jr., and the Critique of Anthropology,* edited by Thomas Biolsi and and Larry J. Zimmerman, 209–21. Tucson: University of Arizona Press.

FENTON, WILLIAM N. 1978. "Northern Iroquoian Cultural Patterns." In *Handbook of North American Indians, vol. 15, Northeast,* volume edited by. Bruce G. Trigger, 296–321. Washington, DC: Smithsonian Institution Press.

GENTRY, CAROLE M., and DONALD A. GRINDE, JR., eds. 1994. *The Unheard Voices: American Indian Responses to the Colombian Quincentennary 1492–1992.* Conference Proceedings. Los Angeles: UCLA American Indian Studies Center.

GIBSON, ARRELL MORGAN. 1980. "Indians and the European Imperial Wars." In *The American Indian: Prehistory to Present.* Lexington, MA: D.C. Heath.

GRAYMONT, BARBARA. 1988. *The Iroquois.* New York: Chelsea House.

GRINDE, DONALD A., JR. 1977. *The Iroquois and the Founding of the American Nation.* San Francisco: Indian Historian Press.

———. 1992. "Iroquois Political Theory and the Roots of American Democracy." In *Exiled in the Land of the Free,* edited by Oren Lyons, John Mohawk, 227–80. Santa Fe: Clear Light.

———. 1994. "Native Peoples of the Northeast." In *Native America: Portrait of the Peoples,* edited by Duane Champagne, 55–74. Detroit: Visible Ink Press.

GRINDE, DONALD A., JR., and BRUCE E. JOHANSEN. 1991. *Exemplar of Liberty: Native America and the Evolution of Democracy.* Los Angeles: UCLA American Indian Studies Center.

HYAMS, MILT. 1990. "The League of Iroquois and the Motive for American Democracy." Student paper submitted for Steve Talbot's class, Native American Studies 130 B, University of California, Davis, March 15.

JOHANSEN, BRUCE E. 1982. *Forgotten Founders: Benjamin Franklin, the Iroquois and the Rationale for the American Revolution.* Ipswich, MA: Gambit.

———. 1993. *Life and Death in Mohawk County.* Golden, CO: North American Press/Fulcrum.

———. 1996. *Native American Political Systems and the Evolution of Democracy: An Annotated Bibliography.* Westport, CT: Greenwood Press.

———. 1999. *Native America and the Evolution of Democracy: A Supplemental Bibliography.* Westport, CT: Greenwood Press.

JOHANSEN, BRUCE E., and DONALD A. GRINDE, JR. 1990. Commentary: "The Debate Regarding Native American Precedents for Democracy: A Recent Historiography." *American Indian Culture and Research Journal* 14 (1): 61–88.

JOHANSEN, BRUCE E., DONALD A. GRINDE JR., and BARBARA A. MANN. 1998. *Debating Democracy: Native American Legacy of Freedom.* Santa Fe: Clear Light.

JOHNSON, TROY, JOANE NAGEL, and DUANE CHAMPAGNE, eds. 1997. *American Indian Activism: Alcatraz to the Longest Walk.* Urbana: University of Illinois Press.

LEACOCK, ELEANOR BURKE, ed. 1972 [1884]. *The Origin of the Family, Private Property and the State,* by Frederick Engels. New York: International.

LYONS, OREN, JOHN MOHAWK, eds. 1992. *Exiled in the Land of the Free: Democracy, Indian Nations, and the U.S. Constitution.* Santa Fe: Clear Light.

MACLEOD, WILLIAM CHRISTIE. 1928. Chapter 19, "The Iroquois Republic: Its Rise and Fall, 1667–1754." In *The American Indian Frontier.* New York: Alfred A. Knopf.

MANN, BARBARA A. and JERRY L. FIELDS. 1996. "A Sign in the Sky: Dating the League of the Haudesaunee." *American Indian Culture and Research Journal* 21 (3): 105–63.

MAYBURY-LEWIS, DAVID. 1997. *Indigenous Peoples, Ethnic Groups, and the State.* Boston: Allyn & Bacon.

MOHAWK, JOHN, ed. [as Akwesasne Notes, ed.], with Oren Lyons and José Barreiro. 1977. *A Basic Call to Consciousness: The Hau de no sau nee Address to the Western World.* Geneva, Switzerland.

———. 1986. "Origins of Iroquois Political Thought." *Northeast Indian Quarterly* (Summer): 16–20.

———. 1989. "International Principles of Indigenous Rights." *Daybreak* 3 (1): 14–17.

MORGAN, LEWIS HENRY. 1962 [1851]. *League of the Iroquois.* Introduction by William N. Fenton. New York: Corinth Books.

———n.d. [1877]. *Ancient Society.* Chicago: Charles H. Kerr.

MURPHY, GERALD (preparer). n.d. *The Constitution of the Iroquois Nations: The Great Binding Law, Gayanashagowa.* The Cleveland Free Net – aa300. http://www.constitution.org/cons/iroquois.htm

NEWMAN, MICHAEL. 1988. "The Iroquois and the Constitution: Founding Feathers." *New Republic* 17 (November): 17–18.

OSWALT, WENDELL H., and SHARLOTTE NEELY. 1999. *This Land Was Theirs: A Study of Native Americans.* 6th ed. Mountain View, CA: Mayfield.

ROSALDO, MICHELLE ZIMBALIST, and LOUISE LAMPHERE, eds. 1974. *Women, Culture & Society.* Stanford, CA: Stanford University Press.

SMITH, DWIGHT L. 1988. "Mutual Dependency and Mutual Trust." In *The American Indian Experience: A Profile,* edited by Philip Weeks, 49–65. Arlington Heights, IL: Forum Press.

STARNA, WILLIAM A., JACK CAMPISI, and LAURENCE M. HAUPTMAN. 1996. "Iroquois Confederacy." In *Native America in the Twentieth Century: An Encyclopedia,* edited by Mary B. Davis, 278–79. New York: Garland.

TALBOT, STEVE. 1994. "Pluralistic Religious Beliefs." In *The Native North American Almanac,* edited by Duane Champagne, 668–83. Detroit: Gale Research.

———. 2002. "Academic Indianismo: Social Scientific Research in American Indian Studies." *American Indian Culture and Research Journal* 26 (4): 67–96.

TOOKER, ELIZABETH. 1978. "The League of the Iroquois: Its History, Politics, and Ritual." In *Handbook of North American Indians, vol. 15, Northwest,* volume edited by Bruce G. Trigger, 418–41. Washington, DC: Smithsonian Institution Press.

———. 1987. "The United States Constitution and the Iroquois League." *Ethnohistory.* 35 (Fall): 305–36.

WALLACE, ANTHONY F. C. 1969. *The Death and Rebirth of the Seneca.* New York: Random House.

WALLACE, PAUL A. W. 1948. *The White Roots of Peace.* Philadelphia: University of Pennsylvania Press.

WRIGHT, RONALD. 1992. *Stolen Continents: The "New World" Through Indian Eyes.* New York: Houghton Mifflin.

GREED AND GENOCIDE
CALIFORNIA INDIANS AND THE GOLD RUSH

During the Gold Rush. Mission Indian basket with the Indians upside down. Gold nuggets placed above the basket symbolizes that gold is more important than the lives of Native people. The nuggets also symbolically create holes in the basket, further attempting to erode the Native people.

One of the last human hunts of civilization, and the basest and most brutal of them all.

—H. H. Bancroft, *History of California*

On January 24, 1848, gold was discovered on the South Fork of the American River at Coloma in California. One hundred and fifty years later, during 1998 and 1999, the State of California observed the sesquicentennial of the Gold Rush. The anniversary, however, was no cause for celebration among Californian Indians. The Spanish mission system, the seizure of California from Mexico by the United States, the influx of thousands of Anglo Forty-niners, and California statehood, all had disastrous consequences for the Indigenous peoples. In this chapter we reexamine this nineteenth century holocaust by documenting the labor exploitation, massacres, sexual assaults, treaty treachery, peonage and slavery, and environmental degradation that led to a precipitous decline of the Native population, and forced Indian identity and culture underground for a hundred years.

CHAPTER OVERVIEW: DEPOPULATION AS GENOCIDE

We begin with the story of California Indians as they were before European entry into the region. Then we describe their experience as conquered peoples under the domination of first the Spaniards, then the Mexicans, and finally the Anglo-Americans that led to their near extinction by the year 1900. The 1849 Gold Rush and the tragic events that followed are an important part of our story, because this is when the extreme genocidal abuses of the Indians occurred. As part of our discourse we also suggest analytical concepts that might assist one in making sense out of this history of oppression. Toward the end of the chapter, we return to a discussion of these concepts to see whether they can indeed explain the depredations against the Native peoples that we have documented. In the last few decades, the Indian peoples of California have been making a remarkable recovery from the tragic days of the Gold Rush. We end the chapter with their story.

The Spanish period of contact introduced a system of religious missions that began in 1769 and ended in 1821. Spanish policy was to convert the Indians to Christianity and to use Indian labor to further Spanish economic aims. The chain of twenty-one Franciscan missions that was established never expanded beyond a narrow section of the California coast, from San Francisco in the north to San Diego in the south. Nevertheless, although limited in its geographic scope, the harsh conditions of mission life resulted in the disintegration of most coastal Indian societies and a significant decline in their population. The Mexican period began in 1821 with the successful revolt by colonial Mexico against Spain, and the subsequent French invasion under Emperor Maximilian. It lasted until 1846 when the Americans were victorious at the end of the Mexican-American War. It was a time of confusion and disarray for the Indians, and it led to further depopulation. The American period commenced with the U.S. defeat of Mexico and the 1846 revolt by the *Americanos* in California. The discovery of gold in 1849, and the rush of miners and settlers that followed the discovery, completely overwhelmed the Native nations. A virulent racism was spawned in the quest for riches, and a holocaust of the California Indians was ensured.

In each of these periods of history we examine the motives, activities, and policies of the non-Indian conquerors of California's Native inhabitants. Special attention is given to the 1849 Gold Rush and the several decades that followed, because this period of California history was the most destructive of the Indians. Unlike other Indians in the Far West, Native Californians often lived and worked with Whites in the early conquest period. This was especially the case during the Spanish and Mexican periods before 1850. The Gold Rush fundamentally changed this relationship when California became marked by a precipitous Indian population decline, unique in U.S. frontier history. The decline in the Indian population of California between the years of 1770 and 1880 is represented in the following graph.

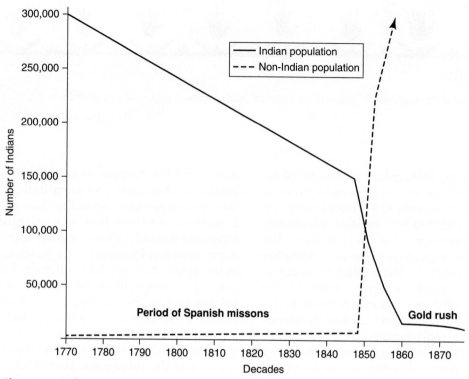

Figure 3.1 Indian and Non-Indian Population Change in California, 1770–1880.

From the graph in Figure 3.1, we see that although the Indian population went into a significant decline during both the Spanish and Mexican periods of history, it was the Anglo period, beginning with the Gold Rush, when the Native population declined almost to the point of extinction; at the same time, the non-Indian population rose dramatically. Sherburne Cook (1978, 91), an expert on California Indian demography, found that between 1770 and 1900, "the Native population experienced a fall from 310,000 to approximately 20,000, a decline of over 90 percent of the original number." The Gold Rush, far from building an independent and wealthy California under U.S. sovereignty, ushered in a period of greed and genocide that decimated the Indigenous inhabitants. The Indian population declined by an incredible 100,000 persons within a decade after the Gold Rush.

In the following pages we document the details of this great depopulation for each of the three historic periods. We also examine the question of whether the drastic population decline corroborates the charge of genocide (the annihilation of a race or ethnic group) that is made by contemporary California Indians and

their allies. (See Costo and Costo 1987; Eargle 1992; and Project Underground 1998.)

ANALYTICAL AND THEORETICAL CONCEPTS

Although it is important to tell the story of the destruction of California's Indian societies and the rapid depopulation that took place, it is even more important to understand how and why it occurred. This is the difference between description and explanation. We therefore look for analytical concepts or theories which might explain the events described in this chapter. We suggest that the genocide definition as formulated by the United Nations, and the *wilding* theory, developed by sociologist Charles Derber, could be helpful in this regard.

Genocide

In terms of world history, genocide is a modern word for an old crime. The Genocide Convention of the United Nations outlaws the committing of certain acts with intent to destroy, wholly or in part, a national, ethnic, racial, or religious group. But what many people fail to realize is that the scope of the Convention is much broader than forbidding the actual killing of such groups. The Convention also includes as genocide "the acts of causing serious bodily or mental harm; deliberate infliction of conditions of life 'calculated to bring about' physical destruction; imposing measures to prevent birth and, finally, forcibly transferring children of one group to another group" (United Nations n.d., 2). Furthermore, the definition includes not only the committing of such acts as punishable, but also conspiracy to commit genocide, direct and public incitement, attempt to commit, and complicity. The Convention further specifies that such acts are genocide whether they are committed in a time of peace or in a time of war.

The Convention on the Prevention and Punishment of the Crime of Genocide was unanimously adopted by the U.N. General Assembly on December 9, 1948, following World War II. It became international law in recognition of the crimes against humanity committed by Nazi Germany, which had adopted a program to systematically annihilate millions of people because of their religion or ethnic origin. The Nuremberg trials of Nazi war criminals, and the ensuing genocide convention, became the legal instruments of world opinion to officially declare: "Never again!"

Those nations ratifying the Genocide Convention are obligated under international law "to prevent and to punish" those guilty of genocide. Ninety-seven nations have ratified the Convention, most of them within a few years of its passage, but it was not ratified by the U.S. Senate until 1985, after almost thirty-six years of delay and intermittent debate. A *New York Times* article of October 15, 1988 reported that "some conservatives in Congress had opposed the treaty on the grounds that its definition of genocide might encourage American Indians to sue the United States Government for their suffering earlier in the nation's history and also that it might result in unsubstantiated charges being brought against the United States by present-day adversaries" (Molotsky 1988). It would have opened the United States to the charge of genocide at a time when it was criticizing the human rights record of the former Soviet Union during the Cold War. Once having ratified the Convention, the U.S. criminal code now includes penalties for genocide. "The maximum penalties are a $1 million fine and 20 years in prison for trying to cause bodily harm, attempting to cause permanent mental impairment through torture or drugs, trying to destroy a group, or trying to prevent births by members of a group" (Molotsky 1988).

Whereas genocide means to kill or to commit physical harm to a national, ethnic, racial, or religious group, the concept of ethnocide (cultural genocide) is defined as the willful destruction of a people's culture or way of life. Unlike the charge of genocide, it is seldom condemned, let alone banned under international law. "On the contrary, it is normally advocated as an appropriate policy. . . . Indigenous peoples are normally looked down upon as 'backward,' so it is presumed that their ways must be changed and their cultures destroyed, partly in order to civilize them and partly to enable them to coexist with others in the modern world" (Maybury-Lewis 1977, 9). As we discuss in this chapter, the religious mission system of the Spanish, and the so-called domestication policy under American occupation following the Gold Rush, with its forced relocation policy, reservation system, and federal Indian boarding school program, can all be construed as examples of ethnocide against the Indians of California.

Wilding

It is not enough to solely describe the individual and collective acts of genocide and ethnocide in California. One needs to understand why such acts occurred in the first place. We therefore offer a theoretical formulation that can explain the structural conditions or underlying causes of Indigenous *ethnic cleansing.* A formulation that may have relevance is sociologist Charles Derber's *wilding* theory, which draws on the theoretical contributions of classical theorists Emile Durkheim and Karl Marx (Derber 1996). Derber has coined the term *wilding* to connote senseless violence and greed with no feelings of remorse or moral responsibility for others. Wilding is defined as rugged individualism run amok.

In his book, *The Wilding of America* (Derber 2002), Derber applies this concept to contemporary society in the United States by describing several kinds of wilders. Wilding includes not only individual wilders who murder for money, and senseless killings without conscience, but also business and corporate wilders like Michael Milken (the "junk bond king"), those responsible for the savings and loan crisis of the 1980s, and politicians who are "bought" with special interest money. A contemporary example of economic wilding is the series of unethical actions by major financial banks and institutions that led to the 2008 collapse of the U.S. economy and ushered in the Great Recession. Some critics would also consider the disregard of international law, the breaking of current environmental and arms control treaties, and the declaration of preemptive war and unilateralism by the George W. Bush administration as examples of political wilding. Last, social wilding occurs when the major institutions of society manifest the characteristics of wilding and it becomes endemic to the entire society.

Derber contends that today we have a national crisis in the United States of violence and greed on both the individual and the national levels of society. Yet wilding is not an entirely new phenomenon on the American scene; it has occurred at other times in U.S. history. The California Gold Rush is a case in point. Wilding completely dominated the economic processes stemming from the Gold Rush, and it also affected the system of California State government, as witnessed by the draconian laws that were passed to indenture and disenfranchise the Native Indians. Wilding also affected the federal government's bad faith treaty negotiations and relocation and reservation policies. In fact, wilding, as Derber defines it, has been the dominant socioeconomic process of the American Indian frontier throughout the history of U.S. expansionism.

We will return to the genocide formulation and Derber's wilding theory at the end of the chapter, but first, in the following pages, we examine these processes in their historical context by describing four different stages of the California Indian experience. Native California as it existed before European entry into the region is our baseline. This is followed by the Spanish mission system period of history; the Mexican period of control; and the Anglo-American period until about 1900. The 1849 Gold Rush and its destructive impact on Native people is the main focus of the American period.

NATIVE CALIFORNIA BEFORE EUROPEANS

Malcolm Margolin, the editor of *News from Native California* magazine, has beautifully described the great diversity of the Indigenous life and environment present in the California region before Europeans came,

> Picture a typical spring afternoon in California 250 years ago. On the prairies of the northeastern part of the state a man, hiding behind a clump of sagebrush, waves a scrap of deerskin in the air, trying to rouse the curiosity of a herd of grazing antelope and draw them within range of his bow and arrow. Along the Klamath River a boy crawls through the circular doorway of a large plank house and walks downstream to watch his father and uncles fish for salmon beneath the redwoods. In the Central Valley a group of women, strings of wild flowers in their hair, wade out into the deep sea of rippling grass to gather roots. As they push forward, herds of elk scatter before them. In San Francisco Bay, two men paddle a rush boat through the quiet channels of a salt water marsh. East of Sierra, families—eager for change and weighed down

> with burden baskets—leave their winter homes in the desert and trek through the pine forests toward thawing mountain lakes and the promise of good fishing. At the edge of the Mohave Desert, men and women plant corn, bean, and pumpkin seeds in the warm, fertile mud of the Colorado River. (Margolin 1982, 34)

The great diversity of the Indigenous peoples of California is illustrated by their aboriginal population of more than three hundred thousand persons, and by their speaking between sixty-four and eighty mutually unintelligible languages (comprising numerous dialects) as dissimilar as English is to Chinese, and representing seven major linguistic families.

The Coast Range and the Sierra Nevada mountain range run through California from north to south. Between the two mountain systems lay fertile valleys in which the majority of the Native peoples lived. The region held an Indigenous population larger than that in any other region of the United States, in large part due to the mild climate and abundance of wild foods, mainly nuts, seeds, and grasses, as well as fish and game.

Native Californians belonged to over five hundred independent tribal groups, small nations, as it were. Their racial and cultural diversity is matched by only several other multiethnic regions of the world, places as distant as the Caucasus, West Africa, New Guinea, upper Burma, Thailand, and southwestern China. While the Yuman people of southern California and the Modocs in the north were warrior nations, those groups in the central part of the region worked and cooperated in peace. The central valley and adjacent country included the Nisenan, Maidu, Konkow, Miwok, and Yokut. The northwestern area included the Tolowa, Yurok, Karok, Hupa, Shasta, Chimariko, Whilkut, and others who lived in the Klamath and Cascade mountains and on the adjacent coast. Their villages (later called *rancherias* in California) held from 30 to as many as 1,000 people, although 250 was about the average (Hurtado 1988a, 15). The 8,000 Pomo, for example, were divided into thirty-four village communities, and the 3,000 Achumawi were divided into eleven. Each group was united by kinship and marriage, religious ceremonies and beliefs, and economic and trade ties.

Ecological and Ethnographic Regions

Aboriginal California can be divided into three main ecological regions that affected the cultures developed by Native peoples who inhabited them. The northwestern region is cooler overall than the rest of California, with a rocky coast and swift rivers rushing down into the valleys from the adjacent mountains, with plentiful rainfall. Sequoias, ponderosa pine, and Douglas fir are found in the high valleys and mountains. The northern area also has many mountain peaks, with Mount Lassen and Mount Shasta still active volcanoes. Both mountains were held sacred by the Native peoples, as they are even today. The mountains and forests contained abundant bear, coyote, deer, wildcat, and wolverine, and before Europeans entered the scene, there were also bighorn mountain sheep and wapiti. Fish, especially salmon and sturgeon in the many rivers, and shellfish along the coast, provided a rich source of food. Languages of the Hokan language family were found mainly in northern California.

Central California includes the central valley, the Sierra foothills, the coast ranges and valleys, the central coast and San Francisco Bay. It is a land of contrast and diversity, "inland lakes and ponds nestled among foothills, spectacular mountains with cascading rivers and streams, broad lush valleys, and coasts rich in shellfish. The variety of plants provided the California basketmakers with a wide selection of fibers, and the especially abundant oaks supplied acorns and hardwood. Fish and game were plentiful" (Garbino and Sasso 1994, 185). Overall the temperature is mild, although it can be hot in the central valley in the summertime. Food was plentiful throughout the entire year, with acorns and seeds as the staple part of the diet. The Penutian language family predominated among the many tongues and dialects spoken.

The third region is southern California. Here the land is dry and the mountains less timbered. There are also fewer rivers, and the climate varies from warm to hot in both summer and winter. Rainfall is scant, and before European entry into the region, the native plants were entirely desert vegetation, such as chaparral, mesquite, and sagebrush, with some oak. Wildlife included the pronghorn antelope, squirrel, rabbit, and kangaroo rat. Shellfish was an important food source along the coast. Acorns and seeds were also food staples throughout the region. Basket-making was an important enterprise. The Shoshonean language family was dominant.

An ethnography is a description of an ethnic group or people. The following section contains an ethnographic example for each of the three California regions described above.

Northern Ethnographic Region

An example of the peoples inhabiting the northern region are the Yurok who lived in the lower Klamath River Valley. (See Garibino and Sasso 1994, 190–7; Pilling 1978, 137–54.) They shared many cultural items with their neighbors, the Karok and Hupa located upstream, and all three groups exhibited cultural influences from the Northwest Coast Indian societies located further north. The Yurok originally numbered about 2,500 linguistically and culturally affiliated persons, who identified primarily as village residents rather than as tribal members. Their fifty or more year-round villages were built along riverbanks, the mouth of rivers, or along the seacoast. "A typical village consisted of six or seven redwood plank houses—smaller and less elaborate than the Northwest Coast houses—and one wooden sweathouse for the men, which also served as their clubhouse and alternate sleeping quarters" (Garbarino and Sasso 1994, 191). The kinship descent group was named after the house site, and spoken of as a family. The house (family) owned the use rights to certain lands, houses, and regalia.

Salmon and acorns, supplemented with deer, seeds, bulbs, and mussels, comprised the Yurok diet. The river, and the sustenance it provided, was the heart of Yurok cultural life. In fact, California before the White man came has been described as a virtual cornucopia of foods. Woodworking and basket weaving were prized skills. The Yurok had no chiefs or priests, but wealth was very important and measured in terms of dentalia, sea shells used as a medium of exchange and trade. To be wealthy meant the ownership of good fishing and hunting lands that could be leased out, and the ability to pay a goodly price (*bridewealth*) for wives. Even so, few men were able to obtain such wealth. The possession of heirlooms, such as obsidian blades or an albino deerskin, and the ability to sponsor a dance ceremonial, were the essential characteristics of a Yurok aristocrat. In addition, the aristocrat, *peyerk* or "real man," had to undergo special training that included a vision quest. There were also female doctors (healers), or "real women" who received their powers from the ancestors in dreams. These specialists comprised about 5 to 10 percent of the Yurok population.

A key part of spiritual life was world renewal, or Fixing the World. When the world or universe was disturbed or became unbalanced, it actually tipped (an earthquake?), and sea animals such as whales came up the rivers. World renewal consisted of a cycle of about a dozen religious ceremonies performed each year to maintain this balance and stave off evil. The Brush Dance, Jumping Dance, and the White Deerskin Dance were an important part of these ceremonies. "All these ceremonial cycles were meant to keep the world in order and running properly for another season and to ensure abundant food and prevent disaster" (Garbarino and Sasso 1994, 195). For the most part, these ceremonies continue to be performed today.

Central Ethnographic Region

The Patwin were typical of the central region. (See Johnson 1978, 350–60; and Kehoe 1992, 404–7). They lived along the Sacramento River and in the nearby hills. Villages held several hundred people who resided in semisubterranean earth lodges. Each locality had a village dance house, also semisubterranean but larger than the other houses. Bark-covered *wickiups* (conical-shaped structures) were used as temporary shelters when hunting or gathering away from the village.

A village chief was selected from a noble family and had the responsibility of overseeing village activities, such as gathering food, trade, and ceremonial dances. A son or brother of a deceased chief was usually chosen as the new chief, but the selection could also be a capable daughter. Other political specialists included a messenger, a council of elders, and a village doctor or medicine man. The Patwin were a ranked society: there were a number of social strata based on social prestige and status (but not on wealth gained by exploiting the labor of others). These social categories included the chief and his noble lineage; craft specialists, such as doctors, traders, or highly successful hunters; common people; "slaves" (who were actually young war captives); "no-account" persons without family ties; and transvestites (men who lived as women). Of all the craft specialties, basketry was the most highly prized (and remains so today among California Indian tribes). Each village was sovereign and had its own distinct territory. Oak groves were village property and an important source for acorns, a food staple. Religious ceremonies and dances with spirit impersonators were central to Patwin collective consciousness and social integration, as it was also for other Central Californian peoples. In addition to these spirit dances, called Kuksu rituals, there were also social dances, special dances such as when a girl becomes a woman (first menses), and a dance associated with gambling games.

Southern Ethnographic Region

The Cahuilla lived in the central portion of the southern California desert (see Bean 1978, and Oswalt 1999). It is estimated that their population ranged between 6,000 and 10,000 when first contacted by the Spaniards and Franciscan Catholic missionaries in the late 1700s. Their villages, located in canyons and on alluvial plains, probably numbered between 150 to 300 persons each, and represented as many as eighty lineages and their respective patriclans (descent traced through the male line). Village land was owned by the lineage, while other lands were divided into tracts controlled by clans, families, and individuals. Buildings ranged from brush shelters to dome-shaped or rectangular houses, fifteen to twenty feet long. The largest house in a Cahuilla village was usually that of the chief, located near a good water source. Close by would be a ceremonial "big house." Other special structures include a communal sweathouse for men and several granaries.

In addition to acorns, a major food source for the Cahuilla was the mesquite bean, with the mesquite groves controlled by the patriclans. Corn, beans, and squash were also raised, with over two hundred plants utilized for medicinal cures. Plant foods were supplemented by hunting, especially rabbits and other small game. The Cahuilla were skilled in both basketry and pottery making.

Social organization featured the division of society into two nonpolitical units or moieties, the Wildcats and the Coyotes. These regulated marriage through exogamy (having to marry outside one's moiety). Social statuses included the hereditary office of the *net* or clan chief. He, in turn, was assisted in his political and ceremonial duties by the *paha*. Another important office was that of the ceremonial talker and singer. The most revered (and feared) persons were the shamans. Shamans were an elite group in Cahuilla society who, together with the *net* and the *paha*, gave important leadership, especially during epidemics and disasters.

The Indian Heritage of California

Without formal laws, courts, or prisons, the world of California Indians was nonetheless well regulated by custom and reinforced by ethical precepts and sanctions. The description of this world as depicted for the Indian peoples of northwestern California by Indian historian Jack Norton is generally representative for the entire region,

> Their daily lives began and ended with songs that were generally prayers. In the intervals between, they were urged, internally and externally, to "keep a good heart,"

"do not think badly of people," "be kind and respectful of the old." "Always," they said, "go up and talk with the elders, say hello, for when you walk away, the old person will say, 'ah, what a fine young man, I hope he lives to be as old as I.'" These urgings and blessings were reinforced by words, rituals, laws and customs during the important religious observances, and in hundreds of stories, gestures, and indirect statements that filled their lives. Proper manners, good breeding, and graciousness were the collective goals. (Norton 1979, 27–28)

The California Indian heritage is, indeed, a rich one. Among the many components of this heritage is that of conservation and environmentalism. The Native peoples *lived lightly on the land,* meaning that both plant and animal foods were respected. They did not overhunt or over-gather. Furthermore, all parts of animal game products were utilized; nothing was ever wasted. For example, not only was "rabbit meat eaten or dried into jerky, the skins were used to weave warm blankets and cloaks, and (as with other small animals) the bones were sometimes crushed into a powder with a mortar and pestle and eaten along with the pounded meat and often much of the viscera" (Margolin 1997/98, 4). Deer hides were made into the sacred Jump Dance and Deerskin Dance regalia, sinews were used as thread, and elk horns were converted into tools, money purses, and spoons. People were considered as part of nature, one of a number of cooperating beings who shared in the workings of the universe. Lowell Bean, a specialist on the Cahuilla, reports that, "a collector never picked all the edible part of a plant; all the seed were not gathered—something was always left over. A protectiveness toward other forms of life was represented by this action" (quoted in Margolin 1997/98, 11).

Today, a controversy exists regarding the function of forest fires, whether our modern institutions should practice fire suppression or let the forest clean itself of brush and tinder. It is instructive, therefore, to learn that the California Natives used fire as a form of range management, and fire ecology was utilized on grassland, woodland, chaparral, and coniferous forest lands. Typical times for burning were from July to October after the seed harvest. "In southern and central California, Indians burned off valley and foothill districts to thin out thicket and to sow, scattering broadcast, grasses from which they would later gather the seed; to promote the growth of clover, which they ate in spring as salad;

and to promote browse for the deer they hunted" (Kehoe 1992, 403).

Interestingly, mining technology was utilized long before the invasion by the Anglo-American miners during the Gold Rush; over one hundred small mines and quarries worked by Native Californians have been identified. Quarrying was common for soapstone, obsidian, salt, and chalk, but never gold. Trade contacts were especially important with the horticultural Indian farmers of the Southwest. Trade routes with the Southwest brought cotton blankets, turquoise, and a little pottery that reached California villages as far up the coast as San Francisco Bay.

THE SPANISH PERIOD (1769–1821)

When the first Spanish explorers first encountered the Native people of California in the early sixteenth century "they universally characterized Indians as shy and friendly people providing travelers with water, food, and hospitality whenever asked" (Castillo 1978b, 101). Spain regarded the Indians as subjects of the Crown but also as human beings with souls capable of receiving Christianity. Twenty-one religious missions were then established in *Alta* (Upper) California, starting in 1774 with Mission San Diego and ending with San Juan Bautista in 1797. (See Figure 3.2.) The mission system, a coercive institution, was a form of the Spanish *reducion* or *congregacion* in which the Indigenous peoples were forcibly gathered from their Native villages into one central site where they could be more easily controlled by armed Spaniards and the Franciscan priests.

In addition to the chain of twenty-one Franciscan missions, the Spaniards also founded *pueblos* or civilian towns, some of which were associated with military garrisons called *presidios;* and *ranchos* (cattle ranches) separate from the missions. The *pueblos,* such as Los Angeles and San Jose, consisted of Spanish settlers, most of whom were retired soldiers, who utilized "Indian labor on a sharecropping or board-and-room basis" (Forbes 1982, 42). The *presidios* or forts served as centers of military control but also depended on Indian labor. The Royal Presidio of San Diego in the 1770s illustrates the typical function of this Spanish institution. It consisted of a stockade with two bronze cannons; one pointing out to sea to protect Spanish interests from rival European powers, and the other pointed at an adjacent Indian village. "Eventually

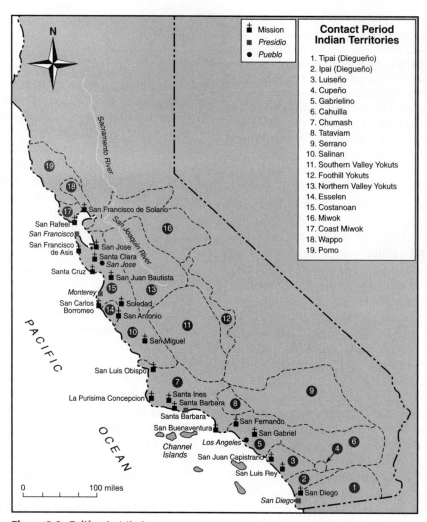

Figure 3.2 California Missions.

the fort protected four major missions and three *asistencias* [Mission auxiliaries] covering a distance of 125 miles to the North" (Schuyler 1978, 74).

The *rancho* as an economic institution underwent a disturbing evolutionary development during the Spanish period. By the 1830s, many observers were describing Indian labor relations in California as serfdom or vassalage, and comparing it to Southern slavery.

Beginning in the 1780s, soldiers and settlers were allowed to graze stock and raise crops in the countryside, using Indian labor entirely. Gradually, these grants of land became more formal; but . . . title to the land always was retained by the Crown, Indian village rights were never quieted by a *rancho* grant, and the ranch owners almost always lived most of the year in town,

leaving his stock and crops in the hands of the Indians working on a sharecropping basis. Gradually, especially after the 1830s, the Indians became serfs, and an economy similar to that of the Deep South of the late nineteenth century developed. (Forbes 1982, 42)

The only other major European presence was at Fort Ross, located ninety miles north of San Francisco Bay. It was an enterprise of Russian mercantile (trade) interests, the Russian American Fur Company, and became a tricultural community of Russian administrators, Aleut fur hunters, and local Pomo Indians utilized as laborers and agriculturalists. There were also some early French fur trapper expeditions in the interior, but it was the Spanish mission system that dominated Indian-European relations in California for the first 150 years.

By 1805, there were twenty thousand neophytes (Indian converts to Christianity) in the Spanish missions. Although Indian persons were recognized as human beings with souls and certain limited rights, Spanish laws nevertheless permitted armed Spaniards to round up the peaceful coastal Indians and impress them into a system of peonage. The Indian lands seized were then held in trust by the Spanish crown under the *encomienda* system with the Indians used as virtual serfs. The *encomienda* was a quasi-feudal arrangement whereby a Spanish "trustee" (Forbes 1982) could collect tribute and free labor from a number of Indians living in a stipulated number of villages, while presumably offering protection and Christian indoctrination. Spanish policy was not to annihilate the Native population as occurred later during the Gold Rush, but rather to absorb it as a labor force for Spanish ranches and the agriculturally-based missions. California became, in effect, a Spanish military colony. "The missions . . . were indeed royal governmental institutions, erected on land belonging ultimately (according to the Spanish viewpoint) to the Crown, although reserved to the Natives with the missionaries as trustees" (Forbes 1982, 39).

Forbes, a historian, describes the evolution of the mission system from its somewhat benign beginnings into an institution of brutal oppression,

> In the early years Natives were ordinarily recruited by the offer of "free" meals and gifts. . . . Subsequently, a standard device was to baptize young children in their home villages and then to require them, as "converts," to enter the mission at ages 5 to 7. Normally the child's mother followed to be with the child and the father followed to be with the wife. By the 1790s, however, the reputation of the missions as places where Indians were "unfree," and as "deathtraps," made it necessary for the missionaries to resort to outright force. . . . Spanish military expeditions brought back *gentiles* (unconverted Indians) as well as *cimarrones* (runaways). Another common variant was to bribe or frighten a village leader into supplying quotas of converts. (Forbes 1982, 40)

Mission life was brutal and harsh. Indian neophytes constructed the mission buildings, herded the cattle, worked the fields, and waited on the mission priests. Men and women were segregated, with the men confined to coffinlike rooms with barely enough space in which to lie down, and the women and girls from the age of seven were housed in bare dormitories called nunneries. Indian marriage and divorce customs were suppressed along with all aspects of Native religion. Anglo-borne diseases easily ravaged the concentrated mission populations. Malnutrition was a persistent problem because mission food was of inferior quality compared to Native diets. Diarrhea was a continual problem for all the missions, in part because the Franciscans often fed the neophytes milk, and Indian genetic makeup lacks the necessary enzyme to digest milk after the age of four or five. Poor sanitation was another cause of diarrhea.

Historical archaeology has discovered the remains of Indian children whose skeletons are deformed, probably from the burden of carrying heavy adobe bricks used in mission building construction. Labor was unpaid, and the neophytes were punished by their religious keepers, the Franciscans, for the smallest infractions. Those Indians who ran away (termed fugitivism), or who resisted, were severely punished if not killed. Typical punishments included whipping with a barbed lash (for both men and women), solitary confinement, mutilation, use of stocks and hobbles, branding, and even execution (Forbes 1982, 39).

The eminent historian, H. H. Bancroft, reported in *History of California, 1884–1890* (see Costo and Costo 1987), on the violence of the Spanish mission system. One account in 1799 by a Franciscan, Antonio de la Conception Horra, accused his fellow Spaniards of brutality in the treatment of the Indians. "The treatment shown to the Indians is the most cruel I have ever read in history. For the slightest things they receive heavy floggings, are shackled, and put in the stocks, and treated with so much cruelty that they are kept whole days without a drink of water" (quoted in Costo and Costo 1987, 69). Costo and Costo (1987, 55) report that a Franciscan priest, Fr. Luis Jayne, of Mission San Diego complained in 1772 to his superiors about the brutality of Spanish soldiers who rape Indian women and destroy Indian fields. Fr. Jayme presented evidence of soldiers gang-raping Indian women. In one incident a blind woman was beaten and carried screaming into the woods to be raped.

> The Indians were so afraid of these soldiers and tried so hard to protect their wives and daughters, that they leave their huts and crops which they gather from the lands around their villages, and go to the woods and experience hunger. They do this so that the soldiers will not rape their women as they have already done so many times in the past. (Costo and Costo 1987, 53)

The problem of rape appears to have been endemic, yet mission officials took little notice of it.

The same Fr. Jayme was later killed in an Indian revolt at San Diego in 1772.

Because stories of the brutal treatment in the missions spread to unconverted tribes, the mission fathers had to rely on the Spanish military to bring in new Indian neophytes. *Presidios* were established in San Diego, Santa Barbara, Monterey, and San Francisco by 1800. Spanish soldiers were also stationed at the missions. Military control was not the only purpose of the *presidio*, however. They "also served as areas where Native labor was exploited and Indian women were forced to entertain Spanish soldiers" (Castillo 1978b, 102).

The invading ruling class of Spanish colonizers was always small in numbers. Initially, the entire coastal strip of California was controlled by a little more than one hundred persons. Even by 1845, on the eve of the Anglo-American Gold Rush, the *gente de razon* (Spanish-speaking persons) never numbered more than four thousand, as against an Indian population of one hundred thousand. "By about 1800, the neophytes were providing much of the support for the Spanish clergy and army, including, especially, food. After 1811 they literally provided the entire support for the province" (Forbes 1982, 41). Although the Spanish encouraged racial mixture, the net effect upon the enslaved coastal Indian populations was the disintegration of Indigenous culture, language, and community. There was also a deep sense of loss and psychological depression.

Disease also ravished the mission Native population. There were several major epidemics during the period of Spanish occupation that included a respiratory epidemic in 1777 at Mission Santa Clara, a pneumonia and diphtheria epidemic in 1802 that raged from Mission San Carlos along the coast to San Luis Obispo, and a measles epidemic in 1806 from San Francisco down to Santa Barbara. Almost 1,600 died in the measles epidemic, and in some missions, children under ten years were almost entirely wiped out. The epidemics also spread inland into the surrounding foothills, as among the Yokuts and Miwok of San Joaquin Valley. "About 45 percent of the population decline during Spanish occupation was the direct result of introduced diseases and sickness" (Castillo 1978b, 104). As a result, by the 1800s, deaths outnumbered births in the missions. Of the more than fifty thousand baptized, most had died, a mortality rate of nearly 70 percent.

The Native population declined by half, from over 300,000 to 150,000 Indians before the Gold Rush began in 1849. The Spanish mission system, far from being the benign, Catholic good work by Franciscan monks as is so often described in church literature, was in reality harsh, cruel, and genocidal.

Missionization often met with fierce Native resistance. The Quechans along the Colorado River mounted a revolt in 1781 that was ultimately successful. Then in 1785 the Tongva attempted to destroy San Gabriel Mission. Uprisings against the missions around San Francisco Bay took place from 1820 through the 1830s, led by Native leaders Yozcolo, Estanislao, Marin, and Quintin.

Forbes (1982, 46) reports that "Sporadic resistance also occurred at San Juan Bautista . . . Mission Santa Clara, and elsewhere during the 1790s and early 1800s, but it was generally put down with ease. More serious, because difficult to combat, were neophyte efforts at poisoning or murdering the Franciscans." "Four padres were poisoned at Mission San Miguel, one of whom died in 1801. In 1811, a San Diego neophyte killed a padre with poison. The next year, Indians at Mission Santa Cruz smothered and castrated a padre. . . . In 1836, southern California Cahuilla Indians kidnapped the padre at Mission San Gabriel and horsewhipped him, as so many of their tribesmen had been whipped" (Castillo 1994, 326).

Among the most noteworthy of the revolts against Spanish colonization was the 1824 revolt at Missions La Purisima and Santa Barbara.

> The reason for the revolt was ill treatment and forced labor imposed by the soldiers and priests, . . . but the immediate cause was a fight that broke out at the flogging of a La Purisima neophyte at Santa Ynez in February. Apparently no one was killed but a large part of the mission buildings was destroyed by fire. That same afternoon as many as 2,000 Indian attacked and captured Mission La Purisima. Soon they were bolstered by reinforcements from Santa Ynez and San Fernando. . . . Meanwhile the news of the uprising . . . reached Santa Barbara. Upon its receipt the neophytes armed themselves. . . . After some futile negotiation with the priests, the neophytes were attacked by the soldiers. A battle of several hours ensued throughout the mission; finally the soldiers withdrew to the *presidio*. The neophytes then sacked the mission and retreated to the back country. . . . A month passed during which the Spanish authorities were able neither to persuade the Santa Barbara Indians to return nor to recapture La Purisima Mission. (Castillo 1978b, 103)

Later, when the Spaniards returned to attack the Indian defenders at La Purisima with hundreds of armed men and four-pounder guns, the neophytes resisted strongly, the battle raging all morning until a cease-fire was negotiated with the assistance of the priests. Many neophytes from San Fernando then joined the rebels at Santa Barbara, and those at San Buenaventura and San Gabriel also showed signs of revolt. At the end of May a truce was negotiated, but as many as four hundred neophytes refused to return. Seven of the La Purisima rebels were executed by the Spaniards, and four leaders of the revolt were sentenced to ten years of chain-gang labor, although two eventually escaped.

Besides outright revolts there were also mass escapes, such as the one in 1795 in which over two hundred Costanoan Indians fled Mission Dolores. "Runaways became so numerous in the early 1800s that, on occasion, large sweeps were made through the Central Valley by troops looking for them; and smaller squads of soldiers were constantly out" (Forbes 1982, 47). Unfortunately, Spanish soldiers were sometimes aided by yet other Indians in capturing the runaways. Nevertheless, the runaway neophytes "introduced Spanish horses, weapons, and military tactics to the unconverted interior tribes and convinced them to stiffen their own efforts at resistance to missionization" (Castillo 1978b, 102). There was also nonviolent resistance, including the practice of abortion, and the infanticide of "children born out of forced concubinage of Indian women by priests and soldiers" (Castillo 1978b, 104).

After sixty-five years of Spanish rule the missions were abandoned in 1834 after Mexico achieved its independence from Spain. The Mission Indians were then left with little economic opportunities to sustain themselves, their populations decimated, and their aboriginal social systems and cultures all but destroyed.

THE MEXICAN-INDIAN PERIOD (1821–46)

As a result of the successful revolt against Spain, Mexico inherited an over extended colonial empire that embraced much of the Southwest in present-day United States, including Alta (Upper) California. In California, however, the young Republic of Mexico took control of only a narrow coastal region, populated by a small population of *Hispanos* (Spanish subjects of whatever race) and the more numerous Indian neophytes who occupied the missions, *presidios*, and civilian pueblos. The vast interior of California remained for a time under the control of free Indian nations.

After the revolution, the 1824 Mexican Constitution formally secularized the mission system. It made the Indians citizens of the new republic and, at least in theory, turned over mission property to them. Yet, in practice, actual Mexican policy towards the Indians

was essentially the same as that of the Spanish. Neither Spain nor Mexico acknowledged Indian ownership of the land, but only the right of occupancy. In spite of an earlier 1821 Act passed by the Mexican government "that guaranteed citizenship . . . and protection of their person and property, Indian neophytes and gentiles alike were seized for forced labor and their property confiscated" (Castillo 1978b, 114–15). In fact, Franciscan resistance and the general political turmoil of the period forestalled secularization until 1833. As late as 1836 the Franciscans continued to mount military campaigns to seize new potential neophytes from the interior for labor at the missions.

It was a time of confusion and disarray for the Indian neophytes. Many lost the promised mission lands to non-Indians. As a result, some of the emancipated neophytes hired themselves out as farm laborers and servants. Others were left at the mercy of the *pueblos* where they were exploited as domestics, plied with alcohol, and left for a life of poverty and debauchery. Others fled to the interior to join traditional Indian communities that were still intact. Some of the former neophytes revolted, as in the Santa Ynez revolt of 1824. Those employed on the *ranchos* became victims of the hacienda system of peonage, bordering on slavery. "By 1840 there were a dozen of these feudal establishments, each with 20 to several hundred Indians, in all perhaps as many as 4,000" (Castillo 1978b, 105).

The *rancho* system, which was carved out of mission lands, accelerated after the legal secularization of the missions in 1834. Many Indians were absorbed into the new *ranchos* as *vaqueros* (cowboys), or as servants. Instead of dividing the land and property between the fifteen thousand surviving neophytes and the clergy, as was originally planned, the Mexican authorities appropriated most of the mission resources for themselves and their relatives. "The entire economy of the Mexican colony now shifted to the large landed estates of wealthy Mexicans" (Castillo 1978b, 105). The Sepulveda Rancho is an example that symbolizes the *rancho* era in southern California. Jose Andres Sepulveda received a huge private estate out of the holdings of the San Capistrano mission in 1837. After Mexican independence and the secularization of the missions, men like Salvador Vallejo, another prosperous landowner, hoped that the former mission Indians would become townsmen and the missions local parishes. Yet, this view did not stop him from becoming wealthy and powerful by enslaving California Natives in order to expand and work his private estate. Sherburne Cook reports that, in 1834,

Vallejo killed over two hundred Wappo Indians and captured three hundred others for his estate (cited in Castillo 1978b, 106).

By the early 1820s, virtually all of the coastal Indians were living in the missions or on the *ranchos*, and the Native villages in the interior valleys were becoming depopulated. The non-Christianized Native peoples of the interior then experienced brutality and violence at the hands of the Mexican colonists, who sought to protect and expand the *rancho* economy. An example of this brutality is the expedition of Jose Maria Amador in 1837. The Amador party invited the Indians, both Christian and non-Christian, to a feast, but as soon as the Indians approached they were surrounded and tied up. Amador later reported,

> [W]e separated 100 Christians. At every half mile or mile we put six of them on their knees to say their prayers, making them understand that they were about to die. Each one was shot with four arrows, two in front and two in the back. Those who refused to die immediately were killed with spears. . . . The Ensign told me to do whatever I thought best (with the others). I answered that I thought all the prisoners should be shot, having previously made Christians of them. They should be told they were going to die and they should be asked if they wanted to be made Christians. . . . We baptized all the Indians and afterwards they were shot in the back. At the first volley 70 fell dead. I doubled the charge for the 30 who remained and they all fell. (Cook 1962, 197–98)

The Indians in the interior did not remain passive but fought back against the depredations of the Mexican *rancheros*. Yozcolo, a former neophyte at Mission Santa Clara, conducted many stock raids during the 1830s before he was finally defeated and killed. "In the central valley the Indian offensive reached a peak in 1845 and then rapidly decreased due to rear attacks suffered from American colonists filling the valley. In the south from 1841 to 1848 warfare became much more intensified" (Castillo 1978b, 106). As much as 6 percent of the Native population decline during the Mexican period can be attributed to warfare casualties.

European-introduced diseases caused most of the deaths among the Indians during the period of Mexican rule. Venereal disease, measles, pneumonia, diphtheria, and other respiratory aliments ravaged the indigenous population until 1827. Smallpox appeared in 1833, along with scarlet fever, cholera, and tuberculosis. The pandemic of 1833 killed an estimated 4,500 Indians, and a smallpox outbreak killed several thousand more. It is estimated that for northern California alone, 11,500 Indians died between 1830 and 1848 from European diseases to which they had no natural immunity. If disease and warfare are taken together, the Mexican period may have been even more destructive than the Spanish period. As a result, by the time of the Anglo-American invasion from 1845 to 1847, there were only about 6,000 ex-mission Indians still residing along the coast, along with 7,000 predominantly Indian-Mexicans. There were also about 700 Europeans, and more than 100,000 Natives remaining in interior California (Forbes 1982, 67).

THE EARLY AMERICAN PERIOD (1846–1900)

The American period in California Indian history commenced with the U.S. declaration of war against Mexico and the Bear Flag revolt by the *Americanos*, the California Battalion, in 1846. It is, of course, longer in duration than either the Spanish or Mexican periods. It is represented by a number of stages, each of which had a somewhat different impact on the Indian peoples, leading to their drastic population decline. The topics examined include the 1849 and early 1850s Gold Rush, the roles of the miners and the military, the part played by disease and starvation, the impact of the unratified treaties on Indigenous sovereignty, the social effects of indenture and slavery, and the deleterious effects of forced relocation and the early reservation system.

Beginning with Jedediah Strong Smith in 1826, Anglo-American fur traders began penetrating California. Britons, French Canadians, and *Hispanos* from New Mexico also entered the Far West and California during this early period. Once an isolated Indian country relatively untouched by the Spanish mission system, the California interior rapidly became part of the international fur trade. Spanish, British, Russian, and American ships also stopped along the northern coast of California after the 1770s for furs and trade. The fur trade also brought malaria and other infectious diseases, which further decimated local Native populations.

Just before the war with Mexico, John A. Sutter established the settlement of New Helvetia (Sacramento) in the Sacramento Valley. "New Helvetia was a large-scale plantation-type enterprise buttressed with coerced Native labor and suffused with violence" (Hurtado 1988b, 35). Sutter and the other Anglo ranchers absolutely depended on Indian labor, but their labor needs weakened the viability of the surrounding Indian communities and made the Anglo ranches vulnerable to attack by starving Indian livestock raiders. In the beginning, Indian labor was plentiful; the Indians worked cheaply, and they could easily be controlled with corporal punishment. White labor, on the other hand, was scarce and expensive.

Indian women were often abused by Sutter, his captains, and the Anglo-American settlers. Sutter's overseer, Heinrich Lienhard, claimed that there was a special room next to Sutter's chambers where a "large number of Indian girls . . . were constantly at his beck and call," and that "Sutter has sexual relations with girls as young as ten" (Hurtado 1988a, 63).

The Mexican war that lasted from 1845 to 1848 ensured the virtual seizure of Alta California from the Republic of Mexico by the United States. As a result of the war, the young Republic of Mexico lost half of its territory, 525,000 square miles, to the United States. The lost territory included California, Nevada, Utah, most of Arizona and New Mexico, and parts of Colorado and Wyoming, for which the U.S. paid Mexico $15 million. Texas, one of the main causes of the war, was annexed in 1845. The war with Mexico, and the Bear Flag Revolt by American settlers in California that followed, brought momentous changes to the Native peoples.

The Gold Discovery

On January 24, 1848, gold was discovered on the South Fork of the American River at Coloma when John Sutter was constructing a sawmill. As word of the discovery went out, *Californios* (former Mexican citizens) and more recently arrived settlers flocked to the hills to wash the sands and gravels of Mother Lode streams and rivers. Two months after the discovery, Alta California, along with Arizona and New Mexico, was transferred from Mexico to the United States under the Treaty of Guadalupe Hidalgo. *Baja* or Lower California was retained by the Mexican Republic. Neither country was aware at the time of the full significance of the gold discovery when the treaty was ratified. By the end of the year, however, President James K. Polk verified the gold discovery in his State of the Union address, and a display of California gold was exhibited in Washington, DC. The stage was now set for the Gold Rush of 1849. A pastoral California, with its Indian population, Spanish missions, and Mexican *ranchos*, was quickly overrun by an invasion of gold seekers from throughout the world, the Forty-niners.

The Treaty of Guadalupe Hildalgo guaranteed the Spanish *Californios* the right to retain their Mexican citizenship, or to become U.S. citizens. Because Indians were considered citizens under the 1824 Mexican Constitution, they theoretically also acquired U.S. citizenship. This legality was totally ignored, however, by the Anglo military administration in California. The 1849 California State Constitution (the Constitutional Convention being dominated by miners) prohibited Indians from voting. A disregard for Indian rights was officially affirmed by Governor Peter H. Burnett in his annual message of January, 1851, when he said that "a war of extermination will continue to be waged between the races until the Indian race become[s] extinct."

Native people could not bear arms, vote, or have a fair trial, or even testify against a White person. In a prizewinning book, *Indian Survival On the California Frontier*, Hurtado (1988a, 98) reports that, "During the first years of the Gold Rush, California Indians were governed only by the regulations of military governors, who did not attempt to extend citizenship rights to them but treated Native people as a distinct class, useful as laborers and dangerous as raiders. . . . The dual concerns of non-Indian landholders—regulating the Indian labor force and controlling livestock raiding—became the principal aims that shaped early United States Indian policy in this region."

Under the Treaty of Guadalupe Hidalgo the United States was supposed to recognize two kinds of Indigenous property rights, traditional *rancho* rights, and open land where Indian title was still intact, including Indian villages and the abandoned missions. Yet, the American authorities immediately violated the treaty with Mexico after taking over California. A land commission was set up in 1851 to decide all cases of lands claimed by Mission Indians under provisions of the Treaty of Guadalupe Hidalgo. Indians were not told of this, so none of them appeared to protest; all of the lands were made public domain and were either opened to settlement or kept by the government. The Indians with traditional rights under aboriginal title lost in several court decisions (probably unconstitutional), which ruled that the Indians were trespassers on the public domain of the United States. The federal government failed to intervene although the state's action was patently illegal under the U.S. Constitution. Instead, both the state and federal governments set about acquiring as much land as possible at the expense of the Indians.

A hard line was also taken against the *rancho* owners of the Spanish land grants, including those whose owners were Indian. These landowners were required to take their deeds and titles to San

Francisco for hearings in order to legally prove title. Many subsequently lost their lands to Anglo speculators and attorneys. By these and similar means, entire Indian communities were destroyed with no recourse in the American courts of justice.

In order to mobilize the dispossessed Indian labor force, the U.S. military government in California decreed that "Indians who did not work for ranchers, or who did not have an official passport, could expect to be tried and punished. Worse, an Indian might be shot on the pretext that he was a horse thief" (Hurtado 1988a, 95). When an epidemic of measles broke out in the Sacramento Valley in the summer of 1847, John Sutter was allowed to replace his dead and dying workforce by using armed force to compel so-called wild Indians to work his ranch. To sum up, Indian-White labor relations in the interior during this transition period produced many of the same dire consequences that Indians had faced under Mexican rule in California, namely, depopulation, labor exploitation, and the weakening of tribal bonds on individuals, but at least the Mexican government and the Franciscans expressed an interest in the Indians' spiritual welfare, albeit within the parameters of Catholic dogma.

The discovery of gold at Sutter's half-finished sawmill on the American River in 1848 ushered in a period of extreme abuse of the Indians, leading to an even more rapid population decline than before. Ironically, it was Maidu Indian workers who helped John Marshall discover gold in the Mother Lode when he was building the mill for Sutter. By the end of that summer, four thousand miners, half of them Indian, were prospecting for gold. Thus, at the beginning of the Gold Rush, Indian labor was used to mine the precious metal. This atmosphere of tolerance lasted no more than a year, however. In the spring of 1849, some Oregon miners were involved in the rape of Maidu women. When Maidu men intervened to stop the outrage, the miners drew their revolvers and shot down three of them (Hittell 1897, 77).

Before the gold discovery Indians outnumbered Whites by nearly ten to one, but by the early 1850s, Whites had come to outnumber Indians by perhaps two to one. Gold fever resulted in tens of thousands of immigrants, young single men, flocking to the California gold fields, hoping to strike it rich and then return to their homes in the East, wealthy. Insatiable greed dominated this non-Indian immigrant population, and unbridled individualism marked the new California society. As a result, the White population steadily rose to more than two hundred thousand,

while the Indian population went into precipitous decline, reaching a nadir of twenty-three thousand by 1880, about 15 percent of its 1848 population.

The Forty-niners were mainly Anglo-Americans, although there were also Mexicans, South Americans, and even Europeans among their number. All, however, were motivated to obtain gold rather than acquire land as settlers. Mexico had valued Indian labor in the missions and on the ranchos, and had therefore attempted to incorporate Native people into the Alta California economy. Not so the Americans. Many Anglo-Americans who came to California after 1848 viewed the Indian people as worthless, and they were appalled by the Mexican custom of sanctioned miscegenation (interracial sexual unions). Many were imbued with a frontier mentality that taught them to despise Native peoples as subhuman *diggers*. California Indians used digging sticks to harvest roots and other food sources from the soil, hence the name, digger, which became a pejorative.

In 1848 the richest gold-bearing regions of California contained the largest concentrations of Native people. The immigrant gold hunters therefore ventured directly into Indian territory, areas which had previously been independent of non-Indian control. By 1852, over $300 million in gold had been extracted from Indian lands, and many millions more remained, over $1.5 billion dollars worth altogether (Bailin 1971, Introduction). There were three major gold mining regions, the central, southern, and northwestern mines. (See Figure 3.3)

At first, a number of Indians were employed as miners or else mined independently. Sutter, for example, began losing his ranching labor force at New Helvetia when some Indians caught the gold fever. Some Indians were at first able to enter the trade system by bargaining their gold for trade goods. Soon, the traders countered by inventing the *digger ounce*, a lead slug that dishonestly outweighed the legitimate weights used to measure the gold brought in by White miners. By this means the Indian miners were cheated out of their hard-earned profits.

In the southern district, Miwok Indians at first washed gold on Weber Creek. The men dug and gave the mud to the children who, in turn, carried it in baskets to the women who lined up on the stream and washed the gold in grass baskets. Soon, however, White miners began driving Native workers out of the central region labor force. "Free White workers vehemently and brutally objected to competition from cheap Indian labor, mostly controlled by California's *ranchero* class" (Hurtado 1988a, 107). Indian laborers

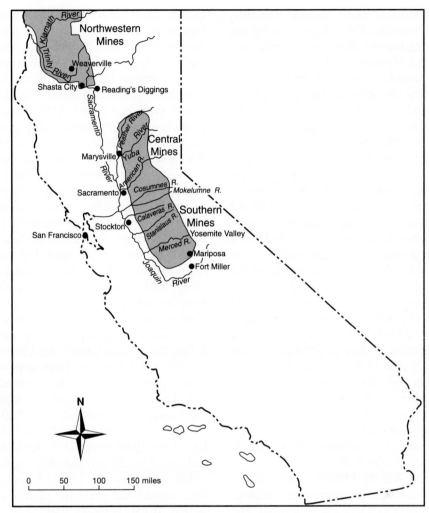

Figure 3.3 California mining regions in the 1850s.

were pushed into the worse jobs or occasionally permitted to work the mine tailings. "To feed their families, some prostituted themselves, while others scavenged through dumps and slaughter pens for the leavings of White miners" (Hurtado 1988a, 108).

Savage Miners and the Military

The Forty-niner Gold Rush initiated a rapid depopulation of California's Native peoples that scarcely diminished in intensity until the end of the nineteenth century. The Indian people were cheated, debauched by liquor and White demands for sex, starved, rounded up and herded on brutal forced marches to small reservations (virtual concentration camps), enslaved in debt peonage, brutally murdered and massacred, and denied civil rights and equal justice before the courts and institutions of Anglo California. Forbes (1982, 69), a historian, writes that "the United States possesses many sordid chapters in it history, but perhaps none is more sordid than that relating to the conquest of California, typified as it is by great brutality and callousness and what closely approaches genocide." Indian historian Jack Norton (1979, 32) reports that in northwestern California, the immigrants shot Indians on sight, often as they were fishing or gathering food, or even as they were seeking to protect their wives and daughters from kidnap and rape. Indian homes were burned and the occupants trapped by settler gunfire. Entire families were trapped and shot in the ravines and caves surrounding their places of habitation. Babies had their heads smashed against trees and rocks. In detailing the massacre of the Yahi, Theodora Kroeber (1969, 84–85) reported that more than thirty Yahi including young children and babies were cornered in a cave at Mill Creek. "They were helpless against the four armed men who forthwith killed them all. Norman Kingsley, as he explained afterwards, changed guns during the slaughter, exchanging his 50-caliber Spencer rifle for a 38-caliber Smith and Wesson revolver, because the rifle 'tore them up so bad,' particularly the babies."

While Sutter was cheating Indians out of their gold-productive lands, and the traders were cheating Indian gold miners with the digger ounce, the Gold Rush came to the lands of the Miwok and Yokut peoples in San Joaquin Valley. Gold mining in these southern mines was spearheaded by James D. Savage, who made treaties with the Yokuts in the winter of 1849. Sometimes characterized as a friend of the Indians because of his treaty-making, he nevertheless didn't hesitate to charge the local Indians a pound of gold for a pound of sugar and sold the beef, given to him by the federal government for distribution to the tribes, for his own profit. He also gambled away the gold that Indian miners entrusted to him for sale in San Francisco. (Project Underground 1998, 3) The miners who followed Savage were not interested in negotiating treaties or paying the local Indians for gold found in their territory. This led to the Mariposa War in December of 1850, when warriors under Chief Tenaya attacked prospectors and burned the trading posts. Savage, in turn, led a force of state militia, called the Mariposa Battalion, into the Sierra Nevada and the Yosemite Valley the following year to put down the Indian rebellion.

While the Yokuts and the Miwoks were battling Savage and the miners in the southern mines, another gold discovery unfolded in northwest California. The incoming miners, spearheaded by Perison Reading, soon overran the local Indian communities, often massacring the inhabitants. Some Indian peoples like the Modocs fought back until they, too, were forcibly overcome and driven to reservations as conquered peoples.

In the early 1870s, the Modocs, led by Kentipoos, also known as Captain Jack, abandoned the Klamath Reservation in Oregon and returned to their ancestral homeland in northern California where they hoped the federal government would give them their own reservation in which to live in peace. In November 1872, when the Army tried to forcibly return the Modocs to reservation confinement in Oregon, Kentipoos and his people fled to the natural fortress of what is now Lava Beds State Park. There, the 150 Modoc warriors and their families successfully held off over 3,000 troops of the U.S. Army for nearly a year. The Modoc resistance fighters lost only one warrior in a series of skirmishes, but the Army lost sixty officers and men, including a general. Eventually,

torn by dissension and without food and water, the Modoc resisters were captured and hanged. "After the execution, the warriors were decapitated and had their heads sent off for 'scientific investigation', and grave robbers later disinterred Kentipoos' body, embalmed it, and displayed it in a carnival in eastern cities" (Waldman 1985, 132). More than a hundred years later, in 1984, after many protests, Kentipoos' skull was returned by the U.S. government's Smithsonian Institution to the Modocs for sanctified reburial.

Local newspapers in northwestern California, like the *Humboldt Times*, beat the drums of Indian war and called for the formation of a volunteer militia to exterminate what were commonly termed "skulking bands of savages." Militia expenses were often subsidized by both state and federal governments. "Almost any White man could raise a volunteer army, outfit it with guns, ammunition, horses, and supplies, and be reasonably sure that the state government would honor its vouchers" (Castillo 1978b, 108). "Volunteer groups grew up, such as the Klamath Rifles, the Salmon Guard, the Union Volunteers, and the Pitt River Rangers. They appeared to be private armies; but, in actuality, were called out, armed, and paid by the State Government. Volunteers received the handsome salaries of from $10 to $15 per day" (Bailin 1971, 17). In both 1851 and 1852 the California Legislature paid over $1,000,000 to those who hunted Indians, thus directly subsidizing the so-called chastising expeditions. "The U.S. Congress eventually reimbursed the state for nearly all of the bonds issued" (Castillo 1978b, 108).

Between 1848 and 1860 there were at least 4,267 Indian deaths attributed to the military, or about 12 percent of the Indian population at the time. Ironically, it was the gold stolen from Indian lands that paid for the ensuing genocide. Towns offered bounties on Indians ranging from "five dollars for every severed head in Shasta in 1855 to twenty-five cents for a scalp in Honey Lake in 1863" (Project Undergound 1998, 5). Flagrant acts of cruelty were many, "Doctor Merriam stated in his testimony before a Congressional Committee that 'On the Klamath and Salmon Rivers, the giant miner's hose nozzles were aimed at Indian villages, dumping houses into the canyons below.' A Mr. Lockhart reported that before leaving Pitt River, 'he had mixed a considerable quantity of strychnine with flour, and placed it where it could be found and consumed by the starving Indians'" (Bailin 1971, 12).

In response to starving Indians who raided settler cattle from time to time, racist reports and editorials appeared in area newspapers. The following excerpt is from a letter to the editor in the *Alta California*, May 21, 1852,

> Your correspondent also labors under a mistake representing the late killing of some 40 Indians at the Upper Crossing as occurring in a "fight." It was a cold-blooded unprovoked massacre. An Indian, sometime in the early part of March, had been shot by a White man at Happy Camp. The Indians on the rivers above were exasperated, and perhaps threatened retaliation. At all events, some miners were alarmed, raided a party, surrounded the Rancheria at the Ferry, and killed every man and some women; then proceeding up the river two miles, surrounded another village and killed every man but one, who escaped wounded, making a total of some 30 or 40 killed. All accounts agree in stating that the attack was wholly unlooked for by the Indians, who from the date of the treaty at Scott's Valley in November, had been perfectly quiet and inoffensive. The facts are given on the authority of the Special Indian Agent in that neighborhood, who investigated the sad affair. . . . It is quite too common for letter writers and editors in California to represent every difficulty which occurs on the frontier, as an aggression or outrage on the part of the Indians, and in justifying the most severe punishment, even their downright butchery.

In 1853 the *Yreka Herald* newspaper called on the government "to carry on a war of extermination until the last redskin of these tribes has been killed. Extermination is no longer a question of time—the time has arrived, the work has commenced and let the first man that says treaty or peace be regarded as a traitor" (Project Undergound 1998, 5). A newspaper report in the *Petaluma Journal* of April 15, 1857, recounted how three or four hundred "'bucks, squaws, and children' had been killed by Whites for running off stock. Most of the women were removed to Round Valley [reservation] but the 'bucks are safely disposed of'" (Bailin 1971, 5). Another report, this time in the *Redding Courier* of September 17, 1859, recounted in great detail the formation of a company of nineteen Whites who had hunted down Pitt River Indians, killing twenty-two warriors, and forty "squaws" and children. The news article went on to say that "the citizens of Pitt River Valley are determined to keep the company in the field until the Indians are wiped out" (Bailin 1971, 5).

Ten years later, the following headlines in the *Eureka Humboldt Times* virtually rationalized the continuing genocide (Norton 1987, 122–23),

- "Let the Indians understand that they as tribes will be held responsible for crimes and no special pain will be taken to find the individual perpetrators.

Any ten will be taken and hung if the guilty are not brought forward." (April 9, 1862)
- "Good Haul of Diggers: Band Exterminated." (January 17, 1863)
- "Good Haul of Diggers: One White Man Killed—Thirty-eight Bucks Killed, Forty Squaws and Children Taken." (April 11, 1863)

The racist sentiments expressed in the newspaper editorials mirrored those of local Whites who wanted to clear the potentially rich agricultural and grazing lands, and gold-bearing deposits of the resident Indian populations. Massacres like the Bloody Island massacre of 125 Clear Lake Pomos in 1849 were the result.

In 1847, Andrew Kelsey and a man known only as Stone purchased a herd of cattle from Salvador Vallejo with the right to pasture the stock at Clear Lake, located in the coastal range north of San Francisco. To run their ranch they employed local Pomo Indians who had worked for Vallejo. Kelsey and Stone imposed harsh discipline on their Indian workers, whipped them for sport, starved their laborers, and even appropriated the wife of their head Indian *vaquero* for themselves. Clear Lake tribal historian William Benson reported in his diaries, "From severe whippings four died. A nephew of an Indian lady who was forced to live with Stone (as his whore) was shot to death by Stone. When a father or mother of a young girl was asked to bring the girl to the house [for sex] by Stone or Kelsey, if this order was not obeyed, he or she would be hung up by the hands and whipped" (quoted in Project Underground 1998, 11).

> Another eyewitness account is the testimony of Thomas Knight, The Kelseys would sometimes go out and get 50, 60 or a hundred of these Indians, and bring them to their place, and make them work for them. They treated them badly, and did not feed them well. . . . The Indians were kept so short of food that they occasionally took a bullock and killed it themselves. On such occasions, if the Kelseys failed to discover the special offenders, they would take any Indian they might suspect, or perhaps one at random and hang him up by the thumbs, so that his toes just touched the floor, in an adobe house they had on the premises, and keep him there two or three days, sometimes with nothing to eat. . . . Sometimes they would kill an Indian outright on the spot for some small offence. In driving them to their place they would shoot any of the old or infirm ones by the wayside.
>
> At the time of the Red Bluff excitement, the Kelseys went up into the Clear Lake region, and got some 80 Indians, and drove them down to Red Bluff to work the valuable mines that were supposed to be there. On getting them there, a long distance from their homes, it was

ascertained that the mines were a sell [worthless], and there was not gold there. The Kelseys then and there abandoned these Indians, who were in a hostile country, with nothing to eat, and they were killed and starved, and finally only some eight or ten of them ever got back to their homes. In revenge they murdered Andy Kelsey, who was in the Clear Lake country, tending a large herd of cattle the brothers had there. (Heizer 1974, 246–47)

To avenge the deaths of Stone and Kelsey the U.S. Army and White volunteers attacked the Clear Lake Pomos in 1850, killing over one hundred of them in a most barbaric manner. This is known as the Bloody Island Massacre. Thomas Knight's account continues: "The two other Kelseys also killed a good many. They were arrested for their inhuman treatment of the Indians, many of those massacred being old or infirm and had never made any trouble, but through some flaw in the law or informality they escaped punishment" (Heizer 1974, 247).

Another brutal massacre occurred on Indian Island (also known as Gunther Island), which is

"Protecting the settlers." Massacre of the Nome Cult Valley Indians during winter of 1858–59.

located just off the Eureka city shoreline, On February 26, 1860, when the peaceful Wiyot people were holding their annual religious ceremonies during the night, they were attacked as they slept by White men who slaughtered them with axes. A Major G. J. Raines, in a report of the massacre to the Assistant Adjutant General of the Army, gave the following account,

I have just been to Indian Island, the home of a band of friendly Indians between Eureka and Uniontown, where I beheld a scene of atrocity and horror unparalleled not only in our own Country, but even in history, for it was done by men self acting and without necessity, color of law, or authority—the murder of little innocent babes and women, from the breast to maturity, barbarously . . . perpetrated by men who act in defiance of and probably in revenge upon the Governor of the State for not sending them arms and having them mustered in as a Volunteer Company for the murder of Indians by wholesale, goaded also by Legislative acts of inquiry into such matters. At any rate such is the opinion of the better class of community as related to me this Sunday morning. I was informed by these men, Volunteers, calling themselves such from Eel River, had employed the earlier part of the day in murdering all the women and children of the above Island and I repaired to the place, but the villains — some five in number had gone—and midst the bitter grief of parents and fathers—many of whom had returned—I beheld a spectacle of horror of unexampled description—babes, with brains oozing out of their skulls, cut and hacked with axes, and squaws exhibiting the most frightful wounds in death which imagination can paint—and this done . . . without cause, otherwise, as far as I can learn, as I have not heard of any of them losing life or cattle by the Indians. Certainly of these Indians, for they lived on an Island and nobody accused them. (Heizer 1974, 259–60)

Major Raines then describes the murdered Indians as he found them in each lodge, the total number being one man, seventeen women, and eleven children. In addition to these dead he reported that eighteen women and an unknown number of children had been carried away by their relatives for burial before his arrival. Another eyewitness described the scene in this way, "Blood stood in pools on all sides; the walls of the huts were stained and the grass colored red. Lying around were dead bodies of both sexes and all ages from the old man to the infant at the breast. Some had their heads split in twain by axes, others beaten into jelly with clubs, others pierced or cut to pieces with bowie knives. Some struck down as they mired [in the water]; others had almost reached the water when overtaken and butchered" (quoted in Norton 1979, 82).

It was later learned that the Indian Island massacre was part of a well-coordinated and premeditated plan by some White farmers and stockmen to exterminate the region's resident Indian population, because that same night three other massacres took place simultaneously, two at the south spit of Humboldt Bay, and the other at the mouth of the Eel River. "One man who had sat on the previous grand jury at Eureka boasted of killing 60 infants with his hatchet at the different 'slaughter grounds'" (Bailin 1971, 5). The total deaths numbered 188 Indians, mostly women and children. The White perpetrators of these barbaric massacres were never brought to justice, and although individual military officers at times spoke out against the depredations, the U.S. Army as an institution backed the interests of the White settlers.

Disease and Starvation

Throughout most of California, the casualties resulting from disease epidemics greatly exceeded those from massacres. "In 1853, five hundred died in Nevada City of smallpox and typhoid. Eight hundred Maidu died of influenza and tuberculosis in the same year" (Bailin 1971, 6). The most common diseases were measles, pneumonia, smallpox, tuberculosis, and venereal disease. Syphilis infected approximately 20 percent of California's Indians, and gonorrhea may have been 100 percent. Venereal disease was contracted mainly from White men who abducted and raped Indian women. *The New York Century* of May 1860, reported that "intercourse of Whites with Clear Lake Indians . . . had laid the foundation for the ultimate extermination of the race by disease . . . of 500–600 'squaws' from ten years old upwards" (quoted in Bailin 1971, 7).

Malnutrition played a tragic role in paving the way for death from disease. The destruction of Native foods sources, either as the indirect effect of gold mining, or as outright theft, contributed to Indian susceptibility to communicable disease. A Special Agent, testifying before a committee of the 66th Congress, gave the following information,

> The first effect of the occupation of the land by the miners was the muddying of the streams by the mining operations and the killing or frightening away of the game, thus cutting off the Indians' fish and game supply. The mining population soon needed gardens, and about the only land suitable was that where the edible roots grew. The stock industry followed very soon, and even the oak trees were fenced in and forbidden to the Indians, as the acorns were needed for hogs. Later the era of wheat came and arable lands passed into private

ownership. The Indians were thus reduced from a state of comparative comfort to one of destitution. (quoted in Bailin 1971, 7–8)

There were also Whites who actively sought out Indian food stores in order to destroy them. On the Trinity River, a principal river for salmon, an Indian food staple, White men took over the entire river. When Indian people attempted to come back for fish upon which they had depended since time immemorial, they were usually shot.

From time to time, Congress authorized purchases of cattle and flour for distribution to the Indians, but more often than not, most of these purchases failed to reach the Indians for whom they were intended. "The system of accountability was such that no voucher was understood to mean what it expressed on its face—500 beef did not mean 500 purchased and delivered but 500 bought, and perhaps 100 delivered and 400 resold . . . private contractors were charging three times the going rate for cattle and delivering it in pieces, not on the hoof, if it was delivered at all. The result—hunger and death all over California" (Bailin 1971, 9).

Sherburne Cook (1978, 93) reports that the years 1845 to 1855 saw a Native population decline from approximately 150,000 to 50,000, or about 66 percent. "This desolation was accomplished by a ruthless flood of miners and farmers who annihilated the Natives without mercy or compensation. The direct causes of death were disease, the bullet, exposure, and acute starvation. The more remote causes were insane passion for gold, abiding hatred for the Red man, and complete lack of any legal control" (Cook 1978, 93).

The mentality that fueled the genocide of the nineteenth century continued into the early twentieth century. Ishi, a Yahi Indian, wandered out of the hills of Tehana County in 1911 as the last surviving member of his tribe. Vigilantes had undertaken raids of extermination against the Yahi and other Indian tribes.

> These deadly raids reduced the Yahi to the handful remaining in Ishi's small band. These few individuals then attempted to hide themselves in the most isolated and rugged reaches of the Mill and Deer Creek valleys of northern California for the next thirty years, raiding mountain cabins for food and crawling under the dense thickets so as not to create any visible trace of their existence. These harsh conditions of life persisted until 1908 when Ishi, alone and emaciated, allowed himself finally to be taken by those from whom he had hidden for so long. (Meyer 1982, 106)

Ishi's story, made famous by Theodora Kroeber, is recounted in *Ishi In Two Worlds.* Ishi, a survivor of genocide, became the living embodiment of a traditional Indian for anthropologists to study (Kroeber 1976). Housed in the anthropology museum, located at that time in San Francisco, he gave demonstrations in flint-knapping and other Yahi skills before succumbing to tuberculosis and dying in 1916. At his request, Ishi's body was cremated, but not before his scientific so-called friends performed an autopsy on the man known as "the last wild Indian" to see what made him different as a so-called primitive man. The idea of an autopsy was abhorrent to Ishi, as the scientists well knew, indeed, sacrilegious in Yahi spiritual beliefs, as it is in many Indigenous and world cultures.

To make matters worse, only in the last few years was it learned that his brain was removed at the time of the autopsy and shipped off to the Smithsonian Institution for "scientific study" (see Hinton 1999, 4–9). Ishi's brain rested, forgotten, on a shelf in a jar of formaldehyde for eighty-three years. At first the Smithsonian declined to return Ishi's brain. Finally, after two years and much public pressure, a petition by the Butte County Native American Cultural Com-2mittee on behalf of all California Native Americans was granted, and the Smithsonian agreed in March of 1999 to repatriate Ishi's brain by sending it home for sanctified burial with his other remains. This episode indicates the depth of the inhumanity of the dominant society toward Native peoples, and that it is institutional in scope, having penetrated the nation's highest scientific institution.

The "Lost" Treaties

The Indigenous peoples of California lost their homeland not only through acts of outright genocide and the scourge of disease, but also by what is known as *domestication policy.* The aim of this policy was to integrate Indians into White society as a brown-skin underclass that included the appropriation of the Indians' land base. The only legal means by which the federal government can acquire Indian lands held under aboriginal title are either by an act of war, or by a treaty of cession or sale. None of these means of acquiring Native lands took place in California. More than 70 percent of Native California was seized by the federal government in 1853 without just compensation as provided under the U.S. Constitution.

In 1851–52 President Fillmore sent three U.S. Indian Commissioners to negotiate eighteen treaties with the majority of California's Indian peoples.

The U.S. Constitution stipulates that only the federal government, and not the states, can make treaties with the Indian nations. Under the terms of the treaties negotiated in California, the Indians reluctantly agreed to surrender their land claims, and the federal government agreed, in turn, to provide some 8.5 million acres of good lands, reservations plus certain goods and services (see Figure 3.4).

> The commissioners negotiated the first two treaties on the Mariposa and San Joaquin rivers, while state volunteers fought the Mariposa Indian war, driving refugees into the arms of the commissioners. Models for subsequent negotiations, the first treaties set aside a large tract of land—as much as several hundred square miles—for the Indians and bound the federal government to provide teachers and farmers for Native people. For two years after ratification, the United States was also supposed to give the Indians thousands of beef and dairy cattle, and brood stock for horses, in addition to flour, cloth, thread, needles, various tools, and clothing. . . . In return, the Indian signatories relinquished their claim to any other lands and acknowledged the sovereignty of the United States. (Hurtado 1988a, 130)

It was the era of the Gold Rush, however, and the greed for gold and California's rich lands motivated the state legislature to pressure the U.S. Senate not to rarify the treaties. Members of the California State Legislature protested that "rich and inexhaustible veins of gold-bearing quartz, . . . have, in the wisdom of these Indian Agents, been considered eligible locations for the untutored tribes of the wilderness, and have accordingly been set apart for that purpose, and the energetic and zealous miner has been rudely ordered by these agents to abandon their claims and obey the limits of the reservations" (quoted in AFSC n.d., 6). The senators argued that the state would lose taxes on the proposed reservation lands worth more than $100 million, but the Commissioners replied it was the poorest land available, and some worth nothing.

The treaties were then conveniently "lost" in the Senate archives and not discovered until 1905. Because the treaties were never ratified, the Indians were forced to give up virtually all of the promised lands and settle for temporary *rancherias* and farms, a mere fraction of the original 8.5 million acres negotiated in good faith with the treaty commissioners. As Hurtado (1988b, 36) explains,

> Then the government established a series of temporary reserves that were supposed to be supported with the

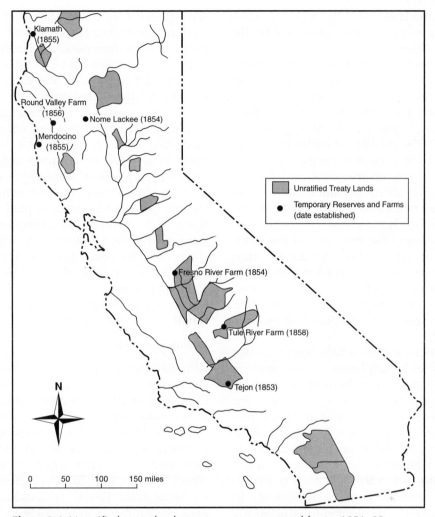

Figure 3.4 Unratified treaty lands, temporary reserves and farms, 1851–60.

crops grown by the Indian inmates. When White settlers needed the reserves, the government would move the Indians to a new location. The temporary reserves failed because Congress did not appropriate enough money to support them, much less provide relief for the tens of thousands of non-reservation Indians who needed assistance in the 1850s. Finally the system was abandoned in favor of reservations established by Presidential order.

Thus Indian lands were criminally diminished from over 70 million acres in 1853, to about 450,000 acres held in trust by the government by the 1970s.

After the eighteen treaties were lost, some California officials proposed shipping the Indians to other states, to eastern Sierra, or to Santa Catalina and other coastal islands. Although Congress vetoed these plans, Native oral historians tell of their people

being shipped to Alcatraz and Goat Island (now Treasure Island), and being dumped into the ocean near San Francisco (*Sacramento Bee* 1997).

The 1887 Dawes (Allotment) Act further reduced California Indian land holdings. Under this Act, tribally owned land was broken up into individual allotments and the supposed surplus released to White ownership. Sixty or so small, scattered plots of land, *rancherias*, were eventually established between 1905 and 1932 on which members of different tribes were mixed together. Then, under the Rancheria Act of 1958 (which applies only to California and was amended in 1964), about thirty-six of these *rancherias* representing over 1,500 Indians were summarily terminated from federal status. This made these former *rancheria* Indian communities vulnerable to an inability to pay taxes and to a lack of protection from fraud by non-Indians, and it required them to relinquish vitally needed services formerly provided by the Bureau of Indian Affairs.

Because the treaties were never ratified, much of California's aboriginal land title was never quieted legally. As late as the 1960s, the Indians still technically owned about one-third of California. Their only redress, however, was through a Congressional Act of 1928 and, later, the 1946 U.S. Court of Indian Claims for the failure of the government to provide the promised reservations and for the illegal taking of their aboriginal lands. Rather than give back a portion of the stolen lands, however, the 1946 law provided solely for a monetary compensation, and at a fraction of the true value of the stolen lands. This kind of justice is like saying that a thief who steals your property doesn't have to give it back and can, instead, merely pay you for its value. Furthermore, the thief (in this instance, the U.S. government) even gets to set the price and terms of the compensation.

Although two claim awards have been made for the illegal taking of Indian lands in California, in 1944 and 1964 respectively, both were patently unfair. The 1944 award was made pursuant to the 1928 Act and a lawsuit filed under it in 1929. It provided for payment of $1.25 per acre for the 8.5 million acres of land promised under the unratified treaties. The total award was for $17 million, hardly a just compensation considering the billions of dollars in gold and resources realized from the stolen lands. To add insult to injury, the government deducted $12 million from the final award as offsets—the goods and services which the federal government claimed to have provided to the Indians—leaving a final award of about $5 million, or $150 per capita. This meant that California Indians paid for all government operations, whether beneficial to them or not, until the 1930s out of this award. Yet the government had made a handsome profit when the disputed lands were originally sold from $2 to $4 per acre to private parties, while compensating the Indians at only $1.75 per acre.

The offsets deducted from the 1944 Indian award included the cost of building and running Sherman Institute, a federal government boarding school in southern California. Boarding schools were set up by the Bureau of Indian Affairs ostensibly to Americanize Native peoples, but in reality to break the ties of Indian children to their traditional cultures, families, and communities; the slogan was "Kill the Indian, save the man." They were run military style

with forced Christianization and the banning of Indian languages, customs, and religion. Indian people, for the most part, hated them. Yet a few years after the award was made, and the Indian claimants were forced to pay for Sherman, the facility was closed to California Indians.

Later, because of the inadequacy of the 1944 award, a new claims case was entered for yet other lands illegally taken. Yet the 1964 award paid only 47 cents an acre for the approximately 65 million net acres illegally seized. Ironically, California Indians were again charged for Sherman Institute even though they had previously paid for it under the terms of the earlier 1944 settlement. An individual claimant received a little over $800 for his or her share of California's great wealth. Some Indians refused their money. Rupert Costo, a prominent Cahuilla Indian and director of the Indian Historical Society, wrote "void" across his settlement check and sent it back to the government.

Indenture and Slavery

Although the enslavement of African Americans in California became illegal in 1849, Indian slavery flourished and actually continued for several years after passage of the 13th Amendment. "Until 1867, an estimated 10,000 California Indians, including 4,000 children, were held as chattel. Only three arrests were made and no convictions for these and similar crimes" (Eargle 1992, 37). On September 26, 1865, the *California Police Gazette* editorialized "that slavery exists in California in precisely the same condition that it did until lately in the Southern states. There the blacks were slaves; here in almost every county Indians are unlawfully held as chattels" (quoted in Project Underground 1998, 8).

Before the Gold Rush and the influx of the miners and settlers, cheap Indian labor was in demand. In their lust for gold and ranch workers the White immigrants first hired Indian workers, and then raided local Native villages for their labor demands. But even after Indian labor was excluded from the mines, this practice of virtual slave labor continued, especially for young women and children. "An estimated 4,000 children were bought and sold. Newspaper accounts of the time noted that while young boys sold for 60 dollars or so, young women could sell for as much as 200 dollars" (Project Underground 1998, 8). In some instances, entire tribes were captured, carried into the White settlements, and sold, according to Thomas Henley, superintendent of Indian Affairs for California in 1863. An editorial in the *Marysville Appeal*, December 6, 1861 describes this practice,

> But it is from these mountain tribes that white settlers draw their supplies of kidnapped children, educated as servants, and women for purposes of labor and lust. . . . It is notorious that there are parties in the northern counties of this state, whose sole occupation has been to steal young children and squaws from the poor Diggers . . . and dispose of them at handsome prices to the settlers, who, being in the majority of cases unmarried but . . . willingly pay 50 or 60 dollars for a young digger to cook and wait upon them, or 100 dollars for a likely young girl. (Sherburne Cook, quoted in Castillo 1978b, 109)

In March of 1850 Senator John Bidwell introduced a bill to the first California State Legislature which mandated that Indian crimes, punishments, and rights were to be adjudicated by justices of the peace in ten Indian districts. The bill would have given limited Indian suffrage, but this was too much for the racist-minded legislature. Instead, a different law, an Act for the Government and Protection of the Indians, was enacted on April 22, 1850. This law, despite its lofty sounding title, while including many features of the Bidwell bill, omitted provisions for Indian justices of the peace and Indian suffrage. This 1850 indenture law introduced virtual Indian slavery, because it ordered that "any Indian, on the word of a White man, could be declared a legal vagrant, thrown in jail, and have his labor sold at auction for up to four months with no pay" (Castillo 1978b, 108). The Act also allowed Indian children to be indentured with the consent of their parents, or if they were orphans.

> The law virtually compelled Indians to work because any Indian found "loitering or strolling about" was subject to arrest on the complaint of any White citizen, whereupon the court was required within twenty-four hours to hire out arrestees to the highest bidder for up to four months. . . . For Indians unable to pay fines, "any White person" could pay the fine or give bond for the Native, then compel him to work for a specified period. Indians would complain to a justice of ill-treatment, "but in no case" could "a White man be convicted of any offense upon the testimony of an Indian." (Hurtado, 1988a, 130)

The Indians who escaped indenture servitude more often than not would end up on reservations that hardly offered a better future. There was no legal redress of grievances under the 1850 law, because Indians were not permitted to testify against Whites.

Commissioner of Indian Affairs William P. Code reported in 1861 that indenturing was just another name for enslavement. The *Humboldt Times* recounted in the same year that a former Indian agent "had gotten eighty Natives apprenticed to him to work the Washoe mines," and the *Marysville Appeal* reported that some White men had persuaded the Tehama County judge to indenture to them "all the most valuable Indians" on the Nome Lackee Reservation (Bailin 1971, 10). Raids to secure Indian slaves became commonplace in some parts of California.

One of the worst practices was the kidnapping of children. The indenture law provided the motive for making Indian children orphans, by killing the parents so that the children could be indentured. Letters from California Army personnel attest to the practice of kidnapping and selling Indian children as a lucrative practice. In a letter dated January 12, 1862, Colonel Francis J. Lippitt reported to the Humboldt military district the following testimony, "Individuals and parties are, moreover, constantly engaged in kidnapping Indian children, frequently attacking the *rancherias*, and killing the parents for no other purpose. This is said to be a very lucrative business, the kidnapped children bringing good prices, in some instances . . . hundreds of dollars apiece" (Heizer and Almquist 1971, 43). Another report, in 1861, noted "that Indians were sold for $37.50 apiece and that one of the traders made $15,000 in the last season's business" (Heizer and Almquist 1971, 43).

As early as 1854 the *Alta California* reported that abducting Indian children had become a common practice. "Nearly all the children belonging to some of the Indian tribes in the Northern part of the state have been stolen. They are taken to the southern part of the state and there sold" (Bailin 1971, 11). The *Sacramento Union* editorialized in 1862 that "there is a class of 'pestilent' whites who systematically killed adults to get their children to sell" (Cook 1976, 313). Heizer and Almquist (1971) also report that California newspapers, the office of Indian Affairs, and other independent observers cited evidence that organized bands of Indian kidnappers, acting independently or following troops on the Indian campaigns, would collect the women and children after a village attack, and that this was one of the main causes of the so-called Indian wars in the late 1850s and early 1860s.

Child kidnapping and Indian slavery continued for fifteen years until 1867 when it was legally overturned in order to comply with the Thirteenth Amendment of the U.S. Constitution abolishing slavery and involuntary servitude. By the end of the Gold Rush there began a general decline in the demand for Indian labor. The valley ranches began to break up, and the labor market was soon flooded with Whites, leaving only subsistence labor and domestic work available to the Indians.

Forced Relocation and Reservations

The so-called humane alternative to extermination was the policy of domestication. This involved rounding up Indian survivors of the Gold Rush, or those occupying homelands and territories desired by the White settlers, and sending them on forced marches to relocation centers, euphemistically called reservations. Not many of these reservations were ever established in California despite the large Native population, because of the unratified treaties. Eventually, five small reservations were created and later added to by additions or extensions. The Hoopa Reservation in northwest California is the largest that was established; Round Valley, just north of San Francisco in Mendocino County, is another. These population relocation centers were an integral part of a policy of ethnic cleansing. Norton (1979, 74) points out that the newly created Klamath Reservation became a virtual concentration camp for the coastal Indians of Northern California, when the Wiyot, Whilkut, Sinkyone, and Chilula Indians of Humboldt County were driven into internment during the years of 1856 to 1861, only to suffer from rotten food, administrative graft and corruption, its hanging tree, and the total brutalization of the Indians. Many hundreds died as a result of the ethnic cleansing operations by the military, because if the Indian refugees did not die or were killed along the way, they found no provisions, houses, or other facilities once they reached their destinations and consequently became victims of disease and starvation.

Brutal atrocities were committed during these death marches. A Mr. Johnson, testifying before a Senate Committee on Indian Affairs of the 75th Congress, described a typical removal operation. Referring to a Paiute woman sitting near him he stated, "Her people were driven by soldiers and officers through the passes of the mountains to the east side without food or water, and when a woman could not carry her children, they were torn from her back and thrown under the bushes. They left their little babies behind . . . but the soldiers came along and speared them, shot them and abused them" (quoted in Bailin 1971, 14).

In 1863, soldiers marched 461 Pomo, Maidu, Konkow, Miwok, Wintu, Wailaki, and Achumawi one hundred miles from Chico to the Round Valley Reservation. Only 277 survived this Trail of Tears.

"Men were shot who tried to escape. The sick, the old, or women with children were speared if they could not keep up, bayonets being used to conserve ammunition. Babies were also killed" (quoted in Project Underground 1998, 10).

At the same time, the organization of *volunteer companies* was encouraged to hasten the policy of Indian removal by attacking Indian villages. "The *Humboldt Times*, the Eureka newspaper, advised 'all classes of our people' to take extra legal steps against the Indians . . . until official 'removal or extermination' could be 'matured'" (Norton 1979, 77). In northwestern California, these volunteers adopted romantic names such as the Humboldt Home Guard, the Hydewille Dragoons, and the Eel River Minutemen.

Once on the reservations, the relocated Indians faced starvation at the hands of crooked Indian agents, who sold government issue cattle intended to feed the Indians and pocketed the proceeds for themselves. One enterprising agent ripped in half the blankets issued to distribute to the Indians and sold the other half for himself. Food fraud was commonplace. Testimony from Joel H. Brooks, an employee of J. Savage, revealed the following admission: Savage received 1,900 head of cattle from local Indian agents in the Lower San Joaquin Valley and was supposed to distribute them to local Indians. Instead, the employee was ordered to "take receipts for double the number actually delivered on the San Joaquin and Kings River, to deliver one-third less than were receipted for to the Indians on the Fresno. He also had orders to sell all the Indian-issued beef he could to miners. He was also instructed to destroy Savage's orders as soon as he read them" (Heizer and Almquist 1971, 83–85).

At Round Valley, the Indians had to survive on only three ears of corn per day; the agent refused to issue beef if he could help it. Another group forced into resettlement were the Yokuts, who were driven to the Fresno Reservation, their villages burned behind them.

In 1872 and 1873, members of the Pit River people in northern California were rounded up like rabbits in a rabbit drive, some sent to the Klamath Reservation in California, others to Round Valley, and still others herded onto a ship where they were promised transportation to a new land away from White men with guns and away from so-called civilization. According to a report by the Pit River Nation (quoted in Heizer and Almquist 1971), the government's plan was to "dispose" of the human cargo in the ocean. The plan worked in almost every instance, with only the strongest making it to shore. These were not the only "shipments" from northern California. Heizer and

Almquist (1971, 29) also report that "in some places the removal of Indians was encouraged by paying bounty hunters for Indian scalps." The *Marysville Weekly Express* reported in April 16, 1859 that "a new plan has been adopted by our neighbors . . . to chastise the Indians for their many depredations. . . . Some men are hired to hunt them, who are recompensed by receiving so much for each scalp, or some other satisfactory evidence that they have been killed. The money has been made up by subscription" (Heizer and Almquist 1971, 29).

Later, in an effort to destroy the Indian family and Indian language and culture, children as young as six years of age were taken from their parents and sent off to federal and mission boarding schools. The schools were run military style with harsh discipline; the children were forbidden to speak their Native language and were severely punished for the least infraction. Christian church attendance was compulsory on Sunday. They were also farmed out to White Christian families for unpaid labor during summer and vacation periods under the guise of civilizing the heathen.

Today, the forcible separation of children from their parents would probably be proscribed by the United Nations 1946 Genocide Convention. "Deliberate massacres, slavery, child prostitution, racism, a system of reservations that starved people to death, made survival of the first peoples of California almost impossible. That any survived is a testimony to their courage and strength as peoples" (Project Underground 1998, 10).

THEORY AND ANALYSIS

In this section we reexamine the analytical concepts that were introduced earlier. First, we consider the charge of genocide against the backdrop of the tremendous decline in the Native population that took place under Spanish and Mexican hegemony, and an even greater decline beginning with the Gold Rush and U.S. domination in the last half of the nineteenth century.

Precipitous Population Decline

The U.S. Secretary of the Interior in his 1937 testimony before a Congressional committee declared that "through starvation and through actual massacre, the population of the Indians in California was cut down to the minimum figure of 20,000. . . . The worlds annals contain few comparable instances of swift depopulation—practically, of racial massacre—at the hands of a conquering race" (quoted in Bailin 1971, 1).

The demographer Cook (1978, 92–93) divides the drastic decline in the Native Indian population into three major stages. The first stage took place from 1769 to 1834 during the Spanish period under the mission system. The major cause of the decline was disease. Cook reports that "within the mission communities, introduced European pathogens were responsible for crude death rates reaching nearly 100 per 1,000 adults and 150 per children" (Cook 1978, 92). It is estimated that the Indian population lost sixty-five thousand people. A valley river traveler wrote in 1833, "From the head of the Sacramento [River] to the great bend and slough of the San Joaquin we did not see more than six or eight live Indians, while large numbers of their skulls and dead bodies were to be seen under almost every shade tree near water, where the uninhabited and deserted villages had been converted into grave yards" (Cook 1976, 212).

The second stage in Cook's analysis extends from the end of the mission system in 1834 to the Mexican War with the United States in 1845. The two demographic processes responsible for population decline during this state were disease and "the opening up of the land to White settlement "(Norton 1987). Two devastating disease epidemics, malaria and smallpox, ravished the Indigenous population in the 1830s. Syphilis was also a factor. Entire village populations were exterminated, and about sixty thousand Indians in all perished from these epidemics.

There were around four thousand Spaniards and Mexicans in California just prior to the Gold Rush, together with an increasing number of White Americans. In the mission areas the Indians' land had been taken over for stock raising and agriculture. In the interior valleys, large land grants were made to White entrepreneurs like John Sutter, John Bidwell, James D. Savage, and George C. Yount. These economic empires destroyed much of the Native subsistence base and forced the Native populations into virtual peonage. Tens of thousands of Indians perished as the result of endemic disease, armed conflict, and the destruction of Native food supplies.

The third, and worst stage took place between 1845 and 1855 during the Anglo-American period of the Gold Rush. This stage witnessed the decline of the Indian population from approximately 150,000 to 50,000. The causes for this rapid decline were described earlier and clearly fall under the definition of genocide. The United Nations defines genocide as the committing of acts with intent to destroy, wholly or in part, a national, ethnic, racial or religious group. In California, these acts were institutional in scope. The sheer scale and enormity of these crimes cannot be blamed on a few White rascals residing on the boundaries of the frontier. Anglo society as a whole in California was guilty of inhumanity as evidenced by the fact that legal rights and protection were denied the Indians well into the 1880s after the initial period of the Gold Rush (Norton 1987, 116).

Following the Gold Rush there was a continuing decline in the Indian population until, by 1900, the U.S. Census reported only 15,377 California Indians remaining. Some authorities believe that this figure for the Indian nadir is too low, but "there is little room for doubt that the minimum level in the population . . . was reached in the decades between 1880 and 1900" (Cook 1978, 93). Since then, the population has begun to slowly recover. The 1928 Roll found almost twenty-two thousand California Indians. Today, California is the most populous Indian state, but this fact is explained as mainly due to the immigration of Indians from other states into the urban areas of Los Angeles-Long Beach, and the San Francisco Bay Area.

Environmental Degradation

An important factor in the precipitous population decline of Native Californians during the American period was the destruction of the environment. Gold mining and White settlement seriously affected the environment upon which the Native population depended for food and livelihood. Mining operations destroyed Native fish dams, polluted salmon streams, and frightened away the wild game.

Plow agriculture prevented communal hunts for rabbit and deer. "Domestic animals changed the plant ecology as the original seed-food grass disappeared and was replaced by European grasses and weeds. Over-grazing brought a period of accelerated erosion and lessened surface water availability. Antelope and bear disappeared; mountain sheep and mountain lion have become almost extinct; deer were reduced in range and numbers. Access to coastal food was reduced" (Shipek 1978, 610). The fences built by White settlers prevented Indian women from access to oak groves for gathering acorns.

The destruction of Native food sources directly contributed to malnutrition and paved the way not only for starvation, but also for susceptibility to foreign diseases. It also fostered stock raiding by starving Natives, and the retaliation by the military and angry Whites upon innocent villages.

Although the environmental destruction and ensuing population decline of the California Indians occurred 150 years ago, gold fever continues to leave a deadly legacy of mercury poison from mining. "And in recent years, another new technology—the use of cyanide to extract gold—has sparked a new Gold Rush by multinational corporations such as Homestake of California, which is digging up the traditional lands of the Pomo in Clear Lake" (Project Underground 1968, 1). The contemporary descendants of California Indians who survived the Forty-niner Gold Rush live on toxic lands and fish in toxic waters. The Pomo Band of Indians at Clear Lake are fighting the Sulphur Banks Mercury Mine that borders their community. Fish are contaminated and the traditional Indian fishery has been ruined. Seventy-five of the tribe's 150 members live at Clear Lake.

Was It Genocide?

Was the near extermination of the California Indians genocide? A number of scholars and California Indians say it was. Certainly the wanton killing, massacres, and slavery that took place during the Anglo period initiated by the Gold Rush was genocidal. In northwestern California especially, as historian Jack Norton (1979) documents, the incidences of genocide were so blatant and hideous that any fair-minded American would weep at the inhumanities inflicted upon the Indigenous peoples who inhabited the lands of California since time immemorial.

Yet, there are also those who indict the earlier Spanish mission system as well. Native American studies professor and artist, Frank Lapena (Nomtipom Wintu) writes,

> The founders of the California missions were not concerned with the traditions, religions, or accomplishments of the Native populations; quite the contrary. Like all colonizers, they were interested primarily in land. Their concern for the Indians was limited to their souls, not their lives; the Church enslaved its converts and was merciless to those who deserted the missions. The Church would have us believe "Indians" were without religion. But in fact when confronted with the sacred activity of the California Indians, the Church tried to destroy it by converting or killing off its practitioners. The justification was that the Indians were animistic pagan savages. (Lapena 1997/98, 17)

In 1987, Rupert Costo (Cahuilla) and Jeanette Henry Costo, founders of the Indian Historical Society and publishers of the journal *The Indian Historian*,

Savages.

brought out a collective work entitled *The Missions of California: A Legacy of Genocide.* The book contains articles by scholars and Indian elders, and resolutions by tribal councils, who charge the Spanish mission system with genocide. An informative part of the Costo book is the section summarizing the United Nations Convention on Genocide in the context of California Spanish mission history (Costo and Costo 1987, 126–29).

The architect of the Franciscan mission system was Fr. Junipero Serra (1713–84), who has become a symbol of eighteenth century feudal forced labor and California Indian abuse. Yet, the Roman Catholic Church has long sought to have him declared a saint. Fr. P. Michael Galvan, writing in the Costos' book, explains that the veneration of the saints is an important element of Roman Catholic theology (Costo and Costo 1987). Through the saints, the Church encourages and supports the faithful in their attempt to live out the gospel as Roman Catholics understand it. The saints are church role models whose faith and life the faithful are called upon to emulate. But should Serra, given the historical record of the California mission system, qualify as a Roman Catholic saint?

The Church's efforts to sanctify Serra became especially vigorous in the early 1980s, only to be followed by widespread Indian protests. The descendants of the Mission Indians of California, although predominantly Roman Catholic, nevertheless found the Vatican project reprehensible in light of the genocidal history of the mission system. The Costos (1987, 189) found that the great majority of the Indian people in California, who know their ancestry and the family stories, what really happened to their people, do not believe Serra is worthy of beautification, or of canonization. The pattern of genocide commenced in California with the mission system, then the exploitative Mexican period, and continued with the American Gold Rush.

California Indians contend that an attempt by the Vatican to canonize Fr. Junipero Serra would serve only to legitimize the Spanish mission system as a saintly institution doing God's work. As can be seen from the facts described in this chapter, this is untrue and represents a gross distortion of the historical record.

Wilding Theory Revisited

How does one explain the virulent racism, in short, the genocide, that was practiced against the Native peoples of California? How can the hierarchy of the Roman Catholic Church justify the oppression of the Indian neophytes under the Spanish mission system?

On what grounds can one rationalize the actions of the Anglo miners and settlers in raping, killing, and enslaving Indians? Or kidnapping children? How could the American founding fathers of California so easily and without conscience deprive Native Americans of citizenship and civil rights? How could federal authorities negotiate Indian treaties supposedly in good faith and then fail to ratify the agreements, hiding them away for decades? Of course, some would contend that these evils occurred in other places and at other times in the history of U.S. westward expansion, but the scale and rapidity by which they occurred in California is without precedent in the history of Indian relations. If one eliminates the obviously fallacious idea that locates causality in the biology or psychological makeup of the non-Indian, then one must attribute the California genocide to historical events and structural causes. Thus, we return to Derber's wilding theory.

What all wilders have in common, says Derber, is a sociopathic personality as a result of being oversocialized in the American Dream. Functionalist theory in sociology contends that deviance is the result of people not becoming sufficiently socialized into the norms and values of society. The major goal of capitalism, however, is material acquisition, and it, in turn, is equated with success in achieving the American Dream. Rather than wilding as a result of not being socialized, wilders are oversocialized in the goal of material success and rugged individualism to achieve it. Derber explains, "A sociopathic society is one . . . marked by the collapse of moral order resulting from the breakdown of community and the failure of institutions. . . . In such a society, the national character type tends towards sociopathy" (Derber 1996, 24–25).

Emil Durkheim, the early French sociologist, feared that the rise of modern industrialism would lead to the breakdown of traditional social solidarity and the weakening of community bonds. Derber, however, contends that Durkheim lacked the politico-economic analysis to explain why wilding is so "startling pervasive among American ruling elites and trickles down to the population at large" (Derber 1996, 16). It is Karl Marx who provides this part of the analysis: "In capitalism, as Marx conceives it, wilding is less a failure of socialization than an expression of society's central norms. To turn a profit, even the most humane capitalist employer commodifies and exploits employees, playing by market rules of competition and profit-maximization to buy and sell their labor power as cheaply as possible" (quoted in Derber 1996, 16). Although capitalism does not inevitably destroy community and social values, Derber believes that rugged individualism in the United States has merged with free market capitalism and the global economy to cause a wilding epidemic. The dream of unlimited wealth and glamour for the rich and powerful opens up endless fantasies and opportunities. This can lead to deviance due to socially prescribed anomie and wilding among elites based on unlimited possibilities of exploitation.

Derber also contends that wilding (individualism run amok) has taken place in earlier periods of U.S. history, only to be followed by periods of correction.

> The Robber Baron era of the 1880s and 1890s, an age of spectacular economic and political wilding, was followed by the Progressive Era of the early 20th century, in which moral forces reasserted themselves. The individualistic license of the 1920s, another era of economic and political wilding epitomized by the Teapot Dome scandal, yielded to the New Deal era of the 1930s and 1940s, when America responded to the Great Depression with remarkable moral and community spirit. The moral idealism of a new generation of youth in the 1960s was followed by the explosion of political, economic, and social wilding in the current era. (Derber 1996, 14)

We suggest that that the Forty-niner Gold Rush in California was one of these periods of social and economic wilding. The lust for wealth in the gold craze became overwhelming, so much so that for many ordinary Anglo-Americans, including those in authority, the usual civility, adherence to law, and moral standards of conduct were tragically set aside. The sociopathic personality came to characterize members of the dominant society and its institutions in California, and the dispossessed Native peoples became its victims. Of course, the Chinese, Blacks, Mexicans, even the Irish, also became the objects of Anglo-American chauvinism and discrimination in early California, but the Native Indians, as we have seen in this chapter, clearly received the brunt of it (see Heizer and Almquist 1971). Their oppression was structural, rising to the level of genocide.

STRUGGLE AND RENAISSANCE

For the next hundred years after the Gold Rush, Indian culture and identity were suppressed or went underground. For many years, it was dangerous to be an Indian in California. Besides homicide, prejudice was commonplace, and structural discrimination by

White institutions, especially the legal and educational systems, actively sought to suppress Native culture, language, and traditions. This continued into the twentieth century. There was a spate of racially motivated murders of Indians in the state as recently as the early 1970s, and one could still find signs that read "Indians and dogs, keep out." Until 1934, Indian religion in the United States was officially banned by federal policy, and Native people could be jailed and fined for practicing religious ceremonies. Miscegenation laws forbidding interracial marriage were still on the books in California until 1948, even though some of California's legally defined Indians were as little as one-sixty-fourth Indian. Many Indian people remained de facto segregated in their own *rancheria* communities and lived in poverty. This state of affairs lasted until World War II.

Despite long-standing religious oppression, the Indians of California have continually sought to preserve their spiritual traditions and ceremonies. In the latter part of the nineteenth century, the Ghost Dance religious revitalization movement swept into California from Nevada. Lasting from 1869 to 1875, it gave hope to the powerless by prophesizing that the White world would disappear and the Indian world, including the dead ancestors, would return. The new rituals at first attracted large numbers of Native peoples to dances held in the semisubterranean earth lodges where their traditional religious rituals had formerly been held. When the predicted disaster failed to occur, the Ghost Dance died out except in the area where the Kuksu religion had been practiced. One variation of the Ghost Dance, the Earth Lodge religion, spread throughout northern and central California. The most lasting ritualistic innovation to occur was the Dreamer or Bole-Maru religion. A new Ghost Dance in 1890, initiated by Wovoka, a Paiute medicine man, had relatively little effect in California. In the 1920s, the Indian Shaker Church reached northwestern California.

Traditional ceremonies continued to be observed in some Native communities, but they were generally concealed from Whites. Today, by contrast, the Hupa openly celebrate their White Deerskin Dance, the Modoc and the Miwuk dance in their Round Houses, and the Chumash sponsor their Big Head dancers, even inviting non-Indians to attend some of their ceremonies.

Secular movements among California Indians did not take place until the beginning of the twentieth century. Indian issues included land acquisition and civil rights. Two early Indian beneficial associations active in California were the Indian Rights Association and the Sequoya League. The League, active until 1911, sought legal protection and emergency assistance for several southern California tribes. Other Indian rights organizations included the Northern California Indian Association, and the Society of Northern California Indians. In the early 1920s the powerful Mission Indian Association arose in southern California. Throughout the next decade it "organized considerable opposition to allotment of reservation lands and promoted participation of women in tribal councils" (Castillo 1978, 715). Some political groups emerged over the issue of redressing the unratified treaties and illegal seizure of Indian lands. Chief among these was the California Indian Brotherhood. A number of White welfare groups, like the Federated Women's Clubs, also joined in this effort. As a result of growing Native political pressure, Congress passed the Jurisdictional Act of 1928 which allowed California Indians to sue the government for redress of land claims. A facsimile of the hated stereotype of digger Indian was burned in effigy about the same time, signaling an end to this derogatory and demeaning stereotype. The 1930s Depression and World War II interrupted these political developments.

After the war, California Indians were greatly disappointed by the outcome of their land claims under the Jurisdictional Act, the Indian plaintiffs received a paltry $5,024,842 after offsets, hardly a fair price for supposedly selling California to the White man. The passage of the Indian Claims Act in 1964 then laid the basis for a second California claims settlement. Starting in the early 1950s, however, the federal government launched its regressive termination and relocation programs. Many California tribes were abolished, their federal status as legal Indians unilaterally ended, and their land protection and government services revoked. Furthermore, the relocation program pressured thousands of Indians from other states to move to California's cities to compete for jobs and services. Paradoxically, the new urban immigrants contributed significantly to the emergence of a sense of Indian pride and solidarity that sparked the New Indian or Red Power Movement of the 1960s and 1970s. Indian community centers, such as the Intertribal Friendship House of Oakland, were formed throughout California's cities.

As a consequence of the unfair land claims settlement and other emergent problems, and also because of the emerging Red Power Movement, New Indian organizations arose in California. The American Indian Historical Society was founded in 1964 by

Cahuilla tribal chairperson, Rupert Costo. It published the important journal, the *Indian Historian*, and a monthly newspaper, *Wassaja,* until the late 1970s. Other important organizations included the California Indian Education Association, founded in 1967, the Inter-tribal Council of California in 1968, and the California Rural Indian Health Board in 1969. Also in 1969, a political uprising among Indian college students led to the occupation of Alcatraz Island in San Francisco Bay. This protest occupation, which was joined by many California Indian young people, elders, and leaders, lasted for eighteen months and drew international attention to a broad spectrum of Indian issues, especially education.

Alcatraz sparked other Indian land occupations around the country, in Washington State, New York, Minnesota, and South Dakota. A notable land occupation in California was by the Pitt River Nation in 1971, which confronted police and endured mass arrests in an attempt to reclaim their traditional lands from Pacific Gas and Electric Corporation. The Pomo occupied an abandoned national defense radio listening station in Sonoma County that resulted in the founding of *Ya-Ka-Ama* (our land). Starting with Indian student demonstrations at San Francisco State University, the University of California at Berkeley, and the University of California, Los Angeles in 1969–70, Native American Studies programs were established in colleges and universities throughout the state. Protests in 1971 at an abandoned Army base near Davis, California, led to the founding of D-Q University which became an Indian tribal community college. In response to these and other protests, the governor of California established the Native American Heritage Commission in 1978. It had the responsibility of monitoring Indian human remains that are uncovered during construction projects, and to pressure universities and state agencies to repatriate Indian remains and associated grave goods to their respective tribes.

Indian political activists from California participated in many of the protest activities of the Red Power Movement that began sweeping the United States in the 1960s and 1970s, the American Indian Movement (AIM) founded in 1968; the 1972 Trail of Broken Treaties and the Bureau of Indian Affairs headquarters takeover; the 1973 Wounded Knee occupation; the International Indian Treaty Council founded in 1974; and the Longest Walk in 1978. In California, young Indians, both those native to the state and other newer immigrants to Los Angeles-Long Beach and the San Francisco Bay area, mobilized in a range of political actions and protests.

In the early 1970s there was a string of racial killings and racially motivated arrests of California Indians. Hooty Croy, Isidro Galley, and Bear Lincoln were unfairly targeted by the criminal justice system. Robert Hahn, a California Highway patrolman, shot and killed William Smith, an unarmed Indian lumberjack. Yet, Hahn was charged only with involuntary manslaughter and released on his own recognizance. Robert Marmon shot and killed unarmed Michael Ferris. Even though Ferris was shot in the back, Marmon, who is White, was charged only with involuntary manslaughter and released on his own recognizance. In contrast, Constancio "Tino" Deocampo, a Miwok and father of five children, had no prior arrests. Yet, when a White man was killed at the Tuolomne Acorn Festival, the alleged murderer identified by witnesses was later released and Deocampo was then charged with first degree murder. No weapon was found, no motive established, and the Grand Jury refused to indict. Even so, the local district attorney continued to harass Deocampo.

The worst racial killing occurred in Santa Rosa, just north of San Francisco. This was the murder of Richard Oakes (Mohawk) by a YMCA caretaker, Michael O. Morgan, on September 20, 1972. Although trial testimony indicated premeditated murder, Morgan was charged with involuntary manslaughter and later acquitted. Oaks, a student leader of the Alcatraz occupation, was married to a Pomo woman and living on the Kashaya Rancheria which borders the YMCA camp. The land on which the camp is located, as well as other so-called valuable real estate in the Santa Rosa area, was once part of the Coastal Pomo domain. Preceding the shooting, there had been a dispute about Indian hunting rights and a long-standing history of animosity towards local Indian people and racist remarks on the part of the caretaker.

Other protest actions included the "G-O" or GO Road Case in northern California. The U.S. Forest Service wanted to complete a five-mile section of a 55-mile long paved road through the Six Rivers National Forest to promote recreational use. The plan was opposed by Yurok, Karuk, and Tolowa Indian people since the road completion represented an impermissible intrusion into the sacred *high country*, the center of their spiritual and ceremonial universe.

Whereas the 1960s and 1970s witnessed the reemergence of Indian pride and political protest, the 1980s and 1990s became a renaissance for Indian culture and traditions. Heyday Books began publishing *News from Native California*, an outstanding quarterly magazine, in 1988. The revivals of other traditions and crafts are frequently featured in the pages of the magazine. Even earlier, in 1964, the first tribally controlled museum, the Malki Museum, was established on the Morongo Indian Reservation. A California Indian Conference, which includes papers and presentations from both academics and traditional Indian people, has been held annually since 1986. The California Indian Basketweavers Association (CIBA) was founded in June of 1991. Initially supported by the National Endowment for the Arts, it sponsors gatherings of weavers in a revival of an important craft tradition.

Biennial language conferences, called Circle of Voices, began in 1992. The Advocates for Indigenous California Language Survival was organized and remains quite active. Its charter is to foster the restoration and revival of Indigenous California languages. Since its inception in 1993, the Master Apprentice Language Learning Program (MALLP or MAP) has helped produce new speakers of over fifteen of the fifty original but endangered California Indian languages.

Beginning in 1981, the Committee for Traditional Indian Health has held annual conferences, most recently at Chau'se, Indian Grinding Rock State Historic Park, in cooperation with the Sierra Tribal Council and the California Rural Indian Health Board. There has been an active program to disseminate knowledge of traditional medicine and healing practices, to provide information on nutrition, and to encourage the use of traditional foods and of diets necessary to maintain good health.

California Indian artists have received prominence and recognition. The Cahuilla Dancers and Singers, the Intertribal Pomo Dancers and Singers, and many other ritual dance groups not only take part in traditional ceremonies, but they are also educating the non-Indian public by performing for local schools and community organizations. There has been a revival of important ceremonies like the Maidu *Weda* or Bear Dance, or Big Time, and other ceremonies that the Mountain Miwok sponsor at Grinding Rock State Historic Park (Chau'se). California Indians also participate in the numerous intertribal pow-wows that take place throughout the state. The oral tradition has returned with a new appreciation of Native storytellers. California Indian scholars are conducting significant research, and writing books and screenplays.

Today, California has 109 federally recognized tribes and 89 non-federally recognized tribes. The state has the second largest number of federally recognized tribes and the largest Indigenous population in the United States. There have been important political and economic gains. Native tribes, long thought to have disappeared or become extinct, have reemerged and, along with other unrecognized or terminated tribes, are today seeking official recognition. These include

California Indian dancer.

the Gabrieleno/Tongva Nation of the Los Angeles Basin, and the Ohlone of the San Francisco East Bay.

The Indian Gaming Act of 1988 provided the basis for the "new buffalo"—Indian casinos—to come to Indian Country. By 1997, California tribes alone were generating $1.5 billion in gaming revenue. Casino profits are underwriting tribal housing, providing employment and income to poor families, founding other economic enterprises, providing college scholarships for tribal youth, and giving free health care and other needed services to their respective tribal nations.

A growing number of California Indian communities are on the way to economic self-sufficiency, although there are still others for whom commercial gaming is not a viable option. Clearly, as the balance of power between Indians and Whites has shifted, ethnocide and wilding have lessened in California. Those tribes without casinos have less political and economic clout to deal with non-Indian people and their institutions than do the gaming tribes. Unfortunately, there has been a backlash in some quarters against the new casinos; unfounded charges are made that the casinos are under the control of criminal syndicates, or that crime and alcoholism rates increase as a result of gambling. Many non-Indians are appreciative of the new job opportunities and the fact that the Indian gaming tribes are making generous charitable contributions from their casino profits to fund community betterment programs in surrounding White towns. Yet, gaming is no panacea for California Indians. In a sense it represents a distorted economy. Will profits from the new buffalo be used wisely? Or will the contagion of economic wilding spread to Indian Country and impede the cultural renaissance that has taken place? Only time will tell.

CHAPTER REVIEW

DISCUSSION QUESTIONS

1. What are the three main ecological or ethnographical regions of California and the names of some of the Indian nations that inhabit them?
2. Describe the California mission system, and the Spanish and Mexican impact on the Native peoples.
3. What are some of the laws, institutions, and practices that led to the depopulation of the Indians during the early Anglo-American occupation period of California?
4. Who is Ishi, and how does his story relate to the depopulation of California's Indians?
5. Define genocide as the concept is applied to international law. What evidence does the chapter supply that would support the charge that the Indians of California have been the victims of genocide?
6. Explain how wilding theory might explain the genocide of the California Indians.
7. What are some of the recent developments that signal the reemergence of California Indian identity and cultural revitalization?

SUGGESTED READINGS

COSTO, RUPERT and JEANETTE HENRY COSTO, eds. 1977. *The Missions of California, A Legacy of Genocide.* San Francisco: Indian Historian Press.

HEIZER, B. F., and M. A. WIPPLE, eds. 1971. *The California Indians, A Source Book,* Berkeley: University of California Press.

LINDSAY, BRENDAN. 2012. *Murder State, California's Native American Genocide, 1846–1873.* Lincoln: University of Nebraska Press.

MARGOLIN, MALCOLM, 1978. *The Ohlone Way, Indian Life in the San Francisco-Monterey Bay Area.* Berkeley: Heyday Books.

MARGOLIN, MALCOLM, publisher, *News from Native California.* Quarterly. Berkeley: Heyday Books.

REFERENCES

ALTA CALIFORNIA. 1852. Letter to the editor, May 21.

American Friends Service Committee (AFSC). n.d. (California Indians.)

BAILIN, ROXANNE. Introduction by Aubrey Grossman. 1971. *One of the Last Human Hunts of Civilization, and the Basest and Most Brutal of Them All.* San Francisco: Image 3 Graphics.

BASSETT, KEVIN ANTHONY. 1990. "The California Gold Rush and the California Indian, An Ethnohistorical Study." A term paper presented to Steve Talbot's Native American Ethnohistory class, University of California, Davis, March.

BEAN, LOWELL JOHN. 1978. "Cahuilla." In *Handbook of North American Indians, vol. 8: California,* volume edited by Robert P. Heizer, 575–87. Washington, DC: Smithsonian Institution Press.

BEAN, LOWELL JOHN and SYLVIA BRAKKE VANE. 1978. "Cults and Their Transformations." In *Handbook of North American Indians, vol. 8: California,* volume edited by Robert P. Heizer, 662–72. Washington, DC: Smithsonian Institution Press.

CASTILLO, EDWARD. 1994. "California Indians." In *The Native North American Almanac,* edited by Duane Champagne, 322–34. Detroit: Gale Research.

———. 1978a. "Twentieth Century Secular Movements." In *Handbook of North American Indians, vol. 8: California,* volume edited by Robert P. Heizer, 713–17. Washington, DC: Smithsonian Institution Press.

———. 1978b. "The Impact of Euro-American Exploration and Settlement." In *Handbook of North American Indians, vol. 8: California,* volume edited by Robert P. Heizer, 99–127. Washington, DC: Smithsonian Institution Press.

COOK, SHERBURNE F. 1962. *Expeditions to the Interior of California: Central Valley, 1820–1840.* University of California Anthropological Records 10 (5): 151–214

———. 1976. *The Conflict Between the California Indian and White Civilization.* Berkeley: University of California Press.

———. 1978. "Historical Demography." In *Handbook of North American Indians, vol. 8: California,* volume edited by Robert P. Heizer, 91–98. Washington, DC: Smithsonian Institution Press.

COSTO, RUPERT, and JEANNETTE HENRY COSTO, eds. 1987. *The Missions of California: A Legacy of Genocide.* San Francisco: Indian Historian Press.

DERBER, CHARLES. 1996. *The Wilding of America: Greed, Violence, and the New American Dream.* New York: St. Martin's Press.

EARGLE, JR., DOLAN H. 1992. *California Indian Country: The Land and the People.* San Francisco: Trees Company Press.

FORBES, JACK D. 1982. *Native Americans of California and Nevada.* Happy Camp, CA: Naturegraph.

GABARINO, MERWYN S., and ROBERT F. SASSO. 1994. *Native American Heritage.* 3rd ed. Prospect Heights, IL: Waveland Press.

GALVAN, FR. P. MICHAEL. 1987. "No Veneration for Serra." In *The Missions of California: A Legacy of Genocide,* edited by Rupert Costo and Jeannette Henry Costo, 168–70. San Francisco: Indian Historian Press.

HEIZER, ROBERT F., ed. 1974. *The Destruction of California Indians.* Santa Barbara, CA: Peregrine Smith.

———. 1978. "Introduction." In *Handbook of North American Indians, vol. 8: California,* volume edited by Robert P. Heizer, 1–5. Washington, DC: Smithsonian Institution Press.

———., and Alan F. Almqist. 1971. *The Other Californians: Prejudice and Discrimination under Spain, Mexico, and the United States to 1920.* Berkeley: University of California Press.

HINTON, LEANNE. 1999. "Ishi's Brain." *News From Native California* 13 (Fall): 4–9.

HITTELL, T. H. 1897. *History of California.* vol. 3. San Francisco: N.J. Stone.

HURTADO, ALBERT L. 1988a. *Indian Survival on the California Frontier.* New Haven, CT: Yale University Press.

———. 1988b. "Indians in Town and Country: The Nisenan Indians' Changing Economy and Society as Shown in John A. Sutter's 1856 Correspondence." *American Indian Culture and Research Journal,* Special Issue: New Perspectives on California Indian Research, 12 (2): 31–51.

JOHNSON, PATTI J. 1978. "Patwin." In *Handbook of North American Indians, vol. 8: California,* volume edited by Robert P. Heizer, 350–60. Washington, DC: Smithsonian Institution Press.

KEHOE, ALICE B. 1992. *North American Indians: A Comprehensive Account.* 2nd ed. Englewood Cliffs, NJ: Prentice-Hall.

KELSEY, C. E. 1906. "Report of the Special Agent for California Indians to the Commission on Indian Affairs." March 21. Retrieved from http://www.csus.edu/anth/museum/pdfs/1906_CA+Special+Agent+Kelsey+Report.pdf

KROEBER, THEODORA. 1976. *Ishi in Two Worlds: A Biography of the Last Wild Indian in North America.* Berkeley: University of California Press.

LAPENA, FRANK. 1997/98. "Dancing and Singing the Sacredness of the Earth." *News From Native California,* 2 (Winter): 17–18.

MARGOLIN, MALCOLM. 1997/98. "Traditional California Indian Conservation." *News From Native California* 11 (Winter).

———. 1982. *The Way We Lived.* Berkeley: Heyday Books.

MAYBURY-LEIS, DAVID. 1977. *Indigenous Peoples, Ethnic Groups, and the State.* Needham Heights, MA: Allyn & Bacon.

MEYER, MELISSA. 1982. Review of "Ishi the Last Yahi, A Documentary History," by Robert F. Heizer and Theodora Kroeber, eds. Berkeley, University of California Press, 1979. *American Indian Culture and Research Journal* 6 (4): 105–7.

MOLOTSKY, IRVIN. 1988. "Senate Votes to Carry Out Treaty Banning Genocide." *New York Times*, October 15.

NORTON, JACK. 1987. "The Path of Genocide, From El Camino Real to the Gold Mines of the North." In *The Missions of California: A Legacy of Genocide*, edited by Rupert Costo and Jeannette Henry Costo, 111–25. San Francisco: Indian Historian Press.

———. 1979. *Genocide in Northwestern California: When Our Worlds Cried*. San Francisco: Indian Historian Press.

OSWALT, WENDELL H., and SHARLOTTE NEELY. 1999. "The Cahuilla, Gatherers in the Desert." In *This Land Was Theirs: A study of Native Americans*, edited by Wendell H. Oswalt and Sharlotte Neely, 145–74. Mountain View, CA: Mayfield.

PILLING, ARNOLD R. 1978. "Yurok." In *Handbook of North American Indians, vol. 8: California*, volume edited by Robert P. Heizer, 137–54. Washington, DC: Smithsonian Institution Press.

Project Underground. 1998. *Gold, Greed, and Genocide.* Research and text by Pratap Chatterjee. Berkeley: Project Underground.

SACRAMENTO BEE. 1997. "California's Lost Tribes." *Sacramento Bee,* Special Report, June 29–July 2.

SCHUYLER, ROBERT L. 1978. "Indian-Euro-American Interaction: Archaeological Evidence from Non-Indian Sites." In *Handbook of North American Indians, vol. 8: California,* volume edited by Robert P. Heizern, 69–79. Washington, DC: Smithsonian Institution Press.

SHIPEK, FLORENCE C. 1978. "History of Southern California Indians." In *Handbook of North American Indians, vol. 8: California,* volume edited by Robert P. Heizer, 610–18. Washington, DC: Smithsonian Institution Press.

TALBOT, STEVE. 1988. "Indian Students and Reminiscences of Alcatraz." In *American Indian Activism: Alcatraz to the Longest Walk,* edited by Troy Johnson, Joane Nagel, and Duane Champagne. 104–12. Urbana: University of Illinois Press.

United Nations. n.d. *The Crime of Genocide.* Pamphlet. United Nations: U.N. Office of Public Information.

WALDMAN, CARL. 1985. *Atlas of the North American Indian.* New York: Facts on File.

SPIRITUAL GENOCIDE
LAKOTA SIOUX AND THE MEANING OF WOUNDED KNEE

The struggle for religious freedom as exemplified by the Lakota Ghost Dance.
(Image inspired by a ledger drawing.)

My father will descend
The earth will tremble
Everybody will rise,
Stretch out your hands

—*Kiowa Ghost Song*

❖ ❖ ❖

Hear me, not for myself
But for my people . . .
Hear me that they may once more
Go back into the Sacred Hoop
And find the good, red road.
Oh, make my people live.

—*Black Elk prayer, 1931*

On June 26, 2002, the Ninth Circuit Court of Appeals in San Francisco ruled that the words "under God" in the Pledge of Allegiance are unconstitutional because they violate the establishment clause of the First Amendment. The court decision resulted an outpouring of sanctimonious criticism and patriotic zeal to "put God back" into the Pledge of Allegiance. Yet this controversy is tragically ironic if one reflects on the more than two hundred years of religious oppression that the Indigenous peoples of the United States have endured, and White America scarcely raised an objection.

Until 1935, the traditional (non-Christian) religions of the American Indians were banned outright on the reservations, and Indian people like the Sioux who practiced their spiritual beliefs and ceremonies could be fined and sent to prison. The *sweat lodge* purification rite and the beautiful Sun Dance religion were outlawed, and many spiritual practices driven underground. At the same time, Christianity was forced upon Native peoples by the missionaries and sanctioned by federal policy. Indeed, it took an act of Congress as recently as 1978, the American Indian Religious Freedom Act (AIRFA), to affirm religious freedom for the Indigenous peoples of the United States. Yet the law lacked teeth, because it contained no civil or criminal penalties (see Talbot 1984). Furthermore, AIRFA did not address the deeper spiritual aspects of American Indian belief and practice, especially the protection of sacred places. Subsequently,

through lobbying and political pressure by Native peoples and their allies, important new legislation was enacted: the National Museum of the American Indian Act of 1989, and the 1990 Native American Graves Protection and Repatriation Act (NAGPRA). The new Indian museum opened in Washington, DC, on the federal mall in September of 2004, and NAGPRA has resulted in the repatriation of human remains and sacred objects in a number of cases. Yet, as LaDuke points out in *Recovering the Sacred* (2005, 106): ten years after its passage, only 10 percent of an estimated two hundred thousand Indian sacred remains have even been inventoried, let alone repatriated; "there are loopholes in NAGPRA so large, and the lack of enforcement so dire, that you can drive an entire collection through it."

The struggle continues in the effort to ensure enforcement of the existing protective legislation and to broaden the scope of Native religious protection, to ensure the right of Native Americans to carry out their spiritual beliefs and ceremonies at places and sites deemed sacred.

THE CONTEXT OF OPPRESSION

In reflecting on the long history of oppression of American Indian religions, one date especially stands out—1890. It was in that year that several hundred Lakota (Western) Sioux were massacred by the U.S. Army at Wounded Knee Creek on the Pine Ridge Reservation in South Dakota. At issue was Indian religious freedom, because those massacred were adherents of the Ghost Dance religion which was seen as a significant threat to White Christianity and authority. It is significant that eighty-four years later, a second confrontation took place between the Indians and U.S. military forces at Wounded Knee. This was the 1973 occupation of Wounded Knee in which the Oglala Lakota were joined by traditional chiefs and the American Indian Movement to protest the ongoing repression on the Pine Ridge Reservation. For seventy-two days, from February 27 through May 8, the protestors and the military shot it out until a stalemate was reached.

Wounded Knee was symbolically retaken in 1973 by Indian people belonging to different tribes but with the goal of reaffirming the sovereignty of the Oglala

Sioux Nation. Spirituality, however, played a key role in Wounded Knee II. Deloria (1974, 253) explains: "The occupation of Wounded Knee . . . was triggered by a deep ethical outrage on the part of many of the Sioux, but the place, itself was not originally sacred to the tribe. Historic events—the original massacre and the succeeding decades of government exploitation of the Oglalas—had made the site one of the most revered places of the Sioux people."

The year 2003 marked the twenty-fifth anniversary of the passage of the American Indian Religious Freedom Act. In observing the anniversary, Native scholars and spokespersons met on October 24, 2003, at Arizona State University's School of Law to evaluate the effect of AIRFA. The proceedings were then published in the Fall 2004 issue of the *Wicazo Sa Review*. In April 2004, a commemorative seminar entitled "AIRFA at 25" was presented at the American Indian Studies section of the 46th Annual Meeting of the Western Social Science Association, in Salt Lake City, Utah. The participants of the two symposia concluded that the First Amendment to the Constitution has never fully protected American Indian religious rights, and that despite progress, a key shortcoming of the 1978 legislation was that it articulated policy rather than compliance.

Among the problems plaguing AIRFA is the fact that it was seriously weakened by two adverse Supreme Court decisions following its passage in 1978. These were *Lying* (1989) concerning the protection of a place sacred to northern California Indians, and *Smith* (1990) involving the use of peyote as a sacrament in the Native American Church (See Native American Rights Fund 1991). These two decisions, respectively, held that the First Amendment does not protect sacred sites from being desecrated by the government, and that peyote use should be criminalized. Fortunately, amendments to AIRFA in 1994 overturned the *Smith* decision. The amendments also legalized the religious use of peyote by Indian worshippers and banned discrimination against Native peoples on the basis of religious practice. The issue of sacred places, however, has remained unresolved and is the most critical item on AIRFA's unfinished agenda. Even though some sacred sites were eventually returned to Indian tribes, there are still over fifty that are currently "threatened by development, pollution, poisons, recreation, looting, and vandalism" (Harjo 2004, 133).

The right of Indian prisoners in state prisons to hold traditional religious ceremonies has also been an uphill battle. The U.S. prison system has become an important place where Indian people reconnect with traditional religious practices, but despite appreciable progress on this issue, there are still prison wardens who are abysmally ignorant of Indian religious beliefs and rights.

The protection of burial grounds and the repatriation of sacred human remains achieved a significant victory when Congress created the National Museum of the American Indian in 1989, and then passed the Native American Graves Protection and Repatriation Act (NAGPRA) in 1990. Despite the progress represented by NAGPRA, some language in the law remains troublesome: the categories "unidentifiable human remains" and "unclaimed human remains" are problematical with respect to the principle of repatriation. There are still tens of thousands of sacred remains stored in anthropology labs, museums, and institutions that fall into these ambiguous categories. The refusal of the courts to return the Kennewick Man to five Northwestern tribes claiming cultural affinity is a case in point. The Ancient One, as the remains are known to the Indian community, is a nine-thousand-year-old male unearthed in 1996 along a riverbank of the Columbia River. Some in the scientific community make the unlikely claim that the remains are of a Caucasian and therefore prove the existence of the White race present in the Americas before the Indians. In a tug of war between the Indian community and the scientists, a court decision gave the remains to the latter.

CHAPTER OVERVIEW

In this chapter we examine the issue of American Indian religious freedom in the historical context of Lakota Sioux relations with White America. The parameters of our discussion are the two Wounded Knees, the massacre of adherents of the religious Ghost Dancers in 1890, and the uprising on the Pine Ridge Reservation in 1973 in which modern-day protestors, joined by Lakota traditional chiefs and religious leaders, returned to the massacre site to make a desperate stand. In documenting this 150-year saga of oppression, we have chosen to highlight the cutting edge of religious and cultural suppression that attempted to destroy the Great Sioux Nation. In this task we focus our attention on the history of Indian-White relations of the Lakota Sioux, whose reservations today lie principally in South Dakota.

In summarizing Sioux-White relations, we show how spirituality has played a pivotal role in Lakota history. For this reason we describe Lakota religious beliefs and practices in some detail, especially the seven sacred rites. Most important, we note that the Lakota always turn to spiritual and cultural revitalization during the greatest periods of their oppression. Finally, as we do throughout this volume, a theoretical formulation is suggested that might explain this history of religious repression. This is the Doctrine of Christian Nations employed by the European colonizing nations in their conquest of the Indigenous peoples of the Americas.

THEORY: THE DOCTRINE OF CHRISTIAN NATIONS

How can one explain the contradiction between word and deed, the stark contrast between the principle of religious freedom that was enshrined in the U.S. Constitution by the Founding Fathers, and the vehement suppression of Indian spirituality? More important, we should ask what can be learned from the history of the oppression of Native peoples that might explain the cause or causes of religious intolerance. An explanatory concept that is now proposed by members of the Indian intellectual community is the Doctrine of Christian Nations (see Traditional Circle in Talbot 2006). Also called the Right of Christian Discovery, it is the doctrine that dominated the ideology of the European invaders of the Americas (see Newcomb 2002, and 2008). It is the proposition that the supposed god-given rights of European Christian nations are legally paramount to those of the Indigenous peoples who occupy the soil. In the United States it became enshrined in the 1823 U.S. Supreme Court decision, *Johnson v. McIntosh*, which ruled that the "right of discovery" by European powers takes precedence over the aboriginal rights of the Indian peoples and nations. It also gave plenary power to Congress to abridge the sovereign rights of American Indian tribes and nations whenever and wherever it was in the interest of the larger nation to do so. It paved the way for the forced removal and relocation of seventy-five thousand eastern and southern Indian peoples to Indian Territory under the 1830 Indian Removal Act. Many thousands died along the trail in this early example of ethnic cleansing. Steven Newcomb (2002) contends that the *Johnson v. McIntosh* court decision "is based on a religiously racist viewpoint that White Christians are superior to heathen Indians." The ruling "contains the promises that the 'first Christian people' (the court's language) have the right to assert 'ultimate dominion' over the heathens" (Newcomb 2002). We will return to this theory in the analysis section at the end of this chapter when it is applied to the religious oppression of the Lakota Sioux.

The theory of Christian dominance over the Indigenous peoples of the Americas is rooted in the directive issued by Pope Nicholas I in 1452 that gave permission to King Alfonso of Portugal to "capture, vanquish, and subdue the Saracens, pagans, and other enemies [and] to put them into perpetual slavery" (Talbot 2006). When applied to the New World, the doctrine dictated that lands which had no Christian owner were considered vacant lands, even though inhabited by non-Christian peoples. The doctrine gave absolute title to, and ultimate dominion over any lands discovered by the Christian nations of Spain, Portugal, France, England, Holland, and Russia. American Indian peoples were denied their aboriginal rights simply because their ancestors were not Christian at the time of the European conquest of the Americas.

Steven Newcomb (Shawnee/Delaware), director of the Indigenous Law Institute at Kumeyaay Community College, explains that the doctrine is directly linked to the Old Testament of the Christian Bible.

> [It] is based on the story of the "covenant" between the deity of the Old Testament and the so-called "chosen people." The covenant was based on land. The land "promised" to the Hebrews by the Old Testament deity was already inhabited by the Canaanites, whom the Hebrews were commanded to dispossess. Eventually, this biblical story was transferred to the Americas. As the British international law scholar, Henry Sumner Maine put the matter: "In North America, where the discoverers of new colonies were chiefly English, the Indians inhabiting that continent were compared almost universally to the Canaanites of the Old Testament." (Newcomb 2002)

A subsidiary concept to the Doctrine of Christian Nations is that of *genocide*. The international Convention on Genocide was adopted by the General Assembly of the United Nations in 1948, although it was not ratified by the U.S. Senate until several decades later. Genocide as defined by the United Nations is the committing of certain acts with intent to destroy, wholly or in part, a national, ethnic, racial, or religious group. The religious discrimination practiced by Western powers against Native peoples may be appropriately called *spiritual genocide*. It was most blatantly practiced in the United States against American Indians during the federal policy of assimilation that lasted from 1887 to 1934. In this chapter, which documents the history of U.S. Indian policy in dealing with the Lakota Sioux, it is suggested that applying the Doctrine of Christian Nations and the concept of spiritual genocide as theoretical constructs has explanatory merit. It can lead to a deeper understanding of this important issue and lead to better legislative remedies and policies.

Closely related to the Doctrine of Christian Nations and spiritual genocide is the concept of Manifest Destiny, that the White race is ordained by a Christian god to rule the world. Manifest Destiny has dominated U.S. foreign and colonial domestic policy with respect to the American Indians, Alaska Natives, and other colonized peoples, such as Puerto Ricans, Samoans, Chamorros of Guam, and Native Hawaiians. This view was codified into law in the 1955 Supreme Court decision *Tee-Hit-Ton v. United States*, that ruled that Indian occupancy is not a property right and can be terminated without compensation at any time by the United States. In Canada, the British Columbia Supreme Court issued a similar court decision in the 1991 Gitksan case, that the Gitksan Indians have no legal standing because of the Law of Nations, or Doctrine of Discovery.

TETON SIOUX SOCIETY AND CULTURE

The Plains of North America as commonly defined was "a region of tall-grass prairies and short-grass high plains extending west from the upper Mississippi River valley to the Rocky Mountains and from the Saskatchewan River valley south to the Rio Grande" (DeMallie 2001a, 1). Implicit in this definition were the vast herds of buffalo (bison) present and the utter dependence of Plains tribes like the Teton Sioux on them for subsistence. Furthermore, buffalo hunting by the eighteenth century had become dependent on the introduction of horses into the area, which revolutionized Teton culture so that they became a nomadic, buffalo-hunting society.

The North American Plains are generally divided into North, South, and Central regions. "The Southern Plains, although not precisely defined, generally refer to the region lying south of the Arkansas River in Kansas and extending southward to include most of Oklahoma, northern Texas, parts of eastern New Mexico, and southeastern Colorado" (Bell and Brooks 2001, 207. It was occupied by the Osage, Kiowa, Wichita, Comanche, and Plains Apache, among others, most of whom, with the exception of the Osage, were not speakers of the Siouan language family. The Northern Plains are situated today in Canada and before 1870 were part of Rupert's Land, an immense area whose rivers and waterways flowed into the Arctic Ocean. In 1870, a substantial portion of this region became part of the new nation of Canada, situated in today's provinces of Manitoba,

Saskatchewan, and Alberta. With the exception of the Santee Sioux refugees, who fled to Rupert's Land following their 1862 uprising, the Northern Plains was occupied by tribes other than the Sioux.

On the Central Plains were the Crow, Hidatsa, Mandan, Northern Cheyenne, and the Sioux. The Western Sioux, or Teton, were masters of the Central Plains, a region encompassing the greater part of the present states of Montana, North and South Dakota, and Nebraska. They were among the most populous peoples of the Plains, numbering in the 4,000–10,000 range and comprising seven divisions or nations. The conquest of the Plains by Euro-Americans was from three directions: Texas and New Mexico from the south, the Canadian prairies from the north, and the Mississippi River from central United States. This chapter focuses on the Central Plains of the United States.

Plains Indians like the Sioux had a reputation as being one of the best light cavalry in the world as mounted horsemen. The importance of the horse to the Sioux is seen in the name they gave it, "sacred dog." The horse affected nearly every aspect of Sioux culture. It was introduced to the Plains by two routes: "along the eastern edge of the Rockies through the Nez Perce and Shoshone tribes, and from the southern Plains through the Comanche, Cheyenne, and Arapahoe. Horses were traded by Indians on the Upper Missouri long before most Indians had ever seen a White trader" (Grobsmith 1981, 9). By the end of the eighteenth century, Plains horse culture was universal, with some tribes becoming horse-rich, as it were. Horses became a medium of exchange and an item against which the price of other trade goods was determined. Before horses, Plains Indians used dogs to draw their sledges (travois) for the seasonal bison hunt.

Warfare on the Plains was characterized by a single mobile raid for women and children, and horses. "These 'hit and run' tactics, often deep within an enemy's hunting territory, confused Europeans who were accustomed to longer campaigns resulting in victory or defeat and ultimately, a transfer of sovereignty or territory" (Swagerty 2001, 267). "By 1830, warfare had been woven into the fabric of Lakota life to the extent that gaining war honors became an end in itself. Striking an enemy ('counting coup') was the basis of the war honor system. Points were assigned for touching—not killing—the enemy" (Grobsmith 1981, 10).

Political Organization

The name *Sioux* is derived from the Ottawa and then borrowed into French as "Nadousessioux," later shortened to the last syllable, "Sioux." It is often asserted that the name means "snake" or enemy, although DeMallie (2001b, 749) denies this interpretation. The Siouan people are comprised of three dialect groupings based on language, and Seven Council Fires or political alliances. The three social groups based on dialects are the eastern or Santee Sioux who speak Dakota, the Northern or Yankton/Yanktonai Sioux who speak Nakota, and the Western or Teton Sioux who speak Lakota. The Santee are comprised of four political groups: Mdewakanton, Wahpeton, Sisseton, and Wapekute. The Yankton and Yanktonai are the fifth and sixth groups respectively, and the Teton the seventh. (See Figure 4.1.)

Despite dialectal differences, all Sioux speakers are intelligible to one another. Although the Santee, Yankton-Yanktonai, and Teton speak different dialects, intermarriage and close personal associations blur these distinctions, and an individual's speech dialect reflects one's own family history and life experiences. The Santee Sioux call themselves

Dakota, and the Teton or Western Sioux, Lakota. The name is usually interpreted as meaning "friends" or "allies." In this chapter we will use the terms Lakota and Western, or Teton Sioux, interchangeably. They are the largest division of the Sioux and the first to cross the Missouri River and become nomadic buffalo hunters.

Of the seven component nations of the Teton Sioux, the four principal ones are the Brule (*sicanju* or "burnt thighs"), the Oglala ("to scatter one's own"), the Minneconjou ("planters by the water"), and the Saone ("whitish people). The Saone, in turn, split into the Sans Arc ("without bows"), Two Kettles ("two boilings"), the Blackfeet ("Black-foot"), and the Hunkpapa ("at the entrance head" or "end of horn"). The number "seven" and the symbol of the "council fire" are a metaphor for the unity of the Sioux people. These seven nations are allied as *Lakota* (friends or allies). Each is also recognized as an *oyate*, or people.

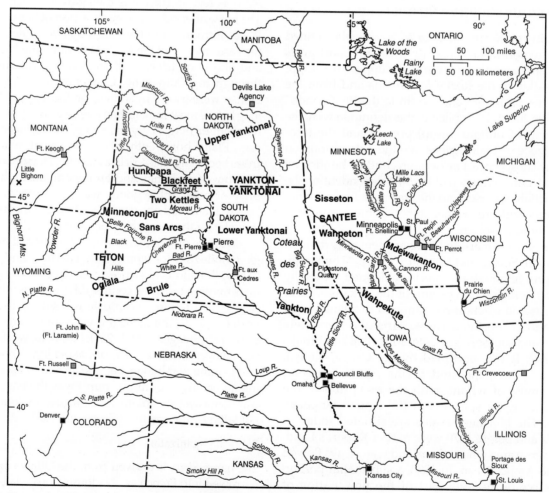

Figure 4.1 Sioux territory, early to mid-nineteenth century.

Lakota might quarrel, but they were never at war with one another in the past, because they were potential relatives. All other Indian tribes were considered as enemies unless peace was made with them, such as the Lakota's relationship with the Cheyenne and Arapaho. White people were called *waisichu*, a word referring to their power, especially with respect to guns. "During most of the year the members of the Seven Council Fires neither hunted nor lived together. Once a year all the divisions came together for the celebration of the annual Sun Dance ceremony, followed by the fall buffalo hunt. Unlike the regular patterns of hunting in small groups, the annual hunt was highly organized and regimented. It was policed by certain societies, which enforced strict rules and guidelines for this major event. After the hunt, the seven divisions returned to their separate locations and did not reunite for another full year" (Grobsmith 1981, 8).

The largest Teton nation is the Oglala, whose descendants today reside on the Pine Ridge Reservation. Next in size is the Brule, who live on the Rosebud, Lower Brule, and Crow Creek reservations. The remaining smaller groups live on the Lower Brule, Standing Rock, and Cheyenne reservations. All are located in South Dakota.

Social Organization

The basic social unit was the *tiyospaye* or lodge group. It could comprise an extended family, or a group of extended families, and number as many as one hundred people. The *tiyospaye* has been translated into English as bands or sub-bands. In the old days, the band averaged from ten to twenty nuclear families who were related patrilineally as a group of brothers—biological, adopted, and parallel cousins. Membership in a band, however, was by choice and reflected the success of a leader in attracting individual families to join his band. Women usually married outside the lodge group into which they were born, but they, like any individual, might consider themselves members of more than one lodge group. Band leaders were called chiefs, a position usually inherited by sons from their fathers. For many contemporary Lakota, the *tiyospaye* still remains a meaningful social grouping.

A camp, or *wicoti*, represented more than one lodge group that usually lived together. It could also include members of other tribes, such as visitors, relatives of the married-in women, and those seeking temporary refuge. Camps were larger and more formal in summer than in winter. At these gatherings,

the lodges of each *tiyospaye* were arranged contiguously in a formal camp circle with their tepee doorways facing the center of the circle, and an opening left in the east of the circle to serve as a formal entryway. The lodge of the leading chief was located on the west directly across from the entryway. "Elsewhere on the enclosed area of the camp circle, men's societies erected tepees for their ceremonies and public dances. Temporary brush shelters in which young men stayed, sweat lodges, and menstrual lodges were placed outside the circle" (DeMallie 2001c, 801).

The various Teton nations always gave the Oglalas the main place in every formal camp of the Lakotas. In fact, when two or more of the seven nations of the Tetons came together, they arranged themselves in the camp circle in preferential order: the Oglalas were first, the Minnekonjous next, the Brules third, and so forth. The same was true for the various sub-bands comprising one of the bands. A council lodge was erected in the center of the camp circle. Some of these practices are still observed in modern Lakota gatherings.

Walker (1982), who lived on the Pine Ridge Reservation for eighteen years at the end of the nineteenth century, lists five basic units of social organization for Lakota society in terms of territory or coresidence. The largest group is the *ontonwepi* (of-own-blood tribal division). The Teton are the principal *ontonwe*, or "camp-on-Plains." Next is the *ospayepi*, tepee divisions or nations. Oglala is the principal *ospaye* among the Teton. Third is the *ti-ospaye*, or bands. Fourth are the *wico-tipi*, or camps. Finally, there are *ti-ognaka*, which are the husbanded tepees.

Teton Sioux encampments were bands consisting of five or six extended families who traveled about independently of one another. At several times a year, especially during spring gatherings and summer buffalo hunts, several of these encampments or villages came together to form a camp circle as described above. Specialized leadership roles included council chiefs and war chiefs as well as conjurers. Chiefs, however, did not possess coercive authority. Their leadership was by way of example, and they were expected to not only give wise counsel, but also display the Sioux value of generosity. There were two types of medicine men: conjurors and curers, the later being herbalists and healers. Another role specialist was the *berdache*, "she-men" who wore women's clothes, seldom married, and who did women's work. Such persons were believed to be sacred and were responsible for important council and ceremonial duties.

The band leader was called chief. He spoke for the council which consisted of the respected adult men. Council decisions were based on consensus and included all things related to the common welfare, including camp moves, relations with other camps and with Whites, hunting parties, war parties, and disputes between camp members. The chief articulated the will of the council, which was then announced publicly by the official crier. The chief was supposed to be generous, putting the general welfare of the people ahead of his own and remaining self-controlled. Camp police called *akicita* carried out the chief's directions. They were appointed by the chief and could punish wrongdoers. They were said to gain their power from the powerful Thunder Beings. The council also appointed "deciders," or magistrates, who were in fact sub-chiefs. They were heads of prominent extended families. "Men were warriors, hunters, and religious and ceremonial practitioners; women took charge of the tepees, cared for their children, processed meat and hides, and cooked the food. Women also filled minor roles in religious ceremonies and some were specialists in herbal medicines" (DeMallie 2001c, 808).

In the Sioux kinship system, father and father's brother were classed together, as were also mother and mother's sister. Father's sister and mother's brother, on the other hand, were called by aunt and uncle terms. Although kinship was traced through both the father and mother, children belonged to the father's social group. Membership in social groups, however, was determined by residence and choice, not descent. Adoption was common and involved the sacred pipe ceremony. Sexual relations were not permitted during courtship. Polygyny (a man having more than one wife) was common. Boys were named after elders in the father's family, while girls were named after relatives in the mother's family. "Everyone was a potential relative. Etiquette required that everyone be addressed by a kin term, rather than by personal name" (DeMallie 2001c, 808).

LAKOTA RELIGION

The early French sociologist Emile Durkheim studied the religious systems of Indigenous peoples and compared them to those of Western societies. In a classic 1915 work he described religion as an integral system of beliefs and practices referring to sacred things, which unite into a moral community called a church by all those who participate in them (Durkheim 1915).

The essence of religion, as Durkheim noted, is not an edifice like a church or temple, or a even a priesthood. Rather, it is a sacred community of believers, the indispensable feeling of collective oneness in worship and faith. Thus the Pipe religion of the Lakota Sioux and other Plains Indians is every bit as strong a religious faith as is Christianity, perhaps stronger, since it is lived "twenty-four/seven" and not just on Sundays, as traditional Indians like to point out.

Religion is not a superstition; nor is it creed or dogma. The Sioux writer Vine Deloria, Jr. was the first contemporary academician to make a serious comparison of American Indian religions and Christianity (Deloria 1973). He pointed out that Indian religions, like Indigenous spirituality the world over, emphasize practice over theology. For example, the swearing on the sacred pipe by Lakota believers is the most serious vow a member of the Pipe religion can make, since the pipe is the most sacred object of the religion. Sacred power, "medicine," the Indians call it, is embodied in the pipe, indeed in all things, but especially in the pipe.

Durkheim (1915) pointed out that in the evolution of the great or world religions (Judaism, Christianity, Islam, Hinduism, etc.), this power became personalized. The sacred object becomes conceived as a superior entity or deity. With civilization, i.e., the rise of politically stratified states with written languages, the sacred power in prayer and practice was written down and interpreted by a priesthood. Thus the Christian Bible became sacred—the word of God—as opposed to a secularly written work. It is what a U.S. citizen swears upon in a court of law, but traditional Indians, like many Lakota, still swear on the pipe as a spiritual pathway to the Creator.

To take another example, in contemporary U.S. society, notarized documents and other official papers have a seal or some ceremonial language to make them sacred, in this sense morally binding. The deeds of property, wills, and other official papers, the U.S. Constitution and Declaration of Independence, all have this sacred quality to set them apart from secularly written documents or works.

There was an earlier time in Western society when Europeans were organized as tribes and clans and the people had religions very much like the adherents of the Indian Pipe religion. The sacred resided not only in human remains (considered sacred in all societies), in certain objects (the crucifix, for example), but also in nature itself, Mother Earth.

James Walker (1991) is the chief source for a detailed compilation of Lakota religious belief and ritual. He enumerated sixteen religious beings or gods for the Lakota, of which the principal ones are "Wi (the Sun), the chief of the Gods; Skan (the Sky), the Great All-powerful Spirit; *Maka* (the Earth), the ancestress of all upon the world and provider for all; and *Inyan* (the Rock), the primal source of all things" (Walker 1991, 50). There are also what Walker terms associate, subordinate, and inferior Gods, such as *Hanwi*, the Moon, and *Ta Tanka*, the Buffalo God. The important point, however, is that they are all the personal manifestations of one Supreme Being, *Wankan Tanka*, "the Great Mystery." In this sense, the Lakota gods are conceived somewhat in the same way as the Holy Trinity for those of the Christian faith, where the Father, Son, and Holy Ghost are separate and yet united into one Supreme Being.

Spiritual Power

Common to the Teton Sioux was a fundamental belief in spiritual "power." Although this power was imbued in all living things, it was nonetheless part of "the Great Mystery," beyond knowing or intellectual understanding. "Humans could share in that power and use it to their advantage by accessing it through dreams or visions, and by participating in rituals" (DeMallie 2001a, 9). Spiritual power was acquired through a vision, usually by men. Such power appeared to the visionary in the form of spirit beings or helpers, often in the form of a bird, such as an eagle, an animal, or natural phenomenon that might transform into a mystical human being. Religious specialists, medicine men or holy men, were individuals who had the greatest experience with this power, those who had garnered more power through a vision than the average person, and who could use that power to advantage in war, hunting, or curing.

Medicine bundles are ritual objects comprised of bird and mammal skins, sacred stones, and other ritual objects, that assisted one in the application of spiritual power. "Religious rituals were focused on individuals' demonstration of power through vision reenactments and on healing through the use of sacred songs and actions" (DeMallie 2001a, 10). The great vision by the holy man Black Elk as recorded by Neihardt is an example. When he was only nine years old, Black Elk was visited by the Thunder Beings "that foreshadowed the special powers he would have to use later in life to cure his people from illness and aid them in war. The vision gave Black Elk remarkable prophetic powers" (DeMallie 1984, 3, 6). There were also important tribal rituals

that invoked spiritual power in a way that could be shared by all participants. The Sioux Sun Dance is such a ritual in which the people come together in a single religious camp circle, not only for individual healing, but also as a ceremony symbolizing tribal unity.

The Sacred Pipe

Lakota ethnogenesis tells of a time when a great flood swept over the Plains, killing all human beings beneath its waves. The bones and bodies of the Sioux peoples turned into hard blood. That blood then became the red pipestone found in a southwestern Minnesota quarry, which then became for the Lakota the *Inyan Sha*, a sacred place. It is said that one young woman survived the flood. She gave birth to twins who became the ancestors of the Great Sioux Nation. This accounts for much of the symbolism of the Pipe religion, since all ceremonial pipes are made from the red pipestone. "The stem is our backbone, the bowl our head. The stone is our blood, red as our skin. The opening in the bowl is our mouth, and the smoke rising from it is our breath, the visible breath of our people" (Lame Deer and Erdoes 1972, 250). The protection of, and access by Indians to the sacred pipestone quarry has been a subject of controversy for many years. It was not until 1939 that Congress finally offered a measure of protection by designating the area the Pipestone National Monument, to be administered by the National Park Service.

Indian culture is replete with religious symbolism in numbers, words, and gestures. For the Lakota Sioux, the number four is *wakan*, or sacred. There are four virtues for men and women. Bravery, generosity, endurance, and wisdom are the most often mentioned virtues for men in traditional culture. For women, they are bravery, generosity, truthfulness, and the bearing of children. In the Pipe religion, there is also much religious symbolism. In using the pipe, the bowl is held in the left hand and the stem in the right. The designs carved into the pipestem are prayers. Where the eagle feather is attached depends on the nature of the ceremony, for example, high on the stem for a curing ceremony, middle of the stem for straightening out some family trouble, and where the handle and bowl touch if for gathering knowledge. The pipe always passes to one's left, taking it from the right, and so forth.

When the sacred pipe is raised in prayer, it forms a bridge from earth though the person to the Great Spirit or Creator. All the universe, all God's creatures, animate and inanimate, are then united in that pipe at the moment of prayer. That is why Indian prayers associated with the Pipe religion always end with the words, "All my relatives." The sacred pipe is at the heart of all other Lakota religious rites, such as the *Inipi* or sweat lodge for purification and prayer, the *Yuwipi*, and the Sun Dance.

In the distant past, a *wakan* (sacred) being, the White Buffalo (Calf) Woman, brought the sacred pipe to the Lakota Sioux in a time of famine. She showed the people how to pray with the pipe, linking through sacred smoke the Sacred Above with the Sacred Below. According to Lakota tradition, it was two hunters who first encountered this sacred being, who appeared to them as a spirit in the form of a beautiful woman carrying a bundle. (It is also said that this being was *Wohpe*, the Mediator of *Skan*, the Sky God.) One of the young men lusted after this beautiful woman dressed in buckskin, failing to understand that she was *wakan*, a spirit. He was immediately enveloped in a mysterious cloud and reduced to a skeleton. The other young man, realizing that the mysterious being was sacred, approached respectfully and was instructed to take a message back to his chief and camp. He was told by the sacred being that she had something of importance to tell the people, and that they should prepare for her coming. He did so dutifully, and when she appeared in camp she took from her bundle the sacred pipe. It was the first pipe received by the Sioux, and it established the kinship between them and the buffalo. When it was smoked the spirits could hear their prayers and send the buffalo. She also taught the Lakota their sacred rituals. Presenting the pipe, she said:

> With this sacred pipe you will walk upon the Earth; for the Earth is your Grandmother and Mother, and She is sacred. The bowl of the pipe is of red stone; it is the Earth. Carved in the stone and facing the center is this buffalo calf who represents all the four-leggeds who live upon your Mother. The stem of the pipe is of wood, and this represents all that grows upon the Earth. And these twelve feathers which hang here where the stem fits into the bowl are from *Wanbli Galeska*, the Spotted Eagle, and they represent the eagle and all the wingeds of the air. All these people and all the things of the universe, are joined to you who smoke the pipe—all send their voices to *Wakan-Tanka*, the Great Spirit. (Brown 1971, 6–7)

She then pointed to the seven circles carved on the bowl of the pipe, declaring that they represented the seven rites in which the pipe was to be used. The Lakota, she said, must follow the good Red Road, the sacred path, and not the "blue" or "black road" that is the path of error and destruction. After yet other instructions, the *Wakan* being departed, but a short distance away sat down and became a young red and brown buffalo calf. Then walking farther still became a white buffalo. Walking still farther turned into a black buffalo. And finally, bowing to each of the sacred four directions, she disappeared over a hill.

This first pipe, Sacred Buffalo Calf Bone Pipe, is still kept by the Sioux Nation as its most sacred possession. It has been cared for generation after generation by a keeper in the Sans Arc tribe and represents a symbol of the unity of the Sioux as a people. Orville Looking Horse is the current pipe keeper for the Lakota. Other sacred pipes made since have copied its manufacture.

Nothing of importance in the traditional Lakota world takes place without the pipe. Lame Deer reports that "Nobody would be foolish enough to tell a lie while the pipe is being smoked. That would surely kill him. And this we believe, even now" (Lame Deer and Erdoes 1972, 257). This is why the *peace pipe* was such an important part of treaty negotiations for the Sioux in their nineteenth century negotiations with White authorities. Smoking and passing the sacred pipe signified to the Indian representatives that everyone's words at the negotiations were true. In this instance, the sacred pipe solemnly sealed the terms and conditions of the treaty which was then "recorded" in the rich oral tradition of a nonliterate culture. For a literate U.S. society, on the other hand, it was the written word, sealed with the signatures (or "X" marks) of the negotiating Indians, and then ratified by the U.S. Senate, that made a treaty official. Little did the Lakota realize that U.S. treaty negotiators sometimes changed the treaty language to favor government interests on their way back to Washington, DC.

The Seven Sacred Rites

In the winter of 1947–48, Joseph Epes Brown (1971) recorded an account of the seven sacred rites of the Oglala Lakota as narrated to him by the holy man Black Elk. Even though not all of these rites are practiced today, they still form the core of Lakota religious ideology. Beginning with the White Buffalo Woman's first visit to the Sioux that gave them the sacred pipe, Black Elk describes the rites in great detail, which had been handed down orally to him by the former Keeper of the Sacred Pipe, Elk Head. The seven rites are the keeping of the soul, the rite of purification, crying for a vision, the Sun Dance, the making of relatives, preparing a girl for womanhood, and the throwing of the ball. According to Black Elk, two of the rites were already known to the Sioux prior to the coming of the sacred woman (although some others dispute it): the *Inipi* rite of purification in the sweat lodge, and the *Hanblecheyapi*, lamenting, or crying for a vision. The sacred pipe ritual was then added to these.

The first rite is the "keeping of the soul." Spirit-keeping is an elaborate ritual that also involves the sacred pipe, and it was brought to the people by the White Buffalo Woman. It was prohibited by the federal government in 1890, and the Sioux were even ordered to release all souls kept by a certain date. In the beginning, according to Black Elk, only the souls of great leaders were kept, but later on, the Lakota kept the souls of almost all good people. By keeping a soul in accordance with the proper rites "one so purifies it that it and the Spirit become one, and it is thus able to return to the 'place' where it was born—*Wakan-Tanka*—and need not wander about the earth as is the case with the souls of bad people" (Brown 1971, 11).

Besides the initial ritual of preparing the sacred bundle of the deceased, the person keeping the souls is forbidden to fight, must pray constantly, and must become an example to the people. In former times, within the tepee where a soul is kept, a woman is designated to care for the sacred bundle. A sacred food is prepared and saved for the day when the soul is released, the execution of which again involves an elaborate ritual and pipe ceremony. "The moment the bundle passes out of the [ceremonial] lodge, the soul is released; it has departed on the 'spirit trail' leading to *Wankan-Tanka*. . . . With this, the rite is finished, and then the people all over the camp are happy and rejoice" (Brown 1971, 30).

Lakota activist Russell Means describes a contemporary example of spirit-keeping. When his mother died in 1980 his brother Ted was asked to keep her spirit.

In our tradition, some of the loved one's hair is used to make . . . an altar—a special place of remembrance. The keeper of the spirit does not participate in social events for four seasons, and during that period or bereavement, stays at home, making offerings to the

altar. The community also honors the person who has moved on to the spirit world, bringing remembrance gifts to put at the holy place. In that way, we keep our loved one's spirit within us. At the end of a year, we have a ceremony to observe the releasing of the spirit from the community to make its passage to the next world. We then have a give away. We distribute all the gifts brought and buy even more to give away. (Means 1995, 494–95)

"*Inipi*, the rite of purification in the 'sweat' lodge, utilizes all the Powers of the universe: earth, and the things which grow from the earth, water, fire, and air. The water represents the Thunder Beings who come fearfully but bring goodness, for the steam which comes from the rocks, within which is the fire, is frightening, but it purifies us so that we may live as *Wakan-Tanka* wills, and He may even send to us a vision if we become very pure" (Brown 1971, 31).

The traditional purification lodge is made of willows, marking the four quarters of the universe and all things of the world—the two-legged, four-legged, winged peoples—are all contained within it. All must be purified in order to send a voice to *Wakan-Tanka*. The heated rocks represent Grandmother Earth, and the fireplace at the center of the lodge is the center of the universe in which the Great Spirit dwells. The special relationship of the Sioux to nature is revealed in the language. The Great Spirit is not only Wakan-Tanka, but is also referred to as *Tunkashila*, "Grandfather"; the sky is "Father"; and the earth is *Unchi*, or "Grandmother."

According to Black Elk, the door to the purification lodge always faces east, the direction that the light of wisdom comes. The sacred fire pit in which the stones are heated outside the lodge, the altar before the door, the manner in which the sweat leader brings in the rocks, administers the water to create steam, prays with the pipe, in short, all these elements and more are executed with the proper protocol and reverence. The participants are encouraged to pray for themselves or loved ones, and "to bring in the ancestors," who may appear as little lights, in order to aid their prayers. "Once within the lodge, the men move around sun-wise and then sit on the sacred sage which had been strewn upon the earth: the leader sits at the east, just inside the door" (Brown 1971, 35). There are four rounds of prayers and sacred songs, with the pipe passed from person to person clockwise; the door is opened briefly between each round to let in the light. "All Sioux ceremonies end with the words *mitakuye oyasin*—all my relations—meaning every living human being on this Earth, every plant and animal, down to the smallest flower and tiniest bug" (Erdoes 1989, 1). In Sioux religious thought, all are bound within the sacred hoop of the universe.

In Black Elk's account of the purification ritual (Brown 1971, 43), he reported that "these rites of the *Inipi* are very *wakan* and are used before any great undertaking for which we wish to make ourselves pure or for which we wish to gain strength; and in many winters past our men, and often the women, made the *inipi* even every day, and sometimes several times in a day, and from this we received much of our power."

The rite is still widely practiced today, not only by the Sioux, but by many Indian nations and individuals in one form or another. It is especially beneficial to those in drug and alcohol rehabilitation since it cleanses mind, body and spirit, and aids in healing.

A third rite is *Hanblecheyapi*, lamenting or "crying for a vision." It was the custom of the Lakota to seek guidance from a vision when undertaking some important thing, or when wishing for something very earnestly. A vision is given by a *wakan* being or spirit and told to the lamenter as in a dream. "No Lakota should undertake anything of great importance without first seeking a vision relative to it. *Hanble* (a vision) is a communication from *Wakan Tanka* or a spirit to one of mankind" (Walker 1991, 79). Before undertaking the rite, it is usual to first purify oneself in the *inipi* lodge.

Black Elk (Brown 1971, 44) recounts that "in the old days we all—men and women—'lamented' all the time [but] only those people who are very qualified . . . receive the great visions, which are interpreted by our holy man, and which give strength and health to our nation." Black Elk also reports that the great chief and holy man, Crazy Horse, "lamented" many times a year. "He received visions of the Rock, the Shadow, the Badger, a prancing horse (from which he received his name), the Day, and also *Wanbli Galeshka*, the Spotted Eagle, and from each of these he received much power and holiness" (Brown 1971, 45).

Black Elk reports that when a person wishes to "cry for a vision," he must go with a filled pipe to a holy man and ask him to be his guide. The old man then offers his blessing to the young man by praying with the pipe to the Great Spirit. In earlier times, on a chosen day, the lamenter would return to the residence of the holy man wearing only a buffalo robe, breech cloth, and moccasins. He again lays his pipe before his guide and asks for his assistance. He must decide on how many days to lament,

but four is customary, especially if he is a young man seeking a vision for the first time. Vision seeking is also a puberty rite, for a boy when his voice is changing to seek how he should govern his life, for a girl by wrapping her first menstrual flow and placing it in a tree.

The medicine man, John Fire Lame Deer, describes his first vision seeking as a young man in the book, *Lame Deer, Seeker of Visions* (1972). He was "locked" in a vision pit and wrapped in a star quilt made by his grandmother especially for the occasion. He also had a pipe together with a bag of *kinnickinnick*, Indian tobacco. "Besides the pipe the medicine man had also given me a gourd. In it were forty small squares of flesh which my grandmother had cut from her arm with a razor blade" (Lame Deer and Erdoes 1972, 13). She had given her own flesh, undergoing pain, to help her grandson pray and be strong-hearted. After several days and nights in the darkened pit, all the time praying, he heard a bird voice, and then a strange, high pitched human voice that said:

> You are sacrificing yourself here to be a medicine man. In time you will be one. You will teach other medicine men. We are the fowl people, the winged ones, the eagles and owls. We are a nation and you shall be our brother. You will never kill or harm any one of us. You are going to understand us whenever you come to seek a vision here on this hill. You will learn about herbs and roots, and you will heal people. You will ask them for nothing in return. A man's life is short. Make yours a worthy one. (Lame Deer and Erdoes 1972, 15–16)

Then his great-grandfather, *Tahca Ushte*, Lame Deer, the Minneconjou chief, appeared before him, and he understood that his great-grandfather wished him to take his name. Lame Deer then recounts that a power surged through him like a flood, what the Sioux call *nagi*, soul, spirit, or essence. "Now I knew for sure that I would become a *wicasa wakan*, a medicine man" (Lame Deer and Erdoes 1972, 16). (The *wicasa wakan*, holy man or shaman, conducts religious ceremonies; the *pejuta wicasa* or medicine man, on the other hand, is a healer.)

The *Wi Wanyang Wacipi*, or Sun Dance, is probably the most solemn and important ritual of the Lakota as well as for many other Plains Indian nations. It is an ancient ritual known to the Sioux before the coming of the White Buffalo Calf Woman. It involves self-torture for the greater collective good.

The Sun Dance is both a prayer and a sacrifice. Dancing from morning until night while tethered to the sacred sun dance pole, even losing consciousness, it also includes piercing the flesh. When the dancers give of their flesh, their own bodies, they are giving the only thing which is theirs alone to give to the Great Spirit. It is the most solemn and important of the seven rites. As Lame Deer explains: "During a vision quest, a man sits alone by himself on a hilltop, having his private communion with Wakan Tanka. The Sun Dance is *all* the people communicating with *all* the spirit powers. It is the *hanblecheya* of the whole Sioux Nation. It is not a macho dance to show how much you can endure. It is a prayer and a sacrifice. One takes part in it in obedience to a vow" (Erdoes 1989, 41).

Nevertheless, the rite, and especially the practice of piercing, enraged the early missionaries, and the federal government obligingly banned the Sun Dance in 1881, making it one of the proscribed Indian Crimes. The Sun Dance then went undergound, and has been revived openly only in recent years.

In the old days, the Sun Dance took place in a lodge of poles resembling a wooden tepee, sixty to one hundred feet in diameter. Today, there is instead an open "shade" for the spectators. The ritual is full of symbolism: "the camp circle represents the universe, the altar the essence of life, the buffalo skull the people's close relationship to this holy animal" (Erdoes 1989, 43).

When a person makes a vow to dance, it may be to heal a sick friend or relative, or to keep a warrior safe in battle. There are elaborate preparations, such as the selection and cutting down of the tree for the sun dance pole: warriors count coup on the tree, and four chaste women do the actual cutting. Tobacco offerings and colored cloth are tied to the pole. Dancers wear long kilts, usually red, and "are naked from the waist up, barefooted, their long hair hanging lose. Not a few have their faces painted. All wear medicine bundles on their chests, and wreaths of sage on their heads and around their wrists. Clenched between their teeth are plumed and quilled, eagle-bone whistles. Dancing, looking at the Sun, the men blow rhythmically on their whistles. . . . They dance from sun-up to sunset" (Erdoes 1989, 44). An eagle claw or sharpened, wooden skewers are fastened to the flesh on the chest or back, with the other end tied to the sacred pole. Women may also be pierced, usually at the wrist, or sometimes at the collar bone. "The high point of the dance [usually on the fourth day] is reached when all the Sun Dancers tear themselves free. All the women make the high, trembling, triumphant, brave heart cry that reverberates from the hills" (Erdoes 1989, 45).

The fifth rite is *Hunkapi*, "the making of relatives." Black Elk attributes the origin of this custom to a Lakota holy man, Matohoshila (Bear Boy), who received a vision about corn, a sacred plant to the Ree (Arikara). Through this rite, peace was established between the Sioux and their former enemies, the Ree. Since then, this ceremony is performed by Lakota who wish to ceremonially adopt a person. Any two individuals, through the *hunka* ceremony, can assume the relationship of a parent and child, brothers, sisters, or brother and sister. In the old days, "this ceremony entitled those for whom it was performed to wear a red stripe painted horizontally across the forehead. All who were entitled to wear this stripe formed a class and considered each other as kindred" (Walker 1982, 63).

There is also the ancient *Tatanka Lowanpi*, or Buffalo Ceremony, for young women. When a young girl becomes a woman, that is, experiences her first menstrual period, she becomes very powerful for either good or evil, because she is *wakan* during this time. In the Buffalo Ceremony she is taught how to take care of herself when she must live apart from others in the "lonely tepee" during the time she is "on her moon," and how to purify herself afterwards. The "buffalo women" form a class distinct from other Lakota women who have not undergone this ceremony.

The last rite is *Tapa Wanka Yap*, "the throwing of the ball." It is a lesser known ceremony, but Black Elk considered it the seventh major ritual. It appears to have originated as a puberty ceremony in which a girl tossed a ball to the four directions. Those catching it receive a special blessing.

Many ceremonies related to the ritual enactment of visions, because vision powers were inert until they were performed. The animal or bird spirit helpers revealed in these visions led to a ceremony in which other visionaries with the same spirit helper participated. This, in turn, created informal societies of elk, buffalo, deer, bear, eagle, and the like. Bear visionaries, for example, received special powers to heal those wounded in war, and these individuals became members of the Bear Society.

Taken altogether, the ancient tradition of the White Buffalo (Calf) Woman, who brought the sacred pipe and taught the seven sacred rites to the people, all attest to the deep religiosity of the Teton Sioux. Then, toward the close of the nineteenth century, at a time of the nadir of their population and their direst needs as a people, the Ghost Dance religion found root among them. Over three hundred of its religious adherents were tragically murdered by U.S. troops in 1890 at Wounded Knee, as will be related later in this chapter.

EARLY HISTORY OF THE TETON SIOUX

To understand how Lakota spirituality has been repressed and religious freedom denied, one must take note of Sioux political history.

The ancestral homeland of the proto-Western Sioux was "west of Lake Michigan, in the area of southern Wisconsin, southeastern Minnesota, northeastern Iowa, and northern Illinois" (DeMallie 2001b, 718). Deer was the principal game animal in the heavily forested parts of the region, and an early French explorer called the Sioux "the nation of beef."

By 1736, most of the Western Sioux were living on the prairie west of the Mississippi River, but warfare with the better-armed Chippewa and Cree forced them to abandon their villages and move westward. Unlike their relatives the Eastern Sioux, the Western or Teton Sioux lived solely by the hunt. They needed to follow the buffalo herds and to be closer to trading posts on the Des Moines, Mississippi, and Missouri rivers. The adoption of horses by the Sioux during this period was a major innovation that fit into the old nomadic buffalo-hunting economy. Horses were used for both buffalo hunting and for carrying baggage. By the early eighteenth century, the number of their villages was reported as between twenty and twenty-seven. During winters, the Teton returned to the wooded areas along the Missouri where the buffalo also sought refuge from the cold. With the coming of spring, the people followed the migratory buffalo herds once again onto the plains.

In the early days, the Plains Indian trade was conducted primarily by the French. This was the case even after the transfer of political sovereignty of Louisiana from France to Spain under the terms of the 1763 Treaty of Paris. It was in Spain's interest to focus attention on English expansionism while maintaining good relations with the resident Indian tribes. It therefore retained, for a time, the French commanders at their posts and allowed French traders to continue their usual trading practices with the Indians. Of the new items traded into Plains Indian country before White settlement, guns were the most important. "From colonial times through the end of the Plains Indian wars of the nineteenth century, availability and prices for guns and ammunition dictated much of the economic relationship between White traders and Indian clients" (Swagerty 2001, 261). While horses appeared before

guns on the South Plains, the reverse was true for the Central and North Plains.

"The Teton were in the forefront of the westward movement of the Sioux . . . [and] by the end of the 18th century, the more southernly Teton tribes, the Oglala and the Brule crossed the Missouri around the mouth of the White River" (DeMallie 2001b, 731). A series of smallpox epidemics among the Arikara in the late 1700s drastically reduced their tribal population and opened the way for the more northern Teton tribes to cross the Missouri. One of the first consequences of White contact was the smallpox epidemic of 1837–38, that was introduced by an American fur company steamboat travelling up the Missouri River. By summer's end, traders were reporting a mortality rate approaching 70–80 percent among the Indians they had encountered.

"During the first half of the 19th century, the westward movement of Sioux groups continued. The Teton, allied with the Cheyenne and Arapaho, pressed westward, driving the Kiowa and the Crow from the Black Hills area and claiming it for their own" (DeMallie 2001b, 732). The first Sioux treaty with the United States was signed in 1805, but warfare between the imperial powers divided the Sioux, the Eastern Sioux siding with the British, while the western groups tacitly supporting the Americans. Four more treaties were signed with the Yankton, Yanktonai, and Teton in 1825.

Estimates of the original Sioux population by White authorities vary considerably, ranging from several thousand to as many as over eight thousand by the Lewis and Clark Corps of Discovery in 1804–5. The two dominant Indian political powers in the region at the time of the Lewis and Clark expedition were the Teton Sioux and the Piegan Blackfoot, but by 1810, the Teton had become the dominant power on the Central Plains. At about the same time, the Cheyenne, who lived around the Black Hills, were also becoming a major force, although they later split into northern and southern branches, the southern branch relocating to the Arkansas River in southern Colorado.

Political Relations (1806–50)

The major frontier institution until 1822 was the *factory* or government trading house; few military posts were built prior to the end of the factory system in that year. The "factors" were in charge of all trade with the Indian nations. The system was also used for distributing presents and annuities. The government's Office of Indian Trade was abolished in 1822 and replaced with the creation of the Bureau of Indian

Affairs. "Until 1834, federal Indian affairs were under the War Department, consisting of superintendents, agents, sub-agents, interpreters, clerks, and mechanics who were political appointees or hired employees of the War Department" (Swagerty 2001, 270).

There were two types of treaties made with the Indian nations on the western frontier before 1835. The first was for "peace and friendship," to ensure nonaggression and amity. A second type was instituted to force the Indian nations to cede portions of their lands and to make room for the relocation of eastern nations when Indian Territory was created in 1825. These 1825 treaties did not succeed in their goals, because the resident Plains Indians resisted the encroachment by White emigrants and the dispossessed tribes from the East. Soon, a more aggressive approach was taken on the Middle Missouri with the Ponca, Teton, Yankton, Yanktonai, Cheyenne, Arikara, Hidatsa, Mandan, and Crow. "At each proceeding, presents were given out, troops paraded in review, cannon were fired, and speeches were made" (Swagerty 2001, 273).

These early treaties were boilerplate, that is, similar in their content and format. Article One specified that the tribe in question acknowledged the sovereignty and protection of the United States and permitted the United States to regulate all trade and intercourse with them. In Article Two, the United States agreed to receive the said Indian tribe under its friendship and protection, and only licensed traders could do business with the Indians in question. These treaties were then supplemented in 1830 with major land cessions from many of the Indian nations. Then from 1836 to 1851, fifteen more treaties were negotiated and ratified by the U.S. Senate.

In the 1840s and 1850s, there were two main routes by which emigrants from eastern United States moved onto the Western Plains: the Oregon Trail into California and the Northwest, and the Santa Fe Trail across the Southwest. By 1850, almost one hundred thousand emigrants had crossed the Plains Indians' hunting grounds bound for California, Oregon, and Utah. This laid the basis for the great treaty councils beginning in 1851 near Fort Laramie that established new reservations. The influx of emigrants also brought Christian missionaries. Beginning in 1819, Congress voted limited appropriations to subsidize missionary work among the emigrant Indians displaced from eastern United States and relocated to Indian Territory and the West.

By 1850, the Plains Indians had become integrated into the capitalist political economy. Buffalo robes were a main item in the fur trade. An average of one hundred thousand robes were produced by Indian women annually in the 1850s. In 1851, Congress implemented a policy of concentrating Indians on reservations away from White settlements and emigrant trails, and appropriated funds to negotiate treaties with the Plains Indian nations. The policy was to civilize (Westernize) the Indians and to restrict them to reservation homelands through treaties and land cessions. Nevertheless, hostilities broke out between the U.S. Army and the Teton Sioux in 1854–55, and the 1860s brought an increase in Indian-White conflict.

Political Relations After 1850

By the late eighteenth century, the territory of the Oglala extended from the forks of the Cheyenne River in what is now southwestern South Dakota, to the forks of the Platte River in western Nebraska. The territory included the Black Hills, which the Teton considered to be the center of their world and sacred, home to powerful spirits. "As buffalo became scarce near the Missouri, the Teton were drawn westward by the abundant herds beyond the Black Hills in the Powder River and Yellowstone River country" (DeMallie 2001c, 794). Of the various tribes comprising the Teton, the Brule were located east of the Oglala. The Saone, who soon divided into five separate nations, were located to the north along the tributaries of the Missouri, from Cheyenne River in present-day northwestern South Dakota and southwestern North Dakota.

By the early nineteenth century, the Teton were slaughtering huge numbers of buffalo for the commercial market in buffalo robes and salted tongues. They were engaged as fulltime traders and had become increasingly dependent on Anglo-American trade goods. "Liquor was being used by traders as a bribe to keep the Sioux loyal to specific trading companies, and its effects on the Sioux were devastating" (Grobsmith 1981, 11). The Brules became split up and disorganized as a result of their heavy drinking and the dwindling buffalo herds. Epidemics of diseases also made their inroads into the Sioux population, coming from the trade centers and emigrants travelling to Oregon and California.

In 1851, the first Fort Laramie Treaty was signed with the U.S. government. In exchange for annuities, the Teton agreed to allow the United States to build roads and military forts that would clear the way for emigrants travelling the Oregon Trail. The latter followed the North Platte River located in the present state of Nebraska, and then northwest into Wyoming, skirting the Powder River country of southern Montana.

The Oregon Trail soon became the focus of hostilities between the Indians and White emigrants when it resulted in the dissemination of Euro-American diseases and driving the buffalo herds away from the Platte River. The hostility of the Indians motivated the federal government to send treaty commissioners to negotiate treaties with the Teton and other tribes. The plan was to confine the tribes to the reservations and away from the emigrants and White entrepreneurs who were pushing the frontier westward. But Indian sentiment again became inflamed when the Bozeman Trail, a short-cut from the Oregon Trail in Wyoming to the gold fields of Montana, was opened in 1862. The new trail disrupted the ability of the Teton bands and their Northern Cheyenne and Arapaho allies to hunt in the Power River country. Hostilities continued after a series of forts were built to protect

the emigrants. The U.S. Army suffered a major set-back when Lieutenant Colonel William J. Fetterman and a detachment of eighty men foolishly allowed themselves to be led into an ambush, and all were killed. In the end, the United States was forced to abandon the Bozeman Trail posts when it signed a new treaty at Fort Laramie in 1868.

The 1868 treaty created the Great Sioux Reservation. It "delineated the boundaries within which the Sioux were permitted to roam: between the northern and southern South Dakota borders and west of the Missouri River. This treaty guaranteed that Indian land was to be entered only with Indian consent and affirmed that the Sioux would cease raiding" (Grobsmith 1981, 11). The Teton, in turn, agreed to permit the building of the Northern Pacific Railroad. Nevertheless, Whites continued to violate the new treaty by trespassing on Sioux lands when gold was discovered in the Black Hills. This led to the military debacle of Custer and his Seventh Cavalry being annihilated in 1876 at the Little Big Horn. The 1868

1868 The Fort Laramie Treaty Outlined the Great Sioux Reservation and the Unceded Indian Territory

1876 The Great Sioux Reservation After the United States Government Took the Black Hills and the Unceded Indian Territory

1889 The Great Sioux Reservation Broken into Smaller Reservations for the Various Sioux Bands

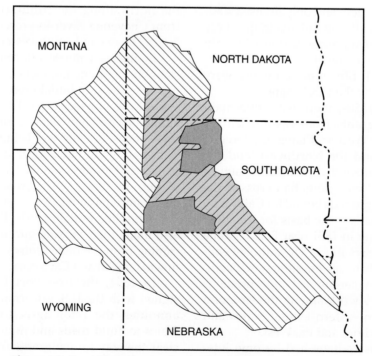

Figure 4.2 Great Sioux Reservation land cessions.

Ft. Laramie Treaty, while it lasted, signaled a major victory for the Teton Sioux. In addition to creating the Great Sioux Reservation, it also acknowledged "the area in Nebraska north of the North Platte and the eastern portions of Wyoming and Montana from the reservation boundary to the summit of the Big Horn Mountains as unceded Indian territory" DeMallie 2001c, 796). It also recognized the right of the Teton to hunt buffalo along the North Platte and Republican Rivers, and authorized the construction of agencies, annuities to the Indians, education, and the eventual allotment of reservation lands. (See Figure 4.2.)

During the next few years, while the new Indian agencies were being built for the different Teton nations, most of the Lakota were still living in the un-ceded Indian territory west of the Great Sioux Reservation, drawn there by the last remnant of the former buffalo herds. In spite of the agreement reached in the 1868 Ft. Laramie Treaty, the U.S. Army entered the fray to fight off Teton attacks as it escorted surveying parties during the summer of 1872 in preparation for railroad construction. The federal government sent a large Sioux Indian delegation to Washington, DC, in an attempt to bring the Teton into submission, but neither Sitting Bull nor any other chiefs who opposed the railroad were included. Railroad construction was completed the following year. A few years later, the United States managed to seize the Black Hills in the Agreement of 1876, although this action violated the 1868 Ft. Laramie Treaty. Treaty language required that any changes be approved by three-fourths of the adult, Sioux male population, which was not done.

BEHIND THE 1890 MASSACRE AT WOUNDED KNEE

It is reported to have been Chief Red Cloud who observed: "They made us many promises, more than I can remember, but they never kept but one. They promised to take our land and they took it." The 1868 Ft. Laramie Treaty guaranteed that all the territory from the Missouri River west to the Wyoming/South Dakota border would belong to the Teton Sioux and the Cheyenne, with the Indians to have sole and exclusive use within those boundaries. They were to have the Black Hills "as long as the grass was green and the sky was blue." Yet, within a few short years the Americans broke the treaty when gold was discovered in the *He Sapa*, holy land of the Teton Sioux and other Indian tribes.

"It is to the sacred lands of the Black Hills that the young men and women of the Plains Tribes went to fast and meditate and receive their vision. Through this vision came their names and instructions to guide their path through life. The Black Hills were, and are, the holiest of lands to the Sioux Nation" (American Indian Movement 1973, 21).

When Lieutenant Colonel George Armstrong Custer led a military expedition of 1,200 men into the Black Hills in the summer of 1874, he broke the 1868 Ft. Laramie Treaty. Ostensibly, the expedition was to locate a new military post, but surveyors in the party confirmed the presence of "gold in paying quantities," prompting a gold rush into the forbidden area. Custer and his Seventh Cavalry had been transferred up from the southern Plains where Custer led the 1868 massacre of Black Kettle and his peaceful Cheyenne on the Washita River. This earned him the name of Squaw Killer, though the Sioux called him Long Hair. The 1874 expedition, in addition to the Seventh Calvary, included "two infantry companies with Gatling guns and artillery, newspaper correspondents to report his exploits, scientists bent on exploring the Sioux' sacred Black Hills, and gangs of White miners lured by the tales of gold Custer claimed he had found the previous year" (Council on Interracial Books 1971, 220).

Hundreds of miners and settlers began invading the area in violation of the 1868 treaty and the government did nothing about it. The invasion into the *He Sapa*, "the heart of everything that is," greatly angered the Sioux, for the region was the "center of the world," a holy place. Yielding to the pressure brought by the gold seekers, the federal government then tried to buy the Black Hills, but the Sioux refused to sell or lease it. Both Crazy Horse and Sitting Bull refused to attend the council called by the federal commission from Washington, DC, seeking to buy the region, and more than twenty thousand Sioux, Cheyenne, and Arapaho camped at the council site to keep an eye on the chiefs in their negotiations with the United States.

When the Lakota refused to sell, the federal commissioners were forced to temporarily abandon their mission. The following year, however, the United States unilaterally condemned the Sioux title to the region, and the U.S. Army was ordered to collect the various Indian bands for deportation to the reservations or be declared hostile. The bands under Crazy Horse and Sitting Bull resisted. "Skirmishes continued through spring and early summer, and ever larger numbers of Indians left the reservations and joined with the 'hostiles' to resist the White invaders.

The Sioux Nation was more closely united than it had ever been before" (Council on Interracial Books 1971, 223).

Battle of the Greasy Grass

The U.S. Army moved in that summer, attacking a large summer gathering of the Teton Sioux and their Cheyenne allies. The location was a creek called the Greasy Grass by the Indians, but designated the Little Big Horn on U.S. Army maps. The conflict which followed culminated in perhaps the most well-known battle between the White invaders and the Indian nations in which Custer and his Seventh Cavalry were decisively defeated. Things had come to a head by the summer of 1876. On June 13, Chief Crazy Horse and his warriors turned back one prong of an army attack led by General George Crook at Rosebud Creek. Crook and his thirteen hundred men were caught by surprise and forced to retreat. The Indians had been holding their annual Sun Dance, a medicine dance for the return of the buffalo, an important religious ceremony. After repelling Crook's attack, the assemblage then moved to Greasy Grass Creek where they were joined by many fellow tribesmen from the government Indian agencies. "Six separate tribal circles—Hunkpapa, Oglala, Miniconjou, Sans Arc, Blackfoot, Northern Cheyenne—extended for three miles along the banks of the Greasy Grass. The village probably counted twelve hundred lodges and mustered almost two thousand fighting men" (Utley 1984, 183). A few days later, the Custer fight took place.

Hungry for glory and blind to all reason, Custer led a force of six hundred soldiers, including over forty Indian scouts and his personal newspaper correspondent, up the Powder River in a two-prong attack ordered by his superiors against the Indian encampment (see Hardorff 1991). Custer divided his men into three companies. The Indian encampment that he foolishly attacked contained twelve to fifteen thousand Indians. The various Indian bands had come together as they had always done for the annual buffalo hunt, for the chiefs to confer among themselves, and to conduct important tribal ceremonies. The U.S. Army attacked from two sides, from both the west and the east. Major Reno's troops, although reinforced by the arrival of Captain Benteen's battalion, were forced to retreat to some nearby bluffs. Custer and his men were quickly cut off and surrounded by the charging Indian warriors on some small hills east of the creek. Within several hours on that scorching Sunday, June 25, 1876, Custer's Seventh Calvary was completely annihilated.

There are several reasons for the Indian victory at the Greasy Grass. One was Sitting Bull's vision. While camped on the Rosebud earlier during the Sun Dance, the revered Hunkpapa chief had experienced a vision predicting many dead White soldiers "falling right into our camp." The people had thrilled to this news, since they put great stock in the power of visions to predict future events. Another reason was the recent arrival of agency Indians; the encampment contained about three times as many warriors as Custer had expected. There was yet another reason why the Indian warriors fought back so ferociously when attacked, first by Major Marcus Reno's battalion from the southwest, and then by Custer's cavalrymen on the east of the Little Big Horn. Enraged by an unprovoked assault on a civilian encampment housing not only women and children, but also holy men conducting religious ceremonies, the warriors counterattacked aggressively. Ironically, this Indian victory in 1876 (just one hundred years after the United States declared its independence from Great Britain) has been officially designated Custer's Massacre by U.S. military historians, while a real massacre a few years later of unarmed Indians by U.S soldiers is termed the Battle of Wounded Knee.

The Greasy Grass battle was a great victory for the Teton Sioux. The Indians fought to assert their hunting rights to the Powder River country as guaranteed to them under the terms of the 1868 treaty, and to be able to hold their large tribal gatherings and religious ceremonies each summer. After the battle, throughout the summer, fall, and winter of 1876, the U.S. Army harassed the Teton as they scattered, some to the Yellowstone country and others back to the agencies on the Great Sioux Reservation. In the spring of 1877, Sitting Bull fled with his followers into Canada. In May, Crazy Horse and his Oglala followers surrendered at Camp Robinson. "Between 1,100 and 1,500 people, including about 300 warriors, made up a column that spread over two miles of prairie. Singing war songs, the van marched into the military quadrangle and drew up before General Crook and his staff. The Crazy Horse hostiles laid down their arms and promised to fight no more" (Utley 1963, 19). Crazy Horse was then treacherously killed while a prisoner of war. The death of Crazy Horse effectively marked the end of armed resistance to White encroachment on Teton lands.

By 1878, the Army's policy of retaliation had driven most of the Teton to the reservations. "In 1881 Sitting Bull brought his followers back from Canada to the Great Sioux Reservation where separate agencies had been created for the different Sioux divisions" (Fowler 2001, 284). The reduction of Teton territory from half of the state of South Dakota to small individual agencies by 1889, and the seizure of the sacred Black Hills by the federal government, resulted in the collapse of Teton land holdings.

Altogether, about eight thousand Sioux gave up between 1876 and 1881 and were herded to the reservations. In 1880 there were an estimated sixteen thousand Teton Sioux residing on the Great Sioux Reservation. They included Red Cloud's seventy-three hundred Oglala and five hundred Northern Cheyenne at Pine Ridge, and Spotted Tail's Upper Brules numbering about four thousand at Rosebud. The bands of other Teton nations were scattered among the remaining agencies.

Americanization and Control Policies

Congress unilaterally ended treaty-making with the Indian tribes and nations in 1871, and the Indian frontier was declared closed. This action further undermined the authority of Teton leaders and their treaty councils. Some federal officials even discouraged Indian leaders from coming to Washington, DC, to air concerns if they did not speak English. The power of respected Indian leaders to represent their peoples was effectively reduced. Federal policy then encouraged the formation of tribal business committees, but these supposedly elected committees held limited authority and were most often under the sway of their respective government Indian superintendents.

In the late nineteenth century, the Indian agents worked diligently to stop Native religious ceremonies, in particular, the Sun Dance, the Ghost Dance, and peyote ceremonies. They also tried to prohibit Indian gatherings and gift exchange. They elicited the cooperation of agency employees and the missionaries to learn about any ceremonies held in secret. They punished Indian transgressors by withholding food supplies from them and their families. "The Peyote religion—which helped individuals adjust to the disappointments and transformations in their social world without rejecting Native religious ideas—spread northward . . . from the Southern Plains" (Fowler 2001, 286). New ceremonies, such as the Grass Dance, soon spread to the Teton Sioux and were represented to the government

Indian agents as harmless social dances. These ceremonies served to reorient the disheartened and oppressed reservation populations to maintain Indian identity and community solidarity. The Ghost Dance, which spread across the Plains in the 1890s, was another matter. Among the Teton, it took on a militant aspect that caused widespread hysteria among local White Americans and was perceived as a threat by the Indian agents.

In 1878, Congress authorized the institution of Indian police. "Police returned truants to government schools, helped to quash dances and curing ceremonies, reported cases of polygamy, gambling, and wearing traditional hair and clothing styles. Violations of regulations could be punished by loss of rations and other supplies, or by incarceration" (Fowler 2001, 286). To enforce the regulations of the agents, a Court of Indian Offenses was instituted by Congress in 1883. It applied to crimes that only Indians could commit. These two institutions criminalized Indian behavior and customs of which Whites disapproved and served to undermine the authority of traditional chiefs and religious leaders. In 1885, Congress passed the Major Crimes Act, which gave states and territories jurisdiction over crimes in Indian communities.

The Dawes Severalty (Indian Allotment) Act was passed by Congress in 1887. It provided each Indian male head of household with individually owned land, usually 160 acres, but with the federal government retaining title for twenty-five years. Reservation land left over after allotment was then sold to Whites. Indians like the Teton Sioux were deemed inferior and peripheral by the dominant White society. The government instituted an Americanization policy in which male heads of Indian households were compelled to take up farming. The Teton and other Indians were supposed to live as nuclear families on individual land allotments. The allottees were to live apart from their extended families, family clusters, and communal lands, and to work on agency irrigation and building projects. The Indian agents were authorized to withhold food rations from those Indians refusing to work as the agents directed. At the same time, the agents had the power to manage the allotted lands and to determine the prices for leasing or sale of the lands. These policies were never totally successful; in spite of the individualization of communal lands, people found ways to pool their resources among relatives and to continue traditional reciprocal relations of gift-giving. The agents then began issuing supplies to heads of households rather than to chiefs and band leaders, and whereas beef initially was issued "on the hoof" (live), agents began to issue it already butchered so that traditional leaders would not be able to legitimate their status in the distribution of meat.

Reservation Life

The Teton Sioux signed many treaties with the United States. The Ft. Laramie Treaty of 1868 provided for virtually all of the land (including the sacred Black Hills), from the Missouri River on the east to the South Dakota border on the west, as the Great Sioux Nation. Subsequent acts and agreements drastically reduced this land base to its present five reservations, and the Teton lost their sacred Black Hills.

Under the reservation system, organized military resistance to U.S. imperialism by the Teton and other Plains Indians ended. The Indian nations, now un-free and powerless, were rendered paupers in their own land. The daily roll call, food ration, and the annuity system checked any further organized resistance. All the old, traditional institutions—the Indian economy, the system of government, kinship groupings and the extended family, Native spirituality and religion—came under attack. In their place, federal authority instituted the 1887 Indian Allotment Act "to break up the tribal mass," as Theodore Roosevelt termed it. Allotment of 160 acres to each family head was said to be a bridge between savagery and civilization, although the Plains were better suited for cattle raising than for agriculture. "The Sioux were told [food] rations would be cut off if they did not cooperate with allotment. In 1889, the first Lakota accepted an allotment. . . . Those who held out altogether and refused to accept allotments soon found their rations cut off. . . . For many Indians it was a choice between accepting allotments or starving" (Grobsmith 1981, 14). Allotment caused ninety-one million acres of communal Indian land to be opened for sale to non-Indians.

Federal policy also ushered in the boarding school system to "kill the Indian but save the man." "In hopes of completing the assimilation process, the church and the federal government together constructed Indian schools to instill western values in children, to teach the English language, and generally to separate the Sioux from their Indigenous tradition" (Grobsmith 1981, 15). School conditions were harsh with strict discipline. The Bureau of Indian Affairs boarding school system made it a policy to snatch six- and seven-year-old children away from their parents and communities. They operated more like jails than schools and were run along military lines. Speaking Indian was forbidden, long hair was cut, civilian dress substituted for Indian clothes, attendance at Sunday Christian services made mandatory for savages, and a lot of corporal punishment meted out. The Sioux medicine man, Lame Deer, reported in his book that the worst admonishment a Sioux parent could give to their children was "Shh, *wasicum anigni kte.*"—"Be quiet or the White man will take you to his home" (Lame Deer and Erdoes 1972, 27).

Children living in boarding schools during the school year were often "farmed out" to White families during the summer to keep them apart from relatives at home on the reservation and to further alienate them from Indian culture. Destitute Lakota families depended on the boarding schools for free room and board during this period in their history. The Indian agent or superintendent was a virtual dictator, and his authority was backed by the Indian police and the code of Indian crimes. This punitive code, amended in 1904, stood in force until 1933. By political power and economic means, the federal government eventually broke the influence of the unprogressive or conservative chiefs one by one.

In dealing with White authority, the Sioux, like other Indian peoples, split in their political strategy into progressives and conservatives, the former cooperating with White authorities in order to gain small concessions or the means to feed their children, and the latter holding out for traditional tribal governance under the old band chiefs and councils, and for retaining aboriginal traditions and religion. Great pressure was also placed upon the Teton to cede lands because of the 1889 Omnibus Bill in Congress that admitted both North and South Dakota to statehood, together with Washington and Montana.

The Court of Indian Offenses attacked Indian beliefs, social customs, and religion. The sacred Sun Dance was banned. Traders and missionaries—Episcopalians, Roman Catholics, Congregationalists, and Presbyterians—flooded the Teton reservations. During the 1870s and 1880s, under President Ulysses S. Grant's so-called peace policy, the government adopted a program of assigning reservations to specific religious denominations. For a time, even the federal reservation schools were given over to the religious missionaries.

By 1890, the Teton realized that the U.S. government had tricked them into making fatal concessions without carrying out its federal promises. There was hunger in Indian camps and even starvation. There were also sickness, epidemics of measles, influenza, and whooping cough. At the Pine Ridge Agency alone, the death rate was 45 persons a month in a population of 5,550. "By the end of the decade, these burdens had plunged the Sioux to depths of despair unprecedented in history. Virtually every meaningful custom had been attacked or proscribed, every institution damaged or destroyed" (Utley 1963, 39). The Lakota had become a bitter and demoralized people.

THE GHOST DANCE RELIGIOUS MOVEMENT

In response to federal betrayal, and in reaction to the dictatorial reservation system, new religious movements swept Indian country throughout the United States. New prophets arose—Handsome Lake, Smohalla, Squasachtum, and Tavibo. Religious revitalization was the attempt to achieve liberation spiritually when it could no longer be achieved through military resistance. It was a spiritual response to the social disorganization and despair brought on by Anglo-American hegemony. As the Lakota holy man Black Elk said, "the nation's hoop was broken." The best known of these prophet-centered revitalization movements was the Ghost Dance. The Ghost Dance religious movement brought a message of hope through spiritual regeneration that quickly spread through the dispirited Indian populations of the Great Basin, the Plains, and Indian Territory.

The first phase of the Ghost Dance appeared about 1870 among the Northern Paiute soon after the construction of the transcontinental Union Pacific railroad through their country that brought destructive changes. "An Indian prophet, 'Wodziwob' (White Hair), had a vision that a big train would bring back the dead ancestors at which time a cataclysm would engulf U.S. society but miraculously leave its material goods behind for the Indians. Then the Great Spirit would return. This event could be hastened by new songs and religious dancing. After a time this early Ghost Dance petered out." (Talbot 1994, 677).

In 1889, a new prophet arose among the Paiute, Wovoka, known also as Jack Wilson. "Wovoka, 'the cutter,' had worked for a non-Indian rancher named Wilson and became familiar with the Christian Bible, learned about Jesus Christ, and watched non-Indian people in their circle dances" (Talbot 1994, 677). His father, Tavibo, was a leader of the Paiute community and a *weather doctor*, a medicine man who would could control the weather. Wovoka, too, became a

weather doctor and led the traditional circle dances. Between dances he preached universal love.

On January 1, 1889, during an eclipse of the sun, while he was very ill, Wovoka experienced a powerful vision. When the sun "died" that winter day he was taken up to Heaven where God gave him a message of peace and right-living. He was considered a prophet by the local Indians and his preaching influenced even neighboring Mormon settlers. Had the Son of God appeared in Nevada, and as an Indian? Using religious paraphernalia from Indian culture, such as red ochre paint and magpie feathers, he taught a new circle dance "to embrace Our Father, God." The celebrants were instructed to move in harmony sunward, singing Ghost (spirit) songs, and to live and work in harmony in actual life.

Wovoka explained that Whites had been sent to punish Indians for their sins, but that they could soon expect deliverance. The ancestors would return along with the game and the old Indian world, and White people would mysteriously disappear. This regenerated Indian world could be visited in the meantime through a new religious dance, by wearing spirit regalia, by singing Ghost songs, and by self-hypnotic trances. A dancer would fall down in a trance, "dying," and then come to life again upon awakening. He would then speak of travelling to the moon or the morning star, coming back with "star flesh" in his fist which had been turned into strange rocks. By these means one could "visit" long-dead relatives and see the promised world. Thus the religious celebrants joyously awaited the coming cataclysm that was supposed to occur sometime in 1890.

Although Wovoka himself never left his native land, Paiute believers and visiting delegations of other Indians soon spread the new gospel. The new religion spread quickly from nation to nation, and soon, the Kiowas, Comanches, Cheyennes, Arapahos, and Shoshonis had taken up the Ghost Dance. The Sioux, when learning of the new religion, sent a delegation to Nevada to talk with the prophet and bring back a report to their chiefs and spiritual leaders. These messengers were Short Bull, a Brule, and Kicking Bear from the Cheyenne River Reservation. "When they finally met Wovoka, he showed them his hat and in it they saw the whole world, their dead relatives alive and smiling, the prairie covered with buffalo. Wovoka also gave them sacred red face paint and magpie feathers, telling them to use these in their dance" (Erdoes 1989, 9). Upon their return they told the people that Wovoka was truly *wakan* (sacred), and what he taught was true, his dance was good.

Meanwhile, the people's spirits were at their lowest point. Dewey Beard, a Lakota living at the time, reported that "the buffalo were gone and all the Indians were hungry. I sat with my father in his tipi when a messenger came and told us that a Savior for the Indians had appeared to an Indian in the far off land of the setting sun, and promised to come again and bring the buffalo and antelope and send the White man from all the land where the Indians hunted in the old times" (Walker 1982, 157). And the Sioux began to ghost dance. "They made themselves special shirts covered with the images of Sun, Moon, stars, crosses, magpies, and eagles, hoping that these would make them bulletproof. They also wrapped themselves in American flags, worn upside down as a sign of distress" (Erdoes 1989, 9).

"The Ghost Dance shared many features with traditional Lakota religion. Performed around a center pole, like the Sun Dance, participants fell into trances in which they interacted with the spirits of their dead relatives. Since giveaways and spirit-keeping ceremonies had been outlawed in 1883, the Sioux had no traditional means of sending the spirits of the dead to the afterworld" (DeMallie 2001c, 815).

Among the Lakota, Wovoka's message of "do no harm to anyone" took a militant turn. The Great Sioux Nation had been broken up and the sacred Black Hills seized in 1877. By 1889, the Teton Sioux people not only had their lands drastically reduced, but they were also experiencing a severe drought. They were forced to eat their seed corn and to butcher even their stud bulls. To make matters worse, Congress had delayed delivery of badly needed food rations. Epidemics of diseases ravaged the population. Local holy men like Kicking Bear took up the Ghost Dance and attempted to give new spiritual leadership to their embittered and despairing people. The Ghost Dance, *Wanagi Wachipi*, thus became a form of spiritual resistance to White authority. Warriors wearing "ghost shirts," it was believed, could even turn back soldier bullets.

Although the new religion was mainly peaceful, hysteria swept the White communities around the reservations. The Indian agent at Pine Ridge urgently wired the U.S. Army to send soldiers to stop the dancing. Three thousand were immediately sent. Meanwhile, Kicking Bear persuaded Sitting Bull at the Standing Rock reservation to allow the Ghost Dance to take place under his protection.

Sitting Bull's Assassination

It was the arrest and murder of the famous Hunkpapa chief, Sitting Bull, on the Standing Rock Reservation on December 15, 1890, that galvanized events which led to the massacre of Ghost Dance adherents at Wounded Knee later that month. The following summarized account based on several sources tells the story.

"The politicians, reinforced by ranking army officers, decide to remove the 'idol,' the strongest symbol of rebellion and traditional Indian customs—Sitting Bull" (Murphy 2004, 49, 51). Accordingly, General Miles recommended that the reservation agent "secure the person of Sitting Bull." The historian, Robert Utley describes what happened when Agent McLaughlin ordered Lieutenant Bull Head, chief of the Indian police, to arrest Sitting Bull at his camp on the Standing Rock Reservation (see Utley 1963, 158–61).

Bull Head assembled twenty-six policemen and two sergeants, together with volunteers. Altogether this force numbered forty-three armed men. Before sunrise, on December 15, 1890, the party surrounded Sitting Bull's one-room log cabin. Two policemen, Red Bear and White Bird, ran to the corral to saddle Sitting Bull's gray circus horse. (Sitting Bull had traveled with William Cody's Wild West Show.) Bull Head, Shave Head, and Red Tomahawk positioned themselves at the door, with Lone Man stationed at one side. Their pounding on the door woke Sitting Bull who called out to them to enter. They did so and Sitting Bull crawled out from under his blankets. "I come after you to take you to the agency. You are under arrest," said Bull Head. At first the old chief meekly submitted to his arrest, replying "How [an expression of assent], let me put on my clothes and go with you." Slowly he dressed himself. "A woman's voice was heard singing: '*Tatanka Iyotake*, Sitting Bull, You were a warrior once. What are you going to do now?'" (Erdoes 1989, 11).

As the police escorted the chief out the door, Sitting Bull's wife began to wail. Once outside, things began to go awry, because the barking of dogs and the cry from Sitting Bull's wife had aroused the sleeping camp. To make matters worse, the prisoner's horse was not yet ready. As the four Indian policemen stood waiting, most of the camp gathered before Sitting Bull's cabin, bristling with anger. One of the Hunkpapa warriors, Catch-the-bear, pushed his way through the crowd. He saw his beloved chief being abducted by his enemy, the policeman Bull Head. Catch-the-bear called out so that all could hear: "Now here are the *ceska maza* [metal breasts], just as we expected all the time. You think you are going to take him. You shall not do it." Turning to the people behind him he commanded, "Come on now, let us protect our chief!" Some of the men began working their way through the police line to be closer to the elderly chief. Sitting Bull's son, Crow Foot, came out of the cabin and began chiding his father: "Well, you always called yourself a brave chief. Now you are allowing yourself to be taken by the *ceska maza*" (Utley 1963, 159). This jibe was too much for the old man. Despite the urging of the police, he hung back and declared "Then I shall not go."

Sitting Bull's horse now ready, the policemen grasped Sitting Bull's arms and began pushing him forward. The people went wild, cursing the policemen, and shouted that they would not take their chief. Catch-the-Bear shouldered his Winchester and felled Bull Head with a single shot. But as Bull Head fell, he, in turn, shot Sitting Bull full in the chest. At the same instant Red Tomahawk fired another bullet into the back of Sitting Bull's head, and the mighty chief of the Hunkpapas died instantly. Lone Man then killed Catch-the-Bear, and a terrible fight ensued. The people attacked the police with knives, clubs, and guns. "In the midst of the melee, with bullets lacing the air, Sitting Bull's old horse sat down and began to perform tricks learned during its days with the Wild West Show. The police were scared. Had the spirit of the dead chief entered the sitting horse?" (Utley 1963, 160).

Within a few minutes the bloody fight ended and the Ghost dancers took refuge in a grove of trees along the river behind Sitting Bull's cabin, shooting another policemen as they retreated. One of the policeman, Red Tomahawk, now took charge. He and the other police dragged Bull Head, still alive but seriously wounded, into the cabin. Inside, they spied the youth, Crow Foot, the murdered chief's seventeen-year-old son, under a pile of blankets. He cried out: "My uncles, do not kill me. I do not wish to die." The wounded Bull Head answered bitterly: "'Do what you like with him. . . . He is one of them that has caused this trouble.' One of the men struck the boy a staggering blow that sent him reeling across the room and out the door. There, as he lay dazed on the ground, two more policemen pumped bullets into him. Tears streaming down their cheeks, they killed him" (Utley 1963, 160). It was a terrible scene: In front of the cabin were eight dead Hunkpapa Ghost dancers, including Sitting Bull, and two dead horses. Four policemen had been killed, with three more wounded, two of them mortally. The regular army soldiers had placed themselves distantly behind the Indian policemen but did not come immediately to their aid when the incursion became

bloody. Finally, the troops began firing into Sitting Bull's camp as his followers fled the scene. But the worst was yet to come.

The Killing Fields at Wounded Knee

After Sitting Bull was killed, four hundred terrorized Hunkpapa followers of the Ghost Dance movement fled south to the camp of *Siha-Tanka*, Chief Big Foot, and his Miniconjous along the Cheyenne River. Meanwhile, panic seized the Sioux Indian agents and the authorities in Washington who now believed that an Indian uprising was in progress. The eastern press sent reporters to the Dakotas, with their dispatches describing the Ghost Dance as a war dance. At the same time, the followers of the Ghost Dance became even more fearful of White reaction and the military response following Sitting Bull's death. Some were for joining the still free Indian bands under Kicking Bear and Short Bull in the region known as the Stronghold. Eventually, one half of the entire U.S. military was thrown against the Sioux to suppress the Ghost Dance religion.

When U.S. Army troops caught up with them, 160 of the Hunkpapa refugees were persuaded to turn back just as they were descending Cherry Creek toward the Cheyenne River Reservation. The rest journeyed on, hoping to find asylum with Big Foot. Big Foot, described as a wise and mild-mannered peacemaker, although sympathetic to the Ghost Dance movement, was afraid that he and his people would also be attacked. They were almost out of food because the government had failed to make its regular autumn issue of food and clothing as required by treaty obligations. A detachment of U.S. soldiers ordered Big Foot to take his people to Camp Bennett. Big Foot's council deliberated whether to go to the soldiers' camp and become prisoners of war, or flee to Pine Ridge. In the end, it was decided to take his Mineconjous, together with the refugees from Standing Rock, many wearing "ghost shirts," to seek shelter and protection from Red Cloud at Pine Ridge.

On December 24, 1890, Big Foot's band of Minneconjous and the Hunkpapa refugees were intercepted and disarmed at Wounded Knee Creek by the Seventh Cavalry, just a few short miles from the Pine Ridge agency. Cavalry men rudely searched the wagons for axes, knives, guns, bows and arrows, and awls, leaving the Indians with no implements to secure or prepare food. "When the soldiers demanded that all Lakota guns be surrendered before any rations were distributed, a struggle ensued between a soldier and a Lakota who wouldn't give up his rifle" (LaDuke 2005, 100). During the scuffle, a soldier was killed. Custer's old regiment, the Seventh Cavalry, immediately opened up with Hotchkiss guns. These early machine guns poured two-pound explosive shells at the rate of nearly fifty a minute, mowing down everything alive—warriors, old people, women, children, ponies, and dogs.

Chief Big Foot and the elders in the council circle were instantly killed. The warriors dashed towards the pile of arms stacked by the cavalry to defend the women and children in hand-to-hand fighting, but they were no match for the army's guns. "Women and children attempted to escape by running up the dry ravine, but were pursued and slaughtered— there is no other word—by hundreds of maddened soldiers, while shells from ten Hotchkiss guns, which had been moved to permit them to sweep the ravine, continued to burst among them. The line of bodies was afterward found to extend for more than two miles from the camp—and they were all women and children" (Andrist 1964, 351).

The Oglala holy man Black Elk, a young man at the time, came upon the scene as the massacre was in progress. He provided this chilling testimony:

> Cavalrymen were riding along the gulch and shooting into it, where the women and children were running away and trying to hide in the gullies and stunted pines. . . . We followed along the dry gulch, and what we saw was terrible. Dead and wounded women and children and little babies were scattered all along there where they had been trying to run away. The soldiers had followed along the gulch, as they ran, and murdered them in there. Sometimes they were in heaps because they had huddled together, and some were scattered all along. Sometimes bunches of them had been killed and torn to pieces where the wagon guns [cannon] hit them. I saw a little baby trying to suck its mother, but she was bloody and dead. . . . There were only about a hundred warriors and there were nearly five hundred soldiers. . . . It was a good winter day when all this happened. The sun was shining. But after the soldiers marched away from their dirty work, a heavy snow began to fall. The wind came up that night and it grew very cold. The snow drifted deep in the crooked gulch, and it was one long grave of butchered women and children and babies, who had never done any harm and were only trying to run away. (Neihardt 1979, 198–201)

Three hundred seventy Indians, 250 of them women and children, were massacred that day. Only about 50 of the Indians survived the onslaught. The soldiers lost twenty-five dead and thirty-nine wounded, a number shot by their own men in the crossfire. "Dead soldiers were buried almost immediately, but it was five days before the frozen Lakota dead were buried. Soldiers and civilians in the burial detail had photographs made of themselves amid the carnage. The Lakota dead were stripped of valuables, then packed into a mass grave" (LaDuke 2005, 101).

Twenty-three medals of honor were awarded the cavalry for what was officially termed their "heroic action" in the "battle of Wounded Knee." Dee Brown, in his classic novel, *Bury My Heart at Wounded Knee* (1970), points out the irony of this national tragedy: The wounded Indian survivors were taken after dark to the Pine Ridge agency. The barracks were filled with soldiers and no one would open their doors to the Indian wounded for shelter. Finally, the Episcopal mission was opened, the benches taken out and hay scattered over the rough flooring. It was the fourth day after Christmas and the season's greenery was still hanging from the church rafters when the first torn and bleeding bodies were carried in. "Across the chancel font above the pulpit was strung a crudely lettered banner: 'Peace On Earth, Good Will to Men'" (Brown 1971, 418).

Rani-Henrick Anderson (2008) has written an excellent and comprehensive account of the massacre, employing the multidimensional historical method. He not only presents the Indian perspective or voice in telling the Great Story of the Lakota Ghost Dance, but also the viewpoints and roles of the other institutional participants—the Indian agents, the army, missionaries, press, and the U.S. Congress. The Indian agents were the worst. They condemned the Ghost Dance from its conception, "demanding that it be stopped, arguing for the arrest of ringleaders, contributing to the general alarm, and finally calling for troops. . . . The army regarded the Ghost Dancers as potential 'enemy combatants' and . . . as religious extremism," although there were schisms within the military (Talbot 2009, 188). General Nelson Miles believed that the Ghost Dance initially had been peaceful, but that "false prophets," especially Sitting Bull, had given it "a combative edge" (Talbot 2009). The Roman Catholic and Protestant missionaries had become active in the 1880s, but found few adherents among the Lakota.

> The Protestant missions, predominantly Episcopalians and Congregationalist, condemned Indian traditionalist religious ceremonies and beliefs as the work of the devil,

mainly through their newspaper the 'Word Carrier' (the Lakota language version being *Inapi Oye*). . . . In terms of the press, there were seventeen reporters on the Lakota reservations, representing half a dozen newspapers that issued contradictory reports about the prospects for peace or war and rumors of the 'Messiah Craze.' Although the newspapers thought they were reporting objectively, alarming headlines and reports more often overshadowed their attempts. . . . [T]he newspapers created the impression that a full-scale war was raging, mainly on Pine Ridge Reservation. (Talbot 2009, 188)

As for the U.S. Congress, it was in recess during the fall of 1890 and took little notice of the Ghost Dance until early December. "It unwisely reduced rations at a time when the Lakota were suffering from crop failure, hunger, and disease. Yet Congress was an onlooker rather than an active participant in the matter of the Lakota Ghost Dance" (Talbot 2009, 188).

By such massacres, treaty fraud, and other genocidal practices, but mainly through starvation—the calculated killing of millions of bison, the Plains Indians' primary food source—the Western Sioux and other Plains Indian nations were defeated and confined to reservations, thereby reduced to the status of captured nations.

EARLY RESERVATION LIFE (1880s–1936)

The social anthropologist Edmund H. Spicer has termed the years from 1871 to 1934 as the "colonial pattern" (1969, 98). The primary colonial agents were the Bureau of Indian Affairs superintendent, the Christian mission church, the federal boarding school, and the White trader. "The means for accomplishing the transformation of Indians consisted of replacing all the collectivities then existing among Indians, specifically, tribal land management, tribal government, . . . tribal religions, and extended families, especially as educational units. The transition was to be brought about without consultation and community interaction" (Spicer 1969, 111–12). The transformation for the Sioux, according to Spicer, took place between 1879 and 1912. To effect the transformation the Indian Agent had two powerful weapons at his disposal: He had food rations to give out at a time when the Lakota needed assistance to stay alive. And he had the Indian police to enforce his regulations and policies. He forbade the old councils and enforced his regulations with the Indian police who were under his control.

Even before the massacre at Wounded Knee, the Lakota had been surrendering to the U.S. Army band by band as the buffalo became scarce. Sioux refugees were unwelcome in Canada, so a return to the reservations was the only option for the defeated Indians. Once on the reservation, the warrior role for men was no longer a viable one. This left religion and politics as the only male roles possible. The Bureau of Indian Affairs fomented political rivalries to increase Agency control by appointing chiefs among the "friendlies," or in bypassing traditional leaders altogether. By the 1880s, the government had established so-called tribal councils at most of the Lakota agencies. Federal policy was to break up the bands into nuclear families in dispersed settlements in preparation for land allotment. The Courts of Indian Offenses, established in 1883, heard cases involving infractions of agency rules and policy. The Indian police and the superintendent-dominated court system replaced the institution of the *akicita*. The Sun Dance, healing ceremonies, and traditional dances were outlawed. Government and religious boarding schools were set up at the reservation agencies. Some Lakota children were sent as far away as Carlisle Indian School in Pennsylvania, and Hampton Institute in Virginia.

In 1888, the government sent its commissioners to break up the Great Sioux Reservation's nine million acres and establish five smaller reservations. The Ft. Laramie Treaty required that any changes receive the approval by three-fourths of the adult male Indian population. The Lakota at first refused. Upon returning the following year, however, the government negotiators were able to gather enough signatures for the Agreement of 1889, but charges of misrepresentation and fraud marred the approval process. Suspicion remained that the drive for statehood by the non-Indians in what became the states of North and South Dakota, Montana, and Washington had manipulated the Agreement.

Economic Life

Lakota economic life on the reservations changed. Beef rations were at first issued "on the hoof," with the cattle hunted down and killed much like the old buffalo hunts. By 1901, due to the outcry by the missionaries at this so-called "barbaric custom," the Indian agents had the cattle butchered and meat rations issued biweekly. The hides were then sold by the agent and the proceeds distributed at the end of the year. Lakota men were required to work on agency building projects for their food rations, a form of involuntary servitude. Reservation Indians were forbidden to carry firearms and the men were required to cut their hair. "Citizen dress" (White man's clothing) was encouraged.

In 1902, the U.S. Supreme Court in *Lone Wolf v. Hitchcock* gave Congress plenary power to overturn treaties. As a result, "lands were increasingly withdrawn from Indian control by the government's preference for leasing to commercial interests and by the inclusion of tribal lands in federal conservation and irrigation projects despite the protest of the tribes" (Fowler 2001, 290). Land allotment at Pine Ridge commenced in 1905 and was largely completed by 1911. Some of the richest agricultural land was removed from the reservation to become Bennett County, with the remaining unallotted land was opened to homesteading. As a result of these corrupt and unfair practices, the Western Sioux lost up to 40 percent of their reservation land base. Tragically, these policies resulted in an ethnic split between the landless mixed-bloods who sold or lost most of their lands, and the "country Sioux," or full-bloods who retained their allotments.

After 1902, as allottees died, the government encouraged heirs to sell their inherited land under the Dead Indian Land Act, the Indian agent allowing the land to be sold for less than the market value. "The Burke Act of 1906 gave the Secretary of the Interior the power to allow certain allottees deemed 'competent' by their agent to receive a fee patent, which permitted them to sell their land and made the land taxable" (Fowler 2001, 290). Then in 1907, Congress passed a law that permitted tribal leaders and individual allotees to lease land to non-Indians. Congress also allowed the Secretary of Interior to sell the land of so-called "non-competent" Indians if they failed to develop their allotments. Competency commissions were set up and fee patents were issued to educated Indians, and those of less than one-half Indian blood, despite the protests of the allottees who then became obligated to pay state and local taxes on their allotments. The vexing problem of heirship emerged. In the first place, federal heirship policy made it possible for women to inherit from their husbands, a role reversal in Lakota culture. In addition, "as allotments were inherited, increasingly large number of heirs owned shares in the allotments, which made it difficult for the land to be farmed or otherwise used by Indians. Instead, the fractionated allotments were sold or leased to non-Indians and the money divided among the heirs" (Fowler 2001, 290).

The allotment problem became a focus of Congressional investigation in 1928 and led to major reform under the Indian New Deal program of the Franklin D. Roosevelt administration. The 1934 Indian Reorganization Act officially ended allotment.

After 1900, federal policy shifted from an emphasis on farming to stock-raising. The Lakota developed large cattle and horse herds. World War I reversed this successful economic pattern when the Lakota were then encouraged to sell their stock and to lease their allotted lands to non-Indian cattlemen. The postwar depression of 1921 caused the cattle market to crash with the cattlemen defaulting on their reservation leases. Mixed-bloods, who had received fee patents to their lands, were encouraged by the government to sell their allotments to speculators and homesteaders. For a short time, dry farming proved a successful enterprise. "The government once again began to encourage the Sioux to farm, although a drought had begun in 1924 and the Indians lacked capital and mechanized equipment to compete with their White neighbors. . . . The financial crash of 1929 ended the agricultural prosperity of the Plains, and the Dust Bowl in the 1930s ruined the economy of the reservations. Gardens were destroyed, livestock died, and to survive, the Sioux sold everything they had—even their dishes" (DeMallie, 2001c, 816).

Economic life did not begin to improve until the creation of the Civilian Conservation Corps in 1933 when its Indian equivalent, the Emergency Civilian Works (ECW), put nearly every able-bodied Indian male to work constructing reservation roads, dams, fire breaks, communal halls, and to start canning projects and gardens. The program ended in 1942 after the United States entered World War II.

Political and Social Life

Reservation life for the Lakota was grim. Deloria (2005) reports that as late as 1926, barbed wire surrounded the Sioux reservations, and troops were stationed in the region in case of an outbreak. On each Lakota reservation the old chiefs at first established treaty councils to deal with government representatives and to pursue treaty claims against the United States under the terms of the 1868 treaty. Political life changed. Erdoes (1972, 174) describes the effect of allotment on Plains Indian tribal governments:

> A man no longer rose to be a chief in the old, natural way. Those who did what the White agent wanted became chiefs and were given fine, two-story houses, so that everybody could see that it paid to do as one was told. Those who disobeyed were removed from office.

The old nomadic democracy of the Plains vanished. The whole attitude of the government was summed up by Hiram Price, U.S. Commissioner of Indian Affairs, in the 1880s: "To domesticate and civilize wild Indians is a noble work."

The kin-based *tiyospaye* became less important and evolved into communities and reservation districts. By 1935, forty-one separate communities had formed on the Pine Ridge Reservation, organized into seven districts; twenty communities developed on Rosebud, and six districts at Lower Brule, each centered around a single community. Mixed-blood communities also developed that focused on ranching, although mixed-bloods did not participate in reservation politics until after the passage of the 1934 Indian Reorganization Act. The districts at Pine Ridge developed into villages with churches, dance halls for traditional dancing, and day schools. "The reservation was a total institution, controlling all aspects of life. The Indian police jealously guarded the borders and no tribal member could leave without a pass from the reservation superintendent. Important economic and political decisions, including land sales and leasing, were made by government agents, whose actions were automatically approved by tribal business committees" (DeMallie, 2001c, 817).

The traditional male role was undermined as women often became the economic mainstay of the family. The old kinship system began to change as the nuclear family rose to prominence and the younger people adopted Anglo kin terms. The kin avoidance patterns, such as mother-in-law and brother-sister avoidance, lessened. Traditional dances continued to be held in outdoor arbors or in district dance halls. Dances that formerly held Indian religious meanings were disguised by eliminating the features objectionable to Whites, and by holding ceremonies on a secular American holiday such as the Fourth of July. Some new dances developed, like the Omaha Dance, which evolved out of the old War Dance, and the Rabbit Dance for couples. The summer Sun Dance "transformed into reservation fairs that celebrated agricultural and domestic arts but also included games and horse racing" (DeMallie, 2001c, 818).

The Indian boarding schools, both those federally established as well as the religious ones, took their toll on Lakota family life and culture. For a time in the 1890s, the government even funded the mission-led schools, although the practice violated the constitutional mandate requiring the separation of church and state. Because it violated the U.S. Constitution, the Bureau of Indian Affairs was eventually forced to abandon the practice, but the psychological and emotional damage to Indian children remained. "Children typically spent half the day working in the school fields, kitchens, laundry, or doing other chores. The children were kept away from their communities as much as possible and punished for speaking their Native language. Upon entering school, children commonly received an English name, including the surname of their fathers" (Fowler 2001, 288). Physical punishment was severe and children often ran away. Mary Brave Bird (formerly, Crow Dog) gives a scathing account of the abuse she experienced at St. Francis Mission School in her book *Lakota Woman,* in a chapter titled "Civilize Them With a Stick" (see Crow Dog and Erdoes 1990, 28–41). Those in the schools formed friendships with children from other tribes, and these associations formed the basis for intertribal cultural borrowings and later political alliances in adult life that social scientists term pan-Indianism.

Religion

Christian churches, mainly Roman Catholic, Episcopal, and Congregational, flourished on the Lakota reservations during the early decades of the twentieth century. Although nominally Christian, many in the older generation continued to practice elements of the traditional religion despite the government's policy of outlawing the old Lakota rituals, such as Spirit Keeping and the Sun Dance. The Pine Ridge and the Rosebud reservations were the most committed to perpetuating traditional religious and healing practices. Conjuring ceremonies such as *yuwipi* and *lowapi* "sings" developed from older forms of traditional religion.

The *yuwipi* ceremony involves a medicine man who is wrapped in a star blanket and tied completely around with a rawhide thong. In a darkened room and amidst the increasing tempo of singing and drumming, the medicine man—the "stone dreamer"—mysteriously frees himself. It is mainly a healing ceremony using the power of the Sacred Stone Rite. A person who requests the assistance of the *yuwipi* man for healing, or to find an object that is lost, usually sends a pipe to him (he never accepts any payment). The *yuwipi* is also a dog feast, because those who participate are fed by the "sponsor" and are required to eat at least one morsel of dog meat.

The *lowapi* sings, on the other hand, take place in a darkened room without the "wrapping up" element and involve healing and prediction.

The Native American Church was introduced to the Lakota in the 1920s. It is also known as the Peyote religion. "Peyotism is a spiritually profound religion and way of life that ranks among the oldest, largest and most continuously practiced tribal religions of the Western Hemisphere" (Echo-Hawk 1991, 8). "Peyote is a small cactus which grows chiefly in the dry country of southern Texas, along the Rio Grande, and below the border in Mexico where the peyote cult is widespread among the Tarahumara, Huichols, and Yaquis" (Erdoes 1989, 36). Peyote is used as a "medicine" (in the Indian definition) by its Indian adherents but was called "the devil's root" by the Spanish priests who accompanied the conquistadores in their conquest of Mexico. The peyote button is chewed during religious ceremonies and can produce an altered state of consciousness that brings the participant closer to God. Contrary to popular belief, it is not addictive; its effects are mild and leave no hangover.

Peyote was introduced into North American tribes by the Comanche chief, Quanah Parker, in the middle of the nineteenth century. "Like the Ghost Dance, the peyote religion was born of despair, helping the poor full-bloods forget hunger and oppression, lifting up the hearts of their women" (Erdoes 1989, 37). It spread north from tribe to tribe and soon reached the Lakota Sioux. It became a pan-tribal religion, part Christian, but retaining a core of traditional Indian religious belief and practice. Two different ceremonial traditions developed, the Half-Moon Way, consciously Indian in focus and held in a tepee, and the Cross Fire Way that is held in church buildings and incorporates the Bible and Christianity into its worship.

RESERVATION LIFE AFTER 1936

The 1934 Indian Reorganization Act (IRA) ended allotment and allowed for the restoration of surplus reservation lands, the limited purchase of land to augment tribal holdings and a tribal credit program. It also provided for local government through elected corporate, tribal councils.

The IRA was the brainchild of Indian reform commissioner John Collier. Collier met with representatives of the Northern Plains tribes in March of 1934 in an effort to persuade the Lakota reservations to accept the new tribal council system of government, but the more traditional Indians remained suspicious, and the Lakota became divided over the issue. The Indian Bureau prepared a model constitution based on elected representation and majority rule. This, however, ran counter to the power lines of the old treaty councils and its system of traditional chieftainships that were still operating on many of the Lakota reservations. As a result, some reservations rejected the government's tribal council system altogether while others adopted it in whole or in part.

The limited authority of the new tribal councils soon became evident. The Secretary of Interior retained veto power in many areas of tribal administration. Furthermore, the councils were in many ways mere advisory councils to the Bureau of Indian Affairs superintendent. Federal policy had merely shifted from direct rule to indirect rule. As a result, the IRA exacerbated factionalism on the Pine Ridge and Rosebud reservations between the mixed-bloods and the full-bloods, and two rival councils formed.

The Johnson-O'Malley Act was also passed in 1934. It provided funds for Indian education, and in addition, a national Indian Arts and Crafts Board was established the following year to encourage arts and crafts development and marketing. The most popular Indian New Deal reform was the Indian Emergency Conservation Works program, previously mentioned, that provided jobs for local reservation Indians. Collier's policy edict that Indian religion and ceremonial life not be interfered with appears to have had little impact on the Lakota reservations. Congress soon eliminated many of the promises made by the Collier administration under the IRA.

World War II and Relocation

With the outbreak of the Second World War, the efforts by pro-Nazi sympathizers to get Indians to resist the wartime draft proved unsuccessful. Plains Indian men serving in the U.S. military ranged from 33 to 70 percent, probably the highest participation rate of any U.S. ethnic or racial group. Thousands left the reservations either for military serve or else to work in defense plants. Almost one-third of all American Indian war casualties were Sioux. As men left the reservations, women assumed many of the tasks formerly held by men, driving tractors, repairing machinery, and herding cattle. Furthermore, returning veterans were profoundly changed when they came home to the reservations after the war.

In 1942, the army withdrew 340,000 acres on the Pine Ridge Reservation for an aerial gunnery range, displacing 128 families. Although technically leased to the military until the end of the war, the Oglala Sioux Tribe did not get back the withdrawn land until 1975, and then only 248,000 acres were returned. The acreage that was returned contained dangerous unexploded ordinance.

Another wartime problem was the Pick-Sloan Project to construct five flood-control dams along the Missouri River. This negatively impacted five Sioux reservations and had a devastating effect on reservation land holdings. Entire communities on Lower Brule and Crow Creek reservations had to be relocated. Cheyenne River Reservation lost the most land and received the least government compensation.

War service had a democratizing impact on the political consciousness of many of the Indian soldiers, who experienced less racism in the armed forces than they had in the reservation border towns. Land and resource loss, however, continued. The leasing of tribal lands to oil and gas concerns was made in the name of helping the war effort. After the war, Indian war veterans had difficulty in finding employment even though they were technically eligible for the G.I. Bill of Rights.

The Indian Claims Commission (ICC) was created in 1946, which allowed Indian tribes to sue the federal government for lands illegally taken in the past. Virtually all Plains tribes filed claims. The Lakota filed their treaty claims with the ICC on August 15, 1950 but did not get a final ruling until 1980. In that year, the U.S. Supreme Court affirmed a 1974 ICC ruling that the Lakota tribes were entitled to $102 million for the Black Hills, which had been seized by the government under the bogus 1877 Agreement. In its ruling, the Court found that "a more ripe and rank case of dishonorable dealings will never, in all probability, be found in our history" (Gonzalez 2001, 134). However, no compensation was given for lost hunting rights, and only $450,000 was awarded for the gold stolen from the Black Hills by trespassing miners before 1877. Although the claims award was the largest ever made to an Indian nation by the U.S. government under the ICC, the Oglala Lakota at Pine Ridge rejected it, demanding adherence to the treaties and the return of the sacred *He Sapa* instead of a money compensation. Tribal attorney Mario Gonzalez sardonically reported: "Today, the Lakota's sacred lands are commercialized. Homestake Mine, the largest gold mine in North America, alone has earned more than $14 billion from gold and silver revenues [in the Black Hills] since 1876. In stark contrast, the Lakota people live in abject poverty on nearby reservations while the U.S. Government and its citizens continue to plunder their land and natural resources year after year" (Gonzalez 2001, 136).

In 1953, the federal policy of termination was instituted under House Concurrent Resolution 108, and Public Law 280 was signed into law. "'Termination' signified the revocation by Congress of an Indian tribe's status as a federally recognized tribe, and therefore its access and that of its members to the programs and privileges accorded such tribes" (Christafferson 2001, 823). The aim was to do away with a number of reservations, to strip them of their resources and shift authority for Indian affairs from the federal government to the respective states. P.L. 280 allowed certain states to take over reservation law and order, but neither policy affected the Indians of South Dakota directly. The federal program of relocation, also initiated in 1953, did have a profound affect on the Lakota as well as many other Indian nations.

The Lakota veterans of World War II and the Korean War returned to the reservations only to encounter joblessness and to find that the skills they had acquired in the military were not required or considered useful. Under these circumstances, many were persuaded to take advantage of the federal government's 1952 so-called voluntary relocation program. BIA relocation officials pressured young married couples to migrate to selected cities where they would, at least in theory, be assisted in finding housing and given employment training and jobs. The relocatees usually ended up in low-paying jobs and housed in low-income neighborhoods, after which government assistance ended. The rationale of relocation was that it would solve the "Indian problem" by draining the surplus Indian population from the reservations and assimilating the younger generation into the blue-collar, urban workforce. Chicago, Los Angeles, and San Francisco were target cities for many Lakota. The return rate to the reservations, however, was very high and often included harrowing stories by the relocatees of being abandoned in the urban centers. "By 1959, 58 percent of those from Rosebud and 45 percent of those from Standing Rock had returned to their reservations" (Christafferson 2001, 824).

An unintended consequence of the relocation program was the Indigenous nationalism and political activism it indirectly spawned. The cultural revitalization that took place among the urban relocatees and their families included disenchantment with Christian denominations, of which they were nominal members, and signaled a return to the religious beliefs and traditions of their grandparents' generation. Urban Indian centers were established, such as the Intertribal Friendship House in Oakland, California, where pow-wows and intertribal activities could take place. Contacts with various racial and ethnic political movements among African Americans, Mexican Americans, and others, as well as the anti-Viet Nam War protests, stimulated political awareness. Many young Indian relocatees concluded that assimilation did not work, and that they did not want to lose their Indian traditions and identity. Many opted to return to the traditions of their grandparents, to reclaim lost lands and to affirm their treaty rights.

Russell Means, a Lakota, who was one of the founders of the American Indian Movement, spent time as a youth in the San Francisco Bay area, and later went on relocation to Cleveland, Ohio. By the 1960s, many Lakotas like Means were participating in what became known as the Red Power movement. (See Means 1995.)

During the 1950s and 1960s, the Oglala Sioux Tribe sponsored an annual Sun Dance, but the ceremony had been shortened to two or three days, and the religious nature of the rite played down. By the 1970s, this began to change. "Men and women grew their hair long, and Sun Dancing and being pierced became important components of being Indian and symbols of political commitment. . . . [During the next few decades] the number of Sun Dances exploded from eight in all of South Dakota in 1978, to 43 on Pine Ridge alone in 1997" (Christafferson 2001, 831).

RETURN TO WOUNDED KNEE

Wounded Knee, site of the 1890 massacre, is located on the Pine Ridge Reservation in southwestern South Dakota. In 1973 it was occupied by Lakota civil rights protesters and their supporters from the American Indian Movement (AIM). The following description is of the reservation at the time of the occupation-protest.

Pine Ridge was originally part of the Great Sioux Reservation, but was split up and reduced by half between the years of 1868 and 1889. The reservation is the homeland of the Oglala Sioux who, at the time of the 1973 occupation, numbered eleven thousand members. The reservation is equal in area to approximately three rural counties, and it is the second largest reservation in the United States. Although the reservation originally comprised four million acres, less than one-half of this area remains in possession of the Oglala today. In 1973, one million acres were owned by Whites and 1.5 million leased to White ranchers at $1 per acre per year by the Bureau of Indian Affairs. The massive land alienation is largely due to allotment under the 1887 Indian Allotment Act. Beginning in 1904, the reservation was divided into 8,275 individual allotments. Only 146,633 acres were allowed to remain in tribal ownership, most of it wasteland. A major problem, a troublesome legacy of the Allotment Act, is heirship, the requirement that the allotment is divided equally among heirs upon the death of the original allottee. Over time, this has led to ownership fragmentation of the original allotment. "The fragmentation of allotted lands through heirship has meant that up to as many as 100 people own one parcel of land. Consequently the parcel cannot be utilized by the Indians as an economic unit. Indians also lack capital. The Indian Agency arranges for the Indian heirs to lease their parcels to Whites, often without the Indians' permission and at low prices. Those at Pine Ridge realize on the average $300 per year, usually received just before Christmas via the BIA Agency Office" (Talbot 1979, 239). The White ranchers, who lease the allotments, make the real money, while the Oglala landlords, traditionalist in values and suspicious of government, live on welfare. (See Figure 4.3.)

In the 1960s, the majority of the resident Indian population were "country Indians," mainly full-bloods who lived in scattered residences, mostly log houses or frame shacks. Some also lived in tents or tepees, and a few Lakotas slept in old cars. Most houses were without running water or electricity, and almost all were heated by wood stoves. In contrast, the community of Pine Ridge Village was peopled mainly by "town Indians," mostly mixed-bloods. It is "the site of the vast agency complex of governmental offices, the federal boarding school and high school, and the Public Health Service hospital. The town is likewise the seat of the tribal council and the Shannon County public school system, and the center of much of the missionary activity on the reservation" (Daniels 1970, 199). "The mixed bloods tend to live in and around [the town of Pine Ridge, where the BIA and tribal government offer as many as 600 job positions. Patronage is the order of the day and the tribal president disperses the jobs—to his friends and family. 'Jobs are so scarce,' said one politician, 'that a janitorial job becomes a political appointment'" (*San Francisco Sunday Examiner and Chronicle* 1973).

The Oglalas live in considerable isolation from their non-Indian neighbors. The nearest large White town is Rapid City, located one hundred miles west from the Pine Ridge Agency. Larger cities are even

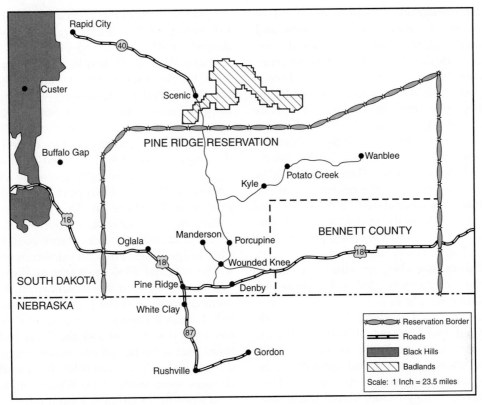

Figure 4.3 Pine Ridge Reservation.

farther away. The main social dichotomy on the Pine Ridge Reservation is between the town Indians and the country Indians. On most Indian reservations there is a class of assimilated Indians who, from necessity or self-interest, cooperate with the government bureaucrats in the neocolonial management of tribal lands and resources. The elected council system instituted under its 1935 IRA constitution displaced the old band structure and made no provision for traditional leadership. It placed control of Oglala affairs in the hands of those who were, in part, acculturated to White culture, reservation members who were often of mixed-blood, and who were not at home in the Lakota language. Although there have been many changes in the last quarter century, this schism has largely remained until today.

The deteriorated social conditions at Pine Ridge include extremely high unemployment. In 1973, a San Francisco newspaper reported that "nearly 70 percent of the Oglala Sioux are unemployed or underemployed, and per capita income is an incredibly low $800 a year" (*San Francisco Sunday Examiner and Chronicle* 1973). This fact led Edgar Cahn of the Citizens' Advocate Center to highlight the following

contradiction: "At the Pine Ridge Reservation . . . $8,040 is spent per family to help the Oglala Sioux Indians out of poverty. Yet, median income among these Indians is $1,910 per family. At last count there was nearly one bureaucrat for each and every family. . . . Over 60 percent of the reservation's work force is without steady employment" (Cahn 1969, 2). "Most people lived in tarpaper shacks without running water, electricity, or indoor plumbing. Some lived in small, ancient log cabins with dirt floors. One family's 'home' was a tiny, ramshackle 1920s trailer. Its owner, with typical Oglala humor [said] his floor space was the size of a 'white man's throw rug.' At least three-quarters of the people were in desperate need of housing. . . . Shannon County, which the reservation is part of, was then and to this day the poorest of all the more than three thousand counties in America" (Banks 2004, 145).

On the eve of the 1973 occupation, most of the country Indians, the rural population, were living on their own land allotments and receiving small lease payments. They were less dependent on tribal employment than was the case for the town Indians. The rural people obtained almost all their food from the government's program of surplus commodities, "from gardens and by gathering wild fruits, and from illegal deer hunting, while in other rural areas some households are deeply involved in a cash economy for such necessities" (Daniels 1970, 203). People usually shopped in the White farm towns bordering the reservation, rather than in the larger towns of Pine Ridge and White Clay, Nebraska. Some shopped even further away "in order to avoid the embarrassing contacts with the mixed-bloods and the 'White people who look down on you'" (Daniels 1970, 203). In spite of the remoteness of the reservation there was a lot of traffic by dilapidated "Indian cars" on poor reservation roads as the people shopped, visited relatives, and attended churches, pow-wows, Sun Dances, and other reservation events.

The political events leading up to the 1973 occupation include the racially motivated and unpunished murders of Native people in Indian country, sometimes by police—Yellow Thunder in Nebraska, Smith and Oakes in California, Shenandoah in Pennsylvania, High Pine in Montana, and Badheart Bull in South Dakota, among others. A series of land restoration protests also had taken place since 1968, such as Fort Lawton, Pitt River, Stanley Island, Mount Rushmore, and the occupation of Alcatraz Island in the San Francisco Bay by Indian college students. In 1972, the Trail of Broken Treaties (TBT) to Washington, DC, ended in the occupation of the Bureau of Indian Affairs headquarters and a standoff with police. The TBT was a national alliance of Indian organizations that led a motor caravan across the country to Washington, DC, to oppose a half dozen anti-Indian bills in Congress that would have curtailed Indian hunting and fishing rights, and limited Indian sovereignty. Although a politically diverse coalition of Indian organizations sponsored the TBT, the militant American Indian Movement (AIM) emerged as a key spokesperson for Indian grievances.

At Pine Ridge, a number of AIM chapters had sprung up, principally because of AIM's popularity after the TBT occupation in the nation's capital, and also because of its leadership in combating racism in South Dakota and Nebraska. When Raymond Yellow Thunder, an elderly Oglala from Pine Ridge, was beaten to death in a racially motivated attack by two White men in Gordon, Nebraska, his assailants were released without bail and charges reduced to second-degree manslaughter. Yellow Thunder's relatives called on AIM, which then led two thousand Indian protesters to Gordon, Nebraska, forcing an investigation into the case.

At that time of the Yellow Thunder murder, the full-bloods on Pine Ridge were engaged in a bitter dispute with the mixed-blood tribal president Richard Wilson. "When Wilson assumed office in 1972, the first jobs available went to his friends and relatives. Wilson followers—among them the toughs known throughout South Dakota as the 'goon squad'—got jobs with the BIA" (Brand 1978, 33). The federal government increased tensions on the reservation when it labeled AIM a subversive organization and secretly gave the Wilson tribal government its full support. Following the TBT protest in Washington, DC, AIM leader Russell Means, who is a Lakota, announced that the group planned to hold a victory dance back home on the Pine Ridge Reservation. Reminiscent of the prelude to the original 1890 massacre at Wounded Knee, Whites living near the reservation, U.S. government officials, and the president of the Pine Ridge tribal council panicked. Instead of Ghost Dancers, this time it was AIM and the "new Indian" movement that were feared and accordingly targeted as dangerous. Wild, completely unsubstantiated charges were made. Two Whites, members of the area's political extremist John Birch Society, spread the rumor that AIM was infiltrated by communists who planned to take over the reservation as a base of operations. AIM members were banned from the reservation; beatings, intimidation, harassment, and arrests became commonplace.

> The crisis came in February 1973, when the Oglala Sioux Civil Rights Organization (OSCRO) gathered a petition to impeach Wilson [the tribal president]. The government sent 80 federal agents to fortify the Pine Ridge BIA compound, and Wilson began deputizing supporters as tribal police. On February 21, he presided over his own highly irregular impeachment trial and acquittal. In response, OSCRO, along with the old treaty council and landowners association, appealed to AIM for help, and on February 28, 1973, some 200 armed men and women occupied the community of Wounded Knee. (Christafferson 2001, 836)

A civil war had come to Pine Ridge, with the federal government providing military assistance to the entrenched tribal council autocracy, including mounting a machine gun on the tribal headquarters and calling in federal marshals. Tribal council president Wilson cancelled all tribal council meetings and deputized a mixed-blood, armed force called the Guardians of the Oglala Nation (GOON), dubbed "the Goon Squad." People were being beaten and shot at by the Goon

Squad, and gatherings of more than three persons were banned on the reservation. The Wilson government had become a virtual dictatorship in the eyes of the traditional Lakota protestors. Russell Means, a Lakota AIM leader who investigated the complaints, reported the following: "I spent two days and nights . . . listening to the litany of horror: Women and girls had been raped by goons, men jailed, whole families beaten by Wilson's police, money and valuables extorted at gunpoint, and homes firebombed by night riders" (Means 1995, 252).

"In early February, 1973, eighty U.S. marshals of the paramilitary Special Operations Group, armed with automatic weapons and backed by armored personnel carriers and helicopters, surrounded the BIA agency at Pine Ridge and fortified the building. Only people approved by Wilson could enter the building" (Means 1995, 251). The Oglala protestors, full-bloods and traditional Sioux, were puzzled why the local BIA superintendent backed the Wilson regime and set about arming it against the traditional Oglala populace. Russell Means believes there was a hidden economic motive: the U.S. government wanted to keep control of the Sheep Mountain Gunnery Range, about one-eighth of the reservation, because of its rich deposits of uranium and molydenum. Another reason was the federal government secret COINTELPRO (counterintelligence) program directed against domestic activist groups like AIM. Backing the Wilson regime would guarantee the reservation not falling under control of what the feds considered dangerous radical political activists with possible links to the Soviet Union. In reality, however, the Oglala protestors were traditional Indians, who considered the real power on the reservation to lay with their chiefs and revered holy men. "They embodied our culture and our aspiration to sovereignty," reports Lakota AIM leader Russell Means in his autobiography (Means 1995, 253).

It was at this time that the traditional Oglala chiefs told the people to go to Wounded Knee and make their stand. Why Wounded Knee? Vine Deloria explains that although Indian religion is based on the sacredness of land, Wounded Knee itself was never considered sacred before the 1890 massacre. "Historic events—the original massacre and the succeeding decades of government exploitation of the Oglalas—had made the site one of the most revered places of the Sioux people" (Deloria 1974, 253). The memory of the Wounded Knee massacre has remained strong in the Lakota consciousness. Deloria (1974, 238–39) writes that a visit to the site was his strongest boyhood memory: "The massacre was vividly etched in

the minds of many of the older reservation people, but it was difficult to find anyone who wanted to talk about it. . . . Many times, over the years, my father would point out survivors of the massacre, and people on the reservation always went out of their way to help them."

The 1973 Occupation

When the occupation of Wounded Knee took place in February, 1973, AIM made three demands: (1) the Senate Committee on Indian Affairs headed by Edward Kennedy should launch an immediate investigation of the BIA and the Department of the Interior for their handling of the Oglala Sioux Nation; (2) Senator William Fullbright of the Senate Foreign Relations Committee should investigate the 371 treaties made with the Indian nations, because the government had failed to fulfill its treaty obligations; and (3) the Pine Ridge Reservation tribal constitution must be suspended and the Oglala Sioux allowed to elect their own officials.

Once the protestors had occupied Wounded Knee village, the site was surrounded and blockaded by federal marshals, the FBI, the Bureau of Indian Affairs police, the federal border patrol, and elements of the U.S. Army. The courts would later rule that the government's action was an illegal blockade.

> The military presence at Wounded Knee was in violation of federal law (18 USC 1385), which stipulates that the use of U.S. military personnel and equipment to quell a civilian disturbance is unconstitutional in the absence of a presidential proclamation or Congressional authorization. Yet the 81 Airborne was there in civilian disguise, and the U.S. Army furnished 16 armored personnel carriers, 400,000 rounds of ammunition, 100 protective vests, a Phantom jet, three helicopters, 120 sniper rifles, 20 grenade launchers, and a host of other equipment. The 200 Indians, on the other hand, had fewer than 50 rifles. . . . A Vietnam veteran inside Wounded Knee later testified: "We took more bullets in 71 days than I took in two years in Vietnam. It was horrible. The Army fired at everything that moved" (Talbot 1981, 63–64).

A federal army had come to Pine Ridge. In alternating periods of cold and hot war, and on-and-off again negotiations, a second massacre of Indian people was narrowly averted.

> There were fifteen armored cars—APCs—one hundred thousand rounds of M-16 ammo, eleven hundred parachute illumination flares, twenty sniper rifles with

night-vision scopes, powerful searchlights, submachine guns, bulletproof vests, gas masks, C rations, ponchos, blankets, and helmets. Low-flying army planes performed photo reconnaissance missions, which frightened some of the older women. They thought we were about to be bombed. . . . A top secret plan called Garden Plot was developed by the Pentagon. Army activity was coordinated by the Directorate of Military Support, an undercover Pentagon unit that was in charge of the army's assistance to law enforcement agencies. (Banks 2004, 171)

The following days were filled with firefights and Indian casualties among the outgunned protestors. Even when food supplies were scant or even nonexistent, the poorly armed protestors carried on their spiritual ceremonies and remained united. Under the guidance of AIM medicine man Leonar Crow Dog, they resurrected the Ghost Dance, "because it was here that in 1890 that Chief Big Foot's ghost-dancers had been massacred by U.S. soldiers" (Banks 2004, 186). Fortunately, the Colonel in charge of the government's military operation rejected the idea of repeating the 1890 massacre, including a request by the FBI to commit two thousand regular army troops to overrun the Indian encampment.

An historic event occurred on March 11 when an independent Oglala Sioux Nation was declared by the protesters. On that date, fourteen of the eighteen tribal chiefs, "traditional and still-respected leaders of their people, as well as eight of twenty members of the Bureau of Indian Affairs corporate tribal council . . . met with the American Indian Movement leaders and declared their independence from the United States government control and domination" (American Indian Movement 1973, 9). The original Oglala government had ceased to be recognized by the United States after the 1890 massacre, and an alien political system, the tribal council form of government, was imposed on the reservation in 1935 under the Indian Reorganization Act. Thus, for the first time since 1890, representatives of the federal government were forced to sit down and negotiate with the "traditional and still-respected leaders" and others who had proclaimed an independent nation. The *New York Times* reported in an editorial: "Perhaps for the first time since the British people's revolutionary war of 1776, the American people gave their support to an armed insurrection against the government of the land. The Lou Harris Poll showed 51% of those questioned supported the

Independent Oglala Nation at Wounded Knee" (*Akwesasne Notes* 1973, 6).

The protestors at Wounded Knee were representatives of many different Indian peoples and nations, although most were Lakota. A liberated zone, an independent Oglala Nation was created despite the blockade. AIM leader Dennis Banks later declared that despite the bullets and the government blockade, he had never felt so free. The common link was spirituality.

Christianity, propagated on Pine Ridge in more than 100 missionary churches, was replaced by a return to traditional Indian spirituality. The once-outlawed religious practices of the Sioux served as a rallying point to unify an otherwise disparate group. No other factor so strengthened the Wounded Knee resistance. Indians smoked the sacred pipe, prayed with the ceremonial peyote and took part in the purifying ceremonies of the sweat lodge. They sought out those who had knowledge about the practices that years before had been forbidden or subjected to the 'civilizing' forces of White missionaries. (Brand 1978, 43)

It was the respected religious leader, Chief Frank Fools Crow, who mediated an end to the confrontation. "On April 5 an agreement, or 'peace treaty' as Means termed it, was actually signed at Wounded Knee. . . . The agreement covered six points, including a government promise to examine all treaties made with the Indians . . . and in particular the 1868 Treaty at Ft. Laramie, and to investigate the functioning of the BIA and tribal governments on the South Dakota reservations" (Hecht 1981, 19). But when the government insisted that the Indians first surrender all their arms before any more discussions could take place, negotiations broke down and the agreement fell apart.

In late April, two of the Indian protestors, Frank Clearwater and Buddy Lamont, were killed by government fire within days of each other. Before the occupation ended, twelve other Indians and two non-Indians were injured, and the Wounded Knee trading post, museum, and Roman Catholic church were destroyed.

As AIM leader Dennis Banks reports: "The stand-down at Wounded Knee took place on Friday, May 8, 1973. On that day, one hundred and forty-six men and women laid down their arms and surrendered. Also surrendered were fifteen inoperable rifles. The Feds lowered our AIM flag and raised their Stars and Stripes while a helicopter flew overhead. One of the marshals made a victory speech" (Banks 2004, 209).

Nevertheless, "when the occupation ended with a negotiated settlement, it was clear that the Oglala Sioux and the American Indian Movement had won a major battle in their continuing effort to press the United States government for recognition of Indian rights and claims" (Brand 1978, 44). As might have been expected, the federal government did not keep its negotiated promises, and the Wounded Knee protestors ended up facing a variety of criminal charges.

Civil War Rages On

Following the end of the occupation, the battle shifted to the courtroom. Wounded Knee "resulted in 562 arrests by federal authorities alone and indictments against 185 persons by federal grand juries. State and tribal charges added to these numbers" (Brand 1978, 83). Of these indictments, nearly half were eventually dismissed, and in the end, only six persons were found guilty of a crime.

The indictments of AIM leaders Russell Means and Dennis Banks became the test cases for both the government and the Indian protesters. On the opening day of the trial of the AIM leaders on conspiracy charges, sixty-five traditional leaders of the Oglala Sioux Nation appeared in court. Many had never been in a White man's court before, some never off the reservation. Most were women and one was ninety-one years old. Some were survivors of the 1890 Wounded Knee massacre. Their spokesman was Frank Fools Crow, who told the court:

> To the American public and to Federal Judge Fred Nichol: we are all Oglala people, landowners and traditional people. We have come to a court we don't know, which doesn't know us, to tell everybody who will listen that we stand with our brothers Russell Means and Dennis Banks. Together we stand with our traditions, our land, our medicine and our Treaty Rights. We represent not only ourselves but the Oglala band, the Sioux Nation and concerned Indian people everywhere. We called our brothers and AIM to help us because we were being oppressed and terrorized. They answered our call. We now call upon all people to honor our people and to honor our Treaty Rights. If Dennis Banks and Russell Means go to jail for supporting the dignity of the Sioux Nation and the promises made to us, you must be ready to send us all to jail. If we cannot live with our brothers in freedom according to our ways and tradition, we are ready to join them in a White Man's prison. (quoted in Talbot 1979, 252)

Throughout the trial, the Indian defense contended that the AIM leaders had acted on their political beliefs, and that the United States therefore had no jurisdiction over the Sioux Nation because of the terms of the 1868 Ft. Laramie treaty. "Nevertheless, the court ruled against the Sioux [claim] although there was not a single item of evidence presented by the United States that it had ever legally taken civil and criminal jurisdiction over the Sioux Nation" (Deloria in Ortiz 1977, book jacket) In the end, however, the presiding judge, angered by the long and expensive trial and extensive government misconduct, dismissed the charges against the AIM leaders and delivered a blistering attack on the chief prosecutor. "The Pentagon had covertly supplied more than $300,000 in arms, personnel and assistance to civilian police agencies during the siege, contravening U.S. federal law, which states that such intervention can occur only by presidential proclamation. 'We don't want the military running the civil affairs in this country, or having anything to do with the execution of laws,' he said'" (Brand 1978, 88).

Hostile relations did not abate after the occupation and the trial of AIM leaders. The violence raged on for the remainder of the decade between the mixed-blood allies of the Wilson tribal government and federal forces, on one side, and the traditional Lakota and the AIM warriors who embraced their cause. Law and order became virtually nonexistent on the reservation.

> Violence on the [Pine Ridge] reservation reached unprecedented heights in the two years after the occupation. There were 23 murders in 1974 alone, giving the reservation a higher murder rate than the city of Chicago. During the 1975 reign of terror, attacks on AIM members and their supporters increased further, finally prompting the Department of the Interior . . . to set up a commission of inquiry into reservation lawlessness. . . . In all, in the first six months of 1975, there were 18 murders and 67 attacks on persons and property on the reservation. (Brand 1978, 119–20)

In 1997, the International Indian Treaty Council (IITC) testified at the United Nations headquarters in Geneva, Switzerland, that as many as three hundred AIM members or supporters died violent deaths or disappeared during the mid-1970s. One of the most egregious of these was the killing of AIM member Anna Mae (Pictou) Aquash.

> In February 1976, the body of a woman was found on the Pine Ridge Indian Reservation in South Dakota. The official autopsy attributed her death to exposure. Both hands were severed and sent to Washington for

fingerprinting, and the body was hastily buried without legal documents. When the FBI identified the woman as Anna Mae Aquash, a Canadian Indian active in the American Indian Movement, friends demanded a second autopsy. It revealed that Anna Mae had been killed by a bullet fired execution-style into the back of her head. (Brand 1978, book jacket)

Born on the Micmac Indian reserve in Nova Scotia, Aquash, a mother of two children, was active in the Boston Indian Council. Later, she participated in the 1972 Trail of Broken Treaties to Washington, DC, and other Indian protests. She soon rose in the ranks of the American Indian Movement to become a skilled and admired activist. "Within AIM she became known as a strongly spiritual person who studied with traditional spiritual leaders whenever possible. She took part regularly in the cleansing and purifying ceremonies of the sweat lodge and was preparing herself in 1974 to take part in the Sioux Sun Dance by praying at dusk and at dawn" (Brand 1978, 115). Unfortunately, Aquash soon became "a person of interest" for the Federal Bureau of Investigation.

The FBI's secret war on dissent, especially Project CHAOS and the COINTELPRO program, included the infiltration and disruption of the American Indian Movement. On the FBI's hit list as being supposedly communist infiltrated were perfectly legal organizations as diverse as the United Farm Workers, the Students for a Democratic Society, the American Friends (Quakers) Service Committee, and the National Association for the Advancement of Colored People. AIM leaders Russell Means and Dennis Banks were tied up in a long, costly court battle, and the organization itself became divided following the Wounded Knee occupation. In this contentious political context, rumors became rife that there were FBI informants within the organization. This suspicion was not unfounded since a highly placed AIM Indian activist, Douglas Durham, turned out to be a White FBI informant masquerading as an Indian. Aquash, whose political activism brought her into a leadership position within the movement, was unfairly accused of being a FBI informant. Shortly before her murder, she had been forced to defend herself before the AIM leadership, and then went underground to escape notoriety and the political pressure. Suspicions as to the cause of her death were that she was either killed by an AIM member, or that her death was orchestrated by the FBI.

Twenty-eight years later, in 2002, two Indian men were arrested and charged with her death. But in promoting his book, *Ojibwa Warrior*, AIM leader Dennis Banks claims that the FBI's informant network was responsible for spreading rumors that Aquash was an FBI informant (Norvell 2004). Banks also contends that the murder of Aquash is tied to an unsolved death on the Rosebud reservation of another Indian woman about whom Aquash knew too much. It is suspected that this death, which occurred a year before Aquash herself was killed, is linked to the career of a young reservation attorney, William Janklow, who later became the attorney general, and then the governor of South Dakota, and, finally, a U.S. Congressman. Banks had prosecuted William Janklow before a tribal court in 1967 for the rape of Jancita Eagle Deer and for threatening her with a gun. Janklow was then disbarred from the tribal court. Eagle Deer was mysteriously struck by a car in a remote part of Nebraska in April 1975, less than a year before Anna Mae Aquash herself was murdered.

Shoot-Out at the Jumping Bull Residence

Even more indicative of the violence was the shoot-out at the Harry and Cecelia Jumping Bull residence near the settlement of Oglala on the Pine Ridge Reservation. By early 1975, a number of AIM supporters had taken up residence on the reservation. In view of the escalating violence and virtual lawlessness, the AIM warriors considered it their duty to protect the Oglala traditional community. The AIM encampment on the Jumping Bull property became known as Tent City. Dennis Banks and his family lived there for a time when he was on trial in Custer, South Dakota, following the Wounded Knee occupation.

On the morning of June 26, two FBI agents entered the AIM encampment, ostensibly looking for a local Indian, Jimmy Eagle, who had been involved in a late-night drinking brawl in which two White farmhands were at first detained and then released unharmed, but minus a pair of cowboy boots. Eagle and two others were accused of kidnapping. Some observers, however, believe that the FBI was simply testing AIM' defenses, and that the kidnapping was a cover story. A gun battle shortly broke out and six hours later, the two FBI men and a twenty-four-year-old Indian man, Joe Stuntz, from the AIM camp, lay dead. "Scores of federal agents surrounded the property and the Jumping Bull house was riddled with bullets, tear-gassed and its interior ransacked by the FBI. . . . What precipitated the shoot-out, or who was responsible for the initial shots, remains unclear to this day, despite evidence given in two related trials" (Brand 1978, 124–25).

Ironically, on the day that the shoot-out took place, one eighth of the reservation, the federal gunnery range, was alienated from Lakota ownership. It was signed over by tribal president Richard Wilson to the National Park Service. This action placed the coal-rich area directly under federal rather than tribal control, and thereby more accessible to the energy corporations.

Immediately after the gun battle, and for the next two weeks, more than 150 FBI agents, including a SWAT team, began combing the reservation to apprehend members of the AIM camp whom they held responsible for the FBI deaths. The agents carried high-powered M-16 automatic rifles and were aided by helicopters, airplanes, jeeps, and dogs. "Two years after the Wounded Knee occupation, armored personnel carriers again became a familiar sight on the reservation. For days following the shoot-out, reservation roads were blockaded and Pine Ridge was in a state of siege. In effect, the FBI had declared martial law on its own authority" (Brand 1978, 126–27). Incredibly, everyone who had been in the AIM camp slipped through the FBI dragnet.

Five months later, a federal grand jury handed down murder indictments for Leonard Peltier and several other AIM warriors in the slaying of the FBI agents. The death of the Indian, Joe Stuntz, however, was never investigated. Throughout the summer and early fall of 1975, the FBI continued its manhunt for the suspects. Some elderly reservation residents were startled to see helicopters landing in their yards and to have their houses ransacked. The manhunt widened to include the entire United States, and RCMP officials in Canada were asked to question Anna Mae Pictou Aquash for the whereabouts of the suspects. She was arrested and threatened. Others were also harassed, arrested and jailed, including Dennis Banks and AIM medicine man Leonard Crow Dog. On February 26, 1976, Leonard Peltier, Darelle Butler, and Robert Robideau were indicted in the deaths of the two FBI agents. Charges against a fourth man were dropped for insufficient evidence. Leonard Peltier (Ojibway/Lakota) was the only one finally convicted (see Mathiessen 1983, and Messsserschmidt 1983). Butler and Robideau were found innocent of the charges against them, the jury finding that they had fired only in self-defense.

Peltier was arrested in Canada and extradited to the United States in chains as a dangerous criminal, although the evidence against him was only circumstantial. Since 1977, he has been serving two consecutive life sentences in a federal prison. Yet, there is no credible evidence that he fired the fatal shots, and the case has all the earmarks of a political frame-up. Indeed, Amnesty International has declared him a prisoner of conscience. Many notables have come to his defense, requesting a new trial based on new evidence that he never fired the fatal shots. They include many members of the U.S. Congress, the Parliament of Canada, the European Parliament, Nobel Prize recipients Archbishop Desmond Tutu and Rigoberta

Prisoner of Conscience, Leonard Peltier.

Menchú Tum, Nelson Mandela of South Africa, the Rev. Jesse Jackson Jr., Mother Teresa, the Kennedy Memorial Center for Human Rights, the Dalai Lama, and the Archbishop of Canterbury, among others (see Lobo and Talbot 2001, 224–25).

Peltier is a spiritual man with a deep sense of justice, who is dedicated to his people's rights and welfare. In a 1999 book, *Prison Writings: My Life is My Sun Dance* (Peltier 1999, 203), he writes:

> This is the twenty-third year of my imprisonment for a crime I did not commit. . . . I can tell you this. We don't ask for vengeance, or even want it. I set aside all accusations because I know all too well what it is to be the accused. I set aside all condemnations because I know all too well what it is to be the condemned. We seek not revenge but reconciliation and mutual respect among our peoples. We may be of different nations, but we are still of the same society, and we share the same land. We all want justice, equality, fairness . . . the very principles on which America is founded and by its own Constitution supposedly bestows on all with its borders, even Indians. Is that too much to ask?

HEALING THROUGH SPIRITUALITY

How should one assess the 1973 occupation? An Indian liberation movement or a civil war? Christafferson (2001, 836) provides this thoughtful assessment:

> The Wounded Knee occupation grew out of a political dispute, and opinions about its significance were equally divided. For many Sioux, Wounded Knee became a symbol of the divisiveness that continued to plague them, and of the violence and lawlessness of AIM which generated hostility toward all Indians. To others, Wounded Knee represented a rebirth of pride and cultural discovery, a willingness to stand up for Indian rights and justice. The intensity of these contrasting positions confirmed the symbolic power of Wounded Knee.

Whatever the final truth, the fact remains that the dispute showed that the appeal of traditional Lakota culture and religion was far from dead, and it provided the ideological and spiritual inspiration for the Wounded Knee protestors. Even more significant is the reconciliation that took place in the 1980s between the belligerents, through Lakota spiritual belief and practice. In a special television presentation of *Frontline* (1990), Duane Brewer, a leader of the Wilson administration Goon Squad, explains how he was gradually persuaded by the traditional people at Pine Ridge to participate in the tribal ceremonies and

the purification sweats. "I got rid of a lot of my anger, and they did, too," he explains. "How can you pray to heal someone in the 'sweat,'" he asks, "and at the same time carry hatred in your heart?"

In the same Frontline program, Milo Yellow Hair underscores the impact of the reservation-based traditional culture and spirituality on the young urban militants: "We were like a library that never got used." The full-bloods had never lost their culture. There were still traditional chiefs and medicine men like Frank Fools Crow and Henry Crow Dog, who became important links to the past. They told AIM that the new movement needed a spiritual foundation, and AIM listened. (Both revered leaders have now passed on to the Spirit World.)

By the decade of the 1980s, many Lakotas saw the performance of the Sun Dance and purification ceremonies as signifying a return to traditional society. "Many disaffected young Indians, largely ignorant of their tribal traditions, had their first taste of Indian religion on Sioux reservations in the Sweat Lodge and Sun Dance arbor" (Archambault 2001, 92). Archambault (2001, 94) credits Indian anthropologist Beatrice Medicine for arguing "persuasively that the Sioux Sun Dance had become a ritual of religious revitalization, initially for the Sioux, and eventually for AIM and far-flung non-Sioux communities, both reservation and urban."

These spiritual practices also became the new battleground in a war against secularization and the co-optation of traditional ceremonies by "plastic medicine men" and "New Agers." In 1993, at an international gathering of U.S. and Canadian Lakota, Dakota, and Nakota nations, about 500 representatives unanimously passed a "Declaration of War Against Exploiters of Lakota Spirituality." It was directed at those who "persist in exploiting, abusing and misrepresenting the sacred traditions and spiritual practices of the Lakota people" (Fenelon 1998, 298). In the same year, "A Statement of Vision for the Next 500 Years" was presented by the Native American delegation at the Parliament of World Religions meeting in Chicago. The Statement began with the words: "We as Indigenous peoples and Native Nations, honoring our ancestors and for our future generations, do hereby declare our present and continuing survival with our sacred homelands" (Fenelon 1998, 310).

The resurgence of Lakota traditional culture and spirituality became a pivotal factor in the Lakota resolve to reject the Black Hills claims award, and to demand instead the return of the *He Sapa*. The centrality of the Black Hills as sacred geography in Lakota religion was described by Vine Deloria in a 1990 interview on the television program *Frontline*. He explained that the Black Hills was considered so sacred that no one lived there; it was the Holy of Holies. The Lakota had the spiritual responsibility of conducting important animal ceremonies that were handed down to them from the beginning of creation. In these ceremonies the land on which these ceremonies took place like the Black Hills is sacred geography. These ceremonies are essential to Lakota spirituality, but can't be performed if removed from their sacred location. When the Lakota become alienated from creation and their sacred geography due to the removal of the Black Hills, social problems were the result; they began to suffer and fight among themselves.

With respect to the 1890 Wounded Knee massacre, healing must take place before there can be a reconciliation between Indian and non-Indian. LaDuke (2005, 110) reports that tribal attorney "Mario Gonzales has begun a campaign to urge the federal government to rescind the Wounded Knee medals of honor" awarded to White soldiers in the 1890 massacre. This, also, is part of the healing process that is taking place. Contemporary Lakotas worry that the spirits of the massacred dead still linger. They are painfully aware that "such ghoulish items as skeletal remains, scalps, and clothing stripped from bodies that lay on the killing fields of Wounded Knee are on display for curious gawkers at museums and historical societies across the country" (quoted in LaDuke 2005, 103). These sacred items must be returned to the Lakota people for sanctified reburial.

Beginning in 1986, the Lakota began commemorating the 1890 tragedy by annually retracing Big Foot's 250-mile route to the massacre site. The *Si Tanka Wokiksuye*, or Big Foot Memorial Ride, was a daunting four-year commitment since it entails a long ride by horseback in the dead of a Northern Plains winter. In 1990, the Ride marked the centennial anniversary by hosting a traditional ceremony that paid tribute to those who died at Wounded Knee, and to bring the descendants of the survivors out of a one-hundred-year mourning period. Alex White Plume, one of the organizers of the Ride, reported: "After the ceremony, we will celebrate a new future. The next seven generations will celebrate *Wolakota*—the people will be stronger than ever. The tree still grows. The unity of the people will mend the hoop" (Simon 1991, 29).

La Duke (2005, 112) writes: "The Lakota people are ready to heal; it is now time for the United States to begin making amends to those who grieve, to those whose land and blood forms the foundation for this country—its prosperity and its awful history. In many way[s], Wounded Knee and the Black Hills, intertwined, remain central and symbolic of all that is wrong with an un-reconciled past."

THEORY REVISITED

In this chapter we have reviewed how the U.S. government waged a multicentury war against the Lakota people. In this genocidal war, Lakota spirituality has been at the centerpiece of the Anglo-American attack. This we have termed *spiritual genocide*. At the same time, Lakota spirituality has been at the forefront of the Indian resistance.

In 1991, a special issue of the *NARF Legal Review* (1991), published by the Native American Rights Fund, assessed the status of Indian religious freedom and the challenges remaining. In the special issue, attorney Walter Echo-Hawk reviews the regressive *Lying* and *Smith* decisions by the U.S. Supreme Court. The 1988 *Lying* decision denied First Amendment rights for tribal worship at sacred sites, and the 1990 *Smith* decision withheld constitutional protection for those practicing the Peyote Religion. Although the *Smith* decision has since been reversed, the issue of sacred lands remains.

In the *Lying v. Northwest Indian Cemetery Protective Association* case, the Supreme Court ruled in favor of the U.S. Forest Service to build a logging road in the Six Rivers National Forest in northern California, an area that is very sacred to three Indian tribes, where Indian doctors have practiced traditional medicine and held ceremonies for hundreds of years. The Forest Service road exposed the sacred area to commercial logging and environmental degradation. In its legal decision, the Court ruled that even the "free exercise of religion" clause did not prevent the government from using its property in any way it saw fit.

A second contribution to the NARF Special Issue is a compelling analysis by Vine Deloria, Jr. of the Indian sacred lands question. Western religions theologians, Deloria argues, fail to comprehend the breadth and complexity of Indigenous spirituality, and the Courts consequently fail to protect it. Unfortunately, neither the 1989 legislation creating the National Museum of the American Indian, nor the Native American Graves Protection and Repatriation Act passed a year later, fully addresses the concerns raised by Echo-Hawk and Deloria.

In the introduction to this chapter, we suggested that the Doctrine of Christian Nations (or Discovery) could provide a theoretical framework for understanding why Native peoples alone have been denied religious freedom in a democracy that prides itself on this basic right. The doctrine was embodied in a key Supreme Court decision as early as 1823, *Johnson v. McIntosh*. Despite the guarantee of the freedom of religion contained in the U.S. Constitution and the Bill of Rights, this doctrine and the 1823 Supreme Court decision have consistently denied sovereignty, territorial integrity, and religious freedom to the Indigenous peoples and nations of the United States. Why did it take Congress almost two hundred years after the founding of the republic to pass the 1978 American Indian Religious Freedom Act? Traditional Indians and Native scholars believe they have the answer.

In a 1992 mimeographed communiqué, the Traditional Circle of Indian Elders & Youth attributed the abridgement of Indian religious freedom to what the Indian movement calls the Doctrine of Christian Nations, and the 1823 *Johnson vs. McIntosh* Supreme Court decision which embodies it (Talbot 2006). The Doctrine explains why it was necessary to legislate the American Indian Religious Freedom Act, and, paradoxically, why it has nevertheless failed to protect traditional Indian religious rights such as access to sacred sites s since its passage. The Traditional Circle concluded that the Doctrine is archaic and should have no standing in contemporary U.S. law (Talbot 2006). Contrary to the separation of church and state provision in the U.S. Constitution, it abridges Indian religious freedom. Furthermore, the doctrine provides the rationale for the U.S. jurisdiction in Indian Country and federal land-taking in violation of Indian treaties.

A year later, the Native American delegation to the Parliament of World Religions meeting in Chicago, Illinois, called on the Roman Catholic Pope to revoke the *Inter Cetera* bull of 1493: "Nineteen ninety-three is the five hundredth anniversary of the *Inter Cetera* bull which was issued by Pope Alexander VI, on May 4, 1493. That papal document called for our Nations and peoples to be 'subjugated' so that the 'Christian empire' would be propagated. Documents of this nature and the policies and doctrines they espouse are an obstacle to the true achievement of justice and human rights for our nations and peoples. We therefore call on Pope John Paul II to formally revoke the *Inter Cetera* bull" (quoted in Fenelon 1998, 287). In 2009 the Episcopalian Church formally rejected the doctrine, and in 2012 the Unitarian-Universalist appeared ready to do the same.

When the Doctrine of Christian Nations is applied by U.S. institutions in both law and policy to a deeply religious people like the Lakota Sioux, the result is spiritual genocide. The international convention on genocide should be amended to encompass the protection of Native spirituality, the religious beliefs and practices of American Indians, Alaska Natives, Native Hawaiians, and others in the Indigenous world. Indigenous religious freedom must be protected, whether in a new convention, or as an amendment to the Declaration on the Rights of Indigenous Peoples that was adopted by the United Nations on September 13, 2007. (See *NARF Legal Review* 2011, 1–8). Furthermore, the U.S. Congress and the courts must overturn *Johnson v. McIntosh* by rejecting the Doctrine of Christian Nations (Discovery) as a basis for American Indian policy. As Indian scholar Steven Newcomb writes: "When the federal government and the Supreme Court use Christianity as a criterion for determining the political and legal status of Indian nations, and then use that criterion as the rationale for unilaterally assuming coercive non-constitutional legislative [plenary] power over Native nations and their lands, *where is the separation of church and state?* [emphasis added]" (Newcomb 1993, 337). This last could be corrected, if not by the courts, then possibly by a joint resolution of Congress. Only then can the deeper spiritual concerns of Native peoples in the United States be protected.

CONCLUSION: THE MEANING OF WOUNDED KNEE

In June of 1979 came the decision by the U.S. Court of Claims to award over $100,000 to the Western Sioux for lands illegally seized in the nineteenth century. "In effect the Court of Claims agreed with the Wounded Knee defendants, Russell Means and Dennis Banks, when they charged at their trial that the federal government had violated the Ft. Laramie Treaty of 1868" (Hecht 1981, 29). Incredibly, the Sioux tribes refused the award, demanding instead the return of their sacred Black Hills. Various bills in Congress since then to settle the dispute have failed, and the Sioux tribes continue to hold out for their spirituality even though interest on the award has swelled the total amount considerably. It is worth noting that the Black Hills may be one of the richest one hundred square miles in the world, estimated as worth more than $800 billion. In this beautiful and sacred region, dozens of transnational corporations have staked claims for uranium and other valuable minerals, and the federal government treats the *He Sapa* as a *national sacrifice area* for the mining corporations. The Homestake Mine alone accounts for half of the entire U.S. gold production.

Robert Thomas, a Cherokee anthropologist, studied Pine Ridge government structure in 1964. He found that nearly all the former institutions on the local level had disappeared except the old Native religious groups, "which have carried over from aboriginal times" (Schusky 1969, 471). Virtually the only Oglala institutions to survive the American conquest and the reservation system were the old, religious groups, the very groups not represented in Pine

Ridge self-government under the Indian Reorganization Act. The significance of the 1973 occupation of Wounded Knee is that the traditional Indians and the Red Power militants joined forces to form a qualitatively new unity in the Indigenous political arena. The glue of this new relationship, following the Indian diaspora caused by U.S. urban relocation policy in the 1950s and 1960s, was the rebirth of traditional Indian culture, and spirituality became the midwife. At Pine Ridge. the Lakota (oral) "library" of traditional culture and religion had survived. It was there for the urban brothers and sisters to "read" (hear) if only they had the opportunity. The return to Wounded Knee in 1973 provided that opportunity.

CHAPTER REVIEW

DISCUSSION QUESTIONS

1. Describe the seven sacred rites or ceremonies of the Lakota Sioux.
2. What were the reservation conditions and events that precipitated the Ghost Dance religious movement among the Lakota?
3. Why should the conflict between the Lakota Ghost Dancers and the U.S. cavalry at Wounded Knee be called a massacre instead of a battle (as the government called it)?

4. What were the reservation circumstances that led the Lakota to return to Wounded Knee in 1973 to make their stand? What were their demands to the government?
5. Give some examples of the violence that erupted on the Lakota reservations following the 1973 confrontation at Wounded Knee. What role has spirituality played in the healing process that has taken place since then?

SUGGESTED READINGS

ANDERSSON, RANI-HENRIK. 2008. *The Lakota Ghost Dance of 1890*. Lincoln: University of Nebraska Press.

BANKS, DENNIS, with RICHARD ERDOES. 2004. *Ojibwa Warrior: Dennis Banks and the Rise of the American Indian Movement*. Norman: University of Oklahoma Press. The most complete and probably the most accurate description (since it is firsthand) of the 1973 Wounded Knee occupation, chapters 13–17.

CHAMPAGNE, DUANE, ed. 2001. "Pluralistic Religious Beliefs." In *The Native North American Almanac,* 718–33. 2nd ed. Farmington Hills, MI: Gale Group.

ERDOES, RICHARD. 1989. *Crying for a Dream: The World through Native American Eyes*. Santa Fe: Bear.

LAME DEER, JOHN (FIRE) and RICHARD ERDOES. 1972. *Lame Deer, Seeker of Visions*. New York: Simon & Schuster.

MEANS, RUSSELL, with MARVIN J. WOLF. 1995. *Where White Men Fear to Tread: The Autobiography of Russell Means*. New York: St. Martin's Press.

TALBOT, STEVE. 1981. *Roots of Oppression: The American Indian Question*. New York: International.

WALKER, JAMES. R. 1991. *Lakota Belief and Ritual,* edited by Raymond J. DeMallie and Elaine A. Jahner. Lincoln: University of Nebraska Press.

REFERENCES

Akwesasne Notes. 1973. "American Public Support for Independent Oglala Nation" *Akwesasne Notes* 5 (3): 6.

American Indian Movement. 1973. *Bulletins* issued by the Lakota Coalition and other documents regarding the Wounded Knee occupation. Rapid City, SD: Red Man's International Warrior Society.

ANDERSSON, RANI-HENRIK. 2008. *The Lakota Ghost Dance of 1890.* Lincoln: University of Nebraska Press.

ANDRIST, RALPH K. 1964. *The Long Death: The Last Days of the Plains Indians.* London: Collier-MacMillan.

ARCHAMBAULT, JOALLYN. 2001. "Sun Dance." In *Handbook of North American Indians, vol. 13, Part 2: Plains,* volume edited by Raymond J. DeMallie, 983–95. Washington, DC: Smithsonian Institution Press.

BANKS, DENNIS, with RICHARD ERDOES. 2004. *Ojibwa Warrior: Dennis Banks and the Rise of the American Indian Movement.* Norman: University of Oklahoma Press.

BELL, ROBERT E. and ROBERT L. BROOKS. 2001. "Plains Village Tradition: Southern." In *Handbook of North American Indians, vol. 13, Part 1: Plains,* volume edited by Raymond J. DeMallie, 207–21. Washington, DC: Smithsonian Institution Press.

BRAND, JOHANNA. 1978. *The Life and Death of Anna Mae Aquash.* Toronto: James Lorimer.

BROWN, JOSEPH EPES (recorded and edited by). 1971. *The Sacred Pipe: Black Elk's Account of the Seven Rites of the Oglala Sioux.* New York: Penguin Books.

CAHN, EDGAR. 1969. *Our Brother's Keeper.* Washington, DC: New Community.

CHAMPAGNE, DUANE, ed. 1994. "Sitting Bull." In *The Native North American Almanac,* edited by Duane Champagne, 1161–62. Detroit: Gale Research.

CHRISTAFFERSON, DENNIS M. 2001. "Sioux, 1930–2000" In *Handbook of North American Indians, vol. 13, Part 2: Plains,* volume edited by Raymond J. DeMallie, 821–39. Washington, DC: Smithsonian Institution Press.

Council on Interracial Books for Children, eds. 1971. *Chronicles of American Indian Protest.* Greenwich, CT: Fawcett.

CROW DOG, MARY, and RICHARD ERDOES. 1990. *Lakota Woman.* New York: Grove Weidenfeld.

DANIELS, ROBERT E. 1970. "Cultural Identities Among the Oglala Sioux." In *The Modern Sioux: Social Systems and Reservation Culture,* edited by Ethel Nurge, 198–245. Lincoln: University of Nebraska Press.

DELORIA, VINE, JR. 1971. "This Country Was a Lot Better Off When the Indians Were Running It." In *Red Power,* edited by Alvin M. Josephy, Jr., 235–47. New York: McGraw-Hill.

———. 1973. *God Is Red.* New York: Grosset & Dunlap.

———. 1974. "Religion and the Modern American Indian" *Current History* 67 (400): 250–3.

———. 1977. Book jacket, *The Great Sioux Nation: Sitting in Judgment on America,* by Roxanne Dunbar Ortiz. San Francisco: American Indian Treaty Council Information Center/Moon Books.

———. 2005. Presentation to an American Indian Studies Roundtable, "Past and Future Paths of Indigenous Activism," 47th Annual Conference of the Western Social Science Association, April 13–16, Albuquerque, New Mexico.

DEMALLIE, RAYMOND J. 2001a. "Introduction." In *Handbook of North American Indians, vol. 13, Part 1: Plains,* volume edited by Raymond J. DeMallie, 1–13. Washington, DC: Smithsonian Institution Press.

———. 2001b. "Sioux Until 1850." In *Handbook of North American Indians, vol. 13, Part 2: Plains,* volume edited by Raymond J. DeMallie, 718–60. Washington, DC: Smithsonian Institution Press.

———. 2001c. "Teton." In *Handbook of North American Indians, vol. 13, Part 2: Plains,* volume edited by Raymond J. DeMallie, 794–820. Washington, DC: Smithsonian Institution Press.

DEMALLIE, RAYMOND J., ed. 1984. *The Sixth Grandfather: Black Elk's Teachings Given to John G. Neihardt.* Lincoln: University of Nebraska Press.

DURKHEIM, EMILE. 1915. *The Elementary Forms of Religious Life.* London: George Allen & Unwin.

ECHO-HAWK, WALTER. 1991. "Loopholes in Religious Liberty: The Need for a Federal Law to Protect Freedom of Worship for Native People." *NARF Legal Review* (Summer): 7–12.

ERDOES, RICHARD. 1972. *The Sun Dance People: The Plains Indians, Their Past and Present.* New York: Random House.

———. 1989. *Crying For a Dream.* Santa Fe: Bear.

FENELON, JAMES V. 1998. *Culturicide, Resistance, and Survival of the Lakota ("Sioux Nation").* New York: Garland.

FOWLER, LORETTA. 2001. "History of the United States Plains Since 1850." In *Handbook of North American Indians, vol. 13, Part 1: Plains,* volume edited by Raymond J. DeMallie, 280–99. Washington, DC: Smithsonian Institution Press.

Frontline. 1990. "In the Spirit of Crazy Horse," a television presentation of *Frontline*, December 18.

GONZALEZ, MARIO. 2001. "The Black Hills: The Sacred Land of the Lakota and Tsistsistas." In *Native American Voices: A Reader,* edited by Susan Lobo and Steve Talbot, 132–40. Upper Saddle River, NJ: Prentice-Hall.

GROBSMITH, ELIZABETH S. 1981. *Lakota of the Rosebud: A Contemporary Ethnography.* New York: Holt, Rinehart and Winston.

HARDORFF, RICHARD G. (compiled and edited by). 1991. *Lakota Recollections of the Custer Fight: New Sources of Indian-Military History.* Lincoln: University of Nebraska Press.

HARJO, SUZAN SHOWN. 2004. "The American Indian Religious Freedom Act After Twenty-five Years. An Introduction." *Wicazô Sa Review* 19 (Fall): 129–136.

HECHT, ROBERT. 1981. *The Occupation of Wounded Knee.* Charlotteville, NY: Samhar Press.

KEHOE, ALICE BECK. 1989. *The Ghost Dance: Ethnohistory and Revitalization.* Case Studies in Cultural Anthropology, edited by George and Louise Spindler. New York: Holt, Rinehart and Winston.

LADUKE, WINONA. 2005. *Recovering the Sacred: The Power of Naming and Claiming.* Cambridge, MA: South End Press.

LAME DEER, JAMES (Fire), and RICHARD ERDOES. 1972. *Lame Deer, Seeker of Visions.* New York: Simon & Schuster.

LOBO, SUSAN, and STEVE TALBOT. 2001. *Native American Voices: A Reader.* Upper Saddle River, NJ: Prentice Hall.

MATTHIESSEN, PETER. 1983. *In the Spirit of Crazy Horse.* New York: Viking Press.

MEANS, RUSSELL, with MARVIN J. WOLF. 1995. *Where White Men Fear to Tread: The Autobiography of Russell Means.* New York: St. Martins Griffin.

MESSERSCHMIDT, JIM. 1983. *The Trial of Leonard Peltier.* New York: South End Press.

MURPHY, PETER G. 2004. "Foucault and Colonial Strategy in Douglas C. Jones's *Arrest Sitting Bull.*" *American Indian Culture and Research Journal* 28 (2): 47–65.

Native American Rights Fund (NARF). 1991. "Special Edition on Freedom of Religion: Today's Challenge" *NARF Legal Review* (Summer).

———. 2011. "United States Finally Endorses Historic United Nations' Declaration on the Rights of Indigenous Peoples." *NARF Legal Review* 36 (1): 1–8.

NEIHARDT, JOHN G. 1979. *Black Elk Speaks: Being the Life Story of a Holy Man of the Oglala Sioux.* Lincoln: University of Nebraska Press.

NEWCOMB, STEVEN T. 1993. "The Evidence of Christian Nationalism in Federal Indian Law: The Doctrine of Discovery, *Johnson v. McIntosh,* and Plenary Power." *Review of Law and Social Change* 20 (2): 303–41.

———. 2002. "The Legacy of Religious Racism in U.S. Indian Law." *Indian Country Today,* April 24, A5.

———. 2008. *Pagans in the Promised Land.* Golden, CO: Fulcrum.

NORVELL, BRENDA. 2004. "Banks Speaks Out" *Indian Country Today* 23 (46, April 28).

ORTIZ, ROANNE DUNBAR. 1977. *The Great Sioux Nation: Sitting in Judgment on America.* San Francisco: American Indian Treaty Council, Information Center/Moon Books.

PELTIER, LEONARD. 1999. *Prison Writings: My Life Is My Sun Dance,* edited by Harvey Arden. New York: St. Martin's Press.

POWERS, WILLIAM K. 1996. "Lakota." In *Native America in the Twentieth Century: An Encyclopedia,* edited by Mary B. Davis, 299–302. New York: Gale.

San Francisco Sunday Examiner and Chronicle. 1973. "For Indians It's a Life With Built-in Failure." *San Francisco Sunday Examiner and Chronicle.* March 18.

SCHUSKY, ERNEST. 1969. *The Right to Be Indian.* Hearings before the Special Subcommittee on Indian Education, Committee on Labor and Public Welfare, 90th Congress. Washington, DC: U.S. Government Printing Office.

SIMON, DAVID J. 1991. "Healing the Sacred Hoop." *National Parks* (September/October).

SPICER, EDWARD H. 1969. *A Short History of the Indians of the United States.* New York: Van Nostrand Reinhold.

SWAGERTY, WILLIAM R. 2001. "History of the United States Plains Until 1850." In *Handbook of North American Indians, vol. 13, Part 1: Plains,* volume edited by Raymond J. DeMallie, 256–79. Washington, DC: Smithsonian Institution Press.

TALBOT, STEVE. 1979. "The Meaning of Wounded Knee, 1973: Indian Self-Government and the Role of Anthropology." In *The Politics of Anthropology,* edited by Gerrit Huizer and Bruce Mannheim, 227–58. The Hague: Mouton.

———. 1981. *Roots of Oppression: The American Indian Question.* New York: International.

———. 1984. "Desecration and American Indian Religious Freedom" *Journal of Ethnic Studies* 12 (Fall): 1–18.

———. 1994. "Pluralistic Religious Beliefs." In *The Native North American Almanac,* edited by Duane Champagne, 668–83. Detroit: Gale Research.

———. 2009. Review of *The Lakota Ghost Dance of 1890. American Indian Culture and Research Journal* 33 (4): 186–89.

———. 2006. "Spiritual Genocide: The Denial of American Indian Religious Freedom, from Conquest to 1934." *Wicazo Sa Review* 21 (2): 7–39.

UTLEY, ROBERT M. 1963. *The Last Days of the Sioux Nation.* Yale University Press.

———. 1984. *The Indian Frontier of the American West, 1846–1890.* Albuquerque: University of New Mexico Press.

WALKER, JAMES R. 1982. *Lakota Society,* edited by Raymond J. DeMallie. Lincoln: University of Nebraska Press.

———. 1991. *Lakota Belief and Ritual,* edited by. Raymond J. DeMallie and Elaine A. Jahner. Lincoln: University of Nebraska Press.

5

RELOCATION AS ETHNIC CLEANSING
The Navajo-Hopi "Land Dispute"

A Navajo rug and Hopi kilt design. The textile design is a symbol that the dispute could unravel each nation regardless of who wins.

Our way of life is our religion and our teaching.

—Mary T. Begay, *Navajo elder*

❖ ❖ ❖

I will never give up either land or life, both of which I hold by my way of worshipping.

—Dan Katchongva, *traditional Hopi*

It was the spring of 1986, and the International Indian Treaty Council (ITC) was holding its annual gathering, this time at Black Mesa on the Navajo Nation in Arizona. Representatives from North and South America, and as far away as Japan and New Zealand, met together to discuss the struggle for Indigenous rights. The ITC would then carry the conference proposals to the United Nations human rights headquarters in Geneva, Switzerland, where they could be incorporated into the draft legislation of an International Declaration for Indigenous Rights. The several hundred attendees had driven the dusty reservation roads, checked in with camp security, and found places to camp around a large circus-style tent that had been erected in a stunningly beautiful area of the mesa.

ITC leaders William Means (Lakota) and Bill Wahpepah (Sak-n-Fox) cochaired the four-day conference. David Sohappy and his wife, Myra (Wapapun/Yakima) had pulled up in their van and found a place to make their camp among the scrub juniper. David Sohappy's court case concerning Northwest fishing rights was pending (see Chapter Seven). Nearby, a Tohono O'Odahm brother and his family from Arizona made camp in the bed of their truck. Across the way, a delegation of Buddhist monks had established their camp, arousing the camp each morning with prayers and bell ringing. The camping places of dozens of other delegates ringed the big tent. Among their numbers was a Maori delegation from New Zealand, who found the slow pace and lengthy discussions of the Indian conference to conform so much to their own cultural traditions that they spent the daily deliberations comfortably sprawled on the ground, taking in the speeches with attentive but half-closed eyes. The acclaimed Acoma Pueblo poet, Simon Ortiz, was there. Floyd Red Crow Westerman, the Dakota musician and actor, entertained the gathering. Indian rights activist, Rigoberta Menchú Tum, reported on the Indigenous struggle in Guatemala. She was to receive the Nobel Peace Prize in 1992.

In the deliberations and conversations over the next few days, there were back and forth translations of the speeches into English, Spanish, Navajo, and at times yet another Indigenous language, depending on the language requirements of the Native delegates. Patience was a virtue as one waited for the translations, and fortunately it was an Indigenous value that the participants shared. The attendees were fed a noon meal, prepared by local Navajo host families, that usually included elk or mutton stew, Indian fry bread, beans, and boiled coffee. Ritual purification *sweats* were held nightly. On the third night of the gathering, the conference delegates relaxed to the enjoyment of a pow-wow in the big tent.

Surrounding the gathering during the hot, tepid days, and the cool, star-studded nights, were the rocky hills of Black Mesa, where one could sense the spirits of long-dead ancient ones amid the ruined vestiges of their adobe homes. Conference delegates were cautioned that picture taking was to be confined solely to the big tent, and were asked to avoid photographing the hills out of respect for the sacred nature of the ancient Anasazi landscape.

A critical issue that was the centerpiece of the conference deliberations was the ongoing land dispute between the Hopis and the Navajos over the partitioning of Black Mesa, initiated by the Navajo-Hopi Land Settlement Act passed by Congress in 1974. The law caused the forced relocation of ten thousand Navajos and several hundred Hopis who found themselves on the wrong side of the partition fence. The mandatory removal of Indian families, mainly Navajos, from their traditionally held lands caused untold hardship and suffering and opened the U.S. government to a charge of ethnic cleansing. The ITC was prepared to take the problem to the

United Nations, but what lay at the base of the land dispute? Why were two traditional Indian peoples, both of whom revere the land as sacred, unable to get along with one another? Was partitioning the disputed land, the Joint Use Area, the best or only solution when it set in motion a virtual ethnic cleansing operation of the largely Navajo residents? Were there contributing external and political factors to the so-called dispute? These are the questions examined below.

CHAPTER OVERVIEW

In this chapter we document the land controversy that arose between two prominent Southwest Indian peoples, the Navajos and the Hopis. As we have done in other chapters, we suggest theoretical formulations that could explain the events surrounding the bitter land dispute. We take issue with the commonly held assumption that partition of the disputed territory was necessary because the two peoples have a history of mutual hostility. A careful examination of the issue reveals that to a large degree, both the dispute and its supposed solution of a land division were imposed upon the two belligerents by U.S. institutions and external forces, aided by the acculturated leaders of both tribes. But partition as a solution to political conflict, like Korea, Vietnam, or occupied Berlin, is never a satisfactory or lasting solution.

We first provide the cultural context and political history of the Navajos in their relations with Hopis and non-Indians. Next, we do the same for the Hopis. We then analyze the land controversy in the context of reservation mineral development and U.S. Indian policy, especially as it has impacted Navajo relocation. Based on this history, it becomes clear that the current animosity generated by the land dispute has its origin largely in federal policy and external economic interests rather than in an inherent culture conflict between the two peoples. In fact, the historical record shows that in spite of the current animosity generated by partition and relocation, there have also been times of friendship and cooperation.

At the end of the chapter, we return to our theoretical questions for an analysis of the conflict in order to gain a comprehensive understanding of the tragedy. Illuminating the causes helps to understand what a humane resolution of the Navajo-Hopi land dispute might be.

A note of explanation is necessary for the use of *tribe* or *tribal* throughout this chapter. We use these terms in no sense as a pejorative, to trivialize Indigenous peoples as lacking in political organization and the civilized arts. Rather, we use them as they are understood by political anthropologists, who define tribes as small-scale sovereign nations, commonly organized at the band or clan level of sociopolitical organization. They "represent small-scale, classless societies, with decentralized, communal, long-termed resource management strategies" (Bodley 1990, 4). They manage local ecosystems for long-term sustained use. By contrast, "States are class-based societies, with centralized management systems that extract resources for short-term profit of special interest groups" (Bodley 1990, 4). People have lived as tribal societies for at least half a million years, whereas states have existed for only the last ten thousand years. Since the advent of the industrial revolution, the birth of mercantile capitalism and its system of colonialism, tribal (Indigenous) peoples have become the victims of so-called progress.

THEORETICAL CONSIDERATIONS

There are several analytical themes to this chapter. First, it must be understood that American Indian societies, like all peoples in the world, are subject to forces of change. Yet, the Navajos and Hopis of the Southwest are what anthropologist and cultural historian Edward Spicer (quoted in Sheridan and Parezo 1996) terms "enduring peoples." He explains that "the persistence of a people did not necessarily depend on the maintenance of racial purity, the retention of a language, or the continuous occupation of a homeland. . . . Enduring people endure despite changes in the language they speak or the place where they live. They persevere because they embrace change and make it their own" (quoted in Sheridan and Parezo 1996, xxvi). They do so through symbols, rituals, words, and their memory of a shared history. Spicer cites as examples the Jewish diaspora from Palestine after AD 70, the Irish Catholic expulsion from Ulster in northeastern Ireland in the seventeenth century, and the deportation of the Yaqui by the Mexican authorities following the 1910 Mexican Revolution. Yet all three groups continue to exist as distinct peoples with strong ties to their original homelands.

A second theme is so-called Indian factionalism. "The term is an American and British expression and is often used to express conflict between parties vying for political control. . . . The factionalism stereotype arises when Americans and British colonists apply their terms of political action to the political processes of American Indian groups and nations" (*Indian Country Today* 2007, A2). The stereotype negatively labels the disputant parties, but explains nothing. When applied to the subject of this chapter, the so-called Navajo-Hopi land dispute, it becomes a victim-blaming label. It implies that the Navajo and Hopi nations cannot get along because of their cultural differences, so that the American state must intervene to settle the dispute, when in reality the two peoples are victims of external, neocolonial forces beyond their control.

In *Victims of Progress* (1990), John Bodley proposes a three-stage theory of Western capitalism's domination of Indigenous peoples: (1) the uncontrolled Indigenous frontier during the early centuries of colonial expansion, (2) the employment of military force to subjugate the Indigenous populations, and (3) the extension of administrative control for direct or indirect rule. Many of the so-called factional disputes among Native peoples have arisen as a result of Bodley's third stage scenario, the extension of colonial or neocolonial rule. In the United States, the War Department was originally in charge of Indian affairs. This authority was transferred to the Department of the Interior in 1849 and given to a specialized agency, the Bureau of Indian Affairs. By the 1920s and 1930s, indirect rule came to be widely accepted by the world's colonial powers as the only valid approach to Native administration. The British set up advisory councils, which had no real power, but it was better politics tactically to rule through these advisory bodies. In the United States, this policy is represented by the 1934 Indian Reorganization Act and the tribal council system it created. Internal political conflict (so-called factionalism) arose within many Indian nations when this neocolonial strategy sought to impose Western political government forms that undermined Indian values and traditional systems of self-rule.

A third theme for understanding the Navajo and Hopi conflict involves the concept of ethnic cleansing. In *Indigenous Peoples, Ethnic Groups, and the State* (1997, 8), David Maybury-Lewis contends that the world's three hundred million Indigenous (or tribal) peoples "are among the world's most underprivileged minorities, facing the constant threat of genocide or ethnocide." Genocide is the physical extermination of a defined category of people, which was addressed by the International Convention on Genocide of 1948 following the horrors perpetuated by the Nazis during World War II. (It was not ratified by the U.S. Congress until 1986, some believe because it would open the United States to the charge of genocide of the American Indians.) Ethnocide, by contrast, is the destruction of a people's way of life. It is "the intended result of policies aimed at incorporating minorities into the dominant culture through coercion or incentive. It is based upon a belief that the Indigenous culture is inferior, and that to replace it by the culture of those who consider themselves superior is desirable, or inevitable. Ethnocide is ethnocentrism put into extreme practice" (Howard and McKim 1983, 397). (Ethnocentrism is the belief that one's own race, culture, or beliefs are superior to those of another people.) In point of fact, the two processes, genocide and ethnocide, often go hand in hand. Ethnic cleansing is the process of carrying out a policy of genocide. We may recall the mass killings in Burundi and Rwanda, and the breakup of the former Yugoslavia, resulting in massive ethnic cleansing operations by the different ethnic components of those nations. More recently, ethnic cleansing has been a tragic reality in Darfur and Iraq.

Ironically, when it concerns Indigenous peoples, ethnocide is not universally condemned. On the contrary, it is normally advocated as an appropriate policy in the colonial management of Indigenous peoples who are looked down upon as backward and incapable of self-governance. "It is the cultures of Indigenous peoples that are regularly threatened, even when their lives are not at risk, and it is to their cultures that they often cling, in order to give meaning and dignity to their lives" (Maybury-Lewis 1997, 9).

In this chapter we describe how two enduring peoples—enduring in large part because of their deep reverence for the land as sacred—nevertheless came to wage a bitter struggle over it. This tragic dispute transpired despite the fact that the traditional members of both groups share many common beliefs concerning Mother Earth, and have even intermarried, cooperated, and shared the land in common in the recent past.

THE NAVAJOS

The Navajo Nation is situated on the Colorado Plateau and comprises 28,803 square miles. It is the largest Indian reservation in the United States and is equivalent in size to the state of West Virginia. The territory of the Navajo domain is "the region bounded on the northeast by the Continental Divide, on the southeast by the Rio Puerto, on the South by the San José and Puerco rivers, on the west by the Little Colorado and Colorado rivers, and on the north by the San Juan River" (Dutton 1983, 73). The reservation extends from the Four Corners area to include a large portion of northeastern Arizona, a smaller part of northwestern New Mexico, and a strip of Utah south of the Colorado River. (See Figure 5.1.)

Much of the land is high desert and semidesert, economically unproductive except for livestock grazing. In some places it takes 240 acres to pasture one sheep for a year. Part of the reservation includes stands of timber. A smaller portion of the reservation is irrigated and can support crops. Elevation ranges from just under 500 feet to 11,300 feet. The ecology includes desert grassland and scrub and piñon-Juniper sagebrush at the lower altitudes; a transitional zone of ponderosa pine and Douglas fir; and spruce, fir, and aspen in the higher elevations.

According to the 2000 U.S. Census about the time of the dispute, the Navajo were the second largest Indian group in the United States, with 269,202 designating themselves as "Navajo alone," and 298,197 designating Navajo in combination with one or more other ethnic categories or "races."

By 2010 these numbers had risen to 286,731 and 332,129 respectively. The reservation, which encompasses a substantial part of Navajo traditional territory, is situated between four sacred mountains: in the east, White Shell Mountain (Blanca Peak in central New Mexico); in the south, Blue Bead Mountain (Mt. Taylor in northwestern New Mexico); in the west, Abalone Shell Mountain (San Francisco Peak in north central Arizona); and in the north, Obsidian Mountain (Hesperus or La Plata Peak in southwestern Colorado).

There are also several off-reservation Navajo communities. The largest of these is the Ramah Navajos, numbering several thousand people, whose land lies southeast of Ramah, New Mexico. Ramah is approximately eighteen by thirty miles in extent, and averages around seven thousand feet in elevation. It was settled by Navajo and Apache exiles who escaped from military confinement in the 1860s at Ft. Sumner under a Navajo patriarch named Many Beads. Today, the community is officially the Ramah Chapter and has an elected representative on the Navajo Tribal Council in Window Rock, the Navajo Nation capital.

Two smaller off-reservation groups are the Puertocito (Alamo) Navajos, and the Canoncito Navajos. The former community developed in part

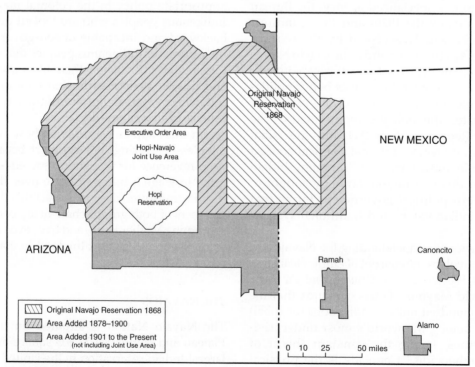

Figure 5.1 Enlargement of the Navajo Reservation, which eventually surrounds the Hopi Reservation.

from Navajo slaves who ran away from their Spanish masters, later congregating at Alamo northwest of Magdalena, New Mexico. They were joined by other Navajos, some of whom fled to escape the roundup by Kit Carson and the Long Walk to Bosque Redondo, which is explained later in this chapter. The second group lives some twenty-five miles west of Albuquerque, New Mexico. They are derived from Navajos who had moved to their present location due to Spanish pressure in the eighteenth century.

In addition to these groups, more than twenty-five thousand Navajos live in the "checkerboard area" of northwestern New Mexico. These are railway right-of-way lands of alternate sections that were then allotted so that each alternate square mile is Indian land (usually 160 acres) with non-Indian sections in between.

The larger reservation, together with its outlying segments in New Mexico, is divided into five administrative districts with the number of council delegates selected proportionally to the population in each district. There are 109 chapters and 37 districts, with two or more chapters making up a tribal election district. In earlier times, the Navajos had an informal system of headmen and clan leaders, the *naat'áanii*, "the ones who orate." Decision making was based on persuasion and consensus.

Origin and Culture

Whereas the origin of most Indigenous peoples found in the Americas is still being debated, it is generally agreed that the Athabascans, from which the Navajos and Apaches are derived, migrated out of northeastern Asia, perhaps as recently as three thousand years ago. The main body, known also by their linguistic name as the Nadene, include the Tlingit, Eyak, and Haida of southeastern Alaska, and Athapascan-speaking groups of interior Alaska. The largest group is comprised of the Athabascans of the American Southwest and northern Mexico from which the Navajos and Apaches are derived. Other Athabascans include smaller enclaves found along coastal California. *Navajo*, rather than being of Spanish origin, is a derivative of a Tewa Indian word meaning "great planted fields." In their own language they call themselves the *Diné* or *Dineh*, meaning "The People." Navajo will be used in this chapter.

Linguistic glottochronology evidence indicates that the divergence of the Navajos from the northern Athabascan groups occurred sometime between seven hundred and one thousand years ago. "Certain of the bands continued southward, some entering

southwestern Texas as the Lipan Apache, others turned westward to occupy chosen locations in southwestern New Mexico and eastern Arizona. And those who were to become known as the Jicarilla Apache and the Navajo found their way westward through mountain passes which brought them into north-central New Mexico, into the upper reaches of the San Juan River" (Dutton 1983, 64).

The region in which the Navajos settled had been occupied by the ancestors of contemporary Pueblo peoples as far back as AD 400–700. For reasons still unclear to researchers, these early Pueblo communities were later abandoned prior to AD 1300, perhaps because of a prolonged drought, or possibly for defense against external enemies. In any case, they moved to higher locations on the mesas where there was more rainfall. The Athabascans, on the other hand, because of their basic hunting and gathering economy, were able to comfortably occupy the abandoned ecological niche as small, foraging bands. The Athabascan Navajos did not constitute an organized tribe. "They lived as a great many different small communities—of from ten to forty families—each living within a defined area of agricultural and grazing land" (Spicer 1962, 213).

The ways-of-life of these two peoples—the Athabascans and the Pueblos—have led to contrasting cultural values, social organization, and economies. Among the Pueblo peoples, of which the Hopis are a representative, "major concern has been for an entire village or community, the group as a whole, with little thought for the individual" (Dutton 1983, 65). In contrast, Athabascans like the Navajos have a cultural system in which the individual, rather than the community, is of primary importance.

Some researchers contend that the Athabascans initially had a patrilineal descent system with patrilocal residence, but definitive evidence is lacking. They also had a shamanistic religion preoccupied with curing and no priestly officers. After contact with Pueblo communities, Athabascan Indians like the Navajos began to change certain elements of their culture. They began to raise corn (maize), and with horticulture, adopted a sedentary residence pattern, which is in evidence today, although wage labor has now become important.

The sacred story of the Navajo creation tells of their southward journey from a northern existence. About 800 to 1,000 years ago, the Athabascans, of whom Navajo family groups are a component, began moving southward. The emergence tradition "tells of their travels from the cold, dark worlds below to one of light and variegated color" (Sheridan and Parezo 1996, 17). At this stage in their cultural development, they were hunters and gatherers who lived in small bands and extended family units, coming together only occasionally to discuss issues of mutual concern. They made "conical skin houses, baskets, harpoons, sinew-backed bows, snowshoes and skin clothing . . . and they used dogs to carry loads and pull travois" (Sheridan and Parezo 1996, 7). This was a period of Navajo clan migrations by the four main matrilineal clans: Bitter Water People, Towering House People, Salt People, and Water Flowing People. Other clans came into existence later as the Navajo increased in population, and as people from other Indian groups married into the Navajos or sought refuge among them. They settled in sparsely populated areas near Pueblo peoples in the canyons of what is now southern Colorado and north central New Mexico. They did not constitute a single, united political entity, but they were united culturally. They considered themselves to be part of *Diné Bikeyah* (Navajo Country), which was ringed by four sacred mountains, the place of Navajo emergence into the present world.

Navajo Life Today

Whereas the Hopis are house-dwellers and horticulturists, the Navajos are basically herdsmen. Agriculture and livestock raising are secondary Navajo activities augmented by money generated from wage labor and revenues from the exploitation of reservation mineral resources.

"The typical Navajo dwelling, the *hogan*, is usually round or hexagonal, sometimes octagonal, constructed of logs and mud, or sometimes of rocks, with a central air vent in the ceiling" (Dutton 1983, 75). It is most often the residence of an older woman, the matriarch of the family. The other structures include small framed houses for the married daughters and their husbands and children. Typically, pick-up trucks are parked nearby. "Near the hogan or under the shelter of a bush-covered ramada, Navajo women may be seen weaving rugs on an upright loom, which was adopted from the Pueblo Indians. . . . Away from their homeland, Navajo Indians are seen at Pueblo ceremonies, especially at Jémez, Laguna, Zuni, and in the Hopi villages. They come to trade and barter, to sell rugs and jewelry, and to take home agricultural products and other Pueblo items" (Dutton 1983, 75). Navajo men seek work, not only on the reservation, but in New Mexico and Arizona cities— Albuquerque, Santa Fe, Gallup, Farmington, and Flagstaff. An increasing number of families spend at least part of their working years in far off cities, such as Chicago, Denver, Dallas, Los Angeles, San Francisco, and Oakland. But it is customary to return to the reservation during family emergencies, for weddings and funerals, and for important ceremonies. Even though many Navajos live and work outside the Navajo Nation, the four sacred mountains continue to mark the boundaries of their spiritual homeland.

Contemporary Navajos live in a complex world that includes dealing with bureaucratic organizations, computers, factories, mines, fast food, and at times, urban living. Overgrazing remains a problem on the reservation, and there are disputes with the Hopis and the Southern Paiutes over mineral and land occupancy rights in the Joint Use Area (which will be explained later in this chapter). Even though small business ownership has grown, the reservation has one of the highest rates of unemployment in the country: per capital income is low and poverty is widespread, forcing many Navajos to seek work off the reservation in the cities. And yet, the Navajos continue to maintain much of their traditional culture in order to walk what they call "the Beautiful Trail."

Spiritual Life

There are three contrasting currents of Navajo spiritual belief and practice: Christian churches, traditional ceremonies, and the Native American Peyote Church. Christian denominations active on the reservation include the Presbyterians, Episcopalians, Mormons, Pentacostalists, and Roman Catholics. Weather control by priests, especially rainmaking, is central in the spiritual and ceremonial life of Pueblo peoples like the Hopis. In contrast, Navajo religion centers on curing ceremonies directed by "medicine people." Rituals are performed to restore physical and mental health, to secure food, and to insure survival. Most of the ceremonies are concerned with the restoration and maintenance of health. A second ceremonial category, the Blessingway group, is concerned with securing wealth and security, blessing a new home, and a girl's puberty ceremony. The underlying basis of Navajo ceremonies is to maintain balance, beauty, or harmony. Two classes of personal forces are recognized, humans and supernatural beings, the Holy People who have great power over people and the earth itself. "The Navajo believes his universe functions according to certain set rules. If one learns these rules and lives in accordance with them, he will keep safe or be restored to safety" (Dutton 1983, 89).

Death and everything connected with it is greatly feared. The spirit world is peopled with ghosts and witches, who take the form of human beings, animals, birds, and various natural phenomena. They appear after dark or on the approach of death. When a person sees a ghost or dreams of one, the proper ceremony must be performed or the individual will surely die. It is believed that a successful ceremonial cure will kill the witch.

Disease and accidental injury are believed to result from attack by the Holy People. The cure can be effected by a special ceremonial chant and sacrificial appeasement to the offended Holy One. Numerous ceremonial chants may be performed until the patient recovers. Generally speaking, each chant has its own special sand painting. "More than five hundred different sand paintings have been recorded, and fifty-eight or more distinct ceremonies" (Dutton 1983, 89). Upon completion of the ceremony, "the patient leaves the hogan, the painting is destroyed in the same order in which it was made, and is deposited to the north of the hogan" (Dutton 1983, 91).

There is a fundamental difference between Navajo and Pueblo religious ceremonies, although both peoples pay deference to "the Sacred." "While Pueblo ceremonies emphasize communal well-being and are sponsored by priesthoods or societies, Navajo ceremonies are held in response to the illness of an individual [the patient] . . . under the direction of a ceremonial practitioner, or singer, who is not part of an organized priesthood" (Griffin-Pierce 2000, 123). Another difference is that instead of a communal religious structure such as a Pueblo kiva, Navajo ceremonies are held in the home of the patient's family, the hogan.

The goal of Navajo ceremonies is to restore the state of orderliness, or holiness, a major theme in Navajo religious thought. "This is why a traditional Navajo greets the Holy People who come with the sunrise with prayers and a pollen blessing" (Griffin-Pierce 2000, 125). The Holy People are closely linked to human beings. What Euro-Americans define as nature, Navajos view as People—mountains, animals, plants, and natural forces. After the emergence, the Holy Wind, a vital energy that animates the universe, endowed all things with life, movement, speech, etc. The act of breathing unites all beings and phenomena. "This understanding imbues the Navajo with a profound sense of connection and responsibility to all other species and beings. Thus, to exploit or destroy any aspect of creation is to harm oneself" (Griffin-Pierce 2000, 126).

"Navajo ceremonies heal by restoring harmonious conditions and right relations in all realms of a patient's life, physically, spiritually, mentally, and socially" (Griffin-Pierce 2000, 131). To accomplish this goal, there are different] kinds of "sings" or "chantways" that can be performed, such as Holyway, Evilway, and Lifeway. The Holyway ritual is to attract the good in order to restore the health of the patient. Most chantways are in this category. "Evilway ritual employs techniques for exorcising Native ghosts and their evil influences. Lifeway ritual treats injuries resulting from accidents" (Griffin-Pierce 2000, 132). Each chant may last two, five, or nine nights. It is said that originally there were some twenty-four chantways, but today, only eight are well known and performed frequently.

Corn is important to Navajo life, and corn pollen is used in ceremonies to symbolize fertility and prosperity. Sand paintings are an integral part of chantway ceremonies. Perhaps the most powerful sand painting is "Mother Earth and Father Sky" (Figure 5.2), because it reflects the complementary principle of Navajo philosophy, "the visual embodiment of humanity's relations to all creation as well as the balancing of maleness and femaleness" (Griffin-Pierce 2000, 137).

It is customary for a Navajo youth to go through an initiation ceremony in order to fully participate in ceremonial life. It usually takes place on next to the last night of the Nightway (*Yei Bichei*) curing ceremony. "Singing occurs for nine nights, sand paintings are made on the last four days, and prayers and other symbolic offerings and rituals are tendered. On the ninth night comes the climax, a drama illustrating an elaborate myth. The Navajo ride in from far and near, make camp, build their fires, and arrange themselves for the night" (Dutton 1983, 92). Navajo actors impersonate the Holy People—Talking God, Water Sprinkler—accompanied by twelve dancers, representing male and female deities. "Monster Slayer, Calling God, Black God, Fringed Mouth, and others may also appear. With these are the singer and the patient" (Dutton 1983, 92). Water Sprinkler serves as a sacred clown. The Mountain Topway, or Mountain Chant, is another frequently held ceremonial. It includes a fire dance. The cost of a ceremonial is borne by the patient and his family, and can be an expensive affair.

In the 1930s, the peyote religion began making inroads among the Navajos, they having learned the ritual from the Utes of southern Colorado. Known more accurately as the Native American Church,

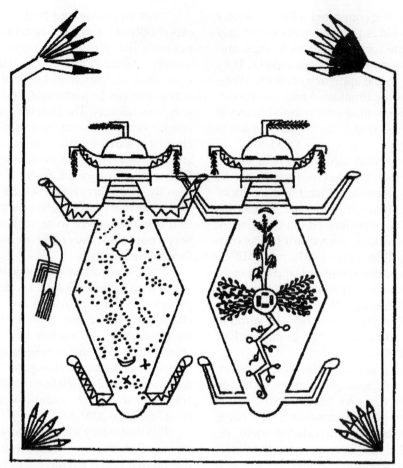

Figure 5.2 Mother Earth and Father Sky.

peyote ceremonies are performed in a hogan or a Plains-type tipi. Emphasis is on the welfare of the community rather than on an individual. By ingesting the peyote button (Grandfather Peyote) as a sacrament, the ritual emphasizes family life, fellowship, and sobriety. At first, the Navajo Tribal Council banned peyote from the reservation, but in 1962, the Native American Church members were exempted from prosecution. It is now a growing religious movement among the Navajo.

The various versions of the Navajo creation story reflect a world in chaos and disorder. Navajo orators tell of "walking and journeys, the landscape and places the hero or heroine passes through. Thus, the theme of Navajos walking the Beautiful Trail . . . in search of harmony, order, and peace" (Sheridan and Parezo 1996, 3).

The Navajo creation took place in a series of worlds, in some accounts as many as twelve, through which their ancestors journeyed before emerging into the present world. "These worlds are identified by number and distinguishing color as well as by the events that transpire in them" (Gill 1983, 502). The Navajos, along with all forms of water, the animals, all vegetation and other features emerged with the aid of supernatural beings. The place of emergence was *Xajiinal*, located in the La Plata Mountains of southwestern Colorado.

In each world the people were instructed to live peacefully and happily, but instead fell prey to quarreling and disharmony and were threatened with destruction. At the last moment they are shown an opening through which they make their escape to the next world above them, but other peoples already occupy the new world. This pattern is repeated for each successive world. Ultimately, they move into the Fifth World, emerging at the center of a sacred land only to discover that the new world is covered by water and inhabited by monsters. The Holy People, immortal beings, eventually come to terms with Water Monster and the water recedes. The winds of the four directions are then called upon to dry the earth.

The next stage involved eliminating chaos. First Man and First Woman do this by using the powers of a sacred medicine bundle to transform some of its contents into holy figures in human-like form. "The stars, moon and sun, food animals, plants, and mountains were created, day and night were distinguished, and time was divided into four seasons" (Sheridan and Parezo 1996, 4). In this ordered environment, Changing Woman is born of the mingling of darkness and dawn and reared by First Man and First Woman. Changing Woman's sacred twins—Child Born of Water and Monster Slayer—defeat the monsters and make the world safe. They are among the better known Holy People. Changing Woman uses her powers to create corn and the first Navajo people. When all is ready, First Man and First Woman construct a ceremonial house, a *hogan*. In the hogan the Holy People arrange the life forms of all living things as in a sand painting. The ceremony lasts all night, and at dawn they are transformed into the Navajo world. Earth People are created and taught the proper customs and habits of how to be human beings. "The first four pairs are the progenitors of the four original Navajo clans" (Gill 1983, 505). Then, the Holy People depart.

In the Navajo worldview, this ordered world stands in contrast to the preemergence condition of disorder and chaos. "The Holy People stressed the importance of ceremonies and prayers to insure that the world and the Diné's travels would be harmonious and orderly. . . . The Diné [Navajos] were taught to search for . . . a state in which all is beautiful, harmonious, and good" (Sheridan and Parezo 1996, 6). This is the world in which the Navajos have lived ever since. The physical beauty of their land in the Four Corners area of southwestern United States is but the outer manifestation of its sacredness.

Social Organization

In the Navajo world, the universe is divided into two categories: holy people and earth-surface people. The latter include Navajos and non-Navajos. There are two types of social solidarity that unite the Navajos as a tribal entity: kin relations among relatives, and systematic exchange or reciprocity among non-kin. These systems of solidarity are complementary. The former is called *k'é*, which means kindness, love, cooperation, thoughtfulness, friendliness, and

peacefulness. "*K'é* is the ideal that orders all social relations" (Witherspoon 1983, 524).

In the past, Navajos lived in small, isolated family groups, and many still do so. The primary social unit is the extended family with kinship traced through the mother's clan. The mother-child bond is the strongest kinship tie in Navajo society. Conversely, the strongest non-kin bond is the affinal relationship between husband and wife. In the Navajo matrilineal kinship system, a grandmother is the center of the extended family with the children belonging to her and her clan. There are sixty or more matrilineal clans. Because of the mother-in-law taboo, "a woman and her husband do not live with the wife's mother. Instead, they erect a home nearby. . . . Thus, one may find several generations dwelling together in proximity: grandmother, mother, daughter, and grandchildren. It is usual for the dwelling, the crops and the livestock to be cared for by the mother and her children, so these are owned by the woman" (Dutton 1983, 75).

Women are the pottery makers and rug weavers; they are the ones who benefit from rug sales and that of their crops and livestock. Men are the silver jewelry smiths. Men also realize income from stock raising or farming, and it is the man who represents the family on public occasions and at ceremonials. Despite close kinship ties, Navajos place great emphasis on the right of the individual. No person has the right to speak for, or to direct the actions of another.

Formerly, in order to deal with outsiders (other Indian peoples and non-Indians), loosely defined local groups were organized around headmen noted for their wealth, influence, ceremonial knowledge, and wise counsel. They were called *naat'áani*—headmen, peace leaders—who knew the Blessingway ceremony. The Blessingway is intended to gain the good will of Navajo supernaturals and to bring good fortune. By the twentieth century, local communities formed around trading posts, schools, and missions. These Navajo communities became formalized when the Navajo tribal council was created, representing more than one hundred local chapters in eighteen reservation districts.

The residence group, or *outfit*, is a basic unit of Navajo social organization. Most residence groups consist of multiple households. "Normally every married couple in the residence group has its own household. . . . [It] can be identified as the group that eats and sleeps together" (Witherspoon 1983, 527). The residence group has an important economic function since it has its own sheep herd, a cooperative enterprise of individual owners. The acquisition of sheep and horses added to the Navajo economic base and pastoral way of life. After 1868, agriculture declined in importance, largely because Colonel Kit Carson destroyed thousands of acres of fields and fruit trees in the early 1860s when the Navajos were rounded up and force-marched on the Long Walk to military confinement at Bosque Redondo. Livestock then became the mainstay of the Navajo economy up to the middle of the twentieth century.

"Whereas the traditional Hopi life is connected to farming, the Navajo spiritual and economic life is intertwined with the health and wellbeing of their animals—horses, goats, and especially sheep" (Mander 1981, 54). Sheep play an important role both psychologically and socially in Navajo culture. It was Changing Woman, it is said, who brought sheep to The People. Pastoral life requires seasonal movements to grazing lands in the mountains in summer, and to the more sheltered lowlands in winter. "The Navajo family moves its herd through the desert region below and beyond the Hopi mesas, from one strategically placed hogan . . . to another along routes chosen for the location of hundreds of sacred sites, among them wells, rock formations, and places where certain herbs are known to grow" (Mander 1981, 54). Until recently, local groups of from ten to forty families under the direction of a headman were economically and politically self-sufficient.

NAVAJO POLITICAL HISTORY

The ancestors of the Navajos emigrated from the north as a group of closely related bands. They had harpoons and the sinew-backed bow, and wore tailored skin clothing. They lived in conical teepee dwellings, used dogs to carry their belongings, and engaged in a subsistence economy of hunting, fishing, and gathering. The social organization was at the band level, with a flexible bilateral kinship system, i.e., they counted both the father's and the mother's sides of their family as kin.

By the time of the arrival of the Spanish, the Pueblo peoples, with the exception of the Hopis on the extreme west, were entirely surrounded by Apachean peoples. The earliest Spanish account that refers to the Navajos as a specific Apachean group was in 1626. Spanish accounts speak of the "Apache de Navajo" as a semisedentary people who planted maize and perhaps other crops, and who moved to areas distant from their fields for hunting (Brugge 1983, 491). They "traded meat, hides, and mineral products, primarily salt and alum, to the Puebloans; lived in 'underground' homes in rancherias" and built special structures for storage (Brugge 1983, 491). "The only distinctively Puebloan traits added to those brought from the north are agriculture and a more formal political structure" (Brugge 1983, 491). They were described as variously friendly, and at other times hostile, to the Pueblo peoples.

The Spaniards did not enter Navajo territory until the early 1700s, although Franciscan missionaries were active earlier. By the late seventeenth century, the Navajos had increased their population and presence in eastern Arizona. They were living in earth-covered houses and growing corn, beans, and squash. They gathered wild foods and hunted. They also engaged in extensive trade networks with other Indian groups and with Spanish settlers. By midcentury, the Spaniards were increasingly putting pressure on the Pueblos. They often attacked the Pueblos, burned their structures, and killed or captured the inhabitants. These depredations led to the Pueblo Revolt of 1680 in which Navajos participated.

Pueblo Influences, Spanish Relations

The Navajos were allies of the Pueblo peoples in the 1680 Pueblo revolt against Spanish rule. After the revolt and the reconquest by the Spaniards in 1692, many Pueblo refugees went to live in *Denétah*, the Navajo homeland, and other Pueblo groups were pushed northward toward the San Juan Basin, bringing them into contact with the Navajos. Intermarriage led to the origin of a new Navajo clan comprised of Pueblo women married to Navajo men and their descendants. The absorption of refugees and comingling of peoples influenced Navajo culture and led to the development of weaving and pottery making, although the Navajo language remained dominant. Navajos adopted the Puebloan style of architecture, manufacturing techniques, and religious paraphernalia, in addition to elements of nonmaterial culture, such as clans, matrilineal descent, matrilocal residence, and the creation story and rituals. "The two major ancestral roots of the traditional Navajo culture, Athabaskan-Apachean and Anasazi-Puebloan, were joined" (Brugge 1983, 493). As a result, Navajo culture became distinct from that of the Apaches, who had less contact with Pueblo peoples. Despite Pueblo cultural influence, the Navajos retained the distinctive hogan as their preferred residence.

The seventeenth and eighteenth centuries saw alternating periods of peace and hostility between the Navajos and the Spaniards. The reconstituted Navajos of the east raided the newly reestablished Spanish settlements on the Rio Grande in New Mexico. In 1745, the Franciscans launched a program of missionization, but Navajos rejected the attempt. The Navajos began raiding Spanish settlements when the Spaniards attempted to convert them to Roman Catholicism and conducted a slave trade of Navajo children. In 1774, the Navajos successfully drove encroaching Spanish settlers from the eastern portion of their land. The region lying between the Rio Grande Pueblos and the Hopi village became known as the Province of the Navajos. "It remained entirely without missions during the whole of the Spanish period and through the Mexican period" (Spicer 1962, 213). Navajo relations with the Pueblo peoples also alternated between friendship and war. Nevertheless, many Navajos visited "Pueblo settlements during dances and traded meat, hides, salt, alum, and later blankets in return for clothing and pottery" (Sheridan and Parezo 1996, 9).

The Navajo economic base changed significantly when they acquired herds of sheep, goats, horses, and cattle from the Spaniards. After 1800 the Navajos began to depend even more on raiding the Spanish villages of New Mexico for sheep, horses, and captives. "A 'Mexican' clan developed among them, composed of descendants of Spanish women captives" (Spicer 1962, 213).

For more than three centuries, to the present day, Navajos relied on sheep, cattle, and horses for the greater part of their economic subsistence. Tending flocks of animals became the mainstay of their adaptation to an arid land, and they gained the reputation of being great traders. Agriculture, animal husbandry, hunting and gathering, and weaving came to form the basis of the traditional Navajo economy. By the mid-eighteenth century, Navajo blankets came to be prized throughout the region.

In 1809, the first treaty between the Navajos and the Spaniards in New Mexico defined the boundary between the two peoples. The Navajo population center was in Canyon de Chelly, but soon the Navajos pressed westward into the regions of Chinle, Black Mesa, Navajo Mountain, Klagetoh, and Steamboat Canyon. The Mexican period followed, lasting from 1821 to 1846. Mexican independence from Spain opened trade with Anglo-Americans and gave New Mexicans a new supply of arms. The

New Mexicans "formed a private army to fight the Navajos. In the continuing warfare, thousands of Navajos and other Indians were captured and sold as slaves in New Mexico" (Sheridan and Parezo 1996, 10).

The Anglo-American Era

The United States annexed the New Mexico Territory in 1846, and the arrival of the U.S. Army troops commanded by General S. W. Kearny signaled the beginning of Anglo-American influence in the Southwest. Under U.S. military pressure, many Navajos began moving into traditional Hopi territory. By 1849, Anglos were already crossing the Southwest in the search for gold in California. "Navajo farms and grazing lands were threatened anew by the arrival of the 'New Men,' Anglo-American settlers and soldiers, in the 1850s" (Sheridan and Parezo 1996, 11). It was common practice for them to abuse and take advantage of the local Indians, especially by encroaching on Indian lands. Despite the fact that three treaties had been signed between the United States and the Navajos, the conflict with the New Mexicans continued in a sporadic fashion.

By 1858, the Navajo populated a wide area "from the Jémez Mountains of the Hopi Country and from the San Juan River to the region south of the Little Colorado" (Dutton 1983, 71). In the years leading up to the Civil War, the Navajos continued to resist both the U.S. Army and settlers. The U.S. government wanted to pacify the region to open it to settlement and mineral development, but the Navajos continued to rebuff Anglo-American aggression. When the U.S. forts and garrisons were left largely unmanned following the outbreak of the war, the Navajos were quick to seize the advantage.

Navajo slavery continued in the New Mexico Territory for a time after the Civil War, although the Emancipation Proclamation had freed Black slaves. The superintendent for Indian affairs in New Mexico himself owned six Navajos. With rare exceptions, the Anglo Indian agents and the U.S. Army were vehemently anti-Indian in their relations with the Navajos. In September 1858, the superintendent of New Mexico told the commissioner of Indian affairs that the Navajos "deserve no mercy at our hands, and should be taught to expect none" (Roessel 1983, 508). Given this hostile atmosphere, it is hardly surprising that on April 30, 1860, the Navajos attacked Fort Defiance, holding it briefly before being repulsed. The New Mexicans pressed into the eastern portion of Navajo territory, sending large flocks of the New

Mexicans' sheep deep into Navajo grazing lands. The newcomers also eagerly expected to find rich deposits of gold, silver, and other minerals.

Ethnic Cleansing

In the fall of 1862, Brigadier General James H. Carleton became the military commander of New Mexico. His mission was to subjugate the Indians and protect the territory from Confederate troops. Arriving on the scene too late to fight the Confederates, he turned his attention to formulating a plan to resettle Navajos and Apaches on a reservation at Ft. Sumner, New Mexico, to force them to become settled farmers like the Pueblo Indians. Colonel Christopher "Kit" Carson was selected to lead the campaign against the Navajos. General Carleton ordered Carson to shoot any male Navajo who resisted, and to destroy all livestock and food supplies. Carson led a force of seven hundred Ute, Pueblo, and New Mexican volunteers into Canyon de Chelly and destroyed not only Navajo sheep, but also their corn fields and peach trees. With their food supplies destroyed, the Navajos either surrendered or fled into Hopi country to avoid capture. "Not only did the Navajo have to contend with the United States Army and Kit Carson, but also their land was filled with other Indians (Ute and Pueblo) and New Mexicans determined to pillage and capture slaves, particularly women and children, to be sold as domestics" (Roessel 1983, 511).

Navajo bands scattered to avoid Carson's attacks, but by December 1864, more than 8,300 Navajo men, women, and children and several hundred Mescalero Apaches had been rounded up and forced to march 250 miles on the Long Walk to Bosque Redondo (Fort Sumner). "People were shot down on the spot if they complained about being tired or sick or if they stopped to help someone. If a woman became in labor with a baby, she was killed. There was absolutely no mercy" (Roessel 1983, 513). "Stragglers were captured by New Mexicans and sold into slavery. More than 300 individuals from the first group of 2,500 perished on the journey" (Sheridan and Parezo 1996, 12). Several thousand Navajos under the leadership of Manulito and Barboncito evaded capture by escaping to hidden canyons at Black Mesa and along the rim of the Grand Canyon.

The story of the Long Walk has become legendary in Navajo oral history and is told in hushed tones from one generation to the next. Spicer (1962, 219) reports that the memory of the Long Walk "stood as an historical incident with as much significance for Navajos as the Civil War . . . for

Anglo-Americans." Almost every Navajo living today has an ancestor or relative who died or encountered the brutality of the Long Walk. Once at Fort Sumner, the Army found the Navajo population much larger than they had anticipated. Arrangements for food and housing were completely inadequate. To make matters worse, "a smallpox epidemic struck in 1865 and 2,321 Navajos were dead within a few months. Less and less of the cropland was planted. Corrupt agents in charge dealt in rations and blankets and the care of the Indians grew worse" (Spicer 1962, 220).

The Navajo Reservation (1878–1934)

The government experiment at Bosque Redondo ended in complete failure. The plan to grow crops failed, and the interred Indians were poorly housed in overcrowded and unsanitary conditions, which led to disease and many deaths. As a result, Carleton was relieved of command on September 19, 1866, and control over the Navajos was transferred from the U.S. Army to the Bureau of Indian Affairs. Among the more vocal critics of Carleton were the superintendent of Indian affairs for New Mexico and Judge Joseph Knapp of the territory's Supreme Court. Knapp criticized Carleton for waging war on Navajos without any legal authority. Those imprisoned, he pointed out, included noncombatants such as the elderly, women, and children.

After four years at Bosque Redondo, the surviving Navajos were allowed to return home after signing a treaty with the United States. Barboncito, the principal spokesman for the Navajos, passionately declared: "I hope to God you will not ask me to go to any other country except my own" (Roessel 1983, 517). Many Navajos attribute their release from bondage to religious ceremonies foretelling their freedom, which they had performed while interred.

On June 1, 1868, a treaty was concluded that established a 3.5 million acre, rectangular reservation for the Navajos "and for such other friendly tribes or individual Indians" in western New Mexico. The Navajos had to give up to any claims to aboriginal rights under the terms of the treaty. In return, the United States agreed to provide seeds and tools for farming, to replace the sheep Kit Carson had killed, and to provide schools and teachers for every thirty children in attendance. These benefits were to be provided for ten years, after which the Navajos were expected to become economically self-sustaining. In reality, the economic struggle for sheer survival by the destitute Navajos in the first years rendered the government's goals inoperable. The seeds and tools usually arrived late, if they arrived at all, school attendance was frustrated because children were needed at home "to help plant the fields, to rebuild the ruined hogans, even to hunt rats and prairie dogs, so the family need not eat their sheep" (Underhill 1963, 231).

There were only four thousand Navajos who survived the Long Walk and confinement at Bosque Redondo to return home to their land within the four sacred mountains. The years following internment were so difficult that many families dispersed throughout the Four Corners area so that by 1879, six million acres outside the reservation were occupied by the Navajos, and many others had moved west to settle among the Hopis. Nevertheless, sheep became the key to the Navajo recovery. By 1878, the sheep herds had multiplied to over seven hundred thousand. With the expansion of the herds, however, grazing land became scarce and led to conflicts with non-Indians on the Navajo eastern boundary. The 1868 Navajo reservation was only one-tenth the size of their former homeland.

The dispersal of the Navajos was exacerbated when the federal government withdrew reservation lands for the Atlantic and Pacific Railroad. This became known as the "checkerboard" area when the federal giveaway to the railroad included odd-numbered sections that "extended forty miles on each side of the main line and absorbed grazing areas and watering holes" (Enders 1971, 25). The sections granted to the railroad contained some of the finest Navajo winter range. The rationale for giving land to the transcontinental railroads, such as the Atlantic and Pacific, was that the generous right-aways would subsidize their construction; the railroads could find coal, wood, gravel, and water for building purposes, and then sell the excess lands to bonafide settlers. In point of fact, much of the excess lands wound up in the hands of large ranching concerns and land companies.

In order to meet the needs of the expanding Navajo population, the government subsequently added to the 1868 reservation by issuing nine Executive Orders and various Acts. Between 1878 and 1933, the Navajo reservation was expanded many times by executive order, eventually encapsulating the Hopi mesas. The executive Order of October 29, 1878, for example, was a rectangular strip of land lying directly west of the 1868 reservation and was meant to compensate the Navajos for land given to the Atlantic and Pacific Railroad. By the early 1880s, there were more than twelve thousand Navajos and the reservation area was three times as large as in

1868. Executive Order of January 6, 1880 added 996,403 acres to the south and to the Arizona-New Mexico border, and another Executive Order of January 8, 1900 added lands comprising approximately 1,517,785 acres that was formerly owned by the Santa Fe Railroad, which was then compensated. (See map, Figure 5.1 featuring additions to the original reservation.)

Sheep as a Way of Life

Sheep have always been at the center of both the Navajo economy and cultural life. Sheep's wool provided much-needed cash for Navajo women who produced the beautifully distinctive and highly prized Navajo rugs. The rugs, along with the silver jewelry crafted by Navajo men, if not used or sold, could be bartered or used as collateral for loans from the traders during hard times. Sheep and horses became mobile wealth, a form of money in the bank. Sheep also became a key social and psychological aspect of Navajo life. "A family's public image, prestige, and status were linked to the size and well-being of the herd" (Sheridan and Parezo 1996, 22). Sheep, although owned by individuals, cemented kinship ties since extended families combined their herds and shared grazing territory. Sheep validated marriages. The wool from sheep used in weaving "also cemented family ties because producing a blanket to keep someone warm was a woman's gift to her husband or son" (Sheridan and Parezo 1996, 23).

In the 1920s, Navajo families experienced the U.S. Army pushing into their lands in western New Mexico. Lacking any papers of ownership for their land, the Navajos and their sheep herds were eventually pushed out to make room for a U.S. Army depot. Official *land creep:* That's how the Army turned "a slice of land used by the Navajos into part of the largest munitions depot in the world. By the time of World War II, the [Fort] Wingate depot would be the repository for 15 million pounds of TNT" (Burnham 2006, B1). "In 1918, the depot began expanding the military area to 22,000 acres, much of it used by the Interior Department as a sheep breeding laboratory. Then the National Forest Service moved in from the south. Through the '30s and '40s, the government fenced land, promising the Navajo they would maintain access to water. When the fence line cut off the local springs, the herders were forced off the mountain" (Burnham 2006, B-2).

As the 1930s approached, sheep remained at the center of Navajo life. Both men and women followed a pattern of going off the reservation to work for several months, or years, but always returning to family lands and herds.

> By 1933, more than 1.1 million sheep and goats were being grazed on the Navajo Reservation, overwhelming the [carrying] capacity of the land. That year, the Bureau of Indian Affairs (BIA) began a program of stock reduction as a solution aimed at reducing stock by 45 percent by the 1950s. The program was to be voluntary and was to consist initially of a 10 percent across-the-board reduction, which large herd owners could meet by culling weak sheep but which would force small owners to sacrifice good stock. (Sheridan and Parezo 1996, 23)

The government's stock reduction policy spelled disaster for the Navajos and led to fierce resistance. "Why should the Government rob us out of our sheep?" complained a Navajo woman. "It is our money" (Sheridan and Parezo 1996, 26). Sheep were needed for feeding guests at ceremonies and for paying singer fees. By 1937, government agents were forcibly destroying Navajo sheep and even threatening the dissenters with jail. Some families with small herds were rendered destitute, and welfare had to be initiated to keep families from starving. The reservation was divided into land management districts, and grazing permits were issued to Navajo herders. "[Government] agents, not understanding that among the Navajos, property was held by women, refused to give them permits. This disenfranchised many women, creating problems within and between families, leaving some women in destitution, shifting sheep from one clan to another, and confusing the inheritance patterns" (Sheridan and Parezo 1996, 28).

As a result of the government's stock reduction program, many sheep were slaughtered and left to rot. Dismayed by seeing their sheep shot and bloating in the sun, the Navajos rejected the Indian Reorganization Act (IRA) in 1935. The IRA set up corporate tribal councils, actually advisory bodies to the Indian Bureau, an innovation of the government's new policy of indirect rule under the New Deal Democratic administration. How the Navajos came to adopt a tribal council system outside the framework of the IRA is explained below.

Tribal Government

Many changes occurred on the reservation after the Long Walk. Traders and the growth of trading posts begin to have an important impact on Navajo life. Compulsory school attendance was another matter. The treaty of 1868 required every Navajo child to attend school, but the Navajos strongly opposed sending their children to distant boarding schools. "Education was looked upon as a threat and a foe to the Navajo way of life as well as a threat to the Navajo family" (Roessel 1983, 522). Nevertheless, the Indian Bureau set about establishing federal boarding schools for Navajo and other Indian children at Fort Defiance in 1882, and at Grand Junction, Colorado, in 1890. Schools were also set up by missionary groups. School discipline was harsh; "ankle chains and solitary confinement were common practices" (Spicer 1962, 223).

A policy of religious oppression dominated the Indian Bureau in the 1920s. Navajos were punished for practicing customs such as polygamy and the execution of individuals for so-called witchcraft.

Other changes among the Navajos included blanket weaving for sale to tourists, silver work artistic development, railroad construction which created new jobs and markets for Navajo arts and crafts, the introduction of wagons, metal plows, roads, automobiles and trucks. The federal government expanded its presence on the reservation, along with health services, missionaries, and missions. The Navajo population increased as did Navajo livestock.

"After their return from Fort Sumner, the Navajo were governed by a band chief, who was appointed by the [government] agent and approved by the secretary of the interior" (Roessel 1983, 523). There were also regional leaders. The agent's authority was supported by the military at Fort Wingate. In 1915 the Indian Bureau divided the reservation into five separate jurisdictions, each with its own agency superintendent and staff. Navajo community councils, called chapters, were created in 1917. As late as 1922, there was no overall political organization among the Navajos. Instead, the traditional *naat'áani* system prevailed, counterbalanced by war leaders, men who knew the Warway ceremony. Nevertheless, the secretary of the interior appointed a Navajo Business Council comprised of influential Navajo men in order to approve oil and timber leases.

When oil was discovered on the reservation in 1922, Secretary of the Interior Albert B. Fall issued a ruling that opened all executive order reservations to oil exploration by oil companies under the 1920 General Leasing Act. This was one of the Indian policies that struck at Indian sovereignty, especially in New Mexico, and led to the protest from the Pueblos and the entry of reformer John Collier and the Indian Defense Association the following year. Collier later became Indian commissioner in 1925 under the New Deal democratic administration of President Franklin D. Roosevelt.

The discovery of oil on the reservation by a subsidiary of Standard Oil forced a revision in the system of Navajo governance. The first council of Navajo men called together by the agent to approve an oil lease refused by a vote of 75–0. When oil pressure continued, "the BIA instructed the local agent to convene a new council and get it to vote permanent 'broad authority to lease the land' to the BIA itself! It took two years to achieve it, but the agent formed a new Navajo council which included regions not formerly represented and gave it more continuing existence; in fact it was the embryo of today's Tribal Council. Its first act, in 1923, was to give away its leasing authority to the BIA" (Mander 1981, 57–58).

Eventually, a forerunner of the modern tribal council was created. The group which came to be called the Navajo Tribal Council consisted of two representatives from each of five districts, usually selected by the local superintendent of each. Despite the Navajo matrilineal tradition, women were not allowed to vote in tribal elections until 1928. The first meeting of the new body was held on July 7, 1923. One of the three tribal leaders was Chee Dodge, a Roman Catholic and wealthy trader and sheepman who spoke English. He became chair of a twelve-member Council and went on to become the widely recognized leader of the Navajos for the next seventy years. The council of advisers was enlarged in 1936 after the five reservation agencies were consolidated into a single Indian Bureau agency. An elected tribal council system was created in 1938. By the 1950s, the tribal council had become an elected, representative organization that functioned under a written constitution. Currently, the Navajo Tribal Council includes a chair, vice-chair, and seventy-four delegates. Women can, and do, serve on the council. Council meetings are held at Window Rock, Arizona, the capital of the Navajo Nation.

When the Indian Reorganization Act (IRA) was legislated in 1935, the Navajos rejected the offer to organize under its provisions because of their animosity to Indian commissioner John Collier. The bitter experience of forced sheep reduction led the Navajos to condemn its architect, the liberal commissioner of Indian Affairs.

World War II and Postwar

More than 3,400 Navajos served in the U.S. armed forces during World War II. Navajo Code Talkers played a key role in the defeat of imperial Japan by contriving a secret code that the Japanese could never break. Another 10,000 Navajos gained a reputation as outstandingly loyal and hardworking employees at shipyards, factories, and defense plants, many working in California. Despite the contribution of Navajo Armed Forces personnel and defense workers, after the war the states of Arizona and New Mexico promulgated a racist policy of prohibiting Navajos and other Indians from voting in state elections. Job opportunities all but dried up after the war, and many Navajos returned to the reservation. The government's relocation program in the 1950s and early 1960s reversed the trend by persuading many Navajos to move to cities, such as Denver, Los Angeles, and the San Francisco Bay area to receive training and job placement. The program ended in failure, however, and Navajo families who had relocated found themselves living in urban poverty. Back home on the reservation, the Navajos were experiencing an exceptionally high rate of youth suicide, and alcoholism was widespread.

Beginning in the 1950s, the Navajos began to develop reservation mineral resources—coal, oil, natural gas, uranium—in addition to forest reserves. Farmland acreage, particularly irrigated lands, increased to a total of 34,800 acres by 1980. Mining companies began prospecting on the reservation, and in 1970, the Utah Construction and Mining Company leased a twenty-five mile long strip of Navajo land to mine coal. The royalty rate of fifteen cents per ton, negotiated by the Bureau of Indian Affairs, was ridiculously low. Nevertheless, the Navajo government launched a program for economic development, and the tribal budget increased significantly. The "Utah oil fields alone generated over $34 million in revenues. . . . Similarly, revenues from uranium mining increased ten fold from 1950 to 1954" (Butler 1996, 381). *Leetso*, "yellow dirt," is the Navajo word for uranium. The Navajo Tribal Council allowed forty-two uranium mines to be located on or immediately adjacent to the reservation. Energy development generated funds to pay salaries to local chapter officials, and new chapter houses were built. A tribal court system was established in 1959, and by 1966, a Navajo legal aid program was up and running.

Uranium mining, however, became a two-edged sword. Former Navajo Nation President Joe Shirley, Jr., has described the uranium mining era as genocide. The largest radioactive accident in the United States was not the Three Mile Island nuclear power plant in Pennsylvania; the biggest radioactive accident occurred on the Navajo Reservation in the early morning hours of July 16, 1979, at Church Rock, New Mexico, when a United Nuclear Corporation containment dam broke, releasing radioactive water and confluent into the Rio Puerco River. The river was called *Toinjoni* in Navajo,"the Beautiful River that Flows," but the pale, muddy water had a putrid smell and was no longer beautiful. "About 94 million gallons of radioactive and chemically toxic waste water and 1,100 tons of contaminated solids were released" (Siskind 1982, 38). Mysterious open sores began to develop on the legs of Navajo sheep and horses shortly after the animals had been in the river. The river had been the source of water for Navajo sheep, goats, and cattle, and for the irrigation of their corn and peach trees, and a playground for Navajo children during the hot summer months. But now the authorities warned them not to eat their animals, and to haul their water from distant wells deemed safe. Later the federal Center for Disease Control said that people could again eat their animals, "as long as they avoid the liver, kidney, spleen and, perhaps, the bone" (Siskind 1982, 37).

The Kerr-McGee Company, the first corporation to mine uranium on the Navajo Reservation, found the leasing arrangement with the tribe incredibly lucrative. There were no taxes at the time, no health,

safety, or pollution regulations, and labor was cheap since there were "few other jobs available to the many Navajos recently home from service in World War II" (Grinde and Johansen 1995, 208). The choice offered the Navajos vis-à-vis exploitation of their energy resources was the same as in the past during the Long Walk—accommodate to the White man's wishes, or starve.

But thirty years after mining began, an increasing number of Navajos were dying of lung cancer. *Leetso* was the cause. A federal inspector found that the ventilation units in the mines were inoperative, and a report dating from 1959 found "that radiation levels in the Kerr-McGee shaft had been allowed to reach ninety times the 'permissible' level" (Churchill and LaDuke 1992, 247). Radioactive uranium tailings wound up approximately sixty feet from the San Juan River. "As Navajo miners continued to die, children who played in water that had flowed over or through abandoned mines and tailing piles came home with burning sores" (Grinde and Johansen 1995, 209).

Uranium mining on Indian reservations has been called "the political economy of radioactive colonialism" (Churchill and LaDuke 1992, 247). About half the recoverable uranium at the time was in New Mexico, much of it in Navajo lands. The city

Navajo uranium miners.

of Grants adopted the nickname "Uranium Capital of the World."

> Navajo uranium miners during the 1940s and 1950s hauled radioactive uranium ore out of the earth as if it were coal. Some ate their lunches in the mines and slaked their thirst with radioactive water. Their families' homes sometimes were built on radioactive earth, and their neighbors' sheep may have watered in small ponds that formed at the mouths of abandoned uranium mines. . . . On dry windy days, the gritty dust from uranium waste tailings piles covered everything in sight. . . . Some miners worked as many as 20 hours a day. . . . Many mine owners didn't even provide toilet paper. When miners relieved themselves, they wiped with fists of radioactive 'yellowcake'—uranium ore. (Johansen 2007, 295)

Over one thousand abandoned uranium mines are located on the Navajo Reservation. The mines and mills are closed, but their radioactive tailings still spread a legacy of death.

As early as 1978, the Navajos were already beginning to trace their lung cancer epidemic to uranium mining exposure. By 1990, about four hundred miners had died of uranium-related diseases. It is believed that lung cancer is the result of the inhalation of radon gas, a byproduct of uranium's decay into radium. The Kerr-McGee uranium mines were never ventilated, nor were the Navajo miners warned of the danger. Because of the uranium-connected deaths, the Navajo Nation in 2005 banned "uranium mining and processing on any sites within Navajo Indian Country."

A much bigger mining lease went to Peabody Coal for strip-mining coal at Black Mesa. The lease involved both the Navajo and Hopi Indians and immediately became controversial because of the disputed land ownership issue and the threat of desecrating Black Mesa. Black Mesa is the Mother Mountain of the Navajo spirit. "If the harmony of the Mother Mountain is destroyed, it is said, the Navajos . . . will die: survival of the people is tied to the survival of the land" (Grinde and Johansen 1995, 122). The Black Mesa desecration issue and the related land dispute between the Navajo and Hopi tribes is examined later in this chapter.

Reservation Life Today

The Navajo Nation has been forced to pay most of the economic, environmental, and social costs of mineral development. "Despite such mineral wealth, the Navajo people are subject to a degree of poverty unequaled by any other minority group in the U.S. . . . The major cause of its underdevelopment is the fact that large corporations siphon off Navajo mineral wealth" (Dutton 1983, 83).

In the 1960s, the Navajos were experiencing an exceptionally high rate of youth suicide, and alcoholism was widespread. On the positive side, the tribe also took over many of the responsibilities previously held by the Bureau of Indian Affairs, and in 1969, the Navajos officially changed their name from the Navajo Tribe to the Navajo *Nation*. By 1990 the Navajo tribal council had established three branches of government—the executive, legislative, and judicial—and the offices of president and vice president, a speaker of the council, and a number of standing committees. Education was emphasized, and the Navajo Community College was opened in 1969, offering associate degrees on several of its reservation campuses. "Even while they were adapting to new ways, however, Navajos did not abandon sheep raising as a way-of-life. Each family continued to have a small herd, and weaving, while not an economically viable occupation for many people, remains part of a very complex economic system" (Sheridan and Parezo 1996, 31).

A governmental crisis occurred in May 1972, when Navajo President Peter MacDonald was convicted of financial mismanagement and sentenced to federal prison. The controversy surrounding his conviction caused a political upheaval on the reservation, dividing the Navajo Nation into supporters and opponents of the tribal president. Even more serious was the Navajo-Hopi land dispute, which began in the 1950s. It is discussed later in this chapter.

By 1980, there were four coal strip mines on the reservation and five giant coal-fired power plants. An area once considered to have the cleanest air in the U.S. became polluted with black smoke and soot. There were thirty-eight uranium mines and six uranium mills. Groundwater tables had become irradiated, and uranium tailings were left in huge uncovered piles around the reservation.

Today, the Navajo dependence on agriculture and livestock has declined and job opportunities on the reservation are scarce. In 1991, over one-third of the reservation workforce was unemployed, and per capita income for the reservation (combining both non-Indian and Navajo residents) was just under $6,000. After the bitter experience with uranium mining, the Navajo government has increasingly tried to entice clean industries to relocate to the reservation. It has also heavily invested in education for its younger citizens. Navajo Community College, the first tribally controlled college in the United States, opened its doors in 1969 and became accredited in 1976. The Navajo Area Indian Health Service is well established on the reservation and is credited with successfully reducing the incidence of infant morbidity and mortality.

The Navajo Nation has been reluctant to join the American Indian gaming industry that generated an estimated $18.5 billion in revenues in 2004. There are currently 411 Native casinos in the United States operated by 224 tribes. In the 1990s, the Navajo Nation rejected Indian gaming, but by 2006, they were poised to open their first casino (Lee 2006, B4).

Despite the changes associated with modernization, the Navajo language is still spoken by most Navajos and, according to the 2000 U.S. Census, a significant number speak only Navajo. At the same time, there is a growing concern that many school-aged children are not fluent in Navajo.

THE HOPIS

The Hopi region has been continuously occupied by Indigenous peoples for thousands of years. Archaeological sites from the late Basketmaker and early Pueblo prehistoric phases are found throughout Hopi country. "Directly descended from the Anasazi cliff dwellers of Mesa Verde and elsewhere, the Hopis have been living exactly where they are now since at least 1,000 A.D. They built their spectacular multistoried apartment villages on the cliff tops of three mesas" (Mander 1981, 54). The Hopi region became one of the three major centers of Pueblo culture, along with Zuni-Acoma and the Rio Grande Pueblos. The Hopi language, comprising four major dialects, belongs to the Uto-Aztecan language family.

The Hopis occupy thirteen villages located in the vicinity of the southern escarpment of Black Mesa in northeastern Arizona. The traditional Hopi homeland, called *Tutsqua*, "extended roughly from the Grand Canyon, south to the Mogollon Rim, west to . . . Williams Mountain, and east towards modern day Ganado, near the contemporary boundaries of northwestern New Mexico and northeastern Arizona" (Feher-Elston 1996, 386*)*. The Hopi villages are located on three mesas, fingerlike projections running south from Black Mesa and westward along Moencopi Wash. On First Mesa are *Walpi*, *Sichomovi*, and the Tewa-speaking village of *Hano*, with the modern community of *Polacca* at the mesa's base. Second Mesa includes *Shipaulovi*, *Mishongnovi*, and

the larger village of *Shungopavi*. Before the twentieth century, only *Oraibi* occupied Third Mesa, but a 1906 factional split led to the establishment of *Hotevilla*, *Bacabi*, and New *Oraibi* (now *Kyakotsmovi*). A summer farming village forty miles to the west divided to form Lower and Upper *Moencopi*. Hopi farms are located below the mesas and beyond the villages within a five-to-ten-mile radius. The Hopis are often said to be the world's most proficient dry farmers because of their ingenious adaptation to an arid environment. They developed plants such as maize and beans, with deep roots in the sandy soil that give high yields. Several farming techniques include two types of flood water farming and irrigation.

Before White contact, the villages were virtual theocratic ministates. Each village was independent and governed by priests called *Moqwis*. A number of Hopi villages still retain this traditional way of governance. Three of the oldest continuously inhabited communities in North America are located on the three Hopi mesas, dating back to A.D. 1200: *Oraibi* on Third Mesa, *Shungopovi* on Second Mesa, and *Walpi* on First Mesa.

Early History and Origins

Before the entry of Europeans into the region, the Hopis were house-dwellers and horticulturists, subsistence farmers, who supplemented their diet with small game. An artistic renaissance occurred in pottery designs during the fourteenth century with the appearance of black-on-orange and orange polychrome designs—"startling sweeping curvilinear motifs; bird, animal, floral, and human representations; and religious masks and ceremonial scenes" (Brew 1979, 517). Paintings on Hopi *kiva* walls, which are part of religious ceremonies, date back to the eleventh century.

When the Spaniards first contacted the village-dwellers of the region, they called each settlement a *pueblo*, and the village dwellers ranging along the Rio Grande River and Hopi country came to be called collectively Pueblo Indians. Today, the Hopis farm, raise cattle, and engage in wage labor both on and off the reservation. Hopi women excel in pottery. Hopi textiles and kachina dolls are also sought after by tourists and collectors.

In their early history the Hopis used coal for cooking and heating, for firing pottery, and for making pigment. It was used to heat both houses and *kivas*, but also held religious significance. Coal beds are found as outcroppings along the mesa rim of Hopi country. It is estimated that some thirty thousand tons of coal were mined in prehistoric times near *Awatovi*, and probably more than one hundred thousand tons along an escarpment of Antelope Mesa. After the arrival of the Spaniards, the Hopis ceased using coal for fuel and turned again to wood for home heating, and sheep dung to fire pottery.

Awatovi was the first Hopi town visited by the Spaniards in 1540. An expedition led by General Francisco Vásquez de Coronado reached the Zuni and the eastern-most Hopi villages and traveled on to discover the Grand Canyon. In 1583, Antonio de Espejo revisited Hopi country in search of mines which had been reported in the area. His visit was a peaceful one. Juan de Oñate, a Spanish colonizer and gold seeker, made several trips into Hopi country at the beginning of the seventeenth century. His was the last recorded visit by the Spaniards for the next twenty-three years.

The Hopis say that their ancestors emerged from under the ground near the confluence of the Colorado and the Little Colorado rivers. It was *Masau'u*, "Lord of this World," who taught the Hopis their culture and who delineated the boundaries of *Tutsqua*. The nearby San Francisco Peaks, north of present-day Flagstaff, are especially sacred to the Hopis, because they are the home of the *Kachinas*, spirits who play a central role in Hopi religious beliefs and ceremonies.

Social Organization

Hopi society is integrated through two interdependent systems of social organization. "The (village) residence sites, the clans, and ceremonial societies are named groups. The households, lineages, and phratries are unnamed groups or named only by reference" (Connelly 1979, 539). The phratry (a kinship class or division) is the largest kinship unit and is exogamous, that is, marriage is forbidden among the members of the clans in the phratry. The cross-clan membership of the ceremonial societies aids in preventing the concentration of excessive power within any one residence group. *Oraibi* in the 1930s had 31 clan houses and 145 households accommodating a population of 963 people.

Traditional Hopi villages are interdependent in their ceremonial ties and obligations. "In the First Mesa area the major ceremonies are in the custody of the mother village *Walpi*, and *Sichomovi* is in a colonial relationship, dependent on *Walpi* for religious initiation. In return, *Sichomovi* serves as a reservoir of available population. . . . The other satellite community on First Mesa, Tewa village, was established in historic times" (Connelly 1979, 540).

At the beginning of the twentieth century, a typical Hopi village consisted of multistoried residence structures, arranged around a central plaza called the *kisoni*. The individual residence, the *kihu*, was matrilineal and matrilocal by custom, that is, kinship and residence was through the women. The Hopi "apartment house" was "a rectangular structure constructed of sandstone and adobe mortar, with a roof built up of layers of timbers, cedar bark and adobe mud" (Hieb 1996, 242). Located either in the plaza, or toward the end of the village was a semisubterranean religious structure, the *kiva*, constructed of similar materials. Other structures were for baking the customary *piki* bread, and for housing tools and farming equipment. Livestock corrals were located at a distance.

The early reservation era included trading posts and mission churches. After World War II, other facilities and businesses appeared. Today, there are gasoline stations, laundromats, arts and crafts shops, schools, and an airport. The Hopi Cultural Center is located on Second Mesa. Century-old trails, ten miles long, originally connected the villages on the three mesas. Today, they have been transformed into modern highways, and beasts of burden have been replaced by trucks and automobiles.

Spiritual Culture

Hopi ceremonies emphasize nonaggression, unity, and cooperation. "Hopi ceremonialism stresses pacification of the natural elements to prevent threatening disturbances in nature. Hopi ideology places equal stress on pacifying, non-aggressive human behavior to counteract the threat posed by competition within the residence unit" (Connelly 1979, 547).

Hopi religious ceremonies have been heavily influenced by the Rio Grande Pueblos and especially the Zuni. The Hopis have a strong kachina (*katsina*) tradition. Curing is controlled by medicine societies operating within the kachina cult. The Kachinas are "benevolent beings who dwell in mountains, springs, and lakes, and who are the bringers of blessings, particularly rain, crops, and wellbeing" (Dutton 1983, 40). Because they are an agricultural people, the ceremonies of the Hopis are primarily for rain.

The kachina impersonators are anthropomorphic individuals who are masked, painted, and costumed. They "appear in the village plazas and *kivas* as impersonators of the spiritual ones enacting esoteric rites and ceremonies" (Dutton 1983, 40). Every person is supposed to be initiated into a ceremonial society, and men take on a lifelong responsibility to impersonate both male and female kachinas. The kachina season begins in November with the enactment of the emergence from the underworld. A major feature is the promotion of fertility and germination in anticipation of the approaching growing season. Then come the curing rites. The dance season draws to a close as the summer solstice approaches.

"Hopi cosmology includes the notion of the evolution of mankind through four worlds, with the final emergence of the Hopis in the Grand Canyon, by way of the *sinapu*, an opening from the underworld below. . . . The *sinapu* is a symbolic medium of exchange and communication between the upper world of the living and the lower world of the spirits" (Hieb 1996, 242). It is an essential element of the traditional Hopi village and the first component to be constructed. The *kiva* replicates this sacred belief by making an opening in the floor representing the *sinapu*, and by the arrangement of the various floor levels.

In traditional culture, women's and men's social space is separate from each other and carefully defined. The *kihu*, once considered women's space, has been altered by changing conditions, but the *kiva* still remains the province of men. Hopi gardens are tended by women, while men care for the corn fields and livestock. "Priests collect snakes and eagles (messengers to sacred space), make offerings at shrines, and go on expeditions for salt" (Hieb 1996, 242).

The basis of Hopi religious beliefs and practices is founded in the creation story of the emergence and Hopi clan traditions. It is given expression in prayer offerings and ritual. "Only those who have been initiated into various societies, or are proper members of the clan, may have access to this knowledge and the sacred objects which embody it" (Hieb 1996, 243). This strongly held belief has led to conflict with non-Hopis who seek to document Hopi sacred culture, or collect its religious paraphernalia for museums or sale. Today, permission for study or publication must be cleared by the Hopi Office of Cultural Preservation.

The Hopi ritual calendar is calibrated to correspond to the summer and winter solstices, "with priestly ceremonies involving the Snake, Antelope *wuwtsim* (the ceremonies of the four men's societies), and women's societies in the summer and fall, and kachina (*katsina*) ceremonies in the winter and spring. The so-called 'social dances,' the Buffalo (winter; hunting) and Butterfly (summer; agriculture) appear immediately following the solstices" (Hieb 1996, 243). Hopi rituals connect the world of the living

with the world of the dead. Corn is the most important ritual symbol and represents the Hopi concern for sustaining life. "Just as the path of an individual moves from birth to death, the Hopi emergence myth and prophecies make clear the Hopi path of life (*hopivotskwani*) (Hieb 1996, 243). Although various Christian missions—Baptists, Roman Catholics, Mennonites, Mormons, and others—operate today on the Hopi Reservation, most Hopis continue to follow their ancient spiritual traditions.

HOPI POLITICAL HISTORY

When the first Athabascan hunters and gatherers entered the American Southwest, the ancestors of the Pueblo peoples had already deserted or were abandoning their settlements throughout the Colorado Plateau. One group of the Athabascan migrants became known as "Apaches de Navajo," and one of the centers of Pueblo concentration was the southern edge of Black Mesa, the heart of the Navajo-Hopi disputed territory today.

In the past, many Pueblo peoples, including the Hopi, Zuni, and Acoma, viewed the Navajos as enemies. Nevertheless, the Hopis, at one time or another in their history, established trade relations with the Rio Grande Pueblos and other Indian peoples in the region, including the Navajos. In the same fashion, "individual Apachean bands or tribes had alliances and trade relations with individual pueblos, even as they were at odds with other Pueblos that were also enemies of their Pueblo trading partners" (Brugge 1994, 4). After the arrival of the Spaniards, "the natural allies for the anti-white faction at most pueblos were their old Apachean trading partners, who remained free of European domination" (Brugge 1994, 4). As early as 1583, when the Spaniard Antonio de Especo led a small party into Hopi country, the Hopis called on their Apachean neighbors to help defend their land.

When the Spanish government took "formal possession of southwestern regions, Spanish saint names were given to the settlements. The Pueblo country was divided into districts and a Catholic priest was assigned to each. The Indians were required to take oaths of obedience and pay homage to the Catholic church and the Spanish crown" (Dutton 1983, 10). In 1598, the Spaniards established their first capital of New Mexico, San Juan de Las Caballeros.

Beginning in 1629, Spanish Franciscan missionaries sought to Christianize the Hopi villages. "Churches were completed at *Awatovi*, the easternmost village, at *Shungopovi* below modern Second Mesa, and at *Oraibi*, the westernmost village, with "visitas" at *Walpi* and *Mishongnovi*" (Spicer 1992, 191). These villages were also provided with schools and probably Spanish village organization. Initially, the Franciscans were well received. The Franciscan friars expanded their conversion activities in the late seventeenth century, concentrating their religious activities at *Awatovi*. The relatively success of the conversion of the *Awatovi* Hopis was exceptional. Spanish attempts to establish missions and *visitas* in other Hopi communities during the seventeenth century were unsuccessful when the Hopis realized that the new religion was not to supplement their existing religion, but was intended to replace it altogether. An early indication of the rejection of Spanish religious conversion occurred when the missionary at *Awatovi* was poisoned.

"Although the religious effect of the Spanish advent on most Hopis was small, the material effect was great. In addition to domestic animals and new food plants, European goods flowed into the Hopi country, although this stream . . . was intermittent and irregular" (Brew 1979, 520). Hopis constructed churches and friaries, "painted decorative murals on the walls, and provided pottery utensils for the kitchen and refectory" (Brew 1979, 510).

When the eastern Pueblos came under Spanish mission control; the masked ceremonies were forced underground, and Pueblo culture was altered. "Tinder was laid for a conflagration. The spark was the seizure and flogging, in 1675, of forty-seven Pueblo leaders accused of fomenting revival of native religion. One of these men was a Tewa from San Juan, Popé. Hiding from the Spanish in the Northern pueblo of Taos, Popé organized a rebellion" (Kehoe 1992, 130). The 1680 Pueblo Revolt drove the Spaniards from New Mexico with great loss of life. The Hopis joined in the revolt, killing their Spanish priests and destroying the churches.

The 1680 Pueblo revolt ended Spanish influence among the Hopis. The Hopis had suffered forced labor under the Franciscan missionaries and had seen their daughters used as concubines by the priests. Joining in the Pueblo revolt, they threw their priests over the mesa cliffs and destroyed churches and visitas. When *Awatovi* was destroyed by anti-Christian Hopis, the men who resisted were killed and the women and children parceled out to the other villages. They remained free until 1692, when Diego de Vargas led an expedition to reconquer Pueblo country.

Between 1692 and 1696, "the Spaniards came back stronger then ever. But not to the Hopis. . . . The kachinas won and the kachinas have held the field ever since. From that time on, Spaniards appeared on the Hopi mesas only as unwelcome visitors, except at *Awatovi*" (Brew 1979, 521). After the Pueblo rebellion, the First and Second Mesa Hopi towns moved to better defensive positions. "There they were joined by Rio Grande refugees. Some of them established their own towns, of which *Hano* on First Mesa and now ruined *Payupki* on Second Mesa are the best known" (Brew 1979, 522).

The Spanish foothold at the Hopi town of *Awatovi* was a tenuous one at best. After Spanish priests left in the fall of 1701, Hopis from other towns destroyed *Awatovi*. Some of the Hopi survivors joined the Navajos, becoming members of the Navajo *táchii'nii* clan. Several branches or sub-clans retain Hopi clan names.

Spanish efforts during the eighteenth century to reestablish their dominance over the Hopis were unsuccessful. In 1741, the King of Spain removed the Franciscans and handed over the task of religious conversion of the Hopis to the Jesuits. Following the failure of the missionization program by the Jesuits, "the Hopis, who were now living in five villages with about eight thousand inhabitants, were more determined than ever to maintain their separate existence" (Spicer 1962, 195).

A final, but unsuccessful attempt to conquer the Hopis took place in 1780 by Governor Juan Bautista de Anza. No major expedition ventured into Hopi country after de Anza, except for a few Forty-niner gold miners passing through to California. "So the Hopis remained isolated on the mesas. Their valiant stand against the return of the Spaniards bears fruit today. They live in enjoyment of their own Indigenous culture where so many American Indian groups have lost all or most of theirs" (Brew 1979, 522).

The eighteenth century saw continuing close relations between the Hopis and some Navajos. When Fr. Silvestre Vález de Escalante made a trip to Hopiland in 1775, he found more than one hundred Navajos living at *Walpi*. In the following year, Fr. Francisco Garcés visited *Oraibi* and noted that the Hopis and Navajos were on friendly terms. When hostilities between the Navajos and Spaniards broke out in 1818 as a result of conflict over grazing lands, some Navajos moved to the Hopi villages for security. In the early 1800s, however, the Hopis were divided in their relations to Navajos. There were those who took considerable risks to help Navajos, "as well as others who would call on aid from the New Mexicans to attack them" (Brugge 1994, 17).

During the period of Spanish rule in New Mexico, two Hopi groups arose to contend for power. "One was a conservative faction, whose members probably relied almost entirely on farming, and who were anti-white, anti-Christian, and pro-independence. This faction seems to have regarded the Navajos as a valuable buffer between themselves and the whites. The other faction relied to some degree on trading and favored good relations with whites. . . . This faction was less friendly with the Navajos." (Brugge 1994, 18).

The Mexican Era

Spanish rule of New Mexico continued until the Mexican Revolution in 1821. The Indians were then declared citizens on equal basis with non-Indians, at least in principle. Life under Mexican rule had little impact on the Pueblos. Mexico never implemented its control of New Mexico following the revolution against Spain. The new republic became embroiled in resisting U.S. imperialistic ambitions, and as a consequence, neglected Hopiland. In the 1830s, there were Navajos living on the mesas throughout Hopi country, and Navajos visited the Hopi villages frequently. Yet, despite these friendly relations, oral tradition tells of a devastating Navajo attack on *Oraibi* about 1837 to avenge the death of some Navajo visitors. Navajo raids of Mexican and other Indian communities increased.

When the Treaty of Guadalupe Hidalgo was signed in 1848, Mexico gave up its claim to territory east of the Rio Grande. It ceded New Mexico and Alta (upper) California to the United States and guaranteed sovereignty to the Pueblos. Since the Hopis were located further west from the Rio Grande, these events had little direct impact on them. The Hopi Way had vanquished the Spaniards, but "the Hopi were increasingly preoccupied with attacks from Mexican, Apache, and Navajo raiders in pursuit of plunder, food, or captives to be sold into slavery in Mexico" (Dockstader 1979, 524).

Although Mexico never controlled New Mexico following its revolution against Spain, a new world opened up following the end of the U.S. war with Mexico in 1849. With the establishment of U.S. authority, John S. Calhoun was appointed official Indian agent for the Southwest, and in 1851 Fort Defiance was established to protect the region against Navajo raids. A smallpox epidemic devastated Hopi villages in 1857–8 and was followed by a period of drought. When U.S. Army troops were reassigned after the outbreak of the Civil War, Navajo attacks increased. Later, Brigadier General

James J. Carleton returned to the area, and assisted by Kit Carson and the U. S. Army presence, ushered in a period of relative peace for the Hopis. This was followed, however, by another drought and a smallpox epidemic. "To escape the pestilence, many Hopi fled to Zuni. . . . During their stay, many major influences entered Hopi culture. . . . Most particularly this is seen in changes of pottery designs, religious influences, and language," including an increasing number of Hopis becoming fluent in Spanish (Dockstader 1979, 525).

In 1858, the Mormons in Utah became interested in the Hopis. This interest led them to found a small colony of Mormons near *Moenkopi*, the westernmost Hopi village. For the most part, unlike the Eastern Pueblos, the Hopis and Zunis experienced relatively few contacts with Whites during the Mexican period. The first intensive contacts with Anglo-Americans were in the 1880s when cattlemen moved into western New Mexico.

Anglo-American Rule

During the Anglo period in New Mexico, Hopis carried on a lively trade with the Navajos, but early in 1854, hostilities again occurred between the two peoples, leading to the death of one Navajo and five Hopis. In 1858, warfare between the United States and the Navajos broke out. At one point it was reported that some Navajos were fleeing toward the Hopi villages. During Kit Carson's scorched earth campaign against the Navajos, Navajo captives reported that there were Navajos with their livestock near Hopi villages and that the Hopi town of *Oraibi* was in league with the Navajos. The treaty of June 1, 1868, ended the U.S.-Navajo wars and the end of the Navajos as an independent people.

Christian missionary activity increased at Hopi villages. Beginning in 1858, Mormon missionary work resulted in a lasting presence among the Hopis and the Southwest generally. The Mormon Church located a mission at *Moenkopi*, a Moravian mission was established at *Oraibi*, and the Baptists founded a mission at *Mishongnovi*. In 1878, Tuba City became the major Mormon outpost in northern Arizona.

Because the Navajo Agency was located at Fort Defiance, far from Hopi villages, an independent Hopi Indian Agency was set up at *Oraibi*. It lasted until 1803 when it was incorporated into the Navajo Agency. The first government buildings were started at Keams Canyon in Hopi country a few years later. "In 1874, the Indian Bureau decided to establish an agency for the Hopis. Offices and a school, run by the Protestant Mission Board, were set up at Keams Canyon. . . . On the First Mesa, nearest to the agency, were the Hopi communities of *Walpi* and *Misshongnovi, Shungopovi,* and *Shipaulovi*—all Hopi villages. On Third Mesa was *Oraibi*—the largest of all—with a population of one thousand. Still farther west was *Moenkopi*, a colony of *Oraibi*" (Spicer 1962, 201–2). "The annual report of the Hopi agent for 1871 described the six easternmost Hopi villages as friendly towards the government, while *Oraibi* was described as hostile and . . . continued to maintain close relations with the Apaches" (Brugge 1994, 25). The local Indian agent issued sheep and encouraged the Hopis to expand their land base for grazing and farming. This brought them into closer contact with Navajos and led to conflict at Keams Canyon, *Awatovi*, and Tuba City.

"The completion in 1881 of the Atlantic and Pacific Railroad resulted in more and more people coming into the country, and the towns of Flagstaff, Winslow, and Holbrook sprung up. Located less than 70 miles from the Hopi villages, they provided entry for a wide variety of outsiders: traders, tourists, and teachers . . . in a period of White supremacy" (Dockstader 1979, 526). The first crack in Hopi hostility towards White authority and culture occurred in 1875. In that year, the English trader, Thomas Keam, took a group of Hopi village leaders to Washington, DC, to meet with President Chester A. Arthur. The *Oraibi* village leader *Lololoma*, formerly hostile to Whites, became deeply impressed by his visit and began to use his influence to persuade his people to send their children to school. Thus began the disintegration at *Oraibi* into two factions known as the Friendlies and the Hostiles. The two factions have also been termed "progressives," and "conservatives" or traditionalists.

The Hopis are unique in that they never signed a treaty with the United States and did not receive official federal recognition until 1882. On December 16 of that year, partly to curb the increasing Mormon presence in the Southwest, "President Chester Arthur delineated by executive order a small rectangle in the center of the Hopi homeland as a reservation, 'set apart for the use of the Moqui [Hopis], and other such Indians as the Secretary of the Interior may see fit to settle thereon.' At the time of the decree, there were several hundred Navajos living on what the United States has declared to be the Hopi Reservation" (Feher-Elston 1996, 388). The creation of a reservation had the effect of confining the Hopis to about 60 percent of their aboriginal land. Despite some

Hopi complaints, the Navajo families living within the borders of the executive order reservation did not move; they continued to reside in the same desert valleys where their ancestors had resided in what later became known as the Joint Use Area. There were occasional quarrels when Navajo herds overran Hopi gardens, but the Navajo agent at the time noted that good feelings existed between the two peoples: "they constantly mingle together at festivals, dances, feasts, etc." (Brugge 1994, 27). For the most part, both Hopis and Navajos observed the new Hopi Reservation boundary.

Causes of Hopi Disputes

A serious force of disruption for the Hopis was the government's 1887 Dawes Severalty (Indian Allotment) Act. It met with firm opposition from Hopi leaders. In March 1894, Moqui village leaders addressed a letter to "the Washington Chiefs" in which they stated that "none of us ever asked that [Hopi land] should be measured into separate lots and given to individuals for this would cause confusion" (Letter by Hopi Headmen 1894). The letter went on to explain Hopi land tenure system based on their matrilineal system of common ownership. It was signed by 123 Hopi headmen with their clan symbols. All the villages opposed the government surveyors who came to Hopi country in 1891 to prepare for allotment. Troops were sent to *Oraibi* to discipline village leaders.

A number of Hopi Hostiles were imprisoned on the prison island of Alcatraz in San Francisco Bay in 1895, following their active opposition to the individual allotment of clan-held land. Earlier opposition against the surveying of Hopi lands in preparation for allotment resulted in the imprisonment of many *Oraibi* men at Fort Wingate (Dockstader 1979, 527, Figure 2). Hopi opposition appears to have had a bearing on the federal government's eventual abandonment of allotment policy in the Southwest.

The government policy of forcibly removing young Indian children from their homes and sending them to distant boarding schools began in the 1880s. From 1880 to 1930, it was the practice of the Indian Bureau to remove Hopi children from their homes and place them under Christian influence, often Mormon. The establishment of a federal boarding school at Keams Canyon in July of 1887 further added to Hopi factionalism. The Tewa-speaking people on First Mesa complied with the order of school attendance, but most families at *Oraibi* refused, as they had also refused to cooperate with the government's 1871 census of population. The boarding school children were forbidden to speak the Hopi language, to wear Hopi clothes, or to keep their traditional long hair styles. "They were given English names . . . and all Hopi customs were outlawed [and] . . . they were required to undergo religious indoctrination, much of it by Mormons" (Mander 1981, 55). Many traditional Hopis refused to allow their children to attend, and a group of Hopi parents were jailed. The school issue, combined with the threat of the allotment program, hardened the resolve of the conservative traditionalists.

Another issue was the appropriation of Hopi religious objects by Whites. "At the World's Columbian Exposition in Chicago in 1893, some of the sacred Hopi ceremonial objects collected by anthropologists and by trader Keams were exhibited. The Hopis reacted strongly against this sacrilege" (Spicer 1962, 203).

The split that had developed between the two Hopi groups came to a head in 1906 within *Oraibi* village when tensions led to a major clash. When the traditional Hopis (Hostiles) invited sympathetic Hopis from Second Mesa to join them at *Oraibi*, the Friendlies sought to evict the newcomers. The dispute led the culturally nonviolent Hopis to engage in an aggressive village push-of-war. After the Hostiles, who numbered about half the village of some twelve hundred people lost, they agreed to leave *Oraibi* and move north to Third Mesa where they built a new village, *Hotevilla*. By 1910 the tribal split was complete. Following the Hopi split at *Oraibi*, the Indian agency went into action "to maintain peace." "The superintendent at Keams Canyon . . . arrested many 'hostile' men, including all their principal leaders and set them to jail for a year" (Spicer 1962, 205). The leader of the Friendles group was sent to a boarding school "to learn civilized ways" When he returned four years later, however, he had become strongly anti-Christian.

World War I and the Depression

From 1910 to 1911, the federal government attempted to allot Hopi lands but succeeded only at *Moencopi* before the effort was abandoned. In 1911, the United States again used the military to force Hopi parents to send their children to the White man's schools. Young Hopi children from the party friendly to the government were taught to distrust Navajos. The government's school policy intensified the anti-White attitudes of the Hopi Hostiles (traditionalists) and further divided the Hopis over this issue. New Mexico was admitted to the Union as a state in January 1912, but it wasn't until 1924 that Congress passed the

Snyder Act making Indians citizens of the United States. Ironically, New Mexico excluded Indians from the right to vote in the state until 1948.

Between 1894 and 1912, Bureau of Indian Affairs day schools were established near the Hopi villages, and a government hospital was opened at Keams Canyon in 1913. Several hundred Hopis enlisted in the armed services during World War I, marking one of their first contacts with the outside world, but the majority adhered to their longstanding noncombatant tradition.

"In 1912, the problem of damage to Navajo and Hopi crops by livestock of the other tribe had become a continuing problem" (Brugge 1994, 30). The sixteen-mile boundary between the two peoples was no longer being observed. Since the federal government had already given tacit approval to the Navajo occupation of land within the 1882 reservation boundary, Hopi expansion was blocked. Some Hopis asked Arizona senator Ralph H. Cameron to make the 1882 reservation exclusive for Hopis. By the 1920s, some Bureau of Indian Affairs agents and officials were recommending that the Executive Order reservation be partitioned between the two tribes. In November of 1930, the first formal negotiation between the two peoples on the land question took place. "Navajo leaders favored splitting the land, while the Hopis argued for the expulsion of all Navajos from the 1882 Reservation" (Brugge 1994, 32). For the Hopis, the area in dispute was the sacred point of their emergence into this, the Fourth World.

The 1930s' Depression took its toll on the Hopi economy. Hopi income was dependent on farming, a modest amount of off-reservation wage labor, and the sale of arts and crafts. For the first time, intoxication became a problem. It was about this time that some non-Indians began perpetuating the "traditional enemy" stereotype that projected an unfavorable image of the "aggressive Navajos" pitted against the "peaceful Hopis."

Indian Reorganization Act

The greatest change during the decade of the 1930s came about as a result of the passage of the 1934 Indian Reorganization Act (IRA). Unlike the Navajos, the Hopis accepted the 1934 Indian Reorganization Act, or more accurately, were unilaterally declared to have accepted it by the Indian Bureau. The Hopi Tribal Council was established after a controversial election in which a minority of Hopis voted to accept the U.S. government-crafted IRA. Most Hopis, traditional in values and protective of their ancient form of village government, refused to vote in the IRA referendum. "What was achieved by coercion in dealing with the Navajos was achieved by simple fraud with the Hopis" (Mander 1981, 58). The Hopi so-called acceptance was marred by the highly questionable voter tabulation employed by the Collier-led Bureau of Indian Affairs. John Collier was the reform Indian commissioner in the Franklin D. Roosevelt New Deal Democratic administration. A federal stock reduction plan, also introduced by the New Deal government, was just as strongly opposed as it was among the Navajos, although eventually, after some dickering, the Hopis were forced to live with it.

An essential feature of the Indian Reorganization Act was the tribal council system of self-government it established. A tribal council system was imposed upon the Hopis after the 1936 referendum vote. This has rendered the elected Hopi Tribal Council unrepresentative and at times dysfunctional in its subsequent history. "The Hopi *Kikmongwis* [village religious leaders] were against the IRA from the start. . . . In keeping with Hopi tradition, the *Kikmongwis* boycotted the referendum and so did the great majority of the Hopis" (Mander 1981, 58). *Old Oraibi* and *Shungopovi* immediately refused to recognize it. The Council was widely viewed as a rubber-stamp body for the Indian Bureau superintendent and was opposed through nonparticipation by five of the traditionally organized villages. The Council was mainly comprised of representatives from the First Mesa villages, coalition groups from villages on Second Mesa, and New *Oraibi*. The Hopis remain divided to this day between the progressives, who endorse an unrepresentative tribal council that is subject to veto power by the secretary of the interior, and the conservatives, traditional villages which continue to govern themselves independently under their religious leaders.

An important debate on the issue of the Hopi IRA referendum took place during 1978–80 in the pages of the *Journal of Ethnic Studies* (see Jorgensen and Clemmer 1978; Washburn 1979; Jorgensen and Clemmer 1980; Clemmer 1980). The debate was initiated by a critical review of a book by historian Wilcomb Washburn. The review by anthropologists Joseph Jorgensen and Richard Clemmer included the question of the Hopi vote count as reported by Washburn in *The Indian in America* (1975). Washburn, now deceased, was a historian with the government's Smithsonian Institution; Jorgensen is a quantitative anthropologist; and Clemmer is an ethnographer who has done extensive Hopi field research.

In their review of the Washburn book, Jorgensen and Clemmer (1980) contend that Washburn ignored the "question of power relations between the dominant and subordinate groups." In the Hopi case, the power relationship was between the Collier-led Bureau of Indian Affairs and the traditional Hopi villages. Collier was determined to bring the Hopis and as many Indian tribes as possible under the umbrella of the Indian Reorganization Act and its tribal council system of government.

In *The Indian in America*, Washburn reported that "fifty percent of the eligible [Hopi] voters came to the polls in October, 1936, and 80 percent voted to accept the constitution authorized under the IRA" (1975, 255). Not so, say Jorgensen and Clemmer. They calculate that "only twenty-seven percent of eligible voters voted 'yes' on the IRA referendum of 1935. The total number of people voting in the referendum was forty-three percent, not fifty-two percent as Washburn asserts" (Jorgensen and Clemmer 1980, 86). The IRA law had stipulated that within a year of its passage in 1935 there would be a referendum election. Each tribe was to discuss the provisions of the act and then vote on whether to accept or reject it.

Jerry Mander, a journalist, found an even smaller number of "yes" votes. "On the day of the referendum, the village of *Hotevilla*, with 250 eligible voters, tallied twelve in favor of IRA and one opposed. In *Oraibi*, out of 73 eligible voters, the total was eight in favor and none opposed. The total Hopi voting population was 2538. Five hundred nineteen Hopis (21%) voted 'yes' while 305 (12%) voted 'no.' One thousand seven hundred fourteen Hopis (67%) refused to vote at all" (1981, 59).

When the IRA bill was initially debated in Congress, part of the debate concerned the voting or ratification by the tribes under the IRA's provisions for self-government. An early version of the bill specified that a three-fifths approval by a tribe's eligible members was required to accept the IRA. The House bill changed this to a simple majority vote, but a supplementary act passed at Collier's insistence resolved the question to "the vote of a majority of those voting." In other words, those Indians not voting would be counted as voting for the new law. No matter how small the number of eligible Indians who voted in favor of the act, by counting the non-votes as "yes," IRA acceptance was virtually assured. This is exactly what happened with the Hopi vote: a minority of Hopis, progressives, voted in the referendum, and voted for the IRA, while a larger number of traditional Hopis were counted as voting for the IRA because they did not vote. The Collier administration ruled that the Hopis voted to accept the IRA and a tribal council system supervised by the Department of the Interior and its Bureau of Indian Affairs. By this means at least seventeen American Indian tribes who actually rejected the Act were considered as being in favor of it. Collier knew that on many reservations the more traditional, full-blood Indians would refuse to participate in the IRA elections. Many Indian tribes which functioned as theocracies, or were still governed under treaty councils of band or clan chiefs, opposed the IRA.

Hopi political divisions as expressed in the progressive–conservative dichotomy can be traced to the flawed 1936 IRA vote. The official Hopi Tribal Council created by the IRA was so weak that by 1943 it was disbanded altogether. It was resurrected by the Interior Department in 1955, in order that a lease could be signed to permit the strip-mining of Black Mesa. "In 1961, the secretary of the interior authorized the Tribal Council to lease Hopi lands," even though the traditional Hopi villages opposed the action (Hieb 1996, 241).

World War II and Postwar

The 1930s also ushered in the federal government's stock reduction program. District Six was established as the Hopi grazing district, which became the de facto Hopi Reservation in a sea of Navajo expansionism. The establishment of the Hopi District Six grazing district resulted in the loss of 501,501 acres of Hopi land, and the boundary issue was again highlighted. Hopi land in District Six officially included territory around all of the Hopi villages except *Moenkopi*, yet it was generally recognized that there were Hopis and Navajos living on both sides of the boundary. Following negotiations to resolve this problem, District Six was increased in size as a partial response to Hopi complaints.

By 1940, there had been irreversible changes on the Hopi Reservation: outside pressures had increased significantly, leading to the major village of *Oraibi* experiencing a decline in population, and completely new villages coming into being. During World War II, jobs were scarce and unemployment high for the Hopis. "Many Hopi people left the reservation for work in the neighboring cities during World War II, and many registered as conscientious objectors, rendering alternative service" (Dockstader 1979, 531). At the same time, the activities of religious missionaries and traders declined. A growing concern was the fact that Navajo families were settling closer to the Hopi villages, their population superiority and political dominance gaining them de facto recognition. Almost every facet of Hopi life was altered. "Architectural changes subtly affected home life, and water-supply programs altered attitudes toward rain ceremonies. The economy changed from a subsistence base with some cash supplement to a completely cash base with a small subsistence support" (Dockstader 1979, 532). And yet, the core of Indigenous life, the Hopi Way, remained.

The postwar period saw significant changes in Hopi culture. In some of the progressive villages, "larger homes with hipped roofs, concrete block walls, large windows, and indoor plumbing appeared" (Hieb 1996, 242). The housing pattern arrangement also changed, with the newer homes built at a distance from the village center. The Navajo-Hopi Long Range Rehabilitation Act was passed by Congress in 1950. It provided $90 million to improve infrastructure on the two reservations—roads, schools, hospitals, water, electricity, and sewers. Traditional Hopis, however, resisted modernizing their villages, primarily to avoid what they saw as the corrupting influence and domination by Western culture and its institutions.

According to Clemmer (1979, 533), the two related issues that dominated Hopi interests in the decades of the 1950s and 1960s were the ceremonial cycle and cultural sovereignty. The ceremonial cycle relates to the land as sacred and central to Hopi life. Hopi elders refer to the land as a shrine "that extends far beyond the Hopi villages to the Grand Canyon, the San Francisco Peaks, the northern reaches of Black Mesa, Zuni Salt Lake, and south of Route 66" (Clemmer 1979, 533). The sovereignty issue relates to the virtual reduction of the 1882 executive order, which reduced Hopi claims to land they had claimed as traditionally and spiritually theirs. When the Navajo and Hopi reservations were divided into grazing districts, the Hopi District Six included only the land immediately surrounding the eleven Hopi villages, and the Hopi settlement of *Moenkopi* was excluded altogether. "The stock reduction procedure shrank the Hopi land base to an almost token faction of the enshrined area venerated in Hopi ceremonies" (Clemmer 1979, 533).

By 1942, "a series of meetings brought elders from all three mesas; and clan functions and duties, religious philosophy, and prophesies were discussed . . . and the start of the counter-campaign to the acculturative pressures of the United States jurisdiction, resulting in emergence of the Hopi

Traditionals as a political entity" (Clemmer 1979, 535). The emergence of the traditionalists had its basis in Hopi origin and migration myth, in which an Elder Brother (*Bahana*) would return to help the people in their time of need. Was the Elder Brother the White man? That was the question.

Two pieces of Congressional legislation had important consequences for Hopi political life. The first was the 1945 Indian Claims Commission Act. This law allowed Indian tribes to sue the U.S. government for land taken without just compensation or due process of law. In response, a delegation of Hopis went to Washington in 1950 to establish the Hopi land claim. They were told, however, that they must revive the Hopi tribal council, which had been disbanded in 1940. Hopi progressives then enlisted the aid of the agency superintendent and persuaded seven of the thirteen villages to select representatives to a revived council. The council was reconstituted in 1951, just in time to retain a lawyer and submit a land claim.

The second law to have important consequences was the Navajo-Hopi Act of 1950. It provided funds for infrastructure improvement and reservation jobs, thus intensifying the federal government's presence on the reservation and legitimating the revived tribal council. Traditional elders opposed the Navajo-Hopi Act and sought political support from outside groups, including the National Congress of American Indians. In 1949, twenty-four ceremonial leaders from four villages sent a letter to President Harry S. Truman in which they rejected the Indian Claims proceedings as a sham, opposed the Navajo-Hopi Act and the activities of the oil companies on sacred Hopi lands, and Hopi military participation stemming from the North Atlantic Treaty Organization. The letter stated in part: "This land is a sacred home of the Hopi people. . . . It was given to the Hopi people the task to guard this land . . . by obedience to our traditional and religious instructions and by being faithful to our Great Spirit *Massau'u*. . . . We have never abandoned our sovereignty to any foreign power or nation" (Clemmer 1979, 535).

The position by the Hopi traditionalists to the 1946 land claims law was logical. They took the view that the land on which they had lived as a people for centuries was sacred. In testimony before Congress they stated: "We, as hereditary Chieftains of the Hopi Tribe, . . . will not ask a White Man, who came to us recently, for a piece of land that is already ours" (Lapham, n.d., 31). "The land could not be lost to the Hopis because that would be contrary to sacred law.

Thus the Hopis could not sue the government for land which the government had taken away because that would be the same thing as admitting that the government rightfully possessed the land and had a right to give it away. . . . Similarly, leases to oil companies and the building of roads . . . would be morally wrong" (Spicer 1962, 206–7).

By 1950, two opposing groups within Hopi society, each with a different political strategy to deal with U.S. political and economic forces had emerged—the tribal council supporters, reflecting sixty years of Christian missionizing influence (especially Mormon), versus the Hopi traditionalists. "Just as the Hopi Traditionals asserted their caretakership of Mother Earth, the tribal council asserted economic interest in Hopi land and resources as a basis for political strength and influence" (Clemmer 1979, 535). Paradoxically, "by 1955 less than 2 percent of all Hopis had become practicing members of the various Christian sects which had been carrying on missionary work for seventy-five years. . . . [T]he religious affiliation of the overwhelming majority of Hopis was still Hopi rather than Christian" (Spicer 1962, 207).

After filing a claim with the U.S. Claims Commission, the Hopi Tribal Council started negotiations with the Navajo Nation for Hopi lands outside District Six. The Claims Court subsequently issued its 1962 *Healing v. Jones* decision, ruling that Hopis had exclusive right to District Six, but only "joint, undivided and equal rights and interests" to the executive order reservation lying outside District Six, designated as the Joint Use Area (JUA).

In 1961, the secretary of the interior authorized the reconstituted tribal council to lease Hopi lands. Intent on pursuing land claims and its economic goals, the Hopi Tribal Council secured leases for mineral exploration and development that brought in more than three million dollars in royalties. One million dollars was paid to the Hopi tribal attorney, and over half of the remainder was invested in constructing an undergarment factory for the B.V.D. Company. The B.V.D. venture was a failure, and the factory closed in 1975. A more successful enterprise was a motel-café-museum complex constructed on Second Mesa, the Hopi Cultural Center.

The Hopi Tribal Council signed a lease with Peabody Coal Company in 1966, allowing for strip mining of twenty-five thousand acres in the JUA. Mining operations began four years later. Traditional Hopis opposed the lease, contending that the Hopi Tribal Council in its present form did not have the legal authority to grant such leases. "At the time of the

1966 vote, the Council was comprised of eighteen seats, proportioned on a population basis, with each village having at least one representative. Only eleven of those seats were filled. Five traditional villages— which did not vote for the constitution in 1935 or sign contracts with [Hopi attorney] Boyden in 1951— refused to send any of the seven representatives they were allotted" (Lapham n.d., 31). The Hopis received an annual royalty of approximately $500,000.

The Peabody Coal lease was in conjunction with a separate lease by the Navajo Tribal Council for mining their portion of Black Mesa. Peabody Coal also negotiated to pump thirty-eight billion gallons of water from underneath Black Mesa for its power plants, even though there were serious concerns that it would lower the water table, adversely threatening Hopi crops and damage the fragile, high desert environment.

The actions and intervention by the Interior Department in securing the Peabody Coal lease was over the objections of Hopi religious leaders who, along with their traditional Navajo counterparts, regard Black Mesa as sacred. It gave credence to the belief that the Hopi Tribal Council was merely rubber stamping the wishes of the Interior Department and mining interests.

In 1970, Hopi village chiefs and ceremonial leaders representing thirteen villages went into federal court in *Lomayakewa v. Morton* to block the strip-mining operations on religious grounds, but their legal action failed on a technicality. "The basis for the suit was that strip-mining violated 'the most sacred elements of traditional Hopi religion, culture and way of life" (Clemmer 1979, 536). The lawsuit contended that the Hopi Tribal Council did not constitute a proper quorum when it signed the lease, and that the secretary of the interior exceeded his authority in approving it.

Hopi farming decreased in the 1960s and 1970s, and the conflict between the traditional Hopis and the Hopi Tribal Council escalated as environmental and political activists rallied to the defense of the Navajo traditionalists at Black Mesa. The 1980s were almost entirely taken up with the land dispute with the Navajos.

By 1990, the Hopi population had nearly tripled, from about 2,200 in 1900 to 7,360. An economy based on subsistence agriculture had shifted to a cash economy centered on wage labor. "Hopis living in Albuquerque, Tucson, or Los Angeles return to the Hopi mesas to participate in the intricate ceremonies of their clans and religious societies.... The symbols, rituals, and words remind people of their identity and distinguish them from others" (Sheridan and Parezo 1996, xxviii). Despite contemporary problems of substance

abuse, suicide, and child abuse, the Hopis strive to maintain their ancient culture and to protect their sacred places and subsistence-gathering areas.

Spicer (1962, 208) sums up the extent of Hopi cultural change as a result of Anglo-American penetration and the government's policy of acculturation. Until the 1880s, he states, they changed very little. But "during the last hundred years of contact with Anglos . . . they had changed profoundly . . . through schools and the growth of communication with Anglo communities. There is no question that the Hopi way had persisted into the 1960s, but it existed within a milieu of very great heterogeneity."

NAVAJO-HOPI LAND DISPUTE

At the base of the Navajo-Hopi land dispute which emerged in the 1970s was the disagreement over two tracts of land: the 1882 Executive Order reservation for the Hopis and "other Indians," and the 1934 Arizona Boundary Bill that added land to the western Navajo Reservation. The compelling desire to develop the vast mineral resources of the 1882 reservation by the two tribes, in addition to the political pressure from corporate America, led to conflicting claims as to tribal land ownership.

The origin of the conflict begins in 1882 when President Chester A. Arthur authorized the withdrawal of 2.5 million acres from the public domain for "the use and occupancy of the Moqui [Hopis] and other Indians as the Secretary of the Interior may see fit to settle thereon" (Kappler 1904, I, 805). In the first place, it is apparent that the setting of the reservation's boundaries as a rectangular reservation was purely arbitrary. Second, the phrase "other Indians" is problematic, although it was a common wording in some of the early Executive Order reservations. The ambiguous language of the Executive Order regarding "other Indians," presumably Navajos, led the Hopis almost a century later to contest joint ownership, claiming instead an exclusive interest in the 1882 reservation based on aboriginal use dating to the pre-Spanish era. The Navajo families living within the boundaries of the 1882 reservation were regarded as trespassers. In response, the Navajos claimed sole interest to those areas exclusive of the Hopi villages on the mesas (largely District Six), about fourth-fifths of the Executive Order Reservation. Which tribe was legally entitled to ownership of the 1882 reservation became a major bone of contention when Peabody Coal negotiated leases for strip-mining Black Mesa.

A contributing factor to the dispute is that the U.S. government has periodically enlarged the Navajo Reservation to accommodate its growing population and the seminomadic, pastoral lifestyle of the people. Beginning in 1878, the reservation was enlarged to 12,271,480 acres by a series of Executive Orders (see map, Figure 5.3) This resulted in the Hopi villages of the 1882 reservation becoming completely surrounded by the much larger Navajo Reservation. The situation was compounded by the deteriorating economic conditions experienced by both tribes during the Dust Bowl and Depression years of the 1930s.

The other, smaller tract of land that also became an issue involves the Hopi enclave of *Moenkopi*. The Arizona Boundary Bill of 1934 established the boundaries of the Western Navajo Reservation as it exists today. Included in the language of the legislation is the disputed phrase, "for the benefit of the Navajos and such other Indians as may already be located thereon." "As in the case of the 1882 Hopi Reservation, the ambiguous phrase 'and such other Indians'

complicated the situation and led to a second controversy between the two tribes" (Enders 1971, 7).

The expansion of the Navajo Reservation through various Executive Orders and Acts of Congress has resulted in four different classes of lands: (1) Land belonging exclusive to the Navajos. This includes the 1868 Navajo Reservation, lands withdrawn from the Tusayan National Forest, lands relinquished by private individuals, and lands purchased with Navajo tribal funds; (2) Land belonging exclusively to the Hopis, i.e., District Six awarded in *Healing v. Jones*—about 20 percent of the 1882 reservation, which includes the Hopi villages of *Oraibi, Shungopovi, Mishongnovi, Walpi,* and *Polacca;* (3) The Joint Use Area established for the common benefit of both the Navajos and Hopis, i.e., four-fifths of the 1882 reservation; (4) Land in controversy as a result of the wording in the 1934 Arizona Boundary Bill.

The boundary issue remained dormant during World War II but emerged again following the war. In the 1950s, Navajos voiced their complaints against perceived Hopi transgressions. Norman M. Littell became the chief attorney for the Navajos. The Hopis, represented by attorney John Boyden, filed a brief with the Department of the Interior in which they claimed exclusive rights to the 1882 Executive Order Reservation. The Navajos countered by presenting archaeological evidence showing a long Navajo occupation in the disputed territory. "Over 350 hogan groups, or sites, had been recorded, and tree ring dates as early as 1622 had been obtained from wood from hogans within the Executive Order Reservation boundaries" (Brugge 1994, 36). The Hopi Tribe, on the other hand, claimed exclusive right to the 1882 reservation largely because it approximated to some degree their aboriginal territory. The Navajo Nation, which had already lost the core of its aboriginal homeland, *Dinétah,* to White settlers, claimed sole rights to four-fifths of the 1882 reservation. They contended that the phrase "and such other Indians" in the 1882 Executive Order meant them. All but one-fourth of the 1882 reservation has been occupied by the Navajos for the past 125 years. Even though the federal government enlarged the Navajo reservation through a series of Executive Orders and Acts, the Navajo population had greatly increased, and the extent of their occupation of the JUA increased as well.

As a result of the land conflict, Congress passed a boundary bill, Public Law 85-547, on July 28, 1958, which authorized the tribal councils of both tribes to initiate claims against each other. A month later, the Hopi tribal chairman filed legal action against the

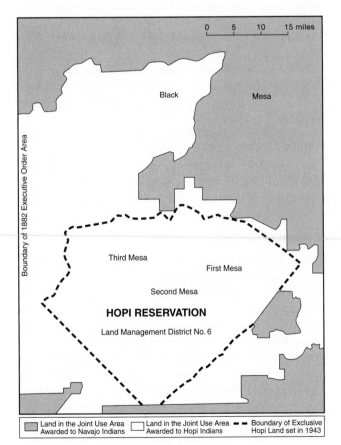

Figure 5.3 Division of the Navajo and Hopi Reservations Joint Use Area.

Navajo tribal chairman. When Dewey Healing replaced the former Hopi tribal chairman, the court case became *Healing v. Jones*, Paul Jones being the Navajo Tribal Chairman. In the legal suit, the lead attorney for the Hopis, John S. Boyden (a former bishop in the Mormon Church), claimed exclusive Hopi jurisdiction to all of the 1882 reservation. The Hopi side also claimed that any Navajo living in the disputed area should be under the jurisdiction of the Hopi Tribe. In opposition to the Hopi claims, the attorneys for the Navajos, Litell, McPherson, and Davis, "asserted that only District Six, an area of 488,000 acres located in the south central part of the 1882 Reservation, including the Hopi villages, was held in trust for the Hopi as an exclusive-use area. The remaining four-fifths of the area was claimed by the Navajo as a restricted area solely for their use" (Enders 1971, 43). It is instructive that Hopi attorney Boyden raised the issue of mineral rights, saying that the disputed Black Mesa area is one of the best oil areas in Arizona.

Healing v. Jones. On September 28, 1962, the U.S. District Court issued its judgment in the case of *Healing v. Jones*. First, the Hopis were to receive exclusive-use area and the title to District Six as the Hopi Indian Tribe. Second, the remainder of the 1882 reservation was to be vested in both tribes on a fifty-fifty basis—the Joint Use Area—the Navajo occupants having acquired squatters rights to one-half interest of the reservation. The court ruled that it had no authority to partition the Joint Use Area (JUA) between the two tribes and allowed the question to be resolved by Congress. The Navajos appealed the decision of *Healing v. Jones*, and the Hopi tribal officials followed with a cross-appeal, but the U.S. Supreme Court concurred with the opinion of the lower court, leaving it up to the government and the tribes to work out a way to jointly administer the JUA. Without a clear title to the mineral deposits at Black Mesa, it was impossible for the government to negotiate a lease with Peabody Coal. The years since 1962 have been taken up with litigation to resolve the conflicting claims regarding both the 1882 reservation and to a lesser degree, the *Moenkopi* boundary area dispute.

During the litigation proceedings, David Brugge, an anthropologist who undertook research for the Navajos, witnessed a number of instances in which stereotypes were projected by Hopi attorney Boyden, in which the Navajos were portrayed as the bad guys in contrast to a romantic image projected of the Hopis. There were "two strongly negative stereotypes of Navajos, one as nomadic raiders encroach-ing on the peaceful little Hopis, and the other as black-hatted despoilers of the environment, the sheep ranchers long depicted in western novels and moving pictures" (Brugge 1994, 103). The negative image of the Navajos served to justify the ethnic cleansing that was about to take place.

The Hopi *Kikmongwis* protested the litigation at every stage. They sued in court at one point, charging that the Hopi Tribal Council had no authority to make mineral leases, but the suit was dismissed. (Leases had been signed with Peabody Coal in 1954 and 1966 at Black Mesa.) In 1971 the Hopi *Kikmongwis* warned: "Our sacred ceremonies depend on contact with the spiritual forces left at Black Mesa by our ancestors. . . . If these places are disturbed or destroyed, our prayers will lose their force and a great calamity will befall not only the Hopi but all of mankind (Mander 1981, 59).

"Lobbying to change the status of the Joint Use Area began in the late 1960s. Attorney Boyden was the spearhead, with help from Peabody Coal, a consortium of Utah bankers, and many of the corporations with interests in Hopi land" (Mander 1981, 60). They raised the specter of a range war raging in Arizona. In 1974, Congress passed Public Law 93-531, the Navajo-Hopi Land Settlement Act, at a time when the nation was distracted by the Watergate scandal. The Act ordered a freeze on any new construction in the JUA and ordered the residents (mainly Navajos) to eliminate 90 percent of their livestock in preparation for the partition of the disputed 1.8 million acres. A plan for partition was then executed in 1977. Ignoring the objections of traditional members of both tribes who revere the land, the law favored the corporate tribal councils and mining interests in setting boundaries dividing the two peoples.

Relocation

When the court drew up lines for partitioning the JUA, more than ten thousand Navajos and one hundred Hopis found themselves on the wrong side of the fence and faced stock reduction and relocation to border towns. Relocation was a wrenching experience for those families who were forced to move from their traditional homesteads, mainly Navajos. Partition also initiated a drastic reduction of livestock, euphemistically called "range management," prohibited building construction and repair, while at the same time encouraging relocation by offering certain benefits (money, housing, counseling) to those who would move voluntarily. A Navajo and Hopi Relocation

Commission was created to assist the relocatees for that purpose. Congress appropriated $37 million, but relocation money was little comfort to those torn from their homes and dumped in border towns, rife with alcoholism, crime, and exploitation.

The so-called voluntary relocation program initiated in 1977 was almost totally rejected by the Navajo residents of the JUA until the government forcibly removed more than 90 percent of their livestock. Since the Navajos depend upon their livestock for subsistence, it was only due to this new scorched earth policy that they were forced to relocate. Forty-six percent of the affected population, or about 1,150 families, were removed between 1977 and 1987. Although hundreds of millions of dollars have been spent on relocation, it has been a complete disaster. The relocated families lost traditional livelihoods and found themselves rendered destitute in racist border towns. The elders became hopelessly homesick, the young fell prey to urban social problems, landlords foreclosed on mortgages to relocatee replacement homes, and families broke up. A 1981 report by the U.S. Navajo and Hopi Indian Relocation Commission found that "35% of the families already relocated had experienced 'marked family instability, financial decline, major debts, mortgaging or selling their new home, had moved back to the reservation, had major health problems, significant depression, suicide, etc.'" (Mander 1981, 61).

Not the least of relocation difficulties are the so-called new lands that were made available in 1987 to the first relocated Navajos after they had experienced problems in relocating to reservation border towns. The new lands, consisting of 365,000 acres, lay south of Chambers, Arizona, and contiguous to the reservation. They include the Rio Puerco, which was heavily contaminated in the Churchrock radioactive containment dam spill in 1979. They are also intersected by Interstate 40 and the Santa Fe Railroad. Those relocated to the new lands were involved in planning for their own relocation; they were allowed to bring their livestock, but water sources for people and livestock were bound to be contaminated, and there was easy access to three liquor stores and little access to police, fire services, local medical services, or telephones, and no school building. Most of all, the new lands did not have the religious significance as did their former lands in the JUA.

Various arguments were put forth to justify a relocation policy that impacted so many Navajo families. It was argued that the Navajos greatly outnumber the Hopis anyway, and being nomads, the Navajos were used to moving about. More serious was the charge that the Navajos had deliberately encroached upon the Hopi domain. Sills (1986, 57) points out that "the bulk of these complaints have come from the Hopis of First Mesa, which is the closest to the BIA agency at Keams Canyon. It is also historically the source of support for the Hopi Tribal Council."

Resistance at Big Mountain

"A center of Navajo resistance to relocation is the Big Mountain area, some thirty miles north of Third Mesa, on a road that leads to the coal mines of Black Mesa" (Feher-Elston 1996, 389). A monstrous, gaping hole was created by strip-mining the area, an ancient aquifer is being drained of its precious water in an arid landscape, plant and animal life is being obliterated, and many Navajos were being forced on a second Long Walk.

The traditional Navajo community at Big Mountain dates back at least to the late eighteenth century. In 1977, the federal government began fencing the partition boundary to force those on the wrong side (mostly Navajos) to relocate. This was when the resistance at Big Mountain began: an elder, Pauline Whitesinger, was arrested for stopping a fencing crew from partitioning her land. Since women by tradition control the herds and grazing lands, it was not unusual for the resistance to be led by Navajo grandmothers. The resistance grew steadily during the next few years and received wide international attention and support.

Big Mountain, rising seven thousand feet, occupies an isolated region of about 150 square miles in the northwestern Black Mesa country. Rich deposits of oil, coal, and uranium underlie Black Mesa and Big Mountain. Since partition, Black Mesa has been intensively mined by Peabody Coal, an affiliate of Kennecott Corporation, a transnational.

Beginning in 1974, there has been a drastic livestock reduction program in effect, a building freeze, and fencing, which caused severe psychological stress and economic hardship to the Navajo residents. The Big Mountain *Diné* and their support committee asserted that the land dispute was created by the federal government and its "puppet tribal councils" to disguise attempts to remove both peoples from an area they have used jointly and peacefully for more than four hundred years. Despite cultural differences, the two peoples have often intermarried. Why, after hundreds of years of living without fences, do the Hopis and Navajos now need to divide up the land? And what about the children of the Navajo-Hopi marriages? To which side of the fence do they relocate? "In 1979, the Big Mountain community, which is affected in its entirety by the Relocation Act, declared its autonomy as 'the Independent *Diné* Nation.' Although the secession was largely symbolic, it clearly illustrates the disaffection of the community of relocatees" (Sills 1986, 59).

There are a number of ways in which relocation violates Indian religious freedom. In the first place, Big Mountain is considered sacred by Navajos and Hopis alike. It is part of Black Mesa, the sacred female mountain in Navajo religious tradition. Big Mountain is enclosed by Black Mesa and a male mountain, the *Lukachusaiss*, to form a sacred hogan. To the Navajos, "the hogan is a home and also a place; to pray; it is like a 'church', and all traditional ceremonies must be held there. . . . It has breath (air). It breathes, so we pray to it" (Wood and Stemmler 1981, 6).

A research report by two anthropologists to the U.S. Congress on behalf of the Big Mountain community explains that "religion at Big Mountain is the same as life, the land, and well-being. The land and the Mountain are Holy, and Big Mountain people are their caretakers. If they are forced to leave the land, they will be forced to leave their religion" (Wood and Stemmler 1981, 2). There are family burial grounds located in the family grazing areas. There is also a variety of herbs, which are used not only pharmaceutically, but also in religious healing ceremonies. There are eagle-nesting sites; eagle feathers are used in ceremonies by both Navajos and Hopis. There are at least two sacred shrines, one which was virtually destroyed by land clearing operations set in motion by the relocation legislation.

The essence of Navajo religion is the relationship between the people and their sacred land. To be forcibly removed from the land is to be denied religious freedom. This is why the Big Mountain Legal Defense/Offense Committee launched a court action on religious grounds to stop further relocation, citing the 1978 American Indian Religious Freedom Act (AIRFA) and First Amendment rights to the Constitution, The suit was rejected by the court on October 18, 1989, however. It ruled that the religious freedom guaranteed under AIRFA was not seriously impaired by relocation, because the Navajos could still practice their religion even if their lands were developed or

they were forced to remove themselves. Clearly, the court did not understand the nature of Indian religious belief and practice.

At the same time that the opposing attorneys and official tribal representatives were locked in litigation, traditional Navajos and Hopis were getting together to try to stop the relocation and the mining at Black Mesa. In June of 1985, for example, Hopi and Navajo elders met in a *Hotevilla kiva* to discuss and reaffirm their long-standing opposition to the Relocation Act. Hopi religious leaders and Navajo elders said the law amounted to cultural genocide and would desecrate the sacred land with energy development. In April of 1986, a meeting was held at the Big Mountain round house between the traditional Hopis and Navajos of Black Mesa. Members of both tribes said that the Relocation Act had created bad feeling between the two peoples, and they denied that the Act had anything to do with any dispute between them. They called for its repeal. A year later, the Big Mountain community hosted a gathering of three hundred people, including traditional elements of the Hopi, O'Odham, and other Native representatives and non-Indian support groups, who together voiced their opposition to compulsory relocation of the Navajos.

Conflict and Litigation

The land settlement act resulted in the JUA being divided between the Navajos and the Hopis as partitioned lands. This led to some hostile confrontations in the new partitioned lands between Navajo holdouts and incoming Hopis. One incident involved a Hopi fencing crew that was confronted by Navajos in 1986, who believed that they were being cut off from needed water. The Navajos removed the fences and held a pistol to the head of one of the Hopi rangers. Hopi cattle have also been shot. On the other hand, "Hopis who have had long-term trading or friendship relations with Navajo families continue to maintain them. . . . Some Navajos say they have Hopi friends, and some that the troubles between the peoples could be settled if both tribes, lawyers, the BIA and the [Navajo-Hopi Indian Relocation Commission] would step aside" (Colby 1990, 22). The Hopis are divided on whether the Navajos should be evicted. Hopi traditionalists, who have opposed the political and legal maneuvers of the progressives on the tribal council, continued to pray for a peaceful resolution, while Hopi progressives threatened to bring in the National Guard to remove any Navajos still on the land.

Neither side was satisfied with the partition of the JUA, although the Navajos were more vocal in their opposition. The Navajo Nation offered to buy out Hopi interests, but the Hopi Tribe refused; they wanted the land, not money. Both tribes have deep religious ties to the land in question, to shrines and other things considered sacred.

The disputed area involves about seven hundred thousand acres of Navajo land that the Hopis claim as their aboriginal homeland. Various legal awards, land adjustments, and appeals continued into the 1980s and 1990s. Financing the mandatory relocation program is estimated to have cost U.S. taxpayers over one billion dollars, in both direct and indirect costs. Because of Navajo resistance and the widespread concern from the public, the issue was mandated to mediation by federal court. In October 1992, the Navajo and Hopi tribes reached an agreement that would end the relocation. The remaining Navajo holdouts could lease Hopi partitioned land for at least seventy-five years, and in return, the Hopis were to receive about 400,000 acres of land near the San Francisco Peaks. But Arizona's non-Indian political leaders denounced the plan.

Congress passed the Navajo-Hopi Land Settlement Act in 1996, which allowed for a longer period of time for the Navajo relocation, "but further paves the way for the destruction of sacred lands and a traditional way of life. Although many Navajo families have since relocated, others have stayed on and, with some traditionalist Hopi allies, have vowed to continue their resistance to destruction of sacred lands and culture" (Waldman 2000, 237). When Bill Clinton was president he issued an Executive Order, the Accommodation Agreement, which set a final date of February 1, 2000, for the relocation of those Navajo residents still remaining on the Hopi Partition Lands (HPL) "Many *Diné* HPL residents entered into AA leases simply to avoid eviction, backed by the promise of higher livestock permits and the lifting of the construction freeze" (Aim4Awareness 1999). In November of 2006, the two tribes reached a final land settlement agreement. Whether the agreement lasts remains to be seen, and is beyond the scope of this chapter.

THEORY REVISITED

There are several factors which have contributed to the Navajo-Hopi land controversy (Feher-Elston 1996, 388): (1) the introduction of sheep and livestock to the region by the Spaniards, which led to Navajo pastoralism; (2) land usurpation of eastern *Dinétah* by the Spaniards and New Mexicans that pushed the Navajos westward into Hopi territory; (3) the growth of the Navajo and Hopi populations, especially the Navajos; and (4) the imposition of the reservation system onto the Navajos and Hopis by the U.S. government in the late nineteenth century. Between 1868 and 1991, the Navajo land base was extended over fifteen times by executive or congressional action. The enlargement of the Navajo Reservation came largely at the expense of what Hopis consider as their traditional land base. At the beginning of the twentieth century, there were only 2,000 Hopis and 7,500 Navajos. Today, the populations have increased to approximately 13,000 Hopis and more than 300,000 Navajos. As a result, both tribal land bases have become ecologically strained. Yet the Navajo land base has been consistently extended, but the Hopi land base has not.

As was explained in the introduction to this chapter, genocide is the killing of a race, a national or religious minority. Ethnocide, a related concept, connotes the deliberate suppression or eradication of a culture or way of life. Ethnocide is the implicit result of the U.S. government's Indian policies, including the Indian New Deal policy of replacing existing traditional governments with the tribal council system. *Ecocide*, another concept, means the annihilation of the environment. It is applicable to the degradation of the sacred land of both peoples caused by the strip-mining of Black Mesa. All three concepts are applicable to the Navajo-Hopi land dispute. Public Law 95-531, the Navajo-Hopi Land Settlement Act, passed in 1974, was an instrument of ethnocide policy, and the mandatory Navajo relocation begun in 1977 became an ethnic cleansing operation reminiscent of the Navajo Long Walk of 1863.

The vast majority of both Navajos and Hopis continue to share a deep respect for their sacred lands—both are enduring peoples. Navajo Nation President Joe Shirley, Jr., played a leading role in the passage of a Navajo law banning uranium mining from the reservation, the Diné Natural Resources Protection Act of 2006. It became a focus of the Indigenous World Uranium Summit, which took place in December 2006, at the Navajo capital at Window Rock, Arizona. A declaration by the summit's more than three hundred participants called attention to "intensifying nuclear threats to Mother

Earth and all life" (*Indian Country Today* 2006a, A2; 2006b, A8).

Despite their mutual reverence for the land, the two peoples have very different views about land acquisition and ownership. For the Hopis, clans and religious societies maintain shrines that delineate the boundaries of their sacred homeland. Hopis did not need to be physically residing on these clan lands in order to claim rightful possession, A key issue for the Hopis is their view that the Navajos have intruded into Hopi land, the 2.5 million acre, 1882 executive order reservation.

The Navajo way, in contrast to that of the Hopis, may in some ways be analogous to homesteading. Land not within Navajo clan boundaries, but within the sacred Navajo homeland, could be entered and settled: "A Navajo house, hogan, could be built upon the land, a ceremony would be held afterward, and the land could be held or used by the Navajo occupants" (Feher-Elston 1996, 388). After their release from Bosque Redondo, the treaty of 1868 confined the displaced Navajos to a small rectangle of land in their former home territory. But an expanding population, the increasing degradation of the land, and the necessity of sheep and goats to have large tracts of grazing land, made the 1868 reservation an inadequate land base for the Navajos. "There is no doubt that much of the Hopi land base has been gradually occupied by the Navajos, as a result of U.S. policy, and much more has been expropriated by the U.S. itself. Hopi demands for restitution of lost lands may be legitimate, but they are made against the wrong party, if justice is of any value. The Hopis, as a people, may deserve restitution, but from whom should it be taken?" (Sills 1986, 65).

It is appropriate to ask if anyone actually benefited from the land dispute. A *Business Week* report found that "eighty percent of the Hopi tribal income derive[s] from present strip-mining operations underway on Black Mesa" (Sills 1986, 60). There is also a revealing conflict of interest by Boyden, the lead Hopi tribal attorney. "The lawyers for the Hopi Tribal Council are Boyden, Kennedy and Romney, a Mormon firm from Salt Lake City and now part of a larger law firm" representing Peabody Coal Company which operates the Black Mesa strip-mine (Sills 1986, 60–61). The Relocation Act was promoted by Boyden, the Hopi Tribal Council, an Arizona congressman, and two U.S. senators. Support also came from an energy consortium, Western Energy Supply and Transmission Associates (WEST), with ties to Peabody Coal, and which included among its members a number of major utility companies. "Besides the WEST members and mining firms like Peabody, large banks, holding companies, construction firms, the States of Arizona and California, perhaps the Mormon Church, and several other major institutions have a major stake in the flow of cheap Indian energy resources" (Sills 1986, 64).

Was there a cultural conflict between the two tribes that made the land dispute inevitable? Actually, there is no inherent conflict between the cultural beliefs and practices of traditional Navajos and Hopis. The conflict obviously came from the acculturated members of both tribes who view energy development as a necessity for survival in a world dominated by a capitalist economy. In such a world, land and its mineral resources are a commodity. The Indians become the colonized, and the corporations and the government agencies become the colonizers. In this context, partition and relocation become the tools of neocolonial policy that seek to exploit Indian lands and resources for profit. The dispute is largely a manufactured one caused by Anglo-American economic penetration and U.S. Indian policies which bypassed, if not outright suppressed, traditional Indian culture and political decision-making.

The reasoning behind U.S. policy in the Navajo-Hopi case is that the land division and forced relocation were necessary because of an age-old dispute between two Indian peoples who have a history of unfriendly if not hostile relations. The historical evidence does not support this view. A summary of the background to the dispute and its progression to the present is presented in Table 5.1 in support of this thesis.

How is one to understand the internal conflict that exacerbated the land dispute issue? In the first place, as Mander (1981, 54) points out, "there is among colonizing cultures an innate desire to exaggerate differences and conflicts among the colonized" (Mander 1981, 54). Dan Bomberry (Cayuga-Salish) put it this way: "They're calling it a Hopi-Navajo dispute, but it's a U.S. law that's forcing the removal, it's Americans that are paying the bills, and it's a U.S. agency actually moving these people. It was the U.S. that shoved the Navajos toward Hopi 120 years ago after killing their animals and putting the Navajos in a concentration camp. And if you want to blame the Hopi council, you've got to realize that those tribal

TABLE 5.1 Historical Context of the Navajo-Hopi Land Dispute

<u>Issue:</u> **The Navajo-Hopi Land Settlement Act was passed in 1974 to settle ownership of the Joint Use Area, "because the two peoples cannot get along."**

<u>Thesis:</u> **The "dispute" is a manufactured one caused by Anglo-American economic penetration and U.S. assimilationist policies which seek to replace Indigenous traditional culture and political decision-making.**

1000 AD	Ancestors of the *Diné* (Navajos) enter the Southwest. They adopt agriculture, social, and religious customs and beliefs from the Hopi and other Pueblo Indians.
1583	Antonia de Espejo reports Navajos living near the Hopi village of Awatovi.
1598	Navajo heartland is *Dinetka,* located in north-central New Mexico. Oñate and his Spanish colonists bring sheep, goats, and cattle to New Mexico. The Navajos begin obtaining these animals, mainly by raiding Spanish settlements.
Late 1600s	The heart of the Navajo homeland is *Dinetka* (Home of the People), located in north-central New Mexico. Navajo culture continues to change.
1680	Pueblo Indian revolt led by Popé. Some Pueblo Indians seek refuge with the Navajos.
1700s	Hopi Indians seek refuge from drought and famine with the Navajos of Canyon de Chelly.
1846	The United States seizes northern third of Mexico and signs the Treaty of Guadalupe Hidalgo. Contrary to the terms of the treaty, Navajo and Hopi lands are condemned as eminent domain and the property of the U.S. government.
1863–1864	The United States establishes a Bureau of Indian Affairs agency at Keams Canyon in Hopi territory. Kit Carson begins an ethnic cleansing campaign against the Navajos. Eight thousand Navajos are forced on "the Long Walk to internment at Fort Sumner (Bosque Redondo). Four thousand Navajos elude the military roundup, including the community at Big Mountain.
1868	The Navajos are released from Ft. Sumner and return to devastated lands. They are forced to sign a treaty in which they retain only a small portion of their original homeland. Additions to the reservation are made in 1878 and 1880.
1880s	The building of the railroad across New Mexico and Arizona causes great dislocation, bringing intoxicants, diseases, and other disrupting forces of White society to "The People" (Navajos). The railroad receives odd-numbered sections of land on each side of its right-of-way, thus creating a "checkerboard strip" in a region with the heaviest concentration of Navajo population.
1882	The Executive Order reservation is established for the Hopis and "other Indians," ostensibly to settle Hopi-Navajo-Mormon land dispute, but really to establish the government's assimilationist program of Americanization and Christianization.
1907	Hopi villages are surrounded by an expanding Navajo Reservation when the Navajos are pushed westward by Whites. Four more Executive Order reservations are created to accommodate Navajo refugees from the New Mexico checker-board lands.
1917	Geological Survey conforms the discovery of a rich coal field underlying Black Mesa.
1923	Oil discovered on Navajo lands near Shiprock, New Mexico. Navajo Tribal Council created by the United States government as a legal entity to make lease arrangements.
1933–1934	Dust Bowl comes to the region, and the government initiates a stock reduction plan. Navajo herds are reduced by 40 percent, causing great hardship to the Navajo, resulting in animosity towards the U.S. government. Both Navajo and Hopi lands are partitioned into grazing districts, with District Six reserved exclusively for Hopi stock-raisers.
1936	Hopis are forced to accept the tribal council system of government under the Indian Reorganization Act. The unfair voting procedure authorized by the Indian Bureau gives rise to the charge of a fraudulent election.
1937	Navajos organize the Eastern Boundary Association to obtain land for 7,000 landless Indians living on the "public domain."
1943	Over one hundred Navajos are deported and their herds slaughtered when the Hopi District Six is enlarged.
1944	The legal question raised as to which tribe owns the 1882 Executive Order reservation.
1946	The Interior Department rules that the Navajos have equal rights to the Hopis respecting the natural resources of the reservation, including Black Mesa. The Indian Claims Commission is set up so that tribes can sue the government for lands illegally taken in the past, but only a monetary compensation is allowed, not the return of the land itself.
1947	Normal Litell of Arlington, VA, becomes the claims attorney for the Navajos. John Boyden of Salt Lake City, Utah, becomes the Hopi attorney. Non-Indian law firms stand to earn millions of dollars by representing Indians in their land claims against the United States.
1955	Boyden files a petition to the Interior Department to overturn the Solicitor General's opinion that the two tribes hold joint ownership of the 1882 Executive Order reservation.
1957	Litell files a legal beief on behalf of the Navajo Tribal Council, recommending that Congress partition the disputed lands.
1958	Congress passes enabling legislation for a court decision on the Navajo-Hopi land ownership case. The Hopi Tribe starts a "friendly" lawsuit against the Navajo Tribe over ownership.
1960s	Boyden is special counsel for the merger of Peabody Coal with Kennecott Copper Corporation. His firm lists Morgan Guarantee Trust as a client, which put up capital for the merger.
1961	Peabody Coal begins lease arrangements of Black Mesa with the Hopis.

1962	The Court's ruling in *Healing v. Jones*: District Six is expanded to become the Hopi Reservation. (Navajo families living inside are ejected in 1972.) The remainder of the 1882 Reservation becomes the Joint Use Area (JUA). The Court refuses to partition the JUA, claiming it lacked jurisdiction.
1963	The U.S. Supreme Court upholds the lower court's decision. There is a tremendous gas and oil exploration boom on Hopi and Navajo lands.
1965	Peabody Coal plans two huge gasification plants on the Navajo Reservation. The Navajos are conned out of their water rights in order for Peabody to slurry coal to the plants.
1972	The district court in Arizona orders drastic Navajo livestock reduction to allow for Hopi use of half of the JUA range. The order also bars Navajo construction in the JUA.
1974	Congress passes the Navajo-Hopi Land Settlement Act (Public Law 93-531), providing for the partition of the JUA and the relocation of Indian members of one tribe living on land partitioned to the other.
1977	The district court in Arizona partitions the JUA. Navajo appeal delays effective date of partition to April 18, 1979.
1987	"New lands" are made available for Navajo relocation. These are along the Rio Puerco, which was badly contaminated in the radioactive spill at Churchrock, New Mexico, eight years earlier.
1989	A sacred lands suit brought by the Big Mountain Legal Defense/Offense Committee under the the 1978 AIRFA is rejected by the court. It rules that Indian religious freedom is not seriously impaired by relocation..
1991	A suit by Hopi traditionalists for a religious government to replace the Hopi Tribal Council is unsuccessful, even though for thousands of years, *kikmongwis* (religious leaders) have been the supreme authority in village affairs.
1996	Congress passes a new Navajo-Hopi Land Settlement Act. The approximately 1,000 Navajos remaining on Hopi partitioned land must sign a 75-year lease with the Hopi Tribe, or relocate.

councils are not Indian institutions. They're American institutions. They were put there by the U.S., created in that form for the purpose of exploiting land" (Mander 1981, 61).

Internal division was clearly a factor in the Hopi situation that pitted the more acculturated Hopi progressives against the Hopi religious traditionalists. In the Hopi case there is also the Mormon factor which was a main contributor to the split with the traditionalists. The largest Christian denomination on the Hopi Reservation is the Church of Latter Day Saints. Ironically, the Book of Mormon teaches that dark skin is a punishment from God. By accepting Mormonism, however, Indians after many generations "shall be a white and delightsome people," according to the Mormon belief. The Mormon Church has historically given a high priority to converting American Indians to its faith.

The unrepresentative Hopi Tribal Council played a leading role in the land dispute. The Bureau of Indian Affairs pressured the Hopis into accepting the IRA tribal council system of government as part of Commissioner John Collier's policy of indirect rule Indian administration. By the 1920s and 1930s, the European colonial powers had come to favor this form of colonial administration since direct rule, especially by the French, had been such an abysmal failure. Collier's reform of creating tribal councils may be understood as a form of neocolonialism. Unfortunately, the BIA-dominated Hopi Tribal

Council was part of the problem and not part of the solution in the Navajo-Hopi land dispute. Today, about a third of the villages on the 2,500 square mile Hopi reservation do not send representatives to the tribal council. Instead, they practice traditional governance by religious and clan leaders.

SUMMARY AND CONCLUSIONS

The Navajos and Hopis who live in the disputed Joint Use Area are among the largest self-sufficient, Indigenous communities still existing within the boundaries of the United States. They are what Spicer (1962) calls "enduring peoples." Yet today, their respective tribal councils are driven by the necessity to fund tribal activities through mineral extraction and energy development. Events precipitated by the 1946 Indian Claims Commission and penetration into tribal territories by the energy corporations have exacerbated intertribal disagreements and led to the polarization of tribal members into progressive and conservative camps. On one side are those who are pro-development and favor the land claims litigation, and on the other side, the religiously oriented traditionalists of both Indigenous nations.

The traditional cultures of the two tribes actually have more in common than they have differences. In both of the Navajo and Hopi spiritual cultures, enormous sacred power is invested in the land as a living being. The land itself is alive, sustaining all living creatures including humans. The land as sacred is therefore held in common; no one owns it. In Western capitalist society, on the other hand, the land is a commodity to be bought and sold.

An important area of culture that differentiates both the Navajos and the Hopis from that of mainstream United States and its institutions is the original system of governance. In traditional Navajo and Hopi cultures, there was no such thing as a tribal council. All political power was local, decentralized, fluid, and usually consensual. "Among the Navajo the only political unit is the autonomous extended family. . . . There is usually a 'headman' (BIA term) who is most often a woman. . . . Among traditional Hopis, central government is even more of an anathema. . . . [E]ach of the Hopi villages was a totally autonomous self-governing

entity" (Mander 1981, 55). Each village was comprised of clans and a *Kikmongwi*, a religious leader, usually male. The *Kikmongwi* has no political authority other than being a wise and respected teacher. As recently as 1991, Hopi traditionalists were pressing the federal government to help them replace their tribal council with a religion-based government. "They charge that the Tribal Council form of government, adopted in 1936, is foreign to Hopis, who for thousands of years gave *kikmongwis*—religious leaders—absolute authority over villages they lived in" (Winton 1991, A8).

Today, the two tribes are internally divided in their strategy for coping with U.S. capitalist society. This has made for the progressive vs. conservative split, especially among the Hopis where the Hopi Tribal Council has aggressively pursued litigation.

CHAPTER REVIEW

DISCUSSION QUESTIONS

1. Compare Navajo traditional culture to that of the Hopis.
2. Compare the history of Hopi tribal government as instituted by the Bureau of Indian Affairs to that of the Navajos. What impact did the 1934 Indian Reorganization Act have on the lives of traditional members of both nations?
3. How can uranium mining on the Navajo Nation be considered a form of genocide?
4. What caused the 1970s Navaho-Hopi land dispute? What role did the mining of Black Mesa play in it? What other factors lay behind the so-called dispute?
5. Describe the resistance at Black Mountain. How has the government resolved the dispute? Why isn't the settlement a satisfactory solution to traditional *Diné* and Hopis?
6. Why is "Indian factionalism" an inadequate concept to explain the Navajo-Hopi land dispute?

SUGGESTED READINGS

BRUGGE, DAVID M. 1994. *The Navajo-Hopi Land Dispute: An American Tragedy.* Albuquerque: University of New Mexico Press.

IVERSON, PETER. 2002. *Diné: A History of the Navajos.* Albuquerque: University of New Mexico Press.

ORTIZ, ALFONSO, vol. ed. 1979. *Handbook of North American Indians, vols. 9, 10, Southwest.* Washington:

Smithsonian Institution, 1979. (Articles by various authors on Hopi history, culture, economy, and intertribal relations.)

SHERIDAN, THOMAS E., and NANCY J. PAREZO. 1996. *Paths of Life: American Indians of the Southwest and Northern Mexico.* Tucson: University of Arizona Press.

REFERENCES

AIM 4 Awareness. 1999. "Kosovo in Arizona? Big Mountain Update." *Aim 4 Awareness,* a Quarterly Information Service of the American Indian Movement. (Double Issue: Spring/Summer).

BODLEY, JOHN H. 1990. *Victims of Progress.* 3rd ed. Moutain View, CA: Mayfield.

BREW, J. O. 1979. "Hopi Prehistory and History to 1850." In *Handbook of North American Indians, vol. 9: Southwest,* volume edited by Alfonso Ortiz, *514–23.* Washington, DC: Smithsonian Institution Press.

BRUGGE, DAVID M. 1983. "Navajo Prehistory and History to 1850." In *Handbook of North American Indians, vol. 10: Southwest,* volume edited by Alfonso Ortiz, 489–501. Washington, DC: Smithsonian Institution Press.

———. 1994. *The Navajo–Hopi Land Dispute: An American Tragedy.* Albuquerque: University of New Mexico Press.

BURNHAM, PHILLIP. 2006. "'Operation Indian Country', Preparing for War." *Indian Country Today* 26 (October 18): B1–2.

BUTLER, KRISTIE LEE. 1996. "Navajo." In *Native America in the Twentieth Century: An Encyclopedia,* edited by Mary B. Davis, 379–84. New York: Garland.

CHURCHILL, WARD, and WINONA LADUKE. 1992. "Native North America: The Political Economy of Radioactive Colonialism." In *The State of Native America: Genocide, Colonialism, and Resistance,* edited by Annette M. James, 241–66. Boston, MA: South End Press.

COLBY, BENJAMIN N., DAVID F. ABERLE, and RICHARD O. CLEMMER. 1990. "The Navajo–Hopi Situation: New Developments." Panel on the Navajo–Hopi Land Dispute, *Anthropology Newsletter,* February: 1, 22–24.

CLEMMER, RICHARD O. 1979. "Hopi History, 1940–1974." In *Handbook of North American Indians, vol. 9: Southwest,* volume edited by Alfonso Ortiz, 533–38. Washington, DC: Smithsonian Institution Press.

———. 1980. "Advocacy, Anthropology, and Accuracy: An Additional Rejoinder to Wilcomb Washburn." *Journal of Ethnic Studies* 8 (2, Summer): 95–113

CONNELLY, JOHN C. 1979. "Hopi Social Organization." In *Handbook of North American Indians, vol. 9: Southwest,* volume edited by Alfonso Ortiz, *539–53.* Washington, DC: Smithsonian Institution Press.

DOCKSTADER, FREDERICK J. 1979. "Hopi History, 1850–1940." In *Handbook of North American Indians, vol. 9: Southwest,* volume edited by Alfonso Ortiz, 524–32. Washington, DC: Smithsonian Institution Press.

DUTTON, BERTHA P. 1983. *American Indians of the Southwest.* Albuquerque: University of New Mexico Press.

ENDERS. GORDON W. 1971. "An Historical Analysis of the Hopi–Navajo Land Disputes, 1882–1970." (May). A Thesis Presented to the Department of History, Brigham Young University. In Partial Fulfillment of the Requirements for the Degree Master of Arts. (Duplicate manuscript. Arizona State Historical Museum, Tucson, Arizona.)

FEHER-ELSTON, CATHERINE. 1996. "Navajo-Hopi Land Controversy." In *Native America in the Twentieth Century: An Encyclopedia,* edited by Mary B. Davis, 386–589. New York: Garland.

GILL, SAM D. 1983. "Navajo Views of Their Origin." In *Handbook of North American Indians, vol. 10: Southwest,* volume edited by Alfonso Ortiz, 502–5). Washington, DC: Smithsonian Institution Press.

GRIFFIN-PIERCE, TRUDY. 2000. "The Continuous Renewal of Sacred Relations: Navajo Religion." In *Native Religions and Cultures of North America: Anthropology of the Sacred,* edited by Lawrence E. Sullivan, 121–41. New York: Continuum International.

GRINDE, DONALD A., and BRUCE E. JOHANSEN. 1995. *Ecocide of Native America: Environmental Destruction of Indian Lands and Peoples.* Santa Fe: Clear Light.

HIEB, LOUIS A. 1996. "Hopi." In *Native America in the Twentieth Century: An Encyclopedia,* edited by Mary B. Davis, 240–43 New York: Garland.

HOWARD, MICHAEL C., and PATRICK C. MCKIM. 1983. *Contemporary Cultural Anthropology.* Boston: Little, Brown.

Indian Country Today. 2006a. "Navajo Nation Battles Yellow 'Monster.'" *Indian Country Today* 26, (November 29): A2.

———. 2006b. "Summit Declaration Demands Worldwide Ban on Uranium." 26 (December 27): A8.

———. 2007. "The Factionalism Stereotype." Editorial. *Indian Country Today,* 26 (January 10): A2.

JOHANSEN, BRUCE E., ed. 2007. *The Praeger Handbook of Contemporary Issues in Native America.* vol. 2. Westport, CT: Praeger.

JORGENSEN, JOSEPH G., and RICHARD O. CLEMMER. 1978. "America in the Indian's Past." *Journal of Ethnic Studies* 6 (Summer): 65–74.

———. 1980. "On Washburn's 'On the Tail of the Activist Anthropologist,' A Rejoinder to a Reply." *Journal of Ethnic Studies* 8 (Summer): 85–113.

KAPPLER, CHARLES J. 1904. *Indian Affairs: Laws and Treaties.* Washington, DC: U.S. Government Printing Office.

KEHOE, ALICE B. 1992. *North American Indians: A Comprehensive Account.* 2nd ed. Englewood Cliffs, NJ: Prentice-Hall.

LAPHAM, NICK. n.d. "Stewardship Or Fraud?" *Clear Creek,* 30–31, 67.

LEE, TANYA. 2006. "Navajo Nation Sets Sights On First Casino." *Indian Country Today* 26 (August 9): B4.

Letter by Hopi Headmen. 1894. Letter addressed "To the Washington Chiefs," March.

MANDER, JERRY. 1981. "Kit Carson In a Three-Piece Suit." *Bioregions, the Co-Evolution Quarterly* (Winter): 52–63.

MAYBURY-LEWIS, DAVID. 1997. *Indigenous Peoples, Ethnic Groups, and the State*. Needham Heights, MA: Allyn & Bacon.

ROSSEL, ROBERT A., JR. 1983. "Navajo History, 1850–1923." In *Handbook of North American Indians, vol. 10: Southwest*, volume edited by Alfonso Ortiz, 506–23. Washington, DC: Smithsonian Institution Press.

SHERIDAN, THOMAS E., and NANCY J. PAREZO, eds. 1996. *Paths of Life: American Indians of the Southwest and Northern Mexico*. Tucson: University of Arizona Press.

SILLS, MARC. 1986. "Relocation Reconsidered: Competing Explanations of the Navajo-Hopi Land Settlement Act of 1974." *Journal of Ethnic Studies* 14 (Fall): 52–83.

SISKIND, JANET. 1982. "'Toinjoni': A Beautiful River That Turned Sour." *Mine Talk* (Summer/Fall): 37–40.

SPICER, EDWARD H. 1962. *Cycles of Conquest: The Impact of Spain, Mexico, and the United States on the Indians of the Southwest, 1533–1960*. Tucson: University of Arizona Press.

UNDERHILL, RUTH. 1963. *Red Man's America*. Chicago: University of Chicago Press.

WALDMAN, CARL. 2000. *Atlas of the North American Indian*. Rev. ed. New York: Checkmark Books.

WASHBURN, WILCOMB E. 1975. *The Indian in America*. New York: Harper & Row.

———. 1979. "On the Trail of the Activist Anthropologist; Response to Jorgensen and Clemmer." *Journal of Ethnic Studies*, 7 (Spring): 89–99.

WINTON, BEN. 1991. "Hopis Push for Religious Recognition." *Phoenix Gazette*, April 3.

WITHERSPOON, GARY. 1983. "Navajo Social Organization." In *Handbook of North American Indians, vol. 10: Southwest*, volume edited by Alfonso Ortiz, 524–35. Washington, DC: Smithsonian Institution Press.

WOOD, JOHN J., and KATHY MULLIN STEMMLER. 1981. "Land and Religion at Big Mountain: The Effects of the Navajo-Hopi Land Dispute on Navajo Well-being." A report to the Congress of the United States, prepared on behalf of the Big Mountain Community. April 5, Flagstaff, Arizona.

THE BIRTH, DEATH, AND RESURRECTION

OF THE CHEROKEE NATION

The seven pointed star represents the seven Cherokee clans: the three words are Birth, Death (Dead person), and Resurrection, "I am awake." These words represent the birth of the Cherokee Nation, the brink of death from the wars with the United States and the Trail of Tears, and the resurrection is the renewal of the Cherokee people.

Native Americans regard their names not as mere labels, but as essential parts of their personalities. A Native person's name is as vital to his or her identity as the eyes or teeth. 'Asgaya-dihi. Mankiller. My Cherokee name in English is Mankiller.'

—Wilma P. Mankiller, Principal Chief, 1985–95.[1]

Probably the best known, and certainly the most populous Indian Nation in the United States is the Cherokee. The Indian scholar Vine Deloria, Jr., (1969, 2–3) satirically observed in *Custer Died For Your Sins*, a best-selling book, that it is popular among many White people to claim Indian blood, no matter how slight, and often from a Cherokee "princess." The fact remains that the Cherokees are well known among the non-Indian public especially because of their adaptation in the nineteenth century to many features of Anglo-American society—literacy, technology, and a form of government resembling that of the United States. This earned them the distinction of being called a "Civilized Tribe," along with the Creeks, Chickasaws, Choctaws, and Seminoles.

Lesser known is the fact that the Cherokees are also distinguished by their relationship to the ancient Mound Builder cultures of eastern North America. The Mound Builders built hundreds of enormous earthen mounds, many of them geometric in shape, and others shaped like animals. (See Chapter 11.) They lived in complex urban settlements with stratified social systems. Some experts believe the Mound Builder civilization equaled if not surpassed the pyramids of Egypt in their overall construction and scope. Advanced mound-building societies lasted for centuries. In the Mississippian phase, they were master farmers, growing corn, beans, squash, pumpkins, and tobacco. They built giant temple mounds, the most famous of which is Monk's Mound in the urban complex of Cahokia, located near present-day city of St. Louis. Cahokia had an estimated population of thirty thousand people (see Waldman 2000, 20–24).

"When the Spaniards of the Hernando Desoto expedition traveled through the southeast of what is today the United States in 1540, they reported seeing temples and mounds and rulers they called 'emperors' and 'queens,' who were carried around by their 'subjects' on litter chairs. They also reported a densely populated region with roads that led to many towns"

(Conley 2005, 17). No specific mention is made of the Cherokees, but Conley (2005, 23) reports that "the Cherokees, under the rule of the Ani-Kutani, almost certainly built mounds, and they probably abandoned the practice after the rule of the Ani-Kutani was overthrown."

According to the 2000 U.S. Census, the Cherokees today constitute the largest Indian "tribe" in the United States, numbering 281,069 individuals claiming "Cherokee only" as their "race" or Indian identity. More than 729,000 selected Cherokee and at least one other "race" or American Indian tribal grouping as their identity. The Cherokees are second only to the Blackfeet in terms of a "mixed race" tribal grouping, with 62 percent designating this census category. Originally a southeastern people, the Cherokees are today divided into three groups: the Eastern Band of Cherokees in North Carolina with over 9,000 members; the Cherokee Nation of Oklahoma with more than 122,000 members; the United Band of Keetoowahs with approximately 7,500 members. "In addition to the federally recognized groups, more than fifty other organizations in at least twelve states claim Cherokee descent" (King 1996, 95).

The Cherokees have been the single largest U.S. Indian tribe chosen in the last two national censuses. The primary reason is their basis for tribal membership, which rejects the federal government's blood quantum requirement for tribal enrollment. Unlike almost all federally recognized Indian nations in the United States, Cherokee enrollment is determined almost exclusively by cultural affiliation. One reason is that adoption was common in traditional culture in the past, not only of other Indians, but of other races as well, following contact with Europeans. More importantly, both the eastern and western Cherokees define tribal membership on the basis of ancestry rather than blood relationship. Enrollment in the Eastern Band requires one-thirty-second degree of Cherokee blood through descent from an enrolled ancestor on the 1924 Baker roll, and the Oklahoma Cherokee through descent from an ancestor on the 1906 Dawes Commission roll.

In the 1930s, Congress and the Bureau of Indian Affairs decided to establish blood quanta for the purpose of tribal enrollment. At the time, blood quantum was set at one-quarter degree, meaning that in order to be a federally recognized Indian, one had to have a full-blooded parent, or parents who are at least half-blood. The conventional wisdom among Whites was that Native Americans were a dying race, and eventually the so-called "Indian problem" would take care of itself when there would be no more legal Indians. The Indians, however, did not vanish as the federal policy makers expected them to do.

The blood-quantum device may be attributed to identity politics, the racial dimension of divide and rule.

> What distinguishes Indians from ethnic minorities is the fact that Native Americans own property—a reservation land base and valuable resources. The blood quantum device defines out of existence many bona fide Native Americans and thereby deprives them of the right to land, resources, and treaty-obligated services that are mandated under federal Indian law. It also separates federally recognized Native Americans from relatives and neighbors who are unrecognized, or who are not considered Indian because of the blood quantum device. As the interracial marriage rate increases, and as more and more Indian adults marry inter-tribally, fewer Native American children can claim enough "blood" of any one tribe or nation to qualify as federally recognized Indians. This trend has been termed *statistical genocide.* (Lobo and Talbot 2001, 8)

The Cherokees, on the other hand, have followed the traditional way of defining tribal membership. In its 1975 constitution, the Cherokee Nation of Oklahoma "took the unprecedented step, still unparalleled by other twentieth-century Indigenous governments, of completely dispensing with blood quantum requirements in its enrollment procedures" (Churchill 1999, 57). Interestingly, Cherokee history confirms this means of determining who is a Cherokee. In the period leading up to the Cherokee Removal of 1838, it was John Ross, "a man 'seven-eighths Scotch-Irish and one-eighth Cherokee by descent,' who served as the primary leader of his people's effort to revitalize their traditional culture, prevent the loss of their homelands . . . and thereby avert mass relocation to Oklahoma Territory" (Churchill 1999, 43). There have also been many

outstanding half-breed Indian leaders in the past among the Comanche, Cheyenne, Oglala Lakota, and Crow Nations.

As to the secret of Cherokee survival, Indian demographer Russell Thornton (1987, 200) has this to say:

> The Oklahoma Cherokee, without a reservation land base, have thus been able to survive tribally by an inclusive definition of what it is to be Cherokee. Their definition allowed relatively large numbers of people with Cherokee lineage but relatively small amounts of Cherokee blood into the tribe. This allowed the tribe to reestablish itself after virtual dissolution and to achieve political power in Oklahoma. The tribe, in turn, has protected a smaller group of full-blood, more traditional Cherokee from American non-Indian ways of life.

CHAPTER OVERVIEW

In this chapter we examine the political history of the ethnic cleansing of the Cherokee people as a result of military pressures from the English colonies, and the removal policy of the United States when Andrew Jackson was elected president in 1828.

By a succession of onerous treaties between 1721 and 1819, the Cherokee homeland was reduced to the mountainous areas of North Carolina, Tennessee, Georgia, and Alabama. In December, 1835, the Treaty of New Echota ceded the last remaining Cherokee lands east of the Mississippi. In exchange, the Cherokees were promised new lands in Indian Territory, today's northeastern Oklahoma.

Their forced removal on a thousand-mile journey in the winters of 1838 and 1839 to Indian Territory west of the Mississippi River became known as the Cherokee Trail of Tears. Some one thousand holdouts who remained in the mountains and avoided this early ethnic cleansing operation by the U.S. government, in time, became federally recognized as the Eastern Band of Cherokee. Those forced to move to Indian Territory, which later became the State of Oklahoma, are the western Cherokee and are today recognized as the Cherokee Nation of Oklahoma.

Of particular interest in the Cherokee story is their response to Anglo-American hegemony. They were the first Indian nation to consciously set about forming a political state, an Indian republic, modeling many of their institutions after those of the United States, but at the same time retaining key aspects of Cherokee culture and a strong sense of their Cherokee nationality. Even more remarkable is that they did this not once, but three times in their history, each time following the destruction of their tribal republic at the hands of the southern states and the U.S. government. The periods of destruction start with the removal policy of the 1830s, which divided their nation and sent the majority of the population on the Trail of Tears to Indian Territory. After rebuilding their political system and society, the Cherokee Nation was again destroyed as a result of the Civil War. They recovered and reestablished their Indian republic, only to be unilaterally liquidated by the federal government when Oklahoma was admitted to the Union as a state in 1907. Once more, however, they began to recover in the 1970s until, today, they have become once again a vibrant Indian nation.

THEORETICAL ANALYSIS AND CONCEPTS

Indian sociologist Duane Champagne (Turtle Mountain Chippewa) has proposed a theory to explain how the Cherokees survived the American holocaust as an Indigenous entity by adapting to Euro-American social institutions without sacrificing tribal identity. "The Cherokees' great achievement was not that they adapted so well to White culture, but that they exerted so great a national impact and yet, being on the beachhead of White expansion, were able to preserve so much that was traditional" (Wardell 1977, xiv). In Champagne's analysis the Cherokees were originally a structurally differentiated society. Each part of the Cherokee culture and social system was autonomous or independent of the other.[2] Traditional, preconquest society was organized around seven matrilineal clans that were autonomous and functionally separate from village government and other Cherokee institutions. Clan function was primarily judicial rather than political, and economic life was left to family households in the Cherokee settlements. The autonomous village governments were the primary political units, but even larger political groups were formed by coalitions of village governments. Religious life was under the care of the clans and specialized priestly lineages, and these were "functionally differentiated from the village headman and warrior leadership roles" (See Champagne 1983; also, Gearing 1962, Mankiller and Wallis 1993, Mooney 1975, and Wright 1992).

Structurally differentiated (segmentary) societies like the Cherokees, in contrast to the non-structurally differentiated Iroquois (see Chapter 2), were able to adjust more easily to European and Anglo-American political pressures. In a series of historic stages, the Cherokees changed their economy by adopting southern plantation agriculture, including slavery. They became literate in their own language, established schools, academies, and courts, and eventually, between 1810 and 1827, formed a national government that was modeled in part on that of the United States, which, in turn, had been influenced by the Iroquois Confederacy. At the same time, the Cherokees kept their language, important aspects of traditional culture, and national identity, thus forming an Indian republic of a new type. Despite this successful adjustment along lines that one might think Anglo-American society would approve, they were repeatedly liquidated as an independent nation. Yet, like a phoenix rising from the ashes each time following the destruction of their nation, they rose again.

TRADITIONAL CULTURE

The name, Cherokee, comes from a Greek word "Chelokee" meaning "people of a different speech." In their own language, the Cherokees called themselves the *Aniyunwiya* (principal or real people), or the "people of Kituhwa" (Keetoowah). Cherokees were known to the Shawnees as the *Keetoowahs*, the name of an ancient Cherokee town located in what is today North Carolina, one of the "seven mother towns." Although accepting the name Cherokee, many prefer "Tsalagi," which is derived from their own name for the Cherokee Nation, *Tsalagihi Ayili*.

The original Cherokee heartland is marked by the Great Smoky and Blue Ridge mountains, through which run major river systems that empty into the Atlantic Ocean, the Gulf of Mexico, and the Mississippi River drainage. Their homeland included what today are the states of North Carolina, part of South Carolina, Georgia, Tennessee, and eventually Alabama. (See Figure 6.1.)

They "also laid claim to a larger domain extending into Kentucky and Virginia, where they hunted deer and gathered raw materials essential to their way of life" (Perdue and Green 1995, 1). The area is blessed with fertile bottomlands and easy transportation routes. "The region contained both wide and narrow valleys suitable for hunting and for farming, as well as extensive chestnut-oak forests" (Fogelson 2004, 337). The region was biologically diverse with complex ecosystems.

The Cherokee language is the sole representative of the southern branch of the Iroquoian language family. Originally, several dialects were

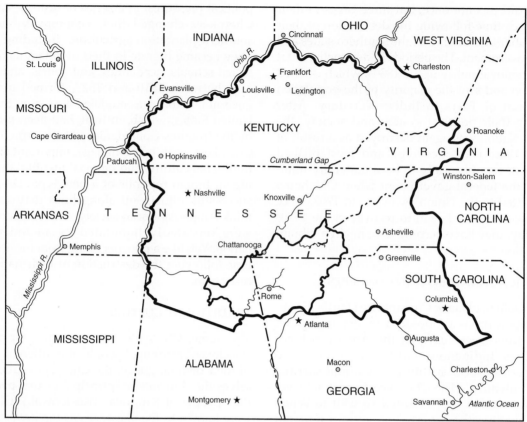

Figure 6.1 Traditional Cherokee territory showing the intersection of state boundaries in violation of Cherokee sovereignty.

spoken, and multilingualism was common. The Eastern dialect was spoken in the Lower Towns of the Cherokee territory. The Middle or Keetoowah dialect was spoken in the towns on the Tuckasegee and the headwaters of the Little Tennessee River. The Western dialect was spoken mostly in the Overhills towns "of east Tennessee and upper Georgia and upon Hiwassee and Cheowa Rivers in North Carolina" (Conley 2005, 26). Today, the Kituwha (Keetoowah) or Middle dialect is spoken by the Eastern Cherokee on the Qualla Boundary Reservation in North Carolina; the Otali or Over-hill dialect is spoken in eastern Tennessee and northern Georgia, which is the primary dialect of the Cherokee of Oklahoma; and the Valley dialect is spoken in the Snowbird community of North Carolina.

The early Cherokees were hunters and farmers. Before the eastern buffalo became scarce, the Cherokees held an annual buffalo hunt. A hunter followed prescribed rituals, including an apology to the spirit of the animal killed. Cherokee traditional culture included maize horticulture, settled villages, and well-developed ceremonials. Economic subsistence relied primarily on staples of corn, beans, and cucurbits, a plant in the gourd family. Horticulture was women's responsibility, while men helped in clearing the fields and harvesting. Many wild plants were part of the traditional diet, including wild strawberries, raspberries, and huckleberries, and wintergreen and gooseberries used in medicinal teas. Also eaten were tree fruits—wild cherries, pawpaws, mulberries, service-berries, and persimmons. Nuts supplemented the diet, especially the chestnut, and the meat of butternuts, black walnuts, and hickory nuts were important ingredients in many Cherokee recipes.

The white-tailed deer was the main game animal, hunted with bow and arrow by the men. Venison was the primary meat in the traditional diet; and all parts of the animal were utilized. By the eighteenth century, deerskins had become the most important export commodity in the trade with the English colonies. Some elk and wood bison were also eaten, along with bears, but never in large numbers. Beavers were hunted to near extinction in the early years of the European conquest. Several different kinds of birds supplemented the diet: geese, ducks, quail, turkeys, and especially passenger pigeons. Eagle feathers were especially prized by the Cherokees, as they are among most Native North Americans. A wide variety of fish completed the Cherokee diet.

Division of labor was solely by age and gender. Women were associated with farming, and men with hunting. A young couple confirmed their marriage by exchanging corn and deer meat. "Girls were socialized at an early age into women's domestic roles as caretakers, cultivators of the fields, collectors, processors, and preparers of food as well as manufacturers of clothing, pottery, basketry and other utilitarian objects" (Fogelson 2004, 344). They were under the strict supervision of older female relatives. Boys, on the other hand, were given a great deal of personal freedom. Adult men traveled to other towns, had hunting territories, and participated in war parties under the mentorship of their mothers' brothers. Marriage was matrilocal, i.e., a married man resided in his wife's community with her relatives. "Postmenopausal women acquired a more audible voice in political affairs. Attaining the status of an elder called for respect and honor" (Fogelson 2004, 346). Death was viewed as a process rather than an event, and was marked by an all-night wake.

The primary unit of residence was the homestead. "These homesteads might be strung out along a river in a narrow mountain valley or tightly clustered in more open terrain, but together they formed a permanent village" or town (Perdue and Green 1995, 2). The latter consisted of "a semi-subterranean and circular or elevated and octagonal structure, located on a pre-existent mound: an open courtyard or 'square ground' surrounded by benches or arbors, and a complex of poles erected for ball games, as prison posts, and perhaps for priestly divination. The ceremonial center might also contain the residence of chiefly priests and other town officials" (Fogelson 2004, 341).

Domestic dwellings were located close by, with the entire complex surrounded by a palisade. Buildings were of wattle and daub, lacking windows but containing a smoke-hole at the top of a thatched roof, and a single door, usually facing eastward. Household clusters included buildings for sleeping and eating, a cookhouse, elevated storage structures, and storage pits. A hot house for ritual *sweats*, for food preparation, and for sleeping during winter (especially by the elders), complemented the structural arrangement of buildings. Fogelson (2004, 341–42) notes that "the shapes and spatial arrangement of household clusters mirrored the larger ceremonial center, which in turn served as a microcosm of the culturally constituted Cherokee universe."

Towns ranged in population from slightly under one hundred to over five hundred residents. As many as several hundred people gathered in the town houses to conduct ceremonies or debate important issues. Traditional Cherokee society was decentralized and egalitarian. Decisions were reached by consensus, even if the matter debated took weeks or month before there was agreement.

The Overhills town of Chota was described in 1673 as built along a river, "with high cliffs on the opposite side of the river, and a twelve-foot high wall of logs around the other three sides of the town. There were scaffolds with parapets to defend the walls" (Conley 2005, 26). Houses were built along streets and the town possessed 150 canoes, the smallest of which could hold twenty men.

Social Organization

Kinship was the glue of Cherokee society. Several generations of a family lived together, "Because the Cherokees were matrilineal—that is, they traced kinship solely through women—the usual residents of a household were a woman, her husband, her daughters and their husbands, her daughters' children, and any unmarried sons (married sons lived in their wives' households)" (Perdue and Green 1995, 2).

The Cherokees were divided into seven matrilineal, exogamous clans: Wild Potato, Deer, Bird, Wolf, Red Paint (or Paint), Long Hair (or Twister), and Blue, sometimes called the Panther clan. All seven clans were usually represented in each Cherokee town, where they were expected to carry out their ceremonial duties and function as agents of social security and social control. A person could venture into a distant town and seek out fellow clan members and expect hospitality. Clans regulated marriage, since one could not marry a person of the same clan; to do so was to commit incest. Most men married women from other towns. Clans were also responsible for avenging slain kin by killing a member of the offending clan, which could lead to chronic feuds and warfare. As an alternative, a war captive could be adopted in place of the deceased clan member, or the offense settled by material compensation and forgiveness.

Clan obligations were so strong, and retribution so swift, that traditional Cherokee culture had no need for a police force or court system. Otherwise, social control in Cherokee society was informal, governed by shame, joking, and ridicule. Fear of witchcraft and sorcery was also a powerful force for social control. Witches were viewed as evil creatures, taking the form of humans and animals who could steal the unexpired life expectancies of their victims. Sorcerers, in contrast, were humans who had knowledge of incantations and rituals to oppose the witches.

The Cherokees endeavored to keep the world in accordance with their "harmony ethic," i.e., keeping the world in balance. This was the primary function of religious observances and rituals.

"People bathed daily for spiritual purification as well as physical cleanliness. The women sang sacred songs as they hoed their corn, and the men observed important rituals, such as asking the deer's pardon and offering its liver to the fire" (Perdue and Green 1995, 4). Men secluded themselves before going to war, and the women did the same during menstruation and childbirth for fear they might overwhelm their opposite and upset the precarious balance of the Cherokee world.

Political Organization

Traditional political organization was dualistic, alternating between a white, or peace group, and a red, or war group. A peace chief, or high priest *uku*, headed the white division. "The *uku* was aided by an executive assistant and advised by seven clan counselors and a committee of elders" (Fogelson 2004, 346). There were also a number of officers to perform various civic and ceremonial tasks. Decision making was by consensus and nonconfrontational.

The question of war or peace was one of the important issues discussed by the village council. Secular matters were discussed under a white flag, led by the chief priest and an inner council of clansmen described above. When a village council deliberated on the question of an offensive war, "the red standard . . . was soon raised, and a new combination of organized groups went into operation," including a war chief, a war priest, and others selected by the warriors (Gearing 1962, 26). The war chief was younger than the peace chief and was assisted by a secondary chief, a war speaker, and messengers. He also "consulted a war council consisting of representatives of the seven clans, as well as a group of war women, or Pretty Women, who might serve as auxiliaries to a war party. The organi-

zation also deployed specially designated scouts and medicine men" (Fogelson 2004, 346).

"The white organization was ascendant in the local town, and its authority was only relinquished to the red organization when the town was under attack. The red organization's natural domain was outside the town: on the warpath, in trading expeditions, on diplomatic embassies, and in coordinating hunting parties" (Fogelson 2004, 346). War leaders gained their status by achievement and inspirational qualities. The position of peace leaders, on the other hand, was more ascribed than achieved. Status was dependent on benevolence, tact, and mutual respect.

Women played an influential role in Cherokee town government by sharing in the responsibilities and rights of tribal organization. Since kinship was traced through the female line, women generally held property rights. (After contact with Europeans, Whites derided the Cherokee for having "a petticoat government"). A powerful Cherokee title was *Ghigau*, "Beloved Woman." Nancy Ward, who played a prominent role in nineteenth century Cherokee history, was designated a Beloved Woman. Women occasionally accompanied the men to war as warriors. Unfortunately, one of the new customs introduced by White people was sexism. It created a lack of balance and harmony between men and women, which ran counter to the Cherokee harmony ethic.

Spiritual Culture

No one knows for certain the origins of the Cherokees before they settled in their Appalachian homeland. One story handed down from the Nighthawk Keetoowah Cherokees of Oklahoma tells of a South American origin, migrating north through Central America and Mexico, traveling farther north before eventually settling in what is now southeastern United States.

In religious oral history, it is related that there were three worlds. There was the world on top, which was the Sky Vault, and then there was also the world underneath of where people now live. The two spirit worlds were populated by powerful beings, and these two worlds were opposed to one another. This meant that the intermediary human world was a dangerous place because it had to maintain the proper balance between the two opposing spiritual forces. "Balance and harmony and purity were therefore all important aspects of the old religion, and there was a rich ceremonial life to help achieve those ends" (Conley 2005, 7). This required an annual cycle of seven major ceremonies, and other special ceremonies whenever events called for them, as well as daily rituals.

The Cherokee creation story relates that in the beginning, it was the little water beetle who created land out of an endless sea by diving to the bottom and bringing up mud. Eventually the earth as we know it became a great island floating in a sea of water. Animals and plants were created first, and human beings later. The first Redman was called Lucky Hunter, the first woman Corn, who was also red. These red human beings came to be called *Yunwiya*, the "real people." The Cherokees believe that there were many worlds before the present one, each ending in a great catastrophe. "It was prophesied that this world will continue only as long as the Cherokees continue to exist as a distinct people upon their own land in accordance with a divine plan" (Fogelson 2004, 347).

Belief and ritual were "premised on the existence of a wide range of spiritual beings who required respect and propitiation" (Fogelson 2004, 347). These beings included monsters and different classes of little people who could intervene in human affairs. There were also sprits of the dead who haunted the night as ghosts, "boogers," or witches. Animal spirits also abounded in the spirit world, and each species had a progenitor responsible for the souls of its faunal descendants. Most diseases stemmed from the displeasure of these animal bosses. "Arrayed against these animal-sent maladies was the power of plants, control of which had to be sought and learned by humans, "hence the value placed on herbalists (Fogelson 2004, 347). Of even more importance was the power of diviners and conjurors who could directly intervene with the spiritual world.

Warfare was a serious and seemingly brutal pursuit in traditional Cherokee society. Warriors prepared for an expedition by fasting and singing sacred songs in the town house. The object of warfare was the surprise attack that often resulted in targeting the most vulnerable victims, including women and children. The rationale behind warfare was the Cherokee world view of keeping the world in balance. Cherokee warriors

> envisioned the world as composed of opposites that balanced each other. Men, for example, balanced women, and hunting balanced farming. By the same token, the Cherokees lived in a state of equilibrium with the non-Cherokees, . . . but if an outsider took the life of a Cherokee, he destroyed that state of equilibrium. For the world to be set right, one of the guilty party's people had to die. Failure to seek vengeance meant that the world remained out of kilter and placed the entire Cherokee people at risk of disease, drought, or a host of other disasters. . . . Once a war party had exacted vengeance and restored cosmic order, however, it went home. Cherokee warriors did not conquer territory or destroy entire villages; they merely sought vengeance and order. (Perdue and Green 1995, 3)

Among the eastern Cherokees, the traditional ceremonial calendar centered on the summer half of the year. It commenced with the first new moon of spring, usually in late March, and related to the ritual preparation for planting the corn crop and weather control. Next was the Green Corn ceremony, a first fruits rite celebrating the ripening of the corn which took place in late July or early August. It involved ritual bloodletting and the drinking and sometimes regurgitation of a specially decocted medicine, climaxed with all-night dancing. A Mature Corn thanksgiving ceremony was celebrated in late August or early September. In the fall, additional ceremonies took place. A medicine dance, the First Great Moon, was held in October. Ten days later, the Reconciliation ceremony took place. It is thought to have marked the Cherokee New Year, because the old fire was extinguished, a new fire ritually lit, old clothing discarded and the town ceremonially cleansed. "The summer ceremonial cycle concluded in early December with the so-called Feast of the Exulting or Bounding Bush" (Fogelson 2004, 349).

During the winter half of the year, there were various dances, although smaller in scale and less involved with religious life. They included various animal dances, such as the Bear Dance and Eagle Dance. The Booger Dance also took place in winter. It represented "a cathartic rejection of Whites and other foreigners along with the biological and social maladies that accompany them" (Fogelson 2004, 349). Winter was also a time for storytelling.

EARLY POLITICAL RELATIONS

The Cherokees were a mountain people, inhabiting the uplands of the Allegheny region of what is now southeastern United States. They considered the Great Smoky Mountains sacred and the heart of their traditional territory. In 1539, the Hernando de Soto expedition landed in Florida and spent three years traveling through the southeastern part of the United States. "On their relentless search for gold, the bloodthirsty Spaniards enslaved, tortured, and killed hundreds, even thousands of Indians" (Conley 2005, 18). They may have visited several Cherokee towns, but if they did so, it was without incident. Twenty-six years later, the Juan Pardo expedition arrived and possibly visited the Cherokees, because there appears to be evidence of Spanish mining operations in the Cherokee country. The Spaniards established a fort along the coast of what is now South Carolina, in part to oppose French exploration.

The first English colony in North America was founded at Jamestown, Virginia, in 1607. This was in the land of the powerful Powhatan Confederacy. After the war between the Powhatan and the English, in which the latter prevailed, several hundred Cherokees attempted to establish a town at the site now occupied by Richmond, Virginia. The alarmed English colonists raised a military force that included one hundred Pamunkey Indian auxiliaries and attacked the newly established Cherokee town but were soundly defeated. This is the first known encounter of the Cherokees with the English. English traders began visiting the Cherokee country in the late seventeenth century. In 1690, Cornelius Dougherty, an Irishman from Virginia, established himself as the first trader among the Cherokees.

When first contacted by the Spaniards, the Cherokees were living in several major geographical groupings that included what is today the western tip of North Carolina, the western corner of South Carolina, and adjacent parts of eastern Tennessee. By the eighteenth century, they "had expanded into northern Georgia and northeastern Alabama; they claimed small portions of Virginia, West Virginia, and most of Kentucky as hunting grounds and buffer zones" (Fogelson 2004, 337). Eventually, Cherokee territory encompassed a vast region of about forty thousand square miles, spanning eight contemporary states. Their territory consisted of three different settlement areas known as the Overhills (or Upper Towns), the Middle Towns, and the Lower Towns (or Valley Towns) (see Figure 6.1). Each had its own environmental niche and was distinguished by a different Cherokee dialect.

In the early relations between the Cherokees and the English colonies, the Europeans became frustrated by having to deal with each Cherokee town separately. This led to the appointment of a *Wro-setasatow*, or trade representative, which "appears to have been the first step toward the central government that would eventually become the Cherokee Nation" (Conley 2005, 27). In 1730, the British sent Sir Alexander Cuming to the Cherokees to affirm earlier land agreements. During his excursion he selected Moytoy of the Cherokee town of Tellico as "Emperor of the Cherokees," but it is highly doubtful that Cuming's accomplishment held any real meaning to the Cherokees. It was some years later in the century before the Cherokees themselves saw the efficacy of having a single leader or governmental organization to represent them when dealing with the colonies and political representatives of England, and later, the United States.

CULTURE CHANGE

Before the American Revolution, the Cherokees were at various times military allies, trading, partners, or enemies of the English colonists. The majority of the Cherokees fought on the side of the English during the Revolutionary War and suffered accordingly when the Americans proved victorious. The English colonists were anxious to acquire Cherokee pelts, especially deer, bear oil, and beeswax.

The early traders married Cherokee women and thus begat mixed-blood families that subsequently became well known in Cherokee political history. Children born of these unions were considered Cherokee, since the matrilineal kinship system considers the children of Cherokee women to be Cherokee despite the so-called race of their fathers. Conversely, many of the Cherokee wives went to live with their non-Indian husbands, contrary to the Cherokee custom of matrilocal residence. Cherokee spiritual leaders opposed their women marrying White men unless the men accepted Cherokee culture and came to live in the Cherokee communities. There were problems for the children of these unions, as well. Former Principal Chief Wilma Mankiller reflects: "They took their father's surnames along with the clan affiliation of their mothers, and became heirs to their fathers' houses and possessions. This caused much confusion and infighting. For the first time in our tribe's history, there was great inequality of wealth. . . . Cherokee society began to erode as many of the mixed-blood youths, swayed by their fathers' religion, decided the old ways were heathen and bad. Mixed-bloods exerted tremendous influence on the tribe. Eventually, they would ascend to the ruling class in Cherokee society, replacing the old form of government" (Mankiller and Wallis 1993, 26).

By 1800, there were many half-, quarter-, and even eighth-blood Cherokees living in the lowlands and along the trade routes. Whites who settled in Cherokee country were mostly Scotch, Irish, and English, and many of the common Cherokee surnames, such as Ross, Blackburn, Taylor, MacGregor, Brown, and Vann, were the result of names inherited through the White male line. "By the 1820s, the mixed-bloods, some of them with blue eyes and light hair, had acquired most of the tribal wealth . . . [and] they held at least 40 percent of the Cherokee government posts. . . . The impact of the mixed-bloods and the influence of Christian missionaries became increasingly evident" (Mankiller and Wallis 1993, 79). The Cherokee census of 1853 listed 16,532 full-bloods and mixed-bloods, 201 Whites intermarried with Cherokees, and 1,592 slaves.

> The more prosperous Cherokees were already on equal terms economically and socially with their White counterparts across the Chattahoochee. They lived in roomy, comfortable houses of brick, frame, and stone. . . . These Cherokees had their furniture and furnishings brought out from the Eastern cities. They wore clothing of the same kind and cut worn by Whites of their economic level. They drove good horses, hitched to fine carriages. They sent their sons and daughters to schools in the [Cherokee] Nation, then to academies and seminaries in South Carolina, Tennessee, and Connecticut. (Fleischmann 1971, 13–14)

As early at the 1820s, the Cherokees, along with the Chickasaws, Choctaws, and Creeks (later, the Seminoles) were becoming known as the Civilized Tribes. These Indian nations had highly developed societies in contrast to the largely illiterate frontier communities in the South. Literacy, education, and the adoption of Western industrial arts and agriculture made them seem civilized to some Whites. In 1819, Congress authorized an annual sum of $10,000 to support and promote the civilization of the Indians. Without fail, the largest proportion of the sum went to the Cherokees. "The five schools in the Cherokee Nation in 1809 had increased to eighteen by 1825. . . . [T]here also were many mission schools" (Mankiller and Wallis 1993, 80).

As more and more White people moved into Cherokee country, the Cherokees became dependent on trade goods, such as knives and hoes made of metal, hatchets, kettles, bolts of cloth, rum, firearms, and ammunition. Guns replaced bows as the primary weapon used for hunting and warfare as the Cherokees moved from subsistence hunting to commercial hunting. Women spent more time than before preparing hides for the deer skin trade. Trade facilitated the movement toward a centralized government, and the position of "trade commissioner," *Wro-setasetow,* came into being, in order to coordinate trade with the colonies.

Log cabins with several rooms began to appear in Cherokee communities, taking the place of traditional dwellings. Cherokees soon became accustomed to settler food and alcohol. They acquired

horses, and some began raising cattle and hogs. Most importantly, the Cherokee ageless concern for keeping the world in balance was altered when the pressure to supply pelts for the deerskin trade resulted in overhunting. Grazing livestock in the canebreaks had a devastating effect on traditional Cherokee basket making.

Slavery, which was unknown before the coming of Whites, also became a feature of Cherokee society when the traders began purchasing Indian prisoners taken in battle. They were sent off to the slave markets to be sold on the block like Africans, where they were then forced to work on colonial plantations, or be shipped off to those in the West Indies. Soon, the Cherokees themselves began to value Black slaves taken as the spoils of war or as runaways. "The British government also presented slaves to influential tribal leaders, calling them 'King's gifts.' During the late eighteenth century, a growing number of the Cherokee elite—mimicking the English colonists—bought and sold slaves for their own use as field workers and servants. By 1790, the Cherokee elite had definitely adopted Black slavery, although the practice never permeated the entire Cherokee Nation" (Mankiller and Wallis 1993, 28).

The spread of European diseases also impacted Cherokee culture and society. In 1738, a smallpox epidemic spread by slave ships killed nearly half of the Cherokee population. Another outbreak occurred in 1739, another in 1759, and again at various times throughout the rest of the eighteenth century. Measles and influenza also ravaged Cherokee settlements. "Many of our spiritual leaders believed the disease [smallpox] was a punishment for having broken ancient tribal laws. . . . Hundreds of our warriors committed suicide after seeing the mutilation and disfigurement that the disease caused to their bodies. Some shot themselves, others cut their throats or stabbed themselves. . . . Many sought relief through death by leaping into huge bonfires. . . . In time, alcohol became even more ruinous than smallpox" (Mankiller and Wallis 1993, 28).

THE CHEROKEE DIASPORA

By 1740, conflicts between Cherokee towns became marked as a result of different Cherokee trade and military alliances made with the competing colonizing nations of Spain, France, and England. France and England went to war in Europe in 1754, the same year Benjamin Franklin assembled colonial representatives at Albany, New York, in an unsuccessful attempt to unite the English colonies in a plan of union and to cement an alliance with the Iroquois against the French. The war between the two imperial powers spilled over into North America where it was called by the English the French and Indian War. It was a war with Indian allies fighting on both sides of the conflict and lasted in North America until 1760. Technically speaking, the Cherokees were allied with England, but through a misunderstanding, Virginia settlers attacked a group of loyal Cherokee warriors returning home, killing twenty-four, scalping and mutilating their bodies. Some Cherokees retaliated against the Virginians in an attempt to restore the balance for those killed and scalped. Some settlers in North Carolina were also killed. From there, the situation deteriorated further, with the Cherokees attacking frontier settlements in South Carolina, and an English army under Colonel Montgomery attacking Cherokee Lower and Middle Towns.

The Cherokees did not understand European-style warfare. Indian wars were sporadic, individualistic affairs, resembling clan retaliation, in order to restore balance. "European warfare was another matter entirely. Europeans fought to obtain territory or to subjugate or even to exterminate entire populations. They brought to America a concept of total war, wherein villages were burned and crops destroyed. . . . Furthermore, they had a fondness for destroying their enemies' homes and stores of food in the middle of winter in order to make the results all the more devastating" (Conley 2005, 52).

The Treaty of Paris was signed February 10, 1763, marking the end of the French and Indian War. The Indian auxiliaries to the conflict were distinguished by their absence from the negotiating table. According to the terms of the treaty, all tribes east of the Mississippi River now came under the complete jurisdiction of England, but the end of the war did nothing to restore peace to the Indian frontier. The English King issued the Proclamation of 1763, making it illegal for the English colonists to cross the Appalachian Mountains into Indian country, but Virginia and South Carolina settlers ignored the Proclamation and began moving onto Cherokee land.

In response to hegemonic pressures from Anglo-American society, the structurally differentiated Cherokee evolved into a political state, adopting many features of Anglo-American culture and its political system. What makes this development especially puzzling is that rather than applauding the Indian achievement, the United States adopted a punitive policy of Indian removal. The policy not only forced the removal of the majority of Cherokee on a Trail of Tears to Indian Territory in 1838 and 1839, but it resulted in dividing the Cherokee Nation into its eastern and western segments. Duane King (2004, 354), an authority on Cherokee history, terms this the Cherokee diaspora. "The saga of the Cherokee in the west reflects a disapora of a people as a result of military conquests in the eighteenth century, treaties with the federal government, discriminatory state laws, military confinement, the forced marches of the removal, the Civil War, land allotment, dissolution of tribal government, economic deprivation in the 1930s, and federal relocation in the 1950s" (King 2004, 354).

The Cherokee diaspora actually started before the Removal Act, as early as 1760 and 1761, when the British armies destroyed the Lower and Middle Towns in the Carolinas, sending "hundreds of refugees westward into the Overhill towns in present-day east Tennessee" (King 2004, 354).

In August of 1794, the Shawnee leader Tecumseh and his Indian and British allies were defeated by the Americans at Fallen Timbers in Ohio. The Cherokees had refused to join in Tecumseh's vision of creating an Indian barrier against further White encroachment, believing that their interests lay elsewhere. Nevertheless, on September 13, 1794, an American infantry company destroyed Cherokee towns, killing about seventy Cherokees, in retaliation for an earlier Cherokee raid on a party of settlers at Muscle Shoals. With their most important towns destroyed and no assistance from their allies, the Cherokees had no choice except to sue for peace. During the American Revolution, Cherokee settlements were repeatedly attacked by the frontier armies of Virginia, North Carolina, South Carolina, and Georgia.

The continual encroachment by the American military and White settlers from the southern colonies persuaded a number of Cherokees to agree to move west. For the remainder of the eighteenth century, many Cherokee moved away from the frontier and began to settle west of the Mississippi River in order to avoid conflict with White settlers. One group living along Chickamauga Creek near present-day Chattanooga, Tennessee, became known as the Chickamaugas. They had fought as allies of the British during the Revolutionary War. They founded Lower Towns near the present Tennessee-Alabama state line, the new towns becoming the staging area from which to launch attacks against frontier settlements. The older towns along the Little Tennessee River, formerly the heart of Cherokee territory, were virtually abandoned by the end of the eighteenth century.

The first pioneers to settle west of the Mississippi River were Cherokees, not Whites. After the first treaty was signed between the Cherokee and the United States at Hopewell, South Carolina, in 1783, some Cherokee families became dissatisfied with the treaty terms. They traveled by dugout canoes to Arkansas, finally settling at a location on the White River. Other Cherokees emigrated to Spanish territory. Among these emigrants were the Chickamaugas who received permission "from the Spanish governor at New Orleans to settle in what was then Spanish territory in the unspoiled hunting grounds in the Arkansas country" (Mankiller and Wallis 1993, 57). While they attempted to gain official recognition of their remaining land base through treaties, Spanish territory provided a refuge for those engaged in the conflict.

"In 1794, a band of Cherokees in present Alabama moved from their home on the Tennessee River to west of Mississippi after a dispute that became known as the Muscle Shoals Massacre. . . . This band of Cherokees was under the leadership of a Cherokee called 'the Bowl.' . . . [He] led his band to desirable land in the valley of the St. Francis River in southeastern Missouri" (Mankiller and Wallis 1993, 57). By 1802, there were about sixty Cherokee families living along the St. Francis River in eastern Arkansas.

Early in 1806, more Cherokees emigrated to Arkansas, taking with them herds of horses and cattle. Catastrophe struck during the winter of 1811–12 when the river valley was rocked by several earthquakes. The event was interpreted by both local Whites and Cherokees as an omen of supernatural displeasure. The Cherokees also believed the quakes were associated with a prophecy by Tecumseh who had warned "that harm would come to Indians who strayed from the path and polluted traditional culture with White influences" (King 2004, 356). In June, a Cherokee prophet, "The Swan," foretold of even greater destruction to the Cherokees should they remain on the St. Francis River. As a result of these prophecies, the Cherokees abandoned their St. Francis River settlements, some moving to the White River, but the majority locating further into Arkansas.

THE LOUISIANA PURCHASE

When Thomas Jefferson became president in 1800, there were already seven hundred thousand White settlers living west of the Appalachian Mountains, including in Ohio, Indiana, and Illinois in the North, and Alabama and Mississippi in the South. The American settlers outnumbered the Indians about eight to one. Jefferson then committed the federal government to promote future removal of the Creeks and the Cherokees from Georgia. With the purchase of Louisiana Territory from France in 1803, a vast new territory became available to the United States. The Louisiana Territory doubled the size of the United States by extending the western frontier from the Appalachian Mountains (which included the traditional Cherokee homeland) across the Mississippi River to the Rocky Mountains. Removal of the eastern and southern Indian nations now became an option, and in 1803, Jefferson recommended to Congress the desirability of removing the resident Indian tribes to west of the Mississippi. Obviously, the goal of assimilating Indians into American culture and society had proven unfeasible due to frontier strife and the insatiable appetite by the ever aggressive Anglo-Americans for Indian lands and resources.

In his message to Congress, Jefferson emphasized two measures that he deemed expedient: first, that the Indians should abandon hunting, and second, that trading houses should be placed among their populations, thus leading to "agriculture, to manufactures and civilization." Congress appropriated $15,000 for that purpose. "Indian removal was necessary for the opening of the vast American lands to agriculture, to commerce, to markets, to money, to the development of the modern capitalist economy. Land was indispensable for all this, and after the Revolution, huge sections of land were bought up by rich speculators, including George Washington and Patrick Henry" (Zinn 2001, 126). Even Jefferson was a land speculator and a merchant, and for that matter, a slaver.

Meanwhile, the Cherokees were adjusting their traditional-based economy to that of the prevailing White society in a remarkable way. As the historian Howard Zinn points out: "With 17,000 Cherokees surrounded by 900,000 Whites in Georgia, Alabama, and Tennessee, the Cherokees decided that survival required adaptation to the Whiteman's world. They became farmers, blacksmiths, carpenters, masons, owners of property. A census of 1826 showed 22,000 cattle, 7,600 horses, 46,000 swine, 726 looms, 2,488 spinning wheels, 172 wagons, 2,943 plows, 10 saw mills, 31 grist mills, 62 blacksmith shops, 8 cotton machines, 18 schools" (Zinn 2001, 136). A government Indian agent declared that the Cherokees were the only people in Arkansas "who appear to have made or are desirous of making any great proficiency in civilization" (King 2004, 356). In 1804, President Jefferson sent Meriwether Lewis and William Clark to explore the newly acquired Louisiana Territory. The Lewis and Clark Corps of Discovery made maps of the new lands and surveyed the Native peoples of the region. The expedition also searched unsuccessfully for a northwest passage, a fabled water route to the Pacific Ocean. An unstated purpose of the expedition, however, was to legitimate the U.S. claim to the new lands under the Doctrine of Christian Nations (Discovery). As European mercantile nations understood international law at the time, it was not enough for a colonizing nation to simply purchase or claim a new territory; the new power must also enter the new land and take possession of it. The Lewis and Clark Expedition legitimated the U.S. claim as the monopolizing trading power. At the same time, according to the Doctrine, the Indigenous nations' "right to the soil" was recognized; therefore, treaties of cession were made with the Indians in order for the colonizer to take actual possession of any of the new lands.

Even larger numbers of Cherokees emigrated to Arkansas in 1807 and 1808 when President Jefferson's resettlement policy was inaugurated, and by 1817, some two to three thousand Cherokees were living in Arkansas. An 1817 treaty "ceded two tracts of land in the east in exchange for an equal parcel of land between the Arkansas and White rivers where most of the Cherokee emigrants lived" (King 2004, 357). Meanwhile, in the Cherokee homeland, the Cherokee Nation divided over the question of removal. In 1819, a new land cession treaty was signed. The number of Cherokees in Arkansas was estimated to be six thousand. Those still remaining in the east and adverse to Removal numbered 12,544.

The voices of women were largely absent from the debate over land cession and removal. "Traditionally, men conducted foreign affairs while women attended to domestic ones. The increasing importance of war and trade in the eighteenth century had magnified this division and shifted political power to men" (Purdue and Green 1995, 122). Nevertheless, Cherokee delegations of women made themselves heard on several occasions on the question of removal when they submitted petitions to the Cherokee National Council in 1817 and 1818. In one petition they said: "We believe the present plan of the General Government to effect our removal West of the Mississippi, and thus obtain our lands for the use of the State of Georgia, to be highly oppressive, cruel and unjust" (Perdue and Green 1995, 126).

Throughout Cherokee history there has always been a strong traditionalist element opposed to land alienation and assimilation. An example is what Champagne terms "the Cherokee fundamentalist movement of 1811–12" led by a mixed-blood prophet named Charley (1992, 103). "All the Cherokee prophets and visionaries were generally fundamentalist, and blamed the loss of game and their ancient lifestyle on the failure of the Cherokee to adhere to the ancient religious beliefs and practices. Charley's special message was that the spiritual 'mother of the nation' had abandoned the Cherokee because they had adopted the agricultural practices and the grain mills of the Americans. The Great Spirit was also displeased that the Cherokee had not kept out American intruders and had not protected Cherokee holy sites" (Champagne 1992, 103). Charley prophesied that non-believers would be destroyed in a hailstorm, but when the prediction failed to materialize, Charley was discredited.

Cherokee leaders have usually listened to their more conservative, or traditionalist citizens. "Between 1810 and 1827, the conservative majority rallied behind Path Killer, the principal chief, and when John Ross . . . was elected principal chief in 1828, he continued to ask the opinions of the conservative leaders and to act in the interest of the conservative majority" (Champagne 1992, 143).

In May of 1828, under pressure from Washington, a delegation of western Cherokee ceded their Arkansas land in exchange for land in the newly established Indian Territory. The delegation was subsequently accused by other Cherokees of "selling out" in a fraudulent treaty, and the U.S. Senate hurriedly ratified the new treaty only three weeks after it had been signed. Nevertheless, "the people who first settled in western Arkansas and then moved in 1828 to northeastern Oklahoma established a distinct Cherokee society that numbered about four thousand by the 1830s" (Purdue and Green 1995, 121).

By 1828, there were already between eighty and one hundred Cherokee families living in Spanish Texas. They were welcomed by the Spaniards as buffers against American encroachment. "Throughout the 1820s and 1830s, they sought legitimacy for their residency, frequently sending delegations to confer with government officials" (King 2004). In spite of the fact that they signed a provisional treaty with Texas in 1836, "they found themselves caught between the conflict between the Mexicans and Americans and between other Indians and non-Indians" (King 2004, 361). Texas separated from Mexico in the same year and declared itself the Lone Star Republic. In May of 1839, the Cherokees were told to leave Texas by President Mirabeau Buonaparte Lamar. Military resistance failed, and the Cherokee survivors dispersed, some fleeing to Mexico, some finding homes among other Texas Indian tribes, and still others to the Cherokee Nation along the Canadian and Arkansas rivers.

EVOLUTION OF THE CHEROKEE STATE

In response to the hegemonic pressures of, first, England, and then the new United States, the Cherokees, for their own protection and survival, evolved into a formidable political state—an Indian republic of a new type. The evolution of the Cherokee state took place in the following way.

In the early 1700s, the Cherokees were still living in the Smoky Mountain area of the contemporary states of South Carolina, Tennessee, Kentucky, and Georgia. On the eastern mountain slopes of the Savannah River system were the Lower Cherokees. On the opposite side of the mountains were the Overhill settlements. Between the two sections were the Middle and Valley settlements, tucked along the Tennessee and Hiwassee river systems. Several dialects were spoken in the sixty-odd settlements. The main coresident unit, however, was the village, not the settlement. Settlements were small, but the village could comprise one or more settlements and number between three hundred fifty and six hundred people. Gearing (1962, 1) believes there were thirty to forty of these politically organized, autonomous villages.

One of the functions of the Cherokee village was to oversee important ceremonies, especially the harvest ceremony, the New Year ritual in October, and the annual renewal ceremony. In between these ritual events were the formal council sessions. "Villagers organized themselves into a single whole by becoming a set of seven clan sections and by activating also another organized group that cut across clan lines, the body of elders or 'beloved men'" (Gearing 1962, 23). There was no formal political system beyond the village. The Cherokees were a jural community, that is, the administration of justice and of rights and obligations was handled solely through the kinship system.

The Cherokee villages, although autonomous and recognizing no higher political authority, did not usually wage war on one another. It was left to the clan system to settle disputes, including blood revenge in the case of murder. By 1720, however, mainly in response to pressures from the prevailing imperial power of Great Britain, the Cherokees slowly transformed their jural community into what Gearing (1962) terms "a Cherokee priest-state." Later, however, in response to the state of belligerency on the frontier, prominent warriors were brought into the tribal councils, and "by the 1760s and 1770s, Cherokee priests were excluded from political and military decisions making. . . . The head warrior of the nation usurped the role of head priest" (Champagne 1989, 42).

It is clear that "pressures from White contact, especially stemming from the deerskin trade with South Carolina, led to an extension of the war organization to deal tribally with external affairs and to a more centralized form of government" (Fogelson 2004, 346–47). Further secularization of Cherokee government continued after 1795 when the United States replaced Great Britain as the dominating power. Finally, in 1827, the Cherokees formally adopted a constitutional form of government modeled after that of the United States.

"Today, Cherokee is the seventh most populous Native language north of Mexico," and it "is most frequently used publicly in religious services" (King 1996, 95). The Cherokees are notable for becoming the first Native American nation to become literate in its own language. This is due to the work of a native intellectual, Sequoyah. Between 1809 and 1821, Sequoyah (Charles Gist or Guess) devised a syllabary for writing the Cherokee language using eighty-five symbols for the basic syllables. By 1832, about half of the Cherokees could read and write in Sequoyah's alphabet. Literacy enabled the Cherokee to codify their laws, publish newspapers, read the Bible, and correspond with one another. It allowed the preservation of esoteric ritual and medical knowledge, and became an important cultural marker of Cherokee national identity.

There are several causes for the evolution of the Cherokee political structure from autonomous villages into a nation-state. The British, for example, found it convenient to deal with a single, central authority to represent Cherokee villages in their trade relations and diplomatic negotiations. It was also in the interest of the Cherokees to centralize tribal political authority, because relations with White settlements were anything but peaceful. Cherokee leaders sought to protect their people from collective punishment and the interruption of trade whenever a trader or settler was killed by a vengeful

Sequoyah.

Cherokee warrior. This had repeatedly resulted in a series of crises for Cherokee leaders. Gearing (1962, 87–88) explains the problem: "One Cherokee, or a few, had harmed a trader; then trade had been cut off. In two of the instances, the loss of the ammunition supply was especially damaging because of a war with neighboring tribes. . . . In short, South Carolina behaved as if all villages together were a political entity sharing group responsibility for the actions by any of its members."

Another stage in Cherokee political development occurred following the American Revolution. "After 1795 the Cherokee responded to American threats to territory and political autonomy with conscious political centralization and economic development. Between 1810 and 1827, in direct response to American political threats, the Cherokee created state political institutions as an instrument to help ensure Cherokee national survival and political autonomy" (Champagne 1983, 758). The Cherokees had lost their hunting lands north of the Ohio River, and by 1800, their seventy-five towns and villages were concentrated east and north of the Creeks in south-central Tennessee, northwestern Georgia, and northeastern Alabama. In about one generation, a new political structure was formed through a concerted action of elders and younger men,

"sometimes assisted by delegations of women whose place continued high in Cherokee affairs" (Spicer 1969, 59). The Cherokees adapted the southern concept of "states' rights" to their own view of tribal sovereignty. This early Cherokee state survived until 1907, when it was unilaterally abolished by the United States government.

When the Cherokees established a central government in 1793, they formalized the titles of principal chief and deputy chief. At the apex of the new political organization were the Most Beloved Men: Path Killer, principal chief; Charles Hicks, the second Most Beloved Man; The Ridge, speaker of the council; a young man named John Ross who later played a major leadership role in Cherokee affairs; and others of lesser importance.

In 1808, they wrote the legislation of the national council and developed a body of codified laws. The first law, passed in 1798, established "regulating companies" called Light Horse Guards, for the maintenance of law and order in all Cherokee territory. In 1810, they legislated against the ancient custom of clan revenge for all crimes except horse theft. This was followed in 1817 with the establishment of a bicameral legislature consisting of a National Committee and a traditional National Council.

In October, 1820, the national council made several major changes in Cherokee governmental organization. The Cherokee territory was divided into eight districts with a legislative body to meet each October at the newly created capital of Newtown.

The legislature was composed of two bodies, the National Committee of thirteen members (forming the upper house), while the National Council (lower house) comprised thirty-two members, four elected from each district. The National Committee oversaw the expenditures of the treasury, heard claims against the Cherokee government, and initiated legislation. The members of the National Committee were elected by the National Council, and the decisions of the National Committee were subject to its approval. The two houses elected the two head chiefs, or executive branch, for terms of four years, and all laws needed the approval of both houses and the two head chiefs. The council also appointed a national treasurer. "In 1825, the council declared that the Cherokee Nation was common property and prohibited its sale under any conditions without authorization from the national council" (Champagne 1992, 136).

In each of the eight districts there was a council house where elected officials met twice a year, and where a judge for the district could transact business. "All the district courts held trial by jury, and were assigned a marshal, constables, and district officers. The Cherokee laws were few, but order was maintained according to the treaty agreements, which were designed to keep the peace on the frontier" (Champagne 1992, 136). Among the laws passed were prohibitions against gambling and intemperance. A national Supreme Court was established in 1822, ten years before the state of Georgia had one. It functioned as an appeals court for the district and circuit courts.

Formal education was encouraged. "The first schools opened in the Cherokee Nation in 1801, and Christian missionaries were welcomed as long as their primary focus was academics instead of religion" (King 2004, 357). By 1825 there were eight schools operated by the American Board of Missions alone, and perhaps another five schools run by other denominations. Thus, a cadre of formally trained young men and women began to play a central role in Cherokee political life.

"American pressure for removal was a major factor that mobilized the Cherokee to centralize and differentiate their government institutions further; Georgia's threats of removal provoked the Cherokee into forming a constitutional government" (Champagne 1992, 137).

A constitution modeled after that of the United States was approved July 26, 1827. It provided for a separation of powers between the executive, judicial, and legislative branches of government. A legal code regulated criminal and economic concerns. A new constitution was formalized on July 26, 1827.

> It created the separation of powers among legislative, executive, and judicial branches. The general council was bicameral, with both houses having elected members. Whereas the national committee had formerly been appointed by the council, now each district elected one member to the committee and three members to the national council. The general council elected the principal chief and the second chief every four years. The court system was maintained and a code of criminal law was defined. . . . A bill of rights granted freedom of religion and the right to trial by jury. (Champagne 1992, 139–40)

At the top of the national structure were two Beloved Men, a president of the National Committee, and a speaker of the National Council. A national capital at New Echota was built in 1825, and a national printing press established. Elias Boudinot became the editor of the *Cherokee Phoenix* newspaper in 1828. In a letter to John Calhoun, a Moravian missionary declared the Cherokees "the most advanced in civilization of any of the Indian tribes without exception" (King 2004, 358).

Despite the remarkable transformation of the Cherokees into an Indian republic, tragedy struck in 1830 with the passage of the Indian Removal Act. This racist policy, spearheaded by President Andrew Jackson and White southern planters, was aimed at solving what they viewed as the Indian problem by forcing Indians nations in the east and southeast to relocate west of the Mississippi River to Indian Territory. Gold had been discovered in Cherokee territory, and the Cherokees came under great pressure from the State of Georgia and its special interests to vacate their rich lands, resources, and plantations. The Cherokee Nation mounted a legal battle, hiring excellent lawyers to represent them on the federal level in countering Georgia's attempt to extend its authority into Cherokee affairs. This eventually led to two major Supreme Court decisions: *Cherokee Nation v. Georgia* (1831), and *Worcester v. Georgia* (1832), which are explained below.

OPPRESSION BY THE STATE OF GEORGIA

Throughout the early 1800s, following the War of 1812, there were increasing pressures on the Cherokees to sell their land. An 1817 treaty "required the Cherokees either to remove westward to present-day Arkansas or to remain in the east but take individual land allotments and live under the laws of the American states" (Champagne 1992, 131). Andrew Jackson, who later became president of the United States, was the chief negotiator. "For the remainder of 1817 and during 1818, American agents, settlers, and the sates of Tennessee, Georgia, and Alabama continued to pressure the Cherokee to remove west. The Cherokee must either emigrate or assimilate" (Champagne 1992, 132). Two years later, the Cherokees were able to secure a compromise treaty which superseded the treaty of 1817. White intruders would be removed from Cherokee territory, but the Cherokees were forced to cede six thousand square miles of land. The Cherokees believed that the treaty of 1819 was a final settlement with the United States, and they were resolved to sell no more land. Between 1819 and 1835 they held fast.

"In the 1820s, it was thought that the formation of an extensive Indian colonization zone in the wilderness area west of the Mississippi would stop once and for all, the clash of cultures over land" (Waldman 2000, 205–6). The proposed solution appealed to both the pro- and anti-Indian constituencies. Those sympathetic to the Indians believed it would create a permanent Indian homeland beyond the Mississippi, closed to White settlement. Those hostile to the Indians argued that it would open new lands to Whites in the East and confine all the Indians to just one area beyond the western frontier. With the support of Congress, Secretary of War John Calhoun in the Monroe administration delineated a new Indian Country in 1825, and by the 1830s, the Jackson administration was calling this area the Indian Territory.

Pressure for removal of the eastern Cherokees came especially from certain southern states, which had drawn their state boundaries through the Cherokee Nation as if it did not exist, even though Cherokee sovereignty had been recognized by federal treaty "for as long as the sun shines and rivers flow." Georgia, South Carolina, and Virginia were among the first to ratify the new U.S. Constitution whose boundaries conflicted with Cherokee territory. North Carolina followed, and then the new states of Kentucky, Alabama, and Tennessee. All were "admitted to the Union, and their boundaries accepted, even though they too ignored Cherokee sovereignty" (Fleischmann 1971, 18).

Georgia was particularly aggressive regarding their land claim to Cherokee territory. The state had surrendered to the federal government its extravagant territorial claim extending west all the way to the Mississippi River. In return, Georgia received a cash payment and a promise that the federal government would extinguish Cherokee and Creek title within Georgia's boundaries. Yet, few Cherokees emigrated from their traditional territory. After ten years of waiting, Georgia grew impatient and began pressing the federal government to discharge its obligation to the state. When Andrew Jackson was elected president in 1828, he promptly ended federal vacillation. Jackson was a seasoned Indian fighter, known as Sharp Knife to the Indians. He told Georgia officials to "build a fire" under the Indians. "When it gets hot enough, they'll move" (Fleischmann 1971, 20). The Georgia legislature accordingly enacted a law preempting Cherokee sovereignty and, at the same time, denying the Cherokee Nation any legal protection within the state.

When Jackson took office as president, he made his position clear in a message to Congress on the issue of Indian relocation: "'I informed the Indians inhabiting parts of Georgia and Alabama that their attempts to establish an independent government would not be countenanced by the Executive of the United States, and advised them to emigrate beyond the Mississippi or submit to the laws of those States.' Congress moved quickly to pass a removal bill" (Zinn 2001, 137–38). "After bitter debate, Jackson's backers in Congress pushed through by a narrow margin, the Indian Removal Act of 1830, authorizing the president to establish districts west of the Mississippi to exchange for Indian-held lands in the Southeast. Jackson immediately signed the bill into law" (Mankiller and Wallis 1993, 87).

Gold was discovered in Cherokee territory in Georgia the same year Jackson took office, and thousands of Whites invaded, destroying Indian property and staking out their claims. "Jackson ordered federal troops to remove them, but also ordered Indians as well as Whites to stop mining. When he removed the troops, the Whites returned, and Jackson said he could not interfere with Georgia authority. . . . The White invaders seized land and stock, forced Indians to sign leases, beat up Indians who protested, sold alcohol to weaken resistance, killed game which Indians needed for food" (Zinn 2001, 134).

One month before Jackson won the 1828 presidential election, John Ross was elected principal chief of the Cherokee Nation, an office he held until his death in 1868. One of the first issues Ross had to deal with was the White-path Rebellion. White-path "was a full-blood member of the National Council, and in 1828, in an echo of the message of Tecumseh and of the Red Stick movement among the Creeks, he began to advocate a complete rejection of all White culture, including Christianity and the new written laws, and a return to the old ways of the Cherokees" (Conley 2005, 132). He soon had a large band of followers known as Red Sticks.

Beloved by his people and a true Cherokee nationalist, John Ross was actually seven-eighths Scot, but in Cherokee culture one's identity depended solely on clan affiliation. Since Ross's mixed-blood mother was a member of the Bird Clan, Ross was a Cherokee by definition and also a member of the Bird Clan. John Ross, with fair skin, reddish hair, and blue eyes, was well educated and an eloquent speaker. Before being elected to office, he had married a Cherokee woman, established a trading post, operated a ferry, and become a successful merchant and planter.

As early as 1817, John Ross was already involved in Cherokee politics, helping to draft the Cherokee Constitution. He opposed the ceding of any more Cherokee land to Whites. On the other hand, he "favored taking 'the White man's road' in the hope that an acceleration in 'acculturation' would fortify the Cherokee Nation, bolstering its position in the eyes of White Americans" (Mankiller and Wallis 1993, 86). Unfortunately, this policy of accommodation weakened Cherokee cultural integration by strengthening the influence of the mixedbloods and diminishing the status of Cherokee women when "the clan system and the timehonored practice of descent through maternal lines began to erode. The Cherokee Constitution further limited women's rights by excluding them from all government offices and prohibiting them from voting" (Mankiller and Wallis 1993, 86).

In the early 1830s, when John Ross became the principal chief, the question of Cherokee sovereign status made its way to the U.S. Supreme Court. The Cherokee attorneys argued that the State of Georgia could not legally enforce its laws in sovereign Cherokee territory, and that the Jackson government had no right to forcibly evict Cherokee people from their own land. But the Court's ruling on March 18, 1831 by Chief Justice John Marshall sidestepped the issue. The landmark ruling of *Cherokee Nation v. Georgia* (1831) redefined Indian political status as a *limited sovereignty*. Chief Justice Marshall ruled that the Indians were "dependent nations," and "that the Cherokee Nation was not a foreign state in the sense that the Cherokees could initiate an original action against the Sate of Georgia in the Supreme Court" (Deloria 1985, 114).

The following year the Court appeared to reverse itself with a second ruling, which was favorable to Cherokee sovereignty. When White missionaries in the Cherokee territory refused to take an oath of allegiance to the state of Georgia, they were arrested. The missionary Samuel Worcester was among those jailed by Georgia. His case was appealed to the Supreme Court in *Worcester v. Georgia* (1832). The Court ordered Worcester freed on the grounds that only the federal government, and not the states, could treat with the Indian nations. "The Court found that Indian nations were capable of making treaties, and that under the United States Constitution, such treaties were the supreme law of the land" (Mankiller and Walliss 1993, 90). But President Jackson refused to enforce the court order and is said to have declared: "John Marshall has made his law, now let him enforce it."

When Jackson failed to enforce the 1832 *Worcester v. Georgia* Court decision favorable to Cherokee sovereignty, the fate of the Indian nation was sealed, and the oppression of the Cherokees intensified: Georgia law forbade the assembly of Cherokees in groups of three or more for any purpose, including religious services. Georgia confiscated the Cherokee national newspaper, the *Cherokee Phoenix*, declaring it subversive. It also proceeded "with a survey of Cherokee lands, the land lottery, and the dispossession of the Cherokee from their own homes" (King 2004, 358). It confiscated Cherokee school buildings, council houses, printing plant for the newspaper and books, and the property of Cherokee leaders who opposed removal. It instituted lotteries to distribute Cherokee property and permitted "Pony clubs" "to raid Cherokee plantations and drive off livestock, to kidnap slaves in the fields, and to destroy crops" (Fleischmann 1971, 22).

The federal government aided Georgia in the harassment by withholding Cherokee annuities and preventing the Cherokees from working their gold deposits. Teams of federal commissioners pressured the Cherokees to accept a treaty of removal.

The two court decisions and Andrew Jackson's reelection in 1832 were enough to convince some Cherokees to move west on their own volition and join the Old Settlers who had emigrated earlier. Those who thought that their chances of remaining in the East was a lost cause, and who advocated negotiation with the government commissioners, became known as the Treaty Party. These leaders included Elias Boudinot, editor of the *Cherokee Phoenix*, Major Ridge, John Ridge, and several others, including John Ross' brother, Andrew Ross. They were among a group of twenty Cherokees who signed the Treaty of New Echota requiring the Cherokee Nation to give up its rich lands in the Southeast. The Removal Act authorized the president to negotiate with the eastern tribes to relocate west of the Mississippi River. Clearly, the designated tribes, including the Cherokees, were coerced in making the journey in what could only be described as an ethnic cleansing operation. Under the treaty's terms, the Cherokees were allowed two years to prepare for removal and then abandon their homeland for Indian Territory west of the Mississippi. In exchange, they were to receive almost fourteen million acres in the West and $5 million to pay all depredation claims and the cost of moving.

"Whatever their motivations, members of the Ridge Party had little support within the Cherokee Nation. Although the tribe was becoming more divided on the issue, the majority of Cherokees adamantly opposed removal. They remained loyal to Chief John Ross and the Ross Party" (Mankiller and Wallis 1993, 91). The Cherokee National Council denounced the treaty as fraudulent, and Ross journeyed to Washington with a protest petition signed by thousands of Cherokee citizens, but President Jackson would not be moved. Congress ratified the removal treaty on May 23, 1836, with a one-vote majority, the northern senators generally voting against removal, and the South supporting it. Ross and several others were briefly arrested for their opposition to removal, and remained in chains for almost two weeks before their release without charges having been filed against them. Not a single elected tribal official signed the contentious treaty of removal, and there was overwhelming opposition among the seventeen thousand tribal population. However, as a result of the fraudulent treaty signed only by the Ridge faction, the Cherokee Nation was forced to relinquish all of its remaining land east of the Mississippi River for $5 million.

In 1835, submitting to Georgia pressure, a small number of the Treaty Party led by The Ridge emigrated, and later, between 1838 and 1839, the majority of the Cherokees under John Ross's leadership reluctantly trekked to Indian Territory. One fourth of the Cherokee population died on the trail as a result of the U.S. government's ethnic cleansing policy. Among those who died on the journey westward was Aualie Ross, the wife of Chief Ross. Cherokee survivors who hid in the hills to avoid removal later became recognized as the Eastern Band of Cherokee.

THE TRAIL OF TEARS

The Trail of Tears means literally "the trail where they cried" in the Cherokee language. "In the roundup and in the stockades, and on the journey of over eight hundred miles, 4,000 Cherokees—more than one-fifth of their Nation—died of cholera, dysentery, fever, exposure, improper care of mothers giving birth, and, especially in the aged, loss of the will to survive" (Fleischmann 1971, 3). An estimated sixty-four villages were affected in which lived about sixteen thousand to seventeen thousand inhabitants. By extension, the Trail of Tears encompassed the cruel fate of all of the Five Civilized Tribes, in which over fifteen thousand Indians died in the forced removal to the Indian Territory. In late 1831, thirteen thousand Choctaws began the dangerous journey, dying by the hundreds on the trail to the Indian Territory. The Chickasaws

followed. "As for the Cherokees, they faced a set of laws passed by Georgia: their lands were taken, their government abolished, all meetings prohibited. Cherokees advising others not to migrate were to be imprisoned. Cherokees could not testify in court against any White. Cherokees could not dig for gold recently discovered on their land" (Zinn 2001, 139). Yet Georgia's unjust laws and policies violated Cherokee sovereignty as guaranteed in their treaties with the United Sates.

In preparing for removal, the government appointed the Stokes Commission to negotiate new treaties to settle the disputes over land between the immigrant Whites and southern tribes like the Cherokees. Of course, these treaties were unfavorable to the Indian nations in question. The Dragoon Expedition and other military units were then ordered to pacify the resident tribes, and to enforce the new treaties and land cessions. Georgia, Alabama, and Mississippi, belatedly ignoring the 1832 *Worcester v. Georgia* decision, began passing laws to extend their states' rule over the Indians and their lands.

"On May 23, 1838, the United States Army under the command of General Winfield Scott and augmented by militia units from the states of Georgia, Tennessee, Alabama, and North Carolina, to a total strength of 9,494 men, began evicting from their homes 19,000 Cherokee Indians and driving them into stockades" (Fleischmann 1971, 3). The Cherokees were incredulous, scarcely believing that civilized people like themselves, many of them their own relatives, would actually carry out the threats, but on May 23, 1838, the roundup began.

Under Scott's orders the troops were disposed at various points throughout the Cherokee country, where stockade forts were erected for gathering in and holding the Indians preparatory to removal. From these, squads of troops were sent to search out with rifle and bayonet every small cabin hidden away in the coves or by the sides of mountain streams, to seize and bring in as prisoners all the occupants, however or wherever they might be found. Families at dinner were startled by the sudden gleam of bayonets in the doorway and rose up to be driven with blows and oaths along the weary miles of trail that led to the stockade. Men were seized in their fields or going along the road, women were taken from their [spinning] wheels and children from their play. In many cases, on turning for one last look, as they crossed the ridge, they saw their homes in flames, fired by the lawless rabble that followed on the heels of the soldiers to loot and pillage. So keen were the outlaws on the scent that in some instances they were driving off the cattle and other stock of the Indians almost before the soldiers had fairly startled their owners in the other direction. (Mooney 1975, 124)

There were "many reports of soldiers dragging Cherokees from their cabins and fields at bayonet point. Homes were looted and crops burned, women and girls were raped. Mixed-blood girls, whom the white soldiers found more desirable, were passed from man to man like bottles of whiskey" (Mankiller and Wallis 1993, 93). "Wagons hired by the Army to haul clothing, bedding, and cooking utensils, from Cherokee homes to the stockades, were seized by roving bands of White men. . . . On the better plantations, men with picks and shovels opened graves in family burial grounds, hoping to find silver and gold ornaments thought to have been buried with the dead" (Fleischmann 1971, 52). In the stockades, sanitation facilities were miserable, consisting of slit trenches, with the camps reeking of excrement, and flies passing from the excrement to food being served. Water supplies were inadequate, if not actually dangerous. "Measles, fevers, whooping cough, chicken pox, dysentery, cholera, swept through the stockades killing Cherokees by the hundreds. Babies were born with almost no chance of survival" (Fleischmann 1971, 61).

The Hitchcock Mission

The forced removal of the Cherokee Nation began in 1838. A Georgia volunteer, who later became a Confederate Army colonel, declared: "I fought through the War between the States, and have seen men shot to pieces by the thousands, but the Cherokee Removal was the cruelest work I ever knew" (Fleischmann 1971, 54). Meanwhile, leaders of the United States were engaged in a "blame game." "Congressmen blamed each other: one side was blamed for ratifying a fraudulent treaty, the other for encouraging the Cherokees to believe they would not have to move. Georgians blamed the Cherokees for not moving during the two-year period of grace. The Army blamed the politicians and the dry weather. Cherokees blamed Andrew Jackson" (Fleischmann 1971, 61).

Although it was denounced in American and European newspapers and hotly debated in the halls of Congress, the ethnic cleansing operation of the southern Indian nations still went forward. The removal was marked by graft and corruption. After confinement in the stockades was completed, several small contingents of Cherokee emigrants set out for the Territory in June under military supervision.

Their experience on the Trail was brutal and devastating, having been marked by deprivation, sickness, deaths of many children, and desertions. This led Cherokee leaders acting for the National Council, two days after the third contingent had left, to propose to General Scott that the emigration be suspended, on the promise that in the autumn the Indians would conduct their own removal. General Scott, anxious to spare the military from condemnation, eagerly accepted the offer. The third contingent, having heard of the new development, now demanded they be allowed to return. Nathan Smith, the Superintendent of Emigration, reported that "they continued to desert some almost every night. . . . These people will have over 300 miles to travel to reach their old homes, and many of them women and children must suffer extremely for want of something to eat" (Fleischmann 1971, 59).

When the Cherokees under John Ross prepared to organize their own emigration to Indian Territory, they passed a resolution once again rejecting the fraudulent 1835 removal treaty, and agreed to retain their constitution and laws upon arriving in their new homeland. The Cherokee emigrants were divided into fourteen parties of about one thousand persons each. Leaders were chosen, a police force organized to oversee the journey, and overland routes were mapped out. The Cherokee leadership decided to increase the number of horses and oxen needed for better transportation to avoid the deaths and deprivation suffered by the earlier emigration parties, even though having to pay for it themselves. Congress, on the other hand, had assumed that most of the emigrants would walk. After a long and arduous journey, the detachments under Chief John Ross arrived at Fort Smith, Indian Territory, in January, February, and March, 1839. Ross recorded that 13,149 members of the Cherokee Nation emigrated under his direction. There were also a few Whites and hundreds of refugees on the Trail who were of African ancestry, free black people and slaves.

It is estimated that 2,500 died in the initial roundup and in the stockades, and about 1,500 died on the Trail of Tears. Altogether, about 4,000 died. More than a thousand evaded capture or escaped, and remained in the mountains to become the nucleus of the Eastern Band of Cherokee.

An irony of Removal was the fact that the federal government charged the tribes for their own removal expenses, the cost of food and provisions, and payments to contractors. These expenses were deducted from the money promised to the tribes for giving up their lands. The job of feeding and transporting the relocated tribes were given out to private contractors, who were friends and relatives of government officials. Much of the suffering and deaths were due to these corrupt contractors who enriched themselves at the Indians' expense.

The abuses suffered by the southern tribes on the Trail of Tears led to the appointment of the Hitchcock Commission in 1841. The Commission's investigation found evidence of "bribery, perjury and forgery, short weights, issues of spoiled meat and grain, and every conceivable subterfuge was employed by designing White men" (Gibson 1980, 338). Once the exhaustive report was submitted to Washington, however, it vanished with the excuse that too many friends of the administration were involved to permit it to become available to Congress or the public.

The early detachments of emigrants to Indian Territory had faced the ravages of drought, but by the time of the Ross party, massive rains plagued the emigrant Cherokees. One eyewitness, a non-Native, was told by "the inhabitants on the road where the Indians passed, that they buried fourteen and fifteen at every stopping place" due to illness and deprivation (Fleischmann 1971, 69). President Martin Van Buren saw things differently. In his December 4, 1838, Message to Congress, he declared: "It affords me sincere pleasure to be able to apprise you of the entire removal of the Cherokee Nation of Indians to their new homes west of the Mississippi. The measures authorized by Congress with a view to the long-standing controversy with them have had the happiest effects, and they have emigrated without any apparent reluctance" (Fleischmann 1971, 65).

INDIAN TERRITORY

Indian Territory originally encompassed the present-day states of Nebraska, Kansas, and Oklahoma. In the years before 1854, the Territory extended "from the Red River to the Missouri, and from the state lines of Arkansas, Missouri, and Iowa to the 100th meridian," the western boundary of the United States at the time (Waldman 2000, 206). In the northern portion, many local tribes, such as the Osage and Kansa, were resettled onto smaller territories to make room for the eastern relocatees. Tribes from the Old Northwest were also settled on this portion of the Indian Territory and included the Potawatomis, Peorias, Wyandots, and Kaskaskias. Other Old Northwest groups, such as the Kickapoos, Delawares, Shawnees, and Sac and Fox, were relocated first in Missouri and Iowa, and then sub-

sequently forced to relocate a second time onto this segment of the Territory. The region south of these groups were given to the Cherokees and the other four Civilized Tribes, the Choctaws, Creeks, Chickasaws, and Seminoles. Those tribes of the western Plains continued to range in their traditional territories, at times coming into conflict with the relocated tribes from the East and the South. To the north of the Indian Territory, in the Missouri and Platte river valleys, were the border tribes, the Iowas, Otos, Missouris, Omahas, and Pawnees. They inhabited the eastern margins of the Great Plains along the major river systems. Further north were the equestrian hunters of the Great Plains—the Western Sioux, Cheyennes, and Arapahoes. (See Figure 6.2)

Added to this conflicting cultural mix was the fact that two of the more heavily traveled routes to the West transected Indian Territory: the Santa Fe Trail, a trader's road, and the Oregon-California Trail, an immigrant road to the Mormon communities in the Great Basin, the Oregon Country, and California. The influx of Whites along these trails added to the difficulty of adjustment by the relocated tribes. Since there was no overall territorial government, military troops and forts sprang up to supervise the tribes and White immigrant travelers and traders. The southern portion of the Territory was divided into three parts: the Cherokees in the north, the Creeks in the center, and the Choctaws in the south. These boundaries were modified somewhat during the late 1830s when the Seminoles and Chickasaws were also relocated to the Indian Territory. "While never a territory in the political sense, it was owned and ruled by the five autonomous Indian republics known as the Cherokee, Choctaw, Chickasaw, Creek or Muskogee, and Seminole nations" (Debo 1968, 3).

Internal Conflicts

Upon arrival in the West, the Cherokees were far from being united. Their population consisted of several divergent groups: the Old Settlers who had emigrated earlier in 1810 and 1817, the Treaty Party, and the Ross Party. The Old Settlers, mainly planters, about eight thousand strong, already had a government in place. They were joined by about two thousand members of the Treaty or Ridge Party who, for the most part, had emigrated voluntarily after approving the 1835 Treaty of New Echota. Third were the members of the Ross Party, who followed Chief John Ross in opposing the treaty, and "expected their government, which represented . . . a clear majority of the Cherokee people, to be transplanted intact from the east" (King 2004, 361). Another element in the

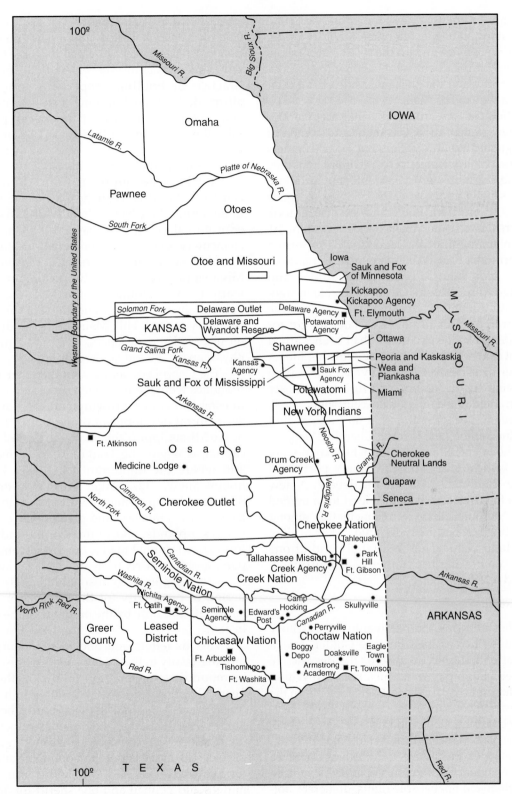

Figure 6.2 Indian Territory before 1854.

factional mix were the Kewetoowahs, who had migrated along with the Cherokee majority under Ross. They were bitter toward the treaty party whom they blamed for their betrayal in signing the fraudulent 1835 treaty, and the subsequent deaths of their relatives on the Trail of Tears.

The Ross Party wanted all tribal members to adopt a new system of government and a code of laws to regulate the entire nation. But the Old Settlers and the Treaty Party joined forces, claiming that they had already established a suitable government. Although several attempts were made to reconcile differences, more than one hundred deaths took place before the factional violence ended. On June 10, 1839, members of all of the factions met to form a new government, but no agreement was reached. Two days later, John Ridge, Elias Boudinot, and Major Ridge were assassinated for their role in signing the fraudulent 1835 treaty. Stand Watie, the younger brother of Boudinot (who later fought for the Confederacy in the Civil War), had been warned of the plot and was able to escape with his life. A month later the Cherokee Council voted amnesty to the surviving treaty signers, and in July, amnesty was also granted to the unknownexecutioners.

For several years the threat of an internal civil war remained among the feuding Cherokee factions. By 1846, however, John Ross and his party were forced to compromise with the Treaty party and accept the fraudulent New Echota Treaty. A new treaty was then signed which provided for a unified Cherokee Nation. Calling for reconciliation among the competing factions, Ross declared: "We are all of the household of the Cherokee family and of one blood . . . embracing each other as Countrymen, friends and relatives" (King 2004, 361).

Cherokee Golden Age

The decades following their arrival in the Territory are often described as the Cherokee Golden Age, a period that ended only because of the destructive forces unleashed in the American Civil War. Within months after the arrival of the last detachments on the Trail of Tears, a constitutional convention was held and a new constitution was adopted on September 6, 1839. An act was passed which stated: "We, the people comprising of the Eastern and Western Cherokee Nation, in National Convention assembled, by virtue of our original and unalienable rights, do hereby solemnly and mutually agree to form ourselves into one body politic, under the style and title of the Cherokee Nation" (quoted in Mankiller and Wallis 1993, 120).

Tahlequah was made the seat of the new Cherokee Nation capital, and a new tribal constitution legislated, which provided for three branches of government as in the old constitution. The Cherokee practice of holding property in common was affirmed. A national printing press was established, and a revived tribal newspaper began publishing. John Ross was elected Principal Chief of the resurrected Cherokee Nation, a position which he held until his death on August 1, 1866.

A Cherokee Supreme Court building was constructed in 1844. With the release of federal funds under terms of the New Echota Treaty, an impressive educational system was set up that included 144 elementary schools and a bilingual curriculum. They founded some of the first schools west of the Mississippi River. In 1851, two institutions of higher learning were founded, the Male Seminary in Tahlequah, the capital, and the Cherokee Female Seminary in Park Hill. Many of the graduates went on to practice as teachers, lawyers, ministers, and physicians in the Indian Territory.

The Cherokees, along with the other four tribal republics were the first, even preceding the Texans, to establish cotton-growing and the now familiar agricultural development of the United States west of the Mississippi. Tahlequah, the Cherokee Nation capital, is where the Trail of Tears ended in 1839, and where the immigrant Cherokees built their homes anew. "Like other Western pioneers, the Southern Indians, many with slave labor, established farms, ranches, and plantations in the virgin valleys, uplands, and prairies of the Indian Territory. They founded towns, businesses, and newspapers, and began river steamer, stage, and freight transport systems" (Gibson 1980, 339). It was a period of prosperity for the Cherokees, a Golden Age shattered only by the outbreak of the Civil War in 1861.

Various letters and documents, many by non-Indians, testify to the achievements of the Cherokees in rebuilding their nation following the Trail of Tears. Ethan Allen Hitchcock noted in his journal, during a visit in 1841, the well-built Cherokee log homes with their ample fields and livestock. Regarding Cherokee government, he wrote: ". . . The people elect the members of the Committee and Council for two years; they elect the sheriffs also, two committees and council and one sheriff for each of the eight districts. The people elect the principal chief and assistant principal chief; and the committee and council act upon the nomination of the judges by the principal chief. They have a Supreme Court and Circuit Courts and other inferior Courts" (Perdue and Green 1995, 171).

The Indian Territory, despite its name, never possessed an integrated territorial government like other U.S. territories. Thus, the idea of the Territory becoming a bonafide state, let alone an Indian state, was never part of the "Indian solution" in the government's removal program. Actual government was administered by the various tribes in question, with tribal organization and government differing widely from tribe to tribe. "Homogeneity and stability were further disrupted . . . by the steady stream of White settlers passing through along the Santa Fe, Oregon, and Mormon trails, especially during the California Gold Rush starting in 1848" (Waldman 2000, 206).

Beginning in the 1850s, as a result of political pressure from the transcontinental railroads, Indian Territory was reduced in size. "In 1854, by an act of Congress, the northern part of the Indian Territory became Kansas and Nebraska territories. And in 1862, the Homestead Act opened up Indian lands in the territories to White homesteaders" (Waldman 2000, 206). A bill to do the same for the southern portion of the Territory was defeated in Congress, but further shrinkage occurred after the Civil War in 1866. The Cherokees, along with the other Civilized Tribes, were forced to accept the terms of Reconstruction because of their involvement with the cause of the Confederacy. This gave the federal government the excuse to appropriate Indian lands and relocate tribes from Kansas within what remained of the Indian Territory.

THE CIVIL WAR

The Civil War in the west was fought partly on Cherokee territory, with Cherokees fighting on both the Union and Confederate sides of the conflict. "Invading troops as well as Native partisans on both sides destroyed property, neighbor killed neighbor, and at war's end the Cherokee Nation had twelve hundred orphans" (Perdue and Green 1995, 174).

Slavery was the major issue in the Civil War, pitting the industrial North against the slave-owning, agrarian South. The issue of slavery also came to dominate the politics of the Cherokee Nation, since an increasing number of Cherokees, mainly the mixed-blood elite, owned slaves. In 1809, less than 5 percent of Cherokees owned slaves. By 1835, the percentage had increased to 8 percent. "After Removal, slave labor helped rebuild the Cherokee

Nation. Those who had access to the ready supply of labor were able to clear land and construct homes and farm buildings sooner and engage in other economic enterprises more readily. The economic disparity between the Cherokee elite and the non-slaveholders increased" (King 2004, 363). By 1860, the Cherokee population was twenty-one thousand and the number of slaves between three thousand five hundred and four thousand.

At the outset of the war, Principal Chief John Ross declared the neutrality of the Cherokee Nation. But by early summer, 1861, the Cherokees appeared to be evenly split on the issue of either making an alliance with the Confederacy, remaining loyal to the Union, or being neutral. Those supporting the Union side included a large number of full-bloods and traditionalists who favored the abolition of slavery, The old Treaty or Ridge Party, headed by Stand Watie and including a secret organization of mixed-bloods (the Knights of the Golden Circle), chose the Confederate side in full support of slavery. Ross, on the other hand, counted on the support of the Keetoowah Society, whose members were pledged to defend Cherokee autonomy. They were also known as Pins, or Pins Indians, because of their insignia of two crossed pins worn under the lapels of their coats and hunting shirts.

The Civil War began on April 12, 1861 when Confederate artillery opened fire on Fort Sumter in Charleston harbor. From the very beginning, the Confederacy was interested in securing Indian Territory. Watie accepted a commission in the Confederate Army, and his volunteers blocked a possible advance by Union forces from Kansas. A battle took place in southwestern Missouri which resulted in the defeat of Union forces. The Cherokee regiment was prominent in the battle, and Stan Watie's prestige within the Confederacy increased. "Unafraid and thoroughly convinced that slavery must end, the Pins repeatedly clashed with Watie and his Confederate Cherokees and Creeks. Pin Indians attacked and burned the homes of southern sympathizers in the Cherokee Nation, and the Watie supporters retaliated with raids on the Unionist faithful" (Mankiller and Wallis 1993, 126).

After Union troops were withdrawn from the forts in Indian Territory, it became clear that Cherokee sentiments were overwhelmingly pro-Confederacy. As a result, on October 7, 1861, Chief Ross concluded a treaty with the Confederate states. "The Creeks, Choctaws, Chickasaws, Seminoles, Osages, Comanches, and several smaller tribes had already aligned with the Confederates" (Mankiller and Wallis 1993, 125).

In early 1862, thousands of Indian refugees, including two thousand Cherokees, were living in southern Kansas in deplorable conditions. Many wanted to enlist in the Union army. "In March 1862, President Abraham Lincoln decided to launch an 'Indian expeditionary force' to liberate loyal Indians beginning with the Cherokee. The force of 5,000 included two regiments of Indian refugees, some 2,000 men, to serve with 3,000 White soldiers from Kansas and Wisconsin" (King 2004, 363).

When confronted by the Union troops, Chief John Ross offered little resistance and briefly became a prisoner of war. He and his relatives were then forced to leave the Cherokee Nation under escort of federal troops. Hundreds of Cherokees went with them or with the Cherokee regiments out of fear of Waite's Confederates. With the departure of federal troops for Kansas, Stan Watie was elected Chief, and all Cherokee males between the ages of sixteen and thirty-five were required to make themselves available for service in the Confederate Army. In 1863, the Ross faction and the Cherokee Home Guard, which supported the Union side of the conflict, held a council meeting at Cowskin Prairie. The Cherokee National Council "abrogated the treaty with the Confederacy, deposed all Confederate Cherokee from office, reaffirmed John Ross as chief, elected Thomas Pegg as acting chief in Ross's absence, and declared the abolition of slavery" (King 2004, 364). In the spring of 1863, Cherokee refugees loyal to the North returned to the Cherokee Nation with a new military expedition. Many Confederate Cherokees fled to Texas. Meanwhile, Stan Watie's men roamed the Cherokee lands at will. "With two opposing armies and governments, the Cherokee Nation was devastated by a ruthless guerilla warfare until the close of the war in 1865" (King 2004, 364). The Civil War officially ended on April 9, 1865, when General Robert E. Lee, representing the South, surrendered to Union General Ulysses S. Grant at Appomattox, Virginia. Stan Watie was the last Confederate general to surrender.

POSTWAR RECONSTRUCTION

The Civil War left the Cherokee Nation devastated. Seven thousand Cherokees had died, at least one-quarter of the tribal population. One-third of all adult women were widows, and one-quarter of the children were orphans. The original purpose of Sequoyah Training School, established by the Cherokee National Council in 1871, was to provide housing and care for children orphaned by the Civil War. A Cherokee census at the time showed only 13,566 Cherokees living in the Nation, a population decline of more than 33 percent from the population at the beginning of the Civil War. Many of the pro-South refugees did not return.

After the war, the Cherokees were regarded with suspicion and treated like defeated Southerners, even though there were those who had not taken sides in the conflict, or even fought with the Union forces. Instead, the entire Cherokee Nation was singled out by a victorious North for collective punishment.

The Cherokee Reconstruction Treaty of 1866 again placed the Cherokees under the jurisdiction of the United States. Cherokee land was seized to make room for other immigrant tribes, who had also been forced to move to Indian Territory. The treaty also abolished slavery, and the former slaves, or freedman, residing in the Cherokee Nation were granted tribal citizenship. Under a treaty provision, one thousand Delawares and seven hundred Shawnees from Kansas also became Cherokee citizens. Despite of the devastation caused by the Civil War, the Cherokee Nation, with a functioning government and 14 million acres of land, was very appealing to the Delawares and other resettled Indian nations. The Cherokee Council opened 32 public schools, two of which were for children of former slaves, and in March, 1868, "Assistant Chief James Vann wrote that at no time in the history of the Cherokee Nation was there such a desire for 'cultivation of the arts of civilization and education'" (King 2004, 365).

In 1866, Lewis Downing, a popular Baptist minister, together with Evan and John Jones, also Baptists, a majority of the revived Keetoowah Society, and certain members of the Southern Party formed a new party of national reconciliation. John Ross had died shortly before the founding of the new party and was succeeded by his nephew, William P. Ross. In the election of 1867, William Ross was defeated by Downing, in part due to the organized effort of the Keetoowah Pins. Lewis Downing died in 1872, followed shortly by the two Joneses, and the Downing coalition dissolved. Most conservatives and the Keetoowah Society then realigned with the National Party, which went on to win the next two Cherokee elections.

Despite reconstruction hardships and internal politics, the Cherokees continued to prosper. In 1870, the *Cherokee Advocate* resumed publication. The following year, the seal of the Cherokee Nation was adopted by the National Council to commemorate the unification conference of 1839. In the center of the seal was a seven-pointed star, symbolizing the sacred number of the Cherokee people, and representing the seven matrilineal clans. A wreath of oak leaves signified strength and everlasting life.

By 1872, the Missouri-Kansas-Texas railroad transected Cherokee territory. The railroad stimulated economic activity and linked the Cherokees to the rest of the continent, but they also gobbled up Cherokee land through the right of eminent domain and brought homesteaders and squatters into the Territory. "Undesirables of every type regarded Indian Territory as a paradise on earth because tribal courts had no jurisdiction over any of the Whites" (Mankiller and Wallis 1993, 131).

A report by Senator Henry L. Dawes of Massachusetts, who visited Cherokee territory in the early 1880s, found the Cherokee Nation flourishing. Every family had a home, and there was not a pauper to be found. The Cherokee Nation was fiscally solvent again; it had rebuilt its own capitol, schools and hospitals. "Countless achievements marked the entire forty-two years between the end of the Civil War in 1865 and Oklahoma statehood in 1907" (Mankiller and Wallis 1993, 133).

Dawes and his congressional supporters, on the other hand, were convinced that collective ownership of Indian land was an abysmal failure. Therefore, in 1887 Congress passed the Dawes Severalty or General Allotment Act with the purpose of promoting the private ownership concept among Native Americans and furthering the assimilation process. "The act called for dividing the lands held in common by Native people into separate parcels, with the heads of families to receive 160 acres each, or a quarter of a mile-square section. Single persons older than eighteen would be allotted eighty acres each, and all other tribal members would receive forty acres each. Any surplus land was to be opened to White settlement" (Mankiller and Wallis 1993, 134).

Initially, Congress excluded the Five Civilized Tribes and a few other tribes from the Dawes Allotment Act. But within two years after its passage, the Territory of Oklahoma was created from the western half of Indian Territory. The new Oklahoma Territory (the word Oklahoma coming from a Choctaw phrase meaning "red people") was not only the new home of other resettled tribes, but it became a desired place for White homesteaders to settle. On April 22, 1889, President Benjamin Harrison proclaimed two million acres at the center of the original Indian Territory as unassigned lands, and fifty thousand homesteaders moved in, including Black settlers. This marked the beginning of the Oklahoma "land runs," much to the detriment of the Cherokees and the other Indian nations. In 1891, under pressure from the federal government, "the Cherokee Nation ceded to the United States all rights and claim to the Cherokee Outlet for a sum in excess of $9 million. Special provision was made for payment to the Freedmen, Delawares, and Shawnees" (King 2004, 366).

The Curtis Act, passed by Congress in 1898, extended allotment policy to the Five Civilized Tribes in Indian Territory. The Dawes Commission began enrolling members on tribal rolls in preparation for individualizing Indian common lands, usually in 110 acre allotments. Many Cherokees, including some members of the Keetoowah Society, actively resisted allotment. The Curtis Act also abolished tribal laws and courts, and made Indian people subject to federal courts. It gave voting rights to hundreds of thousands of non-Native people while denying Indians the same right. It established free public schools for White children in Indian Territory.

The passage of the Indian Allotment Act in 1887, and the Curtis Act in 1898, sealed the fate of the western Cherokees when they and the other Civilized Tribes were terminated as political entities, their tribal lands broken up into small allotments, and the supposed surplus, especially the Cherokee Strip, opened to White settlement in a great land rush. "The opening of the Cherokee Outlet [on September 16, 1893] was the largest land run in American history. More than one hundred thousand land-crazed settlers raced for the forty thousand claims waiting to be staked" (Mankiller and Wallis 1993, 137). Between1902 and 1907, the Cherokee land was allotted and the Cherokee government was formally abolished. The Nighthawks refused to register and accept allotments.

The majority of the non-Indian newcomers moving into Oklahoma Territory pushed for statehood. It took them eighteen years, but they finally achieved their goal in 1907. In the process it was decided to join the two territories into one state. The Five Civilized Tribes attempted to form their own Indian "State of Sequoyah," but their petition was never seriously considered by the U.S. Congress. Instead, the Oklahoma Enabling Act was passed in 1906, making Oklahoma the forty-sixth state of the

Union in November of the following year. "Even then, the Cherokees did not disappear. From traditionalists who found solace performing ancient rituals at ceremonial grounds to highly acculturated individuals who proudly held on to their Indian identity, the Oklahoma Cherokees endured without a land base or a tribe that had governing powers. In North Carolina, a much smaller group that avoided removal maintained both their ethnicity and their land base" (Perdue and Green 1995, 174).

Poverty and Exploitation

When Oklahoma became a state in 1907, the Cherokee Nation was officially dissolved, with its vast surplus lands reverting to the United States government for homesteads. The federal government then divided up the land into individual allotments. For the next sixty years, the Cherokee principal chief was appointed by the president of the United States without the consent of the Cherokee people. The Cherokee Nation remained only as an administrative unit until 1914, with Whites taking over control of former Cherokee lands and businesses. The Cherokees "were relieved of more than six and one-half million acres, and subsequent frauds and swindles by speculators left many individuals landless and penniless" (King 2004, 367). This particular history is recounted in Angie Debo's *And Still the Waters Run* (1968), a classic chronicle of official deceit, skullduggery, and outright theft that deprived the Cherokees and the other Civilized Tribes of their rights to land and self-determination when Indian Territory was absorbed into the State of Oklahoma.

The years following Oklahoma statehood was one of extreme hardship for the nationalistic Cherokees with their distinctive language, customs, and institutions. While the Dawes Commission was engaged in making the tribal membership rolls for the purpose of land allotment, other agencies of government under the supervision of the secretary of the interior were engaged in the administration of the undivided property and the so-called protection of the individual Indian allottees.

Of the five tribal republics, the Cherokees had the largest total population and the most full-bloods. Many Cherokees actively resisted enrollment for the purpose of allotment, especially the Kee-too-wahs and Nighthawks. "As late as 1912, nearly two thousand members of the Cherokee tribe alone steadfastly refused to claim their allotment, and their land was lying idle or in the possession of trespassers. These full-bloods lived in the 'Cherokee hills' in the most extreme destitution, but they refused to accept the per capita payments to which they had become entitled in the final distribution of their property" (Debo 1968, 58). Tribal leaders had hoped that in yielding to the government's allotment policy they still might retain other tribal governmental functions, but this was not to be. Step by step, federal agencies stripped the Cherokee Nation of its administrative authority. The Cherokees lost control of their land rights, court system, revenues, and educational system. The Five Tribes Act of 1906 placed Cherokee schools under federal management. In short, the Cherokee Nation as a political entity was liquidated.

Oil was discovered in the early 1900s, initiating an economic boom in Oklahoma. After 1903, the leasing of mineral-rich Indian lands developed rapidly. The Interior Department assisted the individual Indian allotee in the sale or leasing of his land. Those Cherokees legally permitted to sell their surplus lands included adult White Cherokees, adult Cherokee freedmen, and all mixed-bloods from whom restrictions had been removed. The lust and plunder of Indian lands and resources gave rise to all manner of illegal and reprehensible practices. In her definitive work on the Five Civilized Tribes during this period of history, Angie Debo writes: "The general affect of allotment was an orgy of plunder and exploitation probably unparalleled in American history" (Debo 1968, 91). "Unspeakably greedy people would arrange to be appointed guardians of Cherokee children, and then take control of their individually allotted land" (Mankiller and Wallis 1993, 5).

The allotment grafters were particularly active among the Choctaws, but the Cherokees, too, became victims. The effort by the Dawes Commission to select good lands, especially for the Indian full-bloods, was in accord with the sentiments of the grafters, "who expected to secure surplus land and [were] anxious, therefore, to see the full-blood receive a good allotment. No better plan could have been devised to strip the Indians of their most valuable possessions" (Debo 1968, 95). "Enterprising scouts went into the full-blood settlements, gathered up the Indians, loaded them on trains and brought them in, and sold them to the highest bidder among the real estate dealers, at ten, twenty-five, or even thirty dollars a head. The purchaser then coached his Indians to choose as their surplus the land to which he claimed some sort of possessory title, and secured a lease that was a virtual gift; and the allottee returned to his distant mountain home, content to be relieved of all responsibility for his new possessions" (Debo 1968, 95–96).

One of the worst instances of graft was the plundering of Indian children, especially orphans, of their allotted lands. By 1903, grafters were preying on Indian children by making unconscionable contracts with their parents, usually full-bloods. Later, with statehood, they secured their appointments as professional guardians through the federal courts in order to control the orphans' property. A former United States attorney testified before a Senate committee that there were "less than half a dozen men as guardians for two hundred to three hundred children" (Debo 1968, 112). Restrictions had been placed on nearly all the land of minors during the territorial period, but there was little to prevent the guardian from selling inherited land and squandering the proceeds.

Speculators also engaged in an illicit traffic of "dead claims," land that had become alienable through the death of the original allottee. Two investigations in 1903 found that numerous court officials were connected with the land companies. Furthermore, "every member of the Dawes Commission and nearly every high Interior Department official in the Territory was credited with stock in one or more of these companies" (Debo 1968, 118).

AFTER STATEHOOD

Despite the oppression and impoverishment of the Indians, and the destruction of the five great tribal republics such as the Cherokees, the presence of its Indian population had a profound effect on the consciousness of the citizens of Oklahoma. The name itself, as was mentioned earlier, is a Choctaw expression meaning Red People. The Oklahoma Territory seal showed a frontiersman clasping hands with an Indian. Oklahoma school children were taught to take personal pride in the accomplishments of the five Indian republics as part of their own historic past. "They accepted Sequoyah and Pushmataha as their ancestral heroes, and the 'Trail of Tears' of the Removal exiles rather than the voyage of Columbus became their odyssey" (Debo 1968, 292). Fair-haired citizens proudly bragged of their Indian ancestry because of 1/64th or 1/256th Indian blood.

Yet, an entire generation of Indian children, born after 1906, were growing up in illiteracy and squalor, without land or property, and with no hope for the future.

Debo points to the following paradox of building the new state of Oklahoma: "In the excitement of discovering oil fields, building cities, and placing rich land under the plow, they [the non-Indian citizens] created a philosophy in which personal greed and public spirit were almost inextricably joined. If they could build their personal fortunes and create a great state by destroying the Indian, they would destroy him in the name of all that was selfish and all that was holy" (Debo 1968, 93).

After statehood in 1907, Congress enacted a complex allotment law on May 27, 1908, whose provisions remained in force until April of 1931. "It divided the allottees into three classes: Whites, freedmen, and mixed-bloods of less than one-half Indian blood were released from all restrictions; mixed-bloods of one-half or more and less than three-fourths Indian blood were free to sell their surplus, but their homesteads remained inalienable; and Indians of three-fourths or more Indian blood were restricted in all their holdings. . . . All unrestricted land was declared subject to taxation and all other civil burdens" (Debo 1968, 179). Although the allotment law did not entirely please the avaricious non-Indians as represented in the platforms of the state's Democrat and Republic political parties, it did make more than twelve million acres of land immediately subject to taxation and sale. It also restored the leasing system that the tribal republics had endeavored to correct, and it gave the state's probate courts almost complete control of Indian administration. The true effect of the 1908 law was to enormously increase the opportunities for exploitation of Indian lands through the courts

"The entire Five Tribes area was dominated by a vast criminal conspiracy to wrest a great and rich domain from its owners. In the process of leasing the restricted land or purchasing the unrestricted from ignorant adults or ignorant or corrupt guardians the allottee was overreached by every possible sharp practice or criminal action" (Debo 1968, 197). One stratagem was to win the affection of a young Black or Indian allottee. A marriage would then take place in the real estate office where the deed to the land would be signed over immediately, "and the charmer would walk out of the office, never to be seen again by the allottee" (Debo 1968, 197). The law conferring majority by marriage among minors holding Indian allotments was also abused. Both of these practices were later declared illegal by the courts. Forgeries were common. They were carried out by organized gangs, and very few forgers went to prison. Murder, too, became common. In the traffic of wills, "many sinister stories were told of Indians who died under suspicious circumstances after bequeathing their property to White men" (Debo 1968, 200).

Federal officials were not untouched by the swindling of the Cherokees and other Indians. In fact, many of the swindlers had served for a time with one of the Federal agencies. Eventually, however, federal officials managed to recover a large amount of the property that had been stolen from the Indians. For the next several decades, the most extensive Indian litigation in the history of Oklahoma took place, thirty thousand land suits in all.

In the 1920s, the federal government made an attempt to check the Oklahoma spoils system which was defrauding the Indian estate. The attempted reform centered on the state's probate courts and its Indian guardianship system. An investigation revealed, among other things, excessive padding of expense accounts by court-appointed guardians. In 1927, the Interior Department conducted a survey of the restricted Indians. The following year, the Institute for Government Research published the findings of its landmark Meriam Report. Both reports found "deplorable conditions of ignorance, poverty, and disease that existed in the neglected hill settlements" (Debo 1968, 355). The entire hill country was menaced by famine. "In 1929, land speculators went out through the full-blood settlements and purchased for a mere pittance the shares of inherited land belonging to heirs born prior to March 4, 1906. The object, of course, was to force the sale of the land through partition proceedings as soon as the restrictions in favor of the un-enrolled heirs should expire" (Debo 1968, 361).

The reform administration of Commissioner of Indian Affairs John Collier succeeded in getting Congress to pass the Indian Reorganization Act in 1934. The act authorized tribes to organize under its provisions, set up tribal councils, hold land in common and conduct business, and attaining federal recognition. The Oklahoma delegation worked as a group against the application of the IRA to Oklahoma Indians, especially the formation of tribal organizations and collective land holding. Nevertheless, after drastic amendments to satisfy Oklahoma special interests, the Oklahoma Indian Welfare Act became law in June 26, 1936. It gave Indians such as the Cherokees "the right to engage in business, administer tribal property, elect officers, and manage local affairs. . . . The act also permits the organization of Indians into voluntary cooperative associations for purposes of marketing, consumers' protection, or land management, and authorizes Congress to appropriate two million dollars for loans to such associations" (Debo 1968, 372).

The 1930 U.S. Census found 72,643 Indians of the Five Tribes living in Oklahoma who were "persons of appreciable Indian blood." The Depression and Dust Bowl era of the 1930s increased the misery and oppression of Oklahoma's Indians. One-third of the population in eastern Oklahoma State fled the area, many of them Cherokees. In the 1940s and 1950s, dam building by the U.S. Corps of Engineers created a sportsman's paradise in the eastern part of the state, but tourism failed to benefit the impoverished Cherokees.

A second Trail of Tears, so to speak, took place in the early days of World War II when the U.S. Army enlarged a military installation near Muskogee, Oklahoma. Eighty tracts of restricted Cherokee allotted lands were condemned, claiming the homes of forty-five Cherokee families, who "were given only forty-five days to pack up their belongings and abandon their homes" (Mankiller and Wallis 1993, 63).

In 1949, Angie Debo made a survey of Oklahoma Indian Country at the request of the Indian Rights Association. She found that "the Indians were living in appalling poverty," with the Cherokees "the hardest hit." "Throughout the hills the Indians were living in log cabins as their ancestors had done a century before. Most of them raised gardens, and the women knew how to can vegetables and fruit; but the orchards that had surrounded their dwellings in tribal days had disappeared. They carried their water from springs and did their laundry in the back yard. Although a few of the women were slatterns, the majority kept their crowded, dilapidated houses surprisingly neat" (Debo 1968, xiv). Many of the men worked as unskilled laborers cutting timber, building electric power lines, and constructing flood control dams. The women and children and a few of the men worked in the commercial truck gardens and area berry patches, or picked wild berries for sale. Due to wartime and postwar job opportunities, most of the Indian households had family members working in an Oklahoma city or west coast cities like San Francisco and Oakland, California. In the old Cherokee settlement of Sallisaw, "one hundred families were receiving their mail at the village post office. Seventy-five of these were Indian families. . . . Most of these belonged to the landless generation, and were squatting on the allotments of friends or relatives. Only about one-fifth of the six-mile-square township remained in Indian hands" (Debo 1968, xvi).

In another community there were "five families living on their deceased father's allotment—sixty acres that would hardly have supported one family. Their families were large—one with eleven children, almost unbelievably ragged. The five houses were poverty-stricken hovels, but family pride still existed there, for flowers were blooming in the yards" (Debo 1968, xvi). In yet another case, in which Indian families still owned the land, the families pooled their resources to begin a strawberry-growing operation. "The work animals of the entire settlement totaled one horse owned by an old preacher, and even if farm equipment had been available, the land was too rough for cultivation" (Debo 1968, xvi). After a year of backbreaking toil on forty acres of rocky ground, the families cleared a cash income of only $54. Despite the odds, the cooperative eventually cleared its debt and was able to increase the average annual profit to $600 per family member.

Relocation and Termination

In the 1950s, another exodus from Oklahoma took place under the government's termination and relocation programs. House Concurrent Resolution 108, adopted August 1, 1953, withdrew federal recognition and services for a number of Indian tribes and nations. Ironically, termination was labeled as "the Indian freedom program." "From 1954 until 1962, Congress imposed the policy on sixty-one tribes and native communities, effectively cutting them off from federal services and protection. It was not until 1970 that Congress censured this detestable policy, too late for most tribes that had been terminated" (Mankiller and Wallis 1993, 68).

The government's relocation policy pressured thousands of the younger, supposedly surplus reservation population to relocate to selected metropolitan cities, such as Chicago, Cleveland, Denver, Detroit, Seattle, St. Louis, Los Angeles, Oakland, and San Francisco, with the objective of turning tribal Indians into urbanized proletarians. Ostensibly a training and job placement program, it was largely a failure. (See Chapter 11.) Reservation poverty prompted the move by thousands of Indians, including a significant number of Cherokees from Oklahoma. Once in the cities, however, the relocatees were often abandoned by federal officials and ended up in low-wage, dead-end jobs, urban poverty, and slum housing. Cherokee principal chief Wilma Mankiller, whose family went on relocation to the San Francisco Bay area in the 1950s, reports "that the 'better life' the BIA had promised all of us was, in reality, life in a tough, urban ghetto" (Mankiller and Wallis 1993, 73). The government's attempt to detribalize Indian families and terminate federal services to the reservations and communities was a failure. In the cities, the relocated families "banded together, built Indian centers, held picnics and powwows, and tried to form communities in the midst of large [non-Indian] urban populations. Yet there was always and forever a persistent longing to go home. . . . Most of the relocatees eventually returned to their communities to live and work, some of them trying even harder to strengthen tribal communities and governments. In the end, we survived" (Mankiller and Wallis 1993, 73–74).

Wilma P. Mankiller.

REEMERGENCE OF THE CHEROKEE NATION

Cherokee Nation of Oklahoma

Today, the Cherokee people remain split between the Eastern Band in North Carolina and the Western Cherokee in Oklahoma. Originally thought destined for extinction, the Cherokees of Oklahoma today are second only to the Navajo Nation in population, "with an enrolled tribal membership of more than 140,000, an annual budget of more than $75 million, and more than 1,200 employees spread across 7,000 square miles" (Mankiller and Wallis 1993, xvii). Many tribal members "live in the original territory of the Cherokee Nation, which is located in fourteen counties of northeastern Oklahoma" (King 1996, 97).

The former Cherokee Nation was unilaterally dissolved by the federal government, except for matters of administrative convenience, when Oklahoma became a state in 1907. For the sixty-five years following statehood, the U.S. president appointed a succession of principal chiefs who yielded little real authority, and there was no formal Cherokee government. The Western Cherokee began making a comeback in 1961 when they used money obtained from a federal lawsuit to purchase land and to build a cultural center.[3] They regained the right to elect their own leaders in 1970. They adopted a new constitution in 1975, delineating the three branches of government, and in 1990, the Cherokee Nation of Oklahoma assumed responsibility for running its own affairs with federal funds that were formerly administered by the Bureau of Indian Affairs. "The annual operating budget is more than $66 million, with approximately half of the funds provided by federal programs and the remainder coming from tribally generated sources" (King 1996, 97–98). The land formerly controlled by the tribe in the nineteenth century, however, is no longer a reservation, but, instead, a jurisdictional service area.

"In 1971, W.W. Keeler, who had served as principal chief by presidential appointment since 1949, became the first elected chief since statehood" (King 1996, 98). In 1985, Wilma Mankiller was elected Principal Chief, the first female chief of a major Indian tribe. In Cherokee government, the Deputy Chief presides over a fifteen-member Cherokee Nation Tribal Council. The Council members are elected to four-year terms by popular vote from their respective districts. A judicial branch is comprised of practicing attorneys who are also tribal members. Tribal government includes social programs, development and special services, and tribal operations.

"The Cherokee Nation Enterprises (CNE) operates Cherokee Casinos, a 150-room hotel/resort complex, two golf courses, retail convenience stores and tobacco outlets, and a gift shop" (Cherokee Nation 2004, 10). In March, 2004, CNE purchased Will Rogers Downs, a pari-mutuel horse track in Claremore, Oklahoma. CNE's income is paid to the Cherokee Nation in the form of a dividend. In 2004, the dividends amounted to more than $9 million. The money is used to help fund tribal health, education, and housing programs. Both the eastern and western branches rely heavily on tourism for economic self-sufficiency. A 1990 tribal tax code allows the Nation to tax businesses on tribal lands. Self-governance is the hallmark of the Cherokee Nation's governmental operations.

Eastern Band of Cherokee

Ten years after the majority of the Cherokees were sent westward on the Trail of Tears, those remaining in the mountains of North Carolina gained official recognition by the U.S. Congress, but on the condition that the state in which they resided also recognize their rights as permanent residents. In 1866, North Carolina did so, "and the federal government used money promised under the previous treaty to insure that the tribe would not be dispossessed" (King 1996, 96). By 1876, the Qualla Boundary was established, and during the following decade, Cherokees living in the outlying areas were drawn to it. The Qualla Boundary community was incorporated under the laws of North Carolina in 1889 and was then able to transact business as the Eastern Band of Cherokee Indians. A developing timber industry provided a cash economy for the next few decades.

In 1919, Cherokees who had served in World War I were made citizens, and in 1924, "the band, which had successfully resisted allotment, placed the deeds to tribal land in federal trust to ensure the land would always remain in Cherokee possession" (King 1996, 96). Today, lands held by the Eastern Band include over fifty-six thousand acres in five counties of western North Carolina, and a few acres in eastern Tennessee. In most instances, the possessory title held by Cherokee individuals can only be transferred to other tribal members.

The Cherokee Historical Association was formed in 1948 "to preserve and perpetuate the culture and history of the Eastern Band of Cherokees," and "the outdoor drama, 'Unto These Hills,' made its debut in 1950" (King 1996, 96). There has been criticism in some quarters that the Historical Association is controlled by the University of North Carolina, and that the Cherokee historical drama has been given an unduly Christian slant. In 2000, American Indian playwright Hanay Geiogamah was engaged to revamp the dramatization. Geiogamah, a professor at the University of California, Los Angeles, reported that "the old drama had been performed for 55 years and was replete with historical inaccuracies and an almost nonexistent portrayal of Cherokees and their culture, their music, their humor" (Whitmire 2006). "In the old show, only about a quarter of cast members were Cherokees, and it was routine for whites to play Native parts, often wearing wigs and red makeup" (Whitmire 2006). A second act has been added to focus on the Eastern Band's cultural survival. The end result is a more accurate portrayal of the history and cultural integrity of the Eastern Band of Cherokees.

Today, tourism is the primary industry on the Qualla Boundary. There are over 180 businesses, of which more than two-thirds are owned and operated by tribal members. Although the neon signs, tourist shops, and motels present a garish display, and the main town is literally overrun by tourists during the summer holidays, an impressive Cherokee museum provides a faithful account of Cherokee history and culture.

Over 60 percent of enrolled members live on tribal lands although all members are eligible to vote in tribal elections. The executive branch is comprised of a principal chief, vice-chief, and executive advisor, the former two positions elected by popular vote every four years. "The legislative branch is the Tribal Council, which is composed of two members from each of the six townships. They are elected to two-year terms" on the basis of popular vote (King 1996, 97). The Bureau of Indian Affairs acts as trustee. It operates the schools, the roads, the extension programs, timber resources, and oversees matters relating to realty. The major health programs are managed by the U.S. Public Health Service.

United Keetoowah Band (UKB)

Keetoowah was an ancient principal town in western North Carolina prior to the Cherokee removal. In the 1850s, full-bloods in Arkansas and Oklahoma united to oppose assimilation and to retain Cherokee traditions. The full-bloods united in their churches, mainly northern Baptist, to counter the pro-slavery mixed-bloods from dominating the Cherokee political process. This led to the founding of the Keetoowah Society, in opposition to "the pro-slavery 'Blue Lodges,' later known as the Knights of the Golden Circle (King 2004, 362)." Meetings included ceremonies and dances, since Cherokee traditionalism was inherent to the full-blood way of life. Membership was limited to non-English speaking full-bloods. The Society dominated Cherokee politics until the mid-1880s.

Over time, several groups have variously identified as Ketoowahs, or included Keetoowah in their name, including Redbirth Smith's religious Keetoowah Society, and the Nighhawk Keetoowahs or Nighthawks. During the Civil War, Keetoowahs were pro-Union and Abolitionist. They opposed Chief John Ross because he tolerated slavery and aligned the Cherokee Nation with the Confederacy. "Many of the traditional people believed that the troubles of the Cherokees were a result of the Cherokee people having turned away from their own traditions" (Conley 2005, 196). In 1896, a religious revitalization took place, known as the Redbird Smith Movement. This was in part a reaction to the Dawes Commission taking away the power of the Cherokee Nation to determine its own citizenship. The movement was marked by its religious symbolism.

Although plagued by factionalism in the 1890s, all Cherokees sought a tribal identity distinct from the Cherokee Nation, which had adopted Whites, Cherokee Freedmen, and others after 1839. Keetoowahs opposed the allotment of Cherokee tribal lands and therefore abstained from the general election of January 31, 1899. For this reason they do not appear on the Dawes tribal roll and became ineligible for enrollment in the Cherokee Nation of Oklahoma. In 1905 the Keetoowah Society obtained its own corporate charter.

In the years following 1930, many Keetoowah factions reconciled although tensions remained between the Keetoowah Society and the Nighthawks on one side, and the other Ketoowahs. In 1946, the federal government allowed the Keetoowah to reorganize as a united, exclusively Cherokee tribal entity, apart from the Cherokee Nation. The United Keetoowah Band is legally entitled to determine its own membership, acquire land in trust, and exercise other inherent sovereign powers. Members elect a Council composed of nine District Council members and four executive officers. The Cherokee Nation of Oklahoma has been unsuccessful in absorbing the UKB.

THEORY AND ANALYSIS

In applying Champagne's theory to the Cherokee case, the question remains: what accounts for the Cherokee's remarkable penchant for state-building? Champagne points out that there were several important conditions present in nineteenth century Cherokee society and history of contact that led to institution-building. First, there were the hegemonic threats by the United States to Cherokee sovereignty. Second, there was their incorporation into southern plantation agriculture, mainly the cotton market, which led to class stratification. "About eight percent of Cherokee households became slave-holding plantation owners who produced cotton and other agricultural products for export" (Champagne 1983, 760). The rest of the Cherokee households became small farmers and husbandmen who relied primarily on a subsistence economy "while marketing some products in order to buy manufactured goods" (Champagne 1983, 760). It was the Cherokee planter class who "were influenced in advocating economic and political change and introduced American models of political organization and constitutional government" (Champagne 1989, 51). Third and fundamentally, however, "the Cherokee had two major institutional features that facilitated their capacity to adopt political and economic change: national institutions of social solidarity, and a polity that was differentiated from culture, kinship and the institutions of social solidarity" (Champagne 1989, 52).

In response to Indian demographer Russell Thornton, Champagne (1985) explains why revitalization movements among the Cherokee, such as the Ghost Dance Movement and White Path's Rebellion, or even the Redbird Smith Movement after 1898, never became institutionalized as did similar fundamentalist or traditionally conservative movements among the Iroquois and Delaware. State-building and agricultural development were "the primary Cherokee response to U.S. threats against Cherokee territory and national autonomy," because Cherokee society, unlike that of the Iroquois, was structurally differentiated (Champagne 1985, 128). "In the relatively differentiated Cherokee society, fundamentalist movements failed or were incorporated into the institution-building process; while in the less-differentiated Iroquois and Delaware societies, fundamentalist opposition prevented or fragmented and limited acceptance of political and economic innovations" (Champagne 1985, 129).

CONCLUSION

Several lessons can be learned from the Cherokee experience. One is that Champagne appears to be correct when he theorizes that a structurally differentiated society like the Cherokees can better withstand the assault by the oppressive policies, including ethnic cleansing, of Anglo-American hegemony. We have already seen in Chapter 2, *Hidden Heritage*, that the opposite may also be true in the case of the structurally non-differentiated Iroquois.

Second, the blood quantum concept does not explain the sociocultural processes leading to either acculturation and assimilation, or resistance as a sovereign people. Clearly, the Cherokees as a mixed-race people nonetheless maintained an Indigenous identity, retaining much of their cultural traditions and language throughout their tragic history. A cultural definition is more important in what it means to be a member of a particular Indian nationality than so-called blood quantum.

Finally, the Cherokees have been truly remarkable in their ability to forge an Indian republic of a new type, and then to repeatedly resurrect the institutional fabric of their republic each time it was destroyed or collapsed under pressure from Anglo-American hegemony. The last time was only a little over one hundred years ago when Oklahoma became a state and Indian Territory was abolished. The historian Angie Debo had this to say about the tragic history of the Five Civilized Tribes, including the Cherokees: "The policy of the United States in liquidating the institutions of the Five Tribes was a gigantic blunder that ended a hopeful experiment in Indian development, destroyed a unique civilization, and degraded thousands of individuals" (Debo 1968, x–xi).

CHAPTER REVIEW

DISCUSSION QUESTIONS

1. Explain what Champagne means by the Cherokees being a structurally differentiated Indian people. How was this different from the Iroquois who were discussed in Chapter 2?
2. In traditional culture, before European contact, what was the glue of Cherokee social organization? How were political decisions made?
3. What were some of the changes in Cherokee culture and society that occurred in the eighteenth century as a result of white contact?
4. What were the factors that led to the rise of the Cherokee state? Summarize the structure and function of Cherokee government.
5. What effect did the 1834 Removal Act have on the Cherokee Nation? The American Civil War?
6. What impact did the Oklahoma land rush and statehood have on the Cherokee Nation?
7. What is the political status of the Cherokees today? (Include in your answer the three different Cherokee populations.)

SUGGESTED READINGS

CONLEY, ROBERT J. 2005. *The Cherokee Nation: A History.* Albuquerque: University of New Mexico Press.

DEBO, ANGIE. 1940. *And Still the Waters Run: The Betrayal of the Civilized Tribes.* Princeton University Press.

MANKILLER, WILMA, and MICHAEL WALLIS. 1993. *Mankiller: A Chief and her People.* New York: St. Martin's Press.

MOONEY, JAMES. 1975. *Historical Sketch of the Cherokee.* Chicago: Aldine.

NOTES

1. From P. Mankiller and Michael Wallis, 1993. *Mankiller: A Chief and Her People,* page 3. New York: St. Martin's Press.
2. A portion of this chapter was previously published by the author in 2002 as "Academic Indianismo: Social Scientific Research in American Indian Studies," *American Indian Culture and Research Journal* 26 (4): 67–96.
3. The 2000 U.S. Census gives a number of 281,000 Cherokees. However, the Census asked respondents for the first time to report one or more "races" (White, Black, Asian, etc.) they considered themselves and other members of their households to be. For example, 62 percent of the self-identified "Cherokees" reported at least one other "race" or American Indian tribal grouping. Thus, the 2000 data on race are not directly comparable with data from the 1990 census or earlier censuses. I have not yet seen current information on the number of tribally enrolled members of the Eastern Band in North Carolina, or of the Cherokee Nation of Oklahoma.

REFERENCES

CHAMPAGNE, DUANE. 1983. "Social Structure, Revitalization Movements and State Building: Social Change in Four Native American Societies." *American Sociological Review* 48 (December): 754–63.

———. 1985. "Cherokee Social Movements: A Response to Thornton." *American Sociological Review* 50 (February): 127–30.

———. 1989. "American Indian Societies: Strategies and Conditions of Political and Cultural Survival" *Cultural Survival Report* 32 (December).

———. 1992. *Social Order and Political Change: Constitutional Governments Among the Cherokee, the Choctaw, the Chickasaw, and the Creek.* Stanford, CA: Stanford University Press.

Cherokee Nation. 2004. "Report to the People, 2004." (Tabloid.)

CHURCHILL, WARD. 1999. "The Crucible of American Indian Identity: Native Tradition versus Colonial Imposition in Post-conquest North America." *American Indian Culture and Research Journal* 23 (1): 39–67.

CONLEY, ROBERT J. 2005. *The Cherokee Nation: A History.* Albuquerque: University of New Mexico Press.

DEBO, ANGIE. 1968. *And Still the Waters Run: The Betrayal of the Five Civilized Tribes.* Princeton, NJ: Princeton University Press.

DELORIA, VINE, JR. 1985. *Behind the Trail of Broken Treaties: An Indian Declaration of Independence.* Austin: University of Texas Press.

———. 1969. *Custer Died for Your Sins.* London: Macmillan.

FLEISCHMANN, GLEN. 1971. *The Cherokee Removal, 1838.* New York: Franklin Watts.

FOGELSON, RAYMOND D. 2004. "Cherokee in the East." In *Handbook of North American Indians, vol. 14: Southeast,* volume edited by Raymond D. Fogelson, 337–53. Washington, DC: Smithsonian Institution Press.

GEARING, FRED. 1962. "Priests and Warriors: Social Structures for Cherokee Politics in the 18th Century." In *American Anthropological Association Memoir 93.* Menasha, WI: American Anthropological Association.

GIBSON, ARRELL MORGAN. 1980. *American Indian: Prehisotry to the Present.* Lexington, Ma: D.C. Heath.

KING, DUANE H. 1996. "Cherokee." In *Native America in the Twentieth Century,* edited by Mary B. Davis, 95–98. New York: Garland.

———. 2004 "Cherokee in the West: History Since 1776." In *Handbook of North American Indians, vol. 14: Southeast,* volume edited by Raymond D. Fogelson, 354–72. Washington, DC: Smithsonian Institution Press.

LOBO, SUSAN, and STEVE TALBOT. 2001. *Native American Voices: A Reader.* Upper Saddle River, NJ: Prentice Hall.

MANKILLER, WILMA, and MICHAEL WALLIS. 1993. *Mankiller: A Chief and Her People.* New York: St. Martin's Press.

MOONEY, JAMES. 1975. *Historical Sketch of the Cherokee.* Chicago: Aldine.

PERFUE, THEDA, and MICHAEL D. GREEN, eds. 1995. *The Cherokee Removal: A Brief History with Documents.* New York: St. Martin's Press.

SPICER, EDWARD H. 1969. *A Short History of the Indians of the United States.* New York: Van Nostrand Reinhold.

TALBOT, STEVE. 2002. "Academic Indianismo: Social Scientific Research in American Indian Studies." *American Indian Culture and Research Journal* 26 (4): 67–96.

THORTON, RUSSELL. 1987. *American Indian Holocaust and Survival: A Population History Since 1492.* Norman: University of Oklahoma Press.

WALDMAN, CARL. 2000. *Atlas of the North American Indian.* New York: Checkmark Books.

WARDELL, MORRIS L. 1977. *A Political History of the Cherokee Nation, 1838–1907.* Norman: University of Oklahoma Press.

WHITMORE, TIM. 2006. "'Unto These Hills' Revamped in a Bid to Preserve Cherokee History and Traditions." *Indian Country Today,* July 26: B1.

WRIGHT, RONALD. 1992. *Stolen Continents: The "New World" Through Indian Eyes.* New York: Houghton Mifflin.

ZINN, HOWARD. 2001. *A People's History of the United States: 1492–Present.* New York: HarperCollins.

CRIMINALIZATION OF THE INDIAN
NORTHWEST FISHING RIGHTS AND THE CASE OF DAVID SOHAPPY

Fish design symbolizing the sacred importance of fishing to the traditional cultures of Northwest Indian nations.

God commanded that the lands and fisheries should be common to all who lived upon them; that they were never to be marked off or divided, but that the people should enjoy the fruits that God planted in the land, and the animals that lived upon it, and the fishes in the water. . . . This is the old law.

—Smohalla

Fifteen thousand years ago, American Indians first fished the *Che Wana*, the Columbia River, which separates the states of Washington and Oregon. The Native peoples who lived along the river called themselves People of the Salmon, or simply, the River People. Salmon was the center of life, and spiritual ceremonies and beliefs reflected this dependency and the people's harmony with the river. After the entry of White immigrants into the Northwest in the mid-nineteenth century, treaties were signed which forced the River People to give up millions of acres of their land, but in which they still retained the right to fish "in their usual and accustomed places . . . for as long as the sun shines, as long as the mountains stand and as long as the river flows" (Forder[1] 1989). Yet, as recently as June 17, 1982, a Yakama fisherman, David Sohappy and seventy-five other Indians were arrested for fishing out of season on the Columbia River. Sohappy's front door was kicked down and his house ransacked by local, state, and federal agents. "David, his wife, and his son were arrested for poaching under the Lacey Amendment to the Black Bass Act, which made it a felony to poach instead of a misdemeanor" (Forder 1989). A sting operation, code-named Salmonscam, entrapped the Indian fishermen who openly took salmon in defiance of state regulations, asserting their precious treaty right to fish. David Sohappy, an elder and spiritual leader in the Feather Cult of the Washat or Seven Drums religion, then spent twenty months in a federal prison before being released in June of 1988. Having suffered diabetic strokes in prison, his health broke, and he died in a nursing home three years later.

The Sohappy case exemplifies the hypocrisy and racism of White bureaucracy in its treatment of Native American treaty rights. Sohappy's linear ancestor sold fish to the Lewis and Clark expedition in 1805, but contemporary Indian fishermen were sent to jail in the 1970s and 1980s for taking and selling fish, in spite of treaties guaranteeing them the right to fish. This chapter examines the Northwest fishing rights controversy and the criminalization of the Indian fisherfolk in order to further the special interests of non-Indians and their institutions.

CHAPTER OVERVIEW

In this chapter we consider the following paradox: how is it that the Indian treaties of the Pacific Northwest explicitly guarantee the Indians' legal right to fish "in their accustomed places," yet, at the same time, the fishing tribes have been continually harassed, forbidden to fish, and tribal members arrested and jailed for fishing? How can one explain the criminalization by the authorities of these Indian fisherfolk? To answer this question, we begin our story with a theory suggested by an Indian sociologist who contends that criminalizing the victim, in this case the Indian, is historically linked to a loss of Native sovereignty. In order to demonstrate the relevance of this theory for the Northwest fishing rights issue, we will review the historical context of Indian-White relations in the Pacific Northwest, especially as this history concerns trade and fishing. In 1853, Oregon Territory was divided into the separate states of Washington and Oregon, and the abridgement of Indian fishing rights thereafter took a somewhat different course of development in the two regions. For that reason, each state's history with respect to Indian relations is treated in separate sections of our discourse.

It is also important to describe the nature of salmon and their vital importance to the fishing tribes concerned. Salmon is the cornerstone of the Indian societies of the Northwest, and salmon provide a common link between Native cultures. A discussion of treaties as they concern fishing in the Pacific Northwest is also central to our story, because Indian treaty rights are the basis for the political activism that emerged in the 1960s and 1970s, the "fish-ins" of western Washington State and along the

Columbia River. As a result of the activism in support of Indian treaty rights, a major victory was achieved in 1974 when a federal judge ruled in the Boldt decision that the River tribes were entitled to 50 percent of the salmon catch.

The Columbia River Basin, with its many dams impeding fish migration, receives separate treatment in our narrative. The court-mandated system of separate fishing zones for White fishermen and Indians provides the political and historical context for the notorious Salmonscam by state and federal authorities, that resulted in the arrest of David Sohappy and other traditional Indian fishermen in the mid-1980s.

The chapter ends with a return to theory. The Sohappy case is illustrative of how the River Indians were criminalized by the federal and state governments when their sovereign treaty rights to fish were either ignored or diminished. Also discussed is the White backlash against the Northwest gaming tribes as a sovereignty issue. It is suggested that there may be a theoretical connection between the two economic enterprises, fish and casinos.

THEORY: CRIMINALIZATION OF THE INDIAN

Luana Ross (Salish) (1998), formerly professor of Women's and American Indian Studies at the University of Washington, and now president of Salish-Kootenai College, proposes that American Indians have been criminalized by White society as a result of internal colonialism and a system of racial oppression that has steadily eroded the treaty rights of Indian nations and peoples. This was accomplished by the U.S. courts and Congress steadily eroding Native sovereignty (see Talbot 2002, 71–76). In this chapter we propose that the political struggle by the River People of the Northwest to protect their treaty right to fish may best be understood by Ross' loss of sovereignty theory.

In *Inventing the Savage*, Ross contends that "Native American criminality is tied in a complex and historical way to the loss of [Indian] sovereignty" (Ross 1998, 5). In a section entitled "Colonization and the Social Construction of Deviance," Ross points out that before White conquest, "Native groups all exercised legal systems founded upon their own traditional philosophies," and there were no prisons (Ross 1998, 12–13). "Pre-contact Native criminal justice was primarily a system of restitution—mediation between families, of compensation, of recuperation" (Ross 1998, 14). The subsequent destruction of Native justice systems, and controlling of Indian people

through Anglo-American law is inherently a product of colonialism. Westward migration, the greed for gold, and land speculation by the dominant society provided the motives for the criminalization of the American Indian. As Ross (1998) puts it, "criminal" meant to be other than Euro-American. Traditional tribal justice codes instantly became criminal when the United States imposed its laws, customs, and values on Native people. New laws were legislated as a means of social control that defined many usual, everyday behaviors and beliefs of the Indians as criminal offenses.

Ross's loss of sovereignty proposition draws on colonial theory to explain the particular variant of structural racism that has historically been directed toward people of color in the United States. Colonial theory incorporates race, class, and historical processes to answer the question of why White ethnic groups have overcome their original disadvantaged statuses as immigrant populations, whereas American Indians, Native Hawaiians, Puerto Ricans, Latinos, African Americans, and even Asians to a degree, have not. The theory contends that there is a fundamental difference between the experience of racial minorities and that of European ethnics in the American history. Racial *ethnics*—that is, non-Whites—have been treated much like colonial subjects. Furthermore, American Indian scholars argue that rather than being ethnics, American Indians are Indigenous peoples—mininationalities—with characteristics fundamentally different from those of U.S. ethnic groups. One can make the case that American Indians have been, and continue to be, victimized by a system of internal colonialism, of being oppressed in their own homelands.

In Chapter One of *Inventing the Savage*, Ross documents how Indian sovereignty has been steadily diminished over the last 175 years by Supreme Court decisions and Congressional laws, all of which have defined various traditional acts and beliefs as criminal, or have sought to extend social control over the Indians as an oppressed Indigenous minority, as part of the process of colonization (see Talbot 2002, 75).

The earliest attempt by the United States to gain legal and judicial control over the Indian peoples as independent nations was the passage of the General Crimes Act of 1817. This was followed by the creation of the Bureau of Indian Affairs, in reality a colonial office for Native peoples, first in 1824 within the War Department, and then moved to the Department of the Interior in 1849. Placing the Indian nations in the

Interior Department meant that they were to be managed and controlled in a vein similar to that of lands and resources, rather than in the Department of State as sovereign nations under treaties.

Two early Supreme Court decisions, *Cherokee Nation v. Georgia* (1831) and *Worcester v. Georgia* (1832), reduced the Indian nations to the status of domestic, dependent nations rather than as independent sovereignties. Nations which are dependent as virtual internal colonies do not have the power to determine their own laws and criminal justice systems. A third court decision, *Johnson v. McIntosh* (1823), although not cited by Ross, would also appear to support her thesis (see Talbot 2002, 72; Newcomb 1993). This decision was based on the Doctrine of Christian Nations, by which the right of discovery by European nations was given precedence over the Indians' aboriginal right to the soil, because the Europeans were Christian, while the Indians were considered pagan. In other words, the court relegated the Indian nations to an inferior, even criminal status, because of religious bigotry.

Ross enumerates a series of laws, court decisions, and colonial policies that reduced the Indians' control of their own legal precepts and practices, and further criminalized Indian behavior and culture. These include the Court of Indian Offenses, set up in 1883 to do away with so-called "demoralizing and barbarous Indian customs." Under this policy, Indian traditions and religious practices were termed *Indian offenses* and punished as crimes, with the reservation Indian agent acting as prosecutor, judge, and jury. Starting as early as 1802, a federal ban was placed on serving alcohol to Indians. Although modified from time to time over the years, the federal government did not repeal this law until 1953, following the revocation of state laws dealing with the matter. (Medical scientists have found no genetic evidence that American Indians are physiologically predisposed to alcoholism.)

Until the Indian New Deal of the 1930s, Indians living on the reservations were punished, by fine or imprisonment or both, for failure to follow the Protestant work ethic, for refusing to work at the tasks set by the government Indian agent. The Major Crimes Act of 1885 gave federal courts jurisdiction in Indian country over seven major crimes, later amended to include fourteen felonies when the offenders are Indians. Ross notes that "by taking jurisdiction over crimes, the federal government also assumed the power to punish" (Ross 1998, 19). Indians were officially denied citizenship a few years

later in 1886. Native people were deemed a subject or colonized people, and attempting to vote became a criminal offense.

The 1887 General Allotment (Dawes) Act struck at Indian land tenure when it forcibly broke up communal lands into 160-acre individual plots, and the supposedly surplus lands then made available to White settlers. Over half of the remaining Indian land base in the United States was lost through allotment policy.

The Assimilative Crimes Act of 1889 expanded the number of crimes that could be tried in federal court, but applied only to interracial crimes, not crimes between Indians.

Indian Commissioner W. A. Jones issued a short hair order in 1902, which was directed against Indian customs, such as long hair for men, body painting by both sexes, wearing of Indian clothing, religious dances, and giveaway ceremonies. Indian men who refused to cut their hair, for example, were denied food rations or fired from reservation employment.

Even the 1934 Indian Reorganization Act, sponsored by New Deal Commissioner of Indian Affairs John Collier and the Franklin D. Roosevelt administration, had its negative aspects. By setting up White-modeled tribal councils under Interior Department control, the new legislation bypassed the old treaty councils and traditional political systems which many Indian tribes had managed to retain. The Act turned tribal government over to elected representatives in an English-speaking advisory council system; the traditional leaders were bypassed, and the old systems of governance criminalized. Furthermore, the tribal courts set up under the Indian Reorganization Act became subject to the Bureau of Indian Affairs, with tribal criminal codes modeled after the Anglo-American justice system.

Finally, Public Law 280, passed by Congress in 1953 as part of the government's termination policy, directed a number of states, including Oregon, to assume law and order jurisdiction over most reservations within their borders. It also authorized other states to take over legal jurisdiction if and when they wished to do so. This law was later modified by the 1968 Civil Rights Act to require tribal consent. The Civil Rights Act, while extending certain protections to Indian individuals, nevertheless did so at the expense of tribal jurisdiction. It reduced Indian tribal courts to the status of misdemeanor courts by limiting court sentences to six months' imprisonment and/or fine of five hundred dollars.

In summary, at least five statutory enactments of Congress have directly infringed upon the tribes in dealing with crimes on Indian reservations: the General Crimes Act, Major Crimes Act, Assimilative Crimes Act, P.L. 280, and the Indian Civil Rights Act. The resulting jurisdictional maze has all but eliminated Indian tribal sovereignty in the area of criminal justice. Ross observes that the reservations are the only places within the United States where the criminality of an act depends entirely on the race of the offenders and their victims.

At the end of this chapter, we will return to Ross's theory to explain why the rights specified in the early treaties were denied the fishing tribes, the River People, and how the Indian victims came to be criminalized by oppressive federal and state agencies.

INDIAN-WHITE RELATIONS IN THE PACIFIC NORTHWEST

The Early Years

When George Vancouver first encountered the Skagit and Snohomish Indians of Puget Sound in 1798, he found them already in possession of European weapons, although he and his traders were the first Whites the Indians had ever encountered. Guns had apparently been traded in through Indian intermediaries to the east.

In the early years of trade, European ships anchored in the few accessible harbors along the North Pacific coast. British ships made annual visits to the Northwest as early as 1774, and the American captain Robert Gray navigated the mouth of the Columbia River in 1778 when he began trading with the local Indians. Although the initial meeting between Gray and the Tillamook Indians was a friendly one, Gray later destroyed an entire Vancouver Island village of nearly two hundred houses. Some ship captains were known for their unfriendliness to Natives. The British sea captains furtively sought a northwest passage, hoping to bypass the perilous journey around Cape Horn at the tip of South America. In addition, they, along with the Americans and the Russians, sought to ply a profitable fur trade. "The plan was to obtain furs from Northwest Indians in exchange for gewgaws, then sail for China and barter or sell them for teas and silks sought after in New England" (Roe 1992, 2).

Some of the first Indians encountered by the Lewis and Clark expedition in 1805, in what later became Washington State, were the Wanapums, who lived along the Columbia River from Priest Rapids to the mouth of the Yakima. "They called themselves Soikulks, and they represented, on Clark's map,

about 2,400 souls in 120 lodges which were situated on the Columbia River considerably north of the point where the Snake enters the big river" (Ruby and Brown 1981, 17). "Everywhere there was ample evidence that the natives were a salmon-eating people. The explorers observed their fish-catching and processing paraphernalia and the mixing of roots and berries with the salmon to form a highly nutritious food" (Ruby and Brown 1981, 19). Trade goods were also noted by the explorers. "They found Spanish coins, blue beads, copper kettles, knowledge of many other goods and practices, and perhaps most importantly, a knowledge of White men" (Walker and Sprague 1998, 138). American traders were already doing business in the lower Columbia, and by 1811–12 the fur trade was in full swing.

Originating in British Columbia, the Columbia River flows northward at first, following the Rocky Mountain Trench, and finally reaching Columbia Lake to the south. In the early years before the construction of dams, salmon migrated all the way from the Pacific Ocean to Columbia Lake. Sometimes more than six miles wide, the river serves the drainage of 259,000 square miles of the Northwest before emptying into the Pacific Ocean.

The Indian tribes along the Columbia and its tributaries were astute traders since they had extensive trade networks among themselves before they ever encountered Whitemen. Trade centers were located at various major fishing sites along the great river and its tributaries, including ones at Celilo, The Dalles, and Kettle Falls. (See Figure 7.1.) These large intertribal gatherings were active during the protohistoric period with roots in the prehistoric period. "Around Celilo Falls the Indians prepared fish to be traded to Indians of the Columbia Gorge, who then sold it to ships calling at the Columbia's mouth. The salmon was dried, then pulverized and placed in a basket of grass and reeds, lined with salmon skin, where it was pressed down firmly and covered with another salmon skin, laced tightly together. Several such baskets were stacked up and encased tightly in porous matting to make a ninety to one hundred pound bundle. The fish remained edible for years" (Roe 1992, 125).

The twenty-foot Kettle Falls was the most revered Indian fishing site on the upper Columbia River in what is today Washington State. In late June, local tribes would gather for the First Salmon Dance. The ceremony was presided over by a salmon chief whose duty it was to equitably divide the salmon caught. Not all of the migrating fish were taken; a certain number were allowed to pass above the falls to

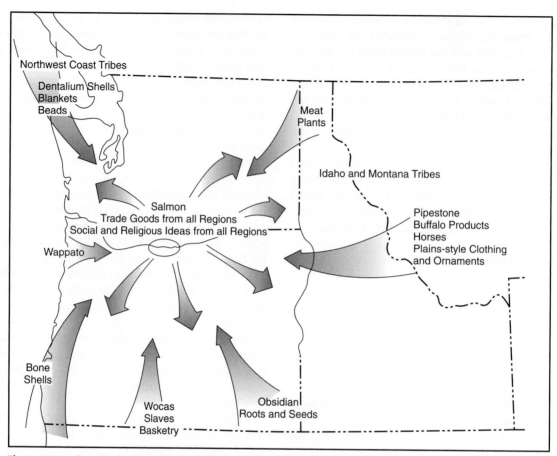

Figure 7.1 Indian Trade Network at the Dalles and Celilo Falls.

spawn upstream. Salmon fishing was a joyous event and was accompanied by secular fun activities, such as dancing, stick or bone games, and horse racing after horses were introduced into the region. The upper Columbia tribes were mariners. They built large canoes and navigated them through the river's rapids and shallows, plying their intertribal commerce and trade. Further down the river, where it now borders the states of Washington and Oregon, Celilo Falls, called the Great Falls of the Columbia, and the eight-mile rapids of The Dalles formed still other major fisheries and trade centers.

After the Louisiana Purchase, when Great Britain was considering setting a boundary south of the Columbia and establishing settlements to shut out the Americans, President Thomas Jefferson decided to send an exploratory party into the western lands. "In 1803, Jefferson secured the princely sum of $2,500 to finance a westward exploration by Meriwether Lewis, Jefferson's secretary, and William Clark" (Roe 1992, 123). They arrived in the region on October 16, 1805, at the confluence of the Snake, Yakima, and Walla Walla Rivers, a traditional meeting place of the local tribes where they negotiated alliances.

The Chinook on the lower Columbia, who already knew some English by the time Lewis and Clark encountered them, quickly established themselves as an intermediary between the European ships and tribes further inland. After 1800, the number of visiting ships declined, and first, the Pacific Fur Company, and then "the Northwest Company monopolized trade in the Columbia Basin until its merger with the Hudson's Bay Company in 1821" (Walker and Sprague 1998, 142). Trade patterns changed only slightly when the fur trade shifted to forts on land, such as Ft. George, Ft. Astoria, and Ft. Clatsop on the lower Columbia. The main trade items were blankets, guns, cloth, steel traps, and various foodstuffs. The Chinook, who were favorably placed in this trade network, were able to control commerce north to Puget Sound as well as to the west and south. They became a nation of traders and monopolized the trade in their region until other trading posts, such as at Vancouver and Nisqually, were opened.

The early European traders had no interest in changing Indian society; they wanted furs, not land. Few in numbers, they were dependent on the Indian peoples to supply the furs. Peaceful relations were an economic necessity. Nevertheless, indirect change with its unintended consequences was inevitable. Contact with Europeans increased social stratification among the trading tribes by increasing economic competition and political influence among Indian leaders in their trade relations. Polygyny increased along with trade wealth, and Indian leaders along the lower Columbia sought to marry their daughters to White traders. Prostitution, which was formerly unknown, became common by the time that Lewis and Clark encountered the lower Columbia Indian nations in 1806.

Indigenous Peoples

The original, Indigenous population of the Northwest Coast before White contact is estimated at approximately 190,000. Sexual contacts between Whites and Indians soon spread venereal disease. Smallpox first struck the coast during the 1770s, followed by less severe outbreaks as immunities were acquired by the survivors. The greatest decline as a result of European-introduced diseases occurred between 1775 and 1801, mainly as a result of smallpox. The initial outbreak infected the entire northwest coastal area from Canada to the Puget Sound, to the mouth of the Columbia River, and probably came from ships engaged in the fur trade. "Small pox appeared again on the central coast about 1801, certainly spread from the Plains via the Columbia Plateau" (Boyd 1990, 138). "A decade before Gray breached the Columbia, the smallpox had raced along that stream as it had up the Missouri River and across the Rocky Mountains to the upper Columbia" (Ruby and Brown 1981, 11). A third epidemic of unknown nature, the so-called "mortality of 1824–1825," infected the central Northwest Coast and the Columbia Plateau. Fever and ague (malaria?) hit the coast tribes in early 1830 and took about twenty-five thousand Indian lives. Another epidemic of smallpox in 1862–63 caused nineteen thousand deaths.

The preoccupation with the fur trade meant less time devoted to traditional Indian fisheries and resulted at times in periods of famine. By the 1830s, the sea otter had become virtually extinct, and trapping shifted to land animals, primarily the beaver. "The fur trade changed the balance between trade and subsistence activities within the Native economy: a predominantly food-gathering society became a fur-gathering society. There was, however, another change: the introduction of limited agricultural production. A gathering society soon became an agricultural one" (Cole and Darling 1990, 131).

There were other changes as well. Intertribal trade fostered the spread of the *potlatch* to the more southern groups of the Pacific Northwest. The potlatch is a social institution in which economic surplus (fish, berries, blankets, furs, and the like) are distributed by wealthy chiefs and clans to other tribal communities in a ceremonial fashion, and the giveaway of possessions is converted to enhancing the chiefly rank of the host and his clansmen and women. The lower Columbia tribes, for example, did not acquire the institution of the potlatch until after 1830.

The changes resulting from White contact in the early years had a devastating impact on those tribes located at the mouth of the Columbia River. The Lower Chinook, Cathlamet, Multnomah, and Clackamus ranged from the ocean coast to a point above the Willamette River, which enters into the Columbia at the site of present-day Portland, Oregon, and Vancouver, Washington. The Upper Chonookan-speaking tribes were those located from this point to a short distance eastward above The Dalles.

The Chinookan villages "were oriented toward fishing and root-and-berry gathering, with extensive economic and political ties among villages, maintained by exchange of goods and alliances through wives" (Silverstein 1990, 536). Fishing, hunting, and gathering formed the core of Native economic subsistence. The five species of salmon, sturgeon, steelhead, along with eulachon and herring, were either eaten fresh or else smoke-dried for winter. Dentalium shells provided a medium of exchange in the extensive Chinook trade networks. After contact with Europeans and Americans, China beads became another form of trade currency.

The Chinook were famous for their elaborate gabled roof, upright cedar plank houses. Winter villages contained fifteen to twenty of these magnificent houses. Larger houses for extended families and chiefly people were forty by one hundred feet in dimensions. Dugout, cedar log canoes of up to fifty feet in length transported people up and down the Columbia River for fishing and trading.

The Lower Chinookans were first contacted by the captain and mate of the American ship *Columbia* on May 18, 1792, and again in the same year by George Vancouver. Lewis and Clark descended the river in the autumn of 1805 and gave the first extensive account by Western observers of these River Peoples and their fishing-trading culture. Fur traders were active in the area in the early period of Astoria in 1811–14, "before large-scale immigration by Euro-Americans to the Columbia and Willamette regions" took place (Silverstein 1990, 535) The fur trade and the cohabitation by the traders with Indian women soon changed the dynamics of Chinookan society when Astoria and Ft. Vancouver became the centers of trade activity.

Rank was the hallmark of traditional Chinookan social organization with society divided between chiefly families at one end of the social spectrum, and slaves at the other end. The majority of slaves were obtained by sale or trade along the coastal tributaries of the Columbia. "Slave raiding increased during the maritime fur trade period," and by the mid-nineteenth century, "Oregon settlers in the Willamette Valley regularly bought slaves from the Chinookans and kept them for farm work" (Silverstein 1990, 543).

Between 1831 and 1855, the Chinookan population was decimated by epidemics of smallpox, measles, malaria, and other White-introduced diseases. Most of the original villages were abandoned, and the survivors, "like their upriver counterparts, were being negotiated onto reservations in exchange for residual fishing rights, many of the treaties for which were never ratified" (Silverstein 1990, 536).

Among the Indian nations further inland on the Columbia Plateau, especially the Cayuse, Nez Perce, Palouse, and Yakama, the introduction of horses from the south radically altered tribal life. Horses had been acquired by the Shoshonis sometime in the 1730s. Their enemies, the Blackfoot, offset their lack of horses with guns obtained from British fur traders. The Columbia Plateau was ideal horse country, and a tribe that possessed horses effectively increased its mobility. "Greater mobility expanded the seasonal round, enabled people to travel greater distances, and provided transport for heavier loads. Tribal gatherings on an unprecedented scale became common" (Walker and Sprague 1998, 139). Villages and bands which were formerly autonomous joined together to become composite bands, and these, in turn, joined together into multi-tribal groupings, for example, to counteract enemy tribes further east, such as the Blackfoot Confederacy. The Walla Walla, Cayuse, and Yakama opened long-distance trade with Indian tribes and Spaniards in California. The goods thus obtained were then exchanged at The Dalles fishery on the Columbia River with other local tribes.

Christian evangelical activity soon became prominent in Puget Sound, and in the Columbia and Willamette valleys, although it was not promoted by the Hudson's Bay Company. After 1834, White settlers began to arrive to acquire land, and the local Indigenous societies were radically altered. "In 1845, over 3,000 immigrants traveled the Oregon Trail, passing through the Columbia Plateau. An additional 2,350 immigrants entered the Oregon Territory in the following year with over 5,000 arriving in 1847. . . . Due to the constant flow of Americans to the Oregon Country, the United States and Great Britain finally resolved their dispute over the boundaries of that area in 1846," fixing 49 degrees latitude as the northern boundary of the United States (Walker and Sprague 1998, 148). The treaty with Great Britain recognized the possessory rights of the Hudson's Bay Company, its subsidiary the Puget Sound Agricultural Company, and resident British citizens, but it ignored all tribal land claims and interests.

Western Washington

Until 1846, the Pacific Northwest that today consists of the separate states of Washington and Oregon and possibly Idaho, was simply Oregon Country, a territory subject to the joint claim and occupation by both the United States and Great Britain. After the two countries resolved their joint claim, a U.S. Congressional Organic Act of 1848 created the Oregon Territory. The Oregon Donation Act of 1850 opened up land to settlement, and a flood of American settlers poured into the Puget Sound and Willamette Valley areas of the new territory. Subsequently, Congress created the Washington Territory in 1853. Isaac J. Stevens was appointed governor and ex officio superintendent of Indian Affairs for the new Washington Territory. A believer in the Anglo-Saxon notion of Manifest Destiny, Stevens set about negotiating a series of Indian treaties in which the title to Indian lands would be extinguished and then opened to Whites in exchange for the creation of reservations remote from White interests and settlements. It is important to note that a common provision found in these early treaties was the Indians' "right of taking fish, at all usual and accustomed grounds and stations . . . in common with all citizens of the Territory" (Marino 1990, 169).

The first treaty concluded was the Medicine Creek Treaty of December, 1854, with the tribes of the lower Puget Sound. Three reservations were created: the Puyallup, near present-day Tacoma, the Nisqually, near Olympia (today the state capital), and the Squaxin on Squaxin Island in southern Puget Sound. In 1857, the Muckleshoot reservation was created between the White and Green rivers for the Salish-speaking bands who had been mentioned in the 1854 treaty. Within a short time, Governor Stevens concluded the Treaty of Point Elliott for other Puget Sound tribes. Stevens then turned to the coastal tribes for yet other treaties. "Still other Indians, both north and south of the Columbia River and throughout the Puget Sound region, continued to live off-reservation, becoming, in time, the 'landless tribes of Western Washington'" (Marino 1990, 171).

Due to the dispossession of the Indians from their lands, and the epidemics of diseases among the Puget Sound and Lower Columbia River tribes, there was a short-lived uprising during the winter of 1855–56. By the 1860s, however, separate Indian agencies had been established to maintain White control. The national Indian program of assimilation was then applied to make farmers out of the former hunting, gathering, and fisher peoples. "Indian agents, many of whom were corrupt, aided by resident farmers, carpenters, and physicians assigned to their respective agencies, embarked on the task of 'civilizing' the Indians. Agriculture and schooling were used as the main tools of the government's reservation policy, but neither appeared to have been adopted enthusiastically by most Indians" (Marino 1990, 172). Some Indians were employed as temporary wage laborers in the White-controlled fishing industry and the canneries, or in the hop fields. Under these exploitative conditions, the Indian population continued to decline, and disease epidemics, malnutrition, and alcoholism took their toll. The 1870 census found only 7,657 Indians left in the region.

By 1879, a dozen or so Indian boarding and day schools were operating, with about three hundred students attending. Nearly all of the Indians of Puget Sound had adopted so called civilized clothing. A Training School for Indian Youth was established in Forest Grove, Oregon, in 1886. Later it was moved to Salem where it became Chemawa Boarding School, which is still in operation today.

Despite the aggressive work of Christian missionaries, many Indian people retained their old beliefs, or developed new forms of spirituality to meet the challenges of conquest and dispossession. The Indian Shaker Church was founded in 1882 by John Slocum, a Squaxin Indian. As a syncretic religion, it combined what the Indians found best or useful in the old Tamahnous religion together with elements of Protestantism and Roman Catholicism. In sum, "after years of Christian control of Indian affairs it became clear that throughout western Washington the traditional patterns of subsistence, kinship networks, and inter-village ties persisted, fostering Indian values and the maintenance of Indian identity" (Marino 1990, 174).

Land allotment to promote the private property concept was instituted as early as 1874 on some of the reservations in Washington. This was followed in 1887 by the Dawes (Indian Allotment) Act which made it federal Indian policy to divide up Indian communal lands. The policy clashed with traditional Indian land tenure. "Many western Washington groups . . . recognized individual or family rights to . . . fishing locations, clam beds, and root beds. The allotment system changed the extent and nature of the ownership of real estate" (Marino 1990, 175). It also resulted in the reduction of the reservations' land bases when surplus lands, those lands left over after the individual allotments, were opened to White settlement. For example, as a result of allotment, the city of Tacoma obtained 50 percent of the Pyuallup Reservation lands, and the U.S. Army expropriated two-thirds of the Nisqually Reservation in 1917.

By the time that Washington Territory was admitted to statehood in 1889, "White-owned commercial fishing and canning operations were well established throughout the Puget Sound region and on the Columbia River, competing among themselves and with the Indians for the seemingly unlimited quantities of salmon" (Marino 1990, 175). Thus began the bitter struggle over Native fishing rights that were supposedly guaranteed in the Indian treaties.

While the right of Indians to fish on reservation lands was recognized, the right to fish off reservation became a major bone of contention. The Lummi lost an important court case in 1897 to a non-Indian commercial fishing company in *United States et al v. Alaska Packers Association*. In *United States v. Winans* (1905), however, the U.S. Supreme Court upheld the Indians' treaty right to fish off reservation at their "usual and accustomed places." The Indians had the right to cross private land, to fish in the river, and to erect temporary houses for curing their catch—the Reserved Rights Doctrine—but the state was allowed to regulate Indian fishing. As a consequence, during the first decades of the twentieth century, the state began limiting Indian treaty rights by increasingly regulating fishing and hunting, both on and off the reservation. Then in 1916, the State Supreme Court ruled against off-reservation treaty rights in two important cases, one involving a Yakama, and the other a Lummi Indian who were exercising their fishing rights without state interference. Thus "the State Court rejected the premise of Indian sovereignty and subjected Indian fishing off-reservation to state regulations" (Marino 1990, 176).

Meanwhile, the potlatch, a traditional giveaway ceremony that fueled the old traditional economy of gift-giving and exchange, was suppressed by the authorities. Even so, the redistribution of goods between Indian families and communities, although modified to suit White conventions, persisted at Indian gatherings such as the winter dances and the Fourth of July celebration. Salmon continued as an important item exchanged during these Indian gatherings.

There were other changes as well during the early years. Native language proficiency declined, intermarriage with Whites took place, alcoholism became a problem (despite its prohibition by the state in 1909), government modeled tribal councils replaced the traditional village government system, the population continued its decline, and many Indian men saw active duty in the two world wars. In spite of the suppression and destruction of much of the traditional culture, Indian people nevertheless continued to try to exercise their fishing rights. In 1951, the Makah tribe successfully "challenged state regulations that prohibited them from fishing off-reservation on the Hoko River" (Marino 1990, 176). A 1957 decision in *State of Washington v. Satiacum,* involving two Puyallup Indians, favored Indian fishing rights in western Washington. In 1963, however, the state Supreme Court upheld the state's right to regulate Indian fishing, and the state subsequently banned Indian fishing in southern Puget Sound. The *fish-ins* of the 1960s were the result. Organized by the National Indian Youth Council, an Indian protest organization, and the Northwest-based Survival of American Indians Association, the fish-ins were modeled after the successful sit-ins against racial segregation by the Civil Rights Movement. In Washington State, the fish-ins were assisted in their protest by Chicanos from Seattle's El Centro de la Raza, and high profile supporters who included African American entertainer-activist Dick Gregory, and actors Marlon Brando and Jane Fonda. They "stopped by to hoist nets and spread the aura of national celebrity, making the Northwest conflict over fish the first widely publicized treaty-rights defense of the late twentieth century" (Grinde and Johansen 1995, 150).

As a result of the success of the fish-ins, the U.S. Supreme Court struck down the state ban on Indian net fishing in 1973, but it still allowed partial state regulation of Indian fishing for conservation purposes. Finally, in 1974, federal Judge George H. Boldt issued a landmark decision in *United States v. State of Washington,* reaffirming Indian treaty-protected fishing rights. The Boldt decision contains six parts: Judge Boldt found that "(1) treaties reserved to Indian tribes fishing rights that are distinct from other citizens; (2) off-reservation Indian fishing rights extended to every place each tribe customarily fished; (3) Indians had reserved rights to a fair share—50 percent—of the harvestable fish exclusive of on-reservation catches and fish taken for subsistence and ceremonial purposes; (4) the state may regulate Indian off-reservation fishing only to the extent necessary for conservation, but not in ways limiting treaty rights to state-preferred times and fishing methods; (5) the state classification of steelhead as a 'game' fish restricted Indian fishing rights and violated the treaties; and (6) fourteen treaty tribes, plus three more upon federal approval [federal recognition], were entitled to share in the decision" (Marino 1990, 176–77) . Following the 1974 Boldt decision, a Fisheries Advisory Board was set up, comprised of both state and tribal representatives, as well as five intertribal treaty councils that represented the original tribes of the 1854–55 treaties. This body then coordinated with the Northwest Indian Fisheries Commission to implement the Boldt decision.

The fishing tribes were already managing their own fisheries. The Lummi had developed a modern aquaculture facility in the early 1970s, and by 1984, sixteen tribes were operating twenty tribal hatcheries. At the same time, the landless Indians, who continued to live as distinct Indian communities, organized the Northwest Federation of American Indians, an intertribal organization. The Federation sought to resolve their landless status and assert their treaty rights. "During the 1950s, under the threat of termination, both landed and landless tribes joined forces in the Inter-tribal Council of Western Washington" (Marino 1990, 178). Eventually, several of the landless groups achieved federal recognition under the 1978 Federal Acknowledgement Program. In the 1970s and 1980s, Northwest tribes shared in the national upsurge of Indian pride and cultural revitalization.

Oregon

Oregon has had a somewhat different history of Indian-White relations than has Washington. The Cayuse War erupted on the Columbia Plateau in

1847 because of the immigration of White settlers into Indian lands. In response, Congress passed the Organic Act of 1848 establishing Oregon as a territory of the United States. The Organic Act also "extended the Northwest Ordinance of 1787 . . . to the Pacific Northwest, which meant that the 'utmost good faith' clause of the ordinance, affirming Indian land title, rights, liberty, and protection from undeclared war, was valid throughout the region" (Beckham 1990, 180).

Although the Organic Act validated Indian land title, it mainly provided land grants of up to 320 acres to "every White settler or occupant of the public lands, American half-breed Indians included, above the age of eighteen years, being a citizen of the United States, or having made a declaration according to law, of his intention to become a citizen" (quoted in Beckham 1990, 180). By 1855 when the Act expired, 7,437 Oregon claimants had filed on 2.5 million acres of Indian lands in western Oregon. The settlers drove the Indians off their claims and out of their villages, fenced off food-gathering areas, decimated the wild game, suppressed the Indians' ecological field-burning management, and allowed cattle to overrun and destroy Native food sources. As a result, the Native peoples encountered starvation and widespread dislocation.

Between 1851 and 1856, there were several attempted treaty negotiations, and even several reservations established. Yet, none of the twenty treaties were ever ratified by Congress, and the early reservations were later abandoned under settler pressure. Few of these early treaty attempts provided for fishing or hunting rights, although one might argue that the Reserved Rights Doctrine should have included them.

The discovery of gold in 1852, in the Rogue River drainage of southern Oregon, led to tragic consequences for local Indian tribes. The Oregon Gold Rush resembled that of northern California with respect to its genocidal impact on Indian communities. Miners formed companies of volunteers who then massacred the Takelma, Shasta, Chetco, and Lower Coquille Indians. Furthermore, "the flood of mining debris took a heavy toll on the important Indian fisheries. The miners drove the Indians from the stream terraces where they had established their villages. . . . Driven by hunger, anger, deception, and a sense of desperation, the Indians fought back" (Beckman 1990, 182). The killing, raping, and enslavement of the Indians resulted in the Rogue River War of 1855.

Two Executive Order reservations were created along the Oregon coast as virtual concentration camps for the Indian survivors of the 1855 war: the Siletz Reservation established in 1855 (originally 125 miles long), and the Grand Ronde Reservation in 1857. The refugee Indians were then driven on death marches to these reservations. As part of the ethnic cleansing operation, "bounty hunters tracked down, captured, or killed Indians hiding in the mountains of southwestern Oregon" (Beckman 1990, 183).

By the 1880s, after the coastal Indians were pacified, a Roman Catholic boarding school was established at Grand Ronde, and a Methodist boarding school at Siletz. Chamawa Indian School, as previously noted, was founded near Salem in 1885. Yet, many Indian people attempted to follow their traditional religious practices, or else founded new religions that sought to combine traditional beliefs with elements of Roman Catholicism and Protestantism. A prophet-based nativistic religion, the Earth Lodge Movement, emerged in 1871 on the two coastal reservations. Its conception appears to have been influenced by the 1870 Ghost Dance of the western Plains, and the Smohalla Washat religion on the Columbian Plateau. The Indian Shaker religion appeared later on the Siletz Reservation in the 1920s.

By the 1860s, Whites were trespassing on the reservations to harvest oysters in Yaquina Bay, as also did settlers in the 1870s on the Alsea and Salmon River estuaries. During the same years, the federal government continually reduced the two coastal reservations. Allotment agreements at the turn of the century and land cessions left many coastal Indian people landless, although some Indians were able to obtain public domain allotments. In the latter half of the nineteenth century, many Oregon Indians "eked out an existence as domestics, hop pickers, loggers, and woodchoppers. Some ran trap lines, processed hides, and marketed tanned leather goods" (Beckham 1990, 187).

During the Indian New Deal of the 1930s, the Siletz and Grand Ronde tribes were able to incorporate under the 1934 Indian Reorganization Act; the Confederated Tribes of the Coos, Lower Umpqua, and Siuslaw did not. Several Oregon tribes filed land claims based on the unratified treaties before the Indian Claims Commission between 1946 and 1951. Tragedy struck in 1954 when the coastal tribes lost their federal recognition and services under the government's Termination Act. This draconian law forced many of the terminated Indians to scatter into the surrounding White communities where they experienced inadequate housing, a loss of federal health and education services, and high rates of unemployment and underemployment. Fortunately, by the late 1970s and early 1980s, federal policy again changed, and they were able to seek federal recognition and receive restoration of some government services and lands. The 1988 Indian Gaming Act allowed the tribes to negotiate tribal compacts with the State of Oregon and construct casinos. A noteworthy record of these developments is the case history of the termination and restoration of the Coos, Lower Umpqua, and Siuslaw Indians by David Beck, *Seeking Recognition* (2009). For coastal tribes, casinos became the new salmon, a unique business opportunity to underwrite a better economic future for tribal members. The same has been true for Washington's Indian tribes. Casino profits, for the most part, are plowed back into the housing, education, health, and welfare needs of their respective Indian communities, and the casinos create employment opportunities for tribal members. Indian casino development has also stimulated local non-Indian business and created resort complexes with hotel accommodations, restaurants, and entertainment centers. A certain percent of tribal casino profits are also generously channeled into charitable donations to service organizations in the wider non-Indian community.

SALMON AS A WAY OF LIFE

When Merriwether Lewis and William Clark explored the Columbia River in October 1805, they found "100 Indian lodges with every member busy catching, drying, or pounding the fish into thin strips to make pemmican for future use," and an estimated fifty thousand Indians taking eighteen million pounds of salmon a year (Cohen 1986, 30). They reported in their journals that they were rarely out of sight of an Indian village. More than fifty Chinook villages lined the lower Columbia for a length of about 150 miles. "The Columbia served as a super-highway for tribes living along it and along the extensive network of tributaries. Canoes could travel nearly 400 miles eastward from the Columbia's mouth, squeezing through a narrow gorge and portaging over a wall of water at Celilo Falls, before the river turned north for another 500 miles to present-day Canada. Along the way, tributaries such as the Deschutes, Umatilla, Walla Walla, Snake, Yakima, Okanogan, and Spokane Rivers greatly expanded the reach of the network, connecting the Columbia to the mountains and high plateaus of present-day eastern

Oregon and Washington, Idaho and Montana, and farther" (Halliday and Chehak 1996, 175–76).

For thousands of years the River Indian tribes of the Pacific Northwest "gathered along the riverbanks and saltwater bays to stake their gill nets, to erect wooden fish traps, or to poise long spears in search of salmon" (Cohen 1986, xxii). Salmon was the heart of tribal culture and fishing a way of life for all tribes in the region. Salmon was "more than food, the fish were vital to the Indians' religion, nourishment for the spirit as well as the body" (Ulrich 1999, 6). Salmon fishing was also a family activity. The Indian child was brought closer to elders, and the child came to understand that the fisherman or woman was a respected member of the tribal community. The salmon was so important to the Indian peoples of the Northwest that when they reluctantly signed away their traditional lands in treaties to the United States, they insisted on retaining the right to fish at their "usual and accustomed places." For the most part, however, these treaties were ignored by the federal government and especially by the state of Washington. Consequently, an important core of Indian culture was suppressed as the states of the Northwest sought to prevent the Indians from fishing at their traditional fisheries.

In the early years, before the dams and canneries, when the salmon were running upstream, the entire Indian community was absorbed in catching, preparing, and storing fish. The men

> utilized an intricate technology employing many kinds of spears, gaffs, dip nets, hooks and lines, and traps and weirs. Women cleaned the fish. Some fish might be boiled while others were split and either spread open for broiling or laid on wooden racks to be smoked, dried, and stored in wooden boxes for later use. Children gathered wood and helped clean fish. . . . Salmon figured prominently in the thoughts, beliefs and rituals of the Indian people. For example, when the Quileute on the Pacific coast divided up the year, they named four of the twelve portions for runs of fish [January and February for steelhead, and September and October for Chinook and silver salmon respectively]. (Cohen 1986, 22–23)

Nisqually astronomy reflected the importance of fish with its many fish images, and the Pleiades constellation was viewed as a species of fish. Indian legends spoke of the close relationship between the human world and that of the Salmon People. Columbia River fishing peoples tell how the supernatural Coyote made human beings and the salmon interdependent. Important religious ceremonies, first-food feasts honoring the salmon, celebrate the renewal of life and express thanks for the salmon's return each year. "Because the 'salmon people' are beings with supernatural power, their arrival must be greeted with respect and ceremony" (Cohen 1986, 24).

Thee are five species of salmon: (1) Chinook, the largest, also called "king salmon," "tyee," or "quinnat salmon"; (2) Coho, or "silver salmon"; (3) Chum, or "dog salmon"; (4) Pinks, the smallest salmon, commonly called "humpbacks" or "humpies"; (5) Sockeye, also called "blueback," or "red salmon." A sixth species, Steelhead is actually an oceangoing trout.

Salmon spend most of their lives in salt water, the ocean, yet their birth, mating and reproduction, and death all take place in freshwater—rivers, streams, and lakes. Salmon are sometimes called the "mystery navigators," because each species will swim hundreds, even thousands of miles away from its place of origin and mix with other fish species and salmon stocks from other states and nations. Yet, each will manage to return to its point of origin to reproduce and die.

Although noted for their strength and endurance, salmon are nevertheless vulnerable to environmental conditions. Only 10 to 20 percent of the "fry" (the early stage of development after the egg stage) and the fingerling stages manage to survive. In order to survive into mature adult fish, salmon must have unimpeded access to and from the ocean, water of the proper temperature, clarity of water, an adequate stream flow, gravel beds for spawning and hatching, sufficient food, and a protective cover from the sun's rays.

Treaties and Fish

Most White Americans fail to understand that American Indian tribes still retain a considerable amount of sovereign status under law. Indian sovereignty is enshrined in the U.S. Constitution and is reflected in the several hundred treaties made by the federal government with Indian nations.

> A treaty is a contract between sovereign nations. The Constitution authorizes the President, with the consent of two-thirds of the Senate, to make a treaty on behalf of the United States.
>
> Treaties are "the supreme law of the land." This means they are superior to state laws and constitutions and are equal in rank to laws passed by Congress. . . . Until 1871 treaties were the accepted method by which the United States conducted its relations with Indian tribes. The United States has entered into more than 650 Indian treaties. Nearly every Indian tribe has at least one treaty with the United States. (Pevar 1983, 32)

Even though treaties are the supreme law of the land, westward expansion in the last century by

Anglo-Americans into the Pacific Northwest created a contradictory policy of recognizing Indian treaty rights on paper while abrogating those same rights in practice. Yet, the U.S. Constitution clearly delineates the sovereign rights of Indian tribes and nations under the Commerce and the Supremacy Clauses. "The Commerce Clause (Article 1, Section 8) provided Congress with the power 'to regulate commerce with foreign Nations, and among the several States, and with the Indian Tribes.' The Supremacy Clause (Article 6) provided that 'all treaties made, or which shall be made, under the authority of the United States, shall be the supreme law of the land; and the judges in every state shall be bound thereby, anything in the constitution or laws of any state notwithstanding'" (Cohen 1986, 32). The 1787 Northwest Ordinance and various trade and intercourse acts further define the power of the federal role in Indian affairs.

An Indian treaty is not a grant of rights to an Indian nation. Rather, it is a grant of rights from them. "The purpose of an Indian treaty was not to give rights to the Indians but to remove rights they [already] had" (Pevar 1983, 32). Therefore, the Indian nation retains any right, such as subsistence hunting and fishing rights, not specifically mentioned in the treaty or federal statute. These rights are known as the Doctrine of Reserved Rights.

Most treaties have two basic provisions. First, the Indian nation signing the treaty agrees to relinquish land to the United States. In return, the United States creates a reservation for the Indians under federal supervision and trust protection. Some treaties also provide the Indian tribes with services, such as medical care, food and clothing, and technical assistance.

In the early years of the republic, Indian nations negotiated treaties with the United States as sovereign equals. They were powerful aboriginal nations and the fledgling United States was relatively weak as a political and military power. This changed following the War of 1812, when the British threat to the young U.S. republic ended. After 1812, the United States was able to take Indian land by force, and Indian treaties were rarely voluntary.

When treaties were being made with the Indian peoples of the Northwest they were involuntary. In other words, the respective tribes had no other options but to win as much as they could in the treaty negotiations. Refusing to relinquish their traditional lands was not an option, but the one right that they tenaciously clung to was the right to fish in their usual and accustomed places.

In 1871 Congress passed a law abolishing treaty making with Indian tribes. Some reservations in the west were then created through Executive Order of the President. Since 1871, Congress has regulated Indian affairs through legislation. The Indians were no longer considered as completely sovereign nations, and Congress was deemed to hold plenary (total) power over the Indian tribes and nations. In *Lone Wolf v. Hitchcock* (1903), the U.S. Supreme Court held that Indian treaties have the same status as federal statutes. Hence, Congress, as the government's lawmaker, has the power to amend or even repeal Indian treaties. As a result, most treaties have been broken or breached by Congress, often resulting in the confiscation of treaty-protected land.

The Fifth Amendment to the Constitution requires that private property cannot be taken by the federal government without just compensation. The Supreme Court has ruled that Indian treaty rights are a form of property protected by the just compensation clause. Thus, when Congress breaks or modifies an Indian treaty, a monetary award is made, although the terms and amount of the award is never fair.

Following the settlement of the international boundary to the Northwest between Great Britain and the United States, the Oregon Donation Act of 1850 was passed. Each settler was offered 320 acres of land, and the Anglo-American immigrants poured into the region. It was then that the federal government began negotiating treaties with the Indians in which the latter were forced to give up millions of acres of prime land to the White settlers. Early treaties with the Indians included the resettlement of those fishing tribes at The Dalles on the Columbia River to the Warm Springs Reservation, some seventy-five miles south and inland. When Washington became a separate territory in 1853, similar means were employed to extinguish aboriginal title held by the Indian nations. The dislocation of Puget Sound Indians by the White settlers almost precipitated an Indian war.

The major treaty-making in Washington took place when Issac Ingalls Stevens became governor and superintendent of Indian Affairs of the territory in 1853. Pressure to obtain land from the Indians came not only from the increasing settler population, but also from plans for a transcontinental railway across the territory. Between 1854 and 1855, a half a dozen treaties were made with tribes representing more than seventeen thousand Indians and involving sixty-four million acres (one hundred thousand square miles) in Washington, Idaho, and Montana. These treaties included the Treaty of Medicine Creek,

Treaty of Point Elliot, the Treaty of Point No Point, the Treaty of Neah Bay, the Yakima Treaty for tribes east of the Cascade Mountains, and the Treaty of Olympia.

Although the Indians of the Northwest relinquished their lands, they retained the right to fish, conceding only to share their off-reservation fishing grounds with the White settlers. All of the treaties stated in nearly identical terms: "The right of taking fish at usual and accustomed grounds and stations is further secured to said Indians in common with all citizens of the United States and of erecting temporary houses for the purpose of curing, together with the privilege of hunting and gathering roots and berries on open and unclaimed lands; provided, however, that they shall not take shell fish from any beds staked or cultivated by citizens" (quoted in Cohen 1986, 38)

The first fish wheel was erected on the Columbia River in 1879. Within a few years there were seventy-nine stationary wheels on the upper Columbia that were operated by different cannery families. "Only one man was required to tend a fishwheel, and the wheel caught large quantities of salmon at costs lower than the prices paid to gillnetters or trapmen" (Smith 1979, 35). The wheels were usually located in prime fishing sites, and therefore conflicted with Indian fishing. Use of fish wheels declined by the turn of the century and were finally banned by the state of Washington in 1934.

By 1883 there were fifty-five canneries on the Columbia River and its tributaries. "Cannery-owned fish wheels and traps came to dot the banks of Columbia and river mouths on Puget Sound" (Cohen 1986, 41). Canning was the process that enabled salmon to be stored for long periods of time, transported over long distances and available for market. Its development, however, seriously curtailed the runs of salmon reaching Indian fishermen. "Indians continued to use fish dipnets in their traditional fishing grounds, but their catches were rapidly diminishing. Gillnetters, trapmen, seiners, fishwheelers, purse seiners, and trollers all competed for a share of the catch as canned salmon became an increasingly important part of the world's food supply" (Smith 1979, 23). In fact, such fierce competition arose among the non-Indian commercial fishermen that fights broke out along the Columbia River between the gillnetters and the trapmen, and later between the gillnetters and the seiners.

One of the consequences of the growth of canneries during the 1880s was the importation of immigrant laborers. Chinese were first employed as cannery laborers in 1872, and by the 1890s the contract labor system was in full swing. A process of ethnic segmentation took place when the Asian immigrants became the main labor source for the canneries, but immigrants from Europe were recruited for fishing. While dipnets continued to be used mainly by the Indians, purse seines were introduced to the Columbia by Austrians. Trollers were more likely to be immigrants from western Europe.

Starting in 1887, Washington State began restricting Indian fishing in its rivers and tributaries, and by the 1920s, Oregon and Washington agreed to jointly manage the Columbia River fishery. At the same time, dam-building, logging, farming, and industrial development placed increasing pressures on the fish environment. "By 1948 some 300 dams . . . had been built in the Columbia Basin, both by private utility companies and by the federal government" (Cohen 1986, 45) As a result, fish runs went into even further decline. With the building of Grand Coulee Dam on the upper reaches of the Columbia in Washington (on the Colville Reservation), 40 percent of fish migration was forever closed off. The 350-foot dam failed to provide any fish ladder or means for the migrating salmon to return to their spawning grounds. Each of the other nine dams on the Columbia River kills an estimated 15 percent of young fish on their way downstream. Celilo Falls, the largest Indian fishery in continental North America, was destroyed when The Dalles Dam was constructed in 1956.

Logjams on the river prevented adult salmon from reaching their spawning grounds, and wood wastes encouraged algae and plant growth that deprive fish of needed oxygen. Clear-cutting along streams exposed the water to the sun; even a small rise in the water temperature proves injurious to salmon which are very heat sensitive. Irrigation by farmers also raised water temperatures by diverting water and slowing stream flows. Migrating salmon became confused when large inland lakes were created as a result of dam-building, instead of the fast-running river that previously existed.

The response by the authorities to decreasing fish runs was to construct hatcheries by using artificial means to produce salmon and steelhead. In retrospect, however, "fisheries biologists today express concern about genetic alterations that hatchery-bred fish introduce into wild runs" (Cohen 1986, 50).

The 1960s Fish-Ins

While the state of Washington was increasingly restricting Indian fishing in violation of treaty rights, federal policy increased its assimilation program.

As a result, Indian off-reservation fishing became criminalized and the Northwest tribes were caught in "the grip of hunger, fear, and prison" (Cohen 1986, 52). The loss of Indian lands under the 1887 Allotment Act resulted in the reservations of western Washington becoming checkerboarded between White and Indian ownership. The Indian tribes typically lost control of lands along the rivers and streams, so that their usual and accustomed places to fish ended up off-reservation on land in control of the White settler population.

For the tribes in Washington, the two main legal issues to emerge were: (1) should Indians have the right to fish at their traditional fishing sites off the reservation; and (2) could the state regulate Indian fishing? By the 1950s, Washington still refused to respect Native fishing rights and was arresting Indians for fishing. Most of the arrests were of Nisqually and Puyallup fisherfolk along their respective rivers in western Washington. In response, in the early 1960s, the tribes started a series of fish-ins in which they "frequently risked their boats, their nets and their fish. They also risked their personal safety in confrontations with [state] game wardens. . . . Indians had secured their right of access to their usual and accustomed fishing grounds, but their right to fish off-reservation without restrictive state regulation remained in jeopardy" (Cohen 1986, 65).

About the same time, Columbia River Indians were challenging Oregon's fishing regulations. When three Umatilla Indians were arrested for fishing in 1958 during a closed season, they took their cased to court and won.

In 1963, the Survival of American Indians Association in Washington organized a major demonstration at the state capitol in Olympia. A protest march took place and an Indian encampment was set up. Ironically, the 1960s fish-ins coincided with a severe fish famine, and the Indians got the blame for the decline in the fish runs. "Instead of pointing to the overabundant, non-Indian commercial fleet, or to dams, or to habitat destruction as reasons for the paucity of fish, the *Seattle Times* ran an increasing number of feature stories blaming Indians for the poor catches during this period" (Cohen 1986, 71). Washington State then introduced two anti-Indian fishing resolutions in the U.S. Congress, but through intense lobbying efforts by the Indians and their supporters, both resolutions failed.

More arrests were made in 1964 as the fish-ins continued. Franks Landing on the Nisqually River became a focal point for the protests and the site of brutal arrests, with game wardens beating the Indian protestors with flashlights and clubs. Two outside groups supporting and assisting the fish-in struggle were the American Friends Service Committee (Quaker-related) and the Native American Rights Fund, an Indian legal advocacy organization based in Denver, Colorado.

"Fish-ins also took place in 1966 at Cook's Landing on the Columbia River. . . . A group of Yakama Indians [River People], acting independently of their tribal council, provided armed guards while tribal fishermen set their nets" (Cohen 1986, 75). The protests at Cook's Landing were unique in that they rejected any kind of state, or even tribal regulation, embracing instead their religiously-oriented, traditional conservation practices that had guided fishing customs for thousands of years.

The 1960s fish-ins resulted in two major court cases, the Puyallup Trilogy, so named because it went to the U.S. Supreme Court three times, and *United States v. Oregon*, the case of Yakima River fisherman Richard Sohappy. In the first case, the treaty right of the Puyallup and Nisqually to fish off-reservation was upheld, but the right of Washington State to regulate Indian fishing for conservation purposes was also recognized. In the Oregon decision, war veteran Richard Sohappy and his uncle, David Sohappy (about whom we will have more to say later), won a court decision of "a fair and equitable share" for Indian fishermen from any given fish run on the Columbia River. The State of Oregon was ordered by presiding Judge Robert Clinton Belloni to manage the fishery so that the Indians could get a fair share of the salmon.

The Boldt Decision

While Oregon began to negotiate the dispute over fishing with its Indian population, the fishing struggle in Washington continued into the early 1970s. Finally, in a major court decision, in *United States v. Washington*, on February 12, 1974, Judge George W. Boldt affirmed the right of the nineteen treaty tribes to fish at their usual and accustomed places in common with White citizens. Most importantly, Judge Boldt ruled that the treaty phrase "in common with" meant a fifty-fifty equal share of the fish catch. A Northwest Indian Fisheries Commission was then set up. Yet, even after the Boldt decision, Washington State continued to criminalize the River Peoples by arresting those who insisted on carrying out their treaty right to fish.

Because of his ruling in favor of the Indians, Judge Boldt became the brunt of an anti-Indian backlash. "Bumper stickers, protests, and petitions were directed against him" (Cohen 1986, 88–89). Washington attorney general Slade Gordon led the attack against Judge Boldt's ruling, and non-Indian commercial fishermen continued to fish illegally. At one point, when Lummi Indian fishermen were physically threatened, the FBI had to step in.

Judge Boldt nevertheless continued to implement his legal decision. A Fisheries Advisory Board was established even while he faced a legal assault by commercial fishing interests. The State Supreme Court attempted to overrule the federal court decision by Judge Boldt, and the federal government was slow to intervene. "As the United States Commission on Civil Rights pointed out after an intensive investigation, the explosive situation following the Boldt decision required a strong federal presence. Instead, the various branches of government chose different ways to deal with the decision" (Cohen 1986, 101).

Part of the backlash against the Boldt decision was the anti-Indian legislation being introduced in Congress at this time. In response, a broad coalition of Indian groups led a cross-country march in 1978 from San Francisco to Washington, DC, termed The Longest Walk, and was successful in helping to defeat the negative legislation. "One of these bills bore the ironic title 'Native American Equal Opportunity Act' and would have eliminated *all* Indian treaty rights" (Cohen 1886, 103).

Since the Washington Supreme Court had ruled in favor of the non-Indian fishing interests and was attempting to block Judge Boldt's fifty-fifty share of the catch decision, it sought to get the U.S. Supreme Court to overturn the federal court decision favoring the Indian fishermen. Finally, the U.S. Supreme Court agreed to review the case, and on July 2, 1979, it upheld Judge Boldt's interpretation of the treaties and his instructions in almost all respects. The major exception was the Court's decision to also include fish caught for ceremonial use and subsistence, as well as fish caught on the reservations, in the 50 percent share.

The Columbia River Basin

The Indian tribes seeking to enjoy their treaty right to fish along the Columbia River faced a somewhat different challenge. Unlike the state of Washington, Oregon and Idaho never made Indian fishing rights a major political issue. Washington, by way of contrast, has been compared to the stance of the Southern segregationists in its opposition to Indian fishing rights and its repression of the fishing tribes.

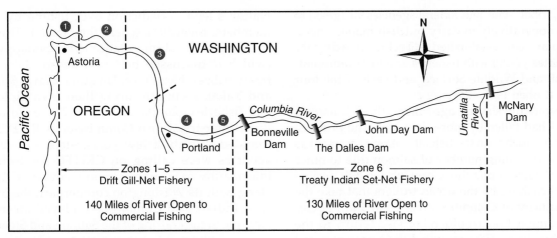

Figure 7.2 Columbia River Fishing Zones.

The Native peoples who fish the Columbia River include the Nez Perce Tribe in Idaho, the Confederated Tribes of the Umatilla, the Confederated Tribes of the Warm Springs (the latter two located in Oregon), and the Confederated Tribes and Bands of the Yakama Indian Nation in Washington State. The Great River that once produced the largest fish runs of chinook salmon and steelhead in the world has been transformed into a great inland lake and center for hydroelectric power. "Dams within the Columbia Basin, impounding the Columbia itself, the Snake, and their tributaries, have reduced by half the habitat accessible to spawning salmon" (Cohen 1986, 118). The most plentiful runs of the past were above what is now Bonneville Dam, located some 150 miles inland from the Pacific Ocean. These are now the most threatened runs. "An important reason for their decrease is that federally-funded hatcheries, built largely to replace upriver runs diminished by the dams, were located in the lower river" (Cohen 1986, 118–19). As a result, non-Indian fishermen are allotted the fish in the lower river, while the upriver Indians must depend on the lesser numbers of wild fish that are able to get past the dams to spawn.

In 1963 a federal court affirmed the Umatillas' right to fish. Five years later, in *Sohappy v. Smith*, Judge Belloni assigned the Oregon tribes "a fair and equitable share" of the state's fish. The federal court ruling was the result of Richard Sohappy and his uncle, David Sohappy, staging a fish-in on the Columbia River. In response to the 1969 Belloni Decision, Oregon set up six zones along the Columbia River to regulate fishing in accordance with the federal court ruling.

The system of zones allowed non-Indians to fish commercially on a 140-mile stretch of the mouth and the lower Columbia River up to Bonneville Dam, Zones One through Five. (See Figure 7.2.) The 130-mile Zone Six above Bonneville Dam was reserved for the Indian fishermen and included the area where Celilo Falls once existed before its destruction in 1957. As it turned out, however, the Indian fishermen actually caught fewer fish than before the 1969 court ruling, because the non-Indian fishermen were able to catch most of the fish entering the Columbia before they reached the Indians' Zone Six.

Destruction of fish runs continued into the 1970s, mainly as a result of logging and four new dams constructed on the Snake River. In addition, a Canadian fishing fleet was taking more than 50 percent of Columbia River Salmon and an even larger share of the Puget Sound runs. By 1974, Indian fisheries were taking no more than 10 to 14 percent of the total Northwest catch. In response to this problem, in May, 1974, "Judge Belloni adopted for the Columbia River the 50-50 harvest allocation and provision for tribal co-management of Judge Boldt's ruling in *United States v. Washington*" (Cohen 1986, 121). A Five Year Plan of joint management for fish stocks was set up. The plan allotted 60 percent of the fall chinook run to the Indian fishermen "for ceremonial, subsistence, and commercial harvest," and 40 percent to the non-Indian fishermen. The formula was reversed for the spring run, with 40 percent going to the treaty fishermen, and 60 percent to the non-Indians. Both Washington and Oregon set management goals for the expected fall and spring runs of the chinook, with additional previsions for the smaller runs of sockeye and coho. The tribes agreed to consider steelhead as sports fish and not to target them. Commercial fishers, tribal, state, and federal agencies all agreed to work cooperatively to carry out fish management. "The plan also established a Technical Advisory Committee (TAC) with fisheries scientists representing Fish and Wildlife Service, and each of the four tribes" (Cohen 1986, 124).

Despite the sharing agreement, the fish harvest by 1981 had fallen by more than half. The problem lay not so much with the fish allocation agreement as with the declining number of salmon due to other factors. Chief among those causing the fish decline was overfishing by the ocean trollers that take the vast majority of Columbia River coho and fall chinook salmon that would otherwise return to the Columbia River. This amounted to 64 percent of fall chinook destined to reach the upper Columbia, and resulted in litigation against the secretary of commerce over the federal ocean fishing regulations. "In *Confederated Tribes v. Kreps,* the tribes charged that the ocean troll season would permit non-Indians to catch too many coho and fall chinook and would thereby prevent Indians from harvesting their share on the upper river" (Cohen 1986, 130). The federal government, however, after initially backing Indian fishing rights, shifted its support to the ocean trollers. When the Department of Commerce found itself the target of litigation by the fishing tribes, it had its National Marine Fisheries agency implement a secret plan to entrap and arrest the traditional River Indians. This hypocritical diversionary target thus fed into a vicious backlash against the Indian tribes and their treaty right to fish.

In the late 1970s, two Washington congressmen, Republican John E. Cunningham and Democrat Lloyd Meeds, introduced regressive legislation to curtail Indian fishing rights. Reaction to the Boldt decision brought on the anti-Indian backlash, although it was less violent on the Columbia than on Puget Sound. Even so, tension was high, with non-Indian fishermen holding press conferences, demonstrations, and carrying signs that read "Down With Treaties," and "Save the Salmon, Can an Indian." Although the Belloni and Boldt decisions eventually brought a belated and reluctant realization by public officials that the Indians must have a say in the Northwest fish management, in the short run, the states continued setting seasons and regulations without consulting the Indians, leading to conflict.

In 1974, the same year as the Boldt decision, the U.S. Supreme Court upheld the Yakama Nation's legal jurisdiction over fishing by tribal members, regardless where they fished. This was to assume critical importance in the Sohappy case (which is discussed below) a decade later. The treaty tribes—Nez Perce, Umatilla, Warm Springs, and Yakama—began hiring their own biologists and fisheries experts, and in 1977, the Columbia River Inter-tribal Fish Commission (CRITFC) was founded. Within a few years, state and federal agencies were calling on CRITFC for technical information regarding salmon recovery. CRITFC, along with its Washington counterpart, the Northwest Indian Fish Commission, played an important role in the crafting of the Salmon and Steelhead Conservation and Enhancement Act. "The new law set up a permanent advisory committee that included tribal representation to create management plans for the Columbia River and Puget Sound" (Ulrich 1999, 158). Despite these encouraging developments, the attack on Indian fishing rights was far from over.

THE CASE OF DAVID SOHAPPY[2]

We return now to the case of David Sohappy and the dozens of other River Indians who were arrested in June of 1982 for poaching salmon under the Lacey Amendment to the Black Bass Act. A sting operation had secretly taken place for fourteen months, from April 1981 to May 1982, involving the sale of 6,100 fish. Sohappy and seventy-five Indian people were subsequently arrested.

For thousands of years, the River People had fished the Great River. "Fifty thousand Indians took 18 million pounds of salmon a year from the Columbia River watershed before 'civilization' began to deplete the runs" (Grinde and Johansen 1995, 145). Salmon were to the fishing tribes of the Northwest that buffalo were to the Plains Indians. Their very existence was dependent upon the fish, and their religion reflected this interdependence with the Salmon People. They lived in harmony with their riverine environment and practiced their own laws of conservation to ensure that the annual fish runs would always be plentiful. An important ceremony took place with the first salmon caught in the yearly run. "The fish was barbecued over an open fire and bits of its flesh parceled out to all in attendance. The bones were saved intact, to be carried by a torchbearing, singing, dancing, and chanting procession back to the river, where they were placed in the water with the head pointing upstream—symbolic of the spawning fish, to assure that there would be runs in the future" (Grinde and Johansen 1995, 146). "In the late 1800s, a prophet arose among the Wanapum band of the Columbia River Indians. He followed the Washat, or Seven Drum religion, and his name was Smohalla. He spoke of a day of great destruction that was quickly approaching and he said only those who followed the strict laws of the Creator would survive. Smohalla spoke of a day when Indians would reclaim what the White Man had stolen. However, in order for this to be possible, the Indians must return to their roots and lead the life the Creator had intended them to live" (Forder 1989, 3). The followers of the Washat religion peacefully resisted the attempts by White authorities to move them to the reservations, clinging instead to their traditional fishing sites and the old way of life on the river. The religion is still practiced along the river today.

In 1855, treaties were signed which pledged that "for as long as the sun shines, as long as the mountains stand, and as long as the river flows," the River People would be able to fish at their accustomed fisheries. Soon, however, White entrepreneurs realized that great profits could be generated by selling Columbia River salmon. Huge harvesting wheels drastically reduced the fish runs, and logging operations began silting up the salmon spawning grounds. By the early 1900s, the salmon were being fished in mechanized, commercial operations even before they reached the mouth of the river.

The year 1933 saw the construction of Bonneville Dam. The dam flooded out traditional villages, burial, ceremonial, and fishing sites. The U.S. Army Corps of Engineers promised funding for new buildings and new fishing sites upstream. To date, this promise has never been fully and honestly carried out. Indian leaders plaintively point out that people have grown old and died waiting for the new homes promised them by the government.

In the early 1940s, David Sohappy and other Wanapum were removed from their ancestral lands at Priest Rapids and White Bluffs, and the area then became part of the Hanford Nuclear Reservation. By 1945, the U.S. Army Corps had built only five in-lieu sites along the Columbia for the displaced River People, although it had promised thirty-seven. Later, the government unfairly specified that the sites were to be used only seasonally for fishing and not for

Indians fishing at Celilo Falls.

permanent housing. But where were the homeless Indians to live? The more traditional Indians refused to move to the reservation; they were River People, and their lives were inextricably connected with the river and the salmon.

The river and the fish have formed the nexus of the River People's lives for thousands of years.

> A respect for nature and the cycles of life have formed the basis of their religion. The fish, the roots, and the berries are honored in their time, beginning with first food ceremonies. Food is only taken in amounts that are needed and all food that is taken is used. By respecting the Creator's gifts in this way, as they have always done, the people are protecting the resources and assured of its return. . . . As the elders explain, if the Indian stopped fishing and holding ceremonies, the fish would not return. These are the old laws of the People taken from the Creator. (Forder 1989, 3)

In 1955, The Dalles Dam was built and Celilo Falls was destroyed—just blown up—and an inland sea created where the greatest Indian fishery in North America had formerly been. With few or no salmon, a number of the River People were persuaded to accept a one-time monetary compensation of $326.8 million and move to the nearby Yakama Reservation. Acceptance of this payment was to plague the people remaining on the river since it was assumed that all the Indians had sold their rights to fish, but this was a misconception.

After the 1974 Boldt decision, the fishing rights battle moved to the Columbia River. In the 1980s, the River People were being denied their unimpeded treaty right to fish in Zone Six, the 113-mile strip of the Columbia River above Bonneville Dam. Over-strict fishing regulations were placed on the Indian fishermen, and most of the fishermen found that they could not subsist under the White-imposed regulations. This was the situation when David Sohappy and other traditional River Indians deliberately ignored state and federal regulations, and fished and traded in the old, time-honored way. It was their intention to test the hegemony of White authorities, both state and federal, in order to secure the treaty right to fish "in their usual and accustomed places."

David Sohappy was born in 1925 and spent most of his childhood going to White Bluff (now Hanford Nuclear Reservation) to fish. His name is derived from "souiehappie," meaning "shoving something under a ledge" in the Wanapum language. David's ancestors traded fish with the Lewis and Clark expedition. He followed the old Washat (Seven Drums) religion his entire life and is a lineal descendent of Smohalla. Sohappy, like other River People, believed that natural law governs the conduct of their lives and the lives of the salmon, which are intertwined.

The Wanapum Band, to which the Sohappy family belonged, remained at White Bluff on the Columbia after the Yakima Treaty was signed in 1855. Almost a century later, in 1942, the remaining families were removed by the government to make way for the Hanford Nuclear Project. "The Wanapum moved upstream and stayed by the river until the mid 1950s, when their last village was destroyed by a public utility district dam. Ironically, the dam was named Priest Rapids after Smohalla" (Ulrich 1999, 127).

David grew up on his grandmother's allotted land on the Yakama Reservation. He was taught to follow the seasonal food cycles of traditional culture consisting of wild game, fish, roots, and huckleberries. Since a young boy, David Sohappy fished for salmon without regard to season or limit; instead, he, like other River fishermen, followed the old, traditional practices of salmon conservation. He believed that to fish is to give thanks to the Creator and to show respect for the Creator's gift of life, salmon.

After he grew up, he worked as a mechanic, married his childhood sweetheart, Myra, and served in the Army Air Corps, rising to the rank of sergeant. After the stint in the Army, he farmed for awhile on the Yakama Reservation, and then held various blue-collar jobs. All the while, he returned again and again to the fishing grounds at Celilo Falls. After Celilo was destroyed, David joined his brother and friends to fish at Cook's Landing, an in-lieu fishing site, during his days off work. When he lost his job at a White Salmon sawmill in 1965, and reflecting on the poverty, alcoholism, and disillusionment of his people, he and his wife decided to return to the old culture entirely where they would be dependent upon no one. He and Myra and their eight children moved permanently to the Great River and went fishing fulltime. They "settled on a sliver of federal land called Cook's Landing, just above the first of several dams along the Columbia River and its tributaries. There they built a small longhouse with a dirt floor" (Grinde and Johansen 1995, 163–64).

David Sohappy believed that only the Creator—not the state, federal, or even tribal governments—controlled his traditional fishing practices. Like other traditional River Indians, he said that the Creator and the Yakima Treaty gave him the right to take salmon and to provide for his family. David believed he could live where he fished, at Cook's Landing on the Columbia River.

No matter the need, he never accepted welfare, unemployment compensation, or surplus commodities. Instead he and his family ate salmon at almost every meal, traded fish for other food staples, and hunted. They were subsistence fishermen. David also provided salmon for tribal ceremonies and conducted religious ceremonies in the family's longhouse.

Other Indian families also spent time at Cook's Landing. "The inlet became the focus of state efforts to control Indian fishing. And it became the centerpiece of the BIA's efforts to remove permanent residents from all the in-lieu sites" (Ulrich 1999, 128). During the 1960s and 1970s the Northwest fishing struggle centered for the most part on the fish-ins in western Washington, and the battle to defend the in-lieu sites on the Columbia became a rearguard action. While the Washington fish-ins were attracting nationwide publicity, David Sohappy fished in silence, using fishing traps he had built from driftwood, until state game and fishing officials raided his camp and beat family members.

In 1968, David Sohappy, his cousin, Richard Sohappy, and a dozen others were arrested and jailed on charges of illegal fishing. The two Sohappys then became the plaintiffs in the landmark federal case of *Sohappy v. Smith*. On July 8, 1969, U.S. District Court Judge Robert C. Belloni ruled that Indian fishermen were allowed to harvest a fair share of the salmon runs in the Columbia River. Judge Belloni's ruling became an important first step toward affirming Indian treaty rights on the river. The decision was also supposed to prevent the states of Washington and Oregon from interfering with Indian fishing, except for conservation purposes. Despite this favorable court decision, the harassment of the Sohappys by state and federal authorities continued.

Meanwhile, the Columbia Plateau treaty tribes—Yakama, Umatilla, and Nez Perce—began asserting their sovereignty by regulating their own fishing seasons and placing restrictions on tribal members. The states, however, ignored tribal authority over fishing and continued to cite Indian fishermen for violating state rules. In 1966 alone, there were over six hundred criminal citations against Yakama fishermen, and Oregon stepped up its enforcement by seizing nets and making arrests.

When the tribes began setting their own seasons and restrictions on fishing, the Indians living along the river like David Sohappy still believed that their right to fish was no more subject to tribal rules than to state rules. David became a thorn in the side of the

Yakama Tribe of which he was a member, because of his opposition to tribal fishing regulations as well as those of state and federal governments. "A leader of the Feather religion, he followed the ways of his Wanapum ancestors" (Ulrich 1999, 160). "With Celilo fishing gone, and with it the chief's authority, some of the River Indians, including David Sohappy, believed only the River People understood the fish well enough to decide when [and where] to fish" (Ulrich 1999, 132). Disenchanted with the tribal governments on the reservations, about one hundred of the River Indians formed the Treaty Indians of the Columbia River, Inc. In 1971, the organization petitioned the United Nations and asked for financial assistance to take their treaty rights dispute to the World Court.

While the River People were making progress in the courts on their treaty right to fish, the Bureau of Indian Affairs was vacillating about its policy on the in-lieu sites along the river. It was simultaneously trying to remove permanent residents, stop the Corps of Engineers from flooding the sites, and at the same time making plans to improve the sites. In 1966, the agency issued rules allowing permanent buildings, but under limited conditions. The following year, it reversed itself by placing a ban on permanent dwellings and announcing that it would remove or demolish any illegal structures. A frequent target were the fish drying sheds. As one resident recalled: "Every time we built dry sheds they burned them down" (Ulrich 1999, 138). Frequently cited as a reason for the BIA's new policy was a sanitation problem of the sites, but other authorities believe that the real reason was to drive the traditional holdouts like the Sohappys off the river entirely. The new rule prohibiting permanent residences was issued "only a few months after the Sohappys and others filed the U.S. District Court suit challenging state efforts to control Indian fishing" (Ulrich 1999, 135).

Key to understanding the determination of the River Indians to protect their occupancy at the in-lieu sites is the promise by the Corps of Engineers to replace the traditional Indian homes and villages that were destroyed by dam construction in the 1930s and 1940s. In 1939 the Corps had promised four hundred acres to accommodate the homes displaced by the construction of Bonneville Dam. This promise was never realized. Little White Salmon site, for example, once planned for 160 acres, became instead the 3.14 acres at Cook's Landing. Cascade Locks, planned for eight acres, was reduced to 1.6 acres. Adding to the problem of landless River People "was the loss of Celilo Falls and dozens of smaller traditional fishing sites on The Dalles and John Day pools" (Ulrich 1999, 137). As a result, instead of the four hundred acres promised, the Corps established only 41.3 acres. To compound its history of broken promises, the Corps in 1970 proposed raising the water level behind the dams, which would flood part of the sites.

In 1972, residents of the in-lieu sites along the river asked Judge Belloni to prevent Oregon from interfering with their spring fishing season. Non-Indians were being allowed to catch the bulk of the salmon originating in the Columbia River, leaving only about 3 percent for the Indians, and less than 10 percent for spawning. Their complaint said that despite the fair share ruling, "Oregon has continued to place restrictions upon the treaty Indian fishery far beyond those necessary for the conservation of the resource" (quoted in Ulrich 1999, 133). In effect, discrimination in Oregon against Indian fishing rights had actually increased.

At Cook's Landing, David Sohappy continued to assert his right under the Stevens' treaties of the last century to fish in the manner of his ancestors. It was a deliberate act of civil disobedience, because he readily admitted to violating federal and tribal fishing regulations. Washington State ignored the court's ruling and continued to harass the Sohappy family. "Usually under cover of darkness, state agents sunk their boats and slashed their nets" (Grinde and Johansen 1995, 164). David later said that he lost more nets than he can remember.

In the early 1980s, fish runs were at an all-time low. A National Marine Fisheries Service (NMFS) study found that forty thousand Columbia River salmon had disappeared while migrating upriver through Zone Six, the region reserved for Indian fishermen. Federal officials claimed that Indian poaching in Zone Six was responsible for the missing salmon. The states of Washington and Oregon had successfully lobbied Congress to pass a law that made the interstate sale of fish a felony. It was aimed squarely at the Sohappys and the River Indians. Using the Indians as the official scapegoat, the NMFS agents teamed up with their counterparts in the Washington Department of Fisheries to prove their poaching theory. Fishery officials then used the excuse of the supposedly stolen fish to justify a fourteen-month, several hundred thousand dollar sting operation code named Salmonscam to entrap David Sohappy and the other Indian fisherfolk living along the Columbia River. "Salmonscam, in turn, was interwoven with efforts to evict residents from the in-lieu site" of Cook's Landing (Ulrich 1999, 160). The sting operation was carried out from April 1981 to May 1982 and involved what was termed the illegal sale of 6,100 fish. The new Lacey Amendment to the Black Bass Act made it a felony to poach fish instead of a misdemeanor. Federal and state officials were at last able to arrest Sohappy instead of merely confiscating his fishing gear and giving him a notice of a violation. Sohappy, who was fifty-seven years old at the time, "would spend the last nine years of his life defending his fishing and his home" (Ulrich 1999, 163). "Sohappy insisted that he fished only for ceremonies and subsistence, supporting an extended family of forty people and supplying salmon for the ceremonies of several longhouses. His living standard could only generously be called moderate. Selling fish was part of the subsistence, he said. Or, as his wife, Myra, explained: 'you can't plop a salmon down when you need gas for the car'" (Ulrich 1999, 160–61).

It is clear that David Sohappy and his people were lured into selling fish by undercover government agents who brandished wads of money. Large, extended families were offered more money than most had ever seen in their lives. The Indian fishermen sold only what they needed to subsist; there were no sales for profit. The River People followed the "old law" of the river, and breaking the White man's law was a way to assert their traditional religious beliefs.

As a result of the sting, thirteen Indians were tried in federal court in Los Angeles, California. The National Lawyers Guild coordinated the defense, but in the end, David Sohappy, his son David, Jr., and his nephew, Bruce Jim, were convicted of selling 345 salmon to undercover agents, each receiving a maximum sentence of five years in federal prison and five years probation. David's religious convictions and traditional fish conservation practices were not allowed as court testimony. The other convicted fishermen received lesser prison sentences. All appealed their convictions. By comparison, those convicted in the national Watergate scandal, which forced President Richard Nixon to resign or face impeachment, received only two-years prison sentences; and Ivan Boeski, a notorious stockbroker, served only three years in prison for insider trading that involved defrauding millions of dollars from investors. The injustice of the Indian case is also shown by the fact that two non-Indian poachers, arrested on January 12, 1987, pleaded guilty to two misdemeanors for selling tons of illegally caught salmon to Washington restaurants and were fined. One received a sentence of only thirty days in prison, and the other got a one-year suspended sentence.

The arrest and eventual imprisonment of the Indian fishermen did nothing to solve the case of the missing fish; the mystery continued to plague the authorities. "Approximately the same percentage of fish continued to disappear after the sting operation. . . . A 50 percent increase in patrol efforts produced arrests and citations for illegal fishing, 93 percent of them non-Indian, but still about half the bright fall Chinook run disappeared" (Cohen 1986, 134). Finally, a study by the National Marine Fisheries Service revealed that the lost fish appeared to be spawning in the tributaries to the Columbia River, such as the mouth of the Deschutes River, before they reached McNary Dam. An additional factor was "an aluminum plant just upriver from The Dalles Dam which had spilled fluorides into the river, confusing those fish it didn't kill" (Ulrich 1999, 159). This led the executive director of the Columbia River Inter-Tribal Fish Commission to declare: "Contrary to widespread publicity concerning presumed large-scale Indian poaching activities, there is no supporting evidence that it is a major conservation problem which explains the loss of some 40,000 fish between Columbia River dams. Blaming Columbia River tribes for these problems is irresponsible, and a disservice to the tribes" (Cohen 1986, 135).

There were those in the Yakama Nation who urged Sohappy to take the Salmonscam conviction into tribal court and plead guilty, but Sohappy's relationship with the tribe was complicated. Although he was an enrolled member and ultimately played a major role in winning judicial recognition of the tribes' treaty rights, he also challenged the Yakama Nation's management of the fishery. "The tribe was rebuffed right after the arrests, when it asked that some of the cases be tried in its own court. It did not again assert its jurisdiction until four years later after Sohappy and four other Yakama tribal members had lost their appeals and were scheduled to report to federal prison" (Ulrich 1999, 164).

Exacerbating the Salmonscam injustice, the federal government moved quickly to evict the Indian families who were living on the in-lieu site of Cook's Landing. The issue of permanent residency on the in-lieu sites had remained unresolved since 1945 when the River Indians originally received the sites from the U.S. Army Corps of Engineers. The sites were supposed to replace the villages and traditional fishing areas flooded out by Columbia River dam construction. For years, a blind eye was cast by the Bureau of Indian Affairs with respect to building permanent structures on the sites where the River People like the Sohappys had taken up residence. Four Northwest senators, however, including the anti-Indian Slate Gordon, wrote to the secretary of the interior, James Watt, to urge him to instruct the BIA to rule that no permanent structures should be allowed on the in-lieu sites. Responding to this political pressure, it then became federal policy to get rid of fishermen termed renegades, and eviction notices were quickly issued by the BIA. The Indians appealed the notices but initially lost in court. Meanwhile, the Salmonscam cases dragged on. The U.S. Ninth Circuit Court of Appeals turned down the Indians' appeal, and the U.S. Supreme Court refused to hear the case. This was when the Yakama Indian Nation passed a resolution asserting jurisdiction over tribal members and their fishing offenses. The federal government resisted tribal ruling and the Sohappys gave up and went to prison.

The flagrant injustice of the David Sohappy case became a symbol of the national struggle for Indian rights in the United States. Myra Sohappy journeyed to the United Nations in Geneva, Switzerland, to seek support from the U.N. Commission on Human Rights to have her husband tried by a jury of his peers in the Yakama Nation's tribal court. A new trial of the Sohappy case to be held by the tribal court was then arranged with the political intervention of Senator Daniel K. Inouye (D-HI) and Senator Daniel J. Evans (R-WA) of the Senate Select Committee on Indian Affairs.

In February 1987, the Indian men convicted in the Salmonscam were returned to the Yakama Nation by the federal authorities to stand trial before a tribal court. This was the first time that David Sohappy had the opportunity to testify as to the religious beliefs that guided his fishing practices. His testimony spoke of the unwritten law of his ancestors and his need to fish according to traditional practices. He argued that if he failed to fish, he failed to thank the Creator, and if he failed to thank the Creator, the fish would not return. Biological experts also testified that the number of fish taken did not detrimentally affect the salmon population. After thirteen days and eight hours of deliberation, the Yakama tribal jury found a verdict of not guilty on all the charges for David Sohappy and the other Indian defendants. The jury also concluded that both state and federal officials had entrapped the Indian fishermen. In addition, the Lacy Amendment was found to have infringed upon

David Sohappy, left rear, and his family.

the religious freedom of the River People, and a letter was sent immediately to then President Ronald Reagan requesting a pardon for all concerned. The government defied the ruling of the tribal court, however, and threatened to cut off federal funding to the Yakama Nation. The Indian defendants were then virtually kidnapped and returned to Minnesota to finish their federal prison sentences.

In federal prison for twenty months, David Sohappy had aged rapidly and his health deteriorated. The sixty-two-year-old spiritual leader suffered several stokes during his months in prison, his diabetes worsened, and he was denied the use of an eagle prayer feather used for religious ceremonies. As a diabetic, he had been used to a diet rich in wild salmon, roots, and berries, but prison food made his physical condition worse. Finally, under increasing international pressure from human rights organizations, including Amnesty International, and with the assistance of Senator Inouye, David was released from federal prison into the arms of his wife, Myra, in June of 1988. Although released early on parole, he still faced probation for at least five years.

A year later, the U.S. Ninth Circuit Court of Appeals ruled against the eviction of the permanent residents of Cook's Landing and Underwood in-lieu sites. This guaranteed that the residents could remain. David Sohappy had beaten the government for what turned out to be his last time. He died in a nursing home in Hood River, Oregon, on May 6, 1991.

Ironically, as was explained earlier, most of the missing fish that Sohappy and his fellow River Indians were accused of poaching were not missing after all. Finding the dams difficult to navigate, the fish had simply spawned in tributaries along the Columbia before reaching McNary Dam.

When David Sohappy was buried, his Wanapum relatives wrapped him in a Pendleton blanket and sang traditional songs as they lowered his body into Mother Earth. His remains were placed with his head towards Mt. Adams so that the early morning sun would warm his face in the spirit world. His attorney, Tom Keefe, Jr., stood by the grave and remembered: "I thanked David Sohappy for the time we had spent together, and I wondered how the salmon he had fought to protect would fare in his absence. Now he is gone, and the natural runs of Chinook that fed his family since time immemorial are headed for the Endangered Species Act list" (Grinde and Johansen 1995, 166).

DAMS AND FISH

The Northwest fishing wars of the 1970s and 1980s victimized the many tribes living in the Puget Sound area and along the rivers of western Washington. It is ironic that the treaties guaranteed the Indians' right to fish in their accustomed places, yet federal and state authorities and agencies, fueled in their policies and practices by racism endemic to White society, continued to harass Native people who endeavored to carry out their treaty rights. The struggle by the Puyallup, Nisqually, and other western Washington tribes for unrestricted fishing at their landings and traditional fishing sites led to the well-known fish-ins of the 1960s and early 1970s, culminating in the Boldt decision. Lesser known is a similar struggle by the River Indians of the Columbia. In the former case, the problem arose from commercial and sports fishermen who were backed by state and federal law enforcement officials. In the latter case, however, the primary enemy to fish, and therefore to the River Peoples living along the Columbia and Snake rivers, was dams erected by special interests that profited from their construction.

"To combat the Great Depression in the 1930s, Franklin Roosevelt unleashed a flurry of major dam-building projects—including Bonneville on the Oregon-Washington border, Shasta in California, and Fort Peck in Montana—culminating in Grand Coulee, which still churns out far more power than any other U.S. dam" (Sharp 2004, 40). Grand Coulee is the mother of all dams. The result for the Northwest was that fourteen major dams turned the fabled Columbia River into a string of man-made lakes, deadly to anandromous fish such as the salmon.

During the Clinton political administration in the 1990s, there was a serious consideration to breech several dams on the upper Columbia to save the salmon. "By blocking fish migration routes and altering water temperatures, dams cause native fish populations to plummet" (Sharp 2004, 38). In the end, however, other measures, half-measures at best, were instituted. The political pressures from agriculture and energy interest groups were too strong for those voices speaking for the salmon and the Indians to overcome. Yet dams are deteriorating not only in the Northwest, but across the nation. By the year 2020, it is estimated that 85 percent of the dams will be at least a half century old; many are already in need of repair. To fix them would cost as much as $10.1 billion over the next dozen years. Hundreds of small dams have already been torn down. The 105-foot-high Elwha Dam in the Olympic Peninsula in Washington State is slated to be one of the first of the big dams to be torn down in order to restore ancient fish runs. But "Elwha and its salmon may need a decade or more to recover from the sediment that will be unleashed downstream" (Sharp 2004, 39).

Today, Celilo Park, a few miles due east of The Dalles, Oregon, marks the spot where the Great Falls of the Che Wana was destroyed in 1957 during the construction of The Dalles Dam. During the first half of the twentieth century, the site was still a major Indian fishery and intertribal gathering ground. Jay Minthorn, a contemporary Umatilla Indian elder, recalls spending part of his boyhood at the falls, camping and fishing with his family: "We sold some of the fish, and we bartered with people in Hood River and Hermiston for apples, melons, vegetables, and buckskins. People would travel for miles to buy Columbia River fish. It was also a religion, because when the first salmon came up, we held a big salmon feast, open to all people, to honor the spring chinook" (Sharp 2004, 42).

In the late 1980s, the author of this text attended a meeting of the International Indian Treaty Council that was hosted by Celilo Village, a small holdout community of the River People. During the gathering, the salmon feast was still respected in the time-honored way, with a ceremonial prayer and blessing. Looking out over the Great River where the Celilo Falls had formerly been, one saw a large lake with dozens of windsurfers on it. Gone forever were the majestic, fast running falls which, from time immemorial, had fed thousands of Indian people and had been a gathering place for the tribes of the greater Northwest to meet and trade. Ulrich, in *Empty Nets* (1999, 194), reports of a conversation one Indian had with a windsurfer: "The windsurfer told George to leave because 'we were here first.' George shook his head. 'No,' he said. 'I was here a long time before you.'" But for the River People there is some good news: Recently the Corps of Engineers, in response to the complaints of the River People about the destruction of Celilo Falls, undertook records research and concluded that the falls might never have been dynamited, but just covered up with the construction of The Dalles dam downstream. An extensive imaging of this section of the river using the latest sophisticated technology revealed, in fact, that this was the case. The falls still exist exactly as they were before being flooded by the dam. The Native fishermen embrace the hope that someday, future generations of their descendants may live to see the falls restored to their pristine beauty and fishery.

Besides the dams, there are other factors contributing to the decline in fish numbers. These include factories like the aluminum plant that appears to have been implicated in the forty thousand missing fish when it dumped fluorides into the Columbia River (the salmon simply found better places to spawn in the river's tributaries). Canneries, especially in the early decades of the twentieth century, involved fish wheels that take more salmon from the river than the Indians ever could. Then there is the Hanford nuclear facility which has not only displaced historic Indian villages and grave sites, but is also responsible for radioactive wastes endangering the river. "Sixty-seven Hanford storage tanks are known to have leaked or are leaking. Tritium is known to have reached into the Columbia River, presaging a radioactive threat to fisheries and millions of residents downstream" (AuCoin 2004).

In June of 2004, the Associated Press reported that the Teck Cominco smelter of British Columbia had dumped tons of highly toxic mercury into the Columbia River for decades. The lead-zinc smelter is located in Trail, BC, about six miles north of the Washington border. Documents reveal that "1.6 tons to 3.6 tons of mercury were discharged into the river each year since the 1940s" (*Register-Guard* 2004). Mercury is a highly toxic metal that can cause neurological damage in developing fetuses. In March 1980, the company was responsible for a 6,300-pound mercury spill into the Columbia that went unreported for five weeks. As a result, "mercury levels in Lake Roosevelt—a 130-mile impoundment of the Columbia behind the Grand Coulee Dam—exceeded drinking water standards. . . . In 1999, the Colville Confederated Tribes petitioned [the Environmental Protection Agency] whether Lake Roosevelt should be declared a Superfund site" (*Register-Guard* 2004).

The logging industry has created serious runoff problems of pollution. Agriculture is responsible for pesticides in the river that kill and harm the fish. Yet, it is the victims, the Indians, who have been blamed for declining fish runs. The Yakama Nation told its Washington and Oregon senators about what had happened to them over the years: "As a consequence, we have seen our grave and village sites destroyed, our fishing places flooded and developed for non-Indian uses, thereby rendering them valueless, and have seen the destruction of spawning habitat for our fish" (Ulrich 1999, 183).

> White people put seventeen dams between salmon and their Columbia and Snake River spawning grounds. White people took river water to irrigate their farms and returned it laden with fish-killing fertilizer and pesticides. White people, mostly logged the forests, grazed cattle on the plains, and build riverside factories, sending silt and pollution into the rivers. White fishermen in the Pacific Ocean caught more than half of the Columbia River salmon. So when the river's salmon runs hit a twenty-year low in 1980, White fishermen and White governments naturally blamed the Indians. (Ulrich 1999, 159)

This accurately sums up what has happened to the Indian way of life on the Columbia River.

Today, the costal Indians of the Northwest are beginning to suffer the effects of global warming. The glaciers are melting, their reservation lands are in danger of flooding, and the rivers are warming. Salmon die when the river water temperature reaches over 70 degrees. But on a positive note, the Native peoples affected are turning to their ancient cultural values to plan ahead for the next Seven Generations.

THEORY REVISITED

The theory of Indian criminalization as conceptualized by Luana Ross (1998), and explained in this chapter's introduction, is a general theory. When applied to the Northwest fishing peoples, it becomes a stinging indictment of the inherent criminality of state laws and policies of Washington and Oregon in overregulating Indian fishing practices, and the criminal neglect of federal agencies to enforce Indian treaties protecting fishing rights. It was only when Indian fishermen repeatedly went to jail in order to bring the issue into the federal courts that fishing rights were finally affirmed in terms of the treaties. Yet, despite favorable court rulings, David Sohappy and the River Indians living in the in-lieu sites were still made the scapegoats in the government's vindictive Salmonscam.

Two major paradigms in the study of social deviance are order (functionalism) theory and conflict theory. A major weakness of functionalist theory is its focus on the individual lawbreaker, resulting in person-blame. Functionalist theory would argue that the Indian fisherfolk are deviants when they break state laws; the inherent injustice of the law itself is not questioned. Conflict theory, on the other hand, focuses on society as a source of deviance; it is society-blame in its approach to deviance. From the conflict perspective one can see that blaming traditional Indian fishermen for breaking unjust laws and regulations is, in reality, blaming the victim. The real story is the unjust nature of fishing laws that violate Indian treaty rights to fish in their usual and accustomed places. So who is the criminal? As Myra Sohappy asks in the documentary film, *River People: Behind the Case of David Sohappy* (1991): "They say we have broken their laws. But what about our laws? The laws of the Creator."

CONCLUSION

The year 2004 was the bicentennial of the Lewis and Clark expedition, although scarcely a cause for celebration by the contemporary Indian peoples of Washington, Idaho, and Oregon. The Corps of

Discovery crossed uncharted territory that was occupied by some fifty Indian nations and became the forerunner of Anglo-American westward expansion in the name of Manifest Destiny that dispossessed the Native inhabitants of most of their rich lands and resources. Yet, despite the wholesale dispossession and depopulation bordering on genocide, the United States recognized the Indian tribes as sovereign nations by signing treaties with them, treaties that forced the Indian peoples to give up most of their lands but which at least protected the right to fish "in their usual and accustomed places." "Thus the United States didn't 'give' them exclusive fishing and hunting rights, subject to interpretation by non-Indian governments or individuals. It only guaranteed to acknowledge and preserve what the Indians already had—albeit on a greatly reduced scale. Tribal nations don't operate enterprises such as casinos or timber because of the benevolence of state or federal government. They do so as sovereign nations doing business on their own land under their own rules and regulations" (Lee 2004).

The Indian Gaming Regulatory Act (IGRA) was passed by Congress in 1988, and most of the tribes in Washington and Oregon in lieu of fishing now have casinos that bring in significant income. By 2002, Oregon's gaming tribes alone generated $370 million in revenue and contributed $8.5 million to local governments and charitable groups. But will Indian gaming replace fish in the Native Northwest? Salmon and other subsistence food-gathering activities have long formed the core of Indian culture. Some traditional Indians oppose casino development because they fear that it will replace Indian culture and values with the capitalist ethic of rugged individualism, in which the almighty dollar becomes the bottom line. But this potential danger, if it becomes a reality, will have to be confronted and solved by Native people themselves, and not by non-Indians and their institutions. This is both the promise and the risk of true self-determination.

POSTSCRIPT: THE "NEW SALMON"

In the Plains states where the Indigenous nations of the past depended on the bison for subsistence, gaming in terms of modern Indian casinos is being termed the "new buffalo." In similar fashion, one might call the development of Indian casinos in the Northwest the "new salmon." Indian gaming enterprises more than any other economic enterprise in recent history are having a great beneficial effect on tribes across the nation. Oregon alone has ten tribal casinos. One of the last to open, the Three Rivers Casino by the Confederated Tribes of the Coos, Lower Umpqua, and Sisulaw Indians, started operations in the summer of 2004. Yet at the time, an organized group of White opponents to the new Indian casino located in the coastal community of Florence, Oregon, evoked racial stereotypes and a vehement attack on Indian sovereignty.

Florence has a population of under eight thousand, of which half are retirees, mostly from out-of-state, many from California. There is an economic divide between the affluent retirees and the local, low-income residents. Fishing and timber industries used to be the economic mainstay of the area, but, today, these occupations have been replaced by tourism, a seasonal enterprise at best. In many ways the new Indian casino in Florence promised to stimulate the local economy and provide year-around, family-wage jobs for the chronically depressed, blue-collar population.

People Against Casino Town (PACT), an organized opposition group, singled out the local Three Rivers Indian community in its attack on Indian federal trust status and the 1988 Indian Gaming Regulatory Act. Eight tribes had already been operating casinos under compacts with the state of Oregon.

The racist nature of the attack by PACT is indicated by the fact that only the Indian community was singled out for the evils of gambling. PACT ignored the state's lottery, video poker, and other gambling games in bars and stores that totaled over $40 million in profits for Lane County alone, where Florence is located. The City of Florence received tens of thousands of dollars from gambling sales in grants and loans. Yet, only the Confederated Tribes Three Rivers Casino became the focus of PACT's wrath.

Ethnic (Indigenous) Cleansing

The history of the Coos, Lower Umpqua, and Siuslaw Indians at the hands of Anglo-American society is a genocidal one that includes an unratified treaty, land dispossession, and reservation imprisonment in the nineteenth century, and termination as a federally recognized tribe in 1954. The tribal confederation was not restored to federal status until 1984. A comprehensive history of the Three Tribes' experience is found in historian David Beck's book, *Seeking Recognition: The Termination and Restoration of the Coos, Lower Umpqua, and Siuslaw Indians, 1855–1984* (2009).

The three affiliated tribes occupied an aboriginal homeland of 1.6 million acres along the central Oregon coast, a fertile land of prime virgin timber, plentiful game, salmon, and shellfish. Despite the bounties of nature, the tribes had the misfortune to live in area coveted by early settlers and mining interests.

To understand how the dispossession of the coastal Indians took place, we begin with the creation of the Oregon Territory in 1846, when the United States and Great Britain divided the disputed Northwest at the forty-ninth parallel. The United States' relation to Oregon's Indians immediately became contentious from this time on because of two laws. The 1848 Organic Act establishing Oregon Territory "followed past legal precedent in guaranteeing that Indian rights and title to the lands could only be extinguished by treaty. The Oregon Donation Act passed two years later, however 'gave any United States citizen title to 320 acres of land for staking and occupying a claim'" (Beck 2009, 15). The land rush was on. Non-Indians staked out and occupied lands that should have been protected by the Organic Act. "The contradictory nature of the two laws coupled with the inability of U.S. Indian Service agents in Oregon to protect tribal rights led to the loss of two and a half million acres of Indian lands" (Beck 2009, 15). In 1855 the Empire Treaty was negotiated by the superintendent of Indian Affairs for the Oregon Territory, but Congress failed to ratify it, and the government never lived up to its terms for compensation and services. Instead, Congress proceeded to open the entire area to White settlement.

When White explorers discovered gold in the far coastal south they and the settlers took Indian land at will. The Indians resisted and the result was the Rogue River War which broke out in 1855, lasting until 1856. Miners and the military forced the midcoastal Indians from their villages, and the refugees were driven under armed guard to Fort Umpqua where they barely survived the winter. The local Indian superintendent cut off food rations, claiming that no treaties had been signed of which he was aware. In 1859 about four hundred remaining Coos and Lower Umpqua Indians were moved further up the Oregon coast north to Yachats where they were forced to subsist on shellfish gathered from the rocks at low tide. In the first five years at Yachats, more than half of the Coos Indians died from exposure and starvation. For nineteen years, until 1875, the United States government imprisoned tribal members on the coast reservation. Some people escaped and returned to their old homes, only to face eviction when the southern part of the reservation was closed and the former tribal lands, including present-day Florence, were thrown open to

White settlement. After release, the Indian survivors returned to the Siuslaw and Umpqua rivers, and Coos Bay to eke out an existence in a hostile world. Many worked as domestic laborers for room and board, as wood choppers, and in the seasonal cranberry harvest. Others eventually intermarried with Whites as a means of economic survival.

In 1916 the three tribes established an elected tribal government, which they have continuously maintained to this day. In 1954, however, they were terminated as a tribal entity without their consent under the Western Oregon Termination Act. The tribes then had to rely on what little resources they could muster to provide at least minimal services for tribal members. Termination was extremely hard on Indian families struggling to survive, and it was psychological devastating to elders.

It was not until 1984 that the Confederated Tribes of Coos, Lower Umpqua, and Siuslaw Indians were again recognized by Congress and restored to federal status. Still, the confederation has yet to be given any restored lands that similar coastal tribes were given upon their restoration. The Indian Casino Regulatory Act was passed by Congress four years later. It provided a window of opportunity for the tribal confederation to undertake economic and social development.

The Confederated Tribes is one of the poorest Indian groups in Oregon. Today, the 720-member confederation owns less than twenty acres in Coos Bay and the recently acquired ninety-six-acre Hatch Tract, site of their Florence casino. Former Senator Gordon Smith (R-OR) sponsored a bill in Congress that would have transferred almost sixty-three thousand acres of the Siuslaw National Forest to the Confederated Tribes, with the Bureau of Indian affairs holding the land in trust. Due to the lobbying efforts of the Oregon Natural Resources Council, however, the bill was rejected in the spring of 2004, and current proposals for a new bill are still unresolved. In the meantime, until a land base is secured, gaming is the only economic option open to the Three Rivers Confederation.

The Controversy

The Confederated Tribes began searching for a gaming site for a casino in 1996. At first, a site in Coos Bay was considered, but because the adjacent Coquille Tribe already operated the Mill Casino in the same area, the Hatch Tract, an Indian property located farther up the coast at Florence, became the desired location. The Hatch Tract soon became a major bone of contention and the focus of the attack by PACT. The Hatch Tract property is the former location of an old Siuslaw Indian village, ceremonial center, and burial ground. It was purchased by the Confederated Tribes from a tribal member in 1998, and the U.S. Department of the Interior subsequently ruled that the property qualified as restored Indian land. This made it eligible as a site for the tribes to build a $20–25 million, temporary midsize casino, which opened in 2004. A new, permanent facility, the Three Rivers Casino and Hotel complex, opened in December 2007. (With the purchase of an adjacent golf course in 2012, the tribal confederation plans to make their casino enterprise a destination resort.)

PACT at first charged that the Hatch Tract did not legally qualify as Indian trust land since it was acquired by the tribes in January 1998, after Congress passed the 1988 Indian Gaming Regulatory Act (IGRA). The IGRA requires that a tribe must come to an agreement with the governor of a state and local communities for gaming on any property acquired after 1988. This stipulation became the basis for a threat by Oregon's governor, John Kitzhaber, to veto the site as potential Indian gaming land. In December 2001, however, the assistant solicitor of the Division of Indian Affairs ruled that the Hatch Tract was legitimate under "the restored lands exception to the prohibition to gaming on lands acquired after October 27, 1988." Because of its historical and cultural significance, and the fact that the property had never left Indian ownership or been on the tax rolls, the Hatch Tract constituted restored lands. In response, the state filed a lawsuit against the Department of Interior asking that the U.S. District Court review the earlier decision by the Department of Interior to allow gaming rights on the Hatch Tract property. A new governor in February 2003, however, decided to drop the lawsuit. Thus, the favorable federal decision allowed the tribes to negotiate an amendment to the gaming compact with the state to designate the Hatch Tract as the Confederated Tribes' gaming site.

Meanwhile, PACT continued an aggressive campaign against the tribes' gaming rights. Over the next several years, PACT mounted lawsuits in an effort to stop casino construction, but all were rejected by the courts. PACT contended that the Oregon Constitution expressly prohibited casinos, and that the Three Rivers Casino was therefore illegal. A legal victory by PACT would have not only invalidated the Florence casino but would probably meant that all Indian casinos in the state were illegal. This would

have dire repercussions not only for Oregon's Indian tribes, but also for the state and local communities that would lose the gaming revenues they currently enjoyed. In a cash-strapped state, hard hit by the Recession, this could pose a serious fiscal crisis. In the short run, however, PACT's hostile actions and propaganda campaign against the Three Rivers casino poisoned public sentiment and divided the Florence community. PACT successfully lobbied the Florence City Council to cancel negotiations with the Three River tribes for a service agreement. After the city rejected negotiations, the tribes forged ahead with construction plans, breaking ground for the casino site, and planning for the Three Rivers Casino to be up and running by the summer of 2004.

Backlash

PACT ostensibly opposed gambling on moral grounds, yet it directed its attack solely on the Indian community and ignored the state lottery and related forms of legal gambling in Oregon. Furthermore, PACT brought in speakers and attorneys from out of state who are associated with a national campaign against Indian sovereignty, viewing it as a form of special privilege based on race. PACT condemned what it saw as the federal role in what they called "the Indian conspiracy," presumably to defraud non-Indian citizens and property owners. It opposed the 1988 Indian Gaming Regulatory Act.

A stridently anti-Indian casino video was circulated in Florence, along with a twenty-two-page packet that included an article attacking Indian identity and sovereignty by William J. Lawrence. The fifty minute video, *Indian Country: An American Crisis* (2000), singled out the Foxwoods Casino operated by the Pequot Indians of Connecticut. The video made a number of false and misleading claims and portrayed Indian casinos as an attack on the U.S. Constitution. It charged that "Indians refuse to integrate" like other "ethnic Americans." Compulsory gambling and suicides are singled out as evils spawned by Indian casinos. In addition to the Pequots, the Miamis and Oneidas are also vilified, and the states of Connecticut, New York, and Illinois are targeted as "battleground states" in the fight against Indian casinos. In New York State the video promotes the anti-Indian group "Upstate Citizens for Equality." Gun rights and Carlton Heston, former president of the National Rifle Association, are mentioned in a favorable light, and the U.S. Congress is blamed "for allowing Indians to steam roll their [White] communities."

The Lawrence (1996) article, with the misleading title "In Defense of Indian Rights," was apparently downloaded from the Internet. Lawrence is identified as Red Lake Chippewa and editor of the *Ojibwe News*. The article contains egregious errors of fact and is pro-assimilationist in perspective. Lawrence uncritically buys into the government's blood quantum definition of who is an Indian and then attacks Indian rights as being race-based and therefore unfair to non-Indians. He contends that Indian tribes are not legitimate governments and that Indians should blend into the mainstream population like White ethnics from Europe did in the past. Lawrence embraced the dissent in *Cohen v. Little Six* by Minnesota Appeals Court judge Jim Randall, who argued that Sylvia Cohen, a non-Native patron at Mystic Lake Casino, should be allowed to pursue a personal injury case against the Shakopee Mdewakanton Dakota Tribe. Judge Randall declared tribal sovereignty "more illusion than real . . . and a throwback to the separate but equal doctrine" (Lawrence 1996).

Clearly, the casino controversy in Florence, Oregon was part of a nationwide attack by certain White interest groups against Indian gaming rights.

Charles E. Trimble, writing in *Indian Country Today* (2003), warned of an impending backlash similar to the one in the mid-1970s following some important gains in Indian Country concerning hunting and fishing rights, such as the 1974 Boldt decision that awarded treaty Indians in Washington and Oregon 50 percent of the salmon catch. Prominent among the anti-Indian groups in the backlash at that time was the Interstate Congress for Equal Rights and Responsibilities (ICERR). Its goals were to do away with Indian hunting and fishing rights altogether, abrogate the treaties, and terminate tribal governments. The justification for the formation of CERR was the supposed special privileges enjoyed by tribal communities, the same bogus justification for the attack on Indian casinos several decades later.

Reflecting on this earlier backlash may help one to understand the resentment by White political conservatives to Indian casino development. Trimble writes: "The backlash of 1976–1977 was triggered by reaction to militant activities in Indian Country, which ignited long-held resentment over what certain interests in western states perceived as privileges and resources available exclusively to Indians at great cost to the federal government. And always an underlying factor, of course, was the lust for Indian lands" (Trimble 2003). Today, the success of Indian gaming has come at a time when most state budgets are strapped financially, and the national economic recovery is a jobless one. The perception that a non-White minority group is progressing while many in the White middle-class are losing ground financially and their privileged social position in society is threatened appears to have fueled the new backlash.

Myths and Stereotypes

There is an unwarranted perception among many White Americans that the rights accorded to Indian tribes, such as gaming, are special privileges based on race, and are unfair to non-Indians, a form of reverse discrimination. On the contrary, Indian rights are based on tribal political status, including treaties, Supreme Court decisions, and federal Indian law. Non-Indians fail to comprehend that Indian tribes are governments possessed of territory whose sovereignty is recognized by the U.S. Constitution. The U.S. Constitution gives Congress the plenary power to regulate commerce with foreign nations, the states, and the Indian tribes. An individual state like Oregon has no regulatory jurisdiction within tribal lands, and tribal governments have the same gaming powers as do state governments. That is why tribal governments (and not individual Indians) can do some things that other groups cannot do. Ethnic groups, for example, do not have a history of sovereign relations with the United States when it negotiated and then ratified treaties with the Indian nations in exchange for North America's rich lands and resources.

Non-Indians often evoke the myth that Indians do not pay taxes. Individual Indians living on a reservation do not pay state taxes, nor taxes on gaming distributions, but they do pay federal income tax. "All Indian people pay federal income, Federal Insurance Contribution Act payments (FICA), and social security taxes" (Spilde 2000, 88). Indian tribes do not pay income taxes, but neither does the state of Oregon nor the city of Florence. The United States does not tax governments on income, and tribes (Native nations) are governments. Tribal governments, on the other hand, do pay into unemployment and disability just like any other government employer. Furthermore, federal law dictates to some extent how tribes must spend their money. Not only do casinos provide jobs for tribal members (In addition to non-Indian employees), but most of the casino profits are ploughed back into tribal services, such as education, health, and housing. Unlike the commercial Las Vegas-type casinos, Indian casinos are not solely for-profit gaming enterprises.

Another myth is that Indians are getting rich because they run casinos (see Spilde 2000, 88–89, and Stevens 2000, 172–73). In the first place, less than 10 percent of gambling in the United States takes place on Indian reservations. Also, one needs to consider that when tribes began to build casinos the average poverty rate on Indian reservations was 31 percent, the highest in the country. Indian unemployment was six times the national average and varied between 70 and 90 percent on some of the larger reservations. Furthermore, only a minority of tribes have casinos. Less than one-third of the country's 558 federally recognized tribes have some form of gaming operations. Many Indian tribes are geographically isolated from potential, urban-based customers, or would have to compete with already existing casinos in order to benefit from gaming as a viable economic enterprise. Still others, such as some of the Iroquois communities, the Hopis (and until recently the Navajos) oppose gaming on their reservations.

In Florence, PACT distributed a Casino Fact Sheet that highlighted its members' concerns. Among the complaints mentioned in the fact sheet (and also in letters by PACT members sent to local newspapers) was that the casino would cause gambling addition to increase, resulting in additional costs to taxpayers. Katherine Spilde, director of research for the National Indian Gaming Association, points out, however, "that casinos are not to blame for gambling addiction anymore than bars are to blame for alcoholism" (2000, 91). Gambling addiction is part of addictive behavior and is therefore not the addict's only problem. Furthermore, "gambling addiction is not widespread despite heavy media coverage. Most tribal governments are sensitive to charges of corrupting the local population and have policies restricting credit lines or monitoring patrons who are known to wager beyond their means" (Spilde 2000, 91).

PACT also charged that gaming jobs would be filled solely by tribal members, and that the casino would cannibalize local businesses and compete with the Florence Events Center. These so-called community concerns also distorted the facts. Two other Indian casinos on the Oregon coast at the time of the Florence casino controversy had in fact stimulated small business development, created jobs, decreased the unemployment rate, and contributed heavily to local community groups and charitable organizations. A stipulation in the tribal compacts signed by the state of Oregon with the gaming tribes in lieu of paying state taxes was that six percent of net revenues from casino profits would be earmarked for charitable giving. About the time that the Coos, Lower Umpqua, and Siuslaw Indians were battling to build a casino, the Mill Casino, operated by the Coquille Tribe at Coos Bay, was already under operation and giving considerable donations to community groups in charitable donations. It gave $130,000 to the University of Oregon and thirteen local community organizations in its 2003 grants, and $400,000 to civic and community organizations in 2004. Oregon's most profitable Indian casino, operated by the Confederated Tribes of the Grand Ronde near Portland, has handed out over $54 million to community groups since its founding in 1997 (Rhodes 2011). A 2004 news article reported that "since the casino opened in 1995, it has transformed the economy of the northwestern Willamette Valley, injecting 1,500 jobs, most held by non-Indians, in a region struggling to overcome the collapse of the timber industry" (Barnard 2004).

PACT predicted increased criminal activity as a result of the Florence casino. Spilde's research (2000, 92) on the White Earth Reservation in Minnesota found that increased criminal activity "reflected the large number of insufficient funds checks written at the casino. While the prosecution of this type of crime demands time, money, and paperwork, these crimes do not represent increased danger to local residents." She also adds that "some anecdotal evidence suggest that crime actually decreases with tribal government gaming due to the availability of jobs and the increase in the standard of living" (Spilde 2000, 92).

Conclusion

Despite the realization that gaming is not an option for all tribes, there is a consensus that it is the only consistently successful economic enterprise in Indian Country today. As early as 2002 the National Indian Gaming Commission reported "that 350 Indian gaming facilities generated almost $14.5 billion in revenue . . . up fourteen percent from the 2001 total of $12.8 billion" (Wanamaker 2003), and Indian gaming was generating over three hundred thousand jobs, many of them to non-Indians. Two hundred thirty-three of the nation's 562 tribes were operating casinos in 28 states by 2009, generating a total of $26.5 billion in income, providing 712,000 jobs, and paying $10.8 billion in local, state, and federal taxes (500nations.com/Indian). In 2012, after two years of decline in North America because of the Recession, gaming revenues overall experienced a slight increase, with the biggest jump in Canada, according to the *Casino City's North American Gaming Almanac*.

The Indian gaming industry now collects 44 percent of all U.S. casino revenue. Gaming provides "tribal governmental revenue to build essential infrastructure such as schools, health, clinics, roads, clean water systems, communication systems, and recreation centers—and also helps fund essential programs such as education, health, child and elder care, law enforcement and fire protection programs, water and sewer service, and many other essential governmental programs" (Van Norman 2003). Each year Indian gaming tribes generate considerable sums of money through gaming for state and local governments, and in specific donations to charitable organizations. The most successful Indian enterprise on the Oregon coast is Grand Ronde's Spirit Mountain Casino, which in 2012 celebrated fifteen years of operation and $56 million in charitable donations. Most important, gaming income allows the Indian nations to explore other avenues of income and commerce, such as fishing, timber, and the arts that may be more in concert with Native traditional values and culture. How about restoring the salmon runs?

CHAPTER REVIEW

DISCUSSION QUESTIONS

1. What role do salmon play in the traditional culture of the fishing tribes or River People of the northwestern United States?
2. Describe the "fish-ins" of the 1960s. What political and economic forces were behind the attempt to curtail Indian fishing? What was the "Boldt decision?"
3. Who was David Sohappy? What happened to him in the government's Salmonscam? Do you think he was ultimately successful in protecting the Indians' right to fish? Explain your answer.
4. What role do dams play in the River Indians' right to fish? What other factors limit Indian fishing? Do you think the new salmon will help or hinder Indian fishing rights in the Pacific Northwest?
5. What are some of the myths about Indian gaming perpetuated by non-Indian opponents of Indian gaming?

SUGGESTED READINGS

COHEN, FAY G. 1986. *Treaties On Trial: The Continuing Controversy over Northwest Indian Fishing Right.* Seattle: University of Washington Press.

CONE, JOSEPH. 1995. *Common Fate: Endangered Salmon and the People of the Pacific Northwest.* Corvallis: Oregon State University Press.

MULLIS, ANGELA, and DAVID KAMPER, eds. 2000. *Indian Gaming: Who Wins?* Los Angeles: UCLA American Indian Studies Center.

River People: Behind the Case of David Sohappy. Produced by Michal Conford and Michele Zaccheo 50 minutes. Released 1991. Filmakers Library. Video cassette.

ULRICH, ROBERTA. 1999. *Empty Nets: Indians, Dams, and the Columbia River.* Corvallis: Oregon State University Press.

NOTES

1. Portions of this section are taken from "Years of Conflict On the Columbia River," by Simon Forder, a term paper submitted to my class in Native American Perception, December 13, 1989, at the University of California at Davis.

2. Many descriptions and details in this section are based on the author's close acquaintance with David Sohappy and his family for over ten years, and also as an Oregon resident and member of the Desecration Commission of the International Indian Treaty Council, a nongovernmental agency in consultative status at the United Nations.

REFERENCES

AUCOIN, LES. 2004. "Nuclear Waste No Problem if we Redefine 'Safe'." *Register-Guard*, Sunday, June 13.

BARNARD, JEFF. 2004. "Oregon Casino Also Major Philanthropist." *Register-Guard*, May 27.

BECK, DAVID R. M. 2009. *Seeking Recognition: The Termination and Restoration of the Coos, Lower Umpqua, and Siuslaw Indians, 1855–1984*. Lincoln: University of Nebraska Press.

BECKHAM. 1990. "History of Western Oregon Since 1846." In *Handbook of North American Indians, vol.7: Northwest Coast*, volume edited by Wayne Suttles, 180–88. Washington, DC: Smithsonian Institution Press.

BOYD, ROBERT T. 1990. "Demographic History, 1774–1874." In *Handbook of North American Indians, vol.7: Northwest Coast*, volume edited by Wayne Suttles, 135–48. Washington, DC: Smithsonian Institution Press.

COHEN, FAY G. 1986. *Treaties On Trial: The Continuing Controversy Over Northwest Indian Fishing Rights*. Seattle: University of Washington Press.

COLE, DOUGLAS, and DAVID DARLING. 1990. "History of the Early Period." In *Handbook of North American Indians, vol.7: Northwest Coast*, volume edited by Wayne Suttles, 119–34. Washington, DC: Smithsonian Institution Press.

FORDER, SIMON. 1989. "Years of Conflict Upon the Columbia River," term paper submitted to Steve Talbot's Native American Studies 70 class in perception, December 13, University of California, Davis.

GRINDE, DONALD A., and BRUCE E. JOHANSEN. 1995. *Ecocide of Native America: Environmental Destruction of Indian Land & Peoples*. Santa Fe: Clear Light. (See Chapter 6, "Fishing Rights: The Usual and Accustomed Places.)

HALLIDAY, JAN, and GAIL CHEHAK. 1996. *Native Peoples of the Northwest: A Traveler's Guide to Land, Art, and Culture*. Seattle: Sasquatch Books.

Indian Casino Facts. Http://500nations.com//Indian Casinos.asp : "500 Nations Indian Casinos SuperSite!" "Indian Casino Facts."

Indian Country: An American Crisis. 2000. November. Video. 50 minutes. Circulated in the Florence, OR, area locally. No other attribution.

LAWRENCE, WILLIAM J. 1996. *In Defense of Indian Rights*. http://media.hoover.org/sites/default/files/documents/0817998721_391.pdf

LEE, BILL. 2004. "Consider Indian Viewpoint During Bicentennial." *Yakima Herald-Republic*, June 17.

MARINO, CESARE. 1990. "History of Western Washington Since 1846." In *Handbook of North American Indians, vol.7: Northwest Coast*, volume edited by Wayne Suttles, 169–79. Washington, DC: Smithsonian Institution Press.

NEWCOMB, STEVEN T. 1993. "The Evidence of Christian Nationalism in Federal Indian Law: The Doctrine of Discovery, *Johnson v. Mcintosh*, and Plenary Power." *Review of Law & Social Change* 20 (2): 303–41.

PEVAR, STEPHEN L. 1983. *The Rights of Indians and Tribes*. New York: Bantam Books.

Register-Guard. 2004. "Plant Dumped Tons of Mercury." *Register-Guard*, June 21.

RHODES, DEAN. 2011. "Spirit Mountain Community Fund." *Smoke Signals*, June 11. http://www.grandoroond.org.

River People: Behind the Case of David Sohappy. Produced by Michal Conford and Michele Zaccheo 50 minutes. Released 1991. Filmakers Library. Video cassette.

ROE, JOANN. 1992. *The Columbia River: A Historical Travel Guide*. Golden, CO: Fulcrum.

ROSS, LUANA. 1998. *Inventing the Savage: The Social Construction of Native American Criminality*. Austin: University of Texas Press.

RUBY, ROBERT H. and JOHN A. BROWN. 1981. *Indians of the Pacific Northwest*. Norman: University of Oklahoma Press.

SHARP, DAVID. 2004. "Dam Nation." *VIA Magazine* (January–February): 36–43.

SILVERSTEIN, MICHAEL. 1990. "Chinookans of the Lower Columbia." In *Handbook of North American Indians, vol.7: Northwest Coast*, volume edited by Wayne Suttles, 533–46. Washington, DC: Smithsonian Institution Press.

SMITH, COURTLAND L. 1979. *Salmon Fishers of the Columbia*. Corvallis: Oregon State University Press.

SPILDE, KATHERINE A. 2000. "Educating Local Non-Indian Communities About Indian Nation Governmental Gaming: Messages and Methods." In *Indian Gaming: Who Wins?*, edited by Angela Mulliis and David Kamper, *83–95*. Los Angeles: UCLA American Indian Studies Center.

STEVENS, ERNIE L. 2000. "Perspective of Ernie L. Stevens, Tribal Councilman, Oneida Nation." In *Indian Gaming: Who Wins?*, edited by Angela Mullis and David Kamper, 172–73. Los Angeles: UCLA American Indian Studies Center.

TALBOT, STEVE. 2002. "Academic Indianismo: Social Scientific Research in American Indian Studies." *American Indian Culture and Research Journal* 26 (4): 67–96.

Register-Guard. 2004. "Plant Dumps Tons of Mercury." *Register-Guard*, June 21.

TRIMBLE, CHARLES E. 2003. "Time for Another Backlash?" *Indian Country Today*, June 25.

ULRICH, ROBERTA. 1999. *Empty Nets: Indians, Dams, and the Columbia River*. Corvallis: Oregon State University Press.

VAN NORMAN, MARK. 2003. "Tribal Governments: Indian Gaming, and the State Budget Crisis." *Indian Country Today*, September 10.

WALKER, DEWARD E, JR., and RODERICK SPRAGUE. 2001. "History Until 1846." In *Handbook of North American Indians, vol 12: Plateau*, volume edited by Deward E. Walker, Jr.. Washington, DC: Smithsonian Institution Press.

WANAMAKER, TOM. 2003. "Gaming is Healthy and Growing." *Indian Country Today*, September 10.

INTERNAL COLONIZATION
NATIVE HAWAIIANS AND THE SOVEREIGNTY MOVEMENT

Two Hawaiian Native figures with traditional designs, holding hands as a sign of sovereignty, with island symbols of the Hawaiian Nation.

UA MAU KE EA O KA 'ĀINA I KA PONO

The Sovereignty of the Land is Always Righteous

❖ ❖ ❖

Hawaiians are not Americans. . . . We are the children of Papa—earth mother, and Wākea—sky father—who created the sacred lands of Hawai'i Nei.

—Haunani-Kay Trask

*A*loha 'Āina, love of the land. This sacred concept epitomizes the contemporary struggle by the Indigenous people of Hawai'i for sovereignty over their beloved islands. As Native daughter, intellectual, and activist, Haunani-Kay Trask explains[1]:

> In our genealogy, *Pa pahānaumoku*—earth mother—mated with *Wākea*—sky father—from whence came our islands, or *moku*. Out of our beloved islands came the *taro*, our immediate progenitor, and from the *taro*, our Chiefs and people. Our relationship to the cosmos is thus familial. As in all of Polynesia, so in Hawai'i: elder sibling must feed and care for younger sibling who returns honor and love. The wisdom of our creation is reciprocal obligation. If we husband our lands and waters, they will feed and care for us. In our language, the name for this relationship is *mālama 'Āina*, care for the Land, who will care for all family members in return. (Trask 1993, 80)

In 1993 the Native peoples of Hawai'i marked the centenary of the overthrow of their Native government and loss of independence with protest demonstrations that resulted in mass arrests. And as recently as May 1, 2008, approximately sixty Native Hawaiian protestors locked the gates of Honolulu's historic Iolani Palace. The palace was the official residence of Hawai'i's last two reigning monarchs before the kingdom was overthrown by the descendants of White missionaries and through the intervention of U.S. Marines. The islands were then illegally annexed by the United States in 1898 over the near unanimous objections of its Native residents. These disastrous events occurred during a period of American expansionism and imperialist ventures outside its continental limits. "No matter what Americans believe, most of us in the colonies do not feel grateful that our country was stolen, along with our citizenship, our lands and our independent place among the family of nations" (Trask 1993, 2).

The protests of the 1990s and 2000s were not the first to take place in recent Hawai'i history. Beginning in 1970, a sovereignty movement evolved from anti-eviction and other land struggles undertaken by small, rural enclaves of Native people in the Hawaiian Islands. These were the remnants of a once thriving Hawaiian civilization that were being threatened by urbanization and commercial and residential development. They were Native communities which continued to carry on many traditional activities such as taro farming, fishing, and speaking the Hawaiian language. It was at this time that the struggle began to focus on asserting Native sovereignty based on the Indigenous birthright to land and sea.

One of the first of these land protests was in 1970 in the Kalama Valley on the island of O'ahu. The Bishop Estate, which is the single largest landowner in Hawai'i, evicted Native farmers in order to construct a high income residential development. The Native resistance engendered an outpouring of support from throughout the islands. Although the protest failed to stop the impending development, it nevertheless underscored the land claims issue for a crescendo of protests that then took place over the next three decades.

In addition to foreign commercial and residential development, the second great colonizing agent in Hawai'i has been the U.S. military. In 1976, the movement for *mālama 'Āina* centered on the island of Kaho'alawe, smallest of Hawai'i's eight major islands. Kaho'alawe is a sacred island with many temples and religious sites, yet it had been used continuously as a bombing range by the U.S. military since World War II. The bombing was finally halted in 1990 due to the protests.

By the end of the 1980s the struggle for Hawaiian sovereignty came to stand for nationhood. The question remained, however, whether a return to an independent Hawaiian government was politically feasible, no matter how just the cause, or whether some other form of a more limited sovereignty was appropriate. For many Native Hawaiians, the emergence of a new political organization, Ka Lāhui Hawai'i (the Hawaiian Nation), offered hope of resurrecting Hawaiian independence.

CHAPTER OVERVIEW

We begin this chapter by highlighting certain analytical and theoretical concepts, especially the theoretical formulation by Hawaiian Studies professor Lilikalā Kame'eleihiwa (1992) .concerning the socioeconomic and spiritual bases for Hawaiian sovereignty, and how what Hawaiians call "the Land" was expropriated by the Americans. The concepts of colonialism, imperialism, and sovereignty are also relevant to the Hawai'i case.

Next, we turn to a description of Hawaiian culture and society as it existed on the eve of Western expansion and conquest. It was a beautiful, unique way of life, in some essential ways reminiscent of that of other Indigenous peoples, yet different in other important aspects. The intrinsic connection of Hawaiian society to the spiritual world, and its reciprocal balance throughout all parts of the social structure based on *aloha*, love for the gods, love for the people, and love for the land is remarkable for its subtle complexity.

The third part of our narrative concerns Hawaiian cultural history in terms of its interaction with Western and United States imperialism during the eighteenth and nineteenth centuries. A key part of this history concerns the loss of Hawaiian sovereignty. How, when, and under what circumstances did it occur? This is an important part of the Hawaiian story, because the contemporary quest by Hawaiian Native peoples in their struggle for survival rests on how to recover their sovereignty as an independent people. Therefore, an historical understanding of when and how sovereignty was lost should have important implications for how it can be regained. This section also includes subtopics that deal with important developments in this history, such as the influence of the American missionaries, the domination by the sugar industry, change in the Hawaiian land tenure system, the overthrow of the monarchy, and, finally, the annexation of Hawai'i in 1898 by the United States of America.

A fourth section is devoted to Hawai'i under colonial rule from 1900 to 1959, after it became a territory of the United States. Why, for example, did the United States, a country founded on the principles of individual freedom and democracy, embark at the end of the nineteenth century on a course of expansionism and imperialism? This part of the chapter provides an analysis of these events, which, in the Hawaiian case, led to the illegal annexation of the islands in 1898.

In the next part of the chapter we return to our analytical concepts by placing Hawaiian history in the wider context of the global colonial system. By 1900 most of the world's peoples were under the yoke of the European colonial nations. It is seldom realized that the United States, although coming late on the world scene as a dominant political power, also became a colonizing nation. For the most part, this was the result of the Spanish American War, when imperialist sentiments at home came to dominate U.S. foreign policy. The seizure of Hawai'i in 1898 is explained within this historical context.

The period of statehood after 1959 saw rapid commercial, military, and tourist development. Although limited political gains were made, the overall economic and cultural impact on the Native peoples and their island environment has been extremely serious. These issues are discussed in a concluding section. At the same time, there has been a significant increase in the political struggle and a rebirth of Hawaiian language, culture, and pride.

We return to a consideration of theory in still another section. Contemporary research by a leading Native scholar, who links the loss of Hawaiian sovereignty to the change in land tenure under the land division that took place in the latter part of the nineteenth century, may provide clues as to how it may now be regained.

Finally, we examine the contemporary revitalization movement and the political options under consideration by the Native people in their struggle for sovereignty and a rebirth of the Hawaiian Nation.

ANALYTICAL AND THEORETICAL CONCEPTS

The analytical concepts that we examine in this chapter to help us understand the contemporary Hawaiian struggle are imperialism, colonialism, and sovereignty.

Imperialism may be defined as "a system in which a nation's authority is extended by territorial acquisition or by establishing economic or political power over other nations" (Wei and Kamel 1998, 18).

A definition in the *Oxford English Dictionary's* 1901 edition is directed specifically to U.S. imperialism: "In the United States, [imperialism] is . . . applied to the new policy of extending the rule of the American people over foreign countries, and of acquiring and holding distant dependencies, in the way in which colonies and dependencies are held by European states" (Osborne 1998, xv).

The related concept of *colonialism* is defined as the military, political, and economic control by one nation over a dependent area and people. The nation which is under foreign control is then referred to as a *colony*. The motive for colonialism is to profit from the dominated nation by reaping the benefits of cheap land, cheap resources, cheap labor, and closed markets. Most often, the apologists for U.S. colonialism speak instead of "America's spheres of influence." The bottom line, however, is that the colonized are deprived of their right to self-determination under international law. This is what occurred in Hawai'i when it was seized by an expansionist United States in 1898 and turned into a de facto colony.

The solution concepts are *sovereignty* and *self-determination*. By sovereignty is meant complete independence and self-government as exercised by a sovereign state or nation. Self-determination is the inherent right of a people or nation to determine its own political status.

We also discuss the research by Lilikalā Kame'eleihiwa on the Hawaiian *Māhele*, or land division, which led to the dispossession of the Native people in 1848 (Kame'eleihiwa 1992). The loss of Hawaiian sovereignty is usually attributed to the landing of U.S. Marines and the overthrow of the Hawaiian monarch by the Missionary Party in 1893, followed by the annexation of the islands by the United States in 1898. Kame'eleihiwa's research, however, infers that this legalistic line of thinking is misleading and superficial. Instead, she traces the loss of sovereignty to the fundamental changes in Hawaiian traditions and land tenure that occurred a half century earlier, leading to the Great *Māhele* (or land division) of 1848–50. An understanding of these historical events is essential if one is to gain a clear understanding of the political course the Native Hawaiians must pursue in order to secure their right to self-determination.

CULTURE AND SOCIETY IN OLD HAWAI'I

The origins of Polynesian Hawaiians can be traced to the skilled sailors and navigators from Indonesia and the Philippines, who migrated to Melanesia in the Pacific Ocean by 3300 BC. New populations of Caucasoid and Mongoloid racial strains then appeared and mixed with the earlier immigrants. By 2000 BC, their descendants began the exploration of the South Pacific. One population group, newcomers into the region who are associated culturally with a ceramic pottery style called Lapita, became the first peoples to occupy Fiji and nearby Tonga. Tonga became the birthplace of the Polynesians and the departure point for the exploration and settlement of the Marquesas and other Polynesian Islands. This was in approximately 1300 BC. These seagoing people began the colonization of a huge geographical triangle that became Polynesia, stretching 3,600 miles south to New Zealand, then 3,000 miles eastward to Easter Island, and finally 2,000 miles northward to Hawai'i, its apex. Within three thousand years, these indefatigable voyagers settled 278 habitable islands and became the most widely dispersed people on earth. The region known as Polynesia encompasses twice the area of the continental United States.

The Marquesan explorers were expert canoe-builders and navigators. Their canoes carried "dried breadfruit, shellfish, coconut meat, dried bonito, *pandanus* flour, drinking coconuts and bamboo stalks filled with fresh water" (Dougherty 1992, 10). They also carried plants for cultivation: sugarcane, taro, banana, breadfruit, sweet potatoes, saplings, as well as special foods (dried fish, whole yams, and dried coconuts) to "feed" the gods, whose replicas they also carried. Livestock probably included dogs, pigs, and chickens. Kindling for fire, and many useful craft items such as cooking stones, bailing buckets, paddles, fishhooks and nets, were among their technological inventory. Skilled navigators, they sailed without compass or sextant, taking their direction from the sun, moon, the stars and their constellations, the winds, and swells and currents.

The Hawaiian Islands were probably settled prior to AD 400 by these Polynesian navigators from the Marquesas. A second migration to Hawai'i occurred about 1100 AD from the Society Islands. They came in oceangoing double canoes, often reaching eighty to one hundred feet in length. There appears to have been two-way contact between Tahiti and Hawai'i during the twelfth through the fourteenth centuries.

With the exception of *Aotearora* (New Zealand), Hawai'i is larger in total inhabitable land area than any other Polynesian island group. The volcanic islands of Hawai'i, a great submarine mountain range, were built up from the ocean floor by successive

Pele, the Volcano Goddess.

eruptions. The islands were created by the goddess Pele, according to Hawaiian tradition. The Hawaiian island chain is 1,523 miles in length, but eight major islands, located in the southeastern part of the chain, account for 99 percent of the land, a total area of 6,425 square miles. These largest islands include Ni'ihau, Kaua'i (the oldest of the islands), O'ahu, Moloka'i, Maui, Lāna'i, Kaho'olawe, and Hawai'i (also known as the "big island," and the youngest in the chain).

The climate is temperate, with temperatures ranging between 65 and 88 degrees Fahrenheit throughout the year. Food, from both the land and the sea, was plentiful before European conquest.

Before European entry into the region the Hawaiian people had highly complex systems of horticulture and fishing. "The combination of diet including *poi*, *taro* tops, coconuts, sweet potatoes, bananas, mountain apples, seaweed, sea foods and, occasionally, chickens, pigs and dogs, along with their daily exposure to sunlight and exercise, gave the Hawaiians everything they needed for outstanding physical development" (Dougherty 1992, 17–18). The custom of bathing and surfing in the ocean helped keep people clean and free of disease. Prevention was the key to good health.

Artists created beautiful images in stone, wood, feathers, and through the custom of tattooing. *Hula* dance performances were dedicated to the various gods and chiefs. An oral tradition of chants and the recitations of genealogies recounted Hawaiian history and emphasized *aloha*, the bond of loving kinship between people, the land, and the natural world. "The earliest Hawaiian history recorded the origins of the islands in the form of competing genealogies which traced the archipelago back to various mythic gods and forces. These genealogies, recited in the form of chants, told of the islands being born, depending on the genealogy consulted" (McMurray 2002, 158).

The most famous of the Hawaiian chants is the *Kumulipo*, a great cosmogonic genealogy. The *Kumulipo* (Beginning in Deep Darkness) is the birth chant of an island chief and his royal family. Composed by a Master of Song in 1700 and transmitted in the oral tradition, its two thousand lines provide an extended genealogy proving the family's divine origin and tracing the family history from the beginning of the world. (See Beckwith 1972). It was translated into English by Queen Lili'uokalani during her imprisonment by the Americans in 1895 at Iolani Palace. It has been compared to the Hebrew Genesis, and to that of the Greeks. It begins in the intense darkness of the spirit world and concludes with the name of the infant chief to whom the name chant and genealogy belong. Such a chant contributed to the prestige of a family of rank. It was recited to Captain Cook, for example, in 1779, at a temple ceremony when he was honored as the god *Lono*.

Names, and hence the genealogies, are a central part of the Hawaiian cultural tradition. The names of the various chiefs and chieftesses are repeated in the chants for successive generations "to enhance and share the honor of the original ancestor. In this process, the name collects its own *mana* [sacred power] and endows the successor who carries it" (Kame'eleihiwa 1992, 21). "Persons especially trained in the memorization of genealogies were important members of a Chief's retinue, because a Chief's ranking in society was determined by the legitimacy of his genealogy" (Mullins 1978, 4).

Nature is personified in Hawaiian culture, which resulted in a great respect for life on the land, in the sea, and in the cosmos. "Our poetry and dance reveal this great depth of sensual feeling—of love—for the beautiful world we inhabited" (Trask 1993, 6). Aggressiveness, possessiveness, and acquisitiveness were considered undesirable behavior, and people were noted for their gentle temperament.

Spiritual Life

Spirituality was a vital part of Hawaiian life, with rituals for everything, from fishing and planting to canoe construction and sporting contests. The various gods and religious specialists had specific duties, and the general populace was governed by a system of special rules, the *kapu* system, which is explained below.[2]

Wākea, Sky Father, and *Papa*, Earth Mother, are the parents of the Hawaiian islands, as well as the ancestors of the Hawaiian Nation. They are also half-brother and sister. According to Hawaiian tradition, their first human offspring was a daughter, with whom *Wākea* slept. As a result of this incest, the *kāhuna*, or priest, provided a religious solution that became a key facet of Hawaiian religious custom. It is known as the *'Aikapu*, or sacred eating, in which men and women are separated in the act of eating.

According to the sacred traditions, *kalo* (taro) is the premature fetus of *Wākea* in the incestuous union with his daughter. Sadly, he was born lifeless and deformed. This male fetus was buried in the ground where he became "quivering long stalk," or *kalo*, when

the first plant sprouted from his mystical body. The next child born of this incestuous union was the first Hawaiian *Ali'i Nui* (high chief). Therefore, "the *kalo* plant, which was the main staple of the people of old, is also the elder brother of the Hawaiian race, and as such deserves great respect" (Kame'eleihiwa 1992, 24).

Kame'eleihiwa (1992, 24–25) contends that there are three historical lessons to be learned from this *Wākea* oral tradition. The first lesson is the strong familial relationship that Hawaiians have to the land. This is called *mālama 'Āina*, "caring for the Land." It is also closely related to *aloha 'Āina*, "love of the Land." The reciprocal relationship of the Hawaiian people loving and caring for the land will result in the land feeding and caring for the people. This harmonious relationship is expressed as *pono*, or "righteous," a universe in perfect harmony.

The second lesson is that of *'Aikapu*, the "sacred eating" prohibition. "Since . . . eating is for men a religious ceremony or sacrifice to the male *Akua* Lono, it must be done apart from anything defiling, especially women" (Kame'eleihiwa 1992, 23). Men therefore prepared food and ate separately from women. Under *'Aikapu*, certain foods were also forbidden for women to eat since these foods, notably the pig, coconuts, bananas, and red fish, are associated with male symbolism. In addition, during the four lunar nights of each month that were set aside for the worship of the four major male gods, men were forbidden to sleep with women.

The third lesson concerns *mana*, or divine power, which arises from chiefly incest. Since the *Ali'i Nui* are considered almost divine, brother-sister marriage or mating among other close relatives in the chiefly class preserves, or actually increases, this sacred power for the benefit of the entire people.

In traditional Hawaiian ideology, the *Akua*, or gods, control all nature—the oceans, volcanoes, land, and the heavens. *Kāne* is the creator, father of human beings and all living things. *Kanaloa* is god of the sea; *Lono* the god of peace, farming, and rain; and *Kū*, the god of war, fishing, and forests. The *'Aumākua* were family gods who helped with fishing, planting, and other daily activities. They "were usually thought to be the spirits of respected ancestors who remained in communication with their descendants on earth" (*Spirit of the Land*, n.d., 3). The *kāhuna* were spiritual leaders and skilled specialists in medicine, canoe building, and various religious items.

Spirituality integrated all aspects of Native Hawaiian life. The people "prayed to one God for their *taro* planting, another for fishing, another for the *hula,* and yet others for different crafts. Each home had an altar for its family Gods or *'Aumākua"* (*Spirit of the Land,* n.d., 4). There were also *heiau,* or temples, where people made offerings in honor of the gods who helped and protected them. Smaller shrines, or *ko'a,* were where the fishermen prayed to the god *Kū'ula* and made offerings for success in fishing.

Mana, or spiritual power, was an important concept. *Mana* was determined by ancestry and social rank, and after death it remained in the possessions of the chiefs and in their bones. The sacred power of *heiau* could be increased by burying the bones of high chiefs on their premises.

The goddess *Pele* and the trickster god *Maui* were related to the history and formation of the islands. Stories or legends about these and other gods, their feats and activities, were usually chanted and performed as *hula* (dance).

The god *Lono* was honored with a four-month series of festivals, the *Makahiki,* which took place annually in November after the harvest and continued into February. It was a time when everyone rested and abstained from work. Warfare was forbidden and the people were encouraged to engage in games of strength—boxing, wrestling, foot racing, chest pushing, hand gripping, spear and dart throwing, sliding, stone bowling, and *hula* dancing.

Warfare was honored under the god *Kū,* but before Europeans arrived, it "was often more symbolic than real—a ritual athletic jousting prefaced by gigantic spouts of poetry and genealogical recitation, by much intimidating gesturing and grimacing. And it could be abruptly ended by the appearance of a Chief so sacred that all the soldiers had to throw themselves to the ground" (Du Plessix Gray 1972a, 53).

Many contemporary Native Hawaiians continue to hold these ancient spiritual beliefs and perform some of the ritual practices. Indeed, in recent years there has been a revitalization of Native culture and traditions as the people's political awareness and participation in the sovereignty movement has developed.

Economic Organization

Each of the eight major islands, or *mokupuni,* were divided into *'okana,* or geographical districts, running upland from the mountains down to the ocean below. (See Figure 8.1.) Each *'okana,* in turn, was subdivided into wedge-shaped pieces of land and sea like the slices of a pie, called *ahupua'a.* "The narrow end of the *ahupua'a* is at a central or inland mountain top, and it broadens out as it progresses towards the

shore and out into the sea" (Dudley and Agard 1990, 1). *Ahupua'a* varied in size from one hundred acres to more than one hundred thousand acres. Ideally, an *ahupua'a* would include everything for subsistence— "timber, thatching, and rope from the mountains, various crops from the uplands, *kalo* [taro] from the lowlands, and fish from the sea" (Kame'eleihiwa 1992, 27). The boundary line between two *ahupua'a* was marked by a carved wooden pig's head, or a pig offering on an altar of stones.

An *Ali'i,* or chief, with an overseer, *konohiki,* were responsible for seeing that there was a constant flow of products moving through the *ahupua'a* to meet everybody's needs. The *Ali'i* oversaw the *'Āina* and was responsible for the upkeep of the extensive irrigation systems that watered the wetland *kalo* fields. The *konohiki,* or land steward, was usually a chief of lesser rank who was responsible for supervising the collection of tribute and the day-to-day activities of the cultivation and fishing. "Due to its range in climate and elevation, the *ahupua'a* usually provided for most of

mokupuni: major island
moku: large districts divided from mountain to sea
ahupua'a: smaller land divisions within each **moku**
'ili: smaller land divisions within each **ahupua'a**
lele: sections of land within an **'ili**

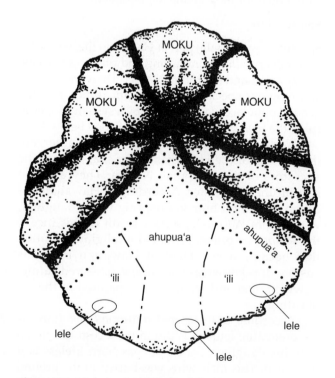

Figure 8.1 *Mokupuni* with its land divisions.

the needs of its people. There were mountain forests with plenty of wood for making canoes, spears, house posts and temple images. At lower elevations farmers planted bananas and yams, and along streams they planted *taro*, sweet potatoes and sugar cane. Usually, each *ahupua'a* had a beach and an area that stretched out into the sea for fishing and catching crabs" (*Spirit of the Land*, n.d., 5).

Each *ahupua'a* was comprised of smaller sections of land, or *'ili*, on which resided the extended families, *'ohana*. The *'ili* varied in size and number from one *ahupua'a* to another. Some paid tribute directly to the *Ali'i* of the *ahupua'a*, while others were independent and paid tribute directly to the *Mō'ī*, or high chief. The *lele* were even smaller pieces of land within an *'ili*. The *'ohana* social unit was the core of the traditional Hawaiian economy. The *'ohana* who lived near the sea exchanged products with the inland *'ohana*, utilizing forrest land, *taro* and sweet potato gardens, and fishing grounds. The *ahupua'a* districts were economically independent, their inhabitants having all of the foodstuffs and necessities of life necessary to subsist. "People did not live in villages: their homes were scattered over the area of the *ahupua'a*" (Dudley and Agard 1990, 2).

"Tribute," in the Hawaiian sense of the term, meant "to make something grow," in this case, "the *mana* or divine power of the *Akua*," so that he in turn can make life grow in the *'Āina* and the people" (Kame'eleihiwa 1992, 29). All of this naturally benefitted the *maka'āinana*, or common people. Tribute collection centered on the *Makahiki* festival in honor of the god of fertility, Lono. Starting in October or November, and continuing for three or four months thereafter, Lono ruled the *'Āina* as supreme *Akua*. *Kū*, the war god, on the other hand, ruled for the other eight months of the year. During the *Makahiki* period, war, human sacrifice, and labor were forbidden.

Among the common people were those who devoted themselves to specialized tasks: some toiled the land, some were fishermen, others designed and built elaborate irrigation systems, and still others were canoe builders, bird catchers, and house builders. The men cooked using underground ovens, while the care of young children was left to the women along with plaiting mats and making cloth from the inner bark of the mulberry tree.

Social Organization

Kinship and social rank were the centerpiece of Hawaiian sociopolitical organization. Rather than organized into socioeconomic classes, the Native Hawaiians were a ranked society based on prestige and social status. At the top of the prestige pyramid were the chiefs, or *Ali'i*. The *Ali'i nui*, or high chief, was responsible to the gods as caretaker of the *'Āina* (land), but private land ownership was unknown. The *Ali'i* competed amongst themselves in terms of rank and the ability to maintain order and foster economic prosperity. Rank itself was derived from *mana* (spiritual power) as set forth in the chiefly genealogies, or from conquest in war. The highest ranking *Ali'i* were advised by a council of chiefs and a powerful *kāhuna* (priestly) class.

The preferred marriage pattern among the *Ali'i* was one where the son of a high chief married a sister or close relative. In this way, the offspring of the union would receive the combined *mana* of both parents and become an even more powerful chief as an adult. The rank in social grades in preferred marriage descended according to the distance in blood between the two parents, provided they themselves were of high chiefly rank. The highest was the union of brother and sister, *pi'o*. That between first cousins, *ho'i*, is next. Less desirable is the union between half-brother and sister, *naha*. The child of a *pi'o* union was an *Akua*, a god. On the other hand, such unions were considered incestuous if they took place among commoners.

The common people, *maka'āinana* (people of the land) were subordinate to their *Ali'i* caretakers, yet independent in many ways. Unlike European feudal society, the *maka'āinana* were not bound to the land as serfs, nor did they owe military service to the *Ali'i*. Land in feudal Europe, by way of contrast, was privately owned by the nobility and the church. The serfs, about 80 percent of the populace, were bound to the manor land with military and other service days due their feudal masters. The erroneous assertion by non-Native supposed "experts" that ancient Hawai'i had a similar feudal system provides a racist justification for the actions of missionary entrepreneurs in destroying the land tenure system and Christianizing the Native people. The *maka'āinana* were also free to move with their *'ohana* to another *Ali'i* if they so chose. The result was that the society's leaders sought to provide for the well-being and contentment of all their constituents. Not to do so would mean the loss of status and thus of *mana* for the *Ali'i*. If anyone in this complex symbiotic system failed in his or her duties, be one *'Ali'i, konohiki,* or *maka'āinana*, it was grounds for dismissal. The *'Āina, Ali'i,* and *maka'āinana* were thus unified mystically in Hawaiian traditional culture.

"Below the commoners were a numerically small group of people known as *'kauwa'* or outcastes. Little is known of their origins or of their true role in Hawaiian society, although they were believed to be slaves of the lowest order" (Mullins 1978, 4).

On the *ahupua'a*, people lived as one large extended family, or *'ohana*. The *'ohana* consisted of blood relatives, others not related by blood but considered part of the *'ohana* nevertheless, and the revered, spiritual ancestors. Members of the *'ohana* are likened to the shoots of the *taro* plant, with its *keiki*, or children, all from the same root. "The family provided for all of the social, economic and educational needs of the individual. Those who lived in the uplands shared *taro*, banana and sweet potato with their *'ohana* by the sea who, in turn, gave them fish and other sea products. Whenever someone was in need, the members of the *'ohana* would come to help" (*Spirit of the Land*, n.d., 5).

The *Kapu* System

Social control was enforced through a moral code of sacred law, the *kapu* system. The system of *kapu* embodied the rules of life; it regulated people's lives and everything from the time for farming and warfare to the proper mating behavior for both the *Ali'i* and *maka'āina* alike. It was the glue of the social system. Commoners could not approach a chief, could not walk in the chief's footsteps, touch his or her possessions, or let their shadows fall on the chief's palace grounds. They were required to kneel or sit when a chief entered an area, depending on the rank of the chief. This was because the chiefs with their powerful *mana* served the Hawaiian gods in their care of the *maka'āinana*.

Everyday activities, too, were regulated by the *kapu*. Women were prohibited from eating the foods reserved for offerings to the gods; they could not prepare meals for the men or eat with them. To promote economic sustainability, the seasons for fishing, for taking animals, and for gathering timber were all strictly controlled by the *kapu* in order to conserve natural resources for the benefit of the entire community. Thus the eating of certain kinds of fish was regulated during certain times of the year in order to conserve the supply. Warfare, too, was forbidden at certain times of the year.

The punishment for breaking a *kapu* was always the same, death, either by strangulation or by clubbing. The rationale was this: "To break the sacred *kapu* was to offend the Gods, and the people believed that the Gods reacted violently toward an offender, most frequently with lava flows, tidal waves, famine, or earthquakes. So to protect themselves from these catastrophes, the people pursued a *kapu* breaker until he was caught and put to death" (U.S. National Park Service n.d.). There was, however, a way to avoid a death sentence. On all of the islands there were religious sanctuaries, *pu'uhonua*. If a *kapu* breaker reached one of these sanctuaries, a ceremony of absolution could be performed by the resident priest. The offender could then return home safely, usually within a few hours or by the next morning.

The *kapu* system did not mean that Hawaiians were prudish about sex: there was considerable sexual freedom. In fact, Hawaiian culture endorsed spontaneous, casual sexual relationships as a prerequisite for permanent unions. This eventually brought them into conflict with the sexual norms of the puritanical missionaries who began to arrive in the early nineteenth century.

HISTORY OF CONQUEST AND DISPOSSESSION

When the first Europeans appeared in Hawai'i in the latter half of the eighteenth century, "the lands were lush and verdant, the seas filled with fish. Life was good. The people were healthy, vigorous, and happy" (Dudley and Agard 1990, 1). All this changed with the arrival of Europeans.

The *Discovery*

Although he might have been preceded by Spanish galleons on their voyages between Mexico and the Philippines, in 1778, Captain James Cook was the first documented Westerner to encounter Hawai'i. Cook made three trips as captain of the British navy ships *Endeavour, Resolution,* and *Discovery* between 1768 and 1779. His first trip in August of 1768 was for the stated purpose of assisting the astronomers of the Royal Society in their observation of the planet Venus in Southern Hemisphere skies. The real reason was for Cook, an excellent navigator, to chart new waters and to lay claim to virgin territories for England. An eerie preview of Cook's future relations with Pacific Islanders took place when he ordered his men to open fire, killing and wounding a number of Native Maori of New Zealand. During Cook's second voyage, begun in October of 1772, he searched for a hypothetical southern continent and more thoroughly explored Polynesia, later venturing into Melanesia.

In his third voyage, 1776–79, Cook further explored Oceania, and also the Pacific Coast of North America, looking for a northwest passage that could open up a direct trade route from England to the Far East. Although portrayed in Western history books as an intelligent and humane man, his biographers nevertheless record that in Tahiti, Cook showed a vicious streak in his dealings with both his crew and the Native people he encountered. For perceived offenses such as stealing, he burned and smashed Native houses and canoes, kidnapped chiefs, and flogged his victims. When this failed, Cook ordered the cropping of ears and the slashing of arms crosswise with a knife. Hawaiians on the coast of O'ahu were the first to sight the two ships under Cook's command, the *Resolution* and the *Discovery*, on January 19, 1778. Cook, however, sailed on and made a landing in Kaua'i to secure fresh water, and also landed briefly at Ni'ihau. Cook then explored the northwest coast and Alaska, and only later returned to further investigate the Hawaiian Islands.

When Cook returned on January 17, 1779, to land at Kealakekua Bay on the Big Island of Hawai'i, it is said that the Hawaiians mistook Cook for the personal manifestation of their god *Lono*, especially since he had arrived during the *Makahiki*, the harvest celebration associated with Lono, and in a bay considered sacred to the god. As a result of this coincidence, as many as 10,000 islanders in 2,500 canoes came out to greet him, with hundreds more approaching gracefully on their surfboards.

In the Hawaiian Islands, Cook found a highly developed society, but this first contact left a tragic legacy of European diseases because of the promiscuous relations between the sailors and Native women. Cook soon overstayed his visit by exhausting the hospitality of the local king who had to provision Cook's ships and also meet the constant demands of the English sailors for food and women. Suspicions begin to arise that Cook was not a god after all.

Trouble arose when *Discovery's* cutter was stolen. Cook and nine marines went ashore in an attempt to take King Kalanioppu hostage, and at the same time blockading the harbor. When a Native canoe was fired on by Cook's men while attempting to leave the harbor, the Hawaiians mounted a furious counterattack. In the battle which followed, four Marines and Cook lost their lives at Kealakekua Bay; between two hundred and three hundred Hawaiians were also killed, including thirty chiefs. The result of this initial Hawaiian contact by Europeans? "Cook left his generous hosts shreds of his lifeless body, a few pieces of hardware, gonorrhea and syphilis" (Dougherty 1992, 41).

Kamehameha I

Throughout the period from 1650 to the end of the 1700s, important socioeconomic changes took place in Hawai'i. As traditional Hawaiian society evolved, it began to be shaped by population pressures and the competition for resources and social status among the chiefs. "The Chiefs of its several islands emerged as a sharply defined upper class and the various *Ali'i*, ambitious for more power and more possessions, turned upon each other and war replaced tranquility in Hawai'i. . . . A stratified society, with a sacred Chief as its head, emerged to preside over a well-defined hierarchy of sub-Chiefs, advisors, priests, craftsmen and commoners" (Dougherty 1992, 20–21). This evolutionary development, possibly already underway at the time of the discovery by Cook, became accelerated by Hawaiian interaction with Europeans and the introduction of trade capitalism.

One of the Hawaiians who encountered Cook at Kealakekua Bay was a young chief named Kamehameha, who took a particular interest in the ship's cannon used by Cook and his men. Later, after Kamehameha became high chief of the northwestern part of the island of Hawai'i, he enlisted the aid of stranded English sailors to use English weaponry and a schooner to conquer the islands of Maui and O'ahu. In April of 1795, Kamehameha landed 16,000 warriors in 1,400 canoes at Waikiki on O'ahu. The *Nu'uanu Pali* battle is considered by many authorities to be the greatest military engagement in Hawaiian history, and the most important event in Kamehameha's struggle to unite the entire Hawaiian island chain under his rule. As Kamehameha I, he conquered and then ruled all the Hawaiian Islands for the next twenty-four years.

Kamehameha's reign (1779–1819) is generally credited as having been a successful one.

> In the midst of a famine, which was partially caused by his sandalwood trading, he took to the royal fields to plant, cultivate and harvest his own *taro* and refused to eat produce from another source. He set out to repair some of the damage his wars of conquest had caused and reestablished some of the almost forgotten tranquility among the ravaged islanders. With his strong Polynesian respect for the Land, he anticipated twentieth century environmentalists by setting standards for the conservation of natural resources. He helped to lay the keel for Hawai'i's early shipbuilding industry. (Dougherty 1992, 46)

The Hawaiian kingdom soon became a respected member of the international community of nations.

During his reign, Hawai'i traded with China, England, the United States, and other nations on a regular basis.

Early Economic Enterprises

Despite Kamehameha's successes, economic changes introduced by the European traders had serious consequences for the aboriginal economy during the early years of the Hawaiian monarchy. Hawai'i became the main stopover in the European trade with the Far East. "Perhaps the greatest side effect of Hawai'i being pulled into the capitalist world market was the spread throughout the islands of firearms. *Ali'i* who were savvy enough to establish good trade links with visiting merchant ships amassed arsenals which allowed them to conquer ever wider territories" (McMurray 2002, 165).

Following the collapse of the North American fur trade, the American-dominated sandalwood market in Hawai'i in the early 1800s became important. Cargoes of sandalwood were shipped to Canton, China, and exchanged for teas and silks, which were then sold at high prices in the United States. Among the traders in sandalwood was John Jacob Astor of New York, an early American capitalist.

Sandalwood, *'iliahi*, is a parasite that attaches itself to another tree. It is a very hard, highly fragrant wood that was in great demand in Asia for fans, and where it is still used as incense, in making hand-carved boxes, in medicine, and as an ingredient for perfume. Harvesting the sandalwood trees in Hawai'i was a brutal task for the Native laborers, to say nothing of the harmful environmental impact on the land. Labor in the sandalwood industry left both men and women physically deformed from carrying the tremendously heavy logs on their backs. Furthermore, the laborers had no time to farm; food grew scarce and the result was famine.

By 1829, the sandalwood forests were denuded, and the bottom fell out of the market. "Within one generation Hawai'i was almost completely stripped of its sandalwood forests. . . . Worse, great numbers of people were brought off the lands and away from their traditional occupations and lifestyles to work the sandalwood trade—the first serious tear in the fabric of traditional society and in the flow of food and services in the *ahupua'a*" (Dudley and Agard 1990, 3). As a result of the economic crisis that followed, the American traders demanded immediate payment on debts still owed by the island chiefs who had gone into debt in their desire to purchase Western goods. When the chiefs pleaded for more time to pay, Astor led the traders' lobby to persuade the U.S. government to engage in gunboat diplomacy by sending two warships to the islands to aid American commerce.

Whaling was another economic enterprise that dominated the Hawaiian market for a time in the early nineteenth century. Fertile sperm whales gathered seasonally in the Arctic off the coast of Japan and along the equator. As early as 1819, the port towns of Hawai'i had become rough, brawling liberty towns, rife with prostitution and vice. Honolulu on O'ahu and Lahaina on Maui became major ports of call for the whaling men. Here they came into conflict with the missionaries and the local authorities. "Shore boats lined the beach and disorderly drunks overflowed jail doors, spilling out on the sidewalk, impeding the progress of early churchgoers" (Dougherty 1992, 75). At one point, with nearly four hundred whaling ships anchored offshore, the sailors at Lahaina rioted on Front Street because of their opposition to the curfews imposed by the pious missionaries.

Cattle were introduced early into Hawai'i, but it was John Palmer Parker who became Hawai'i's first cowboy, or *paniolo*, in 1815. Kamehameha I gave him permission to settle at Kawaihae on the Big Island of Hawai'i in order to hunt the wild herds of cattle roaming the slopes of Mauna Kea volcano. Soon, his cattle empire became the largest in America that was under single ownership. It encompassed 600 miles of fenced grazing land and over 250,000 acres of royal ranch land. The Parker Ranch contained "51,000 head of Herefords, 1,000 quality horses, 132 ranch hands, 213 paddocks, 50 corrals and water reservoirs capable of servicing a small city. In 1816 Parker consolidated his business agreement with the King by marrying Kipikane," the granddaughter of one of Kamehameha's many wives (Dougherty 1992, 66).

Depopulation

The aboriginal population of Native Hawai'i is estimated as having been between eight hundred thousand and one million. Between 1778, when Cook first landed, and 1823, there was a major population decline, by some estimates, of more than 166,000 Hawaiians. In that year, the third year after the arrival of the first missionaries, the Reverend William Ellis made a tour of the Big Island of Hawai'i. He found that foreign diseases had destroyed three-fourths of the Native population. This was mainly due to the impact of the sandalwood trade with its accompanying famine that was then followed by a cholera epidemic in 1804. Dougherty (1992, 50) estimates that "adding those 70,000 cholera deaths to the sandalwood deaths, we arrive at the figure of 135,000 Hawaiian deaths—all during the first 45 years of exposure to the White man." As many as 30,000 of the deaths may have been due to European-style island warfare among the Hawaiian chiefs.

By the 1840s, Hawaiians numbered less than one hundred thousand. This represents a population collapse of nearly 90 percent in less than seventy years. Fifty years later, the Native Hawaiian population had been further reduced to less than forty thousand, a 96 percent genocide rate. A major cause of this momentous population decline were the European-introduced diseases to which the Native peoples had no natural immunity. Not only syphilis and gonorrhea, but also tuberculosis, measles, leprosy, and typhoid fever killed Native Hawaiians by the hundreds of thousands. The destruction of the Native economy, dispossession of the land, and labor exploitation in the sandalwood and sugar economy also contributed to the population decline. As we explain later in the chapter, this catastrophic depopulation was a major cause of the collapse of the traditional Native social system which, in turn, ended Native land tenure and led to the loss of Hawaiian sovereignty.

Liholiho and Ka'ahumanu

Kamehameha's son and heir was Liholiho, but Kamehameha's favorite wife, Ka'ahumanu, with the support of the queen mother, forced him to share power when he inherited the Hawaiian throne. "At the accession of Kamehameha II, she boldly appropriated half of the new King's power and became the first *Kuhina Nui*, or premier, an office that was held only by women until it was abolished in 1886. She was primarily responsible for the overthrow of the *kapu* system. In league with the King's mother, Keopuolani, she convinced Kamehameha II to sit down and eat with the women in violation of one of ancient Hawai'i's most serious prohibitions" (Mullins 1978, 17).

Overturning the *'Aikapu*, or sacred eating prohibition, signaled the beginning of the end for traditional customs and the sanctions that enforced the functions of the social system. With the overthrow of the *kapu* system, Ka'ahumanu was more able to exercise her political authority and rule as chief administer. Finally, "on November 5, 1819, Liholiho, obeying the wishes of Ka'ahumanu, commanded the destruction of all religious images and temples in the kingdom" (Dougherty 1992, 52). Hiram Bingham, the first American missionary to Honolulu, had converted Ka'ahumanu to Christianity. Bingham soon became the chief religious adviser in the Hawaiian monarchy government. After becoming a Christian, Ka'ahumanu enacted a code of laws based on the Ten Commandments. The customs and social structure of the old Hawaiian system began to unravel rapidly.

In 1824 both Liholiho and Queen Kamamalu contracted measles and died. The brother of Liholiho then became Kamehameha III. He immediately abolished all the puritanical laws except those for theft and murder. Viewed by some people as a libertine because of his gambling and drinking, he nevertheless revived the traditional Hawaiian activities of surfing, canoe racing, spear throwing, and *hula*. Even so, missionary influence continued to play a major role in the conquest of Hawai'i.

Christian Missionaries

Calvinist missionaries from Connecticut and Massachusetts came to Hawai'i in 1820. They managed to covert many of the high-ranking Hawaiian chiefs to Christianity and thereby created an ideological bond between the Native people and their foreign colonizers. In a way, "they revived the taboo system, but in a puritanical Protestant form (prohibited dancing, games, activity on the Sabbath; adopted Western dress codes; cracked down on extramarital sex, etc.). They also elevated the missionaries to the position of quasi-priests of the state" (McMurray 2002, 166). Under this pressure, by 1850, most Hawaiians were at least nominally enrolled as members of a Christian church. Many missionaries became permanent residents in Hawai'i, reared families, and came to have a powerful influence over their Native hosts. After several decades, an alliance arose between the missionary descendants and developing Western business interests, principally in the sugar industry. This new alliance became known as the missionary party.

The acquiescence by the Hawaiian chiefs in adopting Western ways laid the basis for religious conversion. After the death of Kamehameha I in 1819, the traditional *kapu* system and the religion which supported it was overthrown. This opened the way for Christianization. As missionary influence grew, King Kamehameha III began to look for advisers who were Western educated, and it seemed natural to recruit missionaries to take positions in the monarchy's government. "By the end of 1844 there were fourteen White men in government service. All three of the most important members of the king's cabinet were White" (Dudley and Agard 1990, 5).

Foreigners came to be called *haole* in the Hawaiian language. The *haole* missionaries in the Hawaiian government were keen to promote the capitalistic economic system with its system of private property and the profit motive. Land ownership in the Western sense was unknown in ancient Hawai'i. Common land use was an integral part of Hawaiian culture, "along with the air, the sunlight, the winds, the waters, and the people. None of these parts was to dominate the others" (Laenui 2001, 143). The Native Hawaiians had experienced only the *ahupua'a* life. In the *ahupua'a* the value of generosity reinforced a system of reciprocity and redistribution as the means of production and the circulation of goods and services. Lacking a cash economy based on the production of commodities for profit (such as sugar), one gave away and exchanged surplus food and craft items, or else redistributed them as tribute through the c chieftainship political system and ceremonial offerings in Native religious rites. Economic reciprocity and redistribution, accompanied by a ranked social system based on the concept of *mana*, were found throughout the Pacific Ocean region before Western colonial penetration. "Under the influence of the missionary party, however, less than thirty years after missionary arrival [in Hawai'i], this Land relationship was overturned." (Laenui 2001, 143).

Land Dispossession: The *Māhele*

Trask (1993, 8) observes that by the middle of the nineteenth century, Native Hawaiian land tenure had been transformed from communal use to private property. This was due to the "gunboat diplomacy" practiced by Western nations and missionary duplicity employed against the Hawaiian chiefs. When Kamehameha III assumed the throne, he was the first Hawaiian king to be educated by missionaries from childhood. His reign from 1825 to 1854 was the longest of any Hawaiian monarch. During these years, *haole* advisers were given citizenship and came to dominate the king's government. For example, Gerrit P. Judd served as secretary for foreign affairs and then as minister of interior. He and other Hawaiian-speaking White advisers to the king pushed through a constitution that was the first step in their gaining control of Hawaiian lands. Their land reform proposal became the Great *Māhele*. Because of its deleterious consequences for Native land tenure, Kamehameha III is often referred to as the Little King by Hawaiians.

The dispute as to whether Hawaiian lands were to remain communal or be divided up into private property began in 1843 when Kamehameha III was forced to temporarily cede control of Hawai'i to Great Britain. "The British consul claimed permanent ownership over Lands sold to him by lesser Chiefs, but those Chiefs had only held them at the king's pleasure" (Dudley and Agard 1990, 4), This international incident helped persuade King Kamehameha III to give in to his *haole* advisers for a division of the lands.

There were Native intellectuals like David Malo who at the time spoke out against the privatization of lands. In 1845 they collected thousands of names of Native Hawaiians on Maui and on the island of Hawai'i in a petition to the king to bar the foreign advisers from government and against private land ownership, but their pleas fell on deaf ears. Once the principle of private ownership of land was agreed to, lands in the Hawaiian islands were divided up as private property. This is known as the *Māhele* of 1848–50, the great division of the *'Āina* that resulted in a virtual giveaway of land as the basis for Hawaiian sovereignty. The traditional land, or *'Āina*, sacred to the Hawaiian people, was then quickly transferred to foreign ownership and the burgeoning sugar plantations. It allowed foreigners to own land, and at the same time led to the dispossession of the Native people. By 1888, three-quarters of all arable land was controlled by *haole* landowners. "Originally the idea was to divide the land three ways: one-third each for the king, the Chiefs, and the commoners. As it turned out, the Chiefs were given about one and a half million acres. Some land was also set aside for the Fort. The king kept about a million acres—the 'crown lands' as they were later called. Most of the rest, roughly another one and a half million acres, was set aside as 'government lands'" (Dudley and Agard 1990, 7).

Dudley and Agard give a useful summary account of the *Māhele* in their book, *A Call For Hawaiian Sovereignty* (1990, 7–17). According to the original plan, two years after the land division, any Native Hawaiian who had lived on their property for the previous ten years could claim between one and two acres of land surrounding their homes. These *kuleana* claims were to come either from the chiefs' lands, the Crown lands, or the government lands. The *kuleana* claimants could also purchase additional, inexpensive property from government lands. In addition, some of the government lands were to be set aside for sale to other commoners who did not qualify for *kuleana* lands. One reason for creating government lands was to generate income for running the Hawaiian government by selling or leasing the land. Yet a provision in the *Book of the Māhele* stated that the government might sell the government lands to Native Hawaiian people at fifty cents an acre. Non-Native Hawaiians were not considered as possible purchasers, with one exception. A year before the final division of the *'Āina* in 1848, some small parcels of land were awarded to non-Hawaiians, who either had held them previously or who merited a reward, but this was the only exception. It is clear that the government lands were intended for Native Hawaiians alone.

At first, Kamehameha III strongly opposed the *Māhele*, but he eventually agreed in part out of his concern for Hawaiian commoners who had become destitute urban refugees from the *ahupua'a*. He believed that giving the *maka'āinana* small plots would encourage them to return to the land as subsistence farmers.

In spite of the possibly good intentions of King Kamehameha III, the *Māhele* was a complete disaster for the Native people. It resulted in the transfer of Hawaiian lands into the hands of a White minority, because the king's government by this time had become dominated by non-Native foreigners. A month before the Hawaiian commoners were to claim their lands, "the Legislature confirmed the decision of the Privy Council allowing all residents, even foreigners, unrestricted rights to buy and sell lands. Under *haole* supervision, the 'government lands,' so carefully set aside 'forever' for his commoners by a loving king, were competed for: cash-poor commoners unaware of the meaning of land-title vs. shrewd *haoles*, some backed with almost unlimited wealth" (Dudley and Agard 1990, 13–14).

The *Māhele* was also doomed to fail because there was no marketing system outside of the *haole*-dominated port towns to support private enterprise by the Hawaiian commoners in the countryside. The entire concept of private land ownership and a profit-oriented, capitalist economy was foreign to the Native Hawaiians who were used to the old *ahupua'a* economic system.

The Hawaiian chiefs were also having problems with the money economy of capitalism. Buying beyond their means and unaccustomed to capitalist business practices, they soon were deeply in debt. Although they lacked money, they did have valuable land as a result of the *Māhele*. Consequently, a law was passed in 1850 "which allowed non-Hawaiian aliens to purchase property, because they [the chiefs] wanted to be able to sell their lands to pay existing debts and to buy more things. But this was like opening Pandora's Box.

From then on, the Chiefs were always in need of more and more money, and were forced to sell off more and more of their land" (Dudley and Agard 1990, 14). Within two years, hundreds of thousands of acres of land had been sold to Whites. "Before the monarchy came to an end forty years later, most of the Chiefs' lands and vast parts of the crown lands and government lands had been sold to Whites" (Dudley and Agard 1990, 15). By 1890, three out of four acres in private ownership were held by non-Hawaiians; a small number of Whites owned one million acres.

The great inequality inherent in the land division process is shown by the fact that the small *kuleanas* distributed to Hawaiian commoners consisted of only one or two acres, while the *haole* missionaries received 560 acres each, and at a nominal cost. Coincidentally, the American Board of Foreign Missions ended its financial support for their missionaries about the same time that the Hawaiian land distribution took place under the *Māhele*. Finding themselves without funding, the missionaries formed the Missionary Party and turned to business enterprise. Their commercial activities eventually evolved into the Hawaiian Big Five, a coalition of five business entities with roots in the Missionary Party that came to dominate every aspect of business, media, and politics in Hawai'i.

"The 'crown lands' and the 'government lands' have become very important to the Hawaiian people today. Native Hawaiians claim that both belong exclusively to them and to no one else, and they want them returned to form part of the land base for the Hawaiian nation" (Dudley and Agard 1990, 8).

Sugar and Ethnic Segmentation

In 1842, President John Tyler announced the Tyler Doctrine, which warned rival European powers that Hawai'i was in the U.S. "sphere of influence." After the *Māhele*, the missionaries and their descendants, and other *haoles*, continued to buy up lands from the chiefs, bought or leased thousands of other acres of government lands, and developed large sugar plantations. Sugar then dominated the Hawaiian economy for the next half century. "Meanwhile, the *Kānaka Maoli* (Native Hawaiians) continued to struggle with disease and dispossession. While some families clung to lands that they had wisely claimed during the *Māhele*, even these fertile taro lands began to lose their productivity as privately funded water projects began to divert water from upland streams to sugar plantations in the more arid areas of the central plains on Maui and O'ahu islands . . . sugar grew at the expense of Native Hawaiian agricultural production" (Wei and Kamel 1998, 133).

With the development of the sugar industry there arose a need for labor, back-breaking toil in the plantation cane fields. Contrary to the myth that Native Hawaiians make poor workers, "more than 50 percent of the able-bodied male Hawaiians were working on Island plantations as late as 1873. On 35 plantations, there were 3,786 laborers. Of these, 2,627 were Hawaiian men and 364 were Hawaiian women" (Dougherty 1992, 133). The Hawaiians were forced to work for low wages and under harsh labor conditions. Due to the depopulation of Native people, however, there was an ongoing labor shortage on the expanding sugar plantations. In response, the White owners turned to importing tens of thousands of contract laborers from China, Japan, Portugal, and several other countries to perform the exhausting work. Over three hundred thousand Asians were brought to the islands between 1850 and 1920 as a cheap labor force, mostly from Japan, Okinawa, and the Philippines, to work for "King Sugar." Ironically, the labor force needs of the sugar industry led in great measure to the ethnic diversity that characterizes Hawai'i today. "In 1853, Hawaiians and part-Hawaiians represented 97 percent of the population of 73,137 inhabitants, while Caucasians constituted only 2 percent and Chinese only half a percent. Seventy years later, Hawaiians and part-Hawaiians made up only 16.3 percent of the population, while Caucasians represented 7.7 percent, Chinese 9.2 percent, Japanese 42.7 percent, Portuguese 10.6 percent, Puerto Ricans .2 percent, Koreans .9 percent, and Filipinos 8.2 percent" (Takaki 1989, 132).

Hoeing and cutting cane meant long hours and arduous work for little money. The immigrants were contract laborers with no rights, who worked under harsh working conditions from 5:00 AM until 4:30 PM. Workers were assigned a *bango*, or number, and were never called by name. The *lunas*, or overseers, were almost always White. A system of differential pay based on both ethnic and gender stratification characterized the plantation system and kept the workforce divided. "In 1902, the daily income of a skilled worker averaged $4.22 for the Caucasian, $1.80 for the Hawaiian, $1.69 for the Portuguese, $1.22 for the Chinese, and $1.06 for the Japanese" (Du Plessix Gray 1972a, 72). Housing was crowded: "Fourteen or more men sometimes slept together in rooms fifteen by twenty feet; the blacksnake whip continued to be used by some *lunas*" (Du Plessix Gray 1972a, 72). Strict discipline was maintained, and workers were fined for various infractions, such as refusal to do

work as ordered (25 cents), trespass (50 cents), insubordination (one dollar), drunkenness (50 cents), gambling in Japanese or Chinese camps (five dollars) (Takaki 1989, 139).

Takaki (1989, 155–56) gives the following description of the racial and ethnic pecking order (ethnic segmentation) of the plantation camps:

> At the top of the hill was the big house, the luxurious home of the manager; below were the nice-looking homes of the Portuguese, Spanish, and Japanese *lunas*, then the identical wooden-frame houses of Japanese Camp, and finally the more run-down Filipino Camp. Moreover, the organization of the housing hierarchy was planned and built around its sewage system. The concrete ditches that serviced the toilets and outhouses ran from the manager's house on the highest slope down to the Filipino Camp on the lowest perimeter of the plantation. The tiered housing pattern and sewage system seemed emblematic: "Shit too was organized according to the plantation pyramid."

It was not until 1900 that a federal law terminated the contract labor system.

Reciprocity and Annexation

Geographically speaking, the U.S. mainland was the logical place to sell Hawaiian sugar because it was closer than any other market. To secure this market, the Missionary Party had two possible solutions from which to choose in order to maximize their profits: a reciprocity agreement, or annexation by the United States. Reciprocity would permit Hawaiian sugar to be imported into the United States duty free, giving the *haole* plantation owners an advantage over other competing sugar producers. Reciprocity agreements, however, were only temporary. The other solution was to get the United States to annex Hawai'i. Annexation would result in a permanent market advantage, because "Hawaiian sugar would be considered domestic rather than foreign and thus not subject to tariff" (Laenui 2001, 143).

During the 1850s, the White planters began to agitate for annexation. King Kamehameha III, however, opposed annexation, and a treaty of annexation drafted by the Americans in his government remained unsigned at the time of his death. His successor, Prince Alexander Liholiho, who ascended the Hawaiian throne in 1854, terminated the annexation negotiations altogether and substituted a policy of sovereignty and reciprocity. The Reciprocity Treaty prepared by his government, however, died in the U.S. Senate, because sugar profits generally had benefited from the ban on southern sugar by the northern states during the U.S. Civil War. The 1867 depression, which occurred after the Civil War, reversed this favorable development and again fostered a demand for reciprocity on the part of Hawai'i's sugar interests.

In 1863, Liholiho died suddenly while on a visit to San Francisco. His brother, Prince Lot, succeeded him as Kamehameha V. He, too, supported Hawaiian independence, and he continued his brother's policy of seeking reciprocity. He also pressed for a four-way treaty with France, Britain, and the United States that would assure Hawaiian independence and neutrality. Meanwhile, the new U.S. minister to Hawai'i, James McBride, advocated as a condition for signing a reciprocity treaty the cession of a port at Honolulu. In 1866, a U.S. warship, the *U.S.S. Lackawanna*, was assigned indefinitely to Hawai'i as a symbol of American dominance. The biggest push for annexation, however, came from the *haole* sugar planters.

When Henry Pierce became the new minister to Hawai'i in 1869, he immediately advocated that the United States be given Pearl River Lagoon (Pearl Harbor) as a naval station in exchange for a reciprocity treaty. Other interests continued to support the call for annexation, seeing reciprocity as a first step.

King Kalākaua and the Bayonet Constitution

Kamehameha V died in 1872 and was replaced by William Lunalilo. The new king's reign lasted only slightly more than a year. Although supported by the Hawaiian people, once elected, he reluctantly gave in to his *haole* advisers and agreed to negotiate a reciprocity treaty which would include the cession of Pearl River Lagoon to the United States. The Hawaiian outcry against this decision caused Lunalilo to reverse himself. Hawaiian public opinion correctly predicted that annexation would mean national death.

A contributing factor to Lunalilo's change of heart may have been the fact that he had personally experienced racial discrimination during a visit to the United States. When he was crown prince, he and his brother, Prince Lot, found themselves victims of segregation laws by being classified as members of the other colored races when travelling by train. Unfortunately, Lunalilo succumbed to tuberculosis and died in 1874. The king's untimely death was a poignant example of the toll that foreign diseases had been taking on the Native Hawaiian people ever since the arrival of Cook a century before.

Civil disturbances in the new towns, such as Lahaina on Maui, and Honolulu on O'ahu, had been a growing problem since the early eighteenth century. Alcohol and prostitution exacerbated the problem of rowdy and drunk foreigners frequenting the sea ports and city saloons. Peacekeeping to protect American economic interests became an excuse for U.S. military intervention. When political disturbances threatened to disrupt the sugar industry, the U.S. military intervened. Such an event occurred following the death of Lunalilo when Kalākaua ran against Dowager Queen Emma for the throne. Lunalilo's supporters and those of the queen engaged in a brief conflict that became a pretense for the landing of U.S. Marines, supposedly to maintain order. In reality, however, it was to support the pro-American Kalākaua against the pro-British Emma Lili'uokalani. Kalākaua became King in 1874, but he was indebted to the Americans for his election. Under Kalākaua, *haole* interests became predominant, and pro-American sentiments dominated the Hawaiian government. Furthermore, U.S. military planners still had their eye on Pearl Lagoon for a north Pacific naval station. President Garfield's secretary of state, James G. Blaine, declared that Hawai'i had become the key to the domination of the Pacific.

An economic crisis arose in the 1880s that left the Kalākaua government debt-ridden. When Kalākaua refused to cede Pearl Harbor, the Missionary Party began a campaign of slander and even ordered an assassination attempt on his life, although it proved unsuccessful. "Following numerous public attacks on Kalākaua's reputation and esteem, the missionary party secretly formed [the Hawaiian League], armed themselves, and forced the king at gunpoint to turn over the powers of government to them. In 1887, Kalākaua signed the 'bayonet' constitution, the name reflecting the method of its adoption. This constitution stripped Kalākaua of power" (Laenui 2001, 144).

After seizing power, the missionary party forced King Kalākaua to give the United States exclusive right to use Pearl Harbor. In return, the U.S. extended the reciprocity treaty for another seven years, which benefited the sugar barons and gave a temporary boost to the Hawaiian economy. It soon became obvious, however, that the new treaty was only a ploy to seize Pearl Harbor, because in 1891, less than four years after ratifying the new reciprocity treaty, "Congress passed the McKinley Act allowing all the sugar of the world to enter the U.S. free of import duty. The United States had Pearl Harbor, but Hawaiian sugar no longer had any advantage over other foreign sugar. This crippled the Hawaiian sugar industry and within a year caused a major depression in the islands" (Dudley and Agard 1990, 19). Dudley and Agard (1990, 50) contend that "there is strong evidence to indicate that the principal purpose for putting the sugar provisions of the McKinley Act into law was to topple the Hawaiian monarchy and to bring the islands under American Control."

In 1891, Kalākaua died somewhat mysteriously in San Francisco while recuperating from an illness. "Rumors still abound in Hawai'i that his death was caused by the missionary party's agents in the United States" (Laenui 2001, 144). His sister, Queen Lili'uokalani, succeeded him.

Lili'uokalani and the Seizure of Hawai'i

By 1887, Hawai'i had treaties and conventions with twenty-one nations, and had established one hundred diplomatic and consular posts around the world. At the time of its overthrow in 1893 "the nation of Hawai'i had a literacy rate that was among the highest in the world. It had telephones and electricity built into its governing palace, 'Iolani,' before the White House had such technology. . . . By 1892, Hawai'i was a vibrant, multiracial, multicultural nation engaged in intellectual and economic commerce with the world" (Laenui 2001, 142).

Between 1877 and 1890, fifty-five thousand new immigrants flocked to Hawai'i, an increase of 33 percent. During the same period, the Native Hawaiian population was reduced by half, while the *haole* population soared. By 1890, Hawaiians made up only 45 percent of the islands' population, while the Whites and Asians constituted 55 percent. An interesting measure taken by the Hawaiian government was the requirement "that voters and political candidates be true citizens, either native-born or naturalized by taking an oath of allegiance solely to the Kingdom of Hawai'i. . . . Chinese and Japanese immigrant laborers and merchants took advantage of the country's hospitality and pledged their allegiance to the Hawaiian kings" (Wei and Kamel 1998, 133). Thus, under the monarchy, to be a Hawaiian citizen one did not have to be Native person.

Soon after her accession, Queen Lili'uokalani received a petition by two-thirds of the registered voters imploring her to do away with the Bayonet Constitution and return the powers of government to the Hawaiian people. The Bayonet Constitution "eliminated the king's power and undermined the Native Hawaiian-controlled legislature by making the House of Nobles accessible only to those with large incomes or land holdings. This constitution also ended citizen-

ship for hundreds of Asian immigrants who, in the eyes of the *haole*, were not considered trustworthy" (Wei and Kamel 1998, 133). By January 14, 1893, the queen had completed a draft of a new constitution. Her cabinet, however, which was under the influence of the Missionary Party, persuaded her to temporarily put off any action. This gave leaders of the Missionary Party, such as Lorrin Thurston and Sanford Dole, time to reconnoiter. Thurston and a dozen others immediately formed a Committee of Public Safety and then met with the American minister plenipotentiary in Hawai'i, John L. Stevens, to plan the overthrow of the Lili'uokalani government. Stevens had long been an advocate for the United States taking over control of Hawai'i. It was agreed that U.S. Marines would land on the pretext of protecting American lives. "The missionary party then would declare itself the provisional government and immediately would turn Hawai'i over to the United States in an annexation treaty. . . . The landing of the marines is now a matter of history. The queen yielded her authority, trusting to the 'enlightened justice' of the United States, expecting a full investigation to be conducted and the United

Queen Lili'uokalani.

States government to restore the constitutional government of Hawai'i" (Laenui 2001, 134).

In 1892, a treaty of annexation was hurriedly prepared and signed by President Benjamin Harrison and sent to the U.S. Senate for ratification. Harrison's Hawaiian policy reflected the growing imperialism of the Republican Party. Before the Senate was able to vote, however, Harrison was replaced by Democrat Grover Cleveland. In his 1893 Inaugural Address, Cleveland had advocated "the non-entangling, anti-colonial foreign policy of the founding fathers" (Osborne 1998, 10). The new president therefore reacted favorably to the pleas by Queen Lili'uokalani's emissaries and appointed a special investigator, James H. Blount, to look into the matter. As a result of the investigation, Cleveland subsequently told Congress that "by an act of war, committed with the participation of a diplomatic representative of the United States and without authority of Congress, the Government of a feeble but friendly and confiding people has been overthrown. A substantial wrong has been done" (Laenui 2001, 145).

For the rest of his term as president, Cleveland refused to send the annexation treaty to the Senate for ratification, and he advocated the restoration of Queen Lili'uokalani's Hawaiian government. The provisional *haole* government rejected Cleveland's decision, however, and Cleveland, in seeming contradiction to his restoration decision, left U.S. troops in Hawai'i's harbors "to protect American lives."

Faced with the pressure by the Cleveland administration in Washington, as well as international criticism, the puppet government of the *haole* conspirators devised a plan whereby they would become a permanent rather than a provisional government. "Sanford Dole, acting as president of the provisional government, announced a constitutional convention of thirty-seven delegates: eighteen elected *and the remaining nineteen selected by him* [emphasis added]" (Laenui 2001, 147). The undemocratic nature of the constitutional convention is also revealed by the requirement that both the candidates and voters for the elected positions had first to renounce Queen Lili'uokalani and swear allegiance to the puppet government. Furthermore, foreigners who supported the *haole* provisional government were allowed to vote, but the Japanese, and especially the Chinese who supported Lili'uokalani, were as a group disenfranchised. Also, "only those who could speak, read, and write English or Hawaiian and could explain the constitution, *written in English*, to the satisfaction of Dole's supporters could vote" (Laenui 2001, 147). As

a result, less than 20 percent of the voting population participated in the election.

The great irony with respect to the founding of American democracy occurred on a summer day in 1894, on the Fourth of July, no less, "while Americans were celebrating their independence day by firing the cannons on their warships in Honolulu harbor, Dole proclaimed the constitution and thus the Republic of Hawai'i into existence," and the overthrow of an independent Hawaiian Nation was complete (Laenui 2001, 147).

During Queen Lili'uokalani's short reign, royalists under the leadership of Robert Wilcox organized to restore Hawaiian sovereignty. "Skirmishes went on for about ten days before the royalists surrendered. After they surrendered, to save them from death, Queen Lili'uokalani formally abdicated her throne" (Dudley and Agard 1990, 62). She was then placed under house arrest and confined to Iolani Palace for many months.

Immediately after the Missionary Party overthrew the Hawaiian monarchy, Hawaiians formed the *Hui Hawai'i Aloha 'Āina*, a protest organization. Together with their women's branch, the association sought to maintain the independence of the Hawaiian Islands by petitioning President Grover Cleveland for assistance in restoring the Hawaiian government. An interesting aspect of the *Huis*, as they were called, was that even though some of the women were married to *haole* men, "their love for their land and nation was apparently greater than their worry about political disagreement with their husbands" (Wei and Kamel 1998, 138).

When Republican William McKinley replaced Cleveland in 1896 and he submitted a treaty of annexation to Congress, the *Huis* swung into action. On September 6, 1897, the *Huis* held a protest meeting at the Palace Square in Honolulu in which thousands of people attended. The association's president warned the crowd "that annexation would open the door for many foreigners to come and take jobs and resources from the Native Hawaiians" (Wei and Kamel 1998, 138). It was at this meeting that a mass petition drive against annexation was initiated. The Petition Protesting Annexation gathered more than twenty-one thousand signatures, an impressive number since the Native population at this time was less than forty thousand.

At another mass meeting of the *Huis* in the following month, it was decided to send delegates to Washington to lobby Congress and the president. "The petition and lobbying by the *kānaka maoli* delegates succeeded in killing the annexation treaty in the U.S. Senate in February 1898 . . . [but] a few months later, in the midst of the war fever stirred up by the Spanish-American War, a joint resolution was passed by Congress supporting the annexation of Hawai'i" (Wei and Kamel 1998, 139). Sanford Dole and the coup-plotters, realizing that a treaty would not get the two-thirds Senate approval required under the U.S. Constitution, circumvented that requirement by settling for a joint resolution of Congress requiring only a majority vote. This was the Newlands Resolution passed on July 7, 1998. It was adopted in the House by 209 votes, of which 178 were Republican, and the Senate then acceded with equal readiness. The Congressional action left in doubt the legality of the annexation since a resolution by a simple majority vote is not legally binding. A treaty which is legally binding, on the other hand, requires a two-thirds vote, but this was never done.

Ignoring the protests by an overwhelming number of Native Hawaiians, and the highly questionable legality of the joint resolution by Congress, "Hawai'i was proclaimed to be a protectorate of the United States without the consent of the U.S. Congress and in violation of international law" (Wei and Kamel 1998,17).

THE COLONIAL CONTEXT

The overthrow of the Hawaiian government and the annexation of the islands which followed are best understood within the context of American imperialism. Americans do not usually think of the United States as a colonial power, but that is exactly what occurred in the context of the 1898 Spanish-American War. The war with Spain, however, was not the first, nor the only time, that the United States had adopted a policy of seizing continental territory and foreign lands, and then incorporating them into the larger nation as "territories." The United States from its earliest years has been an expansionist nation. "Thomas Jefferson, the writer of the Declaration of Independence and third president of the United States . . . doubled the territory of the United States over-night from the French in the Louisiana Purchase. . . . Between 1810 and 1819, also before the missionaries' departure [for Hawai'i], America had fought the battle of New Orleans and taken the Spanish-held area west of it; it had also taken all of Florida from the Spanish; and Americans were poised and ready for their 1821 push into Texas" (Dudley and Agard 1990, 50). An expansion-

ist United States then waged a twenty-five-year long war of skirmishes and battles to subdue the American Indians of the Great Plains. As a justification for this policy of internal colonialism against the Indians, the cry of Manifest Destiny was raised: White Americans were said to be destined by Providence to develop and rule the length and breadth of the continent. "All actions to remove obstacles that stood in their way were therefore morally righteous, including the dispossession and slaughter of Indians" (Dudley and Agard 1990, 52). It was a doctrine that was particularly embraced by the institutional representatives of American capitalism, the military, and the government itself.

Many of the backers of the American Board of Commissioners for Foreign Missions that sponsored the first missionaries sent to Hawai'i were well-known politicians—governors, congressmen, and even a U.S. secretary of state for foreign affairs. Other backers were men who had made their fortunes in merchandising and shipping, and who were looking for new markets for their products and lands to appropriate. Behind the stated goal of sending missionaries to Hawai'i to save "heathen souls" was a hidden purpose: the missionaries would also serve "as goodwill ambassadors, as listening posts in the Pacific, as opinion shapers, as powerful pro-American influences, and as openers of markets" (Dudley and Agard 1990, 51). In the end, their ideological colonialism destroyed the Hawaiian nation by changing the land tenure system through the *Māhele*, and then "buying up and leasing large tracts of land until they or their children owned or controlled all the major business interests in the islands" (Dudley and Agard 1990, 51).

By the 1890s, the United States faced a critical foreign policy debate: whether to remain a self-contained continental republic, or embrace an expansive overseas empire. The illegal annexation of Hawai'i was the opening volley by the imperialist camp in this debate.

The United States is usually portrayed in high school history books as a defender of weak countries and the promoter of democracy, but its real record in the history of world affairs is another matter. The U.S. opposed the 1803 Haitian revolution to free the largely Black population as a French colony. It instigated a war with Mexico in 1846, seizing half the territory of the young republic. It pretended to help Cuba win freedom from Spain, and then occupied Cuba with a military base at Guantanamo, taking over 80 percent of the Cuban economy and retaining the right of intervention through the Platt Amendment. After the war with Spain, it colonized Hawai'i, Puerto Rico, Guam, and the Philippines, and fought a long, brutal war to subjugate the Filipino independence movement. It adopted the Open Door Policy in China as a means of assuring favorable United States competition with other imperial powers for exploiting the Chinese market. It then sent troops to Peking, together with military forces of other capitalist nations, to assert Western supremacy in China, and kept them there for over thirty years.

> While demanding an Open Door in China, it had insisted (with the Monroe Doctrine and many military interventions) on a Closed Door in Latin America—that is, closed to everyone but the United States. It had engineered a revolution against Colombia and created the "independent" state of Panama in order to build and control the Canal. It sent five thousand marines to Nicaragua in 1926 to counter a revolution, and kept a force there for seven years. It intervened in the Dominican Republic for the fourth time in 1916 and kept troops there for eight years. It intervened for the second time in Haiti in 1915 and kept troops there for nineteen years. Between 1900 and 1933, the United States intervened in Cuba four times, in Nicaragua twice, in Panama six times, in Guatemala once, in Honduras seven times. (Zinn 1999, 408)

As former Marine Corps Gen. Smedley D. Butler said in a famous 1931 statement:

"I helped make Mexico safe for American oil interests in 1914. I helped make Haiti and Cuba a decent place for the National City Bank boys to collect revenue in. I helped purify Nicaragua for the international banking house of Brown Brothers. . . . I brought light to the Dominican Republic for American sugar interests in 1916. I helped make Honduras 'right' for American fruit companies in 1903. Looking back on it, I might have given Al Capone a few hints" (Loewen 1995, 220).

The Spanish-American War lasted only ten months during 1898, but it marked the emergence of the United States as a colonial power. The United States had become a major industrial power too late on the world scene to join in the European frenzy to seize large chunks of Africa, Asia, South America, and the Pacific islands as its colonies. The war with Spain at the end of the nineteenth century changed all of that: seized from Spain by the United States were Cuba and Puerto Rica in the Caribbean, along with the Philippines, Eastern Samoa, and the Marianna Islands in the Pacific. "The annexation of

Hawai'i and American Samoa by the United States was closely related to the war," and was an indirect result of rising imperialist sentiment in the United States (Wei and Kamel 1998, 2).

The Spanish-American War was a continuation of the colonial grab for power, for land and markets, this time between a major colonizing nation, Spain, which was in decline, and the newly emergent United States as a "wannabe" colonial power. At its height, the Spanish empire included most of Latin America, much of the Caribbean, the Philippines, and a number of islands in the Pacific Ocean. By the early nineteenth century, most of the Latin American nations had broken away from Spanish domination, but Spain still clung to its possessions in the Caribbean and the Pacific. In the latter part of the nineteenth century, however, even these subject nations were mounting independence movements. In 1868, the Puerto Rican people launched a colonial revolt and declared a short-lived democratic republic. Later, in 1888, the Micronesians of the Pacific Ocean attacked the Spanish governor and his soldiers in Pohnpei. This was followed by the Cuban war of independence in 1895, and the Filipino uprising of 1896.

"By 1898 Spain had become one of Europe's weakest powers, politically and militarily. Independence movements in both Cuba and the Philippines were on the verge of success" (Wei and Kamel 1998, 4). Taking advantage of a Spain weakened by these independence movements, the United States used as a pretext the explosion of the battleship Maine in the harbor of Havana, Cuba, on February 15, 1898, for initiating the Spanish-American War. The result of the war was that the Spanish possessions were seized by the United States, including for a time even Cuba. A number of prominent U.S. political leaders publicly voiced their dream of extending the U.S. "American empire" into the Caribbean, Central and South America, and even the Pacific.

Although Cuba obtained its nominal independence following the war, the Filipinos were sold out by Spain and the United States in the 1898 Treaty of Paris. Under terms of this treaty, the United States bought the Philippines from Spain for $20 million. As many as 250,000 Filipinos subsequently lost their lives in an unsuccessful struggle for freedom against an aggressive United States. The Philippine-American War was much more bloody and protracted than the war against Spain and was marked by a systematic use of torture on the part of the U.S. military.

The expansionist and nationalistic sentiments that existed in the United States during these years laid the imperialist groundwork and rationale for illegally annexing Hawai'i in 1898. The political rationale for American imperialism that arose towards the end of the nineteenth century included the 1823 Monroe Doctrine and concept of Manifest Destiny that signaled the U.S. intention for political hegemony in the Western hemisphere, the Mexican-American War of 1847, the unilateral ending of treaty-making with the American Indians in 1871, and the dispossession of their lands through the 1887 Dawes (Indian Allotment) Act. This last piece of legislation exhausted the remaining vacant lands within the United States and prepared the way for economic expansion. It was followed by the stock market crash or Panic of 1893, in which six hundred banks, seventy-four railways, and fifteen thousand businesses failed. This was an economic depression unparalleled in U.S. history. To restore the stability of its economic system the United States needed to open new markets and acquire new territories. The proponents of insular expansions viewed Pacific islands like Hawai'i "as way stations for exporting surpluses to the boundless markets of China" (Du Plessix Gray 1972a, 70). Hawai'i was called "the Gibraltar of the Pacific."

At the same time, there were voices of opposition to colonial expansionism abroad, as well as growing labor union and racial protests at home. Strange as it may seem, the domestic sugar interests for the most part also opposed annexation, not on principle but out of self-interest. They feared competition from Hawaiian sugar, and if Hawai'i was annexed, then other distant accessions might follow suit as a result of the Spanish-American War. "The output of the Cuban and Philippine cane fields might further reduce the profits of the mainland producers if these former Spanish colonies were transferred to the United States" (Osborne 1998, 135–36). Hawaiian sugar planters also feared "that annexation . . . would interfere with the immigration laws and contract labor system in Hawai'i, both of which they deemed necessary for the survival of the sugar cane industry in the islands" (Osborne 1998, 17). The son of Claus Spreckels, the leading refiner of cane and beet sugar, probably spoke for his father when he told a New York newspaper in 1893: "We can do a more profitable business with our contract labor than we could under the laws of the United States" (Osborne 1998, 18–19).

The American labor movement worried that annexation would lead to the migration of Asian workers to the West Coast as a cheap labor pool, thereby threatening the wages and working conditions of White workingmen. In fact, the common belief in the supposed superiority of Anglo-Saxon peoples and the inferiority of the Hawaiians as people of color was a common thread among many of those who were opposed to annexation during the debate of 1893–94. Still others opposed annexation on principle, that seizing Hawai'i would begin a "drift into colonialism with all its attendant embroilment and injustices," raising the specter of imperialism (Osborne 1998, 136). This was the position of Grover Cleveland and his secretary of state, Walter Q. Gresham, although "no evidence has been found to indicate that xenophobic considerations significantly influenced the shaping of [President] Cleveland's Hawaiian policy" (Osborne 1998, 39).

In 1890, the Sherman Anti-Trust Act was passed to curtail the power of corporate wealth. About this time, also, the Anti-imperialist League was founded. Among the anti-imperialist voices were Jane Addams, founder of the modern social welfare system and the Women's International League for Peace and Freedom; Samuel Gompers of the American Federation of Labor (AFL); progressive industrialist Andrew Carnegie; Moorfield Storey, who later became the first president of the National Association for the Advancement of Colored People (NAACP); and America's best-loved writer, Mark Twain. There were also those who argued illogically that while U.S. expansion within the territory of North America was legitimate, the acquiring of foreign lands outside the continent was contrary to American democratic ideals. In other words, the colonial acquisition of Native Alaska from Russia, the internal conquest of American Indian nations, and the seizure of vast lands from Mexico was all right, but not the seizure of the Philippines and the annexation of Hawai'i.

For those in the imperialist camp, support for the American-Philippine War was whipped up by racist sentiments at home. U.S. military personnel who were engaged in massacring Indians on the Western Plains frontier were mobilized and sent to suppress the Indigenous resistance in the Philippines. In 1896, the U.S. Supreme Court ruled in *Plessy v. Ferguson* that Jim Crow laws were legal, thus sanctioning the system of racial segregation in southern United States. In this context the peoples of America's new possessions were portrayed in vicious racial stereotypes.

The seizure of Hawai'i is inextricably linked to U.S. imperialism. Osborne (1998, 136) points out that within approximately seven months of the passage of the Newlands Resolution annexing Hawai'i, "the

United States acquired Guam, the Philippines, Puerto Rico, and Wake Island." During the Boxer Rebellion in China in 1900, the United States sent troops to Beijing from its naval base in the Philippines. In 1905 it sanctioned Japan's occupation of Korea in return for Japan's support of the U.S. presence in the Philippines. Then in 1903, the United States engineered the secession of Panama from Colombia in order to acquire the Panama Canal and dominate the gateway to the Pacific Ocean, with its naval bastion already in place at Pearl Harbor in Hawai'i. Various military interventions followed in Cuba, Nicaragua, Panama, the Dominican Republic, and Haiti. It is no accident that the recitation of the Pledge of Allegiance was first mandated in 1898 as a compulsory expression of patriotism. Rather than a period of isolationism, as has often been portrayed in the writings of political scientists and historians, this period in U.S. history was an epoch of colonialist expansion under American imperialism.

HAWAI'I UNDER COLONIAL RULE (1900–59)

Two years after Hawai'i was annexed, a new constitution was drafted and approved by Congress. The constitution became the Organic Act of June 14, 1900, that then governed Hawai'i as a territory of the United States until its admission to statehood in 1959. "Territory" is, in reality, a euphemism for *colony*. Residents of U.S. island territories in American Samoa, Guam, and the Commonwealth of Puerto Rico do not enjoy full political rights and can send only nonvoting representatives to Congress. A commonwealth is a territory with limited rights of autonomy and self-government. These de facto colonies are easily subject to economic penetration and labor exploitation by U.S. corporations, and naval and other military bases take up much of the critical land base and damage the fragile island environments.

Immediately after annexation it was hoped that Native people could still achieve a measure of self-determination. Most Hawaiians supported the Home Rule Party rather than either the Republicans or the Democrats. Home Rule members insisted on speaking Hawaiian in the Territorial Congress and swept the first election in 1901. "To regain electoral control of the islands, the Caucasian elite sought a popular Hawaiian Chief whom they could control. They found one in the person of Prince Johan Kūhiō Kalanianāole" (Du Plessix Gray 1972a, 71). They were able to persuade him to become a Republican and run against the Home Rule candidate for

Territorial Representative. He was successful, and the Home Rule Party died out in 1912. The Republicans then controlled Hawai'i for the next four decades.

The Big Five

After Hawai'i became a territory of the United States, Sanford Dole was appointed territorial governor. He, in turn, appointed his cronies to government positions and gave out lucrative government contracts to friends. The Big Five, a coalition of five business entities with roots in the Missionary Party, controlled every aspect of political and economic life in Hawai'i. "Beginning with sugar, they took steps to control transportation, hotels, utilities, banks, insurance agencies, and many small wholesale and retail business. When they teamed up with McKinley's Republican party and the United States Navy, there was virtually nothing left un-exploited" (Laenui 2001, 148). By 1910, the Big Five controlled 75 percent of the sugar, and by 1933, they controlled 96 percent. They came to own every business connected with sugar, including on-island railroad transportation, shipping between the islands, and shipping to and from the U.S. mainland. The cartel totally controlled Hawai'i's economic and political life until the Second World War.

Each of the Big Five businesses had at least one direct descendant of a missionary on its board, and the missionary families controlled everything on the islands through interlocking directorates. By interlocking directorates is meant that an individual on a board of a sugar company, for example, would also be on boards of other business enterprises, thereby ensuring that the policy decisions of these boards of directors would be complementary to their mutual economic interests. "One single family was represented on the boards of directors of eighteen of the forty corporations listed on the Honolulu Stock Exchange in 1928" (Du Plessix Gray 1972b, 52).

Impact on Culture and Traditions

During the period of territorial rule, the Big Five propagated the myth of Anglo-American superiority. Hawaiian children were forced to attend American schools and to pledge allegiance to the United States, and were forbidden to speak the Hawaiian language. Hawaiian parents, feeling the hegemonic pressure of Americanization, discouraged the use of Native language at home. Children were encouraged to adopt an American lifestyle, to adopt White morality, and conform to the White man's laws. "Many heard they were lazy, stupid, and worthless often enough that they came to believe it" (Dudley and Agard 1990, 73). Because of this policy of forced acculturation, many Native Hawaiians became disoriented and marginalized.

Hawaiian traditions and customs, including the Hawaiian names of people and their genealogical connections, were ruthlessly suppressed. "People were coaxed into giving children American names that had no ties with their ancestors—names that described no physical substance, spiritual sense, or human mood; names that could not call upon the winds or waters, the soil or the heat; names totally irrelevant to the surroundings" (Laenui 2001, 137). The people were taught to mimic American habits, to idolize American heroes, and to adopt an American mainland lifestyle.

The *makahiki* celebrations honoring Lono were never observed or mentioned in the schools; Christmas was celebrated instead. The *hula* was forbidden. This was true even for the Kamehameha schools which had been set up under the Bishop Estate specifically to educate children of Hawaiian ancestry. The curriculum and routine of these special schools paralleled that of the boarding school system for American Indians, which, today, are severely criticized as having done irreparable harm to an entire generation of Indian people. "The arts and sciences of Hawai'i's ancestors were driven to near extinction. The advanced practice of healing through the medicines of plants, water, or massage, or just the uttered words, were driven into the back countryside. The science of predicting the future . . . was discounted as superstition. . . . The Hawaiian culture was being ground to dust" (Laenui 2001, 137).

The U.S. military turned the Hawaiian Islands into one vast fortress, converting Pearl Harbor into a major naval port for its Pacific fleet.

[The military] bombed valleys and took a major island (Kaho'olawe) for its exclusive use as a target range. At will, the military tossed families out of their homes and destroyed sacred Hawaiian heirlooms . . . building, in their place, naval communication towers that emitted radiation and ammunition depots that hid nuclear weapons. It declared martial law at will, . . . and imposed military conscription on Hawaiian citizens. . . . The Big Five controlled all shipping. Every aspect of Hawai'i was Americanized. Military strength was constantly on display. Trade was totally controlled. Education and media were regulated. . . . Hawai'i, that melting pot of cultures, races, languages, and lore, changed from a reality to an advertising slogan for politicians and merchants. (Laenui 2001, 137–38)

Tourism replaced sugar plantations, opening the floodgates to millions of visitors each year from the U.S. mainland, Japan, and Europe. "Construction industries changed much of Hawai'i from a lush green paradise, to a cancerous, white, concrete jungle tied together by roadways of asphalt" (Laenui, quoted in Dudely and Agard 1990, 74). Ala Moana in Honolulu became the world's largest shopping center, "a fifty-acre complex of a hundred and sixty shops, steeped in soothing music and warm odors of food and flowers. Open seven days a week—often until midnight—and forever seething with humanity, Ala Moana is a gigantic 'souk,' a Bruchnerian hymn to American consumerism, a perpetual world's fair" (Du Plessiy Gray 1972a, 41).

On ancient burial grounds of our ancestors, glass and steel shopping malls with layered parking lots stretch over what once were the most ingeniously irrigated taro lands, lands that fed millions of our people over thousands of years. Large bays, delicately ringed long ago with well-stocked fish ponds, are now heavily silted and cluttered with jet skis, windsurfers, and sailboats. Multi-story hotels disgorge over six million tourists a year onto stunningly beautiful (and easily polluted) beaches, closing off access to locals. On the major islands of Hawai'i, Maui, O'ahu, and Kaua'i, meanwhile, military airfields, training camps, weapons storage facilities, and exclusive housing and beach areas remind the Native Hawaiians who owns Hawai'i: the foreign colonizing country called the United States of America. (Trask 1993, 2–3)

A Hawaiian Homeland

At the time of the Great *Māhele*, both the crown lands and government lands were set aside by King Kamehameha III. After the Hawaiian monarchy was overthrown by the Missionary Party, the *haole* provisional government sold some of these lands. When Hawai'i was later annexed in 1898, "both sets of lands were 'ceded' to the United States by the Republic of Hawai'i, with the stipulation that they were to be held in trust for 'the Hawaiian people.' Since that time, these lands have been called the 'Ceded Lands.' They comprise about half of the land of the eight major islands" (Dudley and Agard 1990, 64).

Although Native Hawaiians never surrendered their claim to these lands, 20 percent of the lands were transferred to the federal government when Hawai'i became a territory—143,700 acres for military bases and 227,972 acres for national parks. An additional 20,000 acres of the least desirable lands were set aside for homesteading by Hawaiian Natives. With statehood in 1959, the remainder of these lands were transferred to the new state to be held in trust for the Native peoples. It is the entire territory of the Ceded Lands (the original crown and government lands) to which the Hawaiian Native people today lay claim as the territorial basis for a return to sovereign status.

In *A Call for Hawaiian Sovereignty*, Dudley and Agard (1990, 65–71) call attention to the 1921 Hawaiian Homes Commission Act that allows Native Hawaiians to homestead some of the Ceded Lands. Passed by Congress two decades after annexation, the Hawaiian Homes Commission Act placed two hundred thousand acres of crown and government lands into a special land trust for homesteading by Native Hawaiians. This piece of legislation was initiated by the territory's delegate to the U.S. Congress at the time—Prince Jonah Kūhiō Kalanianāole. Congress had come to realize that the policy of forced acculturation was largely a failure. Therefore, returning "the trust lands to Native Hawaiians would 'rehabilitate' the people by giving them farms where they could be self-sufficient, where they could practice initiative, and where they could preserve their Native Hawaiian culture" (Dudley and Agard 1990, 66). These were the officially stated reasons, but there were also latent or unstated reasons that concerned the sugar industry.

Most of the acreage held by the sugar plantations in the early 1900s was owned outright, "but 34,000 acres of their prime agricultural lands were 'government lands' which they had leased from the government over the years" (Dudley and Agard 1990, 66). The Organic Act for the Territory, however, set a ceiling of one thousand acres that could be held by any individual or corporation. Although the plantation owners had been getting around this provision by forming bogus partnerships or corporations, they worried that eventually they would be called to account and taken to court. "Sugar needed Section 55, with its thousand-acre ceiling, repealed from the Organic Act, the constitution of the Territory of Hawai'i" (Dudley and Agard 1990, 67). "Back to the land, back to the culture!" became the rallying cry in the halls of Congress.

There was also a second problem confronting the sugar industry: "Provisions in the Organic Act allowed Hawaiians to homestead prime 'government lands' leased by the sugar plantations, but governors friendly to sugar had consistently renewed expiring leases on the sugar acreage instead of opening up the good sugar lands for homesteading" (Dudley and Agard 1990, 67). Changes in the Organic

Act threatened to open up these leased plantation lands to homesteading for "public purposes." Thus, the sugar industry offered Prince Kūhiō a deal in getting their support for passing his Hawaiian homesteading Act: change the Organic Act to keep homesteaders off the sugar plantation lands, and delete the thousand-acre ownership ceiling. To sweeten the deal, "the mission boys would agree that 30 percent of the revenues which the territory collected in lease rents from the 'government lands' it leased to the plantations would be put into a fund for rehabilitation of the Hawaiian people"—the Home Loan Fund (Dudley and Agard 1990, 68).

The Hawaiian Homes Commission Act looked good on paper, but in reality it was a sham. "Once sugar and forest lands were excluded from consideration, 'what was left was land that no one had ever been able to make productive'" (Dudley and Agard 1990, 68–69). For example, the greater part of the homestead lands on Maui are on the desert side of the island, high up the nine thousand foot peak of Haleakala volcano, beyond the vegetation line. The two hundred thousand acres set aside by the Act as Hawaiian Homes Lands are among the worst lands in the state, and any decent lands given were in remote, inaccessible areas. In addition, the Home Loan Fund had a one million dollar cap, and although raised twice over the years, it has generated less than $14 million. To add insult to injury, by 1990, non-Natives occupied about one hundred thousand acres of Hawaiian Homes Lands and paid an average rent of only $16 per acre per year. As a result, thousands of Native Hawaiians are still waiting for their homesteads, and those who have received them have often had to wait six, ten, or fifteen years for land that was theirs by law. And when they finally receive them, they are unable to grow any crops.

Dudley and Agard (1990, 71) end their analysis by concluding that rather than assisting Native people, "the Hawaiian Homes Commission Act was a response to the needs of the sugar interests." On the other hand, the 1921 Act did officially recognize the right of Native Hawaiians to the Ceded Lands. "This should serve as a valuable precedent in future presentations to Congress, since Congress is the branch of government which will deliberate and formulate the reestablishment of the Hawaiian Nation."

Politics and Ethnicity

One result of American colonialist occupation was its policy of *ethnic segmentation*, an instrument of divide and rule in which the multiracial population of

Hawai'i was split up into separate racial categories "The term Hawaiian was redefined as a racial rather than a national term. Large numbers of citizens were no longer identified simply as Hawaiian but, rather, as Chinese, Japanese, Korean, English, Samoan, and Filipino. The divide-and-conquer tactic was employed even within the Hawaiian community, when Congress declared that 'native Hawaiians' (at least 50 percent 'aboriginal blood') were entitled to special land privileges while others of lesser 'blood' were not" (Laenui 2001, 137). This is the same discredited blood quantum policy that has plagued Native American tribes on the mainland. With intermarriage, fewer Native Hawaiians have enough blood to qualify for their rights as an Indigenous people, and has been termed "statistical genocide." Indigenous identity is also cultural rather than purely racial, and in the Hawaiian case it is also genealogical. (See Kauanui 2008.)

The ethnic status hierarchy in Hawai'i is a product of its earlier immigration history. The first immigrants from Asia were the Chinese. Coming from a competitive culture and lacking a strong national identity with China, they soon left the plantations for the towns, becoming restaurateurs, tailors, laundrymen, or bakers. As immigrants they came as single men and often married Hawaiian women. They also originated the pidgin dialect of Hawai'i, which evolved as a way of communicating with their Native wives.

The Japanese experience was quite different. "The ascent to power of the Japanese in Hawai'i was infinitely more difficult and stormy than that of the Chinese. They were considered subversive by the Caucasian elite, who deeply feared their allegiance to Japan. . . . Their assimilation into Hawai'i's melting pot was extremely slow, for to marry a non-Japanese was considered a dishonor" (Du Plessix Gray 1972a, 73). They began to migrate to Hawai'i's towns in the 1920s to work as machinists, painters, carpenters, fishermen, and shopkeepers, and by the 1930s they were the largest voting bloc in the islands. The Japanese took a leadership role in the unionization of Hawai'i, organizing the first major strike on O'ahu in 1909, and helping to organize thousands of Filipino workers in 1920. Relatively few Japanese were interred in Hawai'i during World War II, because of their large numbers and primary role in the islands' food production. After the war, they began playing a dominant role in state politics. Because of their militancy and the unionization which eventually took place, first on the docks, and then on the sugar and pineapple plantations, they

allied themselves with the Democratic Party. The Democrats replaced the Republicans as the dominant political party in the 1954 territorial elections. The Chinese, on the other hand, tended to be more conservative politically.

In post-World War II Hawai'i, many Native Hawaiians tended to resent the Japanese because they saw them as representing the new establishment. The Chinese were less resented. The Filipinos have been almost as oppressed economically as the Native Hawaiians, initially because of labor exploitation on the plantations, and more recently in the tourist trade as minimum wage workers. Even so, in this ethnic stratification system of income and power, the Polynesian, Samoan, and the Native Hawaiian remain at the bottom.

NEOCOLONIALISM UNDER STATEHOOD

In 1959, Hawai'i became the fiftieth state of the Union, but Native Hawaiians were never really asked for their consent. The United States put forth only one question to "qualified voters" (residents of Hawai'i for at least one year); "Shall Hawai'i immediately be admitted into the Union as a State?" To answer "yes" or "no" meant for Hawai'i to either become a state or remain a territory. There was no box for checking "independence." Self-determination for the Hawaiian people was never an option. This rigged voting procedure for statehood ushered in an era of neocolonialism for Native people and forestalled the aspirations for sovereignty. A research survey revealed that only 43 percent of the islanders actually voted, and only 30 percent of those of Hawaiian or part-Hawaiian blood favored immediate statehood.

Advocates of statehood promised civil rights, including the right to vote in national elections, to own private property, and public education. Yet a half century later, Native Hawaiians remain locked in poverty and homelessness. They have seen the steady desecration and pollution of their sacred islands, and the denigration of their cultural traditions. "Hawai'i is less Hawaiian, culturally, ecologically, and politically. . . . Post-statehood Hawai'i is a tinsel paradise for six-and-a-half million tourists a year, and a living nightmare for our impoverished, marginalized Native people" (Trask 1993, 113–14).

Massive in-migration took place following statehood, with an influx of thousands of Americans from the mainland who brought their own individualistic values, concepts, and materialistic behavior to Hawai'i. "As Americans infiltrated, they took choice jobs with government agencies and management positions with business interests. They bought up or stole, through the manipulation of laws applied by them, much of the land and resources of Hawai'i. They gained power in Hawai'i, controlled greater chunks of the economy, controlled the public media, entrenched themselves in politics, and joined in the brainwashing of the Hawaiians to believe they were American" (Laenui 2001, 137).

The Big Five continued to dominate the economy of Hawai'i. By 1970, Castle & Cooke, one of the cartel members, controlled 208,000 acres of land and about 40 percent of the U.S. pineapple market through its ownership of the Dole Company. It also owned the world's largest producer of macadamia nuts, and it was building hotels and condominiums throughout the Pacific. Another corporate giant in the post-statehood Hawai'i was Amfac, a service-oriented conglomerate. It owned 72,000 acres of Hawaiian land, held long-term leases on 94,000 more, and produced one-fourth of Hawai'i's sugar crop. It also acquired the state's largest hotel chain and a major retail store group.

The Tourist Industry

In the 2000 Census, more than 300,000 of Hawai'i's 1.2 million residents claimed "part Hawaiian or Pacific Islander" as their "race" or ethnicity. In fact, Hawai'i is the most ethnically diverse state in the United States. Yet, despite population growth, tourists outnumber residents by six to one, and they outnumber Native Hawaiians by thirty to one. This rapid growth of the tourist industry has taken place within the last thirty years. While tourism was booming and property values soared, the personal income of the average resident was lower than in any of the other forty-nine states. The median cost of a home on O'ahu, Hawai'i's most populated island, reached $450,000 by the early 1990s. At the same time, more than twenty thousand families were on the waiting list of the Hawaiian trust lands, waiting for housing or pastoral lots.

By the 1990s, Native Hawaiians were protesting three major resort developments in the islands. The commercialization of Native culture has also created a racially stratified, poorly paid servant class of industry workers, who can no longer afford to live in Hawai'i without working two jobs.

Since World War II, tourism has transformed the Hawaiian Islands and, today, has taken the place of the once-mighty sugar industry. Millions of tourists flood the islands annually, many times outnumbering the local residents and bringing millions of dollars in revenues to the tourist industry. Yet this development has not transferred benefits to Native Hawaiians and most other local residents: tourist industry jobs are dead-end, low-paying, and humiliating jobs; land dispossession caused by the development of hotels, resorts, tourist beaches, and golf courses has increased the numbers of homeless or near-homeless island residents; and the cost of living is now the highest of any place in the United States. Not the least of the negative impacts caused by tourism is the destruction of the once-pristine island environment. (Lobo and Talbot 2001, 352)

As early as 1971 the environmental group, Nader's Raiders, reported "that most of the untreated sewage of Honolulu was being dumped into the Pacific less than four miles from Waikiki Beach, spewing forth at the rate of some fifty-five million gallons a day" (Du Plessix Gray 1972b, 66).

Poor Quality of Life

Statistics from the *1998 Native Hawaiian Data Book* confirm that, by 1980, Native Hawaiians had the highest poverty rate in the state, twice that for Whites, and they resided in the poorest neighborhoods in the least desirable land areas. Today, they have the greatest number on welfare; over 50 percent of Native households receive public assistance of some kind. They occupy the worst housing, if they have housing at all.

Native people have the lowest life expectancy of any other minority group in Hawai'i. In spite of a state medical care system, Native Hawaiians have high incidences of heart disease, diabetes, and alcohol and drug abuse. "Hawaiians rank first with most Western diseases for which records are kept; they have the highest death rate from heart diseases, from stroke, from lung cancer, breast cancer, cancer of the stomach, of the esophagus, of the uterus, and of the pancreas. They have the highest infant mortality rate. And they are first with diabetes, hypertension, and kidney failure. . . . All of this adds up: the Native Hawaiians have the shortest life expectancy of all the peoples in the islands" (Dudley and Agard 1990, 77). Before Western contact, when Native Hawaiians ate a traditional diet, they were strong, big, and healthy, and at the same time lithe, agile, and attractive. Hawaiian women were known for their sensual beauty. "Recent studies with Hawaiians who have readopted the traditional diet show a dramatic drop in high blood cholesterol—a major risk factor in heart attacks now so prevalent among Hawaiians" (Dudley and Agard 1990, 100).

The educational situation for Native children in the public school system has been deplorable at best. "The schools that score lowest in the state are schools in which the Hawaiian population is highest. A basic problem is that the 'American' education presented is not culturally relevant for Hawaiians" (Dudley and Agard 1990, 102). As a result, Native young people have the highest school dropout rate in Hawai'i.

Honolulu is the second most expensive city in the United States in which to live. Housing cost are at least 35 percent higher than on the mainland. Today, many Native people in Hawai'i struggle to pay for housing that takes half of their income from minimum wage jobs, or are entirely homeless. Only a few thousand have actually received homesteads. "For decades, the Hawaiian people have fought this dispossession, through courts, through continuing to practice their spiritual beliefs, through active reclamation of lands, and through constant [land] occupations. Hawaiians have 'occupied' trust lands, built homes, and lived on beaches. The state has evicted them and destroyed and burned their homes" (Wei and Kamel 1998, 146).

The lack of affordable housing has been compounded by the presence of tens of thousands of military personnel stationed in Hawai'i. By the 1970s, the defense industry had become the principal part of the state's economy. During the Cold War, no state in the Union was more dependent on the military than Hawai'i. Hawai'i became a major place for "R and R" (rest and recuperation) during the Vietnam War. By 1972, one-sixth of Oahu's population were military personnel and their dependents. Not all of them could be provided with military housing, so the rest competed with Hawai'i's low-income residents for public housing and rent subsidies. "Snubbed by the clannish *haole* elite, they live in Hawai'i in enormous military ghettos, playing golf at military country clubs, swimming at military beaches, buying their food at the PXs, sending their children to schools on the base" (Du Plessix Gray 1972b, 63).

The highest suicide rate in the state is for young Hawaiian men between the ages of eighteen and thirty-four. Alcohol and drug abuse is a serious problem, and linked closely with arrest and incarceration rates. Although Native people constitute about a fourth of the total population of Hawai'i, they are still underrepresented in the college population, where they are one in ten of the students, and they are overrepresented in the state's prisons, where they make up more than half of incarcerated felons. Unlike other ethnic groups in Hawai'i, Natives as an Indigenous people have no other homeland where their language is spoken and their culture is practiced. Hawaiian Natives are culturally different from Westerners and Asians. Despite 150 years of forced acculturation, they remain an "island people whom thousands of years of cultural evolution have formed to interrelate with the Land and the sea and other people in a special way in order to assure their survival. . . . They related to land and sea as family and experience a bond with them which is unknown to Westerners" (Dudley and Agard 1990, 79).

Drug manufacture, "dealing," and addiction are serious problems in Hawai'i. Methamphetamine is the drug of choice. "Hawai'i has the highest rate in the nation of adults who've tried ' ice'; 39 percent of all arrestees test positive for 'ice.' . . . According to the National Drug Intelligence Center's 2003 drug threat assessment for Hawai'i, 'Crystal methamphetamine abuse will continue to represent the most significant drug threat to Hawai'i'" (*Honolulu Weekly* 2003, 6). Tragically, the Native Hawaiian population is not immune to this epidemic, and the homestead lands have become hot spots for "ice."

The problem of self-destructive behavior is compounded by discrimination in the Hawaiian criminal justice system. Native Hawaiians are incarcerated at a much higher rate than are White and Japanese residents. They comprise 20 percent of Hawai'i's general population, yet make up 45 percent of its inmate population. Because correctional statistics count only those with Hawaiian last names to establish the number of Indigenous prisoners, correctional facility workers estimate a Native Hawaiian inmate population closer to 60 percent.

The biased and unnecessary arrests of a disproportionate percentage of the Native population has led to overcrowded prisons. Since 1992, the state has adopted as a solution to this problem the deportation of its excess inmate population, mostly Native Hawaiian, to distant facilities on the U.S. mainland. This removal policy of an Indigenous population is reminiscent of the 1830 Indian Removal Act that sent tens of thousands of eastern Indians on a "Trail of Tears." The forced removal of so many Native Hawaiians from their *'ohana* is equally painful and cruel to both those incarcerated to distant prisons, and to their relatives and communities. At the same time, the state saves money, approximately $50 a day per inmate, by sending inmates to private prisons operated by contracting corporations. Profits exceed $26 million annually for the deportation of inmates. (Sonoda 2000, 5)

CONTEMPORARY STRUGGLE FOR HAWAIIAN SOVEREIGNTY

A Native awakening took place in the 1970s and 1980s that was marked by both political protest and a renewed interest in Hawaiian culture. This Hawaiian renaissance included: "'Keep the Country Country' protests on the Windward Coast of O'ahu in the 1970s; in the standoff at Sand Island on O'ahu where Hawaiians living their traditional way were labeled 'squatters,' were carried away by force, and had their fishing village leveled; in the resistance of the people to being moved off of the seashores at Mākua and at Waimānalo Beach in the early 1980s, and in other protest actions" (Dudley and Agard 1990, 93). There was renewed interest in the traditional *hula*, the Polynesian Voyaging Society was founded, Hawaiian civic clubs were formed, and pro-sovereignty groups were organized.

The 1970 Kalama Valley protest signaled the arrival of social activism for self-determination, and over the next few years there were a series of protests by Native people to resist eviction by large-scale developers. Although fishermen on Mokauea Island who faced eviction successfully negotiated a sixty-year lease to construct a new fishing village, by 1979 the state was evicting Native Hawaiians from their fishing village at Sand Island on O'ahu. The speculative rise in real estate value had put scarce Hawaiian land at a premium price. Within twenty years, homes priced at $10,000 had skyrocketed to $120,000. Consequently, homeless Natives were forced to live in cars and on the beaches. "The state initially looked upon the destitute 'beach people' as a blight hurting the tourist industry" (Dudley and Agard 1990, 115). That view began to change when the evening news carried heart-wrenching scenes of evictions.

One aspect of the new struggle was a demand for reparations for the overthrow of the Hawaiian monarchy. The first protest group embracing this program was A.L.O.H.A. (Aboriginal Lands of Hawaiian Ancestry), founded in 1972. Subsequently, the Hawaiian delegation to Congress entered legislation in 1974 that demanded "a cash payment to the Hawaiian people for loses of lands, resources, rights, and revenues sustained as a result of the overthrow and subsequent annexation by the United States" (Dudley and Agard 1990, 110). A Congressional Study Commission subsequently submitted a report in 1983 recommending against reparations, but many people considered the report hopelessly flawed.

"'Ohana O Hawai'i" (Extended Family of Hawai'i) was founded in 1974. It took the case of the illegal overthrow to international tribunals and the World Court at The Hague, calling for the decolonization of Hawai'i. In 1975, Protect Kaho'olawe 'Ohana (P.K.O.), together with A.L.O.H.A. and another sovereignty group, Hui Ala Loa, made a symbolic landing on the sacred island of Kaho'olawe.

In 1987, the Constitutional Convention for a Hawaiian Nation took place with Native delegates attending from every island. A tentative Constitution was drafted, and Ka Lāhui Hawai'i (Hawaiian Nation) was founded. In 1989, a second Constitutional Convention was held, and Ka Lāhui Hawai'i has met continuously since then. In 1985, another sovereignty group, Nā 'Ōiwi o Hawai'i (Native Hawaiians), sponsored a forum on "Nationalism and Independence at the Kamehameha Schools." Native representatives also attended international meetings on Indigenous rights at the United Nations in Geneva, Switzerland.

At the 1978 Constitutional Convention for the State of Hawai'i, the Office of Hawaiian Affairs (OHA) was established, and in August of 1988, OHA sponsored a Native Hawaiian Rights Conference, which was attended by representatives from several of the sovereignty groups.

Di Alto (2002), writing in a newsletter of the Native American Studies Association, concludes that the Native Hawaiian sovereignty movement of the 1960s and 1970s focused on three main issues: (1) the U.S. military's bombing of the island of Kaho'olawe; (2) the expansion by the tourism industry, business, and non-Native residents into rural areas of Hawai'i where traditional Native populations still resided; and (3) the desire of Native Hawaiians to preserve and transmit their cultural heritage to future generations. Sovereignty was viewed as the solution to these issues, and it remains so today. Native nationalists contend that it is the sovereign right of the Kānaka Maoli (Native Hawaiians) to decide for themselves their political future, something that was not done when Hawai'i was made a state in 1959.

Assault on the Native Environment

A central theme enunciated by the Hawaiian protestors is the protection of the environment, both in its physical as well as its cultural and spiritual dimensions. The main agents in the environmental assault are the military, the tourist industry, official institutions of government, and the *haole* backlash.

The Western idea of environmental stewardship probably comes the closest to the Hawaiian concept of *mālama 'Āina* (love of the land). "The Hawaiian Islands are unique. The most remote island chain in the world, Hawai'i is the site of the world's largest mountain, most active volcano, and highest rainfall. It is also home to over 10,000 unique plants, animals and insects, which populate environments as different as coral reefs, rain forests, and alpine deserts" (Wei and Kamel 1998, 153). Today, however, a growing number of these unique species are either already extinct or critically threatened; sea life, too, is in jeopardy due to commercial fishing off the island coasts and channels. The forests, lands, and waters of a once pristine land have now been degraded, and the introduction of nonnative species, such as cattle and small predators, has effected extensive environmental changes. The introduced changes are so extensive that they have overwhelmed the island environment, making it impossible for the native species to survive or adapt.

An environmental issue that arose in the mid-1980s was the struggle against geothermal drilling in the *Wao Kele O Puna* rain forest on the Big Island. It is the only tropical lowland forest in the United States, "27,000 acres of which are owned by the Campbell Estate, one of the largest land owning estates in Hawai'i" (NARF 2003, 1). The issue is of critical importance since 95 percent of the flowering plants and 97 percent of the animals there are found nowhere else in the world. Because Hawai'i must import oil in order to generate most of its electricity needs, geothermal energy is viewed by those in state government as a cheap, untapped alternate resource.

The Pele Defense Fund (PDF), organized in 1983 by a group of Native Hawaiians, has strongly opposed the geothermal drilling in the *Wao Kele O Puna* rain forest. In the first place, it is a sacred forest region that "has supplied traditional Native Hawaiian doctors with the special herbs and medicines they need for thousands of years. . . . In addition, Hawaiian woodcarvers come to the forest to gather special materials for their craft, and practitioners of the sacred *hula* visit the *Wao Kele* for the materials they need for their traditional performances" (Wei and Kamel 1998, 154). There are also ancient burials and religious structures in the lava tubes beneath the forest that might be damaged from drilling. Furthermore, the volcano where the geothermal company is drilling is the traditional home of the goddess Pele. To drill into Pele's body is a desecration and could result in the angry goddess reacting with a catastrophic event, such as an earthquake, volcanic eruption, or a tidal wave. Even though only several hundred acres would be cleared for drilling in the twenty-seven thousand acre forest, the attendant road construction could be environmentally devastating. The roads would become perfect avenues for alien plants and animals to invade and kill the indigenous wildlife.

The efforts by PDF culminated in a limited victory in August 2002 when the state court in Hilo, Hawai'i, recognized "the PDF members' rights to access, hunt, gather and worship on the Wao Kele lands—part of the bundle of 'traditional and customary rights' protected by the state Constitution. These are rights that pre-date both the formation of the state in 1959, and the overthrow of the Monarchy in 1893" (NARF 2003, 2).

The Military Occupation

The U.S. military has taken over some of the choicest lands, and the Pacific Command, with control over U.S. armed forces in more than half of the world, is headquartered in Hawai'i. By the early 1970s, one out of seven people living in Hawai'i were either in the military or a dependent of military personnel.

For half a century the 45 square mile island of Koho'olawe was used by the U.S. Navy as a bombing range and for military training. Incredibly, a number of *heiau*, shrines, burials, and ancient settlement sites survived the decades of bombing, erosion, and trampling by cattle and goats. There are more than five hundred recorded archaeological sites on the island, and Kaho'olawe's cultural significance to the Hawaiian people is incalculable. It was found to be a key area for learning traditional Hawaiian navigation techniques, with the western end of the island marking the route to Tahiti.

When bombing was brought to a halt and the island finally returned to Native people in 1994, Congress mandated that the Navy must clear the island within ten years of any hazards and unexploded ordinance created by the decades of target practice. Work did not commence, however, until 1998, and only one-tenth of the island's surface had been cleared by the year 2000. The goal of Protect Kaho'olawe 'Ohana, the organization whose protests led to the termination of the bombing, is to eventually replant the entire island, but the erosion and bomb damage make this goal a difficult task. Parts of the island are entirely devoid of soil, reefs are buried by sentiment, and bombing has damaged the water table.

In spite of the Native victory in stopping the bombing of Kaho'olawe, military training activities in Hawai'i have increased since the 9/11 terrorist attack on the United States. Ironically, this national tragedy has complicated the goals of the Native land movement to reduce the military occupation of Hawai'i. The military has expanded its island land usage in the name of pursuing the war against terrorism. Nowhere is this more evident than in Mākua Valley on the island of O'ahu. The conflict by the Native Hawaiian residents and claimants in the valley with the U.S. military has a long and difficult history.

Ancient legends are linked with Mākua Valley. *Mākua* means parents; it is where the Earth Mother, *Papa*, and *Wākea*, the Sky Father, met, and where the *Kānaka Maoli* (Native Hawaiians) were formed from the *'Āina*. It is along this coast where the spirits of the Hawaiian people return to the spirit world at "soul's leap," a point of land jutting out into the waters of the Pacific Ocean. The ocean along Mākua Beach was once a rich resource for sea life, and agriculture was practiced in the lower valley. There are still the remains of several *heiau*. At the time of the Māhele, Mākua Valley was made government land by Kamehameha III, and sixteen *kuleana* were awarded to Native Hawaiians. The rest remained government land that was leased by the government to non-Native Hawaiians for ranching.

U.S. military use of Mākua Valley dates from the 1920s. After the bombing of Pearl Harbor in 1941, the U.S. Army took over the entire Mākua-Kaena Point area. The valley "was transformed from a peaceful cattle ranch into a busy garrison. . . . Structures were demolished by target practice, fences torn down, pipelines cut, fishing holes bombed, and fresh water wells were used as dumps for waste oil. . . . The number of military personnel on O'ahu rose to 400,000, many of whom lived in a tent city in Mākua Valley" (Kelly and Aleck 1997, 8). During World War II, military operations were permitted under Revocable Permit 200, issued by the territorial government. The permit specified that the military was to return the area in a satisfactory condition within six months after hostilities ended, but this was never done. "The Statehood Admission Act of 1959 allowed the Federal government to reserve land for military purposes," and a 1964 Executive Order by President Johnson reserved the interior portion of the valley as Mākua Military Reservation. It also "provided a 65-year lease to the Army for the lower portion of the valley" (Kelly and Aleck 1997, 9).

The coastal area now contains over 40,000 people, with the Army controlling approximately 4,200 acres in the valley. Military training activities include ground maneuvers, amphibious landings, naval and air bombardment strafing, mortar and artillery fire, mustard gas and napalm use. The valley has suffered serious environmental degradation. By 1955, it had become so contaminated that no one could safely return to live in it. A 1992 application by the U.S. Army to the Environmental Protection Agency to conduct open burn/open detonation of waste munitions was withdrawn after a public outcry. Nevertheless, despite the danger from contamination and live-fire training in the upper valley, groups of Native people and other local residents returned to live at Mākua Beach.

In early 2001, when the U.S. Army proposed to resume live-fire operations despite a court order blocking that action, Native Hawaiians long opposed to military activity in the valley sought legal action. They reached an agreement with the Army that allowed training to resume in exchange for a comprehensive environmental impact study. But when the Army's study found no significant environmental impact, over five hundred community members packed a local community center to testify against the Army's findings. Kupuna elders, with both sadness and anger, told how families were inhumanely evicted from the valley and how their homes and church were destroyed. Hawaiian cultural practitioners testified to the riches of the valley prior to the military's occupation. Other testimony included health issues, the lack of information about soil and groundwater contamination, the lack of information on past impacts to Hawaiian culture, community, and the environment. Many testified to the high cancer rate among the Waianae coast and possible links to the toxic contamination in Mākua. Hui Mālama o Mākua is a coalition of concerned organizations that protested the military occupation of Mākua Valley.

The Aloha Industry

Seven million tourists who visit the islands each year create "tremendous pressure on once lavish resources of water, land and sea. As ancient sacred lands are turned into resorts and golf courses, Native Hawaiian culture and arts are taken over and reissued as attractions for tourists from the United States, Japan, and Europe" (Wei and Kamel 1998, 135). Trask (2001, 396) terms the commodification of Hawaiian culture through corporate tourism as "cultural prostitution," because of its negative impact on Native Hawaiian people and culture.

"After decades that saw Hawaiians denying and neglecting their cultural heritage, the early 1970s brought a renewal of interest in traditional Hawaiian music, arts, and crafts" (Dudley and Agard 1990, 107). The *hula* is an example of a beautiful and rare traditional art form that has fallen victim to cultural prostitution. "Hulas were dances that accompanied the poetry of chant. That relationship was inverted

Mākua Valley Protest.

during the decline of traditional Hawaiian culture during the nineteenth century" (McMurray 2002, 169). In traditional Hawai'i, the *hula* was performed for only three reasons: as a sacred offering, to transmit knowledge as a component of the oral traditions, and as a vehicle for providing social and cultural cohesion. Today, in the "Aloha industry," a bastardized version is performed solely for tourist entertainment and industry profit. Young Hawaiians grow up thinking that to dance the *hula* is to dance for tourists.

Hawaiian culture and language were suppressed until the mid-twentieth century. Not only the public school system, but the Kamehameha schools also banned the Hawaiian language during much of its history. Kamehameha schools, named for King Kamehameha I, were funded by Princess Bernice Pauahi Bishop's 1884 will to educate children of Hawaiian ancestry. Until recently, even the *hula* was not allowed.

The money generated from the Bishop Estate to run the Kamehameha schools is derived from old Hawaiian crown lands that were inherited by the descendants of Hawai'i's royal family. Currently, the Bishop Estate owns one-tenth of all the land in Hawai'i. The school curriculum was modeled after the American Indian boarding school system on the mainland that promulgated a policy of forced acculturation. Native Hawaiian children were trained for menial tasks and to emulate middle-class White culture, and taught Calvinist religious precepts. This policy began to change in the 1970s, so that the Kamehameha schools now encourage the students to have a familiarity with Hawaiian language and cultural traditions, including the *hula*. Today, the Kamehamha schools are under pressure to admit non-Hawaiian students, thereby negating the original purpose of the school system. On August 2, 2005, the Ninth U.S. Circuit Court of Appeals in San Francisco ruled that the Kamehameha schools must admit non-Native students, even though the schools receive no federal funding. Native Hawaiians were naturally outraged at the decision.

Hawaiian Language Revival

Despite past policies of acculturation, by the early 1970s, one thousand students had signed up for ethnic studies courses at the University of Hawai'i, many of them in Hawaiian language and culture. Today, Hawaiian language classes are immensely popular at the university. This positive development is part of the Native cultural revitalization movement that has swept the Native Hawaiian community.

The 1896 ban against the Hawaiian language was lifted in 1978 when the state constitution was amended to include Hawaiian as an official language. Since then, it has been making an impressive comeback and is now one of the more popular language courses in the university system. Many young people are also being educated in one of the increasing number of Hawaiian language immersion schools, or in one of the Hawaiian charter schools. It is estimated that by the 2005–06 school year there could be as many as four thousand students enrolled in the fourteen Hawaiian language immersion programs throughout the islands. The Hawaiian language is now required within the State Department of Education curriculum.

The *Aha Pūnana Leo* immersion language pre-schools were founded in 1983 by a group of educators, together with interested families. "The *Pūnana Leo* actually began while it was still illegal to use Hawaiian in the schools. It took a three-year campaign at the state legislature by parents and community members to change the laws, thus ending eighty years of outlaw status for the language" (Hinton 2001, 521). By 1997 there were nine such schools in Hawai'i, with the one in Hilo on the Big Island training the teachers and providing the curriculum. By last count there were a dozen.

In 1987, the State Department of Education began two experimental Hawaiian-language immersion programs that have been very successful scholastically. "End of the year tests showed that children in the two Hawaiian immersion classes, besides doing very well in all other subjects, also tested higher in English than other first graders in the state whose classes were entirely taught in English" (Dudley and Agard 1990, 102). At a Hawaiian-language high school in Hilo, where a number of the teenagers had previously attended the same Pūnana Leo preschool, chanting as an art form is now being revived.

A more recent development is the Native Hawaiian charter school movement. Charter schools are public schools that are freed from many of the regulations that apply to traditional public schools, but that are held accountable for both academic results and fiscal practices. There are now a dozen of these Native charter schools. The mission of the Native Hawaiian Charter School Alliance is to pro-

vide an educational model throughout the Islands, a program that is community designed and controlled, and that reflects Hawaiian cultural values, philosophies and ideologies. The Center for Hawaiian Studies at the University of Hawai'i at Manoa and at Hilo is playing an important academic role in stimulating curriculum development, and the state of Hawai'i provides start-up money for the planning and implementation of a new charter schools.

The immersion schools and the charter school movement offers an alternative to the public school system for parents who want their children to gain a facility in the Native language and a reverence for Hawaiian culture. Although admission is open to children of every ethnic background, the majority of the students are Native Hawaiian. These schools are having a beneficial effect on both the motivation and academic achievement of Hawaiian children.

Another aspect of Hawaiian culture related to language is the renewed interest in Hawaiian genealogy. Hawaiian genealogies are the histories of the people and an integral part of language revitalization. The function of names in the recitation of the genealogies is more than who begot whom. "They are also the mnemonic device by which the *mo'oleo*, or the exploits of the *Āli'i* are recalled. As the list of names are chanted, the adventures of the *Āli'i* are remembered, and these, in turn, form the body of tradition by which their descendants pattern their Chiefly behavior. In times past, when a problem arose, the *Āli'i* usually in council, would send for a *kākā'ālelo*, an antiquarian and genealogist, who would consider the issue and recount all the pertinent *mo'olelo*. Then the *Mō'ī* would know which decision had brought his ancestors success, and would be the path to follow" (Kame'eleihiwa 1992, 22).

"Today, we Hawaiians use genealogical relationships to establish our collective identity via a social network of *'ohana* (family). Our shared genealogy helps us define our *Lāhui* (nation) as an entity distinct from the waves of foreigners that have inundated our islands" (Kame'eleihiwa 1992, 2–3).

The *Haole* Backlash

The grassroots movement by Native Hawaiians resulted in a major victory during the state of Hawai'i's 1978 Constitutional Convention. Called to revise the state constitution, the convention was the dominated by Native activism. Activists forced the adoption of an amendment to provide Native Hawaiians with a pro rata share of the revenues from the Ceded Lands Trust (later set at 20 percent), and created the Office of Hawaiian Affairs (OHA) to manage the revenues. The amendment also created a new category of beneficiaries: "Hawaiian" was now defined as any descendant of the aboriginal peoples of the Hawaiian Islands which exercised sovereignty and subsisted in the Hawaiian Islands in 1778. The amendment creating the Office of Hawaiian Affairs also specified that its board of trustees be comprised of so-defined Hawaiians, and that they be elected by Hawaiians to manage the new agency. These encouraging provisions, however, have since been put in jeopardy by a decision of the U.S. Supreme Court that represents a major blow to the Hawaiian sovereignty movement.

In 1996, in *Rice v. Caytano*, Harold F. Rice, a White rancher, challenged the constitutionality of the voting laws for the election of trustees to the board of the OHA. Rice contended that his civil rights as a non-Native person were violated. On February 23, 2000, the U.S. Supreme Court on appeal ruled in favor of Rice. "The court reasoned that all Hawai'i citizens, regardless of ancestry, should be able to serve as OHA trustees because the requirement that only Hawaiians serve as trustees of OHA is 'a racial classification'" which is unconstitutional (*Indian Country Today* 2001). Under the Fifteenth Amendment, neither the federal nor any state government can deny or abridge the right to vote based on race. The Court ruled that the use of "ancestry" in the Hawaiian case is a proxy for race. The core of the issue, however, lay in the fact that Native Hawaiians have no official political standing in the United States—not even that of the federally recognized Indian tribes on the mainland.

The Court's ruling has also endangered other state programs servicing the Native population, especially those programs specifically financed by the income from the Ceded Lands and administered in trust by the Office of Hawaiian Affairs. "In 2000, in *Arakaki v. State of Hawai'i*, the rules governing election to the board of trustees for OHA were successfully challenged to allow non-Natives to run for office. In *Carroll v. Nakatani*, the income and revenue of OHA came under attack. And in *Barrett v. State* the constitutionality of OHA, the Department of Hawaiian Homelands, and Native Hawaiian gathering rights were contested" (Di Alto 2002, 3). The policy of the George W. Bush administration in opposing federal programs based on race or ethnic criteria has complicated the struggle for Hawaiian rights. Nor has the Barack Obama political administration in Washington advocated any special status for Native Hawaiians.

The Akaka Bill

When President Clinton signed Public Law 103-150, better known as the Apology Resolution, in 1993, many Native activists viewed this event as a major step forward in their long quest for sovereignty. Native leaders believe that only the sovereign control of the *'Āina* and its resources will prevent the Hawaiian culture from disappearing altogether. The Apology Resolution acknowledged that "the Indigenous Hawaiian people never directly relinquished their claims to their inherent sovereignty as a people or over their national lands to the United States, either through their monarchy or through a plebiscite or referendum" (Di Alto 2002, 1). Native optimism was revalidated when Congress voted in 1994 to end its military activities on Kaho'olawe and turn over the control of the sacred island to the state of Hawai'i, to be held in trust for Native Hawaiians until such time as a sovereign Hawaiian entity is established.

In 2000, legislation was introduced into Congress by Senator Daniel Akaka (Dem-HI) to extend federal recognition to Native Hawaiians. This is the "nation-within-a-nation" formula that is similar to the political status of American Indian tribes, whose sovereignty was established in treaties with the United States in years past. Although Native Hawaiians are not governed by treaties, they nevertheless have other legal and historical bases on which to stake their land claims, i.e., the 1.8 million acres ceded to the U.S. government, and the 203,000 acres set aside by Congress in 1920 as Hawaiian Home Lands.

Since 2000 the Native Hawaiian Government Reorganization Act has gone through numerous revisions to appease conservative opposition in Congress. In May of 2003 the Senate Indian Affairs Committee passed an amended version of the Akaka Bill, known as the Akaka-Reid-Stevens Bill. The bill would give Native Hawaiians equivalent legal standing to American Indians and Native Alaskans and lead to the creation of a governing body that would make decisions on behalf of Native Hawaiians in the United States. Under the proposed legislation, a new Hawaiian political entity would be established, the Office for Native Hawaiian Relations, located in the Interior Department. Second, a Hawaiian membership list would be created and then serve "as the voter roll for referendum questions and the election of representatives to the eventual Hawaiian governing body" (Ferrar 2003, 8). Third, "eligible voters on the roll would then elect a Native Hawaiian Interim Governing Council, which would conduct a referendum on the shape of the Hawaiian governing body and then draft its guiding documents. After further votes to ratify those documents and elect representatives to the final governing entity, that body would be officially certified and recognized by the Interior Dept. as the legitimate representative of the Hawaiian people" (Ferrar 2003, 8). The current Office of Hawaiian Affairs, a Hawai'i state organization, would then dissolve itself and transfer all Native trust assets to the new governing body once it is established.

In September 2005, Senator Akaka announced a new version of his Hawaiian recognition bill that represented a compromise with the Bush administration. The new version would have met the administration's concerns over gambling, criminal jurisdiction, military readiness and federal liability. Federal objections and opposition among many Republicans in Congress stalled the Akaka bill. Some Native Hawaiian groups, however, continue to oppose the bill, claiming "they don't need the federal government to assert their rights on islands inherited from their ancestors" (Briscoe 2005).

The Rice decision by the Court signaled a racist backlash against the sovereignty movement and made hollow the promises of the Apology Resolution. The negative ruling in the Rice case has interrupted the Native Hawaiian debate on what should be the appropriate form of Hawaiian sovereignty. "The looming question is whether the rush to close [the Rice] loophole will eclipse prematurely the legitimate discussion under way among Hawaiian people over the numerous details required to put flesh on the framework of Hawaiian self-determination" (NARF 2003, 8).

With the backing of the Obama administration in 2009, supporters of the Akaka Bill were hopeful that at last the legislation would be passed. This did not happen, however, due to conservative opposition in Congress. Furthermore, the U.S. Supreme Court ruled in March of 2009 that the Apology Resolution for overthrowing the Hawaiian monarch in 1893 bears no moral, political or legal weight in stopping the state of Hawai'i from selling 1.2 million acres of lands seized during the illegal regime change before resolving land claims by Native Hawaiians. Finally, in 2011 Senator Akaka announced that he was retiring and would not seek another term. Consequently, the fate of the Akaka legislation is in doubt.

Although the state-based Office of Hawaiian Affairs endorsed the Akaka Bill, there are those in the Hawaiian sovereignty movement who strongly oppose such a remedy. One of them is Professor J. Kehaulani Kauanui of Wesleyan University. In a hearing before the Senate Committee on Indian Affairs in February, 2003, he criticized the original Akaka Bill. Kauanui explained that, in the first place, those who seek such a limited solution do so because of the Rice case and the assault on Hawaiian rights in the courts: "Many Hawaiians and their allies support Akaka's proposal for federal recognition because it is understood as a protective measure against these lawsuits" (Kauanui 2003, 8). While it may seem like a quick fix to afford a measure of protection for Native Hawaiians, Kauanui points out that it would actually limit Hawaiian inherent sovereignty by placing Native people under the direct authority of the secretary of the interior and at the mercy of Congress. Hawaiian rights under the federal recognition model could also leave Native people without a secure land base. Kauanui cites the case of the Supreme Court denying Alaska Native villages the official status of "Indian country," and therefore the legal protection as Indigenous self-governing entities. At the very least, the Hawaiian Nation should have sovereignty over the Ceded Lands, amounting to 1.8 million acres.

Federal recognition following the American Indian model compromises the sovereignty language that Congress has already applied to the Hawaiian case in its 1993 Apology Resolution. The point to remember is that Hawai'i was illegally annexed by the United States, "illegally because the United States never upheld U.S. constitutional law or international law when it purportedly annexed Hawai'i. There was no treaty of annexation" (Kauanui 2003, 9). In fact, the vast majority of the Hawaiian people opposed annexation. For these reasons, Kauanui (2003, 14) concluded his testimony with the following statement: It is "an affront to our collective sovereign rights and full decolonization. The bill is really only a transfer plan of wardship status in the name of the 'trust relationship.' In other words, instead of being wards of the state [of Hawai'i], our people would be considered wards of the federal government." Nevertheless, it must be admitted that until the question of Hawaiian sovereignty is settled, and a political structure is approved and implemented, it will be difficult for Native Hawaiians to oppose the regressive court decisions initiated by the aforementioned Rice case.

THEORY REVISITED

In *Native Land and Foreign Desires* (1992), Kame'eleihiwa contends that it would be incorrect to attribute the loss of Hawaiian sovereignty solely to the acquisition of the islands by the United States. It actually began fifty years earlier when traditional land tenure was radically altered to a system of private property under the *Māhele*. The loss of Hawaiian sovereignty is usually correlated with the Bayonet Constitution and the 1893 overthrow of Queen Lili'uokalani that ended the Hawaiian monarchy and paved the way for the 1898 annexation. On the basis of her research, Kame'eleihiwa contends that the loss of Hawaiian sovereignty began much earlier, when the two-thousand-year-old Hawaiian social system underwent a major change in response to depopulation and Christianization. In old Hawai'i, sovereignty was inextricably linked to spiritual culture and the hierarchical interrelationship of the gods, chiefs, and common people to the land. When the Native Hawaiians lost the *'Āina*, their sovereign birthright was fatally diminished. The attack on Hawaiian sovereignty began when the *haole* missionaries Christianized the chiefly class, undermined the *kapu* system of sacred law, infiltrated the Hawaiian government, and then pressured the monarchy to privatize the land. This was when the fabric of Hawaiian society began to unravel, and that is how sovereignty was taken away.

Kame'eleihiwa presents several schematic representations of Hawaiian social structure as it changed during the course of the eighteenth and nineteenth centuries. Each one is in the shape of a pyramid formed by a hierarchy of social rank. The first, Figure 8.2, is of traditional Hawaiian society as it existed before Western conquest of the islands.

In this representation, the gods (*Akua*), the king (*Mō'ī*), and the chiefs (*Ali'i Nui*) are at the top of the social pyramid, and the common people (*Maka'āinana*) are at the bottom. Social strata of lesser rank and power are grouped in between these extremes in terms of their respective political or religious statuses. The entire social structure, from the top of the pyramid to its base, is characterized by a continuum of the sacred to the profane, with those statuses at the top being sacred (*kapu*), while those at the bottom are *noa* (common or free from *kapu*). The dynamic principle of the social system was the constant seeking of *mana* (sacred power) in order to make the Hawaiian world or universe *pono* (righteous, in a state of perfect harmony).

In this traditional social system, the land, which is sacred, was under the care of the king and his high chiefs. It was their sacred duty to love and care for the land and the people, and in this way to

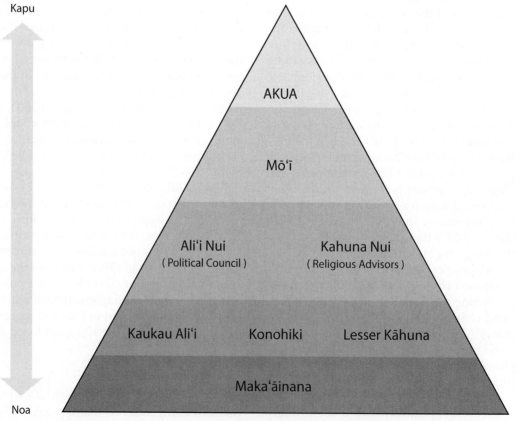

Figure 8.2 Traditional Hawaiian Society.

serve the gods. The traditional Hawaiian land tenure system was based on this divine understanding. Thus, when the social system and its religious underpinnings became undermined by Calvinist influence and Western private property concepts, it underwent a series of changes that gradually rendered it dysfunctional until it eventually broke down altogether. The 1848 *Māhele* was the culmination of this devolution.

When Liholiho as Kamehameha II broke the pivotal religious *'Aikapu* that prevented men and women from eating together (including its wider religious manifestations), his act signaled the growing influence of the missionaries and the beginning of the end for the old Hawaiian religion. Ka'ahumanu, who shared power with Liholiho, was a converted Christian and known as a "free eater." For the next thirteen years during her reign as chief political advisor, she asserted her influence to destroy many of the old cultural traditions. The power of the king was reduced, and the high chiefs upon their deaths began willing the land they controlled to their heirs rather than returning it to the king as tradition had formerly required. *'Ainoa*, or "free eating," became a metaphor for changing any

aspect of Hawaiian culture and society in the search for new ways to achieve *mana*. Below we paraphrase Kame'eleihiwa's explanation (1992, 82) of the impact of the overthrow of this key ritual on the question of Hawaiian land tenure: If there was no sacred eating *kapu*, then the chiefs ceased to be gods, for the proclamation of "free eating" negated the very existence of Hawaiian divinity. If as creators, the gods had before owned the land, and the chiefs were but land stewards to the gods, who now owned the Land? In theory, the answer was that with free eating, ownership of the land was in limbo and the chiefs were no longer land stewards of the gods. As a consequence, by 1825, Hawaiian social structure had noticeably changed. This is represented in the following schematic representation from Kame'eleihiwa in Figure 8.3 (1992, 155).

In Figure 8.3, notice that Jehovah, the Christian god, has replaced the Hawaiian *Akua*, and that missionary Hiram Bingham and other Calvinists now occupy important government offices as religious advisors. Some of the lesser *Ali'i* (chiefs) and *Konohiki* are now merging with the status of the common people, *maka'āinana*, or those without *mana*. After Ka'ahumanu died in 1832, the pyramid arrangement

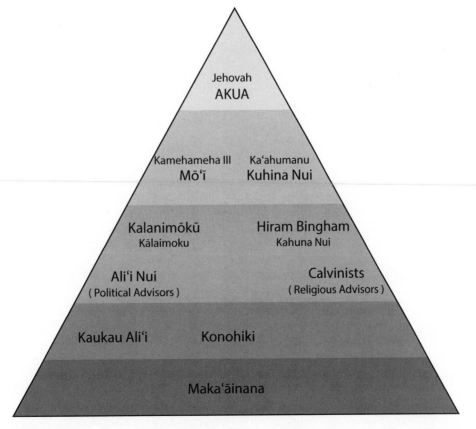

Figure 8.3 Hawaiian Society in 1825.

of social status and sacred authority changed even further. By 1838, virtually all of the religious and political advisors were *haole* with connections to religious or business interests, or both.

Finally, on the eve of the 1848 *Māhele*, a series of Organic Acts fundamentally transformed the Hawaiian traditional government: Cabinet posts were created, governors appointed to administer the various islands, and the Land Commission was created, headed by the Reverend William Richards. In bitter irony, some Native Hawaiians called the White power structure "the missionary monarchy." This structural change is also schematically represented in Kame'eleihiwa's book and is reproduced in Figure 8.4 (1992, 187).

Although *Māhele* is usually translated into English as "division," in the Hawaiian language there is also another connotation, "to share." Kame'eleihiwa believes that in the *Māhele* the chiefs actually intended to share the land and their control of Hawaiian sovereignty with the common people, the *maka'āinana*. After all, the *'Āina* was made by the *Akua* to be held in trust by the chiefs for the people. Kame'eleihiwa's research negates the commonly held assumption that through the *Māhele*, the chiefs

intended to buy their way into the capitalist system. In the end, however, the king, together with the chiefs, was forced to submit to Western pressures to change the traditional land tenure system. Although extremely reluctant to accept the Western system of land tenure, they did so only when they thought they had no other choice.

Kame'eleihiwa also explains the causes for the changes in Hawaiian social structure that led to the collapse of traditional land tenure. The genocidal death rate of the Hawaiian population, mostly from Western diseases, was a major factor in the people losing faith in the *Akua* and the old social system that combined both political and religious institutions. Ninety percent of the Hawaiian Native people died during the early years of Western occupation. Non-Natives, on the other hand, "had broken every *kapu* of the old *Akua* and yet they did not die. Hawaiians adhered to the *'Aikapu* and died by the thousands. White people in Hawai'i got drunk, indulged in sensual pleasures, respected only those Hawaiians who acquired Western goods, and did not seem to possess any *Akua*. Yet White people seemed to hold the secret of life" (Kame'eleihiwa 1992, 80). Native Hawaiians reasoned that, clearly, there must be a new source of

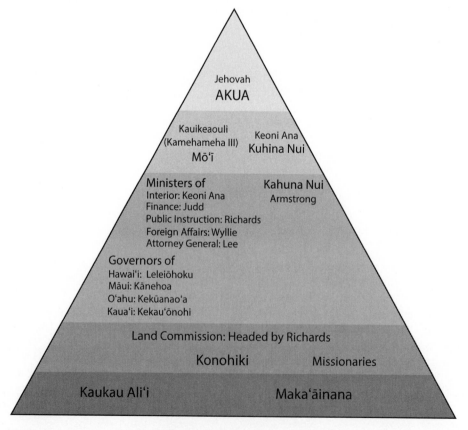

Figure 8.4 Hawaiian Society in 1846 after the Organic Acts.

mana, and maybe the *haole* path of Christianity, materialism, and private property was the way to *pono*, the way to achieve righteousness. "The *Māhele* transformed the traditional land tenure system from one of communal tenure to private ownership on the capitalist model" (Kame'eleihiwa 1992, 8). Thus, Hawaiian sovereignty was actually lost in 1848 during the Great *Māhele*, and not in 1893 when the marines landed in Honolulu, or a few years later when Hawai'i was formally annexed by a colonialist United States.

If the contemporary Hawaiian sovereignty movement is to be successful, it is important to draw lessons from Kame'eleihiwa's research. It becomes obvious that the restoration of sovereignty must include a Native land base, and that the revitalization of the Hawaiian culture and traditions must be an integral part of such a restoration movement if it is to be successful. *Mālama 'Āina*, "caring for the land," and *Aloha 'Āina*, "love of the land," remain the cornerstone concepts that can help restore Native people to their former status as a sovereign power.

Kame'eleihiwa believes an additional ingredient is also necessary for the Native Hawaiian sovereignty movement to succeed. The movement must also adopt the metaphor of *Kū*, the traditional god of war. By this she does not mean to actually go to war against the *haole*, but rather, that Native people must become politicized and take militant action. They cannot not leave the struggle to a modern *'Āli'i*—educators, professionals, and political leaders. The common people, the *Kānaka Maoli* must take action.

CONCLUSION

Self-Determination and Decolonization

After the founding of the United Nations in 1946, Hawai'i was added to the list of Non-Self-Governing Territories that made it eligible for decolonization under international law. The United States circumvented this requirement by pushing aside the question of sovereignty and making Hawai'i a state. In doing so it violated United Nations policies and international law. Hawai'i was never given the right of self-determination, of choosing its own form of government. With statehood secured, Hawai'i was taken off the list of non self-governing territories.

Today, one wing of the Hawaiian sovereignty movement is still calling for decolonization under U.N. protocols. The argument is made that the Hawaiian Kingdom was never legally terminated in

the first place, and some leaders of the sovereignty movement are calling for the restoration of the Hawaiian Kingdom. In 1997, on the anniversary of the illegal taking of the Hawaiian monarchy, Native people were galvanized into action by the discovery of historical records linking their families to the massive resistance of the 1897 annexation. "Today, when people find signatures of *'ohana* among the more than 21,000 people who signed Hui Aloha 'Āina's petition protesting annexation, a powerful political connection is made. Another 17,000 signed Hui Kālai 'āina's petition to restore the monarchy" (Shimokawa 1998, 1).

Sovereignty includes the right of a nation to define its own membership or nationality. Current U.S. government policy prevents this right by practicing a form of statistical genocide, its use of the moribund blood quantum method of denoting Native identity. It confers Native Hawaiian status only on those who have 50 percent blood or more, rather than using a cultural definition of ethnicity. Due to interracial marriage, being Native Hawaiian will soon be defined out of existence, because with each seceding generation there will be fewer pure blood Native Hawaiians. Before *haole* invasion of the islands, a Hawaiian was simply a citizen of the kingdom. The sovereignty movement therefore reserves the right to define its own requirements of nationality as part of the decolonizing process.

Models for Sovereignty?

In *A Call for Hawaiian Sovereignty* (1990, 129), Dudley and Agard suggest three forms that Hawaiian sovereignty could take: (1) Nation within a nation (the American Indian model); (2) trust status under the supervision of the United Nations and the international community; (3) complete independence as a separate nation.

"Some of the sovereignty groups, such as the Office of Hawaiian Affairs and Ka Lāhui Hawai'i, and various individuals . . . are proposing nationhood within the territorial limits of the United States through a treaty or Congressional resolution. . . . They want a sovereign status similar to that of the Native American Indians"(Dudley and Agard 1990, 129). Yet the sovereignty of American Indian tribes is a limited form of sovereignty at best. While this status would give a measure of immediate protection and probably result in some kind of a land base, the new Hawaiian nation would be placed under the supervision of an agency in the U.S. Department of the Interior similar to the Bureau of Indian Affairs, and would have to operate within the American political and governmental system. The problems with this form of limited sovereignty were pointed out by Professor Kauanui in his criticism of the Akaka Bill.

In its 1989 Blueprint for Native Hawaiian Entitlements, the Office of Hawaiian Affairs announced the enrollment of all people of Hawaiian ancestry. The Blueprint also recommended "the return of only 'a substantial portion' of the Ceded Lands, half interest in all resources in submerged lands and offshore waters, back rent for Ceded Lands used by others since 1898, rights to clean water, limited beach access, traditional trail access, fishing, hunting, and gathering rights, freedom for religious practices, and access to historic and cultural sites—along with self-determination and self-governance" (Dudley and Agard 1990, 132–33). Nevertheless, there are Native leaders who believe that these proposed concessions are still too limited in their overall scope and fall short of the right of self-determination.

A second solution calls for the Hawaiian Native people being placed in trust status and eligible for decolonization. Ka Lāhui Hawai'i therefore recommends broadening Hawaiian independence by stages. The Hawaiian land base could be placed on the United Nations' list of non-self-governing territories, and the Hawaiian Nation under U.N. security and supervision. Native people would then "have the right to further determine the kind of relationship they want with the United States. One relationship model being studied is 'free association,' such as is enjoyed by the Trust Territories of the Pacific. This would keep the Hawaiian Nation within the American sphere of influence, but would allow it to interact freely in the international arena" (Dudley and Agard 1990, 135).

The United Nations' Trust Territories of the Pacific Islands (TTPI) were placed in U.S. territorial status following World War II. The United Nations embraced the free association model in 1960, moving the islands from territorial or colonial to self-governing status. In 1986, the TTPI's political status was formalized as Freely Associated States by President Reagan. Today, these island communities constitute the Federated States of Micronesia (including Palau, Ponape, Truk, Yap, and Saipan), and the Republic of the Marshall Islands. The U.N. Security Council terminated the trusteeship status in 1990, and the following year both nations were admitted to the United Nations (NARF 2003, 10–11). The district of the Northern Marianas, on the other hand, separated itself in 1975 from the other trust districts and became a commonwealth in political union with the United

States, the same status that exists for Puerto Rico. Thus there is already a precedent in the case of these Pacific Island trust territories for Hawai'i to eventually achieve a greater measure of independence than is afforded by the nation-within-a-nation model.

The third solution is for the restoration of an independent Hawaiian Nation totally separate from the United States. Actually, this is one of the options afforded by decolonization and trusteeship under the United Nations discussed above. If independence is the option chosen, its form could be either a completely secular Hawaiian nation, or return to a constitutional monarchy.

For the last few years, a number of Native Hawaiians have been occupying public lands on the various islands and are seeking to reinstate the Hawaiian Kingdom. Hawai'i Kingdom supporters contend that Hawai'i's status as an independent nation dates back to at least 1840 when Kamehameha III authorized the Hawaiian Kingdom Constitution. His successor, Queen Lili'uokalani, was in the process of revising this constitution to include universal suffrage when her government was treacherously overthrown. The queen's subsequent protest letter to President Grover Cleveland, and the Memorial Petition signed by thirty-eight thousand Hawaiians in 1897, objecting to the illegal overthrow, proves that Hawaiians never consented to annexation by the United States. "Today, the *kanaka maoli* are rebuilding their government. Following a series of conventions that were held by *kanaka maoli* from all islands, a government pro tem was established in accordance with Hawaiian Kingdom domestic law on March 13, 1999. It was made up of 24 members in the House of Representatives and 24 members in the House of Nobles, thereby reforming the bicameral parliament of the Hawaiian Kingdom" (Taliman 2002).

In July of 2001, a representative for the Hawaiian Kingdom organization filed a complaint against the United States before the Security Council of the United Nations "concerning the prolonged occupation of the Hawaiian Islands since the Spanish American War of 1898" (Crawford 2001). The complaint contends that since Hawai'i was seized illegally under both U.S. and international law, the constitutional monarchy is still the legal government of the islands. The U.N. General Assembly Resolution 1514 mandates that all peoples have the right to self-determination, and Article 73(e) of the United Nations Charter provides for decolonization. The complaint charges that Hawai'i, along with Alaska, American Samoa, Guam, Panama Canal Zone, and Puerto Rico, have a long history of being American colonies, and since 1959, Hawai'i has been ruled as a puppet state.

Whatever the form of sovereignty that is finally chosen (or imposed), all sides in the current debate agree that "the solution to the Hawaiians' problems lies in their return to the Land, and in their reclaiming and developing their traditions and their lifestyle" (Dudley and Agard 1990, 89).

CHAPTER REVIEW

DISCUSSION QUESTIONS

1. Explain how spirituality is a vital part of Native Hawaiian life.
2. What impact did the motives and activities of the Christian missionaries have on Native Hawaiian society and culture in the nineteenth century?
3. What was the Great *Māhele?* How did it change the nature of traditional Hawaiian Native land tenure?
4. What role did the sugar industry play in the colonization of the Hawaiian Islands? The role of the U.S. military? The Big Five?
5. In terms of theory, what do Figures 8.1 through 8.3 reveal as a cause of the loss of Hawaiian sovereignty?
6. What is the Aloha industry, and how does it contribute to Hawai'i as a neocolony of the United States?
7. Briefly summarize how the concepts of imperialism, colonialism, and sovereignty relate to the Hawaiian case.
8. What are some of the developments in the current struggle for Hawaiian sovereignty? Which one of the three models for Hawaiian sovereignty seems the best to you? Which one is the most practical?

SUGGESTED READINGS

'Ai Pōhaku Press. n.d. *Kaho'olawe: Nā Leo o Kanaloa.* Compiled and introduced by Rowland B. Reeve, with a forward by Noa Emmett Aluli. Photographs by Wayne Levin, Rowland B. Reeve, Franco Salmoiraghi, and David Ulrich. Honolulu: 'Ai Pōhaku Press.

American Friends Service Committee, and Office of Curriculum Support, School District of Phildelphia. 1998. *Resistance in Paradise: Rethinking 100 Years of U.S. Involvement in the Caribbean and the Pacific.* Philadelphia: American Friends Service Committee Community Service Division.

BRISCOE, DAVID. 2005. "New Version of Native Hawaiian Bill Announced." *Indian Country Today,* September 28.

KAME'ELEIHIWA, LILIKALĀ. 1992. *Native Land and Foreign Desires: Pebea Lā E. Pono Ali?* Honolulu: Bishop Museum Press.

KAUANUI, J. KEHAULANI. 2008. *Hawaiian Blood: Colonialism and the Politics of Sovereignty and Indigeneity.* Durham, NC: Duke University Press.

LAENUI, POKA. 2010. "The Rediscovery of Hawaiian Sovereignty." Pages 120–28. In *Native American Voices: A Reader,* edited by Susan Lobo, Steve Talbot, and Traci L. Morris. 3rd ed. Upper Saddle River: NJ: Prentice Hall.

MARX, KARL. 1954. [1867]. *Capital.* Translated by S. Moore and E. M. Aveling. London: Lawrence & Wishert.

TRASK, HAUNANI-KAY. 1993. *From A Native Daughter: Colonialism and Sovereignty in Hawai'i.* Monroe, ME: Common Courage Press.

NOTES

1. Hawaiian words that have a long vowel are marked with a dash over the vowel, a macron. We have endeavored to adhere to this and related linguistic markings in the spelling of Hawaiian words but beg the reader's indulgence in the case of linguistic errors.

2. Lilikala Kame'eleihiwā, in her book, *Native Land and Foreign Desires* (1992, 1, footnote), capitalizes the Hawaiian Gods, Land, and Chiefs, because in traditional Hawaiian religious ideology they are all divine. We agree with her in principle, and have left these words capitalized in the Hawaiian.

REFERENCES

BECKWITH, MARTHA WARREN, trans. and ed., with a commentary by. 1972. *The Kumulipo: A Hawaiian Creation Chant.* Foreword by Katharine Luomala. Honolulu: University of Hawai'i Press.

CRAWFORD, SCOTT. 2001. "Hawaiian Kingdom Question before U.N. Security Council." Press Release of July 6, 2001.

DI ALTO, STEPHANIE J. 2002. "The Hawaiian Sovereignty Movement: New Challenges in the New Millennium." *Native American Policy Network Newsletter* 18 (2) (Fall 2002 online edition).

DOUGHERTY, MICHAEL. 1992. *To Steal a Kingdom: Probing Hawaiian History.* Waimanalo, HI: Island Style Press.

DUDLEY, MICHAEL KIONI, and KEANA KEALOHA AGARD. 1990. *A Hawaiian Nation II: A Call for Hawaiian Sovereignty.* With an introduction by John Dominis Holt. Honolulu: Na Kāne O Ka Malo Press.

DU PLESSIX GRAY, FRANCINE. 1972a. "Hawai'i, the Sugar-coated Fortress." *New Yorker.* Part I, March 4.

————. 1972b. "Hawai'i, the Sugar-coated Fortess." *New Yorker.* Part II, March 11.

FERRAR, DEREK. 2003. "Senate Indian Affairs Committee Passes Amended Hawaiian Recognition Bill." *Ka Wai Ola o OHA,* June: 8–9.

HINTON, LEANNE. 2001. "Hawaiian Language Schools." In *Native American Voices: A Reader,* edited by Susan Lobo and Steve Talbot, 520–31. Upper Saddle River, NJ: Prentice Hall. Reprinted from *News From Native California* 10 (Summer 1997).

Honolulu Weekly. 2003. "Tweakerville USA." *Honolulu Weekly* 13 (21) (May 21–27): 6–7.

Indian Country Today. 2001. "Native Hawaiian Grass-roots Movement Born." *Indian Country Today.* May 30.

KAME'ELEIHIWA, LIKKALĀ. 1992. *Native Land and Foreign Desires: Pehea Lā E Pono Ai?* Honolulu: Bishop Museum Press.

————. 2003. "The Akaka Bill: Self-Determination or Predetermination?" *Maluhia Me Ka Pono/Peace With Justice* 7 (1, April): 8–9, 14. Testimony before the Senate Committee on Indian Affairs, February 25, 2003. Published by the American Friends Service Committee, Hawai'i Area Program.

KAUANUI, J. KĒHAULANI. 2008. *Hawaiian Blood: Colonialism and the Politics of Sovereignty and Indigeneity.* Durham, NC: Duke University Press.

KELLY, MARION, and NANCY ALECK. 1997. "Mākua Means Parents: A Brief Cultural History of Mākua Valley." Brochure. Honolulu, HI: American Friends Service Committee, Hawai'i Area Program, December.

LAENUI, PŌKĀ. 2001. "The Rediscovery of Hawaiian Sovereignty." In *Native American Voices: A Reader,* edited by Susan Lobo and Steve Talbot, 141–52. 2nd ed. Upper Saddle River, NJ: Prentice-Hall. (Originally appeared in the *American Indian Culture and Research Journal* 17 (1) (1993): 79–101.)

LOBO, SUSAN, and STEVE TALBOT. 2001. *Native American Voices: A Reader.* 2nd ed. Upper Saddle River, NJ: Prentice Hall.

LOEWEN, JAMES W. 1995. *Lies My Teacher Told Me.* New York: Touchstone.

MCMURRAY, DAVID. 2002, September. "The role of Music and Dance in the Conquest and Rebirth of Native Hawaiian Culture." *Comparative Cultures: Music of Resistance & Cultures of Oppression.* 3rd ed. (Paper). Written for Anthropology 380, Comparative Cultures, a class offered at Oregon State University.

MULLINS, JOSEPH G. 1978. *Hawaiian Journey.* Honolulu: Mutual.

Native American Rights Fund (NARF). 2003. "Cross-cutting Themes in Hawai'i: Native Hawaiian Rights, Perceived Racial Differences, and the Desire to Restore Hawaiian Sovereignty." *NARF Legal Review* 28 (1): 1–11.

OSBORNE, THOMAS J. 1998. *Annexation Hawai'i: Fighting American Imperialism.* Waimanalo, HI: Island Style Press.

SHIMOKAWA, JUNE. 1998. "From Resistance to Affirmation." *Maluhia Me Ka Pono/Peace With Justice* 2 (August). Newsletter of the American Friends Service Committee, Hawai'i Area Program.

SONODA, HEALANI. 2000. "Settler Racism: Criminalization of the Native Hawaiian." *Hawaiian News* 9 (December).

Spirit of the Land: Hawai'i, Continuing Traditions. n.d. Program and teaching guide for a 28-minute video. Produced by Chevron.

TAKAKI, RONALD. 1989. *Strangers from a Different Shore: A History of Asian Americans.* New York: Penguin Books.

TALIMAN, VALERIE. 2002. "Hawaiian Natives Reinstate Kingdom" *Indian Country Today,* August 21.

TRASK, HAUNANI-KAY. 2001. "Lovely Hula Hands: Corporate Tourism and the Prostitution of Hawaiian Culture." In *Native American Voices: A Reader,* edited by Susan Lobo and Steve Talbot, 355–63. 2nd ed. Upper Saddle River, NJ: Prentice Hall.

————. 1993. *From a Native Daughter: Colonialism & Sovereignty in Hawai'i.* Monroe, ME: Common Courage Press.

U.S. National Park Service. n.d. A Sanctuary brochure on the Big Island of Hawai'i.

WEI, DEBORAH, and RACHAEL KAMEL, eds. 1998. *Resistance in Paradise: Rethinking 100 Years of U.S. involvement in the Caribbean and the Pacific.* Philadelphia: American Friends Service Committee, in cooperation with Office of Curriculum Support, School District of Philadelphia.

ZINN, HOWARD. 1999. *A People's History of the United States: 1492–Present.* New York: Perennial Classics/HarperCollins.

9

FIRST NATIONS
CONTEMPORARY INDIGENOUS ISSUES IN CANADA

Hand designs with chains to represent the First Nations being denied their rights on many Aboriginal issues.

Since most American Indian communities are ecocentric, liberation of the environment involves liberation of Native American people.

—Donald Grinde and Bruce E. Johansen, *Ecocide of Native America*

In 2005, the Canadian federal government apologized to the First Nations within its borders for government complicity in linguistic and cultural genocide, and agreed to negotiate a wide-ranging proposal to heal the damage. (First Nations is the preferred term for the aboriginal peoples of Canada.) This apology was a result of a decade and a half of soul-searching among many non-Native Canadians following the tumultuous occupation of the Mohawk settlement of Kanasatake, near Oka, Quebec, during the summer of 1990. The Mohawk warriors' standoff against Canadian Army troops and Quebec police resembled the Wounded Knee occupation in South Dakota during 1973, with the exception that blockades by Native people continued to spread across Canada during 1990. Non-Native Canadians, who often take pride in their civility, were learning that most of the land on which they lived never had been ceded by treaty, and that many of Canada's first inhabitants lived in conditions that resembled the impoverished Third World.

Canada convened the Royal Commission on Aboriginal Peoples during the 1990s, that examined the entire corpus of Native-related law in the country, as well as social and political conditions on Native reserves. The reports issued by the Royal Commission spurred the long-moribund land-claims process in Canada, and began proceedings that could result in compensation for thousands of Canadian Natives who were mistreated in boarding schools. The Royal Commission also outlined steps to recapture Native languages and cultures that had been cruelly suppressed by institutions such as the residential (boarding) school.

At the same time, Canadian Natives were challenging resource allocation in the courts, which provoked a number of rulings that could strengthen their economic base. In the far North, the Inuit won a degree of sovereignty over a new territory, Nunavut, just as many of them were learning that their homeland was imperiled by toxic chemical pollution from southern industries, as well as accelerating warming caused by rising levels of greenhouse gases, also from more southerly latitudes. (See Figure 9.1.)

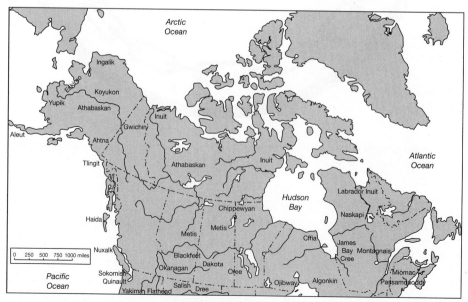

Figure 9.1 Selected Indigenous Peoples of Canada.

Many other First Nations in Canada also face acute environmental problems. The Pimicikamak Cree, for example, assert that for twenty-five years the Manitoba Hydro Power Company has been destroying their traditional lands and society with a series of dams and canals cut through wilderness to divert the flow of rivers upon which their traditional economy depends. Despite the fact that almost C$10 million worth of oil has been pumped out of their land since 1980, the five-hundred-member Indigenous Lubicon Cree community of Little Buffalo in far northern Alberta has inadequate housing, no running water, no sewage, and no public infrastructure. In the Northwest Territories, the Dene (who are related to the Navajo in the United States) have been decimated by uranium mining.

In this chapter we review the current condition and struggles of the Native peoples of Canada. Unlike the United States, the federal government of Canada has issued an official apology to the First Nations, and has paid compensation. Oppressive language policy has been reversed and is having a significant impact on Native cultures. Yet the damaging effects of colonialism run deep, especially as it concerns the threat posed by the degrading environment. All of the official apologies in the world cannot ameliorate the problems of industrial pollution and global warming that affect the lives and cultures of Canadian Natives—without a momentous shift in environmental policy. Such a shift would include a fundamental change in United States environmental policy as well, since the First Nations are, in a sense, the "down-winders" of many pollutants emanating from U.S. soil.

THEORETICAL PERSPECTIVES

The names of Indigenous groups and the case citations of Canada's legal system may sound unfamiliar to a reader from the United States, but in broad brush the concepts and theories being engaged here are very similar. Canadian Native peoples have been emerging from many years of colonialism following invasion of their homelands by European-Canadians. The recovery by Native peoples takes several forms, including the recapture of languages, compensation for abuses suffered in assimilationist boarding schools, and challenges to a legal system that has delayed addressing land-ownership issues.

As in the United States, many of the issues facing Native peoples in Canada have economic bases and involve legal challenges in the courts at all levels. As Canadian First Nations emerge from colonialism they also have been faced with survival issues related to an environment that is being rapidly degraded by industrial pollution. Perhaps nowhere is this more starkly evident than in the Arctic, where Inuit, no more than a generation or two removed from lives lacking sustained contact with the modern industrial world, are now faced with toxic contamination by chemicals brought to them by prevailing winds and ocean currents, as global warming changes their homelands (and, therefore, their lives) beyond traditional reference points of any kind.

Some terms or concepts ventured by Indigenous Studies scholars in the United States also resonate in Canada. One term that comes to mind in this context is Ward Churchill and Winona LaDuke's "radioactive colonialism," specifically with reference to the victimization of the Dene, in the Northwest Territories, by uranium mining, a situation very similar to that experienced by the Navajos in the United States (Churchill and LaDuke 1992, 241–66).

As among Native peoples in the United States, Canadian First Nations struggle to maintain traditional ways of life in the face of *ethno-ecocide*, arguing in the language of the immigrants that is connotatively loaded in favor of development (who could oppose development?), which often devastates their homelands and erodes their traditional ways of life. *Ethnocide* (or cultural genocide) refers to the destruction of Indigenous culture, including language, religion, and traditions. *Ecocide* is the destruction of the Indigenous environment. Joined together, the two concepts become ethno-ecocide, a recipe for the destruction of Indigenous society in Canada.

A vital part in the preservation of Native ways of life is the right to express Native thoughts in Native languages. An example is *pimaatisiiwin*, a Cree term used in northern Quebec in a language which has no separate word for "nature." The word means "a good life," "a continual rebirth," that includes both humans and animals, or by implication, "a way of life" (LaDuke 1999, 51). It does not mean "underdeveloped," because many Native peoples are as "developed" as they wish to be, without toxin-spewing smokestacks, highways, and hydroelectric dams (LaDuke 1999, 49–70). We will return to a consideration of these concepts at the end of the chapter.

HISTORY AND STATUS OF CANADA'S FIRST NATIONS: A PROFILE

The 2006 Canadian census found 1,172,790 people who self-identified as "Aboriginal," about 3.8 percent of the nation's total population. The Native growth rate was six times higher than that of the previous 1996 census, which showed a growth rate of 45 percent.

There are three main categories of Canada's First Nations peoples: Indian, Inuit, and Métis. Dickason (2009, 452), in a comprehensive account of Canada's First Nations, found that much of the recent population growth has been among the Métis and the Inuit according to the 2006 census. The Métis population nearly doubled since the census of 1996 to an estimated 389,785, which constitutes 33 or 33 percent of Canada's total Aboriginal population. In the same period the Inuit population increased by 26 percent to 50,485. And over half a million aboriginal people in Canada are legally recognized as Indians. Yet Dickason contends that given Canada's history racism and of nonreporting its aboriginal population, these figures are probably an undercount. The true total aboriginal population (Métis, Inuit, and Indians) is perhaps double the 2006 census figure, somewhere between two and three million people, or about 10 percent of the total population of Canada.

Before the arrival of Europeans, there were, of course, many thousands more Indigenous people. Some scholars believe that a major decrease in the aboriginal population occurred in the 1500s, as a result of the rapid spread of European-introduced diseases, preceding the actual incursion of Europeans into Native territory.

The imperial designs of two mercantile capitalist nations, France and Great Britain, have left a heavy imprint on the fate of the First Nations of Canada. Beginning in the 1600s, the movement of Europeans across that part of North America that became Canada was initially from east to west, and then later, from south to north. Conquest took place in several stages: first, exploration along the unorganized frontier; second, trade and Christian missionary activity; third, European settlement with the resulting displacement of the Native population; and fourth, administrative control of the subject Indigenous peoples.

In the early historic period, the British created treaties, while the French made few treaties with the Indian nations. Both colonial powers, however, created military alliances with Native peoples to carry out their economic objectives in North America, the French allying with the Mi'kmaq, Malecite, Ojibwa, and Wyandot (Huron), while the British sought support from the Iroquois. The French emphasized the fur trade, intermarried with Indian women, and assimilated the Native peoples into French culture. The British, who were more interested in farming and settlement, usually came as families, bringing their wives with them. They were convinced of their racial superiority over the Native inhabitants.

In contrast to the colonization of the United States, the European invasion of Canada was less populous and slower because of the harsher northern climate, and tended to impact mainly the more temperate, southern edge of Canadian North America. "Indians in the south were enclaved in small reserves and held as irrelevant to the development of Canadian society" (Price 1979, 214). And in the northern arctic and subarctic, the Native peoples were drawn into the fur trade economy with the Europeans.

Today, there are six hundred First Nations bands with an average membership of five hundred persons per band. Each band elects a band chief and a representative band council. There are 2,293 separate reserves, with a total area of ten thousand square miles. Less than 30 percent of the total Native population live off the reserves, mainly in the urban areas of Quebec, southern Ontario, southern Alberta, and the Vancouver area of British Columbia. Many Indians divide their time between jobs in the city and their homes on the reserves. Today these diverse Indian nations are represented by the Assembly of First Nations (AFN), formerly the National Indian Brotherhood.

Language and Cultural Areas

Originally there were approximately fifty different languages spoken, representing eleven language families. Algonkian is the largest, with Cree and Ojibway being the two most representative languages. Algonkian speakers are found in the provinces of eastern Canada, while Cree and Ojibway are spread throughout the south central part of the country. Another large language family is Athabascan, whose related languages are spread across northwestern Canada. Siouan languages are found on the Canadian Plains, and Iroquoian languages are situated around the Great Lakes. Many smaller language families are found in British Columbia. Inuktitut is an Eskimoan language of northern Canada. "Only three—Cree, Ojibway, and Inuktitut—are spoken over large areas today and are considered to have excellent chances of survival" (McMillan 1994, 224).

Today, the Algonkian Indians are scattered in small reserves across a large portion of the country. Deep religious respect for the animals hunted is fundamental to Algonkian culture. This spiritual belief is found among the Ojibway of the western Great Lakes, the Cree of northern Ontario and Quebec, the Inu (Naskapi and Montagnais) of Labrador and adjacent Quebec, and the Mi'kmaq and Maliseet of the east coast Maritime Provinces.

The original Iroquoian societies of the Great Lakes, as represented by the Wyandot (Huron) and Haudenosaunee (Iroquois), were hunters and farmers. The Huron and others were largely annihilated in the Beaver Wars during the early contact period, when the Iroquois Confederation eliminated the Wyandot, Tobacco, and Erie in order to dominate the fur trade. Most Iroquoian peoples of the eastern Great Lakes are today represented by the Six Nations Iroquois, who arrived after the American Revolution. The Iroquoian Mohawk were staunch British loyalists and subsequently fled to Canada under their leader Joseph Brant after the victory by the American revolutionaries. Most settled along the Grand River in southern Ontario. The majority of Canadian Iroquois living today are members of the Haudenosaunee (Six Nations) Confederacy.

The Plains includes homelands of the Blackfoot Confederacy—Blackfoot Blood, and Peigun—and their former foes, the Plains Cree and Ojibway—who hunted the buffalo. When their numbers were reduced by disease and the buffalo were gone, these Indian groups were forced to sign treaties ceding their lands, and then were confined to reserves. Once on the reserves, traditional customs and beliefs, such as the Sun Dance, were suppressed.

The Métis are the product of cohabitation of European (usually French-Canadian) male fur traders with Native women, particularly Cree. They are found mainly in what became the Prairie provinces of Canada. "As the fur trade moved westward, many French-speaking men followed, establishing stable unions with Cree and Ojibway women. Kinship ties from such unions provided alliances that facilitated trade" (McMillan 1994, 235). In the north, English and Scottish employees of the Hudson's Bay Company established similar unions with Cree women. By the end of the eighteenth century, a large mixed-blood population was living around the Great Lakes. A depleted fur trade led many of them to migrate westward, eventually becoming bison hunters and provisioners for the Hudson's Bay and Northwest fur companies. Despite their cultural and religious differences (the French-speaking Métis were Roman Catholic, and the English-Scottish Métis Protestant), they eventually forged a single, ethnic identity. Today, Canada's "forgotten people" are undergoing a cultural and political awakening.

The Canadian Plateau lies between the Rocky Mountains and the West Coast range. Representative peoples included the Kutenai in the east, and the Salish societies of the interior. Traditional economy involved a seasonal round of hunting, fishing, and gathering. The 1858 gold rush in the Fraser Canyon became a major disruptive force, and smallpox and other diseases seriously reduced the Native population of the region. During the 1870s and 1880s, they were confined to small, scattered reserves. Nevertheless, "the Plateau groups never ceded their lands through treaties. Today, land claims are among the most contentious issues, along with such other grievances as legal restrictions on Native fisheries" (McMillan 1994, 231).

The Northwest Coast was the most linguistically diverse and one of the heaviest-populated regions of aboriginal Canada. The Native groups relied on the bounty of the ocean, beach, and rivers for economic sustenance, with salmon the main food source. Large dugout canoes plied the waterways between villages built of large, plank houses, virtual monuments in cedar. In the north were the Haida of Queen Charlotte Island, the Tsimshian on the mainland, and the Tlingit in southeastern Alaska and Canada. Further south were the Kwakiutl, Bella Coola (Nuxalk), Squamish, and others. Northwest Coast peoples place great emphasis on inherited rank and privileges, a major ceremony being the potlatch. Only a few treaties were signed, and these with the Indian peoples of Vancouver Island in the 1850s. The First Nations of British Columbia today are politically active with land rights being the principal issue. A cultural renewal has marked recent decades.

The Canadian subarctic contained Native peoples of the Athabaskan language family, ranging across northern Canada from the west side of Hudson Bay to interior Alaska. The Native peoples were hunters who lived in small, mobile groups, their cultural adaptations differing with the particular environment. They are represented by the Chipewyan in the east, the Beaver in the south, and the Tahltan in northwestern British Columbia. Many Athabascan communities today rely on a combination of trapping, government assistance, and wage labor. "Native political organizations, such as the Dene Nation in the Northwestern Territories, are fighting for recognition of Native land claims and right to self-determination" (McMillan 1994, 234).

North of the tree line are the Inuit, the aboriginal peoples of the Arctic. Inuktitut, the Inuit language, is still widely spoken across the entire region. In earlier times, all groups relied on hunting land and sea mammals and fishing. Caribou and seals were the primary food source. In the Mackenzie Delta, whaling was an important economic activity. In the central Arctic were the Copper, Netsilik, Iglulik, and Inuit of Baffinland, with other groups located in northern Quebec and Labrador. Moravian missionaries were active in Labrador and devised an orthography for writing the

Inuktitut language. The whaling industry collapsed around 1910, and World War II brought a major military presence in the Arctic. When it became increasingly difficult for the Inuit to continue their subsistence economy, the Canadian government pressured Inuit groups to move into administrative settlements, but these small, urban enclaves soon became known as "ghettos of the North." Land claims have become a major issue in the contemporary political struggle. The Inuit of the Northwest Territories have successfully negotiated a self-governing homeland, Nunavut, with a status similar to a Canadian province.

Indians

Beginning in 1850, Great Britain signed a series of treaties with Indian groups whereby it gained control over most aboriginal territory in southern Canada. In exchange, the Indian bands were guaranteed small reserve lands and perpetual trusteeship under the colonial management of the British Crown. Additional reserves were established until 1923. The Indians also received one-time payments and annuities in cash and goods, and the promise of schools and federal services.

When Canada confederated, the Constitution Act of 1867 made the federal government responsible for "Indians and Lands reserved for Indians." The Indian Acts of 1868 and 1876 defined the relationship between the Native peoples and the federal government by setting up an Indian Department, and creating the legal machinery for colonial management. The 1876 Indian Act "provided government control over all aspects of Indian life, and served as a vehicle of assimilation by legally suppressing Native ceremonies such as the Sun Dance on the Plains and the potlatch on the Pacific coast. Although the act was extensively rewritten in 1951 and prohibitions on Native traditions were dropped, the act remains essentially a nineteenth-century colonial document" (McMillan 1994, 237).

The Canadian Indian population was legally divided into three categories: status, treaty, and non-status. A "status Indian" is a person registered or entitled to be registered as an Indian for purposes of the 1876 Indian Act which sets forth a policy of assimilation. Today, "status Indians are members of 633 'bands' across Canada; 'bands' are legal-administrative bodies established under the Indian Act that correspond generally to traditional tribal and kinship group affinities" (Long and Chiste 1994, 335).

"Treaty Indians are those persons who are registered members of, or can prove descent from, a band that signed a treaty. Most status Indians are treaty Indians" (Long and Chiste 1994, 335).

"Non-status Indians are those persons of Indian ancestry and cultural affiliation who have lost their right to be registered under the Indian Act" (Long and Chiste 1994, 335). The most common reason was when a status Indian woman married a non-Indian man; she was then considered enfranchised and no longer an Indian. This inequality, reflecting a racist and sexist bias in Canadian law, was reversed in 1985 when the Indian Act was amended to restore registered Indian status to those Indian women and their children. The reinstatement process resulted in approximately ninety-two thousand Indians being added to the registry.

In spite of reform, the colonial nature of the Indian Act remains essentially unchanged. The administration of Indian lands and finances still lies mainly with the federal minister of Indian and Northern Affairs. Indians are also legally subject to all provincially enacted laws, except where such laws conflict with provisions of the Indian Act or treaty rights. "The socio-economic conditions on Indian reserves have been described as more typical of Third World countries. . . . Indian life expectancy is ten years below the national average. The suicide rate is double that of the general population, and the rate of violent death is triple" (Long and Chiste 1994, 339).

One feature that distinguishes Canada from the United States is that outside of the Yukon and Northwest Territories, the federal government owns very little Crown land area within its borders. As a consequence, land claims by treaty Indians are directed against the provinces.

Inuit

The Inuit were excluded from the terms of the Indian Act until a 1934 Supreme Court decision, *Re Eskimos*. Then they were neglected by the Canadian government until the 1950s, although World War II had already begun to impact their traditional life with the establishment of military bases throughout the North. "The Inuit economy has undergone an enormous change in the last forty years, from a hunting and trapping base to diversification involving tourism, arts and crafts, and development of both renewable and nonrenewable resources" (Long and Chiste 1994, 342).

The Inuit constitute a majority of the population in northern Canada, and they are represented by a strong Indigenous organization, the Inuit Tapirisat of Canada (ITC). The organization was formed in 1971 as the "voice of the north" to press for a land settlement. Today, the Inuit of the eastern Arctic have successfully achieved a self-governing territory, Nunavut, which was created in 1991 (see Figure 9.2). The settlement involved a payment of C$500 million

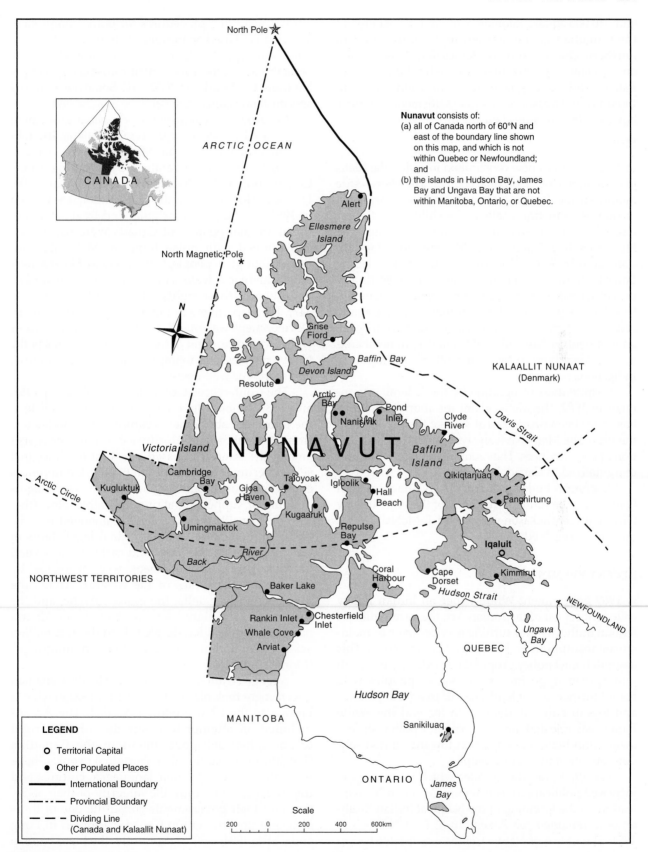

Figure 9.2 Nunavut.

and 350,000 square kilometers of land, a vast area of the Canadian Arctic. Earlier, in 1975, the Inuit of northern Quebec and the James Bay Cree signed an agreement giving them exclusive hunting and fishing rights, language and education rights in Inuktitut, and a cash and royalties settlement. In return, however, they relinquished any further land claims.

Métis

In 1982, Canada's new constitution included the Métis in its definition of "aboriginal people." The Métis reside mainly in the Prairie provinces and the Northwest territories. Sometimes called "the children of the fur trade," the mixed-blood Métis revolted when the Hudson's Bay Company sold their homeland to Canada in 1869. The Red River Resistance was led by Louis Riel, Jr., who sought land title for the Métis and provincial status for the Prairie territories. He attempted to set up a provisional government when Canada refused his demands. He was hanged for treason by the government in November 1985, and is remembered as a national hero to Métis and other contemporary Indigenous peoples.

Despite their recognition by the federal government in 1982, the Métis' claim for aboriginal status has so far been unsuccessful. Unlike the Indians and the Inuit, the Métis have always been under jurisdiction of the provinces. They remain impoverished and marginalized in Canadian society.

A comprehensive history of Canada's First Nations can be found in the book of the same title by Olive Patricia Dickason with David T. McNab (2009), now in its fourth edition.

RECENT EVENTS

A 1969 government White Paper on Indian Policy called for repeal of the Indian Act, the termination of federal authority and turning services over to mainstream institutions and provincial governments. This assimilationist policy proposal immediately met with widespread opposition from Native peoples who feared further loss of lands, loss of treaty obligations, and loss of cultural identity. In the end the White Paper was rejected, and government policy shifted away from blatant assimilation toward limited self-determination for Native peoples.

The 1970s and the decades which followed saw increased political activism among Canadian Natives, leading to the founding of the National Indian Brotherhood, renamed the Assembly of First Nations in 1981. The Office of Native Claims was established in

1974. It instituted procedures for both "comprehensive claims," based on the idea of aboriginal title to the land, and "specific claims," "based on lawful treaty obligations and the government's mismanagement of band assets" (Waldman 2000, 231). Some five hundred specific land claims have yet to be adjudicated.

Confronted by a growing separatist movement in Quebec by French-speaking Canadians, the Liberal government of Prime Minister Pierre Trudeau set out to renovate federalism by adopting a new Constitution and a Charter of Rights, similar to the U.S. Bill of Rights. When the Constitution was revised in 1982, the existing aboriginal and treaty rights of the aboriginal peoples of Canada were recognized and affirmed, with Indian, Inuit, and Métis all identified as aboriginal people, "and a series of First Ministers Conferences were scheduled to work towards a definition of these rights" (Long and Chiste 1994, 347). The Department of Indian Affairs and Northern Development was mandated to carry out measures which would respond to the needs and desires of the Native peoples, and to improve their social, cultural, and economic well-being.

The Conferences took place in 1983, 1984, 1985, and 1987, among the government's first ministers, the four main aboriginal organizations, and leaders from the Yukon and Northwest Territories. Chief among the issues discussed was that of aboriginal self-government. Unfortunately, the Conferences ended without recognizing additional amendments defining or supporting aboriginal rights. Nevertheless, the Constitution Act of 1982, amended in 1984, had a dramatic affect on aboriginal legal status in Canada. "During the 1980s and early 1990s, several immense land claim settlements were negotiated by the aboriginal peoples of the western Arctic, the MacKenzie River delta, the eastern Arctic, and the Yukon. . . . The eight Métis settlements in Alberta have also received fee simple title to the 1.28 million acres of land that comprise their communities" (Morse 1994, 515).

A renewed attempt at federalism by the Canadian government took place on August 16, 1992 in what is known as the Charlottetown Accord. The Accord included an attempt to insert the inherent right to aboriginal self-government in the Canadian Constitution by stating that aboriginal peoples "have the right to promote their languages, cultures and traditions and to ensure the integrity of their societies, and their governments constitute one of three orders of government in Canada" (quoted in Long and Chiste 1994, 349). Significantly, the Métis were to be included for programs and funding under the Indian Act. However, in a national referendum, the Charlottetown Accord was rejected by Canadian voters, including a significant number of Native voters. Some Indian voters did not believe that the promised reforms went far enough. Others feared that Constitutional reform would weaken the treaty relationship, and still others opposed the plan to give the Métis a share of government funding.

Regardless of the significant gains made over the last several decades, Morse (1994, 516) concludes that Canadian Native peoples "are in a significantly weaker legal position than U.S. Indian tribes despite a history of less military conflict, constitutional guarantees, and greater political weight, and the fact that they comprise a five times larger percentage of the Canadian population than do U.S. Indians." Furthermore, overall life expectancy for Canadian Natives is about eight years less than the national average, suicides are six times the national rate, and Natives are incarcerated at more than three times the national rate (Waldman 2000, 231). In recent years, "increased industrial activity and resource development projects in remote wilderness areas has meant new environmental damage, erosion of the Native land base, and disruption of Native ways of life" (Waldman 2000, 232).

The Right to Recapture Indigenous Language

Indigenous language is an integral part of culture and Native identity. The Canadian government's recent policy reversal, from a policy of assimilation to one respecting Indigenous language rights, therefore represents a major achievement in the Native political struggle.

Frank Iacobucci, a former Canadian Supreme Court justice charged with crafting the details of the 2005 National Apology to Canada's First Nations, said he would address one essential human right: the full and equitable restoration of First Nations' linguistic rights. Linguistic rights have been a major part of Canada's attempt to undo the damage of residential (boarding) schools, which aimed to exterminate children's knowledge of their Indigenous languages. The schools took children from their homes and punished them for speaking their Native languages in a determined attempt "to sever normal intergenerational cultural transmission between the children and their families and communities, and to forcibly deny them access to the rich spiritual resources, humor and storytelling that had been part of community life since time immemorial" (Martin 2005 n.p.).

Canada's apology should be followed by programs that include teaching of Native languages in many schools, both as a subject of study and as a language of instruction, including, according to Ian Martin, an associate professor of English at Glendon College, York University, "a right to aboriginal-language immersion programs in communities where the language is seriously endangered" (Martin 2005). Martin also advocates enactment of an Aboriginal Languages Revitalization and Affirmation Act as part of the social-renewal package. "One component," wrote Martin in the *Toronto Star*, "should be the establishment of an Aboriginal Languages Commissioner's office to report annually on the linguistic situation within aboriginal communities (both on and off reserve), and to evaluate steps taken and steps needed to further the goals of the act" (Martin 2005).

In some cases, language revitalization in Canada already has become part of general community life, as at Akwesasne, a Mohawk reserve straddling Canada's border with New York State, where the community newspaper, *Indian Time*, a weekly, carries regular Mohawk-language lessons covering everyday situations, such as the weather: "*Teioweratasehne*, [accent over the second-to-the-last "e"] "It was a windstorm;" "*Ionen'onkion:ne* [accent over the last "o,"] "it was hailing." A quarter of the Mohawks at Akwesasne speak Mohawk with some degree of fluency. Radio Station CKON at Akwesasne (97.3 FM) broadcasts some of its talk shows in Mohawk and receives calls from as far away as the Kanesatake and Kahnawake Mohawk reserves in Canada. Children's books are being published in Mohawk by the Circle of Knowledge Office, Akwesasne Mohawk Board of Education.

Kanien'keha, the Mohawk language, also is being studied by Mohawks at Kahnawake using a computer-based program called Rosetta Stone. The Rosetta Stone method, developed by a Virginia-based company in 1994, uses Native speakers and everyday language on audio, as well as in written text, writing, and speaking exercises. Rosetta Stone has been used for many years to teach European and Asian languages such as Hebrew, Thai, Pashto, and Arabic, as well as Latin. Mohawk is the first American aboriginal language available on Rosetta Stone. The company also is working with the Seminoles of Florida and an Inuit community in northwestern Alaska to develop instructional programs in their respective languages.

The Mohawk reserve at Kahnawake, near Montreal, provided the translators, editors and aboriginal speakers to produce the content. The company provided a template and adapted the software. Rosetta

Stone charged US$240 for a Level 1 package of three hundred hours of instruction, equivalent to one year of in-class training, and another US$170 for Level 2 (Stastna 2004). Only about 10 percent of roughly seven thousand Mohawks at Kahnawake spoke Mohawk in 2005; thirty years before that, more than 20 percent spoke the language (Stastna 2004). Most of the remaining speakers are elderly. The Rosetta Stone Endangered Language Project was part of a five-year, $6.5-million commitment to revive the Mohawk language, part of a broader initiative by the Canadian federal government. The project also included TV and radio programming, adult immersion courses, and workplace language training.

The Lobster War, the Marshall Decision, and Emerging Canadian First Nations' Treaty Rights

A Canadian Supreme Court ruling supporting aboriginal subsistence rights has electrified debate over Native American economic potential and sparked a non-Indian backlash. The immediate flashpoint was the Burnt Church Mi'kmaq Reserve in New Brunswick, where non-Indian lobstermen have trashed several thousand Native lobster traps. Non-Natives also desecrated a sacred site, and at least three people were injured in scuffles associated with the "lobster war."

The Canadian Supreme Court's Marshall decision, announced September 17, 1999, guarantees Canada's first nations access to the natural resources of their aboriginal territories for subsistence purposes, the basis of economic infrastructure. The ruling is similar to some in the United States, notably the historic Boldt decision in favor of Indian fishing rights in the Pacific Northwest, handed down in 1974, and later affirmed by the U.S. Supreme Court. (See Chapter 7.) If anything, the Marshall decision is broader than the U.S. ruling, because it is not restricted to a single resource, such as fish.

As in the Boldt decision, the Canadian Supreme Court in the Marshall case attempted to determine what the original treaties meant to their signers. Both decisions also invoked an aboriginal right to a reasonable standard of living from fishing. In the United States, this standard has been interpreted to include livelihood by commercial sale of fish, which also figures into the Canadian case. As in the United States, the meaning of these terms has been left to judicial interpretation. Boldt's ruling was strictly limited initially to salmon and steelhead (and later expanded to shellfish), leaving little legal wiggle room. In the Canadian case, the scope of the Marshall case was left wide open in the initial ruling, and then tempered.

Two months after its initial decision, the Supreme Court of Canada issued a clarification of the Marshall decision denying that the ruling granted Indigenous communities aboriginal access to forestry, mineral, and oil resources on government-owned lands. The Canadian Supreme Court, in a 6–0 ruling, said that its original decision had been misinterpreted by Indigenous groups, which asserted that it gave the Mi'kmaq free access to all fish and game in eastern Canada and made them immune from government regulations.

The second decision generally restricted the court's action in Marshall to fishing rights. The court also said that Indigenous fishermen on the East Coast of Canada are subject to federal regulations, which could include closure of fisheries, as they exercise their treaty rights to hunt, fish, and gather resources for a "moderate livelihood." The court said that the Canadian federal government could step in to ensure interethnic fairness and recognition of the "historical reliance upon, and participation in, the fishery by non-aboriginal groups" (Caldwell 1999).

The Supreme Court issued its clarification after Nova Scotia Natives claimed rights to large tracts of land throughout the province in a case that could have transformed the logging industry in the same fashion that the 1999 Marshall decision reshaped the Atlantic fishery. Lawyers for thirty-five Natives who were convicted of illegally harvesting lumber told the Nova Scotia Supreme Court in Halifax on February 4, 2002, according to a Canadian newspaper account, "that they have aboriginal title spelled out in eighteenth-century treaties to cut and sell trees on Crown property" (Canadian Press 2002).

As the legal limits of Marshall were being defined by the Canadian Supreme Court, its street-level implications were being played out in Burnt Church, where Indian and non-Indian fishing people jostled over the resources that Canada's legal system sought to allocate. The incidents on the Burnt Church reserve brought back memories for anyone who observed fishing-rights disputes in the U.S. states of Washington and Wisconsin between the 1960s and 1980s. "Substitute 'walleye' for 'lobsters,' and it seems about the same," remarked two activists from Wisconsin. (McNutt and Grossman September 5, 2000). Images of Canadian officials swamping Native boats off Burnt Church recalled similar memories three decades earlier, during the fish-ins at Frank's Landing, Washington.

The Mi'kmaqs, who have some of the highest unemployment rates in Canada (up to 85 percent in some communities), have been testing the Marshall decision in several ways. The most notable assay into Mi'kmaq economic development has been lobster, but some Mi'kmaq also have been catching salmon and cutting timber on Crown (publicly owned) lands as well. Their attorneys have hinted that they believe that even mining activities could be covered under the Marshall ruling. They also assert that the Mi'kmaqs' proper geographic scope for assertion of resource rights is the entire province of Nova Scotia, because the Mi'kmaqs used all of the present-day Canadian province (as well as other adjacent lands) as aboriginal territory.

The landmark case, *R. v. Marshall (No. 1)*, was initiated after a Nova Scotia Mi'kmaq, Donald Marshall, Jr., of Cape Breton, Nova Scotia, was arrested for taking and selling 210 kilograms of eel out of season. The Supreme Court overturned a lower-court conviction of Marshall, finding that Native peoples have a right to fish regardless of season, with or without a license. Marshall knew the Canadian legal system quite well before the Supreme Court ruled on the fishing-rights case that now bears his name. He served more than eleven years in prison for the murder of Sandy Seale; later evidence traced the murder to Roy Ebsary. The long view of legal history clearly indicated that Marshall had been framed by police. The case became the subject of a prizewinning Canadian documentary film.

Marshall's fishing case initially did not fare well in Nova Scotia's provincial courts. During March of 1997, the Nova Scotia Court of Appeal upheld a provincial court ruling that he had illegally caught and sold 210 kilograms of eels. All three appeals-court judges ruled in favor of the federal government's position, against Marshall. Judges in both courts concluded that Marshall couldn't maintain a defense based on the 1760 treaty for having caught eels outside of a season defined by the Canadian government.

On September 17, 1999, however, the Supreme Court ruled 5 to 2 that Marshall should not have been convicted of illegally catching eels because the Treaty of Swegatchy, signed during 1760 as Montreal was being surrendered to the British, gave the Native peoples a right to hunt and fish freely. While references to the Treaty exist in archival documents, all copies of the document's actual text have been lost. "It's a great shot in the arm and a major milestone in the history of the Mi'kmaq people," said Bruce Wildsmith, one of Marshall's attorneys, regarding the Marshall decision. "Mind you, it's only as good as what governments and courts make of it" (Johansen 2004).

The Supreme Court's ruling in Marshall's case caused an immediate impact in Mi'kmaq country. Lobster traps came out of storage. During the fall following the Supreme Court's decision, Native lobster fishermen at Burnt Church set traps after the province's official season had ended. (The official season lasts six months and ends June 30.)

Asked his reaction by two reporters from the Toronto *Star*, Donald Marshall called the non-Indian response "racist." He continued: "If . . . Canadians don't accept what's happened, then it's too goddamned bad. I proved my point, and the truth hurts, I guess." The reporters, Valerie Lawton and Kelly Toughill, wrote that Marshall made this statement with "eyes wet, body shaking and . . . voice trembling." "I proved my point," he said, "and I guess it hurts." (Lawton and Toughill 1999, n.p.)

The Supreme Court ruling in the Marshall case left two important issues open to interpretation. First, what is meant by a harvest suitable for a "moderate livelihood?" In the Marshall case, the Canadian Supreme Court said that the treaty limited the Mi'kmaq's fishing-harvest rights to daily needs, including "food, clothing, and housing, supplemented by a few amenities" (Mofina 1999, A-3).

The second question left unanswered in the Marshall decision was: which particular resources are subject to the decision? While the Mi'kmaqs asserted that logging is covered, some officials of the Nova Scotia provincial government disagreed. For example, Brad Green, provincial aboriginal affairs minister, asserted that the Marshall decision refers specifically to hunting and fishing, but not to logging. (The Supreme Court opinion does refer to "gathering.") Green also asserted that all hunting and fishing rights, Native and not, are subject to reasonable restrictions, such as conservation needs.

As resource-based conflicts surfaced among Mi'kmaqs, their attorneys were preparing to argue in court that the Mi'kmaqs own the entire province of Nova Scotia because none of the province has been ceded by treaty. This is a crucial question in Canada, where the transfer of only a small part of the land was accompanied by treaty negotiations, a much lower proportion than in the United States. By various estimates, roughly 85 percent of Quebec, for example, (most of the province outside major urban areas) never was ceded by treaties. Wildsmith said this is the "next phase" of the Marshall decision. "Nova Scotia and the Maritime provinces are prime candidates for having unceded aboriginal title," said Wildsmith. "They [the Mi'kmaq] were using and occupying all of Nova Scotia and they never did anything in their treaties or otherwise to give up their interest in that land" (Toughill 2000, n.p.).

During early March 2001, a provincial court judge ruled that Native peoples do not have historic rights to vast stretches of land throughout Nova Scotia. In a decision read to about one hundred people crowding his courtroom, Judge Patrick Curran ruled that the Mi'kmaqs were guilty of illegally harvesting lumber in the province and do not possess aboriginal title to those areas of land.

Curran's ruling was not a complete repudiation of the Marshall decision, nor of the treaty on which it was based. This decision meant that Native people cannot harvest trees on Crown land without government authorization. The case was being watched closely by other provinces. "The eighteenth-century Mi'kmaq might have had some claim to coastal lands . . . but those lands did not include any of the cutting sites," Judge Curran said in his ruling (Canadian Press 2001).

"We Are Sorry": Winning Compensation for Residential School Abuses

"On June 11, 2008, the Prime Minister of Canada rose in the House of Commons and made history with three words: 'We are sorry.' . . . The apology was for the many harms wrought on stolen children by the residential schools since the nineteenth century" (Dickason 2009, 427).

Canadian officials sent delegations south of the border to study boarding schools in the United States before establishing their own system, returning with plans for schools that used words such as "firmness" and "discipline" as codes for policies that often utilized beatings and sexual abuse (Milloy 1999, 43). The Canadian minister of Indian affairs, Frank Oliver, forecast in 1908 that the residential school system would "elevate the Indian from his condition of savagery" and "make him a self-supporting member of the state, and eventually a citizen in good standing" (Johansen 2000a, 12).

From the 1870s to the 1980s, generations of aboriginal children were forced to leave their families to attend church-run, government-funded schools meant to prepare them for daily life in mainstream Canadian society. By the early twenty-first-century, hundreds of Canadian Native American were suing churches and the federal government because of maltreatment at these schools.

An estimated eighty-seven thousand people who attended the schools were still alive as of May 2005; roughly twelve thousand had filed for compensation.

The Assembly of First Nations had recommended a C$10,000 payout to each former student, plus C$3,000 for each year each person attended a residential school. The total bill for such a settlement could total more than $4 billion Canadian dollars. This proposal was accepted by Canada's federal government in July, 2005. In the meantime, the Canadian firm Merchant Law Group had won C$350,000 for one client, identified only as "H.L." the largest individual settlement to date, in *H.L. v. Canada (Attorney General)*.

Even after decades, the memories of Native Americans who were forced to attend Canadian boarding schools have a searing quality. "It was like jail," Warner Scout, who was fifty-four years of age in 1999, told the *Calgary Herald*. "The scar will be there for the rest of our lives" (Lowey 1999, A-1). Scout, who is one of the many thousands of Canadian Natives seeking legal redress for boarding school abuses, recalled regular beatings and taunts that he was "an ugly savage" (Lowey 1999, A-1).

More than one hundred thousand Native American students attended residential schools across Canada. Most of these schools were funded by the Canadian federal government and operated by employees of the Roman Catholic, Anglican, Presbyterian, and United churches. Scout was taken from his adopted family to attend the St. Paul residential school, operated by the Anglican Church of Canada on the Blood Reserve near Lethbridge, in southern Alberta. There, he said, "Teaching . . . was beaten into us" (Lowey 1999, A-1). Scout watched as one Indian student was forced to eat his own vomit after he threw up into a bowl of porridge. Students who wet their beds had urine rubbed in their faces, and those who spoke the Blackfoot language had their heads shaven.

Jackie Blackface, who was fifty-two in 1999, recalled being beaten with a tractor's fan belt at an Anglican school on the Siksika First Nation reserve east of Calgary. Federal Canadian law at the time gave the Indian agent on each Native reserve authority to enter private homes and order children aged seven or older into residential schools. Parents who did not cooperate were threatened with time in jail.

Royal Commission on Aboriginal Peoples

Why has a drive to apologize and compensate for the abuses of boarding schools developed in Canada while the issue has been virtually untouched in the United States? The seeds were sown in 1990, during a summer of fire and iron at Oka, Quebec, on and near the Kanesatake Mohawk reserve. That confrontation over a long-ignored land claim reverberated across

Canada during and after 1990, causing intense soul-searching by many non-Native Canadians. This wave of questioning expressed itself in the appointment of the Royal Commission on Aboriginal Peoples, which, in 1996, published a six volume, five-thousand-page report on the many ways in which Native Peoples had been dispossessed of their lands rights during Canadian history. The report presented a twenty-year plan for Canada's aboriginals at a cost of C$38 billion, and First Nations peoples responded enthusiastically.

Part of this report (Volume 1, Chapter 10) documented the abuses of the boarding schools, providing a basis for the establishment of a C$350 million "healing fund" by Canada's federal government, as well as a tidal wave of lawsuits. The healing fund is reserved for community projects, not for individual compensation.

The graphic sexual nature of boarding school abuses shocked many Canadians. Their sense of disgust was not alleviated by the fact that many of the abuses took place at the hands of priests, nuns, and other clerics. The scope of the abuse also has shocked Canadians. The Royal Commission found that abuse was systemic, not occasional or accidental. Thousands of Native young people are said to have died in the schools, and thousands more were scarred for life by physical and sexual abuse. The aboriginal leader George Manuel, a residential school graduate, contends that the schools were "the laboratory and production line of the colonial system . . . the colonial system that was designed to make room for European expansion into a vast empty wilderness needed an Indian population that it could describe as lazy and shiftless . . . the colonial system required such an Indian for casual labor" (Royal Commission 1999).

The Royal Commission on Aboriginal Peoples found that the residential schools' concerted campaign to obliterate aboriginal languages, traditions and beliefs, and its vision of radical resocialization, were compounded by mismanagement and underfunding, the provision of inferior educational services and woeful mistreatment, neglect and abuse of many children—facts that were readily known to the department and the churches throughout the history of the school system.

The Canadian residential school system was designed to transform Native children into Europeans from the ground up, very similar to the U.S. system. In the words of the Royal Commission's report, their purpose was:

[To] release [the children] from the shackles that tied them to their parents, communities and cultures. The civilizers in the churches and the department understood this and, moreover, that it would not be accomplished simply by bringing the children into the school. Rather it required a concerted attack on the ontology, on the basic cultural patterning of the children and on their worldview. They had to be taught to see and understand the world as a European place within which only European values and beliefs had meaning; thus the wisdom of their cultures would seem to them only savage superstition. (Royal Commission 1999)

The main enforcement mechanism in this transformation from so-called permissive aboriginal life to White Canadian discipline was punishment, much of it violent. In 1943, the principal of St. George's School (on the Fraser River, just north of Lyttons, B.C.) disclosed that a set of shackles had been used routinely "to chain runaways to the bed." Furthermore, "At the heart of the vision of residential education—of the school as home and sanctuary of motherly care—there was a stark contradiction, an inherent element of savagery in the mechanics of civilizing the children. The very language in which the vision was couched revealed what would have to be the essentially violent nature of the school system in its assault on child and culture. The basic premise of resocialization, of the great transformation from 'savage' to 'civilized', was violent" (Royal Commission 1999).

In 1936, G. Barry, a district inspector of schools in British Columbia, described a residential school in Port Alberni on Vancouver Island, "where every member of staff carried a strap," and where "children have never learned to work without punishment" (Royal Commission 1999). In 1896, according to the Royal Commission's report, Agent D. L. Clink refused to return a child to the Red Deer school because he feared "he would be abused." Without reprimand from the principal, a teacher had beaten children severely on several occasions, one of whom had to be hospitalized. "Such brutality," Clink concluded, "should not be tolerated for a moment" and "would not be tolerated in a white school for a single day in any part of Canada" (Royal Commission 1999).

The Royal Commission also included a report by a senior official in western Canada, David Laird, on Norway House, recorded during 1907, which described "frequent whippings" over an eight-year period of a young boy, Charlie Clines, for bedwetting. The severity of his punishment was not, Laird asserted, "in accordance with Christian methods." Clines hated the new Anglo world that was being thrust on him so much that he ran away from the school and slept in weather so severe that he lost several frozen toes.

In 1902, Johnny Sticks found his son, Duncan, dead of exposure, after he fled from the Williams Lake, British Columbia, industrial school. Nearly four decades later, in 1937 at the Lejac school, four boys ran away and were found frozen to death on the lake within sight of their community. They were wearing only summer clothes. In both cases, investigations uncovered a history of neglect and violence in evidence given by staff, children, and some graduates. Some students complained that they were given rotten, worm-ridden meat and punished if they didn't eat it.

During 1921, a visiting nurse at Crowstand School discovered nine children "chained to the benches" in the dining room, one of them "marked badly by a strap" (Royal Commission 1999). Children were frequently beaten severely with whips, rods, and fists, chained and shackled, bound hand and foot and locked in closets, basements, and bathrooms.

The Royal Commission reported that in 1919, a student who ran away from the Anglican Old Sun's school was captured, then shackled to a bed with his hands tied and was "most brutally and unmercifully beaten with a horse quirt until his back was bleeding." The man who administered the beating, P. H. Gentlemen, admitted to having used a whip and shackles. Canon S. Gould, the general secretary of the Missionary Society, mounted a curious defense: that such a beating was the norm "more or less, in every boarding school in the country." These men remained at the school after admitting to the beating.

Writing in 1991 of her experience in both Anglican and Catholic schools, Mary Carpenter told an-all-too familiar story: beatings and going hungry. She was forced to stand in a corridor on one leg and to walk in the snow barefoot for speaking Inuvialuktun, her native language. A heavy, stinging paste was rubbed on her face to stop her from expressing the Inuit custom of raising eyebrows for "yes" and wrinkling her nose for "no."

The Aboriginal Commission found that:

> By the mid-1980s, it was widely and publicly recognized that the residential school experience . . . like smallpox and tuberculosis in earlier decades, had devastated and continued to devastate communities. The schools were, with the agents and instruments of economic and political marginalization, part of the contagion of colonization. In their direct attack on language, beliefs and spirituality, the schools had been a particularly virulent strain of that epidemic of empire, sapping the children's bodies and beings. In later life, many adult survivors, and the families and communities to which they returned, all manifested a tragic range of symptoms emblematic of "the silent tortures that continue in our communities." (Royal Commission 1999)

Sexual Abuse

While school supervisors acknowledged and sometimes even took pride in stern discipline, including corporal punishment, they said very little about the deepest secret of the system: sexual abuse of the children. The official files ignore the issue almost completely. Any references were encoded in the language of repression that marked the Canadian discourse on sexual matters. One report at Red Deer School commented that "the moral aspect of affairs is deplorable." Others wrote of "questions of immorality" of "the breaking of the Seventh Commandment" (Royal Commission 1999).

In 1990, the *Toronto Globe and Mail* reported that Rix Rogers, special advisor to the minister of national health and welfare on child sexual abuse, had commented at a meeting of the Canadian Psychological Association that the abuse revealed to date was "just the tip of the iceberg" and that closer scrutiny of treatment of children at residential schools would disclose that all children at some schools were sexually abused (Johansen and Pritzker 2007). A 1989 study sponsored by the Native Women's Association of the Northwest Territories found that eight out of ten girls under the age of eight had been victims of sexual abuse, and that 50 percent of boys the same age had been sexually molested as well (Johansen and Pritzker 2007).

Louis Riel

On January 7, 1998, Minister of Indian Affairs Jane Stewart read a Statement of Reconciliation into the record of Canada's federal Parliament at Ottawa that acknowledged the damage done to the Native population, including the hanging of Louis Riel after he led a rebellion of Indian and mixed-race people in western Canada in 1885. The government apology stopped short of pardoning Riel, a step which aboriginal leaders have demanded for decades. Stewart did, however, apologize for the government's assimilation policies, including the abuses of boarding schools.

"Attitudes of racial and cultural superiority led to a suppression of aboriginal culture and values," Stewart said. She continued:

> As a country, we are burdened by past actions that resulted in weakening the identity of aboriginal peoples, suppressing their languages and cultures, and outlawing

Louis Riel.

spiritual practices. We must recognize the impact of these actions on the once self-sustaining nations that were disaggregated, disrupted, limited or even destroyed by the dispossession of traditional territory, by the relocation of aboriginal people, and by some provisions of the Indian Act. The time has come to state formally that the days of paternalism and disrespect are behind us and we are committed to changing the nature of the relationship between aboriginal and non-aboriginal people in Canada. (Stewart 1998).

Phil Fontaine, leader the Assembly of First Nations, a coalition of nationwide aboriginal groups, said that the apology paves the way for lasting peace between Native peoples and the Canadian government. "This celebrates the beginning of a new era," Fontaine told Inter Press Service. "It is a major step forward in our quest to be recognized as a distinct order of government in Canada" (Bourrie 1998).

On the other hand, some aboriginal leaders were not happy with Stewart's statement. Representatives of Inuit, Native women's groups and Métis said they did not believe the apology was strong enough. They were critical because the statement did not refer in more detail to the wrongs done to their communities. The same groups also maintained that the money involved in recompense was too little, too late. Inuit and Métis leaders, who are not included in Canada's Assembly of First Nations, also complained that Stewart's later statements did not mention specific programs for them.

Among staunch Anglo-American conservatives, Stewart's statement sparked a retort in the Canadian *Financial Post* from columnist David Frum (later a speech writer for President George W. Bush), who wrote, in part: "Let the groveling begin. . . . The descendants of the Europeans have had the good taste never to demand a thank-you from the descendants of the aboriginals. . . . But at the very least they are entitled to refuse to bow and scrape and abase themselves for the sin of having tamed and civilized this inhospitable land" (Frum 1998, n.p.).

Frum's column, published January 13, 1998, drew several indignant letters to the editor, one of which was from Bill Hipwell, a lecturer in political geography at Ottawa's Carleton University. Instead of apologizing, Hipwell suggested, Euro-Canadians should thank Native peoples for several things, among them democratic ideas: "The civilizations of the Mi'kmaq and the Haudenosaunee (Iroquois) Confederacy [which] taught Europeans such basic principles as human rights. . . . Jefferson borrowed liberally from the Haudenosaunee political system" (Hipwell 1998, 18).

Native Litigation

Other non-Indian Canadians complained that the surge of lawsuits for residential school abuse would clog the court system, bankrupt some religious denominations, and strain the Canadian federal budget, requiring new taxes. By the end of the year 2002, according to the Canadian government, more than nineteen thousand Native persons had entered some form of claim, a number equal to roughly 15 to 20 percent of the boarding schools' living alumni. This legal backlog included four class action suits. Indian plaintiffs won all five boarding school abuse trials held during the late 1990s, two in Saskatchewan, and three in British Columbia.

By early 1999, the Canadian federal government had paid out roughly $20 million worth of individual compensation, including awards to several victims of staff at the Gordon reserve in Saskatchewan (which was run by the government without church affiliation). Late in 1998, the federal government and the Catholic Church also reached an out-of-court settlement with eleven men who were abused by Oblate priests while attending St. Joseph's residential school near Williams Lake, B.C., in the 1960s.

In late October 1998, the United Church of Canada, the country's largest Protestant body (including three million Presbyterians, Congregationalists, and Methodists) issued an apology for physical and sexual abuse meted out to Native students at boarding schools it had operated (Associated Press 1998). The apology was made shortly after disclosure of evidence indicating that church officials knew of the abuse as early as 1960 and did nothing to stop it. Peter Grant, an attorney for former students at a British Columbia boarding school, had presented evidence indicating that the vice-principal at the Port Alberni residential school was convicted of indecently assaulting male students between 1948 and 1968. Arthur Plint, who supervised the school's dormitories, pleaded guilty in 1995 to "dozens of sexual assaults," according to the Associated Press (1998) . He was sentenced to eleven years in prison. British Columbia Court Justice William Brenner ruled that both the federal government and the church were "vicariously responsible" for Plint's assaults on Native young people. (Associated Press 1998). "I apologize for the pain and suffering that our church's involvement in the Indian residential school system has caused," the Rev. Bill Phipps, the church's chief executive (or "moderator") told a news conference on October 27 (Associated Press 1998). "We are aware of some of the damage that some of this cruel and ill-conceived system of assimilation has perpetuated on Canada's first nations," Phipps said. "We are truly and humbly sorry" (Mcllroy 1998, 5).

The Anglican and Roman Catholic churches of Canada expressed repentance for their role in boarding school abuses, but, as of 2002, had not apologized, in part because they fear legal liability. The United Church seems to have decided that it will settle with litigants out of court.

The Royal Commission concluded that, "The terrible facts of the residential school system must be made a part of a new sense of what Canada has been and will continue to be for as long as that record is not officially recognized and repudiated. Only by such an act of recognition and repudiation can a start be made on a very different future. Canada and Canadians must realize that they need to consider changing their society so that they can discover ways of living in harmony with the original people of the land" (Royal Commission 1999).

The Royal Commission called for a full investigation into Canada's residential school system, "to bring to light and begin to heal the grievous harms suffered by countless Native children, families and communities as a result of the residential school system" (Royal Commission 1999).

Although not the forum the Royal Commission may have intended, such a public inquiry has begun to unfold, case by specific case, in many Canadian courtrooms. The economic stakes of boarding school compensation in Canada were reflected by the fact that, by late 2002, the Canadian federal government had reserved C$1.7 billion to settle up to eighteen thousand Native residential school lawsuits brought for physical and sexual abuse. The government was planning to require plaintiffs to waive rights to future litigation, including claims based on loss of language and culture.

The Anglican diocese of Caribou, B.C., during 2001 announced plans to close (and to place its assets in trust) following a costly legal fight over compensation for victims of abuse at residential schools in which some of its priests had a role. This was the first Canadian church to give up its corporate identity due to these claims. The churches in the small archdiocese were slated to continue to operate, however. The diocese, which includes about 4,700 parishioners in British Columbia's interior, had legal bills totaling more than C$350,000 from residential litigation, according to a Canadian Broadcasting Corporation report. After more than a decade of battling in court, it has paid out settlements to a small number of victims. All of the diocese's liquid assets had been spent, according to its leaders.

Memories of the residential schools also have changed the ways in which education is delivered to Canadian Native people. Hearing that a Canadian Indian boarding school student had frozen to death as he tried to walk home, Akwesasne Mohawk Ernest Benedict during the late 1960s decided to create a new way to deliver Native American education. The result was the Native North American Traveling College, which brought culturally relevant schooling to many Canadian reserves via caravan. Benedict's traveling college was part of a wave of new approaches to dealing with old problems among the Akwesasne Mohawks. Ray Fadden, for example, created new venues of education for Native young people when he became dissatisfied with the offerings of the Boy Scouts. His family also built its own museum as an alternative to institutional offerings. Benedict also initiated many other self-determination efforts, such as starting the St. Regis Indian Health Service on the United States portion of Akwesasne.

In January 2008, the Canadian federal government approved the landmark Indian Residential Schools Settlement Act and payments began. As part of this agreement, a Truth and Reconciliation Commission was to be appointed. "On 11 June the Prime Minister makes a statement of apology to former students of Indian residential schools in the House of Commons" (Dickason and McNab 2009, 429).

Métis Hunting Rights: The *Powley* Case

The Métis have largely become landless squatters across Canada. In eastern Canada they generally live at the margins of both Indian and Canadian society. In Manitoba, however, they developed a distinct sense of themselves as a people with a right to self-determination. The federal government has continued to insist that the Métis do not come within the terms of its constitutional authority. Early in 2001 the Ontario Court of Appeal ruled that Métis, "as a distinct Aboriginal people, have the constitutional right to hunt for food out of season and without a license" (Dickason and McNab 2009, 334). This concerned an incident in 1993 when two Métis, Steve and Rodney Powley, went hunting and shot a moose out of season. The favorable decision represented the first time that a Canadian appellate court recognized the legal existence of the Métis Nation. Then in September 2003, as a result of the favorable decision in *R v. Powley*, the Supreme Court of Canada affirmed that Métis have rights that are recognized and protected by Canada's constitution.

Governance and Land Rights

The First Nations Governance Act (FNGA) was proposed by the federal government in 2002 as a reform to amend the Indian Act of 1876. Instead, it created a firestorm of criticism and died in Parliament in 2004. Over ten thousand First Nations people participated in the discussion and critique of Bill C-7. "Many First Nations leaders opposed the legislation because it did not recognize the inherent right of self-government, and also was seen as an attack on existing Aboriginal and treaty rights" (Dickason and McNab 2009, 433). The legislation was also opposed by many non-aboriginal groups, such as Amnesty International, and the United, Anglican, and Roman Catholic churches of Canada. "Opposition to the FNGA focused on the vague nature of the proposed legislation and, especially, on the fact that it failed to address the issue of an inherent right to self-government" (Dickason and McNab 2009, 436).

Short of outright self-determination, reforming governance under Canada's Indian Act can be a complicated process. Twenty-one First Nations currently operate under four self-government agreements; the remaining 330 First Nations choose their leadership outside the Act "in a manner according to the different customs of their respective communities. . . . This applies to the 196 that were never moved into the Indian Act system, but also to more than 100 First Nations that had been under the Indian Act but reverted by request to a customary governance model" (Dickason and McNab 2009, 436).

In the last decade, various models of Indigenous governance in Canada have taken shape. Perhaps the best known and most widely acclaimed is Nunavut, an immense Arctic region north and west of Hudson's Bay that was mentioned earlier in this chapter. Eighty-five percent of its population is Inuit, and the territorial government is responsible for all of its citizens, including the non-Inuit. The Inuit in effect have self-government but do not have sovereignty over the region's rich natural resources, the development of which is controlled by Ottawa. But for obvious reasons Nunavut cannot be a blueprint for all of Canada's First Nations peoples, especially for the much smaller Indian reserves and communities that predominate Canada's southern region where the majority of the nation's population reside.

International Indigenous Sovereignty

On September 13, 2007, the United Nations General Assembly adopted the Declaration On the Rights of Indigenous Peoples (UNDRIP) by an overwhelming majority: 143 votes in favor with only four dissenting votes—Australia, New Zealand, United States, and Canada. Australia and New Zealand subsequently withdrew their opposition, and both the United States and Canada have modified their positions in favor of the Declaration. The initial denial of Indigenous rights by the conservative government of Canada, however, may run counter to the nation's constitution, according to Dickason and McNab (2009, 431):

> Domestically, such rights are part and parcel of Canada's Constitution Act (1892), in section 35(1), which states that the "The existing aboriginal and treaty rights of Canada are hereby recognized and reaffirmed." . . . At the same time, the Indian Act (since 1876, as revised), is still on the books, and this federal legislation is racist and colonial, and it takes away the rights of those aboriginal Canadian citizens for whom the nation-state recognizes the same rights under its Constitution. . . . The fundamental issue is one of Indigenous sovereignty.

Ironically, Canada's initial negative vote on the UNDRIP occurred after previous Canadian governments had been instrumental in drafting the Declaration. On April 8, 2008, at the urging of First Nations peoples, the House of Commons "passed a resolution calling on the government of Canada to endorse the legislation as adopted by the UN General Assembly to and called on the government of Canada 'to fully implement the standards contained therein'" (Dickason and McNab 2009, 432).

Sovereignty and First Nations land rights in Canada, as with other Indigenous peoples, are inseparable. This is demonstrated by the militant actions undertaken by Canada's First Nations in the last several decades. "The events of the Temagami block-ades (1988–90) in Northern Ontario, of the summer of 1990 centered on Oka, Quebec, of Ipperwash (1995) and Caledonia (2006) in southern Ontario, and of Gustafson Lake in British Columbia and Burnt Church in New Brunswick will not be erased from history or memory. Nor will the ongoing problems of the Innu of Labrador, the Deh Cho of the North-west Territories, the Lubicon Cree of Northern Alberta, and of the many other outstanding claims be solved by inaction and denial" (Dickason and McNab 2009, 432–433).

ENVIRONMENTAL ISSUES

Canada, which often prides itself on a humane civil rights record regarding Indigenous peoples, has become a major source of Indigenous environmental contamination and conflict. These conflicts span the country from east to west, and north to south. While Canada may have a general reputation for pristine environmental conditions, it also hosts some of the most polluted Native lands in North America. Witness, for example, the Aamjiwnaang First Nation, with a population of 1,900, along the St. Clair River near Sarnia, Ontario, which is ringed by petrochemical factories. Residents there began to notice that something was terribly wrong around 1993 when the birth of baby boys started to become rare. Chemical pollutants affected the hormone levels of pregnant mothers, increasing the proportion of female babies. The number of stillborn babies and children with developmental delays also increased (First Nations' Realities 2005, 4).

During the summer of 2004, an environmental study of the river and a creek that runs through the community revealed extremely high levels of PCBs, nickel, cadmium, arsenic, zinc, and lead. Sharon Fisher, a resident of the area, quit letting her dog Stella, a terrier-poodle mix, play in water behind her home after she gave birth to puppies that were stillborn with no eyes or ears, as well as fleshy paddles instead of paws (Mathewson 2005, 22). Protests broke out among the Native people living on the reserve, asking why they must be forced to live with chemical effluents.

Such concerns have ranged the length of Canada, from the vicinity of the U.S. border to the far north, in Nunavut, where the Inuit have been subject to so much chemical pollution that mothers have been advised, in some cases, not to breast-feed their infants. Along the Arctic Circle, the native Inuit suf-fer major problems ranging from contamination by

persistent organic pollutants such as dioxins and PCBs, among others. Some of the most intense resource exploitation in Canada takes place in remote locations, such as among the Lubicon Cree of north-ern Alberta, whose lands were so inaccessible in 1900 that treaty makers completely missed them. Today, roads have opened their lands to massive oil drilling and logging. The lands of the Cree in Quebec have been scarred by widespread dam building near James Bay that has contaminated large areas with toxic methyl mercury as well as other pollutants. Uranium mining has decimated the Dene in Canada's North-west Territories much as it has ravaged the Navajo in the Southwestern United States. The catalogue of indigenous environmental issues in Canada spans the range of resources—from hydropower, to dia-monds, uranium, gold, silver, and sulfide, aluminum, oil, and natural gas.

The Innu and Cree: North Looking South

Seen from the north, looking southward, the Innu and Cree who live in northern Quebec see an inva-sion of the military, miners, and builders of roads and dams, following over their homelands, bringing development of a type never requested nor desired. The men from the south call the land barren and unproductive, but it has provided sustenance to the Cree, who live east of James Bay, and the Innu, whose homeland (called Nitaassinan, meaning "the land" in Innuaimun, their language) for many thousands of years. (See Figure 9.3.) Historical records recounted by Winona LaDuke in her book *All Our Relations* (LaDuke 1999, 50–53), relate how seventeenth cen-tury Europeans found the Innu living comfortably in robes of moose, deer, and bear, eating a protein-rich diet of animals they hunted. Building roads, dams, and military bases, harbingers of hunters and miners, European-Americans in the twentieth century began to impose a way of life that brought death and cul-tural disintegration to the Innu and the Cree.

The Crees and Hydro-Quebec's Electric Dreams

During the 1970s, planners and engineers at Hydro-Quebec indulged themselves in dreams of an electric empire that would make their utility the biggest supplier of electricity in the world. The utility planned to harness dozens of rivers flowing into James Bay, reshaping the ecology of an area the size of Iowa in the service of electrical generation. At first, the planners at Hydro-Quebec paid very little attention to what might become of the flora and fauna of the James Bay region during what they

Figure 9.3 Aboriginal 'Nitassinan' in the Province of Quebec.

envisaged as the largest earthmoving project in the history of humankind.

The ten thousand Cree and six thousand Innu in the area, scarcely even were recognized as longtime occupants of the land by Hydro-Quebec, soon found themselves challenging the construction project in court. It was a matter of life and death not only for traditional cultures, but also for the peoples themselves. The construction ruined many traditional hunting areas, and replaced them with poisoned earth laced with life-threatening mercury compounds.

The Cree and Inuit of northern Quebec signed a comprehensive claims agreement (formally named the James Bay and Northern Quebec Agreement) with the Canadian federal and Quebec provincial governments in 1975. The Cree entered agreements (in essence, treaties) with the governments of Quebec and Canada, but they soon found the terms of these treaties being violated by the ecological consequences of hydroelectric construction.

The 1975 agreement provided the Cree C\$22 million and the right to continue to hunt, fish, and trap in their usual territories. Not even Hydro-Quebec anticipated that its plans would make a significant portion of the territory unsustainable for any of those activities. In 1979, the first of four projected power stations at La Grande (in H-Q shorthand, LG-1) came on line. With its advent, roughly 4,200 square miles of Cree hunting and trapping grounds were flooded. Three hundred black bears drowned as the reservoirs filled (Biegert 1995, n.p.). Ignoring natural seasonal cycles, Hydro-Quebec's engineers filled their reservoirs just after the bears had put themselves to sleep for the winter, drowning them. The fact that the black bear is the most sacred animal in Cree mythology did not bother them.

During the James Bay project's first phase, large areas of the Crees' homelands were transformed. James Bay I involved nine dams, 206 dikes, five major reservoirs, and the diversion of five major rivers over an area roughly the size of Connecticut. Rivers that once spawned large numbers of fish were reduced to trickles or stopped entirely by the creation of reservoirs behind energy-generating dams. Forests were clear-cut and burned, adding greenhouse gases to the atmosphere. More than ten thousand caribou drowned after Hydro-Quebec's rearrangement of the landscape spilled deep water across their migration routes. Hydro-Quebec called the deaths an "act of God" (Biegert 1995, n.p.). This incident was yet another reminder that while hydroelectricity is often touted as "clean" energy that does not emit pollution or directly increase the atmosphere's overload of greenhouse gases, it is not environmentally benign.

Hydro-Quebec's next project, James Bay II, proposed to dam eight major rivers in northern Quebec at a cost of more than C$170 billion to provide electricity to urban Canada in the St. Lawrence valley, and to the northeastern United States. Little is said these days of the original James Bay project's third proposed stage, the most ambitious electric dream of all. As originally envisaged by the engineers of Hydro-Quebec, the project's second phase (which was successfully impeded by the Cree) was to be followed by an even more ambitious Phase III, a C$100 billion proposal to build a one-hundred-mile dike across the mouth of James Bay, "separating it from Hudson Bay so that the now fresh water from James Bay can be pumped (possibly using nuclear-powered pumps) to the Great Lakes and thence to the Midwestern and Southwestern United States" (Native Forest Network 1994). Formally called the Grand Canal, or Great Recycling and Northern Development proposal, Phase III of the James Bay Project

would have transformed James Bay into a gigantic freshwater lake. According to Hydro-Quebec's plans, fresh water from this reservoir also could be diverted southward through several existing rivers and new canals into the Great Lakes, then into Canada's prairies, as well as the U.S. Midwest and Southwest.

Mercury Contamination and Fish

Just as Hydro-Quebec's electric dreams reached a point of ecocidal fantasy, the Cree and Inuit peoples got in the way. The Crees were called to protest the James Bay project as a matter of life and death, as they faced methyl mercury contamination caused by the earthmoving of the James Bay project's first phase during the 1980s.

Mercury contamination occurs when vast areas of land are disrupted. Plant decay associated with the James Bay's project's earthmoving caused large amounts of ordinary mercury to become methyl mercury, a bio-accumulative poison. Rotting vegetation accelerated microbial activity that converts elemental mercury in previously submerged glacial rocks to toxic methyl mercury. By 1990, many Crees were carrying in their bodies twenty times the level of methyl mercury considered safe by the World Health Organization. Hydro-Quebec did not anticipate the accelerated release of methyl mercury into the waters of the region, contaminating the entire food chain for the Cree, Inuit, birds, fish, and other animals. This type of mercury poisoning can cause loss of vision, numbness of limbs, uncontrollable shaking, and chronic brain damage. By the late 1980s, the Quebec government's health ministry was telling the Cree not to eat fish from their homeland.

Fishing represents more than sustenance for the Cree. Fishing activities are important in knitting family and community. Mercury contamination thus disrupted an entire way of life. Before 1978, concentrations of mercury in 700 millimeter pike was approximately 0.6 microgram per kilogram. After completion of Phase I, the concentrations increased gradually. In 1988 concentrations were 3 milligrams per kilogram, five times the original concentration and six times the maximum permissible concentration for commercial fish (e.g., for human consumption) in Canada (Dumont 1995).

By 1984, the concentration of mercury in the hair of Crees at all ages was much higher than in surveys conducted during the 1970s. During 1993 and 1994, the Cree Board of Health completed an assay of mercury levels in the hair of the Cree. This survey revealed a wide variation in exposure levels among different communities. "If the 6 mg/kg maximum hair concentration recommended by the World Health Organization is used, at least half of the population of several communities is over that limit. In 1984, when Whapmagoostui (Great Whale) was surveyed, 98 percent of the population surveyed had mercury concentrations above 6 mg/kg" (Dumont 1995). Mercury levels increased generally with a person's age. Persons recognized as trappers in their communities consistently tested for higher mercury concentrations. "During the past ten years, the number of individuals with high mercury concentrations has decreased considerably," due in large part to programs persuading the Cree to avoid eating tainted fish (Dumont 1995).

Crees and Inuit Oppose James Bay II

When James Bay II was proposed, the Cree and other Native Americans peoples living in the area not only took the case to court, but also sought to organize the customers of the electric utilities that would receive the power, mostly in Eastern Canada and New England. This activism ultimately convinced an activist nucleus of customers to pressure their utilities to refuse Hydro-Quebec's power on moral grounds.

The Crees became very effective at addressing public forums in New York and Vermont, where a large part of the electricity would have been sold, to tell people that they shared complicity with Hydro-Quebec in the devastation of Northern Quebec. The Crees also urged electricity consumers and utilities to conserve, and to consider other sources of supply. Several non-Indian environmental groups joined with the Grand Council of the Cree against the James Bay projects.

In addition to its toll on the Cree, hydroelectric development ruined wetlands and coastal marshes that were important staging grounds for migratory waterfowl, including several species of duck, teal, and goose. The area also was home to rare and endangered species of freshwater seals, beluga whales, polar bears, and walruses. Anadromous fish, such as the brook trout and lake whitefish, entered the waters of James Bay to spawn from rivers that would have been disrupted or destroyed by additional extensive hydroelectric development under James Bay II. According to the Sierra Club, "Estuaries, heath-covered islands, salt marshes, freshwater fens, sub-tidal eelgrass beds, and ribbon bogs in the James Bay region provide nourishment for huge flocks of geese, ducks, and loons. Tundra on either side of the bays provides habitat for caribou, moose, otter,

muskrat, beaver, lynx, and polar bear. This wildlife, in turn, supports the traditional Cree trappers and fishers of the James Bay region and, along Hudson Bay, the Inuit and Naskapi. The Cree regard their part of the eco-region as a 'garden' providing for all their needs" (Sierra Club n.d.).

The James Bay project was litigated for several years. During September of 1991, a Canadian federal judge in Ottawa ordered a new assessment of the James Bay II project under a process that could give federal authorities the right to stop it. "I conclude that the Crees' right to an independent parallel federal review must be honored," wrote Justice Paul Rouleau (Langan 1991). At the time, the total cost of James Bay I and II was estimated to be $62 billion.

During February 1994, the Supreme Court of Canada ruled that the National Energy Board had the right to examine the environmental effects of the Great Whale Project, essentially the same issue that had been decided by Judge Rouleau two and a half years earlier. Armand Couture, president of Hydro-Quebec, denied at the time that the court's order would have any impact on plans to throw the switch on Great Whale II by the year 2003.

In the meantime, the Crees continued to stoke popular pressure against Hydro-Quebec's efforts to market power from the James Bay projects. Ten Cree and Inuit activists paddled a twenty-five-foot combination kayak-canoe from Ottawa to New York City during the spring of 1990. They crossed the Quebec-Vermont border at the northern end of Lake Champlain and timed their arrival in Central Park to coincide with Earth Day. In mid-April 1993, Native leaders and their supporters bought a full-page advertisement opposing James Bay II in the *New York Times*.

On November 18, 1994 (not too many months after Hydro-Quebec's president Armand Couture had asserted that electricity would begin to flow from James Bay II in 2003), Quebec Premier Jacques Parizeau said that the project was being shelved "indefinitely." He told the press: "We've not saying never, but that project is on ice for quite a while" (Associated Press 1994, 7).

The Great Whale (James Bay II) hydroelectric project was revived on a reduced scale during 2001 after having been shelved seven years earlier. The project was revived with a new twist: a proposal that the Crees, who had played a large role in opposing the project, would eventually become its sole owners. The new proposal involved diversion of the Great Whale River at its headwater, Lac Bienville. At an estimated cost of C$350 million, the river's water would be redirected through ten kilometers of canals into Hydro-Quebec's La Grande hydroelectric complex, increasing the water flow through the turbines. In 1997, Hydro-Quebec had proposed to divert the Great Whale and, for the first time, sought the Crees' consent and offered a minority partnership in the project. This proposal was shelved after 92 percent of Whapmagoostui Crees voted against any development projects on the river (Roslin 2000). The new proposal retained the diversion idea, but proposed that the Crees would own the facility once its debt was paid off. AMEC (the project's builder) would design the facility, arrange financing and retain an ownership share while the debt was being paid off.

The agreement, which later was ratified by the Cree communities of Northern Quebec, allowed the fifteen thousand natives an annual revenue flow and direct participation in any economic development on native land in Northern Quebec. The agreement pledged to pay the Cree C$70 million a year for fifty years. It also included Hydro-Quebec jobs for Crees, an important issue in communities where more than 80 percent of the young people under twenty-five years of age are unemployed. The agreement also promised remediation of mercury contamination, funding for start-up business programs, job training, health and social services, electricity, sanitation, and fire services for Cree communities (Johansen 2010, n.p.).

In return, the Crees promised access to resources (including diversion of the Rupert River for hydroelectric development) and cession of C$3.6 billion in environmental lawsuits. The proposed diversions of the Rupert River were subject to environmental-impact reviews, but the government of Quebec was allowed to make the final decisions. "In effect," according to one analysis, "The Cree will not be able to protest, stop, inhibit, or litigate" environmental outcomes, including the anticipated drying up of parts of the Eastman River and the flooding of trap lines (Johansen 2010, n.p.).

The Cree agreed to drop their environmental lawsuits in part because legal fees were costing them C$9 million a year, but also because many of the cases were faring badly in the Canadian court system. Courts in Quebec had ruled against the Cree on forestry issues, as well as on their opposition to hydroelectric development on the Eastman River (Johansen 2010). The agreement also was important because it saved roughly eight thousand square kilometers of land from being flooded, according to Cree negotiator Coon Come. "We want jobs," he said after the new agreement was negotiated. "We want a

say in where development takes place [and] what happens in our own backyard" (Johansen 2010, n.p.).

The Innu Battle: A Sulfide Mine

The Innu Nation and Labrador Inuit Association have been contending with proposed development of an open-pit nickel mine-and-mill complex at Voisey's Bay, a site that could become the world's largest nickel mine, estimated at 150 million tons of reserves. The Voisey's Bay Nickel Company, a subsidiary of Inco, the largest nickel producer in the world, applied to the Newfoundland provincial government in late May 1997, for permission to construct a road and airstrip at the Voisey's Bay site. Innu and Inuit residents, in response, took their case to the Newfoundland Supreme Court where they sought an injunction to prevent the construction of infrastructure pending an environmental assessment.

Innu president Katie Rich said, "It's too bad we had to go to court. This action is about forcing V.B.N.C. to live up to their public statements about being committed to the environment. The company can't claim to be environmentally responsible when it is trying to detour around the environmental review process" (*Drillbits and Tailings* 1997). The Innu request for an injunction against the mine and mill was rejected by the Supreme Court July 18, 1997. In the meantime, the province already had issued construction permits. Machines and materials were imported, buildings constructed, and four kilometers of roadway cut at the Voisey's Bay (*Drillbits and Tailings* 1997).

On August 20, 1997, their legal appeals exhausted, the Innu Nation and the Labrador Inuit staged a demonstration at Voisey's Bay. That morning, the first Inuit protesters arrived from Nain to establish a protest camp, as more than 250 Innu and Inuit arrived to participate. "Development at the site has gone far enough. Inco is now building a road and an airstrip without Innu and Inuit consent. Without our consent there will be no project!" asserted Rich (*Drillbits and Tailings* 1997). Rich expressed her hope that the protest would remain peaceful. "This is about standing our ground, not about a standoff. The company has never asked for our permission to be here, or asked for our consent for the mine. We have clearly outlined what our consent requires and it is up to them to respond to it. We have lived here for thousands of years and we plan to stay here for thousands more, but we don't want to be living in the mess they will make here by rushing ahead. By standing together with the Labrador Inuit we are saying to Inco and to Brian Tobin [provincial premier] that we will not be bulldozed over on our own land" (*Drillbits and Tailings* 1997).

In addition to the proposed nickel mine, Innu territory has been examined for possible siting of an aluminum smelter. During late July, 2001, the Innu Nation warned potential developers of Lower Churchill hydroelectric projects that a proposed aluminum smelter would require Innu consent. The Innu Nation was responding to the announcement of a new feasibility study for the construction of the Lower Churchill hydroelectric project and an aluminum smelter. Peter Penashue, president of the Innu Nation, responded that the promoters and sponsors of the project must receive the consent of the Innu Nation for any economic project in Innu territory, and that the Innu will only accept "development" proposals that have a sustainable benefit to the Native people. (*Cultural Survival News Notes* 2001).

The Pimicikamak Cree of Manitoba: Imperiled by Hydropower

The Pimicikamak Cree assert that for twenty-five years the Manitoba Hydro Power Company has been destroying their traditional lands and society with a series of dams and canals cut through wilderness to divert the flow of rivers upon which their traditional subsistence economy depends. The Cree signed a treaty in 1977 granting them full compensation for damage to their homeland. They assert, however, that this treaty has not been honored by Manitoba Hydro. Now, the Pimicikamak Cree, who have been experiencing 70 to 80 percent unemployment, have lost their traditional economic base and their cultural and spiritual foundations, leading to an epidemic of suicides (Peterson 2000).

Dams built during the 1970s reengineered Manitoba's two largest rivers and largest lake to serve the energy needs of Manitobans and export to customers in the United States. For twenty-five years, fluctuating waters in Pimicikamak Cree territory provoked by the power company's needs eroded shorelines. According to advocates for the Cree, gravesites have been exposed, islands eroded away, the ecological balance with nature disrupted, and parts of the Native fishing and trapping grounds seriously compromised.

Seven dams were built during the early 1970s in the Nelson and Churchill river systems of Manitoba. A large percentage of game disappeared from the affected area, making subsistence hunting very difficult. Several hundred Native people were displaced into housing projects as their homes were flooded.

The environmental-impact assessment for the Churchill-Nelson project was an after-the-fact matter, initiated after Manitoba Hydro had fixed the configuration, operating regime, and timing of construction for the diversion of the Churchill River into the Nelson River. The unforeseen environmental impacts of the Manitoba projects included:

> Severe shoreline erosion, caused by impoundment of Southern Indian Lake as part of the diversion, led to increased turbidity. This resulted in the collapse of the commercial whitefish industry. Whitefish populations in Cross Lake, another large lake in the Churchill-Nelson river basin, fell 65 percent. In addition, walleye and northern pike in all flooded lakes along the diversion route accumulated mercury levels that exceeded Canadian limits for the protection of human health. Some commercial fisheries were permanently closed, and local residents were encouraged to avoid consumption. The collapse of the commercial fishery placed a severe strain on the social fabric of northern aboriginal communities, forcing them to move and/or to rely increasingly on compensation payments for income. (Canadian Arctic Resources Committee n.d.)

By the early 1990s, studies showed that one in six people in the area was suffering from mercury contamination (LaDuke 1993, A-3). Methyl-mercury contamination was discovered in northern Manitoba during the early 1970s by scientists from the Freshwater Institute in Winnipeg. Similar contamination had not been anticipated by Hydro-Quebec as it began construction of James Bay Phase I at the end of the decade, despite the experiences of a similar utility doing similar construction work, geographically adjacent. Apparently, no one was paying attention.

The Pimicikamik Cree held a Hands Across the Border conference in 2001 to strengthen their campaign to build a coalition of Native nations, farmers, consumers, and environmentalists in the United States and Canada to force the cancellation of utility contracts with Manitoba Hydro requiring a new mega-dam project. Five existing dams in Manitoba have submerged 3.3 million acres of land, including large tracts of boreal forest and extensive animal habitat. The methyl mercury created by construction of these dams has contaminated fish, a staple of the Cree diet, in the Nelson River.

The Pimicikamak Cree of Manitoba adopted a strategy similar to that of the Quebec Cree, who forced Hydro-Quebec to shelve its James Bay Phase II project during the middle 1990s. Representatives of both nations traveled to the United States to convince consumers of the utilities that might purchase the electricity generated by the dams to advocate cancellation of their contracts on moral grounds. As part of this effort, the Pimicikamik Cree lobbied Minnesota public utilities to weigh damage to the Native peoples' ecosystems when purchasing power from Manitoba. Manitoba Hydro maintained that it had spent C$400 million over twenty years to compensate northern communities, but there appeared to be little to show for it. The Cree and other Native peoples asserted that poverty, unemployment, and suicide among the Pimicikamak Cree could be attributed to hydroelectric development (Johansen 2004). George M. Ross, a Cree elder, said, "The south is benefiting at the expense of our misery" (Johansen 2004).

The Inuit: Dioxin and Other Persistent Organic Pollutants

A matrix of geographical and cultural factors have placed the Inuit and other Arctic peoples "at the very top of the natural world's dietary hierarchy" (Cone 2005, 22). In the world of persistent organic pollutants, such a position is extremely hazardous for a people's health. The movements of air masses and ocean currents have turned the Arctic into a chemical garbage dump in an area where the climate fosters a diet of meat-eating animals that store toxins in their body fat.

The Inuit "eat 194 different species of wild animals, most of them inhabiting the sea. Often, on a daily basis, they consume the meat or blubber . . . of fish-eating whales, seals, and walrus four or five links up marine food chains" (Cone 2005, 22). Today, about two hundred toxic pesticides and industrial chemicals have been detected in the bodies of the Arctic's Indigenous people and animals, as well as mercury which is released by coal-burning power plants and chemical factories (Cone 2005, 23). Thus, the Inuit and other Arctic peoples have become "the industrial world's lab rats, the involuntary subjects of an accidental human experiment that reveals what happens when a boundless brew of chemicals builds up in an environment" (Cone 2005, 45). The Inuits' traditional diet, which is otherwise very nutritious (containing an average of forty times the omega-3 fatty acids of typical industrial-world fare, for example) has become a death trap (Cone 2005, 48). While heart disease and prostate cancer are very rare among the Inuit, toxicity-related maladies have exploded in recent years.

Welcome to ground zero on the road to environmental apocalypse: a place, and a people, who never asked for any of the travails that industrial societies to the south have brought to them. The bevy of environmental threats facing the Inuit are entirely outside their historical experience. In addition to toxic contamination, the Inuit also face one of the most rapid rates of global warming on Earth, which is transforming their ice-based society and economy.

ENVIRONMENTAL TOXICITY IN THE ARCTIC

To a tourist with no interest in environmental toxicology, the Inuit's Arctic homeland may seem as pristine as ever during its long, snow-swept winters. Many Inuit still guide dogsleds onto the pack ice surrounding their Arctic-island homelands to hunt polar bears and seals. Such a scene may seem unchanged, until one realizes that the polar bears' and seals' body fats are laced with dioxin and PCBs.

To environmental toxicologists, the Arctic by the 1990s was becoming known as the final destination for a number of manufactured poisons, including, most notably, dioxins and polyvinyl biphenyls (PCBs), which accumulate in the body fat of large aquatic and land mammals (including human beings), sometimes reaching levels that imperil their survival. Thus the Arctic, which seems so clean, has become one of the most contaminated places on Earth—a place where many mothers think twice before breast-feeding their babies, and where a traditional diet of "country food" has become dangerous to the Inuits' health. Most of the chemicals that now afflict the Inuit are synthetic compounds of chlorine; some of them are incredibly toxic. For example, one millionth of a gram of dioxin will kill a guinea pig (Cadbury 1997, 184).

The traditional Inuit diet is high in iron, vitamins, proteins, and omega-3 fatty acids—but also, these days, in several industrial toxins. Beluga whale, for example, has ten times the iron of beef, twice the protein, and five times the vitamin A. Omega-3 fatty acids in the seafood protect the Indigenous people from heart disease. A seventy-year-old Inuit in Greenland has coronary arteries as elastic as those of a twenty-year-old Dane eating Western foods, says Dr. Gert Mulvad of the Primary Health Care Clinic in Nuuk, Greenland's capital. Some Arctic clinics do not even keep heart medications like nitroglycerin in stock. Although heart disease has appeared with the introduction of Western foods, it remains "more or less unknown," Mulvad says (Cone 2004).

In a land with no agriculture, the only alternative to "country food" is airfreighted groceries that are very expensive, and exposes the Inuit to higher risks of various cancers, heart disease, and diabetes

(Gabrielsen 2005, 177–78). This is true across the Canadian arctic, Alaska, and northern Russia, where the collapse of the Soviet state has forced many indigenous peoples to rely on traditional "country food."

"As we put our babies to our breasts we are feeding them a noxious, toxic cocktail," said Sheila Watt-Cloutier, a grandmother who also is president of the Inuit Circumpolar Conference (ICC). "When women have to think twice about breast-feeding their babies, surely that must be a wake-up call to the world" (Johansen 2000b, 27).Watt-Cloutier has a way of bringing scientific conferences to their feet in a most unusual manner, as she injects a human face into otherwise staid proceedings, when she says such things as: "A poisoned Inuk child, a poisoned Arctic, and a poisoned planet are all one and the same" (Cone 2005, 200). Following negotiation of the Stockholm Convention, which outlaws most of the so-called "Dirty Dozen," Watt-Cloutier evoked tears from some delegates with her note of thanks on behalf of the Inuit. The treaty, she said, had "brought us an important step closer to fulfilling the basic human right of every person to live in a world free of toxic contamination. For Inuit and indigenous peoples, this means not only a healthy and secure environment, but also the survival of a people. For that I am grateful. Nakurmiik. Thank you" (Cone 2005, 202).

Watt-Cloutier was raised in an Inuit community in remote northern Quebec. Unknown to her at the time, toxic chemicals were being absorbed by her body, and those of other Inuit in the Arctic. As an adult, Watt-Cloutier ranged between her home in Iqaluit (pronounced "Eehalooeet," capital of the new semisovereign Nunavet Territory) to and from Montreal, New York City, and other points south, doing her best to alert the world to toxic poisoning and other perils faced by her people. The ICC represents the interests of roughly 140,000 Inuit who live around the North Pole from Nunavut (which means "our home" in the Inuktitut language) to Alaska and Russia. Nunavut itself, a territory four times the size of France, has a population of roughly twenty-five thousand, 85 percent of whom are Inuit. Some elders and hunters in Iqaluit have reported physical abnormalities afflicting the seals they catch, including some seals without hair, as well as walruses and seals with holes burned in their skins.

POPs, PCBs, and Dioxins

Persistent organic pollutants (POPs) have been linked to cancer, birth defects, and other neurological, reproductive, and immune-system damage in people and animals. At high levels, these chemicals also damage the central nervous system. Many of them also act as endocrine disrupters, causing deformities in sex organs as well as long-term dysfunction of reproductive systems. POPs also can interfere with the function of the brain and endocrine system by penetrating the placental barrier and scrambling the instructions of the naturally produced chemical messengers. The latter tell a fetus how to develop in the womb and postnatally through puberty; should interference occur, immune, nervous, and reproductive systems may not develop as programmed by the genes inherited by the embryo.

Pesticide residues in the Arctic today may include some used decades ago in the southern United States. The Arctic's cold climate slows the natural decomposition of these toxins, so they persist in the Arctic environment longer than at lower latitudes. The Arctic also acts as a cold trap, collecting and maintaining a wide range of industrial pollutants, from PCBs to toxaphene, chlordane to mercury, according to the Canadian Polar Commission. As a result, "Many Inuit have levels of PCBs, several forms of D.D.T., and other persistent organic pollutants in their blood and fatty tissues that are five to ten times greater than the national average in Canada or the United States" (PCB Working group n.d.).

During the late 1990s, ecologist Barry Commoner and his colleagues used a computer model to track dioxins released from each of their 44,091 sources in North America, a list that includes trash-burning facilities, and medical-waste burning plants. For one year, the scientists followed dioxins as weather patterns scattered them from their sources. Winds took some of the pollution north in a hurry. Riding strong air currents, dioxin molecules can travel four hundred kilometers in one day, according to Mark Cohen, an atmospheric scientist who adapted the model for the study, who works at the National Oceanic and Atmospheric Administration in Silver Spring, Maryland (Rozell 2000).

Dioxins can travel from a smokestack in Indiana, for example, to the breast milk of a woman in Coral Harbour, Nunavut. After riding air currents northward, dioxins drop with snowflakes into Hudson Bay. During the summer, heat may promote evaporation of pesticides in the fields of the American South, feeding a "molecular trickle" of toxaphene, chlordane and other compounds which makes its way to the Arctic, then condenses, and falls to Earth. In water, algae absorb the dioxins. A fish eats the algae; a bearded seal eats the fish, and dioxins build up in the animal's fatty tissue. The woman in Coral Harbour eats the seal meat, and her body transfers the dioxins to the fatty molecules of her breast milk (Rozell 2000; Schneider 1996, A-15). "The Arctic is more than myth and dreams. . . . The fish and whales carry scary amounts of contaminants," Canadian Environment Minister Sergio Marchi said (Schneider 1996, A-15). "This is an important issue for indigenous people in the Arctic," Commoner said. "There's no way of protecting [areas from dioxin fallout]. You can't put an umbrella over Nunavut" (Rozell 2000).

The bodies of some Inuit on the northernmost islands of Nunavut, thousands of miles from sources of pollution, have the highest levels of PCBs ever found, except for victims of industrial accidents. Some Native people in Greenland have several dozen times as much of the pesticide hexaclorobenzene (HCB) in their bodies as temperate-zone Canadians.

One may scan the list of scientific research funding around the world and add up what ails the Arctic. In addition to a plethora of studies documenting the spread of persistent organic pollutants through the flora and fauna of the Arctic, many studies document the saturation of the same area by levels of mercury, lead, and nuclear radiation in fish and game.

"We are the miner's canary," said Watt-Cloutier. "It is only a matter of time until everybody will be poisoned by the pollutants that we are creating in this world" (Johansen 2003). "At times," said Cloutier, "We feel like an endangered species. Our resilience and Inuit spirit and of course the wisdom of this great land that we work so hard to protect gives us back the energy to keep going" (Cloutier, personal communication, March 28, 2001).

Inuit Infants: "A Living Test Tube for Immunologists"

Éric Dewailly, a Laval University scientist (in the Department of Social and Preventive Medicine), accidentally discovered that the Inuit were being heavily contaminated by PCBs. During the middle 1980s, Dewailly first visited the Inuit as he sought a pristine group to use as a baseline with which to compare women in southern Quebec who had PCBs in their breast milk. Instead, Dewailly found that Inuit mothers' PCB levels were several times higher than the Quebec mothers in his study group.

Dewailly and colleagues then investigated whether organochlorine exposure is associated with the incidence of infectious diseases in Inuit infants from Nunavut (1993a, 1993b, 1994, 2000). Dewailly and his colleagues reported that serious ear infections were twice as common among Inuit babies whose mothers had higher-than-usual concentrations of toxic chemicals in their breast milk. More than 80 percent of the 118 babies studied in various Nunavut communities had at least one serious ear infection in the first year of their lives (Johansen 2003). The three most common contaminants that researchers found in Inuit mothers' breast milk were three pesticides (dieldrin, mirex and DDE) and two industrial chemicals, PCBs and hexachlorobenzene. The researchers could not pinpoint which specific chemicals were responsible for making the Inuit babies more vulnerable to illnesses because the chemicals' effects may amplify in combination.

Inuit infants have provided what one observer has called "a living test tube for immunologists" (Cone 1996, A-1). Due to their diet of contaminated sea animals and fish, Inuit women's breast milk by the early 1990s contained six times more PCBs than women in urban Quebec, according to Quebec government studies. Their babies have experienced strikingly high rates of meningitis, bronchitis, pneumonia, and other infections compared with other Canadians. One Inuit child out of every four has chronic hearing loss due to infections. Born with depleted white-blood cells, the children suffer excessive bouts of diseases, including a twenty-fold increase in life-threatening meningitis compared to other Canadian children. These children's immune systems sometimes fail to produce enough antibodies to resist even the usual childhood diseases.

"In our studies, there was a marked increase in the incidence of infectious disease among breast-fed babies exposed to a high concentration of contaminants," said Dewailly (Cone 1996, A-1). A study published September 12, 1996, in the *New England Journal of Medicine* confirmed that children exposed to low levels of PCBs in the womb grow up with low IQs, poor reading comprehension, difficulty paying attention, and memory problems (Jacobson and Jacobson 1996, 783–789).

According to the Quebec Health Center, a concentration of 1,052 parts per billion of PCBs has been found in Arctic women's milk fat. This compares to a reading of 7,002 p.p.b. in polar bear fat, 1,002 p.p.b. in whale blubber, 527 p.p.b. in seal blubber, and 152 p.p.b. in fish. The U.S. Environmental Protection Agency safety standard for edible poultry, by contrast, is 3 p.p.b., and in fish, 2 p.p.b. At 50 p.p.b., soil is often classified as hazardous waste by the U.S. Environmental Protection Agency. Research by the Canadian federal Department of Indian and Northern Affairs indicates that Inuit women throughout Nunavut experience DDT levels nine times the average of women in Canadian urban areas. The milk of Inuit women of the Eastern Arctic has been found to contain as much as 1,210 p.p.b. of DDT and its derivative, DDE, while milk from women living in southern Canada contains about 170 p.p.b. (Suzuki 2000).

The Arctic Monitoring and Assessment Programme, a joint activity of the Arctic nations and organizations of Indigenous Arctic people, found in its study *Pollution and Human Health* that "PCB blood levels in Greenland and the eastern Canadian Arctic were high enough (over 4 micrograms of PCBs per liter of blood) that a proportion of the population would be in a risk range for fetal and childhood development problems" (PCB Working Group n.d.). The last thing aboriginal people should have to worry about is being poisoned by the very food that has always both nourished their bodies and sustained them spiritually. "The process of hunting and fishing, followed by the sharing of food—the communal partaking of animals—is a time-honored ritual that binds us together and links us with our ancestors," said Watt-Cloutier (PCB Working Group n.d.). "Our foods do more than nourish our bodies," Inuit rights activist Ingmar Egede said. "When many things in our lives are changing, our foods remain the same. They make us feel the same as they have for generations. When I eat Inuit foods, I know who I am" (Cone 2004).

Watt-Cloutier, speaking for the Inuit, played a major role in the Stockholm Convention, negotiated in 2001 and implemented in 2005, which banned PCBs, dioxins, and several other persistent organic pollutants. As PCBs and dioxins were are being outlawed, however, a new group of legal contaminants are contaminating the Arctic, including chemical flame retardants (polybrominated diphenyl ethers, or PBDEs), which, like PCBs, scramble hormones and depress intelligence. These new chemicals are now building rapidly in the bodies of the Inuit and the animals they eat (Cone 2005, 207–13). The Inuit thus will be forced to keep a wary eye on the effluent of the industrial world for many years to come.

THE LUBICON CREE: LAND RIGHTS AND RESOURCE EXPLOITATION

The Lubicons were first promised a reserve by the Canadian federal government in 1939, before oil was discovered under their lands. Oil companies flooded into the area in the 1970s, all but destroying the Lubicon society and economy. The story of the Lubicons is a case study of how modern resource exploitation can ruin a natural setting and the Indigenous people who once lived there.

Despite the fact that almost C$10 million worth of oil has been pumped out of their lands since 1980, the five-hundred-member Lubicon Cree community of Little Buffalo, in far northern Alberta, has no running water, inadequate housing, no sewage, and no public infrastructure. The Lubicons have been faced with a choice: rely on an overtly hostile provincial government or move in with another First Nation that can offer them social services. In 1990, after six years of deliberation, the United Nations charged Canada with a human rights violations under the International Covenant on Civil and Political Rights, stating that "recent developments threaten the way of life and culture of the Lubicon Lake Cree and constitute a violation of Article 27 so long as they continue" (Resisting Destruction n.d.).

In 1971, the province of Alberta announced plans for construction of an all-weather road into the Lubicons' traditional territory to provide access for oil exploitation and logging. Road-building plans were undertaken without Lubicon consent, and resisted by the Native band in Canadian courts. At one point, the federal government asserted that the Lubicons were "merely squatters on Provincial crown land with no land rights to negotiate" (Resisting Destruction n.d.).

Having cleared legal challenges, Alberta built the all-weather road into Lubicon territory during 1979. Construction of the road was followed by an explosion of resource-exploitation activity that drove away moose and other game animals, causing the Lubicons' traditional hunting-and-trapping economy to collapse. Within four years, by 1983, more than four hundred oil wells had been drilled within a fifteen-mile radius of the Lubicons' community. From 1979 to 1983, the number of moose killed for food dropped 90 percent from 219 to 19, as trapping income also dropped 90 percent from C$5,000 to C$400 per family. At the same time, the proportion of Lubicon Cree on welfare shot up from less than 10 percent to more than 90 percent. During 1985 and 1986, nineteen of twenty-one Lubicon pregnancies resulted in stillbirths or miscarriages. "In essence the Canadian government has offered to build houses for the Lubicon people and to support us forever on welfare—like animals in the zoo who are cared for and fed at an appointed time," said Chief Bernard Ominayak (Resisting Destruction n.d.).

The Lubicon Lake Cree have a claim to about ten thousand square kilometers in northern Alberta east of the Peace River and north of Lesser Slave Lake. The land was regarded as so remote in 1900 that Canadian officials seeking to negotiate treaties completely ignored it. The Lubicon did not sign Treaty 8, which was negotiated in 1899 and 1900, providing the band no legal title to its land—title they were still seeking to negotiate with Canadian officials a century later.

Oil and Gas Exploitation

During the several decades that the Lubicons have sought legal title to their land base, it has been scarred by oil and gas production as well as industrial-scale logging. While Canadian officials have refused to set aside land for the Lubicons, large oil and gas, pulp and paper and logging companies have moved into the area to exploit its natural wealth (Johansen 2004.).

The Lubicons engaged in negotiations with the federal and provincial governments regarding title to their land three times during the 1990s, but the talks broke off because the two sides failed to agree on the size of the territory and monetary compensation for the Lubicon (Johansen 2004). "It is very worrisome when you are at the table year in, year out . . . with government sponsored and supported resource development . . . subverting the rights you are at the table to negotiate. You have to wonder if there is any sincerity about achieving a settlement," said band advisor Fred Lennarson (Guerette 2001, n.p.).

During the middle 1980s, after the provincial government enacted retroactive legislation to prevent the Lubicon from filing legal actions to protect its traditional territory from oil and gas development, the Lubicon launched a protest campaign against petroleum companies sponsoring the 1988 Calgary Olympics (Guerette 2001). On the eve of the international Olympic event, Premier Don Getty established a personal dialogue with Lubicon Chief Bernard Ominayak which led to the Grimshaw Accord, an agreement committing the province to transfer to Canada the ninety-five-square-mile reserve the Lubicon had been seeking (Guerette 2001).

Oil and gas extraction from Lubicon ancestral lands continued at about C$500 million a year. Not a penny went to the Lubicons. During 1988, after fourteen years getting nowhere in the courts, the Lubicons asserted active sovereignty over their land. A peaceful blockade of access roads into their traditional territory stopped all oil activity for six days. The barricades later were forcibly removed by the Royal Canadian Mounted Police. Alberta's Premier Don Getty then met with Lubicon leaders in Grimshaw, Alberta; the result is an agreement on a 243 square kilometer (95.4 square mile) reserve area called the Grimshaw Accord.

Twelve years later, the provincial government abandoned the agreement. In the meantime, environmental assessments disclosed that more than one thousand oil and gas well sites had been established within a twenty-kilometer radius of Lubicon Lake, on land that had been promised to the Indigenous people. During 2001, Marathon Canada announced plans for a natural gas compressor and pipeline in the area.

Logging Lubicon Land

Forest-industry companies by 2001 held concessions from the provincial government that covered nearly all of the land claimed by the Lubicon not already leased for oil and gas production. The first of the industrial loggers, the Japanese paper company Daishowa, began logging Lubicon land during the 1980s. In 1988, Daishowa announced plans for a pulp mill near the proposed Lubicon territory that would have processed lumber equaling the area of seventy football fields daily. The province of Alberta also granted Daishowa timber rights to an area including the entire Lubicon traditional territory.

An international boycott of Daishowa was launched to protest the company's clear-cutting of Lubicon land. In response, Daishowa stayed off Lubicon land during the 1991–92 winter logging season. Logging later resumed when the company sought to lift the boycott by suing the Lubicons' non-Native allies in Canadian courts. Daishowa's legal action was thrown out of court during the late 1990s as the boycott intensified. Daishowa, which manufactures paper bags, newsprint, and other paper products, retracted its plans to log Lubicon land only after the boycott began to reduce its revenues. Daishowa then again pledged to stay out of Lubicon forests until the Natives' land rights were delineated. At this point, the boycott ended. The company asserted that the boycott had cost it C$20 million in lost sales (Guerette 2001).

THE DENE: DECIMATED BY URANIUM MINING

At the dawn of the nuclear age, Paul Baton and more than thirty other Dene hunters and trappers who were recruited to mine uranium called it "the money rock" (Nikiforuk 1998, A-1). Paid C$3 a day by their employers, the Dene hauled and ferried burlap sacks of the grimy ore from one of the world's first uranium mines at Port Radium across the Northwest Territories to Fort McMurray. Since then, according to an account by Andrew Nikiforuk in the *Calgary*

Herald (from documents obtained through the Northwest Territories Cancer Registry), at least fourteen Dene who worked at the mine between 1942 and 1960 have died of lung, colon, and kidney cancers (Nikiforuk 1998, A-1).

The Port Radium mine supplied the uranium to fuel some of the first atomic bombs. Within half a century, uranium mining in northern Canada had left behind more than 120 million tons of radioactive waste, enough to cover the Trans-Canada Highway two meters (six and a half feet) deep across Canada. By the year 2000, production of uranium waste from Saskatchewan alone occurred at the rate of more than one million tons annually (LaDuke 2001).

The experiences of the Dene were similar to those of Navajo uranium miners in Arizona and New Mexico. Since 1975, following a thirty-year latency period for uranium exposure, hospitalizations for cancer, birth defects and circulatory illnesses in northern Saskatchewan had increased between 123 and 600 percent. In other areas impacted by uranium mining, cancers and birth defects have increased, in some cases, to as much as eight times the Canadian national average (LaDuke 1995).

"Before the mine, you never heard of cancer," said Baton, age eighty-three. "Now, lots of people have died of cancer" (Nikiforuk 1998, 1). The Dene were never told of uranium's dangers. Declassified documents have revealed that the U.S. government, which bought the uranium, and the Canadian federal government, at the time the world's largest supplier of uranium outside the United States, withheld health and safety information from all miners including the Native miners and their families. A 1991 federal aboriginal health survey found that the Deline Dene community reported twice as much illness as any other Canadian aboriginal community.

While mining, "[m]any Dene slept on the ore, ate fish from water contaminated by radioactive tailings and breathed radioactive dust while on the barges, docks and portages. More than a dozen men carried sacks of ore weighing more than 45 kilograms for 12 hours a day, six days a week, four months a year. . . . Children played with the dusty ore at river docks and portage landings. And their women sewed tents from used uranium sacks" (Nikiforuk 1998, A-1).

While many of the Dene blame uranium mining and its waste products for their increased cancer rates, some Canadian officials compiled statistics indicating only marginal increased mortality from uranium exposure. André Corriveau, the Northwest Territories' chief medical officer of health, noted that high cancer rates among the Dene have not differed significantly from the overall territorial profile. He said that the death rate was skewed upward by high rates of smoking (Nikiforuk 1998, 1). The Dene, in the meantime, maintain that the fact that almost half the workers in the Port Radium mine (fourteen of thirty) died of lung cancer cannot be explained by smoking alone.

Until his death in 1940, Louis Ayah, one of the North's great aboriginal spiritual leaders, repeatedly warned his people that the waters in Great Bear Lake would turn a foul yellow. According to "Grandfather," the yellow poison would flow toward the village, recalls Madelaine Bayha, one of a dozen scarfed and skirted "uranium widows" in the village (Nikiforuk 1998, A-1).

The first Dene to die of cancer, or what elders still call "the incurable disease," was Old Man Ferdinand in 1960. He had worked at the mine site as a logger, guide and stevedore for nearly a decade. "It was Christmastime and he wanted to shake hands with all the people as they came back from hunting," recalled Rene Fumoleau, then an Oblate missionary working in Deline. After saying goodbye to the last family that came in, Ferdinand declared: "'Well, I guess I shook hands with everyone now,' and he died three hours later" (Nikiforuk 1998, A-1).

According to Nikiforuk's account, others died during the next decade. Victor Dolphus' arm came off when he tried to start an outboard motor. Joe Kenny, a boat pilot, died of colon cancer. His son, Napoleon, a deckhand, died of stomach cancer. The premature death of so many men has not only left many widows, but interrupted the handing down of culture. "In Dene society it is the grandfather who passes on the traditions and now there are too many men with no uncles, fathers or grandfathers to advise them," said Cindy Gilday, Joe Kenny's daughter, and chair of Deline Uranium Committee (Nikiforuk 1998, A-1).

"It's the most vicious example of cultural genocide I have ever seen," Gilday said. "And it's in my own home." (Nikiforuk 1998, A-1) According to Nikiforuk, "Watching a uranium miner die of a radioactive damaged lung is a job only for the brave." He referred to Al King, an eighty-two-year-old retired member of the steelworkers union in Vancouver, British Columbia, who has held the hands of the dying. King described one retired Port Radium miner whose chest lesions were so bad that they had spread to his femur and exploded it. "They couldn't pump enough morphine into him to keep him from screaming before he died," said King (Nikiforuk 1998, A-1).

In exchange for their labors in the uranium mines, the Dene received a few sacks of flour, lard, and baking powder. "Nobody knew what was going on," recalled Isadore Yukon, who hauled uranium ore for three summers in a row during the 1940s. "Keeping the mine going full blast was the important thing" (Nikiforuk 1998, A-1).

The Dene town of Deline was described by one of its residents as:

> practically a village of widows. Most of the men who worked as laborers have died of some form of cancer. The widows, who are traditional women were left to raise their families with no breadwinners, supporters. They were left to depend on welfare and other young men for their traditional food source. This village of young men are the first generation of men in the history of Dene on this lake to grow up without guidance from their grandfathers, fathers and uncles. This cultural, economic, spiritual, emotional deprivation impact on the community is a threat to the survival of the one and only tribe on Great Bear Lake. (Gilday n.d.)

REDRESS FOR COLONIALISM REVISITED: CONCLUDING THOUGHTS

And what of the future? Canada in some ways has a leg up on the United States with its efforts to compensate boarding school abuses and make good on a history of colonial neglect of Native peoples. Efforts to reclaim languages, to provide Native peoples the rudiments of a decent living, and to clean up the environment have become a matter of national policy-making in Canada. The same issues exist in the United States, but the U.S. federal government has taken little initiative toward redress. Efforts to apologize to Native peoples in the United States under the rubric of making good for the outcomes of colonialism and ethno-ecocide have been discussed in Congress, and discarded. Momentum toward redress in the United States (such as the effort to address the Individual Indian Money Accounts funds mess in *Cobell v. Norton*, for example), have emerged outside of government, often despite it, in an adversarial manner. The idea that government has a duty to support the basic rights of its citizens (especially victims) still resonates (at least to an extent) in Canada. In the United States, where government today mainly has become a shill for economic privilege, this idea has been mainly lost.

The grassroots nature of change in Indigenous communities is not a bad thing, however; it is congruent with decolonization movements in general, and especially salient for Native peoples, most of whose societies have been maintained by ideas that nurture a unique worldview (Tuhiwai-Smith 2001). Such responses have (and will continue to be) a seed of First Nations' nation-building in response to a history of European-American political domination (Champagne 1985). When pollution crosses national borders, however, local action will not suffice. The Inuits' leaders have become international diplomats, for example, to impress on the world community the urgent need to outlaw dioxins, PCBs, and other toxins that threatened their lives and cultures. Inuit testimony played a crucial role in forging the Stockholm Convention on Persistent Organic Pollutants, negotiated in 2001, which is now being implemented. Canadian Natives have on their own initiative adopted the mantra of the Green Party: "Think globally, act locally." From international to local, peoples struggling to survive and to preserve their traditions will find solutions through a variety of Indigenous strategies.

In the final analysis, the First Nations of Canada, along with their American Indian counterparts in the United States, are fighting to liberate Mother Earth "from totally Eurocentric conceptions of the environment" (Grinde and Johansen 1995, 278). In opposing the ethno-ecocide policies of Canadian society, they are asserting their right to self-determination, and therefore the liberation of their diverse peoples and nations.

ADDENDUM: IDLE NO MORE

Idle No More is the latest protest movement originating among the aboriginal peoples in Canada, comprising the First Nations, Métis, and Inuit peoples, and their non-Indigenous supporters. It has become one of the largest Indigenous political movements in Canadian history and has spread among its supporters internationally.

After the Canadian election in May 2011, the government of Prime Minister Stephen Harper introduced a number of omnibus bills that seriously endanger aboriginal rights. One bill in particular, Bill C-45 of December 14, 2012, overhauls the Navigable Waters Protection Act, thereby weakening environmental safety and compromising aboriginal land rights. Many of the affected waterways in Bill-45 pass through land reserved for the First Nations. The oppressive legislation led to a series of marches and protests by aboriginal peoples regarding treaty rights and other grievances.

On December 11, 2012, Attawahpiskat chief Theresa Spence joined the movement by fasting until the Harper government and a representative of the Crown agreed to a summit meeting to address the oppressive conditions of the Indigenous peoples of Canada and revisit the treaty relationship. This led to an immense outpouring of Native protests across Canada, known as the Idle No More Movement. Protestors charged that Bill C-45 undermines centuries-old treaties by changing the approval process for leasing lands to non-aboriginal outside interests that favor resource extraction over environmental oversight. The manifesto of the Idle No More Movement says in part: "Currently this [Harper] government is trying to pass many laws so that [aboriginal] reserve lands can also be bought and sold by big companies to profit from resources" (Vowel 2013, 8).

Spence, the chief of a First Nation in Ontario, first hit news headlines when she declared a state of emergency over dismal housing and health conditions on her reserve. "Then, on December 11 [2012] Spence announced her 'hunger strike' on Ottawa's Parliament Hill the day after international Idle No More Indigenous protests took place in communities across the country. She vowed she was willing to die in her attempt to mend the broken relationship between Aboriginal people and Ottawa" (Ball 2013, 13).

The Idle No More Movement has since spread internationally through the social media and included "flash mobs" performing round dances in shopping malls during the December, 2012, Christmas shopping season.

Idle No More Protest.

Chief Theresa ended her fast on January 24, 2013, "after First Nations leaders and heads of the Liberal Party and New Democratic Party (NDP) signed a 13-point Declaration of Commitment that laid out the priorities, needs and demands of aboriginals in Canada" (Indian *Country Today* February 20, 2013, 6). However, neither Prime Minister Stephen Harper nor a representative of his Conservative government signed the agreement. But Harper in a meeting with Assembly of First Nations (AFN) officials did promise to continue the dialogue.

CHAPTER REVIEW

DISCUSSION QUESTIONS

1. Name the three major groups of First Nations peoples. What are their approximate numbers and locations in Canada?
2. What are the three different kinds of Indian legal status in Canada? Explain.
3. Who was Luis Riel and what was he known for in Canadian history?
4. Name some of the Indian tribes and give their approximate locations.

5. Explain the environmental issues involving the Cree and James Bay Hydro-Quebec.
6. What are some of the environmental issues facing Canada's aboriginal peoples? The Inuu of Labrador? Pimicikamak Cree? Inuit? Lubicon Cree? Dene?
7. Who is Theresa Spense, and what is her role in the Indigenous struggle?

SUGGESTED READINGS

Assembly of First Nations [Canada]. 1990. *Towards Linguistic Justice for First Nations*. Ottawa, Ontario: Education Secretariat, Assembly of First Nations.

Canadian Press. 2002. "Natives Lay Claim to Nova Scotia Forests." *Toronto Globe and Mail*, February 5, A-6.

CHAMPAGNE, DUANE, ed. 2001. *The Native North American Alamanac*. 2nd ed. Farmington Hills: MI.: Gale Group. A reference work with relevant articles on Canada's First Nation peoples.

DICKASON, OLIVE PATRICIA, with DAVID T. MCNAB. 2009. *Canada's First Nations: A History of Founding Peoples from Earliest Times*. 4th ed. Oxford University Press.

"First Nations' Realities: Poisoned Land." 2005. First Nations Health Bulletin Summer 2005 Special Issue: Safe Homes, Safe Communities, 4. http://www.afn.ca/cmslib/general/HB-SM-05.pdf

LADUKE, WINONA. 2010. "Indigenous Environmental Perspectives: A North American Primer." In *Native American Voices: A Reader*, edited by Susan Lobo, Steve Talbot, and Traci L. Morris. 376–87. 3rd ed. Upper Saddle River, NJ: Prentice Hall.

LAGHI, BRIAN. 2001. "Policy for Land Claims Abject Failure." *Toronto Globe and Mail,* January 2, n.p.

LAWLOR, ALLISON. 2001. "Strict Enforcement Planned at Burnt Church." *Toronto Globe and Mail*, August 28.

MOFINA, RICK. 2000. "Study Pinpoints Dioxin Origins: Cancer-causing Agents in Arctic Aboriginals' Breast Milk Comes from U.S. and Quebec." *Montreal Gazette*, October 4, A-12.

Native Americas. 1995. "NATO and Innu Set for Showdown in Eastern Canada." *Native Americas* 12 (Fall): 10–11.

PRATT, WILLIAM HENRY. 1987. *Battlefield and Classroom: Four Decades with the American Indian, 1867–1904*, edited by Robert M. Utley. Lincoln: University of Nebraska Press.

PRICE, JOHN. 1979. *Indians of Canada: Cultural Dynamics*. Salem, WI: Sheffield.

TALBOT, STEVE. 2010. "First Nations: Indigenous Peoples of Canada." In *Native American Voices: A Reader*, edited by Susan Lobo, Steve Talbot, and Traci L. Morris. 36–41. 3rd ed. Upper Saddle River, NJ: Prentice Hall, 2010.

REFERENCES

Associated Press. 1994. "Quebec will Shelve Huge Hydroelectric Project Indefinitely." *Omaha World-Herald*, November 19, 7.

Associated Press. 1998. "Canada's United Church Apologizes for Abuse at Indian Schools." *Associated Press Canada*, October 28.

BALL, DAVD P. 2013. "A Journey of Support," *Indian Country Today* 3 (2, January 23): 13.

BIEGERT, CLAUS. 1995. "A People Called Empty." In Rainer Wittenborn and Biegert, "Amazon of the North: James Bay Revisited." Program for Show, Santa Fe Center for Contemporary Arts, August 4 through September 5, 1995, n.p.

BOURRIE, MARK. 1998. "RIGHTS: Canada Apologizes For Abuse of Native Peoples." *Inter Press Service*, January 8. http://www.ipsnews.net/1998/01/rights-canada-apologizes-for-abuse-of-native-peoples/

CADBURY, DEBORAH. 1997. *Altering Eden: The Feminization of Nature*. New York: St. Martin's Press.

CALDWELL, BRAD. n.d. "Fisheries Law: Papers and Articles: R. v. Marshall: Supreme Court of Canada Recognizes Aboriginal Treaty Rights to Trade in Fish." Reprinted from November 1999 issue of *Westcoast Fisherman*, in admiraltylaw.com http://www.admiraltylaw.com/fisheries/Papers/treatyrights.htm

Canadian Press. 2001. "Court Rules Natives Don't Have Logging Rights." *Toronto Globe and Mail*, March 8.

———. 2002. "Natives Lay Claim to Nova Scotia Forests." *Toronto Globe and Mail*, February 5, A-6.

Canadian Arctic Resources Committee. n.d. "Sustainable Development in the Hudson Bay: James Bay Bio-region." Environmental Committee of Sanikiluaq, Rawson Academy of Aquatic Science. http://www.carc.org/pubs/v19no3/2.htm

CHAMPAGNE, DUANE. 1985. *American Indian Societies: Strategies and Conditions of Political and Cultural Survival in American Indian Societies*. Cultural Survival Report 21. Cambridge, MA: Cultural Survival (December).

CHURCHILL, WARD, and WINONA LADUKE. 1992. "The Political Economy of Radioactive Colonialism" In *The State of Native America: Genocide, Colonization and Resistance*, edited by M. Annette Jaimes, 241–66. Boston: South End Press.

CLOUTIER, SHEILA WATT. Personal Communication, March 28, 2001.

CONE, MARLA. 1996. "Human Immune Systems May be Pollution Victims." *Los Angeles Times*, May 13, A-1.

———. 2004. "Dozens of Words for Snow, None for Pollution." *Mother Jones* (January–February). [http://www.hartford-hwp.com/archives/27b/059.html]

———. 2005. *Silent Snow: The Slow Poisoning of the Arctic*. New York: Grove Press.

Cultural Survival News Notes. 2001. "Innu Respond to N.F. Hydro/Alcoa Announcement." *Cultural Survival News Notes*, July 26. http://www.cs.org/main.htm

DEWAILLY, ÉRIC, PIERRE AYOTTE, SUZANNE BRUNEAU, SUZANNE GINGRAS, MARTHE BELLES-ISLES, and RAYNALD ROY. 2000. "Susceptibility to Infections and Immune Status in Inuit Infants Exposed to Organochlorines." *Environment Health Perspectives* 108: 205–11.

————, S. BRUNEAU, C. LALIBERTE, M. BELLES-ILES, J.-P. WEBER, and R. ROY. 1993a. "Breast Milk Contamination by PCB and PCDD/Fs in Arctic Quebec. Preliminary Results on the Immune Status of Inuit Infants." *Organohalogen Compounds* 13: 403–6.

————, S. DODIN, R. VERREAULT, P. AYOTTE, L. SAUVE L. and J. MORIN. 1993b. High Organochlorine Body Burden in Breast Cancer Women with Oestrogen Receptors. *Organohalogen Compounds* 13: 385–388.

————, J. J. RYAN, C. LALIBERTE, S. BRUNEAU, J.-P.WEBER, S. GINGRAS, and G. CARRIER. 1994. "Exposure of Remote Maritime Populations to Coplanar PCBs." *Environmental Health Perspectives* 102 suppl. 1: 205–209.

DICKASON, OLIVE PATRICIA, and DAVID T. MCNAB. 2009. *Canada's First Nations: A History of Founding Peoples from Earliest Times.* 4th ed. Canada: Oxford University Press.

Drillbits and Tailings. 1997. "Innu Begin Occupation To Halt Construction At Voisey's Bay." *Drillbits and Tailings,* August 21, n.p.

DUMONT, CHARLES. 1995. "Proceedings of 1995 Canadian Mercury Network Workshop. Mercury and Health: The James Bay Cree." Cree Board of Health and Social Services. Montreal, 1995, in Water Science: National Water Research Institiute. Canada's Leader in Freshwater Research. http://www.ec.gc.ca/inre-nwri/

FRUM, DAVID. 1998. "Natives Should Do the Thanking: The European Settlement of North America Aided Their Lifestyle." *Financial Post,* January 13: n.p.

GABRIELSEN, GEIR WING. 2005. "The Arctic Paradox: The Traditional Diet of Inuits has Health benefits but Exposes Them to Dangerous Levels of Pollutants." *Nature* 436 (July 14): 177–78.

GILDAY, CINDY KENNY. n.d. "A Village of Widows." *Arctic Circle.* http://arcticcircle.uconn.edu/SEEJ/Mining/gilday.html

GRINDE, DONALD A., and BRUCE E. JOHANSEN. 1995. *Ecocide of Native America.* Santa Fe: Clear Light.

GUERETTE, DEB. 2001. "No Clear-cut Answer: Timber Rights Allocation on Lubicon Land a Worrisome Development." *Grande Prairie Daily Herald-Tribune,* March 5, n.p.

HIPWELL, BILL. 1998. "Apology Should Have Been a Thank You." *The Financial Post* [Ottawa, Ontario], February 3, 18.

Indian Country Today. 2013. "Spence Ends Fast." *Indian Country Today,* February 20, 6.

Inter Press Service. 1993. *Story Earth: Native Voices on the Environment.* San Francisco: Mercury House.

JACOBSON, JOSEPH L., and SANDRA W. JACOBSON. 1996. "Intellectual Impairment in Children Exposed to Polychlorinated Biphenyls *in Utero.*" *New England Journal of Medicine* 335 (11, September 12): 783–89.

JOHANSEN, BRUCE E. 2000a. "Education: The Nightmare and the Dream: A Shared National Tragedy, a Shared National Disgrace." *Native Americas* 12 (4): 10–19.

————. 2000b. "Pristine No More: The Arctic, Where Mother's Milk is Toxic." *The Progressive* (December): 27–29.

————. 2003. *The Dirty Dozen: Toxic Chemicals and the Earth's Future.* Westport, CT: Praeger Publishers.

————, ed. 2004. *Enduring Legacies: Native American Treaties and Contemporary Controversies.* Westport, CT: Praeger Publishers.

————. 2010. *Native Americans Today: A Biographical Dictionary.* Santa Barbara, CA: ABC-CLIO.

————, and BARRY PRITZKER. 2007. *Encyclopedia of the American Indian.* 4 vols. Santa Barbara, CA: ABC-CLIO.

LADUKE, WINONA. 1993. "Tribal Coalition Dams Hydro-Quebec Project." *Indian Country Today,* July 21, A-3.

————. 1999. *All Our Relations: Native Struggles for Land and Life.* Cambridge, MA: South End Press.

————. 2001. "Insider Essays: Our Responsibility." *Electnet/Newswire,* October 2. http://www.electnet.org/dsp_essay.cfm?intID=28

LANGAN, FRED. 1991. Canadians Negotiate Power Project. *Christian Science Monitor,* September 18

LAWTON, VALERIE, and KELLY TOUGHILL. 1999. "Chiefs Call Temporary Truce in Fish War." *Toronto Star,* October 7, n.p.

LONG, J. ANTHONY, and KATHERINE BEATY CHISTE. 1994. "Aboriginal Peoples in Canada." In *The Native North American Almanac,* edited by Duane Champagne, 334–54. Detroit: Gale Research.

LOWEY, MARK. 1999. "Alberta Natives Sue Over Residential Schools." *Calgary Herald,* January 3, A-1.

MARTIN, IAN. 2005. "Restoring Linguistic Rights for Aboriginals." *Toronto Star,* June 3, n.p.

MATHEWSON, GEORGE. 2005. "Toxic Creek Worries Band." *Sarnia [Ontario] Observer* in *Anishinabek News* (North Bay, Ontario), April, 22.

MATTEO, ENZO DI. 2002. "Damned Deal: Cree Leaders Call Hydro Pact Signed in Secret a Monstrous Sellout." *Now Magazine* [Toronto], February, n.p.

MCLLROY, ANNE. 1998. "Canadians Apologize for Abuse." *Manchester Guardian Weekly,* November 8, 5.

MCMILLAN, ALAN D. 1994. "Canadian Native Distribution, Habitat, and Demograhy." In *The Native North American Almanac,* edited by Duane Champagne, 223–43. Detroit: Gale Research.

MCNUTT, DEBI, and ZOLTRAN GROSSMAN. 2000. Midwest Treaty Network, Madison, Wisconsin. Personal communication, September 5.

MILLOY, JOHN S. 1999. *A National Crime: The Canadian Government and the Residential School System, 1879–1986.* Winnipeg: Manitoba University Press.

MOFINA, RICK. 1999. "Treaty Ruling Causing 'Chaos': Federal Cabinet May Suspend Top Court Ruling on Native Fishing." *Ottawa Citizen,* September 28, A-3.

MORSE, BRADFORD W. 1994. "An Overview of Canadian Aboriginal Law." In *The Native North American Almanac,* edited by Duane Champagne, 510–516. Detroit: Gale Research.

Native Forest Network. 1994. "Quebec-Hydro Project May Destroy James Bay." Victoria, British Columbia: Friends of the Earth. http://jinx.sistm.unsw.edu.au/~greenlft/1994/137/137p14.htm

NIKIFORUK, ANDREW. 1998. "Echoes of the Atomic Age: Cancer Kills Fourteen Aboriginal Uranium Workers." *Calgary Herald*, March 14, A-1, A-4. http://www.ccnr.org/deline_deaths.html

PCB Working Group. n.d. "Communities Respond to PCB Contamination: Their Stories are Here." Accessed March 22, 2013. http://www.learningace.com/doc/5278671/88318dba028abb0096268d22debcee37/ipen-pcb

PETERSON, DIANE J. 2000. "Two Twin Cities Churches Protest Hydro Power Injustices." *Earthkeeping News* 9 (July/August). http://www.nacce.org/2000/manitoba.html

PRICE, JOHN. 1979. *Indians of Canada: Cultural Dyamics.* Salem, WI: Sheffield.

"Resisting Destruction: Chronology of the Lubicon Crees' Struggle to Survive." n.d. http://www.rob.00go.com/Lubicon%20News.htm

ROSLIN, ALEX. 2000. "Crees Revive Hydro Project." *Montreal Gazette*, January 21. http://www.montrealgazette.com/news/pages/010121/5036705.html

Royal Commission on Aboriginal Peoples. 1999. Parliament of Canada, Parliamentary Information and Research Service. PRB 99-24E. http://www.parl.gc.ca/Content/LOP/ResearchPublications/prb9924-e.htm

ROZELL, NED. 2000. "Alaska Science Forum: Dioxins: Another Uninvited Visitor to the North." Geophysical Institute, University of Alaska Fairbanks. November 9. http://www.gi.alaska.edu/ScienceForum/ASF15/1515.html

SCHNEIDER, HOWARD. 1996. "Facing World's Pollution in the North." *Washington Post*, September 21, A-15. http://www.washingtonpost.com/wp-srv/inatl/long-term/canada/stories/pollution092196.htm

SIERRA CLUB. n.d. HUDSON BAY/JAMES BAY WATERSHED Eco-region. http://www.sierraclub.org/ecoregions/hudsonbay.asp

STASTNA, KAZI. 2004. "There's No M For Mohawk; Language Fading, Software May Help Delay Disappearance." *Montreal Gazette*, April 27. http://www.canada.com/montreal/montrealgazette/news/story.html?id=5eee6167-9773-4255-8dd1-d2ed62249a62

STEWART, JANE. 1998. "Notes for an Address by the Honourable Jane Stewart Minister of Indian Affairs and Northern Development on the Occasion of the Unveiling of *Gathering Strength—Canada's Aboriginal Action Plan.* Ottawa, Ontario. January 7. Aboriginal Affairs and Northern Development Canada. https://www.aadnc-aandc.gc.ca/eng/1100100015725/1100100015726

SUZUKI, DAVID. 2000. "Science Matters: POP Agreement Needed to Eliminate Toxic Chemicals." December 6. http://www.davidsuzuki.org/Dr_David_Suzuki/Article_Archives/weekly12060002.asp

TOUGHILL, KELLY. 2000. "Mi'kmaq Own Entire Province, N[ova] S[cotia] Court Told." *Toronto Star*, December 9, n.p.

TUHIWAI-SMITH, LINDA. 2001. *Decolonizing Methodologies: Research and Indigenous Peoples.* London, UK and Dunedin, New Zealand: Zed Books.

VOWEL, CHELSEA. 2013. "The Natives Are Restless. Wonder Why?" *Indian Country Today*, January 16, 8–9.

WALDMAN, CARL. 2000. *Atlas of the North American Indian.* Rev. ed. New York: Checkmark Books.

10

EXPERIMENT IN "RED CAPITALISM"
OIL VERSUS ALASKA NATIVE LAND AND SUBSISTENCE RIGHTS

Oil drop with Suqpiaq petroglyph symbolizing the Alaska Native subsistence struggle against capitalist development. The drop of oil has "removed" part of the leg from the petrogylph representing the destruction of Native land and culture.

All aboriginal titles, if any, and claims of aboriginal title in Alaska based on use and occupancy, including submerged land underneath all water areas, both inland and offshore, and including any aboriginal hunting or fishing rights that may exist, are hereby extinguished.

(Alaska Native Claims Settlement Act P.L. 92-203, Sec. 4b)

❖ ❖ ❖

Everybody is subsistence here in the village.

—Vincent Kvasnikoff, English Bay, Alaska

"Who speaks for the eagle?" Onondaga Faithkeeper Oren Lyons wanted to know. At the historic United Nations international conference on the rights of Indigenous peoples in 1977, it fell to Oren Lyons to issue the Haudenosaunee (Iroquois) "A Basic Call to Consciousness." Lyons, a traditional chief of the Onondaga Nation (Iroquois), was advocating for the natural world which is an integral part of Indigenous culture and society. "I see no seat for the eagles," he said. "We forget and we consider ourselves superior. But we are after all a mere part of creation." (Barreiro 2007, 40).

Thirty years later on July 7, 2007, Faithkeeper Lyons and other Native American traditionalists were still asking the same question when Native and non-Native leaders attended a Mother Earth program at the National Museum of the American Indian in Washington, DC. Former Vice-president Al Gore spoke at the gathering, "thanking Indians for reminding humanity how we're all 'connected to the natural world'" (Barreiro 2007, 36). Gore's much acclaimed film, *An Inconvenient Truth*, had won an Oscar at the Hollywood Academy Awards ceremony the previous year for the best documentary. Scientific evidence for the climate change crisis is now beyond dispute. "Current evidence point toward increased drought, more frequent severe storms, the drop of water levels in lakes and rivers, and a rise in sea level. The northward migration of warmer temperatures is bringing change to vegetation, growing seasons, and animal behavior, as well as diseases and pests that attack humans, plants, and animals" (Barreiro 2007, 38). The six hundred Iñupiat Eskimo residents of Shishmaref, Alaska, are experiencing their village falling into the rising Chukchi Sea. Shishmaref may be the canary in the coal mine, an indicator of what is to come.

Perhaps the greatest climate change danger to Indigenous peoples is the threat to a traditional subsistence way of life, a living gained by hunting, fishing, and gathering in a respectful and spiritual way. "The Arctic Region's climate is changing very rapidly, resulting in widespread melting of glaciers and sea ice and shortened snow season. . . . For Native Alaskans this can turn into a serious loss of subsistence food and animals central to their culture" (Barreiro 2007, 38). The climate threat to Alaska Native subsistence, however, is compounded by events emanating from the 1968 Alaska oil discovery and development, and that of the Alaska Native Claims Settlement Act (ANCSA) of 1971. The latter is the immediate danger faced by the Native peoples of Alaska.

CHAPTER OVERVIEW

In this chapter we examine the events leading up to the 1968 oil discovery and development in Alaska and the passage of the 1971 Alaska Native Claims Settlement Act, which brought into focus the immense giveaway of Native lands and a corporate model of land ownership and administration imposed on Alaska Native communities. The primary historical focus is the decades of the 1960s and the 1970s, although the actions emanating from the oil discovery and land claims legislation had unforeseen implications for the Alaska Native struggle for subsistence rights in the 1980s continuing to the present.

In the last decades of the twentieth century, Alaska represented the American frontier, the capitalist development of an area one-fifth the size of the entire United States, 686,412 square miles. But what kind of development? Development for multinational oil corporations, impersonal and located in far-off temperate capitals? Development for Alaska's state entrepreneurs and business interests with their historic disregard of Native interests? Development for the non-Native working class who hoped to benefit from jobs stemming from the oil boom? "Or development for the Indigenous peoples, the Alaska Natives, who today are 15 percent of the state's population, but who have been treated (according to some Native activists) as 'niggers in parkas?'" In point of fact, even before the oil boom, the history of Alaska has been "an account of the expropriation of land and resources by people and businesses located outside Alaska and the dislocations and dependencies these actions caused among Natives" (Jorgensen 2003, 95).

It was clear that by the 1960s Alaska was at the crossroads of tremendous economic change that would have a major impact on the lives and traditions of Alaska Natives. A major issue to emerge in the 1980s and 1990s was the question of Native subsistence rights in the crucible of capitalist development. In order to understand the significance of the recent impact of the oil discovery and subsequent legislation to settle the Native land claims, we provide a historical perspective of earlier economic changes in the nineteenth and early twentieth centuries that did not have the same consequences.

THEORETICAL PERSPECTIVES

Our major concept in this chapter is *subsistence*. Subsistence in the Indigenous world means more than the minimum necessity to support life. It means living close to nature, growing or gathering one's food, or obtaining it by hunting and fishing, with little reliance on a cash economy. Of course, a Native person must own or have legal access to the land and waters on which subsistence activities take place.

Alaska Natives who follow a subsistence economy have a totally different view of the natural world than do non-Native, rural Alaskans.

Alaska Native peoples have traditionally tried to live in harmony with the world around them. This has required the construction of an intricate subsistence-based worldview, a complex way of life with specific cultural mandates regarding the ways in which the human being is to relate to other human relatives and the natural and spiritual worlds. . . . Native peoples developed many rituals and ceremonies with respect to motherhood and child rearing, care of animals, hunting and trapping practices, and related ceremonies for maintaining balance between the human, natural, and spiritual realms. (Kawagley 1995, 8)

Professor of anthropology Deanna Kingston, who is King Island Eskimo, explains the spiritual importance of the animal world in the following way (Kingston 2001): Animals have thought, free will like people, and they give themselves up to humans who are worthy. The hunter is obligated to give back to the animals he hunts by performing rituals, or dancing to entertain the animals, to reciprocate for the animals having given their flesh and fur. Life and death is a circle. That is why there is name recycling among the Eskimos, and along with the name the soul is also reincarnated. Animals are reincarnated in the same way. Hunters perform rituals so that the animal spirit can return home to be reborn. Environmentalists want to conserve animals, but Eskimos say that animals are a finite number who recirculate. If game is scarce, it is because humans are not acting right or doing the required rituals. These strongly held beliefs and practices are absent in the subsistence activities of non-Natives.

A related concept for understanding Indigenous subsistence is *cultural ecology*. It is defined as the adaptation of human beings to their physical environment: the customs, beliefs, and roles related to getting food and shelter. There are various biotic zones in Alaska in terms of its fauna and flora, landscape, and weather. The state has a rich and varied ecology, and the different economic adaptations found among its Native peoples correspond to these biotic zones. Depending on the biotic environment, the aboriginal population density varies a great deal. The Bering Sea and arctic tundra areas in the far north support few persons. A setting of coniferous forest in the Interior also has a limited potential for settlement. Only in the grasslands of the Aleutian biotic province does the population density increase, reaching its peak in a north Pacific forest environment of southern Alaska and the southeastern panhandle. "The people of the Arctic and sub-arctic have adapted to these ecosystems and still maintain a viable, sustainable subsistence economy. The worldviews of the peoples of these regions recognize that *the land is a giver of life*" (Kawagley 1995, 12, emphasis added).

The spiritual aspect of Native peoples' beliefs and practices in relation to their land is rarely understood by non-Natives, but it is key to the struggle by Alaska Natives for subsistence rights. In *Recovering the Sacred*, Indian environmentalist Winona LaDuke (2005) explains that in each Indigenous culture there are certain things, such as mountains, lakes, religious objects, fish, and animals that are part of the sacred landscape.

This is the concept of "the Sacred" in Native American spiritual culture. LaDuke defines it as "the relationship of peoples to their sacred lands, to relatives with fins or hooves, to the plant and animal foods that anchor a way of life" (LaDuke 2005, 12). In Alaska, these sacred relatives include the whales, fish and game, roots and berries. "The Sacred" lies at the heart of what subsistence means to Native peoples. "The term 'subsistence' in Alaska . . . is not just about getting food on the table; it is also the proper way of conducting social relations among humans and between humans and animals" (Bodenhorn 2000, 133). "The Sacred" is to know something more with the spirit than with the other senses (Beck and Walters 1977, 6). It is not only something made or declared holy; it is also something that is shared, a collective experience necessary in order to keep the oral traditions and sacred ways vital. It lies at the heart of Indigenous culture.

We hypothesize that "the Sacred" in Alaska Native subsistence complex is also informed by anthropologist Edward Spicer's concept of *social and cultural integration* (Spicer 1959/60). He defines the two processes as linking different components of the *society* (the behavior of groups of people interacting in a defined territory), and *culture* (material items, techniques, customs, values, and beliefs). Social and cultural linkage are necessary for the functioning and internal cohesion of a people-hood (society), and its

way of life (culture) respectively. An example of social linkage is the Civil Rights Movement when viewed as an attempt by African Americans to make social practice in the South consistent with American democracy. An example of cultural linkage is the United States of fifty years ago when the Christian Bible served to link many activities from planting to village government. We propose in this chapter that the subsistence complex of activities and beliefs may be the linking mechanism that integrates Alaska Native society and culture. Curtailing or suppressing the subsistence rights of Alaska Natives could have negative consequences for the continued maintenance and well-being of Indigenous culture and society.

In the following pages we explore the struggle for land and subsistence rights by the Native peoples of Alaska in its ethnohistorical perspective.

THE INDIGENOUS PEOPLES OF ALASKA

Alaska is more than twice the size of Texas and is bordered on the east by Canada, the north by the Arctic Ocean, and the south and west by the Pacific Ocean and Bering Sea. It has nineteen mountains over 14,000 feet, including Mt. Denali (McKinley), the highest peak in North America at 20,320 feet.

There are several major groups of Indigenous peoples in Alaska who are commonly termed Eskimos, Aleuts, and Indians, and who are collectively called

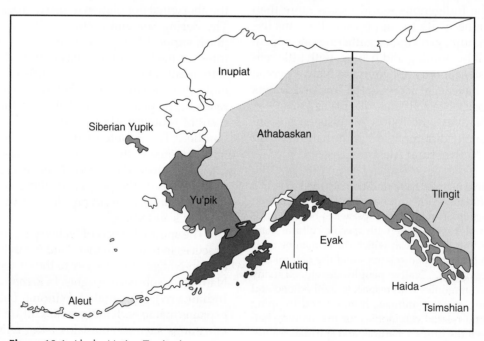

Figure 10.1 Alaska Native Territories.

Alaska Natives. Anthropologists hypothesize that the peopling of Alaska was from Asia across the Bering Strait, first by the Indians, and more recently the Eskimos. Native scholars dispute the Bering Strait hypothesis as far too simplistic and Eurocentric. What is clear, however, is that whatever their origins, Alaska's Native peoples have made unique and efficient adaptations to their arctic and subarctic environments. These cultural adaptations are now being modified in unhealthy ways, and some are seriously in jeopardy of being lost altogether. (See Figure 10.1)

Eskimos

The Eskimo category includes four ethnically related Indigenous peoples who are distinguished by differences in homeland, language or dialect, traditions, and identity. At the time of historical contact and conquest, three-fifths spoke the Inupi language or dialect, and the remainder spoke Yupik. Both related languages are still widely spoken today. Significantly more than half of the total Eskimo population of the circumpolar region of the planet are found in Alaska. The remainder are found in northeastern Siberia of the Russian Federation, northern Canada, and Greenland.

The traditional territory of the Iñupiat Eskimos, or "real people," of northern and northwest Alaska stretches from the U.S.-Canadian border along the coast of the Arctic Ocean and the Bering Sea coast from Kotzebue Sound to Unalakleet. The region consists of low-lying coastal tundra, with many streams, rivers, and lakes. "This plain and the foothills found farther inland contain herds of migratory caribou, and the mountains beyond the foothills are home to bears and Dall sheep. . . . Berries and some edible plants occur throughout the region" (Bodenhorn 2000, 131). The coastal waters are rich in marine life, especially the Bowhead and Beluga whales on which the people have depended for survival for the bulk of their subsistence diet for at least two thousand years. A Point Hope Iñupiat told the Eskimo Whaling Commission in 1988: "We eat the animals of the sea. We eat animals of the land. We have two sources for our subsistence, we who live on the shores" (Bodenhorn 2000, 133). Their aboriginal population was about 2,900 in 1840 when first contacted by commercial non-Native explorers and whalers, and the population lived in small extended family settlements. "In addition to permanent winter settlements, there were other strategically located sites used during certain times of the year either for hunting or fishing" (Craig 1996, 274). Today, the Iñupiat territory in Alaska has a total population of twelve thousand and includes

the modern communities of Nome, Kotzebue, and Barrow. Despite the availability of some wage jobs related to the oil fields, the need for subsistence activities remain important. "Our culture is built around hunting, fishing, and food gathering; these subsistence activities are still a big part of our life as we lack industry in our villages to support a cash economy lifestyle" (Craig 1996, 276).

"In 1958 the Atomic Energy Commission (AEC) actively sought Alaskan support for Project Chariot, which would create a deepwater port near Cape Thompson by detonating atomic bombs many times more powerful than Hiroshima" (Craig 1996, 275). Protests by the Iñupiat and other Alaska Natives led to the cancellation of the dangerous project, but thirty years later it was found that "the AEC had dumped 15,000 pounds of radioactive materials from Nevada at the site. In the meantime, several members of a family whose campground is the Cape Thompson site died of cancer" (Craig 1996, 275). The radioactive waste was simply buried in a hole in the ground and covered with gravel.

A second great Eskimo nation are the Yup'ik (Yupiit)) of southwestern Alaska, whose land extends "from Prince William Sound on the Pacific coast of Alaska to both sides of the Bering Strait and from there 6,000 miles north and east along Canada's Arctic coast into Labrador and Greenland. . . . Today, nearly 20,000 Yupiit live in western Alaska, scattered among seventy small communities of from 150 to 600 inhabitants each" (Fienup-Riordan 2000, 241, 248). These villages are found principally along the coast and three mighty river systems, the Yukon, Kuskokwim, and Nushagak. "The sub-arctic tundra environment nourishes a rich array of plants and animals, and the Bering Sea coast supports rich fauna" (Fienup-Riordan 2000, 249). The richness of the biotic environment allowed for a more settled way of life than in other parts of the Arctic. "Along the coast, harvesting activity focused on seals, walrus, beluga whales, ocean-going and freshwater fish, migratory birds, small animals, berries, and greens. . . . Upriver hunters also pursued larger animals, including moose, caribou, and bear" (Fienup-Riordan 2000, 249).

A Yup'ik writer, John Active, explains the spiritual bond between humans and nonhuman life in his culture:

> Our closeness to nature is religious, we call it spirituality. The Yup'ik believe that everything has a spirit. Animals, birds, and plants have an awareness, and we treat them with the same respect we have for ourselves. . . . [W]e

treat them as guests. We talk to the fish and animals. We tell them we caught them because we need them to survive, and we will eat them with care. We thank them for having been caught and we believe their spirits will return to their makers and report on how they were cared for. If the animals were treated well, then their makers will provide more of the same. Yup'ik spirituality is being aware and conscious of everything around including animals, plants, and the environment. (Active 1996, 718)

Since 1964, a regional nonprofit corporation, the Association of Village Council Presidents (AVCP), has represented fifty-six villages in the Yukon-Kuskokwim Delta. The main issue that it is currently dealing with is subsistence rights.

We should also mention a third Eskimo people, the Siberian Yup'ik, who people St. Lawrence Island (part of Alaska) and the Russian coast across the Bering Strait. "Saint Lawrence Island lies about 40 miles to the southeast of the Siberian mainland but about 125 miles from that of Alaska" (Hughes 1984, 243). We include them here because both before and after the Cold War with the former Soviet Union, there was trade and communication between those in Siberia and the Alaska Yup'ik to whom they are related. The Chukotka, Autonomous Region of the Russian Federation is inhabited by several groups of Native and non-Native peoples. The coastal Yup'ik and the inland reindeer herders, the more numerous Chukchi, constitute the two most numerous Native groups of the region. The Siberian Yup'ik depend on sea-mammal hunting, the most important of which are the walrus and several species of seal, now endangered by the threat of global warming. Bowhead whales are taken during open-water season, and seals during the winter sea-ice season. Other subsistence activities include gathering berries and grasses on the tundra, gathering eggs of ducks, geese, and other birds, and river fishing.

A fourth group are the Alutiiq, or Pacific Eskimos, although their self-designation is *Sugpiaq* ("real person"). They are sometimes mistakenly referred to as Aleut, the aboriginal people of the Aleutian Islands who have a different culture and language.

The Alutiiq include several culturally and linguistically related peoples who have inhabited the regions of the Alaska Peninsula, Prince William Sound, the lower Kenai Peninsula, and Kodiak Island for at least seven thousand years. The Kodiak Alutiiq are also called the Kontiagmiut. Their aboriginal population is estimated as between ten thousand and twenty thousand people, with Kodiak Island being one of the most densely populated Indigenous areas north of Mexico.

In the 1980s the descendants of the Pacific Eskimos were living in fifteen villages and five towns, as well as scattered among the larger cities of Alaska and the other states. The current Alutiiq population is about five thousand. They retained a strong Russian influence in language, religion, and culture. American influence became predominant by the mid-nineteenth century. After 1936, several villages formed Indian Reorganization Act governments. In 1964 a severe Alaska earthquake devastated several of their villages. Since the passage of the Alaska Native Claims Act in 1971, the Alutiiq have been represented by three different regional corporations, including the Bristol Bay Native Corporation. A cultural revitalization movement took place on Kodiak Island in the mid-1980s. In 1989 the *Exxon Valdez* ran aground in Prince William Sound and spilled nearly eleven million gallons of crude oil, resulting in a tremendous loss of sea life upon which the people depend for their maritime livelihood and subsistence economy. The region has never fully recovered.

Unanangan

The Unanangan, or Aleuts, of southwestern Alaska occupy a long and narrow land base, the Aleutian Shumagin and Pribilof Islands, reaching from the Alaskan mainland westward toward the International Date Line. It is believed that the Aleut people separated from the proto-Eskimo stock 4,500 years ago to form their own peoplehood and linguistic grouping. In 1900 they occupied small villages, each comprised of six or seven sod houses, and located either on the Bering Sea or the north Pacific Ocean coasts. Each village had an assigned hunting area.

The 1867 purchase of Alaska by the United States had little impact on the Unanangan until World War II. After the Japanese attack on the Aleutian Islands, the United States decided to relocate all the Native islanders supposedly to protect them from the invaders. "The people were interned in southeast Alaska in camps which were mostly located in abandoned canneries. There was no heat, scant food, and little medical care. Disease brought on by unsanitary conditions of the camps took the lives of many people, those most susceptible again being the elders and children" (Swetzof 1996, 665). Tuberculosis became endemic. After the war, the Unanangan were allowed to go home, but it took months to arrange transportation, and the people found their villages destroyed, and their churches and homes ransacked by the U.S. military. Today they heroically strive to maintain their Native communities and traditions while at the same time adjusting to contemporary economic options and conditions.

Indians

This is another umbrella category devised by non-Native people to identify the Indigenous peoples of the Interior and southeastern Alaska who are different in both physical appearance and culture from the Eskimos and Aleuts. They include the many Athabascan-speaking communities of south-central and interior Alaska, and the Tlingit, Haida, and other Indians who people the panhandle of southeastern Alaska that reaches along the Pacific coast from Mount St. Elias to the Nass River, including Sitka and other islands of the Alexander Archipelago.

The traditional homeland of the Athabascans in south-central Alaska include Cook Inlet, Kenai Peninsula, Prince William Sound, and the temperate Matanuska Valley. Those of the Interior inhabit the broad plateau between the Alaska Range north of Anchorage and the Brooks Range above the Arctic Circle. This plateau consists of rolling hills and watery tundra, covered with small spruce trees. In 1900, winters were spent in semisubterranean homes in small villages along the Yukon and the upper Kuskokwim rivers and their tributaries. During the summer, families moved to fish camps, principally taking varieties of salmon which were dried for preservation, with a sufficient amount stored for winter. Other foods included moose, caribou, black and brown bear, beaver, porcupine, many kinds of fowl, fish and sea mammals, and roots, berries and plants. Contemporary Athabascans continue to rely on these foods to supplement their modern diets, although the rapid growth of the non-Native population in the Greater Anchorage and Kenai Peninsula regions have decreased the plant, fish, and animal habitat.

The major Indian populations of southeastern Alaska include the Tlingit and Haida. "The Tlingit occupied nearly all of what is today southeastern Alaska, portions of northern British Columbia, and part of the Yukon Territory of Canada. In the mid-eighteenth century, some Haida migrated into southeastern Alaska and their descendants have been neighbors to the Tlingit for several generations" (Olson 1996, 635). The Haida came to Alaska from the Queen Charlotte Islands in Canada. They were under the care of the Presbyterian Church and settled principally at Hydaburg with the cooperation of the U.S. Bureau of Indian Affairs. The Alaska and Canadian Haida communities have been shaped by different historical experiences and national policies. Nevertheless, their traditional economy is based on fishing, hunting, clamming, and gathering wild berries and dulse (red alga). These cultural activities continue to reaffirm Haida cultural identity.

Southeastern Alaska is a region of high, rugged mountains and a rain forest terrain, and many large glaciers. Before conquest by non-Natives, the Tlingit lived in temporary wooden houses during the summer and in huge cedar structures in winter, housing up to fifty people of a clan. Famous for their skill in carving, Tlingit totem poles have been called "monuments in cedar." Each family was identified with a clan totem, such as the wolf or eagle. The Tlingit are also known for their elaborate ceremonies and competitive feasting, the most important being the potlatch. The staple food was fish, especially salmon. During the summer, men fished and women gathered and preserved berries, plants, and roots. The precontact population is estimated as between fifteen thousand and twenty-five thousand persons. Approximately twenty thousand persons today consider themselves Tlingit, although at least half of this number reside in the states of Washington and Oregon.

In 1935 the U.S. Congress passed the Tlingit and Haida jurisdictional act, which authorized the two peoples to sue the United States for the loss of their tribal territories taken from them without compensation. In 1958 they were awarded a $7.5 million judgment by the Court of Claims, although payment was not implemented until 1971. The paltry amount of the award and the many years of delay in receiving it persuaded Alaska Native organizations to take their blanket land claims to the U.S. Congress rather than the Court of Claims.

Although contemporary Tlingit are among the more acculturated of Alaska Native peoples, they remain proud of their cultural heritage. "Over the last thirty years, there has been a gradual Tlingit cultural renaissance. The memorial for the dead, which some refer to as the potlatch, is still an important Tlingit social and religious event" (Olson 1996, 636). In addition to the Sealaska Corporation, a for-profit regional corporation focusing on economic development, there is also the Sealaska Heritage Foundation, a nonprofit corporation sponsoring Tlingit oratory, an acclaimed theater group, and a postsecondary scholarship program.

THE $200 BILLION DOLLAR THEFT

In 1968, oil was discovered at Prudhoe Bay off the northern coast of Alaska in what was estimated at the time to be the largest field yet found in North America, a 9.6 million-barrel reservoir that could supply one-eighth of the domestic oil supply of the United States. Oil development brought the world's major oil giants at the time—British Petroleum, Atlantic-Richfield, Humble Oil, among others—into direct conflict with the aboriginal land, resource, and subsistence rights of Alaska Natives.

The Alaska oil development, including the construction of a mammoth pipeline through Native villages and across Native lands, highlights the basic confrontation between monopoly capitalism and the Fourth World, the world of Indigenous peoples. By the 1960s and 1970s, multinational energy corporations were on the move all over the globe, penetrating the resource-rich lands of Indigenous peoples, such as those of the Australian Aborigines, the Natives of New Guinea, Indian lands in South America, and Indian reservations of the United States.

In 1974 the United Nations declared a new international economic order. The U.N. declaration stated that a people's sovereignty over raw materials was the essence of development, the cornerstone of not only political rights, but also economic independence from exploitation by the multinationals and freedom from neocolonialism. The question remains: what rights do Indigenous peoples have, since they are without states and are unrepresented at the United Nations? An American Indian activist complained in the 1960s that Red, meaning Indigenous peoples, is the only color not represented at the United Nations.

With the discovery of Alaskan oil, many officials and establishment spokesmen were emphatic not only about their expectations of rapid development of the new state of Alaska, but they also made optimistic predictions of jobs and wealth for Alaskan Natives. When Atlantic Richfield announced on March 13, 1968, its discovery of rich oil deposits beneath the tundra at Prudhoe Bay, it was hailed as a new day for Alaska's Natives.

A Demographic and Economic Profile

What was the socioeconomic situation of Alaska Natives at the time of the oil discovery? The U.S. Census estimated a population of fifty-three thousand for Alaska Natives in 1960. Of this number, 52 percent were said to be Eskimo, 34 percent Indian, and 14 percent Aleut. More than 70 percent were living in 178 towns and villages, half of which had a population of 155 persons or less. Another 25 percent lived in the urban areas of Anchorage, Fairbanks, Juneau, Ketchikan, Kodiak, and Sitka. There was also migration to regional urban centers in Native districts, such as Kotzabue, Bethel, and Barrow. Only one thousand Indians lived on two small Alaska reservations. Alaska Natives were living in cities, towns, and villages spread throughout half-million square miles across four time zones, a region greater than the combined regions of the nineteen easternmost states in the Lower Forty-eight. Most of the Native communities could be reached only by air. Even the capital of Juneau, located in southeastern Alaska, could be visited only by airplane or ship.

Extracting a living from the arctic and subarctic environments has always been difficult. But with the colonization of Alaska, and especially the more recent penetration by mining, oil, lumber, and land development interests, the ecological balance has become threatened, with dire consequences for the Native way of life. Alaska Natives rely on hunting, fishing, and gathering as an essential means of subsistence, in addition to the symbolic function and meaning that such pursuits signify for the maintenance of Indigenous identity and culture. Since the oil discovery, the traditional land base needed for subsistence activities has been seriously curtailed.

According to the 1960 U.S. Census, the average age of death for Natives was thirty-five years, and infant mortality was 54 percent, with respiratory diseases accounting for the largest number of deaths; tuberculosis alone was the worst in the nation. Electricity was an unheard of luxury. The 1970 U.S. Census still found deprivation among Alaska Natives, with Native incomes ranking far below that of Whites, and even that of African Americans. The average Native family received only two-fifths of the income considered acute privation level. The median income for single Whites was $3,706; for Blacks, $2,761; and for Natives and others combined, only $1,573. In summary, there had been no gain in the relative socioeconomic position of Eskimo and Indian people, no decrease in the extent of economic discrimination. In the decade leading up to 1970, Alaska Natives were disproportionately impoverished in comparison to the White majority of the state.

In the early 1970s, at the time that the Alaska Native land settlement was legislated by Congress, Alaska had the highest unemployment rate in the nation, with an astronomical 80 to 90 percent unemployment in the Native villages. The employment rate for Alaska Native workers in the oil fields was dismal; Native workers routinely were denied jobs. In some areas, such as Bethel on the Kuskokwim River, the only employment opportunities were the seasonal jobs of fire fighting and cannery work. Consequently, about 25 percent of the Native workforce was required to migrate regularly to urban areas in search of work, including as far away as Seattle, Washington.

By the 1970s, the huge military bases in Alaska, oil prospecting activity, commercial fishing, and the general penetration of capitalism had sharply curtailed the possibilities of the traditional subsistence economy of Alaska Natives. At the same time, living costs were 30 percent higher than in any of the other states excluding Hawaii. Rent alone was 97 percent higher, and the cost of living in rural Alaska, which was 90 percent Native, was double that of the Lower Forty-eight. The median family cash income hovered around $1,000 annually. Company stores extracted maximum profits for their merchandise. Many nutritional necessities, such as milk, fresh fruits, and vegetables, were rare in rural Alaska.

Alaska is a land filled with natural bounty that continues to be a vital factor for the Native livelihood, although land ownership or access to it is needed for a subsistence-based economy. The Alaskan Federation of Natives estimated that for some regions in Alaska, a village of two hundred people required as much as six hundred thousand acres to survive. Many Eskimos in the Arctic still hunted whale, walrus, and seal in coastal waters, and caribou in the tundra. They gathered murre eggs from the sea cliffs in July and took duck and geese in the summer. Athabascan Indians continued to rely on the moose, beaver, muskrat, rabbit, and black bear, which they hunted in the white spruce and birch forests of the Interior. The many lakes provided them with ducks and geese, and at their summer fish camps they took several species of salmon. Dried or jerked salmon was the main winter food staple. When the waters froze over, pike was caught through the ice. Wild blueberries were plentiful in July, and cranberries in September. In short, with their extremely meager sources of cash income from wage work eaten up by skyrocketing store prices, the Native peoples still relied on the land and the seas for much of their food needs.

When Native land use became threatened by encroaching capitalist development, and as living conditions worsened, ancient land rights became even more important. As a result, political militancy and organizational unity grew among the Alaska Natives. In 1966 the Alaska Federation of Natives was founded and blanket land claims were filed with the U.S. government. This legal maneuver effectively held up the building of an oil pipeline to transport the oil treasure from Prudhoe Bay for several years until the Alaska Native Claims Settlement Act (ANCSA) was passed in 1971. ANCSA was officially billed as America's generous gift to Native Peoples, and the land plus money settlement—forty-four million acres and $900,000—was heralded as a model solution for the Indigenous world. But was it really?

In accepting the land claims legislation as crafted by Congress, Alaska Natives sought to lessen their poverty and powerlessness, while at the same time maintaining their cultural traditions and Indigenous identity. But like the history of treaty-making with the Indians of the Lower Forty-eight, the capitalist political economy of Alaska was being developed at the direct expense of its Native peoples. Joseph Jorgensen (1978, 10), an applied anthropologist, terms the particular politico-economic niche, which the American Indians occupy in U.S. society, as *neocolonial,* in reference to exploitation that is both economic and political, but no longer colonial in the pure sense of the term. This kind of exploitation is the hallmark of capitalist encroachment upon Native peoples' labor, lands, and resources. It is the legacy of the old Indian frontier, and today, Alaska is the last frontier of the United States.

The problem of Native land claims became urgent for mainstream America only after the oil discovery. The extraction of the oil, in addition to natural gas and other minerals, necessitated the immediate settlement of the long-standing question about aboriginal land title in Alaska. As one observer put it: "Alaska developers . . . like all capitalists, define a "problem" as anything against their interests and "urgency" as how much money is involved. These individuals and corporations also have a word for the "solution" that is profitable to them: it is called "progress" and is enforced by their political-economic-military machine called the U.S. Government. The Natives define their solution as justice; and after all the patient and bitter years of experience, they are still losing" (Weber 1972, 1).

DISCOVERY IN THE TWENTIETH CENTURY

Although the Native peoples of Alaska were invaded by a variety of conquest agents with different economic aims and options over the last two centuries,

TABLE 10.1 Important Dates in the Alaska Native Struggle

1821	Russia colonizes Alaska.
1867	Russia sells Alaska to U.S.
1884	U.S. Congress passes Organic Act.
19th century	Period of whaling, fur seal, and sea otter exploitation.
1886	Alaskan gold rush begins.
1891	Sheldon Jackson introduces reindeer herding.
1910s	Typical village settlement includes a Bureau of Indian Affairs agent, a school teacher, a trader, and perhaps a missionary.
1920s	Trapping becomes important, especially of arctic fox.
1940s	Alaska becomes a military territory during World War II.
1950s	Distant Early Warning (DEW) Line is built.
1958	Alaska becomes a state. U.S. government unilaterally withdraws 103 million acres from aboriginal lands.
1960s	Blanket Native land claims are filed covering 296 of Alaska's 375 million acres.
	Alaska Native Declaration of Independence is circulated.
1966	Alaska Federation of Natives (AFN) is founded.
	Secretary of Interior Udall freezes land until Native land claims are settled.
	Oil exploration results in major discovery at Prudhoe Bay in Arctic Ocean off the coast at Barrow, AK.
1971	U.S. Congress passes Alaska Native Claims Settlement Act.
1973	U. S. Congress passes pipeline legislation, initiating the building of the 800-mile Alaskan pipeline from Prudhoe Bay to the Port of Valdez on the Pacific Ocean.
1980s–1991	Alaskan Natives lobby for 1991 Amendments and Indian Reorganization Act status but have only limited success.

the question of Native land rights was never seriously addressed until the 1968 oil discovery. Pushed this way and that by the economic forces unleashed by non-Native invaders, Alaska Natives still had the land on which to depend for subsistence when things got tough. Table 10.1 and the following historical profile illustrates this truth.

Russian Fur Trade

The first Whites in Alaska were Russian fur traders and whalers who killed large numbers of game and practically exterminated the sea otter. As the trade in sea otter pelts grew, investors in European Russia underwrote independent trappers called *promyeshlenniki* to harvest pelts on their behalf. Aleuts were coerced to hunt sea otters to depletion along the Alaskan coast. In the process, many Aleuts were killed. Soon, however, imperial Russia stopped this practice, punishing some of the worst traders. The tyrannical tenure of Lord Baranov of Sitka, for example, came to an end when he died in transit to Russia for imprisonment. The Russian government then gave the trading monopoly to the Russian American Company (RAC). The RAC was comprised of private investors, including some in the Czar's government. Imperial Russia had come to realize the immense

value of the fur trade and of the Native peoples as commodity producers, as hunters of fur-bearing animals and sea mammals.[1]

The Russian Charter of 1821 specified that all creoles (mixed-bloods) and tribes who were dependent upon the Russians for a livelihood were to be considered citizens with all the rights and privileges thereof. With regard to the more isolated northern Indians and Eskimo groups, the Russians required their agents "not to make any effort to conquer them . . . avoid anything which might create in these people suspicion of the intention to violate their independence" (O'Mahoney 1975, 15). The Czarist government, being a mercantile fur-trading nation in Alaska, did not see itself as possessors of the land itself. Land titles were unknown; only the right to trade or to have chartered trading companies existed.

Alaska was "sold" to the United States by Russia in 1867 when Secretary of State William Henry Seward purchased Russian America from Czar Alexander II. It was known as "Seward's folly" at the time, but Secretary of State Seward knew what he was doing when he advocated buying Alaska. He was acting in the interests of U.S. capitalists who coveted not only the lands and resources of Alaska, but also a trade route to the Orient. "Seward, a former governor and senator from New York, manifestly believed in Manifest Destiny, and for years he had believed that acquiring Russian America was part of it. As early as 1852, Senator Seward had persuaded his colleagues to support the American whaling industry by sending the navy to chart Bering Strait" (Mitchell 1997, 24).

Russia sold what it neither legally possessed nor entirely controlled, its trading interest being confined mainly to the Aleutian chain and Southeast Alaska. Czarist Russia also sold what it could no longer hold onto as a fur colony. This was due to its weakened political position among the other European trading nations, and the emerging economic power of the United States of America.

Technically speaking, Russia sold to the United States only the right to tax and govern, and not the land itself, but the Treaty of 1867 did not clearly recognize the rights of all the Alaska Natives. It guaranteed the rights of citizenship under the United States to those Russians who chose to remain in Alaska and to the "civilized tribes," those Natives who had come under Russian influence, but it denied these same rights to the "uncivilized tribes" of the Interior. Later, the Organic Act of 1884 by the United States did recognize Native land rights but with a caveat; Section 8 stipulates that "the Indians or other persons in said district (Alaska) shall not be disturbed in the possession of any lands actually in their use or occupation or now claimed by them but the terms under which persons may acquire title to such lands is reserved for future legislation by Congress" (Federal Field Committee 1968, 427). In the following years, several other acts of Congress and state and federal court decisions protected the land occupation and subsistence rights of Alaska Native peoples.

Whalers

American whale men had a primary impact on Alaskan and Siberian Eskimo groups in the nineteenth century. Foote (1964, 16) estimates that more than 5,000 ships, carrying at least 150,000 men, visited northern arctic waters between 1835 and 1915. By 1852, the peak year of the industry, the whaling fleet from Boston and New Bedford "had increased to 278 vessels, with a catch valued at $14 millions" (Jenness 1962, 5). Lesser known is the influence of numerous French, German, and British trading schooners, which traded each summer for baleen, walrus, ivory, furs, and other Native-produced products. The Russian-American Company in the early nineteenth century sought to develop the whale fishery in arctic waters. Before its decline, several

Eskimo entrepreneurs entered into the business of commercial whaling for profit rather than for use as in aboriginal culture. At Point Barrow, one Eskimo maintained five or six boat crews.

Like the earlier fur seal and sea otter exploitation of Aleutian and northern Pacific waters by the Russian trading companies, these trading contacts by whalers had a devastating effect on the Native populations; alcoholism and foreign diseases became widespread. It is estimated that after 1850, half of the entire coastal Eskimo population was wiped out. There was also sexual exploitation of Native women by the all-male crews and personnel of the whaling and trading companies. The spread of venereal disease among Alaska Natives is directly attributed to this fact.

Sea mammal life was also decimated by this early form of capitalist development, but the exploitation had little impact on the land ownership question. Neither the Russians nor the Euro-Americans were interested in owning or occupying the land, but only in reaping the bounty of the seas and the land, although they needed the Native inhabitants to hunt and transport the pelts, or seal mammal products, and to work their ships.

The "international competition in the salmon and fur-seal fisheries, and a mounting interest in the mineral resources of Alaska, combined with the pressure exerted by certain missionary societies" were influences responsible for the passage of the first Organic Act in 1884 by the U.S. Congress (Jenness 1962, 7). The Act established a skeleton administrative apparatus for the Alaska Territory, all positions appointed by the U.S. President. Of special significance was the fact that it affirmed Native rights over land, the United States having purchased from Russia only the rights to tax and govern. It specifically stated that "the general land laws of the United States are not extended over the country," and that "the squatter rights of Indians and others are recognized" (Jenness 1962, 8).

Among the Act's provisions was education. It set up thirty-five schools for Alaskan children regardless of race, the majority at this time being Natives. The schools were under the administration of Sheldon Jackson, a prominent Presbyterian missionary. Jackson's early role in shaping Alaska Native educational policy lasted into the twentieth century. The school system included both secular and missions schools, with the government at first subsidizing the religious-run schools. The main educational thrust of these schools, as far as Native children were concerned, was the policy of assimilation, forced adaptation to the White-Anglo, Lower Forty-eight standard—"the education to be provided for the natives of Alaska should fit them for the social and industrial life of the white population of the United States and promote their not-too-distant assimilation" (quoted in Jenness 1962, 9). In 1895, following federal enforcement of the Constitutional principle of the separation of church and state, the government subsidy for the mission schools was ended, but both systems—the secular day schools run by the government and the mission schools—were still operating prominently at the time of the oil discover and the 1971 Alaska Native Land Settlement Act. Both school systems continued to follow the policy of assimilation.

Reindeer Herding

In 1891 Sheldon Jackson persuaded Congress to buy and import reindeer into Alaska to form the basis of a substitute for the Native economy that was being destroyed. Jenness (1962, 35) reports that by 1917, the herds numbered ninety-five thousand, and by 1931 it is estimated that approximately thirteen thousand Eskimos depended on reindeer for their livelihood, the hides and meat used for their own needs and consumption, as well as providing income received from their sale.

Reindeer herding in Alaska, introduced as a possible substitute for the fast disappearing caribou, did not fare well. In the first place, herding practices were not compatible with traditional caribou hunting by Native people. The domesticated reindeer tended to wander off and mix with the wild caribou. It became easier for the Native hunter to hunt the reindeer on the tundra, just as they had traditionally hunted wild game. An additional factor was World War II, when the military alert against Japanese militarist aggression and wage labor opportunities related to the war effort drew people away from herding. Many reindeer were slaughtered for winter parkas (clothing). Most importantly, the introduction of reindeer herding (or hunting) did not require private land ownership, and the question of Native land title did not arise. Another reason for the decline was the competition afforded by the U.S.-based beef-packing industry and their Alaska trading post outlets. Locally produced reindeer would potentially sell at cheaper prices and undercut the control by the States-based beef monopoly.

Gold Rush

It was not until the gold rush, beginning in 1896 and lasting into the early 1900s at its peak years, that minerals were first extracted from Alaska. Mining claims by American miners simply ignored the question of mineral rights, or whose land was being trespassed upon. Native peoples were not yet an organized political force with whom Whites had to contend. Gold was discovered in southeastern Alaska in 1897, and in the following year "more than 100,000 people headed for the Klondike—of whom 40,000 reached their destination" (Jorgensen 2003, 97). In response, Congress extended the 1872 Mining Claims Act to Alaska, which allowed prospectors to stake claims to property "owned" by the federal government. Of course, as it became clear with the oil discovery and the land claims issue a century later, the federal government did not hold clear title to Alaska, but this was unrecognized at the time. In 1898 gold was also discovered at Nome on the Bering Sea coast, and the community quickly grew to 20,000 people. Fairbanks, located in central Alaska, had a similar population increase.

Congress passed an Alaska Homestead Act in 1898, which provided land free and for purchase, although most land in Alaska is not arable. The Act also offered rights-of-way for various kinds of transportation, including railroads. Mining camps and "boom towns" sprung up along Alaska's great waterways. Athabascan Natives along the Yukon River cut and sold firewood to the paddle-wheel steamers that plied the river, as well as for industrial mining operations, and worked as pilots for the ore-bearing ships. Later, when the richest of the gold strikes gave out, the mining settlements crumpled into the tundra and the miners disappeared. Even so, the mining companies had reaped untold millions of dollars from Native lands, in addition to sweating the miners who, for the most part, had gone to the Alaskan frontier because of unemployment and hard times back home in the Lower Forty-eight.

Alaska Natives never owned or operated any of the industrial mining concerns, and when the boom was over, the miners departed with no lasting effect on the Native land ownership question. Mining in Alaska devolved into industrial businesses controlled by interests outside of Alaska. The Alaska Syndicate, comprising Guggenheim, J.P. Morgan, and Kennecott, "built a rail line to serve its copper mine, docks in Cordova to move ore to its smelters in the Lower Forty-eight, and purchased the twelve largest canning operations in Alaska" (Jorgensen 2003, 98). The Syndicate monopolized copper mining while also seeking to control Alaska's salmon industry. In 1910 an influenza epidemic drove destitute prospectors, small entrepreneurs, and sundry non-Native camp-followers from Alaska.

By the beginning of the twentieth century, "the new White mining settlements, the flourishing salmon industry in Bristol Bay, the multiplying herds of semi-domesticated reindeer, and the decline in numbers of the whale and walrus—these had transformed the Eskimo economy" (Jenness 1962, 13). The old land-based, subsistence economies of the Natives had been altered. One hundred percent subsistence off the land and sea was no longer to be obtained because of the wanton destruction of sea and land life which had taken place. Some Native people turned to wage labor. There was some seasonal employment in the salmon fisheries, although most labor was White, imported from the States, and there was casual labor in a few settlements and on the Yukon River boats. The majority, perhaps 75 percent of the Native population, turned to fur trapping. A different kind of economy was created through trapping in that it was commodity-producing, but Native land ownership was not an issue.

Other Economic Changes

From the history so far related in this narrative, it is clear that there have been major economic changes in the past which had consequences for Native land use, some far-reaching, but which did not bring into question the fundamental issue of land ownership.

The introduction of repeating rifles toward the end of the last century substantially changed hunting technology and with it Native social organization. Hunting practices became more individualistic and less cooperative. Because of the introduction of firearms, both the numbers of sea mammals and the caribou diminished significantly. A supply of wild meat was no longer available as it had been in former times. There were more than one million caribou in Alaska in the 1920s, whereas by the 1960s on the eve of oil development there were only about 160,000 left. Since the break-up of the large herds in the Copper River area and elsewhere in south-central and interior Alaska, there are even less today. This is one of the fears expressed by contemporary Native spokesmen as a possible consequence of the pipeline construction with its access roads, and the opening of formerly isolated areas which have traditionally been the breeding and feeding grounds for large animal herds.

By 1914 almost every northern Eskimo settlement had its Bureau of Indian Affairs school, its non-Native school teacher, and perhaps also a White fur trader and a White missionary as well. White settlement remained the heaviest in subarctic Alaska, in the rainy southeast panhandle area and in the Bristol Bay region, both noted for rich timber and fishing resources.

Trapping

A new economic pattern began to flourish by 1920, the trade in fox pelts. Trapping rapidly became a main source for cash income; the money was very good while it lasted, but its pursuit as an economic activity decreased the traditional forms of economic life which were collective in nature. Chance (1966, 16) explains its impact on the North Slope Alaska Eskimos:

> Traditional Eskimo hunting patterns had been based on strong cooperative ties maintained between members of related or quasi-related families. Trapping, in contrast, was a much more individualistic enterprise involving at most two related families. Furthermore, it was a winter occupation . . . a period previously devoted to extensive activity, such as informal visiting between friends, story telling, and an almost continuous round of entertainment in the Eskimo *karigi* or dance houses. Once having committed themselves to a cash economy based on trapping, the Eskimo frequently spent much of the long dark winter living in lonely driftwood cabins along the coast, far removed from friends and relatives. The consequent reduction of the cooperative bond between kin and enforced winter isolation quickly affected village cohesion.

It is worth noting, however, that Strong (1973, appendix) believes that the importance of fur trapping in the over-all North American economy has been overdrawn. He points out that the northern fur market deals with luxury furs—martin, sable, lynx, fox, beaver, high quality squirrel, and muskrat—intended for the well-do-do consumer of fashion, and not the mass market. Yet in many places until the end of the 1940s, "the fur industry was the major branch of the economy in the areas of Alaska populated by Eskimos, and also in the Canadian Far North" (Fainberg 1965, 29).

Trapping had two important implications economically for the Alaska Native fur-trapper: First, when it was profitable, it was one of the few sources for obtaining cash, (needed for rifles, certain food stables like coffee and flour, and other European-derived necessities), but at the same time the Native family maintained its basic dependence on hunting, fishing, and whaling for its food and clothing. Second, the fur trade nevertheless was the single most exploitative economic enterprise ever introduced to the Native Peoples in the American North. Strong reproduces a chart from Bergeron (1971, 12–13) showing that the Indigenous trapper expends 65 percent of his labor in the production of luxury fur but realizes only 0.01 percent of the profits. The trading company hardly does anything at all in terms of productive labor, yet realizes on the average 60 percent profit. The artisan worker, who "produces" the coat or finished fur product, exerts 30 percent of the total labor involved but is also exploited by the fur capitalist, realizing only 5 percent of the value of the finished product. Finally, the merchant, who sells the finished produce, fur coats and hats, to the consumer, expends little if any labor on the product, but through this control of the market realizes 30 percent of the profit.

Until after World War II, prices for furs were fairly high. However, there were always fluctuations, and there was a very serious decline in the prices for raw furs by the time of the 1960s oil discovery. The growth of fur farms and the development of synthetic furs have taken over most of the U.S. market, and the extravagant prices charged for luxury furs prevented the expansion of the industry. "Even as late as 1914, on the eve of the First World War, the Eskimos of Kotzebue and Barrow, in far northern Alaska, received on the average $15 for every white fox pelt, and paid only the Seattle price, $1.00 or $1.30, for a 50-lb. sack of flour which, then as now, was the main item in the trapper's diet. But during the war the value of all pelts slumped, whereas staple goods became dearer" (Jenness 1962, 15). Only in the Pribilof Islands, where there is a large fur seal herd, is the value of raw furs of any significance in Alaska Native economic life today.

The decline in the numbers of fur-bearing animals and the going out of fashion of the long-haired furs (primarily the Polar fox) were factors leading to the decline of trapping in Alaska. Fainberg (1965, 29) reported in the 1960s that "during the past 15 to 17 years, the annual take of Polar fox diminished from an average of 15,000 skins to 3,000 to 4,000." Prior to the Second World War, a trapper earned a thousand to several thousand dollars per season. Following the war, the annual income from the fur trade in northern Alaska, dropped precipitously to a few hundred dollars per season.

EARLY ATTEMPTS TO SETTLE THE LAND QUESTION

From the early days of U.S. occupation of Alaska until World War II, there were several attempts made by friend and foe alike to settle the question of Native land ownership. These attempts included proposals

to establish land allotments, or reservations and townships exclusively for Alaska Natives, but both Natives and the majority of Whites opposed these plans at the time. Nor was the idea of corporations entirely new to Alaska Natives. Under the Alaska Reorganization Act of 1936 (ARA), the secretary of the interior established six land and water reserves in Alaska between 1941 and 1946 to promote "community economic development through corporations, and self-government through constitutions," but "the creation of these reserves did not result in the economic development of Native resources" (Soza 1989, 2789-A).

Proposals to establish reservations for Alaska Natives were also largely unsuccessful. When a U.S. land agent and an Alaskan territorial judge proposed that a reservation be established in the vicinity of the Tanana River, the Tanana Chiefs (a federation of Athabascan villages) categorically rejected the idea as preposterous and inimical to their aboriginal land claims. Furthermore, White interests generally opposed the creation of reservations for a different reason, namely their wish to usurp Native lands altogether. Their opposition, however, was cloaked the pretence of opposing racial segregation.

There are only two reservations in Alaska: the Metlakatla-Annette Island reservation of 86,741 acres, set up in 1881 for Tsimshian Indians who had emigrated from Canada under the Anglican missionary William Duncan, and the small Klukwan reserve of 894 acres, created in 1957. Neither are based on treaties but only on Acts of Congress. About two dozen reserves were created between 1905 and 1943 by Executive Order, Administrative Order, and under the Indian Reorganization Act, but none of them have the same legal status as similar Acts of Congress reserves do in the Lower Forty-eight. The important point is the following, as summarized by Strong (1973, 64): "At the date of settlement of the Alaska native land claims [1971], less than one percent of the State of Alaska was under any form of Alaska Native ownership or control . . . and there was a strong sentiment among the white sector of Alaska's residents against 'giving Indians back Alaska.'"

Tlingit-Haida Land Claims Settlement

The Alaskan Native Brotherhood, the one significant intertribal organization before statehood, was the first Native political group to bring up the land claims issue. In 1934 an Act of Congress creating the U.S. Court of Claims enabled the Tlingit and Haida

Indians of Southeast Alaska to sue the U.S. government for compensation for the lands which had been stolen from them in past years. Since they were included among the "civilized tribes" referred to in the 1884 Organic Act, their land rights under United States law should have been without question. Yet it took thirty-five years, from the date of the suit in 1935 to 1970, before their claim was settled and compensation awarded. Ironically, no land was returned to the Indians. Instead, an extremely low payment of $7,500,000 was awarded. This meant that the Tlingit and Haida received only about 45 cents an acre for their coastal lands, forests, and salmon fisheries. Considering the immense size of the land claim they were forced to give up, most of which today forms the Tongass National Forest, the largest forest in the United States, and considering the timber profits derived by U.S. and Japanese timber companies from the lumber sold, the Indians were forced to sell their birthright dearly.

The lesson of this miscarriage of justice was not lost upon other Alaska Native peoples when they developed their strategy for blanket land claims in the 1960s. They decided to carry their battle to Congress rather than to the U.S. Court of Claims, because the Tlingit-Haida claim had been so unfairly adjudicated.

Summary

We have reviewed the several different land use patterns which were introduced into Native Alaska—the taking of the fur seal in the Aleutian Islands and southeast Alaska by the Russians; whaling, chiefly by Americans in Arctic waters; mining along the Yukon River and the Interior of Alaska; the Christian missionary-federal government program of reindeer herding; and trapping, with the trading companies introducing the company store in the "bush" settlements. With the possible exception of reindeer herding, all of these economic enterprises were exploitative of the Alaska Native communities and disrupted their traditional subsistence patterns. These foreign economic patterns exploited the Alaskan environment and utilized Native workers as commodity producers. In the early years, they led to genocidal conditions as a result of the deadly disease epidemics spread by White contact. Yet, when one economic option after another became closed to them, the Native peoples still had the land and their traditional means of subsistence livelihood on which to survive, although their ecological adaptation to the environment had been modified, as for example, by the introduction of guns for hunting.

The Caribou Eskimos of the Interior were forced to migrate to the northern coast, and there, along with remnants of the coastal Eskimos abandoned by the whaling industry, reconstituted themselves as an Indigenous entity, in some cases returning to their ancient villages. The same processes took place among the Southwestern Eskimos along the Kuskokwim River. When reindeer herding or trapping failed, they somehow managed to continue to live from migratory fish, bird life, and their old pattern of living off the land. This was also true for the Ahtna or Copper River Athabascans of the Interior, when so many had died due to early disease epidemics, forcing them to move to new locations. They, too, managed to survive by living off the land. The option to make this kind of adaptation, however, became increasingly difficult with the outbreak of the war with Japan, and the Cold War with the Soviet Union that followed.

WORLD WAR II AND THE EARLY POSTWAR PERIOD

With the advent of World War II, Alaska came under military administration, and all Native claims to the land were disregarded because of the national emergency. The excuse was Alaska's strategic geographic location in relationship to Japan, as well as its importance as a supply route for Soviet defense of the Eastern Front. The government withdrew huge areas of land for military purposes, resettled most of the Aleut peoples to the Alaskan mainland under near genocidal conditions, and took other actions which ignored the traditional land claims of Alaska Natives. Yet during this time of national emergency, Alaska Natives fought and died in the war even though they had few civil rights as American citizens.

The overwhelming presence of the military establishment during and after World War II opened wage labor opportunities for Alaska Natives, but racial segregation was still the policy of the U.S. military. In Anchorage, Native people still could not enter bars or eating places, this despite the democratic character of the war itself. Paradoxically, the Eskimo Scout Division of the Alaska National Guard had been created, because Native soldiers were absolutely essential for guarding Alaska's frontiers due to their intimate knowledge of the vast territory and their ability to survive in what for the non-Native soldier was an alien environment. From 1941 to 1945 "over a billion dollars was spent on war construction in Alaska." (Fainberg 1965, 27).

To be sure, there were individual White Alaskans who did take an interest in Native welfare. There were the workmen—seamen and those in the trades—who remained in Alaska or returned to it after World War II, because they preferred the natural beauty of the region and its way of life. In many cases they married Native women, formed labor unions, and often took a more progressive attitude toward Native workers. The territorial governor, Ernest Gruening, became disturbed by the blatant discriminatory practices of Alaskan businessmen. Racial segregation had taken root during the Gold Rush days and "revealed itself openly in hotel, motion-picture theatres, and elsewhere down to 1944, when the territorial government passed three laws forbidding racial discrimination, in the administration of mothers' pensions, in the treatment of juvenile offenses, and in admission to hotels and other public places" (Jenness 1962, 20). In 1945 the Alaskan Territorial Legislature passed the Anti-Discrimination Act, giving Native peoples equal rights, at least in principle, with White citizens.

Military development had important social consequences for Alaska, not the least of which was the rapid increase in the Territory's population from immigration. During World War II there were 150,000 military personnel stationed in Alaska, one-fourth of the entire state population. Alaska Natives worked on the highways, airports, and other military construction. In the decade following the war, the value of military construction in Alaska remained quite high, nonmilitary development representing only one-quarter of that spent by the military. One of the largest of the postwar construction projects, in which many Native people found employment in blue-collar trades, was the building of the chain of distant-early-warning-radar stations, or DEW Line, through Alaska, Canada and Greenland. This was to prevent the perceived Soviet threat. In 1953–55 another long military pipeline was constructed. For the post-World War II decade and into the 1960s, the military presence absolutely dominated the economy of Alaska and therefore the lives of Native peoples.

Besides the military personnel, there were carpenters, machinists, longshoremen, and other civilian workers who went north, seeking employment during the military boom. This was in addition to those already employed in the fishing industry in south-central and southeast Alsska. "As a consequence, the population of Alaska increased from 72,500 to 128,000 between 1940 and 1950. In 1954 there were more than 200,000 persons in Alaska, and the figure had reached 226,000 by the 1960 census" (Fainberg 1965, 28). By 1970–71, on the eve of the passage of the Alaska Claims Settlement Act, about 40 percent of the state's population was either in the military itself or indirectly employed through military contracts. Before the war, the Alaskan Native population was only slightly less than that of White Alaskans, but by 1970 the total population had reached 302,361, of which 50,885 (perhaps a conservative figure) were Native. Alaska Natives had become a minority in their own land.

Although the bulk of the new population from the Lower Forty-eight took up residence around the military bases, predominantly in the Anchorage area of south-central Alaska, the impact of military construction was far-reaching, even in the more distantly located Native communities. Fainberg (1965, 28) reports that "during the war and post-war years, many Eskimos have abandoned their habitual homes and moved to the outskirts of Anchorage, Fairbanks, and other centers of military construction." In fact, Eskimo intrusion into Fairbanks, Alaska's second largest city, caused some interethnic rivalry between them and the local Athabascan Indians. Despite Fairbanks's control by Whites, the Indians had long considered the city, perhaps since the early Gold Rush, the de facto Athabascan capital. Not only did Native peoples flock to the White-dominated urban centers, but they also migrated to the larger Native settlements where there were military-related installations, such as Barrow, Kotzebue, Unalakleet, and Bethel. These regional centers tripled and quadrupled in size and population, although Barrow, the largest of these, never exceeded 1,300 people.

There were other effects of the military boom as well. During the 1940s and 1950s, the economic way of life changed for many Native people from a subsistence to a commodity-exchange economy. The chief impact upon the Native Peoples was the shift in subsistence patterns: seal, whale, furs, caribou, and even fish had either been drastically reduced in numbers so as to no longer constitute a dependable means of subsistence livelihood by traditional methods, or else they had been monopolized and their production taken over by White entrepreneurs. Jenness (1962, 38, 40) gives this assessment of the wartime changes affecting the Eskimo population of Alaska:

> Fishing and sea mammal hunting, fur trapping, reindeer herding, handicrafts, and occasional wage-employment— these occupations helped keep the wolf of hunger from the Eskimos' doors but provided no more than mere subsistence; they did not improve the diet, build houses as

comfortable as white Alaskans, or supply the material and social amenities the latter enjoyed. Contact with the whites had increased the number of Natives' necessities and desires without furnishing sufficient means to satisfy them; and between Eskimo living conditions and those of white Alaskans yawned a wide gap. The latter enjoyed better education, better health, and firmer associations with the outside world. To reach equality with them the Eskimos needed a much stronger economy; and no sure base or bases for such an economy had . . . come into view. . . .

Military operations in and around Nome placed the grazing grounds of 5,000 reindeer out of bounds to their Eskimo owners and indirectly sentenced to destruction the entire herd; but the same operations stimulated so great a demand for Native curios and fur clothing that in one year, 1944, ivory carvers and the Nome Skin Sewers Cooperative Association sold about $200,000 worth of goods to the armed forces.

The situation described by Fainberg (1965, 30) for Eskimos in the workforce is probably also true for most other Alaska Natives: "The Eskimos needed wage work in order somehow to survive. On the other hand, for military construction in Alaska the Eskimos represented a source of cheap labor, well adapted to local conditions. . . . Thus, in recent years more than 60 percent of the native population of Alaska has worked for hire, although for the most part not on permanent but on seasonal jobs." Fainberg (1965, 30) also recounts the work history of a typical Eskimo worker: "A Point Hope Eskimo, Attungoruk, related in an autobiography recorded by Van Stone, that from 1946 to 1951 he worked in at least eight different localities. He worked in the gold fields, on the Alaska Railroad, as a dishwasher at an air base, as a longshoreman and elsewhere. Van Stone comments that the biography of Attungoruk is typical of the younger Alaskan Eskimos."

The nature of Native employment and its duration depended on one's geographical location in Alaska, whether one worked as a fisherman or in the summer cannery operations, in the gold fields, mines, or in military radar construction. By 1954, even the relatively isolated Kuskokwim Eskimos had wage income exceeding that from trapping. There was also some Native craft development with sales to the increasing local White population as well as through the usual trade outlets. The Eskimo bone carvers of St. Lawrence Island are an example. Yet the central feature of the new wage economy was its instability. Native workers who no longer could depend entirely on the land and sea for their means of subsistence were at the mercy of military policy within its Cold War context, and the haphazard or unplanned nature

of capitalist development in Alaska. Native welfare was never a priority policy consideration.

DEVELOPMENTS SINCE WORLD WAR II

Statehood

Alaska was a territory until 1958. Outside interests, such as mining and salmon canning industries, controlled Alaska and were opposed to statehood. The leading newspapers—Juneau's *Alaska Daily Empire*, Ketchikan's *Fishing News*, Fairbanks' *News-Miner*, and Anchorage's *Anchorage News*—all opposed statehood. But the winds of change led to a territorial referendum in 1946 favoring statehood, and President Harry S. Truman became its leading advocate. Governor Ernest Gruening and Alaska's delegate to Congress, Bob Artlett, were also proponents of statehood for Alaska. An opponent was "Judge" Winton C. Arnold who argued that statehood would conflict with aboriginal land claims, but after statehood became a fact he argued against Native land claims. For years, southern Democrats and conservative Republicans had blocked statehood for Alaska and Hawai'i. One argument was the supposed communism of the longshoreman's union (ILWU), which was trying to organize cannery workers in both Alaska and Hawai'i.

A constitutional convention took place in 1956, Congress voted statehood in 1958, and President Dwight Eisenhower signed the statehood proclamation on January 3, 1959. The discovery of oil on the Kenai Peninsula in 1957 by Richfield Oil (ARCO) may have influenced political forces undecided about statehood. Alaska became the seventh oil-producing state of the Union.

Oil Discovery at Prudhoe Bay

In 1968 Atlantic-Richfield discovered a vast oil deposit on the North Slope at Prudhoe Bay, and Alaska quickly became the number two oil-producing state behind Texas. Prudhoe Bay's 9.6 billion barrels of oil could supply one-eighth of the entire U.S. domestic oil supply. Including offshore and outer continental shelf deposits, Alaska's total energy resources were conservatively estimated by the Alaska Department of Natural Resources as 77 trillion cubic feet (Hanrahan and Gruenstein 1977, 123). If one added the Naval Petroleum Reserve No. 4, there would be a potential of 133 billion barrels of oil on-shore on the North Slope of Alaska alone. At prevailing oil prices in the early 1970s this was worth about $4 trillion. About 95 percent of the Prudhoe Bay oil field was controlled by four oil giants: Exxon, Atlantic-Richfield (Arco), Standard Oil of Ohio, and British Petroleum.

Hanrahan and Gruenstein (1977, 2) summarized Alaska's economic resources at the time as follows:

> Cradling hundreds of billions of dollars worth of oil, natural gas, timber, coal, gold, silver, gemstones, uranium, copper, moybdenum, nickel, lead, zinc, tin, tungsten, fluorite, iron, mercury, antimony, platinum-group metals, barite, zeolite and chromite, among others. Alaska probably exceeds the rest of the nation in the potential value of its resources. Its national wealth is, in fact, so vast that the second least populous state will probably have more impact on the lives of Americans over at least the next half century than any of the other forty-nine states.

The presence of oil deposits in Alaska was not new knowledge; the first White explorers had recorded oil seeps, and the Eskimos of the North Slope had long made use of petroleum products from these seeps.

Filing Native Land Claims

With the passage by Congress in 1946 of the Indian Claims Commission Act, and another Act in 1949 enlarging the jurisdiction of the Court of Claims, the door was reopened for filing Native claims in Alaska against the U.S. government. The Court of Indian Claims was set up to settle Indian claims in the Lower Forty-eight, but its impact on Alaskan Native land rights had a snowballing effect: the large number of Native claims filed in the 1960s was instrumental in effecting the final land settlement of December 1971.

There had been previous attempts by Alaskan Natives to establish land claims before the 1960s. A Tanacross claim by Athabascan Indians was first filed in 1917, filed again in the early 1940s, again in 1961, and a fourth time in 1963 (ISEGR 1967, 12). But the government's Bureau of Land Management either lost the claims or simply failed to act on them. The Tanacross Natives were later astounded and dismayed when the new state of Alaska at the New York World's Fair, ignoring Tanacross claims, began offering tracts of Tanacross land at Lake George for sale as vacation resorts. Fortunately, through the intervention of the Alaskan Federation of Natives, Native-hired attorneys were able to block some of the land thefts like this one.

The impetus for filing blanket land claims by Alaskan Natives to obtain clear title to their aboriginal lands was the granting of Alaskan statehood in 1958. What most alarmed Native leaders was the provision in the Statehood Act granting the new state the authority to select 103 million acres from "vacant, un-appropriated, unreserved" lands. The blanket claims asserted the right of the Native peoples of Alaska to own, develop and manage the lands their ancestors had used and occupied since time immemorial. By April 1, 1968, there were forty of these recorded claims, covering 296 million of Alaska's 375 million acres.

Despite the giveaway of 103 million acres, the Alaska Statehood Act also acknowledged in principle the Native peoples' right to their lands. The Act stipulated that "the state . . . agrees and declares that it forever disclaims all rights and title . . . to any lands or other property (including fishing rights), the right of title to which may be held by any Indians, Eskimos, or Aleuts." The question remained: Whose interest would come first? The conveying of land title to the Native peoples, or the unilateral withdrawal of 103 million acres by the state of Alaska? Would state interests (business, land speculators and petty entrepreneurs), in collusion with the non-Native state legislature and executive, predominate regardless of whether the state's land withdrawals conflicted with aboriginal title?

Native Declaration of Independence

By the 1960s, although the ratio of Whites to Alaskan Natives had widened significantly in favor of the former, Native peoples remained a significant population segment throughout Alaska. Indeed, in the northwest and southwest regions of Alaska they easily predominated. The non-Native population was centered primarily at Fairbanks in the Interior, in the greater Anchorage area in south-central Alaska, and to a lesser extent in Juneau, the capital, in southeast Alaska. (Although the non-Native part of the population has continued to increase vis-à-vis the Native population of the state, the regions of Native population concentration continue to hold true today.)

By the time of statehood, the economic situation for Native peoples had steadily worsened. Employment was down from the war and postwar wage boom. Laws, hiring practices, and development plans by private companies and the state agencies were formulated that were economically disadvantageous to Alaskan Natives. Native rights and interests were all but ignored.

> Salmon companies dammed and depleted many streams for more profits, with the aid of state government. The

cost of living in Alaska climbed while Native employment remained miniscule because of racial discrimination. In those areas where Indians were allowed jobs, they were prohibited from organizing for decent wages and conditions. Governmental structures were imposed which robbed the Native peoples of self-determination without providing essential benefits or protections. The distant state capital [Juneau] either ignored the interests and needs of Alaskan Natives entirely or appointed a few bureaucrats . . . to ignore them. (Weber 1972, 3)

Viewed in this light, it is not surprising to find the rapid growth of political militancy among Alaskan Natives. In the mid-1960s an Alaska Native Declaration and Petition (ADNP) was circulated among Native activists listing their grievances of the Native People against the federal-state power structure in Alaska. More important, it asserted the right to self-determination, calling for the formation in Alaska of a separate Native state, or lacking that, a return to territorial status under Native control. The proposal for a separate Native political territory was not seen at the time as realistic by most Native people, but the list of grievances and the spirit and political thrust of the document had an ideological impact on the thinking of Alaskan Native leaders.

The Declaration starts off with language taken from the U.S. Declaration of Independence, thereby drawing attention immediately to the two parallel cases of colonial abuse.

> When in the course of human events, it becomes necessary for one people to dissolve the political bands which have connected them with another, and assume among the powers of the earth, the separate and equal station to which the laws of nature and of nature's God entitled them, a decent respect for the opinions of mankind requires that they should declare the causes which impel them to separation.

> We hold these truths to be self-evident—that all men are created equal; that they are endowed by their Creator with certain inalienable rights; that among these are life, liberty and the pursuit of happiness. That, to secure these rights, governments are instituted among men deriving their just powers from the consent of the governed; that whenever any form of government becomes destructive of these ends, *it is the right of the people to alter or to abolish it, and to institute a new government . . .* [emphasis added]. (ANDP n.d., 1)

This is the Declaration's basic premise—powerful ideas and sentiments today just as they were more than two hundred years ago when the early British colonists declared their independence from King George's Great Britain.

The Declaration then lists the abuses suffered by the Native peoples of Alaska: "The history of the United States Government and the State of Alaska is a history of repeated injuries and usurpations, all having its direct object the establishment of an absolute tyranny over the Native people of Alaska and over villages of Alaska" (ANDP n.d., 2). The Declaration itself is lengthy, but selected examples from the document bearing out this assertion are the following (ANDP n.d., 2–5):

1. The state capital is located two or more time zones from the major part of the state with no road links. . . . The state government is controlled by people from non-Native areas and has been unresponsive to the needs, demands and petitions of Native People. . . .

2. The state and federal governments have mocked Native People by distinguishing them as without sufficient capital to determine their own affairs while at the same time boldly and without legal authority taking unto themselves the land and minerals, which have been in the use, possession and ownership of the Native People for longer than non-Native civilization has existed;

3. The state government has deprived Native People of their right to a jury of their peers in . . . major criminal cases by holding such trials at locations at which only non-Native juries are gathered;

4. The state and federal governments have ignored and suppressed the use of Native languages, even in the conduct of local government;

5. The state and federal governments and non-Native corporations and commercial interests have brazenly destroyed Native cemeteries and homes, have uncaringly injured the landscape and initiated erosion problems, and now seek to continue this activity in wildlife refuges and similar places—all without compensation to the Native owners and without concern for the cycle of pollution and continuing damage now in progress. . . .

After listing a number of abuses (of which the above are but a few examples), the Declaration continues (ANDP n.d., 5–6),: "In every stage of these oppressions . . . we have petitioned for redress, in the most humble terms; [but] our petitions have been answered only by repeated injury." The document then proposes as a solution that Alaskan Native peoples be given political autonomy. The proposed boundaries of the new state or territory, embodying the principle of Native political autonomy, include those regions of heaviest Indigenous concentration: to the north and east of Fairbanks and west of Anchorage. Only the south-central region and southeastern Alaska are to be left to the state under White authority. The Native petitioners conclude their document with the following statement: "We hereby assert our right under the First Amendment peacefully to assemble and to petition the Government for a redress of grievances" (ANDP n.d., 7).

Although many Natives signed the petition, it seems to have been ignored by the public officials to whom it was addressed. Nor were its proposals acted upon, specifically that a presidential commission meet with an all-Alaskan Native Congress to investigate the validity of the assertions and requests, and to actually set up the new Alaska Native State.

Land Freeze

It was the total ignoring of Native grievances and land claims that led to the formation of Alaskan Native regional organizations starting in the 1960s, and the founding of an umbrella group, the Alaskan Federation of Natives (AFN), in 1966. Another reason for Native political action was Project Chariot. "Project Chariot refers to the plan of Edward Teller, the father of the hydrogen bomb, to create a deepwater port by detonating underwater thermonuclear devices near the Iñupiat village of Point Hope, on the coast of northwestern Alaska" (Maas 2003, 168). Teller's proposal was blocked, and Native leaders obtained the assistance of the Association on American Indian Affairs to persuade Secretary of the Interior Stuart Udall to impose a freeze on the withdrawal of lands by the state until Native land claims were settled.

A report by the Institute of Social, Economic and Governmental Research at the University Alaska (ISEGR 1967, 6) further explains why the Native people organized at this particular time:

> One factor that cannot be ignored was the growing awareness by the Natives of their political strength. Adult Natives comprise about one-fifth of the voting population, and 1966 was an election year. Political candidates spent extra days visiting the far-flung Native villages, and their stands on the land claims issue made headlines. Land rights proved the cohesive that pulled

the several Native associations in the state together, and in October, 1966, the groups met in Anchorage to form a statewide association. A land claims bill was drawn up at this meeting and subsequently submitted to Congress.

Land rights were not the only matter of concern to the new AFN association; active committees were formed on topics such as education, health, and employment.

The legal base for the Natives' land claims case was strong: they had never sold their land, lost it by treaty, or been defeated in war, so their right to land under original title or occupancy had never been extinguished. These are the only constitutionally legal means by which the U.S. government can extinguish aboriginal title to the land. In creating the 1946 Court of Indian land claims, the government in effect admitted its unlawfulness in taking western Indian lands without compensation, and it set up the legal machinery to rectify this expansionist oversight.

There is also the constitutional procedure stipulating that only the federal government, and not an individual state, can end aboriginal land title. The new state of Alaska was violating this constitutional procedure by arbitrarily seizing Alaska Native lands under the Statehood Act. Therefore, as a result of the AFN's legal action in filing blanket land claims, the then secretary of the interior, Stuart Udall, on December 21, 1966, ordered a freeze on all further land transfers to the state of Alaska until Native claims were settled by Congress.

Legal arguments for Native land title were based on international law; the 1887 Treaty of Cession from Russia; the Organic Act of 1854, which brought civil government to the Territory of Alaska; the Statehood Act; and past court decisions honoring Indian land claimants. These, in addition to the constitutional provisions previously cited, made the Native claims case a strong one legally. Yet Secretary of the Interior Udall failed to make much of a legal argument for Native rights when he issued his land freeze decision. In August of 1967 he rather lamely informed Alaska's Governor Walter Hickel of only the moral question involved. "In the face of the Federal guarantee that the Alaska Natives shall not be disturbed in their use and occupation of lands, I could not in good conscience allow title to pass into other' hands" (quoted in ISEGR 1967, 5).

In the mid-1960s Atlantic Richfield, British Petroleum, Humble, and Sinclair oil corporations leased land on the North Slope near Barrow, Alaska, paying only $412 million for leases probably worth as much as $200 billion. Beginning in March 1968, and continuing through 1969 came the discovery of a vast oil deposit at Prudhoe Bay on Alaska's North Slope, "a development that inflamed the intense interest of major oil companies, the ambitions of state politicians and capitalists and the attention of Washington" (Weber 1972, 5). Under Governor Walter Hickel, a self-made Alaskan millionaire with interests in Atlantic Richfield, the state government auctioned off oil exploration rights to the North Slope to major oil companies for a cool $900 million, while hundreds of Native people picketed against the unilateral leasing of their lands. By right, the $900 million should have gone to the North Slope Eskimos. The Native protest was in Anchorage where the state auction of Alaskan lands was taking place.

About the time that AFN filed their blanket land claims, shortly after oil was discovered, Secretary Udall was collaborating in a scheme to dispossess the Navajo and Hopi Indians of their water, coal, and land rights, a plan concocted by the Interior Department's Bureau of Land Management and large coal corporations, utility companies, and water and power interests (see Chapter 5). In the Alaska case, it seems likely that he was also acting in the interests of the national and multinational oil corporations who sought a clear title to Alaska oil, and against local Alaskan state entrepreneurs and smaller venture capitalists, who were anxious for pipeline construction to commence so as to reap residual profits from the oil boom.

The 1966 freeze did not include federal lands already under lease, nor state-owned lands, including tidal and submerged lands, so it was of little help in protecting the land rights of Alaskan Natives (ISEGR 1967, 5). In fact, at the time the freeze was imposed, the state of Alaska had already been granted patent to 5.2 million acres, had received tentative approval to 7.9 million more (and was receiving revenues from these same lands), and had applied for 17.8 million more acres. Irrespective of the conflicting Native land claims, the North Slope oil fields were already claimed by the state. The state used the rationale that it was merely exercising its option provided in the Statehood Act to select lands in the so-called public domain.

Weber (1972, 9) sums up the situation in Alaska at the end of 1969: "The oil companies were drilling away, Alaskan developers and statesmen were counting their prospective millions, politicians were squirming to find a way around the land freeze to get more mineral-rich land, Washington was claiming that 'national defense' needed Alaska's oil, and the Natives (remember the Natives?) continued to struggle for subsistence in rural villages."

The land freeze was set to expire at the end of 1970s. Yet before it expired, five million acres had already been patented to the state, along with twelve million acres tentatively approved as state lands, and the Senate and House Interior committees had approved a right-of-way for a trans-Alaska pipeline to extend from Prudhoe Bay in the north to the Port of Valdez in the south. All this was executed without any promised compensation to Native claimants.

There were those at the time who supported Native land rights, but their voices went unheeded. The Honorable Arthur J. Goldberg, formerly of the U.S. Supreme Court, stated that justice was all on the side of the Native peoples: "[Alaska Natives] have conclusive legal and moral claims to most of Alaska's 375 million acres. Since 1825, when Chief Justice John Marshall, in the case of Johnson V. McIntosh, announced that America's original inhabitants are the rightful occupants of the soil with legal as well as just claims to retain possession of it, the Alaska Natives have neither sold, nor ceded their lands, nor have they lost them in war" (Research Institute of Alaska 1970, 296).

The irony of the Vietnam War—the fact that billions were being spent by the nation on the war but scarcely anything for Native peoples—was not lost upon some of the Native leaders who were making land claims. An Athabascan Indian, speaking at a peace rally in 1972, told the crowd: "The money spent only ten days of fighting in Vietnam would buy for Alaska Natives and the poor: 70,000 low-cost housing units, over 300 hospitals with 125 beds each, 1800 public health centers, over 10,000 new classrooms, high schools in every part of the state, and a fully paid college education for every Alaska Native. . . . And for want of the money being thrown down the drain in Vietnam, Alaska Natives will no doubt be cheated of fair compensation for their land claims" (John 1971, 36).

The Oil Pipeline

The development of the North Slope oil deposit led to the decision in 1969 to build an eight-hundred-mile hot oil trans-Alaska pipeline from Prudhoe Bay in the Beaufort Sea to the southern Port of Valdez on the Pacific Ocean. A consortium of companies was formed, including British Petroleum, SOHIO, Mobil, Phillips, Union, and Ameranda Hess, in what

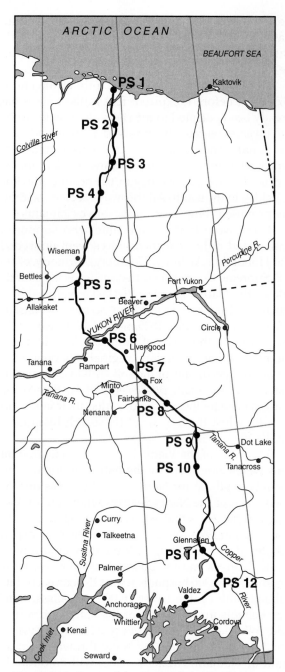

Figure 10.2 Route of the Trans-Alaska Pipeline

oil for companies, and a 90 percent revenue return allowance from the federal treasury for the State of Alaska" (Weber 1972, 6).

The "iron corridor," as the pipeline was called, immediately became a subject of controversy. It directly affected Native land claims because much of the claimed land would be used for its construction. (See Figure 10.2.) There was also a question of its impact on the Native way of life, on hunting, fishing, and gathering, and the potential problems of a hot oil pipeline on the arctic permafrost, and haul roads destroying the natural habitat. A pipeline to Valdez meant that single-hulled super oil tankers would be negotiating treacherous waters with the possibility of an oil spill in the valuable fishing grounds off Valdez and Cordova in south-central Alaska. In fact, twenty years later, on March 29, 1989, the unthinkable happened when the oil tanker *Exxon Valdez* ran aground in the Valdez Arm of Prince William Sound, spilling its cargo of crude oil that despoiled 1,200 miles of coastline. Hundreds of thousands of seabirds and marine animals died as a result. The spill all but ended the subsistence-based economy of local Native villages and seriously curtailed the fishing livelihoods of Native and non-Native fishermen alike.

To construct the pipeline, forty-eight-inch diameter pipe was ordered from Japan and stored on the sunken shoreline of Valdez, which had been partially destroyed by the Great Alaska Earthquake of 1964. Some observers questioned the selection of Valdez as the pipeline's terminus given the possibility of another earthquake, but construction plans went ahead anyway. Alyeska Pipeline Service Company became the contractor, with an estimated pipeline cost of $900 million. Because of litigation initiated by Alaska Native villages and environmental groups, actual construction did not begin until 1974. At the peak of construction, there were twenty-four thousand workers employed on the pipeline—the majority from outside Alaska. Construction included a 360-mile haul road in northern Alaska, twelve pumping stations, twenty bridges over major streams, a 2,300-foot bridge over the Yukon River, three permanent airfields and eight temporary airfields, "fifteen permanent access roads, an eight inch gas pipeline to the four northern pumping stations, nineteen construction camps, as well as the Valdez terminal" (Strong 1977, 9). At the peak years of its construction, the pipeline dominated the Alaskan economy.

became the Alyeska Pipeline Service Company. "Billed as the answer to America's growing domestic oil needs as well as those of 'national security,' it was really a scheme designed to get the oil to market at a fantastic profit. In addition, profits would even increase further due to federal subsidies on domestic

Strong's research (1977, iv) found that despite many serious construction problems (such as pipe weld tests having been falsified by a subcontractor), the Alaska pipeline nevertheless produced some positive benefits, such as employment and job training for Alaska Natives, with Native workers joining unions, and business opportunities becoming available for Native regional corporations. On the negative side, large-scale projects based on nonrenewable resources rarely provide permanent employment for local inhabitants. Pipeline wage work opportunities were limited to the unskilled and semiskilled categories, caribou herds and fish on which Native people depended were threatened, and inflation brought on by the influx of out-of-state pipeline workers quadrupled food prices.

Role of the State of Alaska

In October 1970, the year the land freeze was to expire, there were federal, state, and local elections in Alaska. As the election season approached there was a flurry of activity by businessmen and politicians to unite White and Native interests around a compromise land claims bill and then to get on with the construction of the pipeline, from which many of the well-to-do investors who had bankrolled the general political campaign stood to profit. But despite the electioneering rhetoric of "unity," it soon became clear that the expiration of the land freeze was eagerly anticipated by those same interests and the prospect of the big land grab to come. The new secretary of the interior, former Alaskan governor Walter Hickel, repeatedly declared that pipeline construction would begin in the early spring of 1971. The real issues in Alaska during the election campaign facing the citizens, both Native and non-Native, never came up. Presumably the pipeline construction would cure all ills. The important problems of controlling the oil capitalists, protecting Native lands and communities, and rolling back unemployment were rarely mentioned. Unemployment stood officially at 12 percent in Alaska. It was as high as 25 percent in Fairbanks, which was mostly White, and up to 85 percent in Bethel, mostly Eskimo. Alaska had the highest median income of any state, but it also had and has the highest cost of living of any of the continental states, producing only 5 percent of its food needs in 1970. Rural poverty, mostly Native, was phenomenal. Family income for the Eskimo in the Arctic region averaged as low as $390 per year.

Meanwhile, despite the land freeze, the state of Alaska was moving in on the lands claimed by Native peoples. The Native citizens of Ouzinkie woke up one December morning in 1970 to find their gardens, located one-fourth mile from town, staked out in five-acre recreational tracts. The state was making the land available to Whites under open-to-entry leases. Ouzinkie is a fishing village, a fourth-class city on Spruce Island about forty miles from Kodiak. Hearings had not been held as was legally required, and the state's officials had not so much as even consulted with the Ouzinkie Advisory Planning Board before unilaterally classifying the land as vacant. Fortunately, the Ouzinkie people were able to obtain the services of the Alaska Legal Services. A lawsuit was filed against the state in Superior Court, and the state withdrew its claim to the land it was attempting to sell rather than risk a test case on the Native versus state land rights issue in court. The state attorney general knew that under the law the state might lose and the door would then be open for other Native lawsuits regarding Native lands seized by the state, lands involving valuable minerals, including oil and gas. There were other cases similar to the one at Ouzinkie.

Related Events at the National Level

In 1970–71 the situation of Alaska Natives worsened also because of national developments. Walter J. Hickel, no longer Alaska's governor, was appointed by President Richard Nixon to the important post of secretary of the interior. This gave him direct responsibility for protecting the environment, as well as being the trustee, through the Bureau of Indian Affairs, of Native American lands and resources. Hickel's anticonservation and anti-Indian record was so negative that his appointment caused considerable controversy during the Senate confirmation hearings. Many testified against his appointment, but in the end he was confirmed. It was widely suspected that the oil companies in Alaska had manipulated the appointment.

At this time there seemed little possibility that the litigation on behalf of Alaska Natives would substantially hinder pipeline construction. Native leaders worried that there was not enough legal help to wage battle in the courts once the land rush started. They realized that litigating land rights could be a long and protracted one, the outcome of which was uncertain. Meanwhile, the land-grabbers would be able to fully entrench themselves. That is why Native leadership saw a compromise land set-tlement through Congressional action as the best route for them to follow. Proving aboriginal use and occupancy of the land could be a complicated process. Native hunting, fishing, berry and trap-ping grounds, grave sites and other religious and historic areas are not marked by "no trespass" signs, by fences, or by mapped boundaries. A necessary prerequisite was the recognition by Congress of aboriginal land use in principle, which it had not yet done.

Hickel as governor of Alaska had consistently fought the land freeze in favor of immediate pipeline construction. When the freeze was initiated in 1969 he brought suit in the Federal District Court seeking to compel the secretary of interior to complete the trans-fer of some twelve million acres of Native land to the state. The land freeze was supposed to continue until Congress acted on Native claims, but Hickel indi-cated upon his nomination to the Interior Department that he would honor the land freeze, Public Land Order 4582, only for the duration of the Ninety-first Congress, after which he would continue the transfer of the "public domain" (Native-claimed lands for the most part) to the state of Alaska.

Hickel later sought to mollify Native outrage by indicating he would institute a partial freeze on eight townships around each Native village. His main pur-pose in offering a partial freeze was to nullify two impending court injunctions: one brought by conser-vationists, and the other by the Athabascan village of Stevens through whose territory the pipeline was to pass. Stevens Village had refused this modification of the land freeze and the grant of right-of-way for the pipeline as Hickel had requested. One of their main objections was the failure of the pipeline company to comply with an agreement to employ Native work-ers. Friends of the Earth charged in 1971 that the promise of Native jobs in the oil boom was a sham. (One oil company ad showed a happy Eskimo hold-ing a tube of oil.) In the first place, the oil companies promised jobs to Natives only because they had to as a condition for running the pipeline over Native lands. Second, Native jobs in a boom/bust oil econ-omy would probably be temporary. Non-Native workers were already being flown in from the Lower Forty-eight to work on the pipeline. Furthermore, oil development would do irreparable harm to the unique cultures of the Native peoples by endanger-ing the land and wildlife. The situation had already deteriorated to such an extent that five Native villages were suing the oil companies for violation of land-use agreements.

Ecology Hearings

There was a problem with Hickel's plans succeeding and those of the business interests which he repre-sented. The Natives and the ecologists obtained a court injunction to hold up the pipeline construction with its companion roadway, based on the National Environmental Policy Act passed by Congress in 1959. The Act stated that projects on federal land must be scrutinized for their environmental consequences before they are undertaken. This delayed construc-tion of the pipeline until federal hearings could be held on the matter. Even so, construction materials continued to be stockpiled and other development plans by the oil companies went forward to the extent they could legally do so.

On February 24, 1971, an environmental hearing was held in Anchorage. The general line of the "boomers" who testified for the pipeline was that it was patriotic to build it to help supply U.S. energy needs. Their testimony was opposed by the conserva-tionists and Natives, who cited dangers to the envi-ronment and the land rights of Alaska's Indigenous peoples whose lands the proposed pipeline would cross. At the hearing only three speakers out of sev-eral hundred submitted testimony in favor of settling the Native land claims issue before the problem of oil transportation could be settled. (The author of this book was one of those who did so.)

Along with oil fever, racism in Alaska increased during this period. Bumper stickers on cars pro-claimed "Oil feeds my family," and it was rumored that the then governor, Keith Miller, was overheard in an Anchorage restaurant singing "the only good Indian is a dead Indian." The assassination of the Kennedys and the Rev. Martin Luther King Jr. had resulted in a national movement for gun control. In conservative Alaska, however, the favorite slo-gan was "The West wasn't won with a registered gun." A Native humorist came up with an appro-priate answer: "It was lost as we know with a regis-tered bow!"

Meanwhile, petty entrepreneurs—merchants and those companies which had built up their inven-tories of equipment and supplies in expectation of quick profits to be made from the pipeline construction—began to experience loses through the delay in construction, some forced into bankruptcy. The conservative-controlled media blamed the

Natives and "outside preservationists" for the small business failures and, indeed, for all of Alaska's many ills. Unemployed non-Native workers were told that the Natives were to blame. Many White workers had been persuaded to come to Alaska to share in the pipeline construction and the oil boom through false or misleading advertising put out by state agencies and the Alaska Chamber of Commerce. They were never told of the environmental impact issue, nor the Natives' aboriginal land rights controversy.

Under these deteriorating social conditions, political pressure was increased on Congress to take action in the matter of Native land claims. The pressure to settle the land claims problem was felt by all parties concerned, from the oil company presidents down to the leadership of Native organizations and the state's political representatives. Each conflicting interest group wanted Congress to strike a compromise Native land claims settlement, but each group also had its own view of what constituted a fair settlement.

It was not until April 29, 1974, almost six years after the Prudhoe Bay oil discovery, and several years after a Native land claims settlement (discussed below), that pipeline construction was able to begin. The pipeline would have to cross 350 streams and major rivers, four earthquake zones, six mountain ranges, and hundreds of miles of frozen tundra. The technological obstacles were immense, let alone the issue of aboriginal land rights. Regardless, there was tremendous desire to start construction immediately without adequate study of the technological problems involved, including the effect of the pipeline on tundra ecology, or considering alternative methods of getting the oil to market—by sea tanker, by a trans-Canadian pipeline, or by a suspended pipeline. Construction took place over several years, and by mid-1977 the first oil was flowing. The eight-hundred-mile pipeline was originally slated to cost over $2 billion. According to news reports, the cost rose to $5.98 billion in 1974, and by 1975 it had risen to $6.4 billion.

THE LAND CLAIMS SETTLEMENT: WHO OWNS ALASKA?

The Alaska Native Claims Settlement Act (ANCSA) was signed into law by President Richard M. Nixon on December 18, 1971. ANCSA was passed as the result of hearings, maneuvers, and bargains made among the various politicians and corporate power-holders about the fate of Alaska Natives. The land claims settlement was seen by Congress and the Nixon administration "as a means to assimilate Alaska Natives into the larger society. Natives, on the other hand, largely viewed ANCSA as a vehicle of economic self-determination" (Gibbs 2007, 491).

ANCSA granted Alaska Natives forty-four million acres (10 percent of Alaska) and $962.5 million in compensation. The land distribution was made to twelve Native for-profit regional corporations and 203 village corporations rather than to existing Native political entities. In each of the Native regions, a new economic corporation was formed with the explicit purpose of making money. "The size of the regional corporations ranged from Ahtna, Inc., with about 1,000 shareholders, to Sealaska Corporation, with about 16,000 shareholders. . . . Because Cook Inlet Region [CIRI] was based in Alaska's largest city, CIRI became a 'melting pot' for all Alaska Native groups. Many Alaska Natives from other parts of Alaska who moved to Anchorage signed up for CIRI" (McClanahan 2007, 2). Village corporations received 22 million acres of land with surface rights. "The regional corporations received full title to 16 million acres of land and the sub-surface estate in the 22 million acres patented to the villages. . . . Two million acres were set aside for other purposes, including cemeteries and historical sites" (Gibbs 2007, 492). The number of Alaska Native shareholders enrolled in the corporations totaled more than seventy-eight thousand at the time of ANCSA's passage. A thirteenth corporation was established for Alaska Natives living outside of Alaska, mainly in the Seattle urban area, for those who could no longer claim Alaska residence. They were to receive a pro rata share of the financial settlement only. (There were an estimated twenty thousand Alaska Natives living in the Lower Forty-eight and elsewhere in the world.) The four million acres held as five reserves as trust lands, established under the 1936 ARA, were revoked. The only remaining reservation in Alaska was Annette Island, which had been established in 1891 for the Tsimshian Indians.

Not to be overlooked is the fact that Native hunting and fishing rights were extinguished under ANCSA. Section 4b of the Act states: "All aboriginal titles, if any, and claims of aboriginal title in Alaska based on use and occupancy, including submerged land underneath all water areas, both inland and off-shore, and including any aboriginal hunting or fishing rights that may exist, are hereby extinguished." In 1980, nine years after ANCSA, Congress passed the Alaska National Interest Land Conservation Act (ANILCA), which set up a subsistence priority for "rural Alaskans," including Alaska Natives. Its implementation soon encountered serious problems, however. "Alaska's subsistence policy remains mired in politics pitting state vs. federal governments, rural vs. urban residents, and most unfortunately, Natives vs. non-Natives" (Thornton 1998, 29).

ANCSA was widely heralded as the most generous land settlement ever made to an Indigenous people, yet 44 million acres represented only a small portion of Alaska's 375 million acres. The AFN originally asked for 60 million acres of land to insure traditional hunting and gathering customs; $900 million dollars for extinguishing claims to their other 300 million acres; and a 2 percent annual royalty on oil revenues to insure continued income for future generations. Under ANCSA, the acreage desired by Native leaders was cut by a third, and traditional hunting and fishing rights were made vulnerable to state regulation. Furthermore, the Natives would initially be allowed to choose only a small portion of their land around their villages in the amount of 18 million acres; then the state would be allowed to select its 77 million acres as granted in the Statehood Act. Only then would Alaska Natives be allowed to complete their land selection. This stipulation effectively prevented Alaska Natives from choosing valuable mineral, oil, or timber lands. "Perhaps worse, a 20-year grace period was the only restraint imposed on the state [of Alaska] before it could tax undeveloped corporate land—then foreclose for tax delinquency and remove from Native ownership" (Burnham 2003a, 1). (This was corrected by Congressional legislative amendments, discussed later in this chapter.)

It should be noted that the cash settlement of $962.5 million was not paid as a single lump sum, but was to be paid out in a series of payments over a number of years. The money was to be paid from an Alaska Native Fund established by the U.S. Treasury. Congress was to pay $462.5 million over an eleven-year period, and the state of Alaska was to pay 2 percent of its mineral revenues until a balance of $50 million was reached.

The money part of the settlement was funneled into the newly formed Native corporations, with boards of directors, annual corporate reports, proxy fights, and Native shareholders. In a historical depar-

ture from U.S.-Indian relations, Congress authorized the creation of corporations instead of reservations to receive the monetary part of the land claims settlement. ANCSA also "permitted multinational corporations to build docks in Valdez on Prince William Sound, a pipeline to move oil from the North Slope, and to drill for and pump oil from beneath the shallow waters of Prudhoe Bay" (Jorgensen 2003, 99).

The role of the newly-created regional corporations was elevated to a powerful one, both financially and administratively, over the powers of Native village leadership, thus tending to undermine traditional authority in favor of middle-class-oriented, business-trained executives. This led to grumbling among those in the villages that the corporation offices were being filled by "Brooks Brothers Natives." The 2 percent oil royalty proposed by the AFN was eliminated from the final legislation, apparently because sharing corporate profits on a continuing basis with Native people, even if the land is theirs, was too much for corporate interests and their Congressional allies to swallow.

ANCSA required "that the Secretary of the Interior make firm decisions, within nine months after its enactment, on the withdrawal from other uses of up to 80 million acres of federally-owned land for study purposes for possible additions to national parks, forests, wildlife refuges and wild and scenic rivers" (U.S. Department of the Interior 1974). The Interior Department later announced that it was designating 90 million acres from which the Natives could select "their 40 million," but it was reserving vast areas for national parks "in the public interest." While this action assured the Natives of their full acreage, it also allowed them even less chance to get good lands of known economic value, such as oil, copper, or timber.

Interestingly, the Sierra Club, a conservation group, actively lobbied for the withdrawal of "no less than 80 million acres for permanent protection in federal ownership"—about 25 percent of the State of Alaska. Their position was that areas of scenic beauty and wildlife habitation should be protected from the rapacious economic interests represented by the state, which wished to obtain mineral and other lands in their 103 million acre package. The Sierra Club naively recommended that nearly all of the 80 million acres should be under protective management of the Department of the Interior. Yet any politically aware person knows that the Interior Department, with its bureaus of Land Management, Forestry, Fisheries, Mines, and Indian Affairs, is a badly compromised advocate for the public interest. Edgar Cahn documented this point conclusively in *Our Brother's Keeper* (1969, 157): "The U.S. Department of the Interior is a chamber of the mighty. Oil and gas billionaires, lumber barons, ranchers and corporate farmers, sportsmen and recreation interests, hydroelectric and mining promoters number among its customary clientele and constituency. All have intimate relationships with the Department, all work amicably with Interior officials to cultivate a relationship of mutual accommodation." Reserving 80 million acres under federal control is equivalent to reserving future mineral and resource expropriation by corporate developers at the public's expense. Once designated as public lands, oil, gas, copper, timber and similar corporations pay no land taxes and are not responsible for the land's upkeep.

It is interesting to note the kind of investments that were initially made by the newly created Native corporations. McBeath and Morehouse (1980, 62, 64) report that the Arctic Slope Regional Corporation bought the department store at Barrow and built a hotel-restaurant. Sealaska Corporation constructed an office building in Juneau, the state capital. Calista Corporation built a high-rise hotel in Anchorage, Alaska's largest city. Aleut Corporation purchased two crabbing and fishing boats. With respect to the village corporations, the Togotthele Corporation of the Athabascan Indians at Nenana invested in a sawmill and log home-building enterprise; and the Bethel Corporation built a million-dollar hotel and apartment building. Many of the smaller village corporations purchased village stores. But "not all investments in new enterprises have turned a profit, and a few corporations have experienced heavy losses during their early years of investments . . . some have made poor investment choices . . . and some have developed large bureaucracies and payrolls which have further eroded capital resources. The potential profitability of many long-term ventures in real estate, minerals, fisheries, and timber is, however, yet to be determined" (McBeath and Morehouse 1980, 64).

By way of contrast, the many nonprofit Native regional associations have played an important role in providing "a variety of social programs supported by grants, or contracts from government agencies or foundations, and new nonprofit organizations have formed in the wake of the settlement act. . . . Thus, the [preexisting] Native associations continue as nonprofit corporations, conducting programs in such areas as health, education, housing and employ-

ment assistance in their regions" (McBeath and Morehouse 1980, 65–67). An example is the Cook Inlet Native Association, which operated a Native Assistance Center in Anchorage to help Natives new to the city find jobs, locate housing, and find special services. These nonprofit associations also play an advocacy role for Native issues.

FAILURE OF THE CORPORATE MODEL

[*Note*: The following assessment of the economic viability of the regional and village corporations, i.e., the Settlement Act's corporate model, is for the first two decades after ANCSA was passed, i.e., until the early 1990s.]

The land title to forty-four million acres, one ninth of the total area of the state, included both surface and subsurface rights. There were two requirements for eligibility as an Alaska Native for enrollment in a corporation: possession of one-fourth or more Alaska Indian, Aleut, or Eskimo blood, or declare that she or he is regarded as an Alaska Native by a Native community. The Alaska Native is then enrolled with one hundred shares in a *regional corporation* and, if a village resident, an additional one hundred shares in a *village corporation*. A Native village corporation was defined as any tribe, clan, group, village, community, or association comprising twenty-five or more eligible Natives, or "Native groups" in the case of urban enclaves. All Native lands were exempted under the Act from property taxes for twenty years from the 1971 date, as long as they remain undeveloped. The Native shareholders were prohibited from selling or transferring their stock during this period. Non-Natives who inherit stock during this period were denied voting rights until 1991.

The conventional wisdom is that the ANCSA represented an unparalleled victory for Alaska Natives, but a closer examination paints a different picture. In the first place, only 90 million acres of Alaska's total 375 million acres were designated as available to Alaska Natives from which to select their 44 million. As a result, the poorest of Alaska's lands went to the impoverished Natives. The remaining acres were either retained by the federal government or given away to the state of Alaska and the energy monopolies.

Second, in the fabulously oil rich North Slope, the Iñupiat Eskimos received only surface or hunting rights to most of their area. The underground oil treasure went to the non-Native energy corporations.

Not one cent of the $1 billion land claims settlement went to the fifty-five thousand impoverished Alaska Natives. Instead, $462.5 million would be paid out over an eleven-year period to shareholders of twelve Alaska Native corporations, which were to dispense it somewhat like the government's antipoverty programs.

Third, many of the federal withdrawals, ostensibly for national parks and wild life areas, conflicted with Native subsistence-based economies and traditional usage of their aboriginal land base. This was the case for the proposed Wrangell Mountain National Park, which would be carved out of the historic homeland of the Ahtna (Athabascan) Indians in the Chitina River Valley and the Chisana-Nabesna country. The region is spectacular for its glacial landscapes, wilderness river valleys, high peaks, and wildlife. Some of it is also rich in copper and other minerals. It would be an easy step for mineral rights to be transferred from the federal government or the state and then to the mining corporations, to the complete neglect of Native interests.

Fourth, more or less overlooked by Native leaders at the time of its passage, ANCSA not only extinguished claims to most of Native traditional lands and all subsurface resources on land not transferred to them, but it also extinguished Native claims to the control of wildlife, whether on Native land, state land, or Federal land, by vesting regulatory authority over wildlife in various federal and state agencies. There have been other problems as well.

In *The Dynamics of Alaska Native Self-government* (1980), McBeath and Morehouse undertook a comprehensive analysis of the changes in rural Alaska from the granting of statehood to 1980. They note that the "shared wealth" provision of ANCSA has caused some problems and leading to litigation. Section 7(i) specifies that "70 percent of all interest received by regional corporations on delayed distribution of their timber resources and subsurface estate are to be divided annually among all twelve regional corporations" (McBeath and Morehouse 1980, 61). Some corporations complied, but others brought lawsuits. By mid-1978, these regional corporations had received $374 million under ANCSA, with about half going to village corporations and individuals.

In the early 1980s the Canadian justice Thomas Berger surveyed the opinions of Alaska Natives in sixty-two villages for the Alaska Native Review Commission regarding the impact of ANCSA at the Native grassroots. In *Village Journey* (1985) he concluded that the real intent of Congress in passing ANCSA was the assimilation of Native Peoples by transferring aboriginal lands to regional and village corporations rather than to tribal entities. "The land that ANCSA conveyed does not belong to Alaska Natives, it belongs to these corporations. . . . Congress wanted Alaska Natives to become shareholders and businessmen, to become part of the commercial and corporate mainstream of America. . . . But these corporate structures put the land at risk. For Native land is now a corporate asset. Alaska Natives fear that, through corporate failure, corporate takeover, and taxation, they could lose the land" (Berger 1985, 6–7). "Both village Natives and urban Natives believe the land should be passed on to their children. This spiritual and cultural relationship with the land is the bedrock of Native culture" (Berger 1985, 75).

Anthropologist Gary Anders (1985, 10) also warned of the danger of the capitalist corporate model for Alaska Natives: "Forced acceptance of the profit motive and the attendant requirements of individualism and competition undermine long standing cultural values which operated to minimize conflict and equitably distribute basic economic goods. Establishment of new corporate institutions with the hierarchical organization of technicians, managers, and executive decision-makers has replaced traditional leadership patterns that bonded Natives into cohesive groups." Anders argues that there is a direct parallel between ANCSA and the 1887 Dawes Allotment Act under which American Indians of the Lower Forty-eight lost half of their land base. "The Alaska Natives face the oil companies in much the same manner as the Indians after the enactment of the Dawes Act faced railroad companies" (Anders 1985, 5).

Berger (1985, 85) also makes the connection between ANCSA and the Allotment Act: "ANCSA has many parallels to the [Dawes] General Allotment Act. It places the land in fee title, it makes land alienable and taxable. Although ANCSA has not divided the ancestral lands of Alaska Natives into individual parcels, it has made Native land a corporate asset and divided its ownership into individual stock certificates. These shares are not tangible like land but, after 1991, they can be sold. Even if shares are not sold, corporations could lose their lands through bankruptcy, corporate takeovers, and tax sales."

Furthermore, the corporate infrastructure created under ANCSA is part and parcel of the historical colonial penetration of Alaska and the equivalent to the tribal councils created under the 1934 Indian Reorganization Act.

ANCSA created a corporate model for a land claims settlement in which "the Alaskan Natives were to be turned instantly into corporate executives and stockholders and [would be] required to use their cash payments and the natural resources of their land holdings to extract cash profits from their Native corporations" (Bodley 1982, 90). This experiment in Indigenous "Red capitalism" was supposed to lift Alaska Natives out of poverty, generate rapid economic growth, provide jobs, and pay generous dividends. By March 1985, however, fourteen years after passage of ANCSA, only two-thirds of the land had been transferred to Indigenous title, and the Alaska Bureau of Indian Affairs predicted that it could be another forty years before all of the land surveys are finished and the land transfer completed. To make matters worse, the ANCSA money was received in the late 1970s just as high inflation and the 1981 recession hit, decreasing the value of the money payout. The 1985 world collapse in oil prices and the U.S. recession forestalled any economic success by the regional corporations when they had just begun to move assets into active business operations, such as oilfield service, seafood processing, construction, real estate, and marine transportation.

> Between 1981 and 1986, their holdings of stocks and bonds dropped from 39 percent of their total asset base to 24 percent. . . . At the start of the 1990s, the corporations seemed to cluster into three groups. The first group consists of those recovering from heavy loses and with few assets: Aleut, Bering Straits, Bristol Bay, Calista, Chugach, and Koniag. The second group—Ahtna, Doyon, Nana, and Sealaska—has consolidated operations, focused on natural resource development where possible, and established financial portfolios as major sources of ongoing income. The third group—Arctic Slope and Cook Inlet—were continuing major business expansions and active participation in oil, gas, broadcasting, and real estate. (Colt 1996, 15)

The corporations as a whole lost money in seven of the first seventeen years of operation.

Recognizing that natural resources are distributed unevenly, Section 7[I] of ANCSA required that the regional corporations share 70 percent of their net revenues from timber and subsurface resources with the village corporations and shareholders not enrolled in village corporations. Between 1972 and 1990, $98 million in sharable net revenues was generated, 95 percent of which came from Arctic Slope, Cook Inlet, and Sealaska. Several corporations have made shareholder employment a priority. Both

Arctic Slope and Nana employed roughly 20 percent of their shareholders. The regional corporations have also "contributed significant funds to scholarship, cultural preservation, and social service programs" (Colt 1996, 17).

Government delays in transferring the lands, corporate power struggles, and poor management of the regional corporations kept dividends low, and significant Native employment failed to materialize. There was also the danger that non-Natives could take over the corporations when Native stock became available for sale in 1991. According to the ANCSA provisions, the assets of the twelve regional corporations would become taxable in December, 1991. Alaska Native shareholders could then sell their stock, if they wished to do so. Thus, there was the danger of (1) corporations going bankrupt because they could not come up with money for taxes; (2) shareholders selling their stock, their ancestral rights to the land and its resources; or (3) corporate takeovers by non-Native outside interests.

The danger of shareholders selling their shares existed because only half of the Alaska Natives residing in the state live in small, remote, rural villages, communities which still have strong ties to the land. It is estimated that 25 percent of all shareholders do not live on Native lands: one-half live in Anchorage and Fairbanks, one-fourth live in Seattle, and the rest are scattered throughout the other states. This is the group which might be more easily inclined to sell their shares in 1991, especially given the fact that by the mid-1980s many of the corporations were already in serious financial trouble and were paying little if any dividends. Surveys showed that as many as 40 percent of Alaska Natives said they might sell their stock in 1991 if they were economically hard pressed.

Then there are the village corporations. Under the ANCSA provisions, each village corporation was to receive so many thousand acres of surface estate, including a core village township of six square miles, at least 640 acres (one square mile) of contiguous sections. The village corporation was to receive a one-time money compensation for "lands lost"—from $10,000 to $100,000. It should be noted, however, that the village corporation owns its mineral wealth only on the land directly beneath the village, and not in the much larger surface estate. With the settlement slanted in favor of the regional corporations, it is not surprising that by the mid-1980s an angry dissident group representing some eighty villages was demanding that the Native lands be taken from the corporations and placed in the care of the traditional tribal councils.

Alaska grew by 19.2 percent between 1980 and 1983 to 479,000 residents, giving it the nation's highest rate of growth for a state, although the state lost population in 1983 due to a downturn in oil prices. By 1990 there were at least 78,000 Eskimos, Aleuts, and Indians in Alaska, constituting about 16 percent of the total state population. More than half of Alaska Natives live in small rural villages. It is expensive to be a rural "bush" Native in Alaska. In 1985 the proportion of household income spent on imported fuel oil and electricity by Alaska Native villages was 43 percent. "Electricity ranged between ten and 15 times the average cost for a typical city . . . [and] fuel oil, which must be transported in during the summer months on barges or flown in during the winter should supplies run short, costs up to six times the Anchorage price" (Anders 1985, 8). There has been growing energy dependence at extremely high costs by the Native peoples at the same time that billions of dollars of oil, 25 percent of the entire U.S. domestic supply, is being pumped from underneath their feet, so to speak.

Although Alaska Natives constituted about 15 percent of the state's population in 1990, they were almost completely lacking in the capital needed to compete with non-Native business enterprises, and to raise their standard of living through their own efforts. The money grant in ANCSA was intended to provide that capital. Alaska Natives were expected to sell their aboriginal birthright as represented in land claims and take over all services and expenditures previously provided by the state. But by the late 1980s it had not worked out that way. While several regional corporations were successful, many others were on the brink of bankruptcy. Poverty among Alaska Natives was widespread in 1986. A report by the Institute of Social and Economic Research at the University of Alaska found that Alaska Natives made up about 40 percent of the enrollment in the state's core public assistance programs. Broadly speaking, Alaskans who qualify for public assistance could not have assets worth more than $2,500, and in some cases were limited to assets of less than $500.

On the other hand, an unlooked for but encouraging development in reaction to ANCSA was the emergence of Native political organization and a cultural renaissance. The series of hearings held throughout the state by the Alaska Native Review Commission and Justice Berger's subsequent report,

Village Journey (1985), played an important role in the emerging Native political consciousness. There was a growing awareness that the for-profit corporations created by ANCSA were culturally inappropriate for Alaska Native villages. In 1983 the Alaska Native Federation Convention adopted a resolution charging that Western business corporations are foreign to Native culture and in many ways inconsistent with Native values.

The 1991 Amendments

A major bone of contention with ANCSA was the fact that Alaska Natives born after passage of the Act were excluded from its provisions. "The conflict between for-profit corporations and Native values emerged as 1991 approached. Natives became alarmed that the expiration of the restrictions on the sale of stock could lead to non-Native control and ownership of Native lands. At the 1982 AFN Convention, Natives voted to make the '1991' issue its top priority and to seek amendments to ANCSA to protect Native land" (Gibbs 2007, 493).

As the anniversary date of 1991 approached, as many as twenty thousand children and young people were being denied their aboriginal right to share in the land claims settlement. They could not enroll and receive corporate shares in the land claims settlement, although they could inherit or purchase shares. They would as a class of persons own and control nothing relating to their Native heritage, including no stake in the village corporations held by their elders. As a result of the inequities suffered by the New Natives (as they were called), Alaska Native organizations pressed for corrective legislation. In response to their concerns, Congress passed the 1991 Amendments to ANCSA, with President Ronald Reagan signing them into law on February 3, 1988.

The new legislation as passed by Congress, however, did not fully measure up to Native expectations. The Native American Rights Fund (NARF 1988, l) warned that the legislation would prove inadequate: "While partially satisfying their primary goal of protecting the Native corporations and their land, they failed to deal with fundamental flaws in the system, and permit the continued treatment of Alaska Native governments as second class Indian tribes."

The primary goals of the 1991 amendments as originally proposed by Alaska Native groups were: (1) to ensure continued Native ownership of the corporations and their land, (2) to offer a way out of the corporate system through a tribal option, and (3) to authorize issuance of stock to Natives born after 1971. The Amendments as passed helped to protect Native ownership of the corporations by extending the restrictions on sale of stock for an indefinite period of time, but the amendments also authorized individual corporations to lift the restrictions at their discretion. The "tribal option" part of the House and Senate bills, also known as the "Qualified Transferee Entity" or QTE, was dropped entirely from the final legislation. "The QTE section would have authorized Native corporations to transfer land to tribal governments without having to pay dissenting shareholders" (NARF 1988, 3). Tribal or village governments would have become empowered with money and lands presently controlled by the regional Native corporations if the constituents voted to do so.

The Amendments as passed allowed for the issuance of stock to the New Natives, but as McClanahan (2007, 1) points out, it was done "through the creation of a new type of stock, known as 'life state stock.' This stock is valid only during the shareholder's lifetime and cannot be passed on. Only a few corporations have extended stock ownership to those born after 1971." Another provision of the 1991 Amendments as passed authorized the regional corporations to issue new voting stock to non-Natives; the stock may even be given greater voting power than the existing Native-owned stock, which could lead to the possible loss of Native control of the corporations.

On the positive side, the 1991 Amendments "provides automatic 'land bank' protections to land owned by a Native corporation so long as the land is not developed, leased or sold to third parties. This protects Native regional corporation lands from taxation, squatter rights, bankruptcy and involuntary dissolution. On the other hand, the corporations could lose their land if is pledged as collateral for a loan. It could also simply be sold and lost by the corporation through unwise business decisions" (NARF 1988, 2). The land bank provisions do not provide protection for developed lands. "Thus, the core areas of villages where people live will be exposed to loss through taxation, bankruptcy and other forms of judicial foreclosure. . . . In short, the 'land bank' is a decent stop-gap measure, but still offers manifold opportunities for erosion of the Native land base" (NARF 1988, 3).

At best, the 1991 Amendments provided only stopgap protection for Native shareholders and their corporations. They fall far short of what Alaska Natives wanted or deserve. Nowhere in the legislation is there mention made of Alaska Native subsistence rights.

DOES "RED CAPITALISM" WORK?

According to a 2004 report by the University of Alaska Anchorage, the health and social conditions of Alaska Natives have improved somewhat since the 1960s but still lag behind those of non-Natives. Sanitation, housing, and medical care have greatly improved in rural Alaska over the last few decades, but Alaska Natives still die younger and more violently than non-Natives. "While Alaska Natives are better educated than ever and more are working, their per-capita is half that of non-Natives, and Natives are three times more likely to live in poverty. . . . One out of five Alaskans, or 119,000 people, claimed Alaska Native heritage in the 2000 U.S. census," and the numbers are growing (University of Alaska Anchorage Report 2004, A5). Nearly 45 percent are nineteen or younger. Nearly 43 percent live in Alaska's urban areas, primarily because of better full-time work opportunities. Per capita income averages $13,000, compared to $25,000 for non-Natives. Nearly 75 percent have graduated from high school, but the dropout rate has risen sharply since 1998, as it has also for non-Natives. Although Alaska Natives are living longer than before, their average longevity falls seven years short of the national rate of 76.5 years. They suffer higher rates of accidental death, suicide, and homicide, of diabetes and hearth disease, and of fetal alcohol problems than non-Natives. Fewer than 50 percent of Alaska Natives have fulltime jobs. Full-time jobs are more easily found in Alaska's urban areas, but a little more than half the Native population is still rural where work is harder to find.

One would suppose that because of the money and land claims settlement under ANCSA, the current status of Alaska Natives would have shown significant improvement, but the institutional structure and operations of the Native regional corporations, which control most of the land and the money, remains problematic. David Maas (1994, 299), writing in the mid-1990s, reported that the performance of the Native corporations in the first twenty years has been mixed at best.

Four of the corporations reported cumulative losses between 1973 and 1990, and eight increased their assets. But six of these achieved a positive balance only through the sale of their net operating losses to large outside companies for tax write-offs. Profitable corporations have relied on the development of their natural resources or investments in securities or the oil and gas industry. . . . Of the nearly $1.4 billion of assets held by the twelve corporations, half consists of buildings, equipment, and real estate; 18 percent is invested in securities; 20 percent is held in escrow by the Internal Revenue Service; and the rest consists of parcels of land, insurance policies, and miscellaneous payments.

The benefits paid to stockholders were minimal. At-large stockholders (those not affiliated with a village corporation) had received only $6,500, and village stockholders a mere $1,500—not enough to cover a winter's heating bill. Only two corporations, the Arctic Slope Regional Corporation and the Northwest Arctic Native Association, were employing a significant number of Native shareholders.

Anderson and Aschenbrenner, writing in the *NARF Legal Review* (1988, 1) a few years earlier, gave this assessment: "Although the [land claims] settlement has provided economic benefits to some Natives, most corporations, especially in the villages, struggle to survive. . . . The Native corporations are business entities whose major asset is ancestral lands. As with any profit corporation, the assets must be risked in order to perpetuate corporation existence. For most of the isolated Native villages, located hundreds of miles from the road system and accessible only by boat or plane, there are simply no economic development opportunities available."

The fact remains that the Alaska Native corporation is a strange kind of business arrangement. For example, no other corporation in the United States is required to share its revenue with twelve other corporations. Joseph Jorgensen (1995, 61), a quantitative anthropologist at the University of California at Irvine, gives the following assessment: "Beginning with the implementation of ANCSA, the corporations were undercapitalized and the shareholder populations were under-trained, undereducated, and inexperienced in corporate ownership and control. The villages are located long distances from markets, are dependent on naturally-occurring resources for access to markets, and are subject to high costs for transportation and goods. Most of the villages have poorly developed infrastructures and meager political influence." The problems were exacerbated by the plunge in oil prices in 1985, the plunge in the price of salmon in 1989, the reduction in public money transfers under the Reagan administration budgets, and by the reduction in oil sales by the state of Alaska during the oil slump. By the early 1990s, the regional corporations as a whole continued to flounder. They "have not become the instruments to propel Natives into the world market economy as fully integrated capitalists. . . . Ownership of the means of production within Alaska is outside Alaska. . . . Until 1971, Natives were given the dole. After 1971 they were mandated to create undercapitalized, for-profit, shareholder corporations" (Jorgensen 1995, 63).

In a more recent assessment, Maas (2003, 170–71) writes that the twelve regional corporations have unquestionably become an important force in Alaska, with economic activities encompassing "oil and gas services, tourism, catering, investments, real estate (in and out of the state), timber harvesting, construction, and government contracting." But with few exceptions, these activities have not benefited shareholder distribution nor Native employment opportunities. Only 15 percent of regional corporation jobs are held by Natives, mostly menial and unskilled work, and employment opportunities in the 180 village corporations make even fewer jobs available. Between 1995 and 1997, the average shareholder dividend for ten of the regional corporations (excluding Sealaska and Cook Inlet) was only $486. Alaska Natives under ANCSA have not become "Red capitalists."

The Sealaska regional corporation is owned by more than sixteen thousand Tlingit, Haida, and Tsimshian shareholders in the resource-rich Alaskan panhandle. "Even with diversified investments in timber, telecommunications, plastics in Mexico, and Indian gambling in California, profits at Sealaska have been spotty. The company posted losses of $120 million in 2000 and $22 million in 2001" (Burnham 2003b, C1). In 2002, however, Sealaska reported a profit of $40.5 million and was able to pay a dividend to its Indian shareholders.

Rosita Worl (Tlingit) is president of Sealaska Heritage Institute and a board member of Sealaska Corporation. In an interview with *Indian Country Today* (Burnham 2003a, D2) she admits that ANCSA was seriously flawed. First of all, Natives born after 1971 couldn't become shareholders unless they inherited stock. Second, stock inheritance was diluted through multiple heirs to sometimes include non-Natives. Aboriginal subsistence rights (hunting and fishing) were extinguished throughout the state, and this came as a stunning surprise to many Natives. Consequently, there has been a discussion among Native leaders about the retribalization of

Native lands and rejecting the corporate model altogether, but this idea has been rebuffed by government authorities. ANCSA created a disconnect: the corporations were given economic power tied to a land base but no political authority, while the Native tribes or villages held no land but had political authority. Fortunately, Native land loses have been minimal to date, but this may not be the case in the future.

Flanders (1989, 299) concurs that the conglomerate model for the Alaska Native corporations is fundamentally flawed:

> Conglomerates were popular at the time that Congress passed ANCSA, but they have since fallen out of favor as a corporate strategy. In particular, companies found it impossible to manage operations in different industries, especially when the economy was contracting. ANCSA corporations have encountered the same difficulties. . . . Native corporations are in an especially difficult situation because they are trying to find viable investments in an economy prone to booms and busts at the same time that they are trying to fulfill the real social and economic needs of their shareholders.

Since the 1970s, conglomerates have lost their productivity in part because managers found it difficult to manage multi-industry firms.

The Alaska Native corporations could have invested their money into trusts or a portfolio of investments that would have guaranteed a steady return on their money over a period of years, but none did so. Instead they bought up a number of dissimilar enterprises. NANA Regional Corporation based in Kotzebue "invested in a bank, formed joint ventures for oil exploration and lead-zinc mining, and run a jade factor, a seafood processing plant, and a hotel" (Flanders 1989, 303). The managers of Alaska Native corporations have had difficulties in finding viable economic enterprises; in a number of instances the economic enterprises purchased by the corporations turned out to be money-losers. The investment problems have been even greater for the village corporations. Since they hold only surface rights, their investment opportunities are limited to timber or the land itself. Many of the village corporations are located in the Arctic beyond the tree line, and exploiting the land conflicts with the interests of shareholders who depend on the land for subsistence. The village corporations "had the option of becoming non-profit corporations providing social and education services of their shareholders. None did" (Flanders 1989, 307).

Flanders concludes his analysis by drawing the parallel to the deleterious effect that the 1887 General Allotment Act had on the Indian tribes of the Lower Forty-eight. Allotment embraced the family farm as the engine for Indian prosperity and reform. "It turned out that the allotments were too small for efficient farming and were divided into even smaller parcels as they passed through the generations. Many Indians sold their allotments to non-Natives, who consolidated them into larger holdings. Some Native corporations may go the same way, though for somewhat different reasons. *The great irony is that both the family farm and the conglomerate are now fading from America* [emphasis added]" (Flanders 1989, 310).

THE THREAT TO NATIVE SUBSISTENCE

The history of subsistence rights in Alaska is complex. The state is unique for giving a subsistence priority in its wildlife management to rural citizens, whether Native or non-Native, although the subsistence needs of the two populations are very different. "The Alaska Statehood Act [of 1959] required that as a condition of entering the federal union, Alaska must disclaim all right and title 'to any lands or other property (including fishing rights)' of Alaska Natives. The state of Alaska ignored this provision of the Statehood Act and began to enforce its fish and game management laws on all Alaskans, without recognizing any preexisting rights of Alaska Natives" (NARF 1999, 1). Then in 1971, ANCSA officially abolished aboriginal hunting and fishing rights in Alaska even though "the final House-Senate Conference Committee Report that accompanied ANCSA explained clearly that Congress expected that both the Secretary of Interior and the State 'take any action necessary to protect the subsistence needs of the Alaska Natives'" (NARF 1999, 1–2). In anticipation of federal legislation, the state passed a rural subsistence priority law in 1978, giving priority to "subsistence users" but failed to define "users." Two years later Congress passed the Alaska National Interest Lands Conservation Act (ANILCA), whose Title VIII became the federal counterpart to the Alaska subsistence law as applied to federal lands, primarily national parks and wildlife refuges.

> Since the State and the Secretary [of the Interior] had failed to protect Native subsistence after ANCSA, Title VIII of ANILCA required that subsistence uses by "rural Alaska residents" be given a priority over all other (sport and commercial) uses of fish and game on federal public lands in Alaska.

As a compromise, Congress allowed the State to continue managing fish and game uses on federal public lands, but only on the condition that *the State of Alaska adopt a statute* that made the new Title VIII "rural" subsistence priority applicable on state, as well as on federal lands. And if the State ever fell out of compliance with Title VIII, Congress required the Secretary of Interior to reassume management of fish and game on the federal public lands [emphasis added]. (NARF 1999, 2)

Congress did not enact a racial preference specifying Alaska Natives "in part because of the State's opposition. All parties assumed that 'rural' would work; and the Native community had to compromise in order to get a preference that the State could carry out. . . . Title VIII offered the State the option of continuing to regulate subsistence on federally owned public lands (in addition to its own jurisdiction over state and private lands), if the Legislature would enact and implement within one year 'laws of general applicability' which are consistent with and which provide for the definition, preference, and participation specified" in the federal law (AFN 1998, 2).

ANILCA required the state of Alaska to recognize and enforce the Title VIII provision, but the rural preference clause conflicted with the state constitution, which declares that Alaska's natural resources belong equally to all its citizens. "As a compromise, Congress allowed the State to continue managing fish and game uses on federal public lands, but only on the condition that the State of Alaska adopt a statue that made the new Title VIII 'rural' subsistence priority applicable on state, as well as on federal lands. And if the State ever fell out of compliance with Title VIII, Congress required the Secretary of Interior to reassume management of fish and game on the federal public lands" (NARF 1999, 2).

In 1982 the Alaska Boards of Fisheries and Game adopted the rural residency standard by regulation. Two years later, Athabascan elder Katie John sued in federal court, claiming that the federal government had failed to protect her right to subsistence fishing as guaranteed under ANILCA. In response, in 1986, "the Legislature amended its subsistence statute to limit the definition of 'subsistence uses' to residents of 'rural areas,' thereby complying with Title VIII . . . [but] State compliance with Title VIII of ANILCA came to an abrupt halt on December 22, 1989, when the Alaska Supreme Court . . . struck down the 1986 subsistence users; the rest of the 1986 statute, giving

preference to subsistence over other *uses*, remained intact" (AFN 1998, 3). The court ruled that the definition of "rural" in the state subsistence law was out of compliance with ANILCA, because the natural bounty of wildlife was for the "common use" of all Alaskans. The court's action was in response to a court challenge of Title VIII by representatives of Alaska's sport hunting and fishing organizations. In 1990, because the state was no longer in compliance, "the federal government took over subsistence management of game and the gathering of plant resources on federal areas." Fisheries management remained with the state due to the pending Katie John lawsuit. By 1999, "Congress . . . effectively blocked a federal takeover of subsistence fisheries management, and likewise the subsistence priority of Native villages" (NARF 1999, 2).

The complexity of Alaska's fish and game regulations at this time is illustrated by the fact that four different user groups competed for the salmon runs in south-central Alaska's Copper River: commercial, personal use, sport, and subsistence. A reporter for the *New York Times* compared the subsistence debate to affirmative action, "creating similar racial tensions. The Natives say the issue is their civil rights, while the sportsmen say the Natives are demanding 'special rights' and unfair quotas" (Verhovek 1999, A13). Tlingit leader Rosita Worl summarized the subsistence status of Alaska Natives in the 1990s as follows: "Native subsistence protection had been diminished to rural geographical regions, excluded Native communities engulfed by urban development, and included non-Native rural residents" (Worl 1998, 77).

It is not surprising that Alaska Natives overwhelmingly supported an amendment to ANILCA that would clearly recognize a Native subsistence priority. In 1997 when the governor of Alaska appointed a seven member Subsistence Task Force that excluded Alaska Natives, nine hundred Native representatives gathered in Anchorage in a Subsistence Summit. The Summit adopted guiding principles and made a dozen policy recommendations. They sent a delegation to Washington, DC, with their recommendations, but their voices were ignored. Worl explains the importance of subsistence rights to Alaska Native peoples: "Subsistence is more than an issue of allocating fish and wildlife resources. Subsistence represents the economic wellbeing of communities which have a minimal cash economy, it embodies their cultural values which recognizes a

Subsistence fishermen dip their nets in the Kenai River to catch salmon.

special and spiritual relationship to their land and animals and unifies them as tribal groups through hunting, gathering, distributing, and sharing their harvests" (Worl 1998, 78).

The main thrust of ANILCA was to set aside national parks, including the Arctic National Wildlife Refuge (ANWR). The pressure by the energy monopolies and conservative politicians to open ANWR to drilling has become a recurrent issue that endangers not only the pristine tundra environment, but also threatens the political unity of Alaska Natives. The Alaska Federation of Natives is at odds with many of the tribal governments with respect to drilling in ANWR, the "Sacred Place Where Life Begins," as the Gwich'in Indians call it. The AFN with its 207 corporations passed a resolution in support of drilling for gas and oil, while the Gwich'in and a growing number of tribal governments, including the Tanana Chiefs Conference, are opposed. Grassroots Natives charge that the Alaska Federation of Natives is run mostly by urban executives who are too reflective of corporate interests.

The Gwich'in are a hunting people, and the 130,000 Porcupine River caribou herd travels hundreds of miles each year to calve in Gwich'in territory on the Arctic Refuge coastal plain. Grizzly bears, musk oxen, wolves, golden eagles, and tundra swans all call this unique place home for at least part of the year. A Gwich'in Native of Fort Yukon told an interviewer: "I don't think the word 'subsistence' exists out here. . . . In my language, the closest thing I can come to what you are talking about is—we would say *Tee terra'in*. It means . . . people working together and sharing to accomplish something, to accomplish common goals" (Anderson 1998, 40–41).

Global Warming and Environmental Pollution

The survival agenda of today's Indigenous peoples of the Arctic not only includes the struggle for their traditional subsistence rights, but also encompasses reversing "rapid global warming, stratospheric ozone depletion, and levels of chemical pollution so noxious that mothers have been warned to avoid to breast-feeding their babies" (Johansen 2007, 269).

Climate change has been rapid in the Arctic, detectable within a single human lifetime. Eighty percent of the glaciers in Alaska are melting. The weather is growing noticeably warmer and the polar ice is retreating, threatening the mammal and fish species, and therefore the Native peoples' subsistence economy. Polar bears are in trouble. They must obtain their food of ringed seals from the ice, but with the ice pack retreating from the coastal shoreline, the bears find it too far to swim and are subject to drowning if not starvation. The Arctic's rapid thaw endangers the lives of Native hunters; some of the rivers with their fish stocks have dried up. "Erosion and flooding affect 86 percent—or 184—of Alaska Native villages to some degree, according to a 2003 report by the U.S. Government Accountability Office" (D'Oro 2007). "Six hundred people living in the Alaska Eskimo village of Shishmaref . . . in the far western reaches of Alaska, have been watching their village erode into the sea. The permafrost that had reinforced its coast is thawing. . . . In Kotzebue, Alaska, the town hospital was relocated because it was sinking into the ground" (Johansen 2007, 283–284).

There are about two hundred toxic pesticides and industrial chemicals that have been found in the bodies of people and animals living in the Arctic. These include mercury, which is released by coal-burning power plants and chemical factories in the temperate zone, but which has migrated northward. The Environmental Programme's Governing Council of the United Nations has officially recognized the Arctic as a barometer of the earth's environmental health. "To environmental toxicologists, the Arctic by the 1990s was becoming known as the final destination for a number of manufactured poisons, including, most notably, dioxins and polychlorinated biphenyls (PCBs), which accumulate in the body fat of large aquatic and land mammals (including human beings), sometimes reaching levels that imperil their survival" (Johansen 2007, 272). To compound the problem, the cold temperatures of the Arctic slow the natural decomposition of these toxic chemicals. The fear of toxic contamination has led Iñupiat hunters to closely inspect their game animals in the butchering process. A scientist from the National Marine Fisheries Service "has trained several groups of villagers in Nome, Barrow, and other Alaska settlements to take samples as part of their regular hunts" (Johansen 2007, 278). Some Alaska Natives are avoiding traditional foods altogether out of fear that fish and wild game contain pesticides, heavy metals, and other toxins. A study by the University of Alaska Anchorage found that pregnant women who eat traditional foods may be exposing their fetuses to dangerous pollutants.

When the oil tanker *Exxon Valdez* foundered on a reef outside the Valdez Arm of Prince William Sound in March of 1989, "an oil slick and oil balls" from eleven million gallons of crude oil "drifted with tides and currents throughout large portions of Prince William Sound, southwest down the Kenai Peninsula to Kodiak Island, and then northeast into Cook Inlet" (Jorgensen 1995, 1). When Native claimants sought damages they ran into a legal problem because the 1980 ANILCA provided protection for all rural residents of Alaska, not Natives alone. Yet the proportion of Native households gaining more then 50 percent of their diets from wild resources was twice that of non-Native households (Jorgensen 1995, 34). Tragically, many Native people of Prince William Sound no longer eat traditional foods because of the oil spill contamination.

SUBSISTENCE RIGHTS: THE STRUGGLE CONTINUES

The struggle by Alaska Natives for their subsistence rights has been a long and bitter experience. Alaska Natives do not have the legal protection of hunting and fishing rights that Indian nations of the contiguous states have held under the treaty relationship. Section 4(b) of the 1971 ANCSA specifically extinguished aboriginal hunting and fishing rights in Alaska. A new fish and game department began enforcing fishing and hunting regulations on White sportsmen and Natives alike on a "first come, first served" basis. The situation came to a head when the pipeline boom of the late 1970s created an urban, non-Native population explosion.

> Throughout the five-year process of enacting ANCSA, the primary focus was on land ownership, but the issue of subsistence also pervaded the process. Congressional findings in the final Senate bill emphasized protection of "Native subsistence hunting, fishing, trapping, and gathering rights." If enacted, it would have required the Secretary of the Interior to designate public lands around Native villages as "subsistence use areas" . . . and, under certain circumstances, to close them to non-subsistence uses. But both provisions were dropped by the conference committee because the Congress, the oil companies, and the State of Alaska didn't want to delay the land settlement (i.e., the pipeline) in order to deal with subsistence. (AFN 1998, 1)

The new state regulations "created conditions of hardship for subsistence hunters, particularly for Natives living in interior areas where sources of animal protein other than caribou are not available and where stores frequently do not stock meat products" (McBeath and Morehouse 1980, 88). When a state study found a diminishing of the caribou herd in northern Alaska and attempted to curtail the number hunted, this led to a "caribou crisis" for the Iñupiat Eskimos of the North Slope Borough. The Borough then made its own study and found that the herd was near its normal size.

The North Slope Borough comprises eight small Iñupiat communities in a region of eighty-nine thousand square miles stretching northward from the foothills of the Brooks Range to the Arctic Ocean. The people follow a traditional lifestyle that is heavily dependent on the subsistence harvesting of marine and land mammals, fish, and migratory birds. Caribou are considered their single most important terrestrial subsistence resource. The annual cycle of subsistence activities is a core value of Iñupiat culture. Subsistence hunting puts food on the table in a region where the cost of living is extremely high. "Furthermore, because most rural communities do not have banks, local businesses often take a percentage of paychecks in order to cash them" (Brower and Hepa 1998, 38).

A new crisis occurred in early 1977 when the International Whaling Commission (IWC) proposed a moratorium on the hunting of bowhead whales. The whale ban deeply impacted Iñupiat social and ceremonial life, as well as depriving the people of an important food source. The Borough again swung into action. Supported by the Arctic Slope Regional Corporation, it organized a new Alaska Eskimo Whaling Commission which questioned the IWC research. "At a special December meeting of the IWC in Tokyo, attended by a delegation of Iñupiat whalers and state officials, the U. S. succeeded in persuading the IWC to lift the moratorium in exchange for a subsistence quota of twelve whales taken (or eighteen whales struck) for Alaska Eskimos" (McBeath and Morehouse 1980, 90).

The Iñupiat look forward to spring when the first migratory waterfowl arrive. This is the time when waterfowl are historically hunted in the Delta, but such hunting has been illegal since 1918 under the Migratory Bird Treaty, and swan hunting is illegal in any season in the Delta. The enforcement of the waterfowl law has been largely ineffectual due to local resistance, but in 1961 there was the famous incident of the Barrow Duck-In. "When several Native men including a state legislator were arrested for spring bird hunting, 300 Iñupiat (138 of them holding dead eider ducks which they claimed to have taken illegally), gathered in the community hall.

Faced with arresting much of the community, enforcement agents backed down" (Morrow and Hensel 1992, 44).

Approximately fifteen thousand Yup'ik live in some fifty villages in the Yukon-Kuskokwim Delta of Southwest Alaska. Subsistence hunting, fishing, and gathering are an essential part of their local diet and identity. "Subsistence harvests in the Delta are among the highest in the state, in some villages reaching an annual per capita of up to 1100 pounds . . . the generic word for food and for fish is the same" (Morrow and Hensel 1992, 39). Seals, walrus, and beluga whales are also hunted avidly, and sea mammal products are widely shared and traded. Large and small land animals are hunted; berries and both edible and medicinal herbs are gathered. Preserved food stocks see the population through the winter, but by spring they begin to run low, and people hunger for the plentiful waterfowl which come to nest in the watery Delta.

There have been similar conflicts between Alaska Natives and the state of Alaska involving subsistence practices and Alaska's fish and game regulations. An underlying factor in some of these controversies is the shrinking Native land base. The land allocated to the Native corporations under ANCSA, especially for the villages, is inadequate to sustain subsistence activities on which most village Alaska Natives continue to depend: "Although, as property owners, Natives have the exclusive right to wildlife on their own land, they have no rights as Natives for hunting, trapping, or fishing reserved for them over the ninety percent of Alaska in which their rights were extinguished" (Berger 1985, 92).

After the state failed to come back into compliance with ANILCA in 1990, federal management regulations excluded marine and navigable waters from the government's jurisdiction, leaving fish stocks without protection. Under ANILCA, the title to these waters had been guaranteed to the state of Alaska. It was then that Alaska Natives brought suit in U.S. District Court, claiming that the term "public lands" in the ANILCA law included navigable waters. In 1984 Katie John and Doris Charles, two Athabascan elders, asked the Alaska State Board of Fisheries to open Batzulnetas, a historic upper Ahtna village and fish camp, to subsistence fishing. Their request was denied despite the fact that downstream users were permitted to take hundreds of thousands of salmon for sport and commercial uses. Attorneys for the petitioners from the Native

American Rights Fund "filed suit against the State in late 1985 pursuant to Title VIII of ANILCA to compel the State to re-open the historic Batzulnetas fishery" (NARF 2001a, 6). A year later the state added rural preference to its fish and game statute. However, in 1989 the Alaska Supreme Court ruled against the state law that limits subsistence uses to Alaska's "rural residents" as violating the "equal access" provisions of the State constitution. Consequently, in 1990, the federal government assumed responsibility for subsistence management of fish and wildlife on federal public lands in Alaska. "A dual management structure commenced with the federal government regulating subsistence on federal lands (60 percent of the state) and the state retaining authority over state (30 percent) and private (10 percent) lands" (Thornton 1998, 30).

Federal authority was later extended to certain navigable waters in Alaska following a 1995 federal court ruling in *Katie John et al. v. United States of America*. Public lands in Alaska include navigable waters on or adjacent to federal conservation units. The 1995 decision found that Katie John and the other plaintiffs had been illegally denied their right to subsistence fishing by the state of Alaska and the federal government. In 2001 the Ninth U.S. Circuit Court of Appeals upheld the lower court's decision, ruling that "the federal government has the obligation to provide subsistence fishing priority on all navigable waters in Alaska in which the United States has a federally reserved water right" (NARF 2001b, 2). Following the court's ruling, "with strong pressure from Alaska tribes, the Governor of Alaska decided not to seek review of the decision in the U.S. Supreme Court and ended the State's opposition to Native subsistence fishing in navigable waters (NARF 2001a, 5).

On August 27, 2001, Alaska governor Tony Knowles informed Katie John, the subsistence plaintiff, of the good news. Katie John (Athabascan) at the time was an eighty-six-year-old, a mother of fourteen children and adopted children, with 150 grandchildren, great grandchildren, and great-great grandchildren. A few weeks before making his decision, the governor met personally with Katie John at her village home of Mentasta, located at the headwaters of Copper River in southeast Alaska. He said "I learned more that day than is written in all the boxes of legal briefs in this long lasting court battle. I understand the strength, care and values that subsistence gives to Katie John's family, and to the thousands of similar families from Metlakatla to Bethel, to Norvik to Ft. Yukon to Barrow" (NARF 2001b, 1).

Rural Alaskans, who comprise about 20 percent of the state's residents and 49 percent of the Native population, annually harvest an estimated 43.7 million pounds of usable wild foods, or about

Athabascan activist Katie John.

375 pounds per capita. In comparison, urban Alaskans consume only about 22 pounds of wild food per capita. "Although subsistence hunting and fishing accounts for only about two percent of the total harvest of fish and wildlife in Alaska (compared to 97 percent for commercial fisheries and one percent for recreational hunters and fishers), this harvest provides a significant proportion of the protein consumed in many rural communities" (quoted in Haynes 2003, 280–81).

On April 17, 2002, Rosita Worl (Tlingit) of the Sealaska Heritage Institute testified at a U.S. congressional hearing in support of Alaska Native subsistence hunting and fishing rights. The federal protections under the Alaska National Interest Lands Conservation Act of 1980 must be maintained, she said. "ANILCA has offered the only measure of protection for subsistence against the State of Alaska, which has refused to recognize a rural subsistence hunting and fishing priority" (Worl 2002, 10). She explained that sharing is a key value of subsistence and the survival of Alaska Native communities. Not only does sharing ensure the survival of the entire community, but it also acknowledges the status of elders by giving them "special shares and parts of an animal. . . . Sharing with elders functions in many ways like the social security system in which individuals receive retirement benefits. Single women, who act as head of households, also receive special shares" (Worl 2002, 4).

An important ideological component of Native subsistence activities is the belief that "wildlife has spirits and that Native people have a kinship or special relationship with them. This relationship obligates Native people to adhere to certain codes of conduct and to treat animals in prescriptive ways to ensure success in future hunts and to assure that animals will return to be harvested" (Worl 2002, 5). Native subsistence is a group activity "based on some form of kinship whether it is along a bilateral kinship system characteristic of the Iñupiat and Yup'ik, or a clan or some other group membership such as that adopted by the Siberian Yup'ik of St. Lawrence Island or the Athabascans of Interior Alaska" (Worl 2002, 5–6).

At the time of Dr. Worl's testimony, the state of Alaska had not yet adopted an amendment to its constitution to give a subsistence priority to rural Alaska, let alone to Native people. This led to the state's flawed "all Alaskans" subsistence policy, which gives preference to every one of Alaska's 610,000 residents.

In 2006 the Alaska Federation of Natives set forth its federal priorities. Regarding subsistence the AFN candidly stated: "Today, the only significant protection for our way of life is Title VIII of the Alaska National Interest Lands Conservation Act (ANILCA), which provides a priority for 'subsistence' over sport and commercial uses of fish and game to residents of rural Alaska," but that "powerful anti-subsistence forces at work in Alaska seek to weaken or even repeal this law" (AFN 2006, 1).

CONCLUSION: THEORETICAL CONCEPTS REVISITED

The issue of Alaska Native subsistence rights is intrinsically related to the land settlement as mandated by the 1971 ANCSA; if the Native land base is inadequate, then subsistence is impacted. ANCSA is seriously flawed in other ways as well. In an interview with *Indian Country Today*, Rosita Worl told a reporter: "Natives born after 1971 couldn't become shareholders [in the Native corporations] unless they inherited stock. Stock inheritance was diluted through multiple heirs, sometimes including non-Natives. What's more, aboriginal subsistence rights (hunting and fishing) were extinguished throughout the state, what came as a shock to many tribal people. Perhaps worse, a 20-year grace period was the only restraint imposed on the state before it could tax undeveloped corporate land—then foreclose for tax delinquency and remove from Native ownership" (Burnham 2003a).

The Native corporations are required by law to share 70 percent of their profits from subsurface and timber sales with resource-poor regional corporations. This odd arrangement has been dubbed "corporate socialism." Fortunately, adds Worl, nothing so far has been lost because of bankruptcy, debt, or taxes, but some village corporations have transferred their lands to the tribes at the risk of not being protected by either ANCSA or Indian trust status. There is a disconnect between the tribes which have governance but no land, and the corporations which have land but no governance. In 1996 the U.S. Supreme Court ruled that ANCSA lands are not considered part of Indian Country, thereby depriving the Indigenous peoples of Alaska protections that Indian nations have in the contiguous forty-eight states.

A major problem for Alaska Natives has been proving that Indigenous subsistence should take priority over that of urban, non-Native Alaskans, because current federal and Alaska state laws currently forbid such a distinction. There is, however, a fundamental difference. As Davis Maas of the University of Alaska points out, Native subsistence is much more than merely putting food on the table; it is an integral part of Native existence:

> The average person in rural areas consumes 375 pounds of wild foods a year. In the interior and the arctic the averages are twice as high. Subsistence resources are also used for clothing, transportation, heating, housing, and arts and crafts. Traditional values of sharing, cooperation, reciprocity, respect for elders, spirituality, and consensual decision-making continue. . . . Customary rules guide the distribution and consumption of subsistence foods. Many Natives consider themselves first and foremost hunters and fishers. There is evidence, too, that subsistence economies are not only resilient, but also growing in some villages. (Maas 2003, 170)

We return to the concept of *cultural ecology*, as explained in the introduction to this chapter. The cultural adaptations made by the Native peoples to the varied biotic environments of Alaska became impacted upon the entry of non-Native peoples and Western institutions. Nevertheless, as Alaska Natives were compelled under colonial conditions to respond to new, often exploitative economic options, they retained for the most part their ability to fall back upon traditional subsistence activities for survival. With the oil discovery in 1968 and the passage of the Alaska Native Claims Settlement Act in 1971, this option became problematic. To a large degree, Alaska Natives continue to rely on a subsistence-based economy. Over the millennia there has been a unique adaptation to the physical environment of the Arctic and subarctic. Despite significant acculturation, Alaska Natives have not abandoned their traditional pursuits of subsistence hunting, fishing, and gathering. Subsistence production still provides an important part of protein consumed in Native villages and a significant portion of caloric intake.

In addition to the nutritional aspect, subsistence plays an integrating role in *Native identity*, both socially and culturally. "Hunting, fishing, gathering define a seasonal cycle of cultural activities and the products from these activities are the key to intimate sharing patterns, village celebrations, and religious ceremonies"—in short, what it means to be a Native (Langdon 1986, 32). As was pointed out earlier in this chapter, unlike rural Whites, Natives have a spiritual connection to the nonhuman world. This remains true even for urban-based Natives no longer able to engage in the full round of subsistence-based activities. Sharing subsistence foods and participating in village ceremonies whenever and wherever one can is an integral part of being Native.

The importance of "the Sacred" in Alaska Native subsistence is informed by anthropologist Edward Spicer's explanation of *social and cultural integration* (Spicer 1959/60), discussed at the beginning of this chapter. Subsistence activities link key components of Native social organization, such as kinship relations, sharing, and ceremonies. In similar fashion special Native terms and language mirror a belief system that links human subsistence activity to the non-human world of game, fish, plants, and berries. This cultural linkage around subsistence-based foods has a sacred quality that was described in the introduction of this chapter in the discussion of Winona LaDuke's book, *Recovering the Sacred* (2005).

In the academic year 1970–71 the author of this book worked as a counselor for the Alaska Native Program/EOP of Alaska Methodist University in Anchorage. During the following summer, he led a group of students on an informal field trip through the Athabascan villages of the Copper River area. We were struck by the hospitality of the Native villagers in hosting the student delegation, sharing their knowledge about local issues, visiting their fish camps along nearby rivers. Invariably, upon our departure from a village we would receive bountiful gifts of dried "red" and "silver" salmon. The villagers were generous to the core in sharing what was to be their winter's supply of subsistence food, so much so that our group had very little need to purchase additional food on our journey. The point here is that the "salmon gift" was more than just food: it was the sharing of a cultural symbol, a bond of Native solidarity between the villagers and the students.

We therefore conclude that subsistence activity is more than feeding a family. The practice of sharing game among relatives and fellow-villagers (social linkage), and common spiritual beliefs and values about sharing what is sacred (cultural linkage), serves to integrate Alaska Native society and culture. Native subsistence activities, beliefs and values are the cornerstone, the linchpin, of Alaska Native society and culture. Moreover, as we have repeatedly emphasized in this chapter, the subsistence complex is integrally related to the land itself, which is viewed as sacred. Take away the land base, and/or suppress subsistence activities, and Native society and culture could unravel or be gravely weakened, leading to *ethnocide*.

Why have the dominant U.S. society and its institutions been so reluctant to recognize Indigenous subsistence rights in Alaska? A major impediment is explained by Professor Steve Langdon of the University of Alaska. He suggests that there is "a contradiction in contemporary Alaskan Native economy and society that derives from the relationship of the essentially subsistence economy of the villages with the economic institutions established by the Alaska Native Claims Settlement Act of 1971" (Langdon 1986, 29). The pursuit of one cannot proceed without the denial of the other. This fundamental contradiction manifests itself "from factional fights within village corporations to battles between one regional corporation and another" (Langdon 1986, 29). Yet at the time of its enactment in 1971, ANCSA was widely hailed as possibly the most comprehensive and generous plan to settle aboriginal claims ever made. Even the *Tundra Times*, a Native-owned-and-operated newspaper, characterized ANCSA as "the beginning of a great era for the Native people of Alaska" Langdon 1986, 33).

In an important sense, ANCSA's potential for success lay in the structured relationship between the village and regional corporation, but this relationship is a contradictory one and problematic from the point of view of subsistence rights.

> Since regional corporations hold sub-surface rights under village lands within the region, it is possible that resource extraction deemed appropriate by the regional corporation could damage local fish and animal resources and would therefore be opposed by the villagers whose village corporation land the regional corporation is exploring and/or developing. Similarly, ANCSA allowed regional corporations to select lands of their own, many of which are adjacent to village corporation lands. Development activities on these lands might have effects on subsistence activities of nearby villagers. (Langdon 1986, 36)

The presumption of a congruence between villagers and corporate shareholders is unwarranted.

Another problem is that the shareholders in a village corporation may in fact be Native residents of large urban centers such as Anchorage or Fairbanks, or even cities outside Alaska. The cash and credit needs of such a "village shareholder" may conflict with the long-term interests of the village itself in terms of investment of its capital for its own long-term interests and development. There is also a potential conflict between those village shareholders who depend on subsistence, and the village corporation itself, which holds fee simple title to lands on which fish and animal resources are found. The village government must retain its corporate status and must find a viable economic use of its land base instead of subsistence, because the 1971 claims settlement allowed for village lands to be taxed after twenty years.

In spite of these potential problems, Langdon concludes "that village corporations will be dominated by the subsistence interests of local villagers for the immediate future. The key question for most villagers . . . is how to ensure that they retain their lands and access to nearby state and federal lands for subsistence pursuits" (Langdon 1986, 43).

Finally, Langdon (1986, 43) warns that it is not only the internal contradictions of ANCSA that threaten Native subsistence rights, but also external forces—the "accelerating demand within the state, national, and world economies for resource development, increasing demands by non-Native Alaskans for lands in rural areas, and increasing demands by urban populations for the fish and animal resources of rural areas."

Based on the information presented in this chapter, one must seriously question the success of the government's unique experiment in "Red capitalism" for settling aboriginal land claims in Alaska. Alaska Natives may not be able to count on the viability of their weakened corporations for any significant economic assistance and in winning the struggle for subsistence rights. On the other hand, political organization, especially in terms of the village associations and tribal governments, has been strengthened, Indigenous awareness sharpened, and political sophistication increased.

CHAPTER REVIEW

DISCUSSION QUESTIONS

1. Name the major groups of Indigenous peoples in Alaska, and their locations.
2. What were some of the economic activities that impacted Alaska in the nineteenth and early twentieth centuries, but which did not raise the question of Native land ownership?
3. What effect did World War II, and the economic boom which followed have on Alaska Natives and their way of life? And statehood?
4. Describe how the oil discovery in 1968 at Prudhoe Bay, and the trans-Alaska pipeline, impacted the question of Alaska Native land and subsistence rights.

5. In terms of Native land and subsistence rights, what were the limitations of the 1971 Alaska Native Claims Settlement Act? Did the 1981 Amendments adequately address these limitations? Explain your answer.
6. Explain why the state of Alaska's "all Alaskans" subsistence policy fails to protect Native subsistence rights.
7. How is the Alaska Native view of "the Sacred" related to the struggle for subsistence rights? In what way are subsistence rights the linchpin of Native society and culture?

SUGGESTED READINGS

BERGER, THOMAS R. 1985. *Village Journey: The Report of the Alaska Native Review Commission.* New York: Hill and Wang.

FREEMAN, MILTON M. R. 2000. *Endangered Peoples of the Arctic: Struggles to Survive and Thrive.* Westport, CT: Greenwood Press.

MITCHELL, DONALD CRAIG. 1997. *Sold American.* Hanover, NH: University Press of New England.

SENUNGETUK, JOSEPH E. 1971. *Give or Take a Century: An Eskimo Chronicle.* San Francisco: Indian Historian Press.

TALBOT, STEVE. 2010. "Alaska Natives Struggle for Subsistence Rights." In *Native American Voices: A Reader,* edited by Susan Lobo, Steve Talbot, and Traci L. Morris, 389–95. 3rd ed. Upper Saddle River, NJ: Prentice Hall.

NOTE

1. For a history of Russian Alaska and the later U.S. military occupation after purchase, see Mitchell 1997, Chapter One.

REFERENCES

ACTIVE, JOHN. 1996. "Yup'ik." *Native America in the Twentieth Century: An Encyclopedia,* edited by Mary B. Davis, 717–18. New York: Garland.

AFN (Alaska Federation of Natives). 1998. "Subsistence Chronology, A Short History of Subsistence Policy in Alaska Since Statehood." Rev. ed. http://www.alaskool. org/projects/ansca/subsistence_chron/subchron.htm

———. 2006. "AFN 2006 Federal Priorities: Subsistence." http://www.nativefederation.org/2006FedPriorSubsistence.php

ANDP (Alaska Native Declaration and Petition). n.d. *Alaska Native Declaration and Petition.* (Mimeograph document, mid-1960s.)

ANDERS, GARY C. 1985. "A Critical Analysis of the Alaska Native Land Claims and Native Corporate Development" *Journal of Ethnic Studies* 13 (1): 1–12.

ANDERSON, BOB, and LARE ASCHENBRENNER. 1988. "Amendments Provide Stop-Gap Protection for Native Land and Corporations." *NARF Legal Review* 13 (2): 1–5.

ANDERSON, DAVID B. 1998. "A View from the Yukon Flats" *Cultural Survival Quarterly* 22 (3): 40–43.

BARREIRO, JOSÉ. 2007. "A Call to Consciousness on the Fate of Mother Earth: Global Warming and Climate Change." *National Museum of the American Indian*, Fall.

BECK, PEGGY V., and ANNA L. WALTERS. 1977. *The Sacred: Ways of Knowledge, Sources of Life*. 'Tsaili, AZ: Navajo Community College Press.

BERGER, THOMAS R. 1985. *Village Journey: The Report of the Alaska Native Review Commission*. New York: Hill and Wang.

BERGERON, LEANDRE. 1971. *The History of Quebec: A Patriot's Handbook*. Toronto: New Canada.

BODENHORN, BARBARA. 2000. "The Iñupiat of Alaska." In *Endangered Peoples of the Arctic*, edited by Milton M. R. Freeman, 131–49. Westport, CT: Greenwood Press.

BODLEY, JOHN H. 1982. *Victims of Progress*. 2nd ed. Mountain View, CA: Mayfield.

BROWER, HARRY, JR., and TAQULIK HEPA. 1998. "Subsistence Hunting and the Iñupiat Eskimo." *Cultural Survival Quarterly* 22 (3): 37–39.

BURNHAM, PHILIP. 2003a. "Corporations: Native Style." *Indian Country Today*, October 1, Part One, D1–D2.

———. 2003b. "Sealaska and Corporate Socialism." *Indian Country Today*, October 8, Part Two, C1–2.

CAHN, EDGAR. 1969. *Our Brother's Keeper*. Washington, DC: New Community Press.

CHANCE, NORMAN. 1966. *The Eskimo of North Alaska*. New York: Holt, Rhinehart and Winston.

COLT, STEPHEN. 1996. "Alaska Native Regional Corporations." In *Native America in the Twentieth Century: An Encyclopedia*, edited by Mary B. Davis, 13–17. New York: Garland.

CRAIG, RACHEL. 1996. "Iñupiat." In *Native America in the Twentieth Century: An Encyclopedia*, edited by Mary B. Davis, 274–76. New York: Garland.

D'ORO, RACHEL. 2007. "In Many Villages, Alaskans Face Physical and Cultural Erosion," *Indian Country Today*, January 10.

FAINBERG, L. A. 1965. "The Contemporary Situation of the Eskimos (1940–1960) and the Problem of Their Future in the Works of American and Canadian Ethnographers." *Soviet Anthropology and Archaeology* 4 (1): 27–45.

Federal Field Committee. 1968. *Alaska Natives and the Land*. Washington, DC: U.S. Government Printing Office, October.

FIENUP-RIORDAN, ANN. 2000. "The Yupiit of Western Alaska." In *Endangered Peoples of the Arctic*, edited by Milton M. R. Freeman, 247–66. Westport, CT: Greenwood Press.

FLANDERS, NICHOLAS E. 1989. "The Alaska Native Corporation as Conglomerate: The Problem of Profitability." *Human Organization* 48 (4): 199–312.

FOOTE, DON CHARLES. 1964. "American Whalemen in Northwestern Arctic Alaska." *Arctic Anthropology* 2 (2).

GIBBS, DANIEL R. 2007. "Alaska Native Claims Settlement Act." In *Encyclopedia of American Indian History*, vol. 2, edited by Bruce E. Johansen and Barry M. Pritzker, 491–93. Santa Barbara, CA: ABC-CLIO.

HANRAHAN, JOHN, and PETER GRUENSTEIN. 1977. *The Lost Frontier: The Marketing of Alaska*. New York: W.W. Norton.

HAYNES, TERRY L. 2003. "Ethical Issues and Subsistence in Alaska." *Kroeber Anthropological Society Papers* 89/90: 273–86.

HUGHES, CHARLES C. 1984. "Asiatic Eskimos: Introduction," and "Siberian Eskimo." In *Handbook of North American Indians, vol. 5, The Arctic*, edited by David Damas, 243–61. Washington, DC: Smithsonian Institution Press.

ISEGR (Institute of Social, Economic, and Governmental Research). 1967. *Native Land Claims. ISEGR* 4 (November). University of Alaska.

JENNESS, DIAMOND. 1962. *Eskimo Administration: I. Alaska*. Arctic Institute of North America, Technical Paper No. 10 (July), Montreal, Canada.

JOHANSEN, BRUCE E. 2007. "The New Inuit." In *The Praeger Handbook on Contemporary Issues in Native America, vol. 2*. Westport, CT: Praeger.

JOHN, ADAM. 1971. "Alaska Indians Make the Connection." Speech to the Fairbanks Native Community Center, printed in *Memo*, a quarterly publication of Women Strike for Peace, Fall issue, 36.

JORGENSEN, JOSEPH G. 1978. "A Century of Political Economic Effects on American Indian Society, 1880–1980." *Journal of Ethnic Studies* 6 (3): 1–82.

———. 1995. "Ethnicity, Not Culture? Obfuscating Social Science in the *Exxon Valdez* Oil Spill Case." *American Indian Culture and Research Journal* 19 (4): 1–124.

———. 2003. Review of *Alaska, an American Colony*, by Stephen Haycox (Seattle: University of Washington Press, 2002), *American Indian Culture and Research Journal* 27 (3): 95–99.

KAWAGLEY, A. OSCAR. 1995. *A Yupiaq Worldview: A Pathway to Ecology and Spirit*. Prospect Heights, IL: Waveland Press.

KINGSTON, DEANNA. 2001. Lecture to Steve Talbot's anthropology class, Oregon State University, August 9.

LADUKE, WINONA. 2005. *Recovering the Sacred: The Power of Naming and Claiming*. Cambridge, MA: South End Press.

LANGDON, STEVE J. 1986. "Contradictions in Alaska Native Economy and Society." In *Contemporary Alaskan Native Economies*, edited by Steve J. Langdon, 29–46. Lanham, MD: University Press of America.

MAAS, DAVID C. 1994. "Alaska Natives." In *The Native North American Almanac*, edited by Duane Champagne, 293–301. Detroit, MI: Gale Research.

———. 2003. Review of "Take My Land, Take My Life: The Story of Congress's Historic Settlement of Alaska Native Land Claims, 1960–1971," by Donald Craig Mitchell (Fairbanks: University of Alaska Press, 2001), in *American Indian Culture and Research Journal* 27 (1): 167–72.

MCBEATH, GERALD A., and THOMAS A. MOREHOUSE. 1980. *The Dynamics of Alaska Native Self-government.* Lanham, MD: University Press of America.

MCCLANAHAN, ALEXANDRA J. 2007. "Alaska Native Claims Settlement Act (ANCSA)." http:litsite.alaska.edu/aktraditions.ansca.html

MITCHELL, DONALD CRAIG. 1997. *Sold America: The Story of Alaska Natives and Their Land, 1867–1959.* Hanover, NH: University Press of New England.

MORROW, PHYLLIS, and CHASE HENSEL. 1992. "Hidden Dissension: Minority–Majority Relationships and the Use of Contested Terminology." *Arctic Anthropology* 29 (1): 38–53.

NARF (Native American Rights Fund). 1988. "Amendments Provide Stop-Gap Protection or Native Land and Corporations." *NARF Legal Review* (Spring): 1–5.

———. 1999. "Alaska Native Subsistence." *Justice Newsletter:* 1–6. http://www.narf.org/pubs/justice/1999spring.html

———. 2001a. "Executive Director's Message." *Native American Rights Fund Annual Report.*

———. 2001b. "Katie John Prevails in Subsistence Fight." *NARF Legal Review* 26 (2): 1–6.

OLSON, WALLACE. 1996. "Tlingit." In *Native America in the Twentieth Century: An Encyclopedia,* edited by Mary B. Davis, 645–37. New York: Garland.

O'MAHONEY, JOSEPH C. 1975. *Russian Administration of Alaska and the Status of the Alaskan Natives.* Senate Document 152. Washington, DC: U.S. Government Printing Office.

Research Institute of Alaska. 1970. *Alaska Survey and Report:1970–71.* Anchorage: Research Institute of Alaska.

SOZA, ROMONA E. 1989. *Alaska Natives and Federal Indian Policy* (University of Washington, 1988), *Dissertation Abstracts International* 49 (9): 2789-A.

SPICER, EDWARD H. 1959/60. Course on "Culture Change." Department of Anthropology, University of Arizona, Tucson.

STRONG, B. STEPHEN. 1973. Chapter Seven, "Stage III: Period of Direct Dependence Upon Commodities, 1950–1971." Manuscript.

———. 1977. "The Social and Economic Impact of the Trans-Alaska Oil Pipeline Upon the Alaska Native People." *Report to the Northern Social Research Division, Department of Indian Affairs and Northern Development,* Government of Canada.

SWETZOF, PAUL R. 1996. "Unangan." In *Native America in the Twentieth Century: An Encyclopedia,* edited by Mary B. Davis, 665–66. New York: Garland.

THORNTON, THOMAS F. 1998. "Alaska Native Subsistence: A Matter of Cultural Survival." *Cultural Survival Quarterly* 22 (3): 29–34.

University of Alaska Anchorage Report. 2004. "Alaska Native Status Improves, but Still Lags." *Indian Country Today,* June 9.

U.S. Department of the Interior. 1974. News release, August 1.

VERHOVEK, SAM HOWE. 1999. "Alaska Torn Over Rights to Live Off the Land." *New York Times,* July 12, A1, A13–A15.

WEBBER, LAURA. 1972. "The Alaskan Land Settlement: An Old Story." Student paper, Native American Studies, University of California, Berkeley.

WORL, ROSITA. 1998. "Competition, Confrontation, and Compromise: The Politics of Fish and Game Allocations." *Cultural Survival Quarterly* 22 (3): 77–78.

———. 2002. "Alaska Native Subsistence: Cultures and Economy." Testimony presented to the U.S. Senate Committee on Indian Affairs, Oversight Hearing on Subsistence Hunting and Fishing in the State of Alaska. Washington, DC, April 17.

THE TROUBLE WITH STEREOTYPES
NATIVE NATIONS AND THE URBAN TRADITION

Indian stereotypes regarding the urban tradition. The icon above also shows the stereotype of what "traditional Indians" are: feathers and long hair.

Urban assimilation . . . threatens to accomplish the destruction of Indian culture as efficiently as cavalry raids and massacres.

—Russell Means

Urban is a person, not a place.

—Susan Lobo

During the decades of the 1950s and 1960s, tens of thousands of Native Americans moved from reservations and villages to U.S. cities. They were pressured to relocate by the Bureau of Indian Affairs in order to implement the government's policies of tribal termination and urban relocation. But instead of assimilating into the mainstream society, as did the European immigrants of earlier decades, and as governmental authorities assumed would be the case, most American Indians and Alaska Natives continued to maintain an Indigenous identity. Furthermore, their patterns of social and cultural interaction in the cities continued to be primarily with other Native relocatees rather than with non-Indians and their institutions. The enigma of the "urban Indian" became a source of research by social scientists for the next half century, and it is a subject of this chapter.

CHAPTER OVERVIEW

We begin this chapter with a discussion of *ancient urbanism* as found in North America and Mesoamerica at the time of the Spanish conquest in the fifteenth century. Then we turn to a discussion of *contemporary* or *modern* urbanism in the United States and Canada.

It is important to point out at the outset that urbanism is not a new phenomenon in the history of Indigenous America. On the eve of the European discovery at the end of the fifteenth century, there were more people living in the Americas than in Europe, and many were living in huge urban complexes. Indigenous cities such as Tenotchtitlán, the Aztec capital, "were far greater in population than any contemporary European city. Tenochitlán, unlike any capital in Europe at the time, had running water, beautiful botanical gardens, and immaculately clean streets" (Mann 2005, book jacket). Anthropological demographer Henry Dobyns estimates that there were as many as 90 to 112 million people inhabiting the Western Hemisphere, but as a result of the European conquest, 90 percent perished, mainly from imported diseases to which they had no natural immunity. That is a death toll of 80 to 100 million people, "the largest human holocaust in history and about 20 percent of the world's population at that time" (Johansen 2005, 121).

The 1,200 Native languages and 180 linguistic families in North and South America attest to the thousands of years that Indigenous peoples have inhabited the Western Hemisphere, whereas only four language families exist in Europe. In his book, *1492, New Revelations of the Americas Before Columbus* (2005), Charles Mann questions how so many languages could have developed in the time frame that is usually estimated by scientists for the presence of Indigenous peoples in the Americas. The common wisdom among archaeologists is that small groups of paleo-Indians chased large mammals like the mammoth across the Bering Strait land bridge from Asia to Alaska about thirteen thousand years ago at the end of the last Ice Age, and then, through overhunting, were responsible for the mammalian extinction that followed. Vine Deloria, Jr., humorously critiqued the Bering Strait thesis and blaming paleo-Indians for the mammalian extinction as patently ridiculous (Deloria 1995, chapters 4 and 5). In fact, recent archaeological sites found in South America place human habitation in the Americas much earlier. The oldest known human settlements may be those located in present-day Chile, which are believed to date back at least thirty thousand years. Complicating the picture is the fact that, according to genetic evidence, the peopling of the Americas consisted of more than one migration. In any case, Indigenous urbanism in the Western Hemisphere took place at a comparatively early stage in world human cultural development.

In this chapter we highlight some of the ancient centers of urban development, such as the Mound Builders and Aztecs in North America, and the Mayas in Mesoamerica. We call this *ancient urbanism*. These urban developments underscore the fact that Indigenous urbanism is far from being a recent phenomenon in the Americas. Second, we examine the contemporary migration of Indigenous people to cities in the twentieth century, the modern *urban Indian*. Forbes (2001, 5) observes that "huge numbers of First Nations people reside today in cities such as Buenos Aires, Lima, La Paz, Quito, Guatemala City, Mexico City, Toronto, Denver, Chicago, Los Angeles, San Francisco-Oakland, and so on." The First Americans have gone through periods of urbanization at various times in their histories. In fact, urbanism has been a major aspect of Native American life from ancient times to the present, although as a result of different socioeconomic forces and cultural processes.

Today in the United States, more than two-thirds of the Native American population lives in urban, metropolitan areas of the country, and a related process has occurred in Canadian cities. In this chapter we refer to this phenomenon as *contemporary urbanism*. The latter has taken several forms or subtypes. First, there was an early stream of Native American emigrants from the reservations to U.S. cities in the early decades due to reservation land loss and poverty stemming from the 1887 Indian Allotment Act. In Canada the Indian Act, among other effects, disfranchised Native women, forcing thousands into urban poverty. A larger Native American immigrant wave began in the United States in the 1950s when multitribal, urban Indian communities were formed as a result of the U.S. governmental policies of tribal termination and urban relocation. At the same time there are also Native communities that have existed for decades as self-contained urban enclaves, and we include several noteworthy examples in this chapter.

Some of the first scholarly studies of contemporary Indian urbanism in the United States in mid-twentieth century were published in the *American Anthropologist* and *Human Organization*, journals of the American Anthropological Association and the Society for Applied Anthropology respectively. These early studies were then republished in several edited works. One of the first was *Native Americans Today* (Bahr, Chadwick, and Day 1972). The motivation for this volume, as stated by its sociologist editors, was "the almost incredible dearth of information about Indian people today," given the fact that half

or more of all Indian people had left the reservations and were living in urban areas. In "An End to Invisibility," coeditor Howard Bahr (1972, 404–12) examined the reasons for the prevailing fiction that urban Indians are not "real Indians," as some academicians of the period seemed to imply. The subject of the urban Indian was at first all but ignored by anthropologists who had concentrated their studies on reservation Indians. Demographic information on Indian urbanism was fragmentary; the urban Indian was an invisible person. This has changed within the last several decades with the emergence of the field of Native American Studies as researchers, including some anthropologists, began making up-to-date and more compelling studies of contemporary Indian urbanism. An overview of their research is presented in this chapter, and in Part IX of the third edition of *Native American Voices: A Reader* (Lobo, Talbot, and Morris 2010, 398–434).

In summary, we examine Native American urbanism, both ancient and contemporary, and consider the socioeconomic and cultural processes that may account for them. Selected concepts are introduced that we believe can assist in the analysis of Indian urbanism, and we return to them in the conclusion to this chapter.

ANALYTICAL CONCEPTS

As described in this chapter, ancient urbanism is distinguished by the Indigenous peoples and nations who populated the Americas before Columbus. Their societies built huge urban complexes and are distinguished by ceremonialism and intensive cultivation. Contemporary urbanism, on the other hand, as found in contemporary Canadian and U.S. cities, has a different line of development that is the result of an Indigenous response to internal colonialism. Contemporary Native nations and peoples comprise an oppressed minority in the countries in which they reside. This chapter will highlight the differences.

Identity is a key concept. Clearly, this was the case for the proud, ancient urban civilizations of Central America, such as the Olmecs, Mayas, and Aztecs. Their pride and intellect led to nation-building and great contributions in agriculture, math, and astronomy. We will examine the factors leading to this remarkable development.

In an analysis of contemporary Indigenous identity, Hilary Weaver (2010) examined three facets: self, community, and external identity. "Identity," she writes, "is the combination of self-identification and the perception of others" (2010, 30). Identity is multi-faceted. For some, clan affiliation is primary. "For others, identification with a tribe or region like the Northern Plains, is most meaningful. Still others espouse a broader identity as Native or Indigenous people" (Weaver 2010, 30). At its core, "Indigenous identity is connected to a sense of peoplehood inseparably linked to sacred traditions, traditional homelands, and a shared history as Indigenous peoples" (Weaver 2010, 31).

In the past, researchers who examined contemporary Indian urbanism usually employed the concept of *acculturation* to explain the phenomenon. The common wisdom among government policy pundits was that the so-called Indian problem is the result of Native peoples' reluctance or failure to adapt and adjust to the dominant Anglo-American society and its institutions. Acculturation in the American Indian context refers to the extent that Native peoples give up their sacred lands, tribal languages, spirituality and cultural traditions, and adopt English, Christianity, and the capitalist work ethic. It was assumed that Native Americans are an ethnic minority like "hyphenated Americans" (Irish-Americans, Italian-Americans, etc.), and that they would eventually follow the European immigrant experience of acculturation. This supposedly natural process could be accelerated by government policies and programs, such as tribal termination and a federally funded relocation program, which sent thousands of Native people to U.S. cities during the 1950s and 1960s.

A variant of acculturation rationale, termed "national integration," is found in Mexico as its national Indian policy. Paradoxically, this official policy has emphasized assimilation for its Indian peoples at the same time that the country celebrates national pride in its ancient Indian heritage. Not surprisingly, the policy has yielded contradictory results. David Edmunds summarizes this policy in an article reprinted in *Native American Voices: A Reader* (Lobo, Talbot, and Morris 2010, 42–43). We shall return to his critique in our conclusions to this chapter.

A section of this chapter is also devoted to *urban Indian enclave* communities. Webster's New Collegiate Dictionary defines an enclave as "a territorial or culturally distinct unit enclosed within foreign territory." But this does not mean that most urban-based Indian communities are clustered, and it is not the same as an urban ghetto. As Susan Lobo (2009, 4) points out, "the assumption by some researchers that

Indian peoples in cities must live clustered in urban neighborhoods, ghettos, or enclaves, and that this is synonymous with an Indian community, still continues to persist." In fact, most urban Indian communities are dispersed and based on a network of relatives. "Those cities such as Oakland, Los Angeles, and New York that were relocation sites tend to have a more tribally heterogeneous population compared to those that were not relocation cities and that grew through self-motivated migration from nearby reservations" (Lobo 2009, 5). Nevertheless, we have found several examples of urban Indian communities that, due to particular socioeconomic and historical circumstances, have existed for decades or more years as unified resident populations. We refer to these cases as urban enclaves.

To understand why many if not most relocated Indians did not fully acculturate and readily assimilate into Anglo-American society, we should differentiate the concept of an Indigenous people from that of an ethnic minority. Native peoples are not a solitary ethnic group like the European immigrants who came to the United States in the past. There were three waves of European immigration to the United States. "The first wave of immigrants arrived between 1790 and 1820 and consisted mainly of English-speaking Britons. They became the dominant stream of Anglo-Americans who came to dominate the country's political, religious, and cultural institutions. The second wave, mostly Irish and German, came in the 1840s and 1850s and challenged the dominance of Protestantism, which led to a backlash against Catholics. The third wave, between 1880 and 1914, brought over 20 million, mostly Southern and Eastern Europeans who found factory jobs in the large cities" (Eitzen and Zinn 2007, 205). In the 1920s the United States adopted a *national origins* rule to severely limit immigration from Eastern Europe and Asia. The *new immigration* began in 1965 when the United States abandoned the quota system. The new population now consists of immigrants from the Third World, especially Asia and Latin America, with millions present in the United States illegally.

The characterization of Native peoples as urban immigrants within the United States in mid-twentieth century has an entirely different history and is another phenomenon altogether. In the first place, Native Americans are the original inhabitants of the Americas and not a solitary ethnic group emigrating from Europe or abroad. Native peoples living today are the dispossessed descendents of the original Indigenous nations of pre-Columbian America. They comprise many different tribes and segments, mininationalities if you will. And as Indigenous peoples, their tribally specific creation stories, languages, and traditions are rooted in sacred homelands which lie within the Americas and are still held in deep reverence.

ANCIENT URBANISM

Jack Forbes of the University of California at Davis contends that "urban life has been a major aspect of American life from ancient times. . . . It may well be that the Americas witnessed a greater process of urban development in pre-1500 C.E. times than did any other continent, with the growth of the most elaborate planned cities found anywhere. In fact, the evidence seems to indicate that from about 1600–1700 B.C. until 1519–1520 C.E. period, the largest cities in the world were often located in the Americas rather than in Asia, Africa, or Europe" (Forbes 2001, 5). University of Southern California professor Joan Weibel-Orlando (2008, 308). echoes Forbes' assessment: "Urban residence is neither novel to, nor nontraditional for Native Americans. Great city centers had been established throughout North (Cahokia, Chaco Canyon), Central (the great Mayan Toltec, and Olmec complexes), and South (Incan urban centers) America long before Western European contact."

Forbes explains that urbanism in the Americas, as opposed to urbanism in other continents, is distinguished by four main characteristics: multiethnic populations speaking different languages; an urban population that is kinship-based, such as the *capulli*-style neighborhoods of the Aztecs; "metropolitan areas that include areas of countryside or villages or barrios associated intimately with a ceremonial or market center as opposed to distinctly separated urban-rural zones"; and megacities such as the Aztec capital of Tenochtitlán (Forbes 2001, 6). "One of the special characteristics of American life in such diverse regions as Peru, Mesoamerica, and the Mississippi Valley is the very early development of ceremonial centers, usually featuring mounds of pyramid-like structures. . . . Many of these mounds become huge (as at Cahokia, Teotihuacán, Cholula, and Moche), rivaling the largest pyramids of the ancient Kemi (Egyptian) people" (Forbes 2001, 7). Rather than farmlands, these ceremonial and market centers were surrounded by small to medium towns or hamlets, forming a single unit.

In 1928 the historian William Christie MacLeod criticized the Euro-American belief of American Indians as nomads. The prevailing stereotype at the time was that the Indians wandered aimlessly about the North American landscape as hunters and gatherers. This view provided a convenient rationale for English settlers to seize Indian lands, since the Indians, it was said, did not occupy the land for any productive purposes. MacLeod (1928, 17) gave the following rejoinder:

All land suitable for agriculture or productive of wild roots, fish, or animals, therefore was in demand. It was valuable. Did the Indians run helter-skelter over it, with no, or only vague, ideas of ownership? Were they nomads in the usual sense of the term? They were not. All Indians, even the Labrador hunters, the tribes of the buffalo-covered plains, and the Eskimos, lived in villages. True, the hunters, and sometimes their families, might have to be away from their villages for months during the hunting season, but always for at least a part of the year the whole village gathered in its permanent home.

In addition, the Indians east of the Mississippi River, along with many peoples of the American Southwest, were settled horticulturists rather than foragers, although they supplemented their diets with hunting and gathering.

Christie also noted that "the average American tribe was a very small city-state. It had extensive territories over which it hunted, but it usually lived in a single village of from five hundred to three thousand population. Many tribes, however, comprised a number of villages totaling ten thousand or more inhabitants" (MacLeod 1928, 21). The main point is the following: "At the time of Columbus the great majority of Native Americans were found south of the Rio Grande. They were not nomadic, but built up and lived in some of the world's biggest and most opulent cities" (Mann 2005, 15).

Centers of Urbanism and Cultural Development

Urbanism defined in its wider sense is not a new phenomenon for Native America. We begin, therefore, with the story of the Americas before Columbus. By way of introduction, it is important to understand that the Neolithic Revolution that occurred in the Middle East about eleven thousand years ago had a second, completely independent rebirth in the Western Hemisphere a thousand years later. There were at least two centers of the Neolithic Revolutions in the Americas, one in Andean South America and the other in Mesoamerica. Great urban centers were a key hallmark of the American development. Circa 1400, these two major orbits were characterized by

> intensive irrigation; large and densely populated settlements, including cities built around impressive works of architecture, such as temples or palaces; craft products, such as pottery or weaving, clearly made for high status elites; and massive evidence of an ideological superstructure through which the goals of these elite-ruled orbits were manifested to the population at large. One such interaction area of high contour was the Central Andes, in what is today Peru and Bolivia . . . the heartland of the Inca Empire. . . . The other area was Mesoamerica, located in the highlands of present-day Mexico and Guatemala and in the adjacent lowlands. This was the area inhabited at the time of the Spanish Conquest by the Aztecs and the Maya. (Wolf 1982, 58–59)

We confine our discussion in this chapter, however, to examples of ancient urbanism in North America and Mesoamerica.

In North America, one such urban center with a complex development of religious life, local government, and artistic expression was in the southwestern United States where ancestors of the Pueblo Indians lived along the Rio Grande and the Little Colorado rivers in the region of the present-day states of New Mexico and Arizona. They are divided by convention into the Western and Eastern Pueblos. These Pueblo peoples lived in large communities of contiguous, masonry buildings of three to four stories. There were also desert farmers with developed irrigation systems, the Pima-speaking Indians of southern Arizona, ancestors to the present-day O'Odham (Pima and Tohono), whose agricultural accomplishments date back to the third century.

A second center was in the southeastern United States, from the lower Mississippi Valley east to the Atlantic coast—the Natchez, Choctaw, Creek and others, with the Cherokees sharing in this cultural growth later in the historical period. The town government of the Creek villages was a basically democratic form of government that could absorb numerous other peoples. These nations were later termed by the United States as the Five Civilized Tribes when they became literate in their own languages. Antecedent to these examples of urbanism in eastern and southeastern United States was the older Mound Builder civilization that is described later in this chapter.

The third major center was that of the Haudenosaunee (Iroquois) nations in what later became New York State (see Chapter Two).

The fourth center was in the region of present-day Mexico and Guatemala. It includes principally the Mayans and the Aztecs and is the region with which we begin our narrative.

URBANISM IN MESOAMERICA

Mesoamerica includes the greater part of present-day Mexico, Guatemala, and Honduras. The region extends from 22 degrees to about 10 degrees latitude and is bounded by the coastal plains along the Atlantic Ocean in the east and by the Pacific Ocean and its coastal plains in the west. To the north lie the desert-like lands of northern Mexico. Between the two mountain ranges are three high plateaus, "the most important and fertile of which is the plateau of Mexico, the Mesa Central, where it is thought that a population of between six and twenty million were living on the eve of the Conquest. . . . At the center of this high plateau lies the Valley of Mexico." (Katz 2000, 25). The Aztec capital of Tenochtitlán, site of present-day Mexico City, became one of the truly great urban centers of the ancient world.

Mesoamerican urbanism is associated with the American food revolution, the domestication and cultivation of plants, especially maize, and with irrigation. At least half or more of the world's foods were developed by the Indigenous peoples of the Americas. "Maize was domesticated in Mexico by about 5000 B.C. and spread into the southwestern U.S. by 2000–1500 B.C. By 700–900 C.E. the widespread production of maize began to revolutionize Mississippi Valley life-ways" (Forbes 2001, 8).

Olmecs

The origin of Mesoamerican urban development appears to have begun in the Olmec-Tulapan region on the Gulf of Mexico and correlates with the oldest date in the Mesoamerican calendar, 3113 or 3114 BC. The Olmec culture, originating in the present-day Mexican state of Vera Cruz, is considered to be the "mother culture" of the urban civilizations of Mesoamerica, appearing in central Mexico as early as 1800 BC. The Olmec tradition of scattered ceremonial centers found its highest expression in the culture of the Maya. It reached its peak of development in the lowlands rather than on the plateau, with La Venta and Tres Zapotes becoming regional commercial centers under the domination of a priesthood, which rose "to become overlords of the whole of the surrounding districts, and finally also engaged in military conquest" (Katz 2000, 41).

Mesoamerican urbanism spawned the complex development of what political anthropologists term the chieftainship state. In Mesoamerica, the great urban civilizations were variously dominated by either a priesthood or a warrior caste. Although most had religions that included human sacrifice, their economic and scientific accomplishments were many. "They invented a dozen different systems of writing, established widespread trade networks, tracked the orbits of the planets, created a 365-day calendar (more accurate than its contemporaries in Europe), and recorded their histories in accordion-folded 'books' of fig tree bark paper. . . . The Olmec, Maya, and other Mesoamerican societies were world pioneers in mathematics and astronomy. . . . Perhaps their greatest intellectual accomplishment was the invention of zero, which first recorded evidence occurred in a Maya carving from 357 A.D." (Mann 2005, 18–19).

Toltecs

In the first century AD, on the Mexican plateau in the northeastern part of the Valley of Mexico, the most impressive ancient civilization and urban complex in the Americas took place, Teotihuacán, the home of the Toltecs, revered as the traditional burial place of the gods. The complex was constructed "with carefully planned designs featuring avenues and plazas arranged in a systematic manner totally unknown in most European cities of the time" (Forbes 2001, 15). At its zenith in the fifth and sixth centuries, Teotihuacán was larger than Rome at the time of the Caesars, even though its population was only one-fifth that of Rome, and its influence extended thousands of miles throughout Mesoamerica and beyond. Teotihuacán possessed a ceremonial area of seven square miles and a population between 125 and 250 thousand people. Most famous among its structures are the imposing Pyramid of the Sun (over 210 feet high), the Pyramid of the Moon, and the Temple of the Feathered Serpent.

The city's economic base of agriculture was sustained by an ingenious irrigation system where water sources are diverted to the fields by a series of small channels dug out of the surrounding hillsides. Katz (2000, 51) believes it is also possible that the Toltecs "were already familiar with the very productive *chinampa* system of artificial islands in the skein of lakes in Mexico, which was later used by the Aztecs."

The city was a major spiritual and education center, as well as a center for trade and manufacture. Although thought to have been a religious center,

Teotihuacán could not have existed nor extended its immense influence throughout the region without its warriors. "On the eve of the Spanish Conquest, five distinct ruling groups had developed in Mesoamerica: a warrior caste that slowly turned into a hereditary aristocracy, which usually supplied the ruler; a priesthood; a mercantile caste; a tribal aristocracy and—in the early stages—a state bureaucracy with ever-increasing powers" (Katz 2000, 53–54).

In spite of its obsidian mines and products and its wide political cultural outreach, Teotihuacán disintegrated by AD 1700. Its fall is associated with the decline of the Maya cities in the tropical forests of the Petén. After its demise, various warlike states contested with one another, and the center of cultural development spread northward to Tula outside the Valley of Mexico. It became the Toltec capital, "an epicenter of groups of warriors, traders, cultivators, and priests employing the Toltec name and symbols as charters for conquest and colonization" (Wolf 1982, 67). The ruins of Teotihuacán have been preserved and are located today just forty miles from Mexico City.

In the Valley of Mexico itself there were five city-states striving for dominance. One of these, Azcapozalco, ruled by the Otomi-speaking Tepanec, was later overthrown by the Aztecs, who at the time were a mere band of mercenaries in service to the Tepanec. In the midst of Toltec military struggles and ensuing political strife, the long-ruling king, Topilzin Quetzalcuatl, was forced from office in about 987 AD. He fled with his loyalists to the Yucatan Peninsula, promising to return, a prophecy that later played a role in the Spanish conquest of the Aztecs. He apparently conquered the Maya city of Chichén Itzá, which he then rebuilt in the image of Toltec architecture.

Mayan City States

For two thousand years the Mayan civilization developed over an extensive area of southern Mexico and Mesoamerica. Renowned for monumental architecture, the Mayan civilization arose at a time when Europe was entering the Dark Ages. Of special note is the majestic Temple IV of the ruined Maya city of Tikal, which, until the construction of the first skyscrapers in the late nineteenth century, was the tallest building in the Americas. The Mayan urban complexes, including Palenque, Tikal, and Copan, occupied three distinct regions of Mesoamerica: southern tropical rain forest lowlands, the Guatemala highlands of mountain and valleys, and northern Yucatan consisting of desert scrub and limited water sources. There were numerous independent Mayan city-states with no one city being the central hub of all Mayan society. "Although some of them were the first Mesoamericans to meet Spaniards, other Mayas were the last to be subdued. One state kept its independence in the Petén jungle until 1697—more than a century and a half after the rest had fallen—while smaller groups lived free in remote parts of the same forest until the twentieth century" (Wright 1992, 49).

The classic period of the Maya, 250 AD to 925 AD, "is distinguished by a spectacular flowering of architecture, sculpture, painting and learning. The architecture of the Mayan centers was monumental. They contained great plazas bordered by tremendous pyramids, temples and palaces. . . . Wide roads suitable for religious processions lead into these central plazas. The centers are in some respect reminiscent of Teothuacan" (Katz 2000, 60). The center of the Mayan civilization during its classic period was the Petén jungle where more than a dozen great cities flourished, with Tikal becoming the greatest of them all. The city covered twenty-three square miles; its urban core included three thousand buildings and a population as large as one hundred thousand people at its height. "Five temples with ornate stone temples on their summits still rise 20 feet into the air," with Temple IV being "the tallest structure in the Americas until the Washington Capitol dome was built eleven centuries later" (Wright 1992, 49–50). To support their cities, the Maya developed a unique system of intensive agriculture in which a network of canals and raised fields allowed large populations to thrive in a jungle environment. The newly discovered urban center of Calakmul covered as much as twenty-five square miles. It had thousands of buildings, dozens of reservoirs and canals, and more than a hundred monuments.

Mayan achievements in art, writing, architecture, astronomy, and mathematics rival those of ancient Egypt or classical Europe. The Maya are famous for their advanced system of mathematics. "A group of mathematicians and astronomers developed a system that, among other things, could have predicted an eclipse that would darken the skies over a thousand years in the future, without instruments, only by using the naked eye" (Kearns 2007, B3). Mayan astronomical predictions required years of careful observation of the sun and moon, and they built their temples in relation to these observations. The Maya also constructed an elaborate calendar system, actually two calendars, a ritual calendar of 260 days, and a solar calendar of 365 days for farming. The latter was more accurate than the Julian calendar in use in Europe at the time of the Spanish conquest, and sophisticated enough to make leap-year-like corrections. The year 3114 BC in the Maya calendar represents the beginning of time or creation.

One of the Maya's most striking achievements was hieroglyphics, a system of writing that combined phonetics and ideographs. The hieroglyphics are found on more than one thousand stone stelae that had been erected in the center of Mayan cities. The stone stelae record the family history of Mayan kings and queens. Tragically, of their thousands of ancient books, only three survived Spanish bonfires, the Dresden Codex being the most famous of these. The Mayan writing system is very complicated, with eight hundred differing glyphs based on words (logographic) and some signs representing syllables. The Maya Code has only recently been broken by Maya specialists, and contemporary Maya are now rediscovering their history and culture by learning to read their ancient language.

Maya development appears to have been influenced by the Toltecs of Teotihuacán. Maya inscriptions record that on January 8, 378, the warlord Fire Is Born and his warriors arrived in Waka, an ancient Maya city-state, as envoys from the great Toltec power in the highlands of Mexico. Under his reign, the Maya reached an apogee lasting five centuries. Maya cities like Tikal made alliances, fought wars, and traded for goods over a territory that stretched from what is today southern Mexico through the Petén to the Caribbean coast of Honduras. "Mediating between the heavens and earth were the Maya kings—the *kuhul ajaw*, or holy lords, who derived their power from the gods. They functioned both as shamans, interpreting religion and ideology, and rulers who led their subjects in peace and war" (Gugliotta 2007, 81).

Although Mayan cultural development was influenced by the Toltecs, the Mayan centers never reached the population density of Teotihuacán. Rather, they were ceremonial in function with the people of outlying villages flocking "into these centers only on religious occasions, on feast days and market days. Otherwise they were inhabited only by the upper classes, their servants and a few peasants" (Katz 2000, 70). The Mayan centers were probably priestly city-states or theocracies.

About a century before the Spanish invasion, the Mayan heartland went into a steep decline for unknown reasons. Most authorities believe that drought, deforestation, and overuse of the land, plus an over-burdening upper class, were contributing factors. Unlike Teotihuacán, which had intensive agriculture and sophisticated methods of food production, the Maya had a culture where agriculture was comparatively undeveloped. Between the third to the ninth centuries, warfare among rival superpowers ravaged Mayan cities, and human sacrifice became widespread. There is archaeological evidence of destructive battles between Mayan city-states towards the end of the civilization's decline.

Although Hernando Cortés passed through several lowland Maya kingdoms in the 1520s during his conquest of the Aztecs, he never attempted to conquer the Maya. It fell to Pedro de Alvarado to become the conqueror of Guatemala. Joined by his Indian allies, the Tlazcalans, he ruthlessly defeated the Quiche and Cakchiquel Maya in his lust for gold, destroying their cities in the process. "The Mayas of Guatemala entered the long period of resistance, sometimes passive, sometimes armed, that continues to this day" (Wright 1992, 60–61). As a result of the Spanish invasion, the Mayan elites were either eliminated or incorporated into the new colonial system. This left the Maya-speaking population as a relatively undifferentiated mass of rural peasants, devoid of their civilization's rich accomplishments, and through Hispanization, illiterate in their own languages. Nevertheless, there are over six million Maya living today with much of their culture still intact.

AZTECS OF MEXICO

The Valley of Mexico became the center of one of the world's most impressive civilizations—the Aztec Confederacy or Empire, that lasted almost two hundred years until destroyed by the Spanish conquest in the early 1500s. The Aztec, or *Mexica* legacy is the core culture of the Mexican people and also an integral part of the multiethnic population of the United States, especially in the Southwest and California. The Mexican people are the descendants of an American civilization that rivaled ancient Greece and Rome in Europe.

Historical Background

Nine thousand years ago, an agricultural revolution took place in the Valley of Mexico. Maize, or corn, and then beans, squash, and chili (high in vitamin C) were developed and cultivated. Central America, especially in the highlands of Mexico and Guatemala, became one of the world's four or five primary centers of plant domestication.

Beginning about AD 900, there were a number of migrations into the Valley of Mexico from Atzlán, a mythic homeland located, according to some accounts, north of the Mexican plateau. These were the Chichimecas. The Toltecs were the first of the Chichimec invaders to establish hegemony in Central Mexico from AD 968 to AD 1156. Yet other accounts place Atzlán to the west of Mexico, possibly in the present Mexican state of Nayarit bordering the Pacific Ocean. Aztlán means "land of egrets." Legends recount that the early Aztecs were driven from one infertile region to another and forced into military service by successive overlords. They migrated south to the Valley of Mexico around 1200 AD during the fall of the Toltec Empire. For fifty-two years they struggled to survive as hunters and gatherers at Atelelco, and then at Tizapan in the southwestern part of the Valley of Mexico, part of the territory of the city state of Culhuacan.

In their search for the promised land the Aztecs were led by their High Priest, Huitzilopochtli, who died along the journey and became deified as their spiritual patron. Huitzilopochtli advised the Aztecs through a vision to search for an eagle perched on a cactus, warming itself in the sun (the eagle being a symbol of the sun), and there they should build a city and establish themselves as the lords of the region. In the year 1325 the Aztecs found an eagle on a cactus on a small uninhabited island in Lake Texcoco. "The region now settled was an island in the middle of the lake district of the Valley of Mexico, which they called Tenochtitlán. This island—the site of today's Mexico City—was to become their capital" (Katz 2000, 136–37). There they built a temple to honor Huitzilopochtli. They took the name of Mexica, a term associated with Huitzilopochtli. (See Figure 11.1.)

The island had amazing potential. It was impervious to attack and bordered Atzcapotzalco, the major city state in the Valley of Mexico. The marshes of Lake Texcoco were drained, filled in, and connected to produce bumper crops by employing the *chinampa* system. "Chinampas are narrow strips of land . . . almost completely surrounded by canals. They produce several crops a year and remain amazingly fertile century after century" (Farb 1968, 169). The *chinampas* increased Aztec wealth and economic power, and the political alliance with the Tepanecs of Atzcapozalco increased their influence in the valley. Within a century after founding their capital city, the

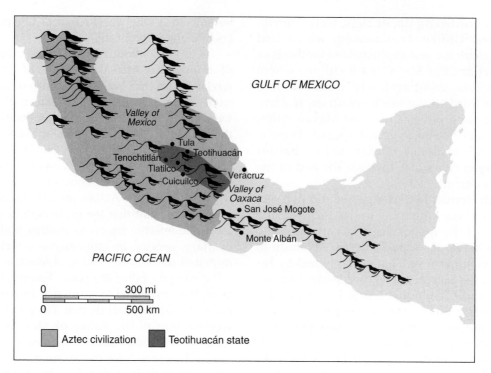

Figure 11.1 The Aztec Empire.

Aztecs had become one of the most important city states in the region.

Aztec Social Organization

The Aztec Empire was a tribute-gathering organization with extensive trade networks. The Aztec emperor was known as Tlatoani, or "Great Speaker," who was chosen by the Aztec nobles. The society was highly stratified with each class identified by a certain type of clothing. Slavery existed but was not hereditary. Religion was vitally important, necessitating constant "flower wars" to gain captives for human sacrifice and to intimidate potential enemies. Aztec gods represented various aspects of nature and society. Huitzilopochtli was the patron of Tenochtitlán and the god of war. Quetzalcóatl was the creator god and patron of rulers and priests. Tlaloc was the god of rain, fertility, and lightning. Aztec religion involved daily human sacrifice in order to ensure the survival of the sun.

The Aztecs believed that everything is temporary and destined for oblivion. Time was reckoned in cycles, unlike the European linear system. Among their many accomplishments was an intricate calendar system, as represented in the elaborately incised Sun Stone (Mexican calendar stone), which has survived the Spanish conquest. It provided the Aztecs with a guide for the planting seasons and agriculture, but it was also used ceremonially to understand the balance and cycles of nature.

There are two systems of reckoning time in Aztec science. The first count is the *Xiuhuitl*, or *Xiuhpohualli*, consisting of eighteen months of twenty days each, the number twenty being the base number in the ancient American world instead of the European ten. Eighteen multiplied by twenty is 360, the degrees of a circle, but the earth does not revolve around the sun in a perfect circle and actually takes 365.25 days. These extra days were considered useless and unlucky by the Aztecs and counted in a period called *Nemontemi* (useless) (Sanchez 1998). The *Xihuitl* count of the solar year is roughly equivalent to the Gregorian year.

A second count as represented on the Sun Stone is *Tonalamatl*, or *Tonalpohualli*, the sacred time or Sun paper count. "Each day is called a Tonal and the day a person is born on is considered their *Tonalli*, or destiny influence. The *Tonalamatl* consists of 13 count of 20 symbols to give a total of 260 days" (Sanchez 1998). It repeats every 260 days and is used to keep track of which god should be honored on which day.

The Aztecs solidified their power through a policy of constant warfare, crushing their rivals to gain tribute and also captives for religious sacrifices. The eighth ruler of the Aztecs, Ahuítzotl, died in 1502. By the time of his death,

> he had conquered most of the peoples southward to Guatemala and northward to the borders of the deserts; he ruled much of Mexico from the Gulf to the Pacific Ocean.... New aqueducts carried water from the mainland to the island capital; giant causeways, engineering marvels, were built to span the lakes. The fabulous Great Temple (on the site of Mexico City's Zócalo and the National Palace) was erected—and dedicated by the sacrifice of twenty thousand captives. The crafts and literature were encouraged, and many new schools established." (Farb 1968, 168)

Tenochtitlán

When the Spaniards first entered Tenochtitlán, the Aztec capital city, they were amazed and astonished by its magnificence. It already had a population of 200,000 to 300,000 people, larger than any city with which the Spaniards were familiar in Europe, several times larger than London and much cleaner. Professional garbage collectors scoured the city's streets and plazas, and the temples and buildings were plastered a dazzling white. Its canals rivaled Venice. Three causeways supplied the city with water, and there was a steady commerce of merchant canoes laden with food and merchandise. It was not possible to pass from house to house except by drawbridges or in canoes. The temples, towers, and fortresses were gleaming white, with a great plaza and market place in the center of the city where multitudes of people gathered daily as they went about their various duties and errands. The Spanish soldiers, although familiar with the ancient capitals Europe, nevertheless marveled at the sight of such order and development that was superior to anything they had previously witnessed in their travels.

Despite their admiration the Spaniards considered the Aztecs barbarians and thought only of seizing their riches and forcing them to become Christian. Aided by enemy tribes to the Aztecs, a smallpox epidemic, and a myth of the coming of a White god, the Spaniards destroyed the Aztec Empire in two years. But when the Aztecs first encountered the Spaniards in the early 1500s, it was a powerful empire under the rule of Moctezuma II, whom the Spaniards called Montezuma.

The Aztec Empire was actually a loose federation of three autonomous city-states— Mexico (home of the Mexica), Texcoco, and Tlacopan. These three city-states lay in a great valley, seven thousand feet above sea level, surrounded by volcanoes and icy peaks.

Tenochitlán, as the leading city of the Triple Alliance, provided the conquered regions with military protection in exchange for a wide variety of goods that were obtained from thirty-eight tributary provinces. Numbering more than sixhundred thousand citizens, Tenochtitlán and Tlateloco, together known as Mexico, was the largest city in the Americas, and one of the largest then existing in the world. It covered more than six square miles. "The two cities grew into one, but each had its own central square, temples, nobility, and royal palaces. Tenochtitlán's great plaza, measuring more than a quarter of a mile on each side, held some eighty shrines. Tlateloco's was almost as big, but much of it was taken up by a marketplace . . . one was the political hub of the Empire, the other its commercial core" (Wright 1992, 20).

Tenochitlán, "the Place of the Fruit of the Cactus," was the largest of nineteen island communities on Lake Texcoco, and it was connected to the mainland by three causeways. The city itself was divided into a progression of coresidence units, beginning with four quarters, or "great neighborhoods." Each quarter was further divided into its constituent residential wards, or "small neighborhoods," in which the *calpulli* (a clan-like kinship unit) resided. There were twenty for the entire city. Each had its own "streets" or smaller kinship units, temples, markets, and administrative buildings. Each street had its individual family plots consisting of several *chinampas*. The *capulli* had its own temple, and some of the more prestigious ones had schools for military education. Land was owned in common but was under control of the *capulli*.

In addition to the nobility and the commoners, there were also displaced persons without citizenship who worked for the Aztecs, and also a small number of slaves. The division of labor was complex and included warriors, merchants, goldsmiths, lapidaries, and feather workers. The merchants and craftsmen were organized into hereditary guilds.

Government started at the *capulli* level. "Speakers" were elected from each of the twenty *capulli* to serve in the High Council. In turn, other representatives were elected to the National Council to advise the Aztec head of state. At the time of the Spanish invasion, Montezuma was head of state, much like a Roman emperor, but he was also the high priest. A complex legal code integrated the criminal justice system. It was applied by judges, with one chief judge at the top. There was a network of lower and higher courts. Police enforced the laws and legal decisions.

Flower Wars

Contemporary Western writers have universally condemned the Aztec custom of human sacrifice, conveniently forgetting the institution of European serfdom, the feudal practice of drawing and quartering, burning women at the stake as witches, the torturing of thousands of victims by the Inquisition, the persecution of the Jews, Huguenots, and others, to say nothing of the savagery of the conquistadors who chopped off hands and feet, tore Indians apart with their attack dogs, and committed many other atrocities. It is true that the Aztecs sacrificed tens of thousands of prisoners in their "flower wars," "flower" being a metaphor for human blood, but they never tortured. Human sacrifice was the rationale to obtain potential victims in Aztec flower wars and was reinforced by religious ideology. "According to Aztec lore, the universe had been destroyed four times; to create the sun and moon for this fifth epoch, two gods committed suicide, hurling themselves into a fire. Now, to keep the sun moving and the whole cosmos working, all the gods needed a diet of human hearts and blood—thus explaining the Aztec necessity for wars, prisoners, and human sacrifice. Every detail of Aztec life centered on their religion. Church and state were one" (McDowell 1980, 720).

Death was thought to bring to ordinary folk a difficult series of trials before eternal peace could be obtained. Warriors and sacrificial victims, on the other hand, could enter immediately into the highest paradise, the House of the Sun. Unlike Greco-Roman civilization, the Aztecs were not a fully developed slave society; conquered enemies could be put to work tilling the crops and doing the low status jobs of Aztec society. The religious rationale for human sacrifice, therefore, was a functional means of subduing and weakening potential enemy tribes, rationalized by an elaborate, religious ideology. While one may rightly condemn this bloody custom, it should be viewed in the full context of the many outstanding accomplishments by this early civilization. Who knows where Aztec social development may have led if it had not been destroyed by Spanish aggression?

Destruction of the Aztecs

The conquistador conquest of the Mexica civilization set the stage for a hemispheric slaughter of hundreds of thousands of Indigenous persons in Mesoamerica. It started with the massacre in the main temple of Tenochtitlán during a religious festival that the Aztecs celebrated in honor of their god, Huitzilopochtli. It was the most important of their religious celebrations. The dancers and singers were completely unarmed. They had only their religious paraphernalia of embroidered cloaks, turquoises, lip plugs and necklaces, heron feathers, and objects made of deer hoofs. The drummers, old men, brought their gourds of snuff and timbrels. Nevertheless the Spanish soldiers attacked the musicians first. The singers, the water carriers, horse tenders, food preparers, sweepers, and even the spectators, were killed with the slaughter continuing for three hours.

Later, when the Aztecs mobilized to drive the Spanish conquistadors from their midst, they fought ferociously to the last warrior in their capital city. By this time, however, smallpox, obtained from the Spaniards, was ravaging the city in epidemic proportions. The Aztecs had no immunity to European diseases, thus they died in droves. With broken spears from the weakened Aztec warriors, and the city's plaza and temples red with blood, the besieged Aztec empire came to its tragic end.

MOUND BUILDERS OF EASTERN NORTH AMERICA

Much earlier than the Aztec civilization in central Mexico were the Mound Builders, located in eastern United States. (See Waldman 2000, 20–24.) It is there that ancient Indigenous peoples built impressive earthen works or mounds. Thousands of such earthen works dot the landscape from Florida to Wisconsin. Some were as high as ten-story buildings; others were effigy mounds—hundreds of feet long and shaped like birds, serpents, and human beings.

Until the 1890s, scientists refused to believe that the ancestors of present-day Indians were capable of such architectural achievements. It was variously theorized that they had been built instead by a mythical Mound Builder civilization derived from either the Celts, Carthage, the Vikings, the Lost Tribes of Israel, or even Atlantis. Today, we know that it was the ancestors of contemporary Indians who were responsible for the impressive Mound Builder culture. In reality, there were several culturally similar but different developments of mound-building in what is now the eastern United States.

The First Mound Builders

A development which archaeologists call the Adena culture started about 1000 BC and lasted to AD 200. The Hopewell culture was a new period of mound-building, which arose about 300 BC and lasted to AD 700. Although the two cultural traditions coexisted for five centuries, their exact relationship is unknown.

The Adena centered on the Ohio Valley, along the Ohio River and into the territory that is now Kentucky, West Virginia, Indiana, Pennsylvania, and New York. Although the Adena people were hunters and gatherers, their earthen works reflected a high degree of social organization. In the later part of development, high mounds were constructed over multiple burials, the dead usually placed in log-lined tombs. Often, too, these earthen monuments were surrounded by rounded walls or ridges known as "sacred circles." The Great Serpent Mound in Peebles, Ohio, for example, is a low, rounded embankment, about four feet high and fifteen to twenty feet across, and extending 1,330 feet in the shape of an uncoiling snake with jaws and a tail. Seen from the air, its proportions and symmetry are perfect, indicating that the Adena people were not only artists but mathematicians.

The Hopewell were similar in many respects to the Adena, but their mound-building was generally on an enhanced scale—more and larger earthen works, richer burials, intensified ceremonialism, greater refinement in art, a stricter social class system and division of labor, agriculture, and a far-flung trading network. There was obsidian traded in from the Black Hills of present-day South Dakota and the Rockies, shells from the Atlantic and Gulf coasts, mica from the Appalachians, silver from Canada, and alligator skulls and teeth from Florida.

Many of the mounds, covering multiple burials, stood thirty to forty feet high. Large effigy mounds often stood nearby, as did also geometric enclosures. Some of these earthen walls were fifty feet high and two hundred feet wide at their base. The enclosure at Newark, Ohio, covered four square miles. Art flourished. The grave furnishings included large ceramic figures, copper headdresses and breast ornaments, obsidian spearheads and knives, mica mirrors, conch shell drinking cups, pearl jewelry, hammered gold silhouettes, incised and stamped pottery, and elaborately carved stone platform pipes with naturalistic human and animal sculptures.

Temple Mound Builders

Beginning about AD 700, and lasting into the post-contact period of European colonization, a new and even more impressive mound-building culture arose, the Mississippian or Temple Mound Builders. The huge temple mounds were ceremonial centers for adjacent villages and were centered along the Lower Mississippi Valley and encompassed most of southeastern United States.

The Temple Mound Builders were master farmers who grew corn, beans, squash, and tobacco. They had a complex social structure and a rigid caste system with a death or southern cult. They were probably influenced by Mesoamerican developments via the Gulf of Mexico. Priests and nobles lived on the higher mounds; merchants, craftsmen, hunters, farmers, and laborers lived in the surrounding huts.

The largest and most famous Temple Mound site is Cahokia in Illinois near present-day St. Louis, which flourished in the eleventh century AD on an alluvial plain below the junction of the Mississippi and Missouri rivers. The village area extended for six miles along the Illinois River and contained over one hundred temple and burial mounds. It sustained an estimated maximum population, including outlying villages, of seventy-five thousand. "At one time, there were more than two hundred packed-earth pyramids, or 'mounds,' at Cahokia and its suburbs. More than half of these were built in a five-square mile zone that was designed with reference to the four sacred directions and the upper and lower worlds. The pyramids were arranged around vast open plazas and were surrounded, in turn, by thousands of pole-and-thatch houses, temples, and public buildings" (Pauketat 2009, book blurb, Chapter One). The largest mound, Monk's Mound, was built in fourteen stages over 250 years. Upon its completion it covered sixteen acres at its base, which is broader than the Great Pyramid of Egypt, and stood on hundred feet high. Other important centers of Mississippian culture include Moundville in present-day Alabama, Towah and Ocmulgee in Georgia, Spiro in Oklahoma, and Hiwassee Island in Tennessee.

By the early seventeenth century the Mississippian Temple Mound centers had been abandoned. Overpopulation, drought, political strife, or perhaps diseases spread by early European contact, may have been responsible. At least one Native American representative of the Temple Mound people survived into the eighteenth century until their extinction by the French. They were the *Natchez* who lived along the lower Mississippi River near New Orleans. The Natchez had a central temple mound with a nearby open plaza and satellite mounds. The Natchez chieftain, called the Great Sun, lived on one of these. On others lived the queen mother and the Great Sun's brothers, also called Suns, from whom were chosen the war chief and head priest, and his sisters. A complicated caste system included the nobles and honored men as an upper caste, with the commoners and slaves as lower castes. Yet all grades of nobility had to wed commoners. In 1729 the Natchez revolted against the French colonists who were living in their midst. Eventually they were defeated by the French, who sold many captured Natchez survivors into slavery in Santo Domingo in the Caribbean. Other refugees settled among the Chickasaws, Creeks, and Cherokees where they gained reputations as mystics because of their ancient religious cult.

Over one hundred thousand of these impressive Indian mounds were built east of the Mississippi River. Although many have been destroyed, some survive and can be visited today by those interested in the Native American heritage. The Egyptians are hailed because of their pyramids, but some scholars believe the Indian mound-building to go far beyond the Egyptian achievements in their overall scope. Rather than turn to Mesopotamia and Egypt in the ancient world as examples of impressive early civilizations, those of us living in North America would do well to acknowledge our own hidden cultural heritage—the astounding Mound Builder civilization.

CONTEMPORARY INDIAN URBANISM IN THE UNITED STATES AND CANADA

Native American urban communities have long been a feature of U.S. cities. As early as in the 1880s American Indian members of Laguna Pueblo began leaving their tribal homelands to work for the Atchison, Topeka, and Santa Fe Railroad, and establishing satellite communities along the route. Indian ironworkers founded settlements in Brooklyn, New York City, Buffalo, Cleveland, and Detroit. "Each settlement had its bar, community hall, and church" (Wells 1996, 278). Mohawk high steel workers from Canada and the United States lived in the Canarsie section of Brooklyn, New York. LaGrande (2002, Chapter One), in his study of the urban Indians of Chicago, points out that Native people were already migrating to the city in the first decades of the twentieth century as a result of land dispossession, the 1887 Indian Allotment Act, reservation poverty, and unemployment. Nevertheless, by 1950, Native Americans were still predominantly reservation-based or rural (86.6 percent). By the 1950s following World War II, however, urban migration vastly increased due primarily to the formulation and implementation of two U.S. government policy initiatives: federal termination and tribal relocation.

House Concurrent Resolution 108, *termination*, ended federal supervision, protection, and services to selected tribes. From 1954 through 1960, sixty-one tribes, *rancherias*, allotments and communities were unilaterally terminated by the federal government. The policy violated treaty rights and is an example of the egregious plenary power doctrine of Congress.

A second onerous policy of Congress was *relocation*. It initiated a federal program that provided young Indians with transportation to selected cities where they were to receive employment assistance and job placement. Twelve metropolitan areas were designated as target cities. In 1962 the program was renamed the Employment Assistance Program when educational and training components were added.

As a result of these two government programs, tens of thousands of American Indians and Alaska Natives moved to metropolitan areas of the United States in the 1950s and 1960s. This led many researchers to conclude that Indian acculturation and assimilation would take place, similar to the pattern of European immigration in earlier decades. It was predicted that soon there would be no "real Indians" left, that an entire generation of Native Americans would become urban like millions of European immigrants before them. The federal rationale for relocation was to resettle the supposedly surplus reservation Indian population in U.S. cities. Younger families were relocated, leaving older Indians on the reservations. Eventually those remaining on the reservations and in rural Indian country would die, and those resettled in the cities would acculturate to the mainstream culture. To carry out relocation policy, the Bureau of Indian Affairs (BIA) maintained employment assistance centers in Chicago, Cleveland, Dallas, Denver, Los Angeles, Oakland, San Jose, Tulsa, Oklahoma City, and Seattle. From the very beginning, however, the program ran into trouble. Thirty-five thousand Indians entered the program during the 1960s, but nearly one-third returned home, "often after discovering that promises of jobs and decent housing was illusory" (Pevar 2004, 12). Some tried relocation a second or even a third time.

The impetus for reservation Indians to relocate to the cities was reinforced by the government's termination program, which was in effect from 1953 to 1968. By 1962, Congress had passed fourteen tribal termination bills. For those tribes affected it meant the "termination of the tribe's trust relationship with the United States and, as a consequence, its loss of federal benefits and support services, the destruction of its government and reservation. Heralded as the policy that would set Indians free, termination brought Indian tribes to the brink of total disaster" (Pevar 2004, 11). One hundred and nine tribes were terminated, forcing tribal members into the nearby towns and cities to eke out a living without treaty-mandated federal assistance. The U.S. government withdrew federal recognition from tribes in California, Florida, New York, Oregon, and Texas, including the timber-rich Menominee of Wisconsin and the Klamath Indians of Oregon.

Termination policy soon came under intense criticism from Indian activists. "The Red Power movement that emerged in the 1960s emphasized themes like pride in Indian culture, tribal sovereignty, and Indian self-determination, and led to demands that the policy be changed" (Burt 1996, 222). In 1970, responding to widespread political pressure, President Richard M. Nixon rejected termination policy, and in 1975 a new policy of Indian self-determination was ushered in. On April 20, 1988, termination was officially repealed by Congress. A number of the terminated tribes—but not all—were eventually restored to federal status.

Relocation may be seen as a policy of proletarianization, since the employment training and job placement was entirely into low-end, blue-collar jobs, such as auto body repair for men, and typing and file clerk jobs for women. There were no opportunities for preprofessional training to become a physician, lawyer, or teacher. Relocatees could attend college but had to pay their own tuition and registration fees. Instead of acculturating, however, the result was entirely opposite to what the government planners intended. The relocates established Indian centers in most of the designated cities and continued to maintain tribal identities and ties to their respective reservations and communities in Indian Country.

Early Urban Indian Research

In the 1960s, academic researchers were just beginning to note, let alone investigate, the urban Indian phenomenon. One of these researchers who did investigate was the action anthropologist Joan Ablon. In her research of American Indian relocatees in the San Francisco Bay Area, Ablon found that rather than assimilating, the relocates chose instead to associate "primarily with other Indians of their own or differing tribes in both informal and formal social interaction" (Ablon 1972, 413). Pow-wows featuring traditional Plains Indian dancing and singing were a monthly affair. Interaction with Whites was relatively superficial. Social interaction for some took

place in "Indian bars," which were also places where Indians could cash checks. Home visiting was another social activity, especially for members of the larger, more traditional tribes, such as the Turtle Mountain Chippewa, Navajo, and Sioux. Formal Indian interaction included baseball and basketball teams, religious groups, and political organizations. The most influential organizations at the time of Ablon's study were the Oakland Intertribal Friendship House, the San Francisco American Indian Center, the Four Winds Club, the Oakland American Indian Baptist Church, the San Jose Dance Club, and the American Indian Council of the Bay Area. The Santa Fe Indian Village in nearby Richmond, California, formed a century earlier by Indian railroad workers and their families, was for many years a self-contained Indian entity.

Robert K. Thomas, a Cherokee researcher also active in the 1960s, noted two main cultural responses by the urban Indian migrants: First was the growth of a generalized Indian culture, or pan-Indianism, as both a unifying and a divisive cultural force of the new urbanism. "In the last decade [1960s], American Indians have moved to urban centers and Plains Indian communities are forming around Indian centers in some of our larger cities. In most cases, the tone for these activities at these centers is set by people who have had previous experiences in pan-Indian—that is Pan-Plains—activities, and these symbols become symbols of a forming Indian community in the city" (Thomas 1968, 134). At the same time, in opposition to Plains pan-Indianism, an alliance was formed among some of the Eastern Woodland tribes and Southwestern Indians around traditional culture. "In recent years the traditional factions of the Seminole, Iroquois and the Hopi have joined forces, and now there is a new social type arisen on the American scene, the traditional Indian" (Thomas 1968, 135). With respect to pan-Indianism, Thomas attributed its origin to the Indian boarding schools in which Plains Indian culture, with its feather headdress and pow-wows among related characteristics, came to dominate. By the mid-nineteenth century, "almost every tribal group has pow-wows, a pow-wow committee, a women's club, and a veterans' organization" (Thomas 1968, 132).

An element of the new urban Indian community was the growing nationalism and cultural militancy among younger Indians, particularly college students, who were organizing Indian clubs and Indian youth councils. Thomas noted this growing political activism, or nationalism, among Indian youth in the

1960s as the "tip of the pan-Indian social movement" (Thomas 1968, 137). This ran counter to the White stereotype of the Indian being passive and nonconfrontational.

Another early researcher of Indian urbanism was John A. Price, who undertook a demographic analysis and brief history of Indian migration to Los Angeles, California (1972, 428–439). He noted that the total number of Indians in California doubled in the 1950s, and by 1960 the number of urban Indians had increased by three to four times. An immigration wave had begun around 1955, with the majority coming from Arizona, New Mexico, South Dakota, North Dakota, and Montana, augmented by Native California Indians. There were representatives of over one hundred tribes, predominantly Navajo, Sioux, and the Civilized Tribes (Cherokee, Creek, Choctaw, Chickasaw, and Seminole). Although Plains Indians predominated, there were also members of eastern seaboard people, such as the Nanticokes. Price estimated a total Los Angeles Indian population at the time of about twenty-five thousand. The new immigrants were younger, had lesser skills and lower income, more often lived in central Los Angeles, were fluent in an Indian language, and associated with other Indians more often than with Whites. Twenty percent were active in formal Indian associations (athletic leagues, churches, clubs, and community centers). Twenty-nine percent associated solely with other Indians, while 67 percent associated with both Whites and other Indians. Forty-five percent preferred living in a mixed neighborhood.

Another academic work coming out at this time was *The American Indian Today*, edited by Stuart La Vine and Nancy O. Lurie (1968). One of its contributors was Shirley Hill Witt who, echoing Thomas, also noted the factors leading to "Indian nationalism" that emerged mainly among urban Indians in the 1960s (Witt 1968, 93–127). In addition, she pointed out that even before the government's termination and relocation programs in the 1950s, there was already an Indian migration to cities in progress. During World War II, for example, an estimated forty thousand Indians left the reservations to work in wartime industries, and others became farm workers. At the end of the war, most Indian industrial workers and war veterans returned to their reservations only to find deplorable living conditions, discrimination, and astronomical unemployment. As a result, thousands returned once more to the cities.

Murray L. Wax's *Indian Americans: Unity and Diversity*, published in 1971, includes a chapter entitled "Indians in the Cities." In addition to providing data on the urban Indian migration of the 1950s and 1960s, he also identified distinct urban tribal enclaves that had persisted for years. These include the Mohawk of North Gowanus living in Brooklyn, NY, and the Sioux camps bordering Rapid City, South Dakota. The existence of urban Indian enclaves that pre-date the mid-twentieth century urban migration is important to note.

Recent Research

The 2010 U.S. Census found 5.2 million people reporting American Indian and Alaska Native as a component of their "race" (1.7 percent of the total U.S. population of 308.7 million). Of this number, 2.9 million said they were American Indian and Alaska Native (AI/AN) alone. "The American Indian and Alaska Native in combination population experienced rapid growth, increasing by 39 percent since 2000" (Norris, Vines, and Hoeffel 2012, 1–5). This rate is almost twice as fast as the U.S. population generally and continues the trend noted in the previous census. (The AI/AN population had previously increased by 26 percent between 1990 and 2000.)

"In the 2010 census, 41 percent of the American Indian and Alaska Native alone-or-in-combination population lived in the west," with California and Oklahoma having the largest number who identified as American Indian and Alaska Native (Norris, Vines, and Hoeffel 2012, 5–6). New York City with 112,000 had the largest population of American Indian and Alaska Native alone or-in-combination, followed by Los Angeles with 54,000. Among cities with 100,000 or more population, Anchorage, Alaska, had the greatest proportion of AI/AN (12 percent), followed by Tulsa, OK (9 percent), Norman, OK (8 percent), and Billings, MT (6 percent) (Norris, Vines, and Hoeffel 2012, 11). Seventy-eight percent of the AI/AN population live outside of the traditional American Indian and Alaska Native areas. This continues the trend noted in the 2000 U.S. Census, which found 66 percent of the AI/AN population living in urban areas. Yet, most off-reservation AI/AN continue to maintain contact with their home reservations, *rancherias*, villages, and Native communities.

The 2006 Canadian census found 1,172,790 people identifying as "Aboriginal." This number is 3.8 percent of the total population of Canada and reflects a remarkable growth rate that is six times higher than the non-Native population (Dickason 2009, 451–52). Of this number, 54 percent reside in urban areas, with the largest concentration found in Winnepeg—

with an aboriginal population of 68,380 or 10 percent of that city's citizens. Other Canadian cities with high numbers of Native people are Vancouver, Saskatoon, Prince Albert, Edmonton, and Calgary. An estimated 40 percent still live on rural reserves. Weibel-Orlando (2008, 313) reports that Canadian government authorities deliberately made the reserves small and scattered them among White communities to encourage acculturation.

It is within this demographic context that studies by social scientists have taken place within the last few decades. A selection of some of these new studies were reprinted in an edited volume by Susan Lobo and Kurt Peters, *American Indians and the Urban Experience* (2001). It was the first major academic work devoted entirely to the study of urban Indians. Lobo, the volume's lead editor, contributed a key article in which the title frames the issue: "Is Urban a Person or a Place?" (2001, 73–84). The article is an ethnographic description of "urban Indian country" based on her experience as coordinator of the Community History Project at the Inter-tribal Friendship House in Oakland, California. Urban Indian characteristics, she found, include a proliferation of organizations, a community that is multigenerational and multitribal, one that has increased economic and class diversity, and which has a recognized urban history. Most important, unlike federally recognized tribal membership based on blood quantum for identity, urban Indian membership is more fluid, based instead on informal consensus. There are four criteria: ancestry, appearance, cultural knowledge, and community participation. Does one have Indian relatives and ancestors, and is one a functioning member of an Indian extended family? Does a person look Indian? Is the person knowledgeable of Indian cultural traditions and values? Does the person come out for urban Indian events and activities and contribute to the community's well-being? (Lobo 2001, 81)

A key finding in Lobo's research is that of the urban Indians' sense of community based on a network of relatedness. She argues that the contemporary urban Indian community "is not essentially a place, but rather it is characterized by relationships that bond people together and is therefore one of the ways that identity is established." It is "a widely scattered and frequently shifting network of relationships with locational nodes found in organizations and activity sites of special significance" (Lobo 2001, 71). Furthermore, "the federal government's image of a tribe as a bounded entity within a geographically rigid, demarcated territory or reservation, govern-

ment by a body of elected officials . . . is not transferred to urban Indian communities" (Lobo 2001, 77). The sense of community is a fluid one, with Indian people moving in and out of the city, making return visits to their rural home territories or reservations, or sometimes return there for good. The urban Indian community remains linked to Indian Country. Thus, the urban Indian is "a person and not a place."

Other contributions in *American Indians and the Urban Experience* flesh out the contemporary Indian urban experience. For example, Terry Straus and Debra Valentino (2001) discuss the "retribalization" of urban Indian communities by focusing on the historical experience of Indians in Chicago. They argue that "the rift between urban and reservation people is artificial and imposed. . . . Chicago has been a meeting ground for Indian people since before the fur trade. . . . 'Urban' is not a kind of Indian. It is a kind of experience. . . . There are urban areas on or closely bordering many reservation; there is a lot of movement between urban and reservation communities" (Straus and Valentino 2001, 86–87). The authors also point out that "Indian activism, from Alcatraz on, found its origins in the city and served to strengthen urban intertribal communities," but that despite their urban origins, Indian political activism soon became reservation centered (2001, 88). Thus what began as an urban Indian movement eventually returned to its reservation roots.

A year after the publication of this edited work, Lobo, joined by an urban Indian coordinating committee, brought out *Urban Voices: The Bay Area American Indian Community* (2002). This beautifully illustrated book presents the findings of the Community History Project of the Oakland Intertribal Friendship House. "In the 1950s, Native people from all over the United States moved to the San Francisco Bay Area as part of the Bureau of Indian Affairs Relocation Program. Oakland was a major destination of this program, and once there, Indian people arriving from rural and reservation areas had to adjust to urban living. They did it by creating a cooperative, multi-tribal community—not a geographical community, but rather a network of people linked by shared experiences and understandings" (Lobo 2002, book jacket). The Intertribal Friendship House became a sanctuary and gathering place for Indian people and their activities.

LaGrande (2002) has undertaken a definitive social history of urban Indian life in Chicago. His comprehensive research substantiates the findings of Straus and Valentino. LaGrande's study spans a thirty-year period (1945–75), during which time, Chicago's Indian population increased from roughly five hundred to ten thousand, and a new Indian identity was forged—a generalized Indian identity, or pan-Indianism. Among LaGrande's findings are the following: In late 1951, the BIA opened relocation offices Los Angeles, Denver, Salt Lake City, and Chicago. These were soon followed by offices in the San Francisco Bay area, St. Louis, Joliet, Waukegan, Cincinnati, Cleveland, and Dallas. "Initially, it [relocation] gave relocates to Chicago four cents a mile if they drove themselves or the cost of bus or train fare up to $50. After relocatees arrived in Chicago, the BIA provided $25 per week for heads of families and $10 for each additional family member for two weeks. Later the BIA increased the length of subsistence payments to three weeks and then four and also increased the amount given for subsistence. . . . The BIA would send some of the money to a relocatee's reservation before the move so a bus or train ticket could be purchased" (LaGrande 2002, 52–53).

"Chicago alone received almost five thousand relocatees and the greater Chicago area six thousand, accounting for about 20 percent of all relocatees during the eight year period" (LaGrande 2002, 75). The relocatees came from the Upper Midwest (the states of Michigan, Wisconsin, Minnesota), and the Northern Plains (North Dakota, South Dakota, Nebraska, and Montana). In terms of regions from a national perspective, New York City served as the relocation center for the East, Chicago for the Midwest, and Los Angeles and other California cities for the West. At first, Chicago was the most popular relocation site, but by 1954, Los Angeles had overtaken it, and a year later Greater Los Angeles was drawing half of all Indian relocatees.

Relocation saw the massive emigration from the reservations of young Indians to the designated cities, because the relocation program was officially designed for those between the ages of eighteen and thirty-five. This, of course, disrupted the traditional Indian extended family, which is made up of a network of multigenerational kin. In both housing and employment, Indian migrants to Chicago in the 1950s faced problems. Chicago neighborhoods were already occupied by other racial and ethnic groups, and there was a serious lack of housing following World War II. Indian relocatees moved from one area to another before "Uptown" became the primary location where they clustered by the end of the 1950s.

LaGrande reports that approximately 35 to 45 percent of relocatees to Chicago during the 1950s soon returned to the reservation. "Many Indian people who lived in Chicago from a few months to a few years never thought of the city as their true home.

Social, psychological, and spiritual ties to the reservation remained vital and strong. Nagging long-term feelings and tension were often replaced by a welcome sense of peace when Indian people returned to their reservations. Most who decided to leave Chicago, then, did so because of homesickness and loneliness. Single people tended to succumb slightly more often than families, yet no group was untouched" (LaGRande 2002, 131–32). Relocatees who stayed in Chicago made periodic trips back to their reservations. There was a Fourth of July exodus as early as late June, and also a return for the Christmas season. West coast relocation data found that members of the more traditional tribes, such as the Navajo and the southwestern Pueblos, also returned to their reservations for religious ceremonies. Nevertheless, the people who increasingly became known as urban Indians, both by themselves and by the reservation residents, were becoming a distinct group with their own experiences and struggles. This outcome became apparent with the rise of the Red Power Movement of the 1960s and 1970s, which emanated from the cities.

Another recent study is by Deborah Davis Jackson (2002), who studied the urban Indian community of an upper Great Lakes city that she calls "Riverton" (not its real name). The book's title, *Our Elders Lived It*, is a metaphor for the younger urban Anishinaabeg who define their Indian identity in terms of their elders. Riverton's economy is based on the automobile industry, and the ebb and flow of Indian immigration has varied accordingly. Approximately eighty percent of the county's Indian population is Aishinaabeg. The book provides an insight into urban Indian identity:. "The elder Anishinaabe had been raised in communities where the values, perspectives, social norms and habits that constitute the Indian way had been instilled within them, and the subtle features that characterized the Anishinaabe way of life in these rural communities were implanted in the children through constant daily interaction with community members of all ages" (Jackson 2002, 17–18). For the Aninishaabe families, identity is a matter of community. In this respect, Jackson's findings agree with Lobo's research for the San Francisco Bay area. On the other hand, Jackson found that some members in the Riverton Indian community were relative newcomers to an Indian identity. They traced their ancestry to tribes other than Anishinaabeg, and adopted the material trappings—long hair, dress, adornment, pow-wows and ceremonies, and the like—of a pan-Indian identity.

Another important study is the edited work by Krouse and Howard, *Keeping the Campfires Going* (2009), on the activist role of Native women in urban Indian communities in the United States and Canada. Six of the ten essays were reprinted from a 2003 issue of the *American Indian Quarterly*. In the introduction, the editors write: "Research on urban American and Canadian Indians began in the 1960s with a focus on assimilation and the assumption that urban Indians would blend into their urban surroundings. . . . Not until the 1990s did the focus begin to shift to the vibrant communities that Indian people had created in the cities. . . . [Furthermore] Native women have been instrumental in the shaping of identity and community in the city, in mobilizing resources to benefit their communities, and in fighting the poverty and discrimination that too often afflict Indian people" (Krouse and Howard 2009, ix–x).

Canada

Of special note is the fact that several essays in *Keeping the Campfires Going* deal with Indian women's urban roles in Canada. These include the article on Native women organizing in Thunder Bay, Ontario, by Nancy Janovicek; Native women in downtown Vancouver, BC, by Dara Culmane; and women's class strategies and activism in Toronto, by Heather A. Howard. The 1996 census of Canada found a population of almost eight hundred thousand First Nations (Indigenous) peoples—Indian, Inuit, and Métis—3 percent of the total national population. "Over half a million are legally recognized as Indians. In addition, the Inuit are estimated at 41,000, and the Métis slightly more than 210,000" (Talbot 2010, 36). The Indians, whose traditional lands lie in the southern part of Canada, are confined to reserves. Today "there are 2,293 separate reserves, encompassing a total area of 10,000 square miles. Less than 30 percent of the total Native population live off the reserves, mainly in the urban areas of Quebec, southern Ontario, southern Alberta, and the Vancouver area of British Columbia" (Talbot 2010, 37). "Until 1985, women lost their federal Indian status when they married non-status or non-Native men. These women were then forced to leave their home reserves, resulting in slightly larger numbers of women than men migrating from rural reserves to urban areas" (Krouse and Howard 2009, xiii).

The factors leading to Indian urbanism in Canada are somewhat different from those in the United States. Although there was no government-sponsored relocation program as in the United States, there has been the threat of termination. In 1969 the Canadian government released a White Paper on Indian policy that included a proposal to terminate the Indian Act, arguing that the elimination of special rights would foster Indian participation (i.e., acculturation) in Canadian society. In response, Indian leaders organized and successfully impeded the implementation of the proposed termination policy. "The defeat of the White Paper was a catalyst for the revival of Native activism in the 1970s, but Indian leaders' defense of the Indian Act curtailed Native women's efforts to protect their rights. The central goal of Native women organizing was the removal of Section 12(1)(b) from the Indian Act. Under [this section] a woman's status was determined by marriage, not by familial association or blood. Between 1958 and 1968, 4,605 women were removed from the Indian registry" (Janovicek 2009, 58–59).

The opening essay, "Urban Clan Mothers," in *Keeping the Campfires Going* is by Susan Lobo (2009), who underscores the major contributions by urban Native women. Lobo explains the key role of older, respected, and influential women in the urban Indian population of the San Francisco Bay area of fifty thousand. These women she calls "urban clan mothers." Although residence is dispersed in the city, there is a community network of the many organizations and activities in which urban Indians participate. It is the key households of older women that serve to link the community network of Indian activities. "These household gathering spots often provide short-term or extended housing and food for many people, health and healing practices and advice, a location for ceremony, emotional and spiritual support, entertainment, and transportation and communication resources. They are also vital spots of linkage with rural communities and tribal homelands. The women who head these key households and extend many services to community members are strong but low-profile activists" (Lobo 2009, 2). Lobo also points out that the clan mothers are active in leadership positions in local Indian organizations. Their homes serve as stopover points in the ebb and flow of Indian migrants on the move.

In summary, the essays in the Krouse and Howard volume document the important roles and activism of urban Indian women. This is the book's major contribution. It serves as counterpoint to the political activism of Indian men that is better known. Readers may be familiar with names like Dennis Banks (Ojibway), Russell Means (Lakota), Clyde and Vernon Bellecourt (Ojibway), and other leaders of the American Indian

Movement, but the activist narratives of Indian women are lesser known. Lanada Boyer Warjack (Bannock-Shoshonee) was a relocatee to the San Francisco Bay area before she became a leader of the 1969 Alcatraz occupation. Another relocatee and Alcatraz veteran was Madonna Thunderhawk (Lakota), who became a leader of the Black Hills Alliance, and Women of All Red Nations (WARN). Yet another woman leader from the Bay Area urban Indian community and Alcatraz was Wilma Mankiller, who later became the beloved chief of the Cherokee Nation, the largest of the 565 federally recognized Indian tribes of the United States. One must also include Winona LaDuke (Anishinaabeg), noted environmental activist and author, and twice the Green Party candidate for vice-president of the United States. The list goes on.

URBAN ENCLAVES

A unique feature of Indian urbanism in the United States has been the formation of uniquely Indian communities as enclaves within mainstream cities and metropolitan areas. Webster's New Collegiate dictionary defines an enclave as "a territorial or culturally distinct unit enclosed within a foreign territory." The aforementioned urban tradition volume by Lobo and Peters includes two examples of urban Indian enclaves. Octaviana Trujillo (2001, 49–68) discusses the Yaqui community of Guadalupe on the outskirts of Phoenix, Arizona , and Kurt Peters traces the history of Santa Fe Village in Richmond, California (2001, 117–26).

Guadalupe Village

This large urban Indian community was founded by Yaqui refugees from Sonora, Mexico, at the turn of the nineteenth century, and today occupies a one square mile area on the urban fringe of Phoenix, Arizona. In the introduction to her article, Trujillo (2001, 50) reminds us that "urban, socially interdependent communities, characterized by a high degree of cooperation and specialization, have been found historically throughout the Americas." The Yaquis, in fact, have a history of urban living since their contact with Jesuit missionaries in Mexico during the 1600s. Guadalupe Village, although not a product of ancient urbanism, is nevertheless a well-integrated community with a rich ceremonial life, Yaqui traditions, and institutions. At the same time it is trilingual and tricultural in character, having interacted with Mexicans and Mexican Americans as well as with Anglos for the many decades of its existence.

The traditional homeland of the Yaquis, or Yoeme (their own name for themselves), is in the southern part of the state of Sonora, Mexico. Yaqui preference for urban living can be traced to the influence of Spanish Jesuits, who persuaded them "to organize and settle in eight pueblos, similar to European towns, by having them build eight mission churches along the length of their country" (Trujillo 2001, 50). The eight mission communities were deemed sacred and eventually housed several thousand inhabitants instead of the few hundred living under their former *rancheria* settlement pattern. A new governmental system and realignment of family groups took place. There was also a blending of Christian and Yaqui religious beliefs, a phenomenon termed syncretism by social scientists. Yaqui governors and other officials administered the new towns, conferring with the Jesuit church officials.

Due to secular Spanish encroachment into their sacred towns, the period of peaceful change ended in 1740 when the Yaquis, joined by their Indian neighbors the Mayos, revolted. Although the Yaquis had welcomed the Spanish priests in the early 1600s, they fiercely resisted later attempts by Spanish secular authorities to regulate them. The revolt was eventually crushed and the Jesuits (whom the Yaquis had spared) were expelled by Spain from the New World. After Mexican independence from Spain in 1821, Mexican authorities attempted to tighten secular control over Yaqui country and seize their lands. For the remainder of the nineteenth century, the conflict between the Yaquis and the Mexican authorities escalated into a war that reached genocidal proportions. The Yaqui armies were defeated in 1887 and Mexico began a campaign to deport the people and destroy their culture, which led to the Yaqui diaspora. Many Yaquis were transported to the brutal henequen plantations of Yucatan and into virtual slavery. "There were still at least 15,000 Yaquis in the world, but they were nowhere in command of anything that they would have been willing to call their own local communities. Thousands of their families had been forced apart, so that they were living as individuals, or in broken parts of families in Mexican or in North American communities. They had become the most widely scattered Native people of North America" (Spicer 1980, 158). (See Figure 11.2.)

Yaqui refugees began crossing the border into the United States as early as the 1880s. "The major migration of the historical era came during the years 1900–1910. The Yaqui uprising of 1927 in Mexico led

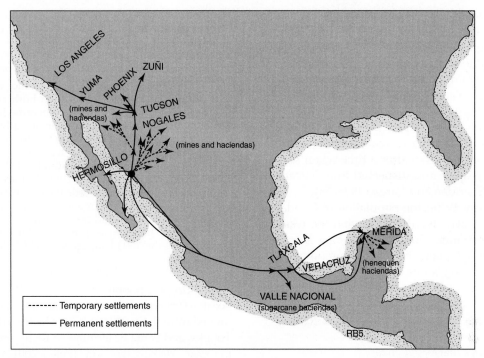

Figure 11.2 The Yaqui Diaspora.

to another wave of northerly migration. By the 1950s there were approximately four thousand in Arizona. For the most part, they were escaping deportation to Yucatan or seeking employment when conditions in Sonora had become extremely difficult" (Trujillo 2001, 54). At first, the Yaquis in Arizona owned no land and were forced to establish themselves "as squatters in barrios at the edge of cities or in work camps, neither assimilating into the dominant society nor returning to their homeland permanently" (Trujillo 2001, 54). Nevertheless, Yaqui urban settlements soon took root in Arizona—Barrio Libre and Pascua in Tucson, a Yaqui enclave in Marana twenty miles north of Tucson, and Guadalupe Village on the outskirts of Phoenix and Tempe.

The establishment of Guadalupe as a permanent residence began in 1910 when a Friar Lucas acquired forty acres for the Yaquis to build a permanent settlement on the edge of Phoenix. "The first settlement . . . was encouraged by the Salt River Valley Water Users Association in efforts to increase the labor supply for the large new agricultural enterprises being developed in the Salt River region" (Spicer 1980, 241). Today, Guadalupe is a mixed Yaqui-Mexican-American community, with the older generation speaking both Spanish and Yaqui, and the younger generation becoming facile in English. Yet, remarkably, after

many decades of experiencing the tremendous population dispersion and suffering caused by the diaspora, the Yaqui refugees who fled to Arizona have preserved their rich syncretic religion, cultural traditions, and a penchant for urban living.

The Yaqui religion is a mixture of ancient Yoeme beliefs and Spanish seventeenth century Christianity. Yaquis were fascinated with the story of Jesus as a healer. They adopted many seventeenth and eighteenth century Roman Catholic customs, including the elaborate public observances of Lent and Holy Week, but the celebrations also include many elements of ancient Yoeme traditions. Although they had been pushed out of their Mexico homeland, and the refugee population was required to adapt to new economic conditions in Arizona, their cultural traditions were never forgotten. "The sacred peaks marking the tribal boundary, the eight towns on their sacred locations, the hills and canyons and other places where mythical and legendary events took place—these became a part of the ritual language and were regularly referred to in sermons. The homeland continued to exist in the world of words and symbols" (Spicer 1980, 342).

Flowers pervade Yoeme culture. The Yaqui believe in an enchanted world called the Flower World, which is always filled with animals and beautiful flowers. People can visit this world by dreaming and singing special deer songs. The deer songs are the most ancient of Yoeme songs. During the Deer Dance, "little brother deer" leaves his home in the Flower World to visit in this world. Yaqui "rituals are the single most important expression of Yaqui Indigenous identity. Yaqui rituals are one of the ways in which the Yaquis have survived persecution and diaspora . . . and they helped Yoemen in the refugee communities of Arizona recreate a vital social and cultural life of their own after a time when families had been torn apart and dispersed from Yucatan to California" (Sheridan and Parezo 1996, 55).

By the early 1970s, the population of Guadalupe had reached nearly five thousand, and the residents voted to incorporate. Today, Guadalupe is a huge, vibrant—although poor—bilingual community, on the way to adding English as a third language. Over 60 percent are unemployed, and most residents live below the poverty level. Yet, the Yaqui (Yoeme) are what Edward Spicer terms "an enduring people" (1980).

Santa Fe Indian Village

Another selection in *American Indians and the Urban Experience* traces the history of Laguna Pueblo railroaders who founded an Indian enclave in Richmond, California. It became known as the Santa Fe Indian Village (Peters 2001).

In 1886, the Atlantic & Pacific Railroad received a federal grant to build a rail line along the thirty-fifth parallel from Albuquerque, New Mexico, to the Arizona-California border. When railroad construction was blocked by the location of Laguna Pueblo, which lay squarely in the railroad's path, an innovative accommodation was reached between the two parties. "They agreed that the railroad could pass through the Laguna territory unmolested, with one stipulation: the railroad would forever employ as many of the Lagunas to help build and maintain the system as wished to work, so long as the governor of the pueblo granted the workers his approval" (Peters 2001, 117). Every year thereafter, the Lagunas and the new purchaser of the railroad, the Atchison, Topeka, and the Santa Fe, met to reaffirm the terms of the agreement, which the Laguna people call "watering the flower."

Dozens of Laguna men, and often their wives, took employment with the railroad. True to its promise, the company provided housing for the Pueblo workers and their families next to towns through which the line ran—Gallup, N.M., Winslow, Ariz., and in California, Barstow, Riverside, and Richmond. The railroad set up rows of boxcars for housing, each modified with windows, bedrooms, a living area and a kitchen with a wood cookstove. Often two, and sometimes three, boxcars were joined together to make one home. In later years the boxcars provided water to the kitchen area, although even in the 1960s many did not have indoor plumbing; families shared a communal bathhouse. . . .

The boxcars became known as colonies of the Laguna Pueblo, and functioned as such both culturally and politically. Children born there became known as boxcar babies. They attended public or Catholic schools in nearby towns. . . . At schools in California and Arizona, Laguna children mingled with students of all races and backgrounds, becoming fluent in English and broadening their awareness of the world. With free train passes, boxcar families not only rode the rails between the colonies and the Pueblo, many traveled to places they almost certainly would not otherwise have seen in the era before highways—Los Angel[e]s, Albuquerque, and even the 1893 Chicago's World Fair. (Fauntleroy 2012, 46)

During the Shopmen's Strike of 1922, the Lagunas became strikebreakers when "more than a hundred men moved from the pueblo in New Mexico to the Atchison, Topeka, and Santa Fe terminal in Richmond, California, to replace striking workers" (Peters 2001, 118). After the strike ended, some of the Lagunas remained at the Richmond terminal, but others went home or to other railroad centers. To buttress the insufficient supply of Laguna railroad workers in Richmond, the Laguna Pueblo governor asked the nearby Acoma Pueblo for replacements, and so the Acoma workers became part of the growing Indian village in Richmond.

World War II saw a population boom in the Richmond community as many more Indians and non-Indians alike migrated to work in the Kaiser shipyards, the existing railroad shops, the Standard Oil refinery, and the Ford assembly plant. A similar pattern took place among the other railroad settlements of Indian workers at Gallup, Winslow, Barstow, and Los Angeles. Among the railroad labor pool were many Laguna women, who held skilled, blue-collar jobs.

Yet with all the outside influences, the powerful unifying forces of traditional Pueblo culture, ceremony, language and many age-old ways of life continued in the colonies. Keresan [language] continued to be spoken among adults and in families, at least through the first few decades of the 20th century. The feast days of St. Joseph, March 19th and September 19, were celebrated in the colonies as they were at home. Dances took place . . . [and] the Pueblo's unique tradition of "throw days" or "grab days" took place at the colonies as well. On days honoring certain saints, Laguna members named for those saints stand on rooftops and toss down gifts of food to neighbors, relatives and friends below. (Fauntleroy 2012, 46)

Boxcar women in the colonies baked bread in the traditional manner using outdoor ovens or *hornos.* Men hunted deer in groups as they had done in the Laguna Pueblo. Each colony had a formal governing structure in accord with the Laguna constitution. Keresan was the official language of colony meetings, and the leaders were required to report annually to the tribal council back home at Laguna Pueblo.

"The village at Richmond was . . . headed by an annually elected governor. Village men were thereafter required to attend meetings to vote on matters involving their home pueblo during which only their native language was spoken. . . . The village developed a reputation as a focal point for entertaining returning Native American military men passing through the San Francisco Bay Area" (Peters 2001, 119, 121). The village had an orchestra, and the railroad workers and their families actively participated in other Indian community events in the San Francisco Bay area, such as those of the Four Winds Club. One Laguna informant told ethnohistorian Kurt Peters: "'We had our own recreation hall [a converted boxcar] where our own Indian people put up dances that could not be seen by the white people. We were able,' she said, to maintain 'our own ways' in the train yards. . . . Lagunas relied on many rituals, including the annual 'watering the flower', in the maintenance of identity" (Peters 2001, 122).

The Santa Fe Village came to an end in the mid-1980s, although the reasons for its demise are not entirely clear. Apparently there had been some conflict between the Laguna founders and the Acoma newcomers. More likely, however, the breakup of the community was due to a complex of factors, including technological changes making railroad employment less labor intensive. A local newspaper reported: "Today the Santa Fe Indian Village has been torn apart [and] the last two families, one from the Acoma Pueblo and the other from the Laguna Pueblo, have moved" (quoted in Peters 2001, 123).

For many decades, the village had functioned as a satellite to the distant Laguna Pueblo in New Mexico. "They [the Indian railroad workers and their families] adapted themselves selectively to surrounding non-Native American functions, yet clung to tradition, returning often to their pueblos for nurturing celebrations and rituals" (Peters 2001, 124).

Piscataway Nation

Only fifteen miles south of Washington, DC, on the Potomac River in southeast Maryland, lies Moyaone, ancestral capital of the Piscataway Indians. The Piscataway are a tribal nation that is neither state nor federally recognized, and they have no formal reservation. Today, they are comprised of three groups: the Piscataway Indian Nation at Moyaone, the Piscataway-Conoy Indians, and the Cedarville Bank of Piscataway Indians, all based in southern Maryland. Piscataway means "where the waters blend."

At one time the Piscataway were the most populous and powerful Indigenous nation of the Chesapeake Bay region, and their origins date back ten thousand to eleven thousand years ago. Moyaone has been the capital of the Piscataway high chief for centuries. It was noted by the English when Captain John Smith arrived in 1608. According to historian James Rice (Lutz 2008): "From around 400 on, this was an urban place, with people living close to each other and working at specialized occupations. . . . It wasn't until 1650s and 1660s that European settlements on the river compared in size to the native towns they were replacing." The Piscataway numbered twelve thousand people and Moyaone was the main village and seat of their principal chief. Today, only a few hundred remain. Originally they occupied millions of aces which now make up the District of Columbia, much of Maryland and a good portion of Virginia, and they held a string of villages along the Potomac River. "The White House is built on the site of a Piscataway village and so is the U.S. capitol" (Willoughby 1983).

Today, a scattering of Piscataway families continue to live in their Chesapeake Bay homeland, but Moyaone is still revered by all Piscataway as the ancient seat of their people where the principal chief, the Tayac, resides. Tayac became a family name of the descendants. Billy Redwing Tayac is currently the traditional chief of the Piscataway Indian Nation. He is the son of Chief Turkey Tayac, who led the tribe through a cultural revitalization movement before his death in 1978. It was said that he was an encyclopedia of traditional knowledge. He "shared his knowledge of his native language with scholars, joined archaeologists studying the Moyaone settlement, and encouraged the preservation of the land as a National Park" (Lutz 2008). Chief Turkey's life is documented in a moving and informative video, "The Flickering Flame," produced by the Piscataway Indian Nation (1999).

Moyaone contains the sacred burial ground of the Piscataway people. The Piscataway ancestral remains are believed to be on a long journey to the spirit world. The ancestors intercede to help the living, so the unsanctified removal of the remains is considered to be an act of desecration. Thus the protection of Moyaone is paramount to Piscataway spirituality.

Desecration of sacred human remains is the issue addressed by the passage in 1990 of NAGPRA, the Native American Graves Protection and Restoration Act. Unfortunately, Moyaone is among the seventy-five percent of the Indigenous sacred sites in the United States that are no longer in possession of the Indian nations (LaDuke 2005, 14). It is estimated that over seven thousand of Piscataway ancestors have been dug up and removed from the sacred burial grounds. It is the most documented archaeological site east of the Mississippi River, and the only Native American religious site within a radius of five hundred miles of Washington, DC. It lies entirely within the Piscataway National Park, a 4,200-acre area which also contains the National Colonial Farm. Access to, and use of Moyaone is controlled by the National Park Service and the Accokeek Foundation, and not by the Piscataway Indian Nation. And yet, access to Moyaone has not always been as easy as it is today. In the 1960s and 1970s, during the Red Power Movement, local racism and government hysteria made access extremely difficult. It took an act of Congress to get Chief Turkey buried in the sacred burial ground. The Alice P. Furguson Foundation owned the sixty acres encompassing the Colonial Farm and Moyaone. The Foundation rigidly controlled access to Moyaone and did everything it could to keep the Indians out. Furthermore, White officials became unduly alarmed when Indian ceremonies were conducted at Moyaone.

Because the Piscataway lacked a reservation, Chief Turkey thought the best option to protect the twenty acres of Moyaone was to incorporate it into the national park system. There was an informal arrangement with the government, with the promise by then Secretary of the Interior Stuart Udall that Turkey could be buried there. But when the chief died in 1978 the Piscataway were told that no such agreement existed. It took almost a year of negotiation and finally an act of Congress before Chief Turkey's remains were interred at Moyaone. A sacred cedar tree today marks the grave site. Paradoxically, a National Park Service anthropologist told the 1985 annual meeting of the Society for Applied Anthropology in Reno, Nevada, that Mayaone became sacred only when a contemporary Indian elder was buried there. But this belies the fact that Mayaone has always been sacred ground. Piscataway Park, covering five thousand acres, was created primarily to preserve an unblemished view from Mount Vernon, George Washington's home, on the Potomac River. Ironically, Moyaone lies directly across the river from Mount Vernon.

At Moyaone, the Piscataway continue to observe the four natural cycles (seasons) of Mother Earth: summer, the Green Corn ceremony; fall, the Feast of the Dead; winter, the Midwinter festival; and spring, the Awakening of Mother Earth ceremony. Piscataway ceremonies are full of important symbols. The sacred red cedar tree with its tobacco ties carries the spirit of

Piscataway Chief Billy Tayac and his son Mark.

Chief Turkey Tayac, who is buried at Mayaone. "The spirit posts, which mark the four directions, protect the cedar tree and the people who are buried under it. The fire sends our prayers to the ancestors and to the Creator. Part of celebrating the Awakening of Mother Earth is celebrating springtime and new life, and sometimes there are special naming ceremonies for babies" (Tayac 2002, 34).

In 1999, at the groundbreaking ceremony of the National Museum of the American Indian, Piscataway Chief Billy Tayac, with his son, Mark, offered tobacco and sang traditional songs to bless the site of the new facility. Hundreds of Native peoples from North and South America attended the gathering of dignitaries on the National Mall to celebrate that historic day.

In her book about a Piscataway Indian boy, Gabrielle Tayac, historian at the Smithsonian's National Museum of the American Indian, reports: "Today our tribe is allowed to use Moyaone for ceremonies, but when we drive onto the property we have to be escorted by national park rangers. It seems strange that my people are restricted on the land that we have lived on for thousands of years. But I'm glad we can at least still go to Moyaone. Many places that are sacred to other American Indian tribes are not always as well protected or can't be used at all anymore" (Tayac 2002, 28).

POLITICAL ACTIVISM, ALCATRAZ, AND BEYOND

We end our discussion of urban Indians by taking note of the political activism by urban Indians that took place in the 1960s and 1970s in what became known as the New Indian or Red Power Movement. The activism was in response to Indigenous oppression and took the form of promoting Native treaty rights and the revival of traditional culture. In California it grew out of Indian student-led strikes and demonstrations on San Francisco Bay area university campuses in support of the fledgling Native American Studies programs. It was also a reaction by young Indian relocatees to the U.S. government's programs of acculturation as promulgated in its termination and relocation policies. The political activism was marked especially by its many land occupations, starting with the Indian occupation of Alcatraz Island on November 20, 1969, led by Native students from San Francisco State University, the University of California, Berkeley, and the University of California, Los Angeles.

The Indian Occupation of Alcatraz

"We are Indians of All Tribes—We hold the Rock!" The occupation on Alcatraz Island in San Francisco Bay began on the night of November 9, 1969, when fourteen Indians and Eskimo university students secretly landed on the former prison island. They were forced by U.S. Marshals to leave the following day but vowed they would return, next time to build an independent community. Their act crystallized support because Native American people in the United States nurse many grievances stemming from their status as oppressed Indigenous non-white, mini-nationalities. Native Americans viewed the landing as symbolic of a spiritual rebirth and as a first step towards rebuilding the land base, a persistent theme since the original invasion by European Powers and the expansion of the Yankee Republic across Redman's America.

In the second landing, which took place on November 20, the liberation group comprised more than 80 men, women, and children. This time they had come to stay. For nineteen months they resisted all government attempts to dislodge them, including threats, hunger, cold, loss of jobs or college status, and federal "deals," before they were finally overwhelmed and evicted. During this time the island's population averaged 100 residents, representing fifty tribes and including Indians and Eskimos from Alaska, Canada, and North America. More than 12,000 supporters, Indian and non-Indian, visited "the free land of Alcatraz," as the protestors called their community, and demonstrated their solidarity by contributing money, food, supplies, and labor, The range of supporters included both individuals and organized groups, from ordinary citizens to movie stars, from Indian community organizations to ecology groups and trade unions (Talbot 1978, 83)

In the November occupation, a coalition was formed that included California Indians, along with the more numerous representatives of out-of-state tribes (see Castillo 1997, 121–22). They were joined by non-student Indian adults, including families. One of the many innovations instrumented by the Indians of All Tribes governing council was an Indian-run school for the island's children, a school with voluntary teachers who emphasized the children's Indian cultural heritage in addition to the "three Rs." Also, the occupation group was soon visited by traditional Indian elders who gave spiritual support and advice. Radio Free Alcatraz began broadcasting from the island, educating tens of thousands of its listeners in the San Francisco Bay Area with its messages on Indian history, culture, and the Indian political agenda. The island residents also published a newsletter, and there was a literary explosion of writing, poetry, and art.

Alcatraz

As lightning strikes the Golden Gate
and fire dances the city's streets,
a Navajo child whimpers the tide's pull
and Sioux and Cheyenne dance lowly on the ground.

Tomorrow is breathing my shadow's heart
and a tribe is an island, and a tribe is an island
and silhouettes are the Katchina dancers
of my beautiful people

Heart and heaven and spirit
written in a drum's life cycle
and a tribe is an island forever,
forever we have been an island.

As we sleep our dreaming in eagles,
a tribe is an island
and a tribe is a people—
in the eternity of Coyote's Mountain.

—blue cloud

Island Administration

Three months after the November occupation, the student protestors, who had incorporated as Indians of All Tribes with a seven-member governing council, submitted a $300,000 planning grant proposal for Alcatraz in which they voiced their resistance to the U.S. government's programs of acculturation and assimilation:

> One of the reasons we took Alcatraz was because the students were having problems in the universities and colleges they were attending. This was the first time that Indian people had ever had the chance to get into a university or college because relocation was all vocation oriented. . . . We all realized that we didn't want to go through the university machinery coming out white-oriented like the few Indian people before us, or like the non-Indian people who were running our government, our Indian government, or our Indian affairs. . . . We didn't want to melt with the melting pot, which was the object of federal relocation programs. We wanted to remain Indians. That's why Native American studies became a prime issue . . . why we wanted our own Indian university. (Indians of All Tribes 1970, 4–5)

The grant proposal also explained another key objective of the Indians of All Tribes, to help their people back home in Indian Country: "We were also concerned about . . . what was happening on the reservations as well, because while we were physically away, we still had our own families and people in our hearts and on our minds, the problems they were facing . . . because we were trying to get the necessary tools so we could return to our reservations some day. . . . In the meantime . . . we needed a place to get together in the city so that we didn't become victims of assimilation" (Indians of All Tribes 1970, 5–6).

In addition, an all-Indian support organization was established, the Bay Area Native American Council (BANAC). BANAC provided a voice for the approximately forty thousand Indian adults and their families of the San Francisco Bay Area, those who could neither quit their jobs nor neglect family responsibilities to join the largely student occupiers on an unheated island during wintertime, but who could still provide needed logistical, political, and spiritual support.

The Alcatraz occupiers elected seven representatives to serve on the island council. They were in charge of three areas: (1) service, in the nursery, school, medical clinic, general maintenance, kitchen, security, and the like; (2) planning, such as higher education and curriculum development, a cultural complex with a museum and archives, ecology center, Indian legal rights, and vocational education; and (3) administration and community organizing, which included an advisory board, contact with reservations, public relations, and finances. But as time wore on without the negotiations with the government being resolved, dissentions appeared within the island's leadership. One internal controversy concerned drugs and alcohol, and the presence of a handful of Indian street people who had taken up residence on the island. But the attitude of the island's administration was that it was better for them to be on Alcatraz with their brothers and sisters than on the streets of San Francisco, left at the mercy of the police and the elements.

Historical Context

Alcatraz was a federal prison until closed by Attorney General Robert Kennedy in 1963 as too costly, inefficient, and inhumane. In mid-nineteenth century, Anglo-Americans converted the island into a fort after successfully seizing California from Mexico. Alcatraz became a disciplinary barracks and then a military prison. In the early 1870s, the Paiute leader, Winnemucca, was imprisoned for spreading the Wovoka doctrine among his people. Wovoca taught religious resistance to Euro-American conquest. It was the origin of the Ghost Dance among the Plains tribes. Alcatraz later held Philippine war deserters and conscientious objectors during both world wars.

In 1940, an elderly Tohono O'Oham chief was imprisoned for failure to comply with the Selective Service Act and allow the young men of his village to register for the draft. The chief and his people did not speak English and believed their village to be a part of Mexico. He died shortly after release from prison at the war's end. Imprisonment had hastened his death.

In March of 1964, a handful of Sioux Indians from the San Francisco Bay Area briefly occupied the island. They sought to establish a land claim under the terms of an old treaty entitling Sioux Indians to federal lands that are declared surplus by the U.S. government. Although their claim was rejected by the government and they were removed from the island, knowledge of the 1964 invasion provided inspiration to the Indian student liberators five years later. Interestingly, one of the 1964 Indian participants was Russell Means (Oglala Lakota), who later became a major figure in the American Indian Movement (AIM).

Since 1963, Alcatraz had stood vacant, the paint peeling from its damp walls and the steel guard towers rusting, a grim monument of man's inhumanity to man. The government offered it to the City of San Francisco, which began dickering with billionaire financiers to submit plans for development. A Texas oilman, Lamar Hunt, proposed a futuristic space monument and commercial exploitation of the island. The public, however, was sickened by the profit-motivated and tasteless development plans. When the Indians took matters into their own hands and reclaimed Alcatraz, putting forth their own humane proposals, the public response was generally enthusiastic. "Who needs an Astrodome in San Francisco Bay?" sang songwriter Malvina Reynolds in her ballad for Alcatraz.

Negotiations by the government with the island's Indian leaders during the nineteen-month occupation were intense and drawn out. A variety of federal agencies was involved, but principally representatives from the General Service Administration and the National Council of Indian Opportunity. President Richard Nixon's aides for minority affairs were early negotiators. Nixon, who intended to have a favorable Indian policy during his tenure, wanted to keep negotiations peaceful, although the U.S. Coast Guard maintained a blockade of the island throughout the occupation. The Nixon administration wanted to avoid another Kent State tragedy where protesting students were shot down by the National Guard. At one point, government authorities proposed making Alcatraz a federal park with an emphasis on Indian culture. In response, hundreds of Indians flocked to the island to challenge the Interior Department's intention to turn Alcatraz into a national park. Government negotiators, in turn, rejected the Indians' $300,000 planning grant proposal. Six months into the occupation, the Nixon administration began to take a tougher stance: the

"feds" cut off telephone service, electricity, and water supplies to the island (Garvey and Johnson 1997, 166). By August 1970, the government was considering a secret plan to take the island by force, if need be, code-named Operation Park. The Indians remaining on the island expected as much.

Meanwhile, the militant example of the Indian Alcatraz occupation spread throughout the country, and other land occupations soon followed. In November of 1970, scores of Indians and Chicano activists liberated an old Army communications Center near Davis, California, and founded an Indian and Chicano education center, D-Q University. Brief occupations also took place in 1970–71 "at Fort Lawton and Fort Lewis in Washington, at Ellis Island in New York, at the Twin Cities Naval Air Station in Minneapolis, at former Nike Missile sites on Lake Michigan near Chicago and at Argonne, Illinois, and at an abandoned Coast Guard lifeboat station in Milwaukee" (Johnson, Champagne, and Nagel 1997, 32). More important, however, was the founding of the American Indian Movement (AIM) in 1968 as an urban Indian rights group in Minneapolis, Minnesota, and its subsequent development into a nationwide Indian protest organization. It is of interest to note that Dennis Banks, founder of AIM, visited Alcatraz during the 1969–70 occupation. Major all-Indian protest actions included the 1972 Trail of Broken Treaties Caravan to Washington, DC, with its Twenty Points Indian manifesto, and subsequent takeover of the Bureau of Indian Affairs, the seventy-four-day occupation of Wounded Knee on the Pine Ridge Reservation in 1973, and the coast-to-coast Longest Walk in 1978 to protest anti-Indian legislation being considered in Congress.

The Crucible of Activism

The West Coast generally, and the San Francisco Bay Area in particular, was a hotbed of protests in the 1960s and early 1970s, and this provided the wider context for the Alcatraz occupation. The cultural revolution was in full swing, with San Francisco becoming the de facto hippie capital of the United States. Cesar Chavez led the United Farm Workers' grape boycott in California's valleys, and chapters of La Raza and SNCC (Student Nonviolent Coordinating Committee) were active on college campuses. The national headquarters of the Black Panther Party were in Oakland, California. The anti-Viet Nam movement was in full swing, with huge marches reaching from the San Francisco Embarcadero all the way to Golden Gate Park. The Reverend Dr. Martin

Luther King Jr. spoke at a large rally at the Oakland Coliseum. University student activism was intense at both Berkeley and San Francisco State universities. The Berkeley students launched their Free Speech movement when the university administration sought to curtail student political activity. Finally, in the fall of 1968, both campuses erupted with boycotts of classes and demonstrations in support of creating ethnic studies programs. At San Francisco State, the Third World Liberation Front called a strike with a list of demands, including the formation of a School of Ethnic Studies. The counterpart Third World Strike at Berkeley led directly to the creation of a Department of Ethnic Studies, encompassing Asian, Chicano, and Native American studies, and today offers a doctoral program. But the activism at the time was not without widespread arrests and beatings of student demonstrators on campus by police.

In truth, Native Americans have a long history of struggle that includes cultural revitalization movements. In the eighteenth and nineteenth centuries, these movements were mainly religious in character. (See Talbot 2001, 718–33.) The 1880s Ghost Dance movement is an obvious example (discussed in Chapter 4). In the twentieth century, Indian activism has most often been secular, but with an emphasis on preserving Native spiritual traditions and values, as well as presenting Indigenous grievances and interests. The founding of the National Indian Youth Council in Chicago in 1960, and the Survival of American Indians Association in Washington State in the 1960s to preserve Indian fishing rights, are noteworthy examples. A comprehensive overview of American Indian activism during this period is the edited work by Troy Johnson, Duane Champagne, and Joane Nagel, *American Indian Activism: Alcatraz to the Longest Walk*. In an introductory overview chapter (Johnson, Champagne, and Nagel 1997, 9–44) the editors provide a comprehensive survey of "organization and protest in the urban environment."

Some of the events that directly contributed to Indian student militancy on the Berkeley university campus preceding the Alcatraz occupation, for example, were the books they were reading. Harold Cardinal's *The Unjust Society* (1969) appeared in Canada, and Vine Deloria's *Custer Died For Your Sins* (1969) became a best seller in the United States. A third work, *Our Brother's Keeper* (1969), an exposé of U.S. Indian policy by Edgar Cahn, came out in the same year. There was also the visit by the traditional Iroquois traveling college, the White Roots of Peace, to the Bay Area college campuses. The students were also moved by the film, *You Are on Indian Land* (National Film Board 1969), a documentary of the Cornwall Bridge blockade by Mohawks at the international border between Canada and the United States in support of their Jay Treaty. The main student leader of the Alcatraz occupation, Richard Oakes, was a Mohawk Indian.

Many of the Indian students had come to the San Francisco Bay Area on the government's relocation program. This was the case for another student leader, LaNada Boyer (Bannock-Shoshone), formerly LaNada Means. She was the "first Native American student to be accepted at U.C. Berkeley through special admissions of the Economic Opportunity Program" (Boyer 1997, 89). Some students were members of California Indian tribes, and a few were war veterans. In "Reflections of Alcatraz," Boyer recounts how she left her reservation at Ft. Hall to go on the government's relocation program. She writes: "We were not aware that the federal government's plan to 'drop us off' in the cities was another insidious method of depriving us of our reservation lands and membership in our own tribes. Some of us knew that non-Indians were exerting intense political pressures to gain more of our lands for their economic benefit" (Boyer 1997, 88).

A major objective of the student protestors for Alcatraz was to establish a center on ecology, including "a place for our spiritual leaders and our medicine men to come. . . . We also plan to have our own library and archives to help us document the wrongs which have been done in this country and the wisdom that has been lost. Also . . . a place where we can practice our own dances and songs and music and drums, where we can teach our children" (Indians of All Tribes 1970, 8–9).

End of the Alcatraz Occupation

Despite the earnest proposals presented by the Indian occupiers, negotiations with the government went nowhere. "After a year and a half the government's cautious response had worked. The occupation had begun to run its course. . . . The approaching election of 1972 set the stage for the government to seriously consider the removal option" (Garvey and Johnson 1997, 179). Despite the promise by the government representatives not to attempt a removal while negotiations were in progress, the U.S. Marshal Service, armed with handguns, M-130 carbines, and shotguns, was mobilized on June 11, 1971. Other law enforcement personnel were also put on standby notice, and the removal began. "Three hours after the White House gave authority to remove the Indians from Alcatraz, the islanders, who were enjoying 'a beautiful sun baked afternoon,' were surprised by three Coast Guard vessels, a helicopter, and about twenty to thirty armed U.S. Marshals. The federal action met with no resistance and took less than thirty minutes. The fifteen Indians were frisked, and the six men, four women, and five children were put in protective custody. The press was not notified or allowed on Alcatraz during the removal" (Garvey and Johnson 1997, 176–77).

The Indian occupation of Alcatraz was over, but the legacy of political activism was not. The Red Power Movement had begun in the cities, but it then spread to the reservations, Native villages and communities from Alaska to the Lower Forty-eight. This is exemplified principally by the seventy-one-day occupation of Wounded Knee on the Pine Ridge Reservation in 1973 (discussed in Chapter 4). Most important, the return of the urban militants to Indian Country resulted in a vital new component to the movement, a spiritual rebirth under the tutelage of the traditional elders and medicine men, and a revitalization of Indian culture and spirituality throughout Redman's America.

ANALYSIS AND CONCLUSIONS

Ancient Urbanism

Ancient urbanism is closely associated with the American food revolution, the domestication and cultivation of plants, especially maize, and irrigation. At least half or more of the world's foods were developed by the Indigenous peoples of the Americas. Maize was domesticated in Mexico by about 5000 BC and spread into the North American southwest by 2000–1500 BC. This ancient development formed the economic basis for the development of huge urban complexes in the Americas, a second Neolithic revolution equal to, if not surpassing that which occurred in the Fertile Crescent region of the Old World. The American Neolithic occurred in two different places: along the Andean coast of South America culminating in the Inca civilization (beyond the scope of this book), and in Central America, principally with the Maya and Aztec civilizations.

Ancient American urbanism in Mesoamerica is also distinguished by *ceremonialism*, with a combination of kinship and political stratification based on rank. The ancient urban complexes were principally the residence of priests and a kinship-based military elite organized at the tributary mode of production. The Spanish conquest of this region resulted in an unusual phenomenon whereby the modern Latin American states acknowledge the magnificent accomplishments of these early civilizations, yet the contemporary Ladino (mixed race) population, although Indigenous by blood, have become an Hispanicized people. This anomaly is especially noted in Mexico.

Today, there are as many as ten million Indians living in Mexico who retain their native languages and identities, and the ancient Indigenous heritage with its impressive monumental ruins is celebrated at the national level. Yet the Mexican government's policy for its contemporary Indian population has been one of "national integration" (acculturation). Unlike the United States and Canada, Mexico attempted to break from the genocidal Indian policy of its colonial past. But "having achieved independence from Spain in 1820, Mexico formulated provisions designed to accelerate the integration of Indian people into the mainstream of Mexican society" (Edmunds 2010, 42).

The term *Mestizo* refers to the cultural fusion or blending of the Spanish and Indian into a sociocultural amalgam that is present-day Mexico. Yet more than one million Mexicans still speak *Nahuatl*, the old Aztec language. The concept of *mestizaje* and its associated concept, *Indigenismo*, was promoted by Lazaro Cardenas, the reputed Mexican champion of Indian rights. Paradoxically, Cardenas saw *Indigenismo* as a means for assimilating Indians into the body politic of Mexico. But *Indigenismo* and its ethos of *mestizaje* became a means of reducing the political power of the Native peoples and nations of Mexico, even denying their Indigenous existence altogether. Alexander Ewen (2001) has coined the term, *Indianismo* as a counterpart to *Indigenismo*. *Indianismo* is defined by Ewen as "the Indian way." It supports Indian identity and the struggle for Indigenous rights, as exemplified by the Zapatista Maya Indian rebellion that began in January of 1994.

Ironically, Indigenous oppression is again underway today as seen by the illegal immigration problem from Mexico, because the so-called Mexican refugees are, in fact, Indian by blood. The Mexican Indian underclass is being driven off their lands due to Mexico's integration policy, and by the economic distress caused by the North American Free Trade Agreement (NAFTA). In addition, the Mestizo and Indian underclass is caught in a deadly war of competing drug cartels versus the government's armed forces.

Contemporary Urbanism

Another kind of urbanization examined is the *contemporary* kind described in this chapter for the United States, mainly as a result of the government's programs of reservation termination and relocation in the 1950s and 1960s that sought to empty Indian reservations of their populations and drive tens of thousands of Native peoples into the cities. It was a policy of forced acculturation on a grand scale, a sociocultural ethnic cleansing, even surpassing the earlier policies of suppressing Indian culture and identity through the institution of the federal Indian boarding school. The objective of the boarding school was to make Indians into brown-skinned Whites, so to speak. Indian students, many as young as six years old, were harshly punished for speaking "Indian," forced to attend Christian religious services and submit to a regime of military discipline.

In introducing analytical concepts at the beginning of this chapter, we referred to Weaver's three kinds of Native *identity*—self, community, and external. Weaver contends that "identity is the combination of self-identification and the perception of others" (Weaver 2010, 30). Moreover, "Indigenous identity is connected to a sense of peoplehood inseparably linked to sacred traditions, traditional homelands, and a shared history as Indigenous peoples" (Weaver 2010, 31). Indigenous identity is therefore multifaceted, but residence, whether in the city or on the reservation, is not the deciding factor. Identity is not location or geography, but instead it is shaped by ancestry, by kin and community ties, and by knowledge of and participation in Indian culture. As Susan Lobo (2001) contends, an urban Indian is a person, not a place.

In the United States, the ability by Indigenous peoples—Indians, Alaska Natives, and Hawaiian Natives—to define their own membership (identity) is made difficult by law and policy. With respect to the Indian category, there is no single legal external definition of who is a Native person. "Each government (tribal, state, and government) determines who is an Indian for purposes of that government's law and programs" (Pevar 2004, 8). Federally recognized tribes have the power to define their own membership, but there are two problems. First, Indian iden-

tity is determined in terms of a pseudoracial definition, i.e., the blood quantum device. Usually a person has to be at least one-fourth Indian, or "quarter blood," in order to be tribally enrolled in a federally recognized Indian tribe—for example, have a "full-blooded" grandparent, or a parent who is "half-blooded." Blood quantum, however, ignores cultural affinity as the essential aspect of identity, i.e., the self and community aspects of Indian identity as defined by Hilary Weaver (2010) and discussed by Susan Lobo (2001) for urban Indians earlier in this chapter.

A second problem is the fact that not all Indian tribes are federally recognized. Since 1978, nearly 250 tribes have petitioned the Bureau of Indian Affairs for federal acknowledgement, but few have been approved (Pevar 2004, 310). During the termination era of Indian affairs federal recognition was withdrawn from 109 tribes and bands, including 38 California *rancherias* and numerous bands in coastal Oregon, their legal and sociocultural rights as Indigenous persons summarily abolished. In the United States, the legally recognized definitions of who is an Indian, Indian tribe, and Indian country are neither clear nor entirely logical.

The situation in Canada, although different, is equally complex. The First Nations are divided into the pseudoracial categories of Indians, Inuit, and Métis, with the former further subdivided into status, nonstatus, and treaty Indians (see Talbot 2010, 36–41). Thus, Indigenous identity is imposed on First Nation peoples by government colonial policy rather than by the Native peoples themselves.

The term *acculturation* is often used interchangeably with *assimilation*, although conceptually speaking they have different although related meanings. Acculturation refers to adopting mainstream Anglo-American culture, while assimilation refers to integration into the social institutions and economic fabric of U.S. society. In her study of Upper Great Lakes Indian urbanism, Jackson (2002, 74–75) explains the two concepts in the following way: "The term 'assimilation' is usually used to mean the loss by an individual, of the markers that serve to distinguish him or her as a member of one social group, and the acquisition of traits that allow that person to blend in with, and succeed in, a different social group. . . . The term is virtually always used to refer to members of a minority group, or a colonized people, becoming absorbed in the majority, or dominant, society." Acculturation and assimilation obviously have implications for Indigenous identity.

In the European immigrant experience, assimilation typically took place in three generations. The first generation enters the country as an exploitable, immigrant workforce. By the second generation, the group's members have learned English and acquired the basic skills needed for a blue-collar workforce. The third generation acquires further education to enter white-collar professions and, most important, intermarries outside the original ethnic group. The ethnic language is gone and the third generation becomes monolingual in English. The final outcome is the loss or dilution of one's original national identity and culture.

Clearly, this has not been the experience of Native peoples of the United States and Canada. In the first place, they are not emigrating from a foreign country; they are instead the First Nations of the Americas. True, there have been significant inroads into the number of Native language speakers in some tribes, but after several centuries of Euro-American attempts to stamp out Indigenous cultures, it is remarkable how many Native speakers remain. In fact, since the rise of the new Indian movement of the 1960s and 1970s, Indian country has seen a rebirth of Indigenous language programs in colleges and universities.

For many urban Indians, facility in a Native language is not an option for maintaining an Indigenous identity. Nevertheless, a binding tie to kin and tribal communities continues to persist among urban Indians. For many there also remains a strong connection to one's sacred homeland, sizeable areas of the United States, which Native peoples still retain as tribal reservations, California *rancherias*, Native Hawaiian "crown and government lands," and Alaska Native villages.

Assimilation for Native Americans, as with other people of color, is often blocked by racism. Jackson reports that Anishinaabe people in Riverton, no matter how acculturated they are, still face racism. "Becoming assimilated in outer appearance through clothing and manner, language and religion, was not enough—the bottom line remained that 'once an Indian, always an Indian'" (Jackson 2002, 79). Even those relocatees who had come to embrace an identity as labor union industrial workers were blocked from fully assimilating because of their non-White appearance. The important point here is that although acculturation made inroads into an earlier generation of Indian adults who had been socialized in the Indian boarding school system (the parents of the young urban activists of the 1960s), they still found themselves blocked from fully assimilating into the White urban population due to a system of racial and ethnic segmentation. In California in the 1960s, for example, Native Americans had the lowest ranking of any population segment in terms of income level, and were relegated to living in mixed-race, low-income neighborhoods. California's antimiscegenation law prohibiting interracial marriage was not overturned until 1948, when the state's Supreme Court ruled such laws unconstitutional.

The 1960s and 1970s Red Power Indians rejected the false premise of the U.S. government's acculturation and assimilation policies and turned, instead, to their grandparents' generation with whom to identify as Indians. It was this older generation that in many cases still retained the language, spiritual knowledge, and customs of traditional Indian society—the essence of what it means to be an Indigenous person.

"In the 1960s a new type of Indian had emerged in cities such as Chicago. . . . Sometimes called 'pan-tribal' or 'pan Indian' or 'ethnic', this identity began to partially replace traditional, strictly tribal, identities" (LaGrande 2002, 161–62). The epitome of *pan-Indianism* in Chicago, as in other target cities, was the pow-wow. The pow-wow itself was the hallmark of a pan-Plains culture, which had its origin in the Indian cultural mix of an earlier boarding school era. "Although a pan-Indian spirit grew among Native Americans in Chicago during the early 1960s, its intensity varied by tribe" (LaGrande 2002, 166). The Chippewas in Chicago tended to retain ties with their home communities and reservations, and the Navajos also were initially reluctant to become fully involved in pan-Indian activities.

In his autobiography, AIM activist Russell Means (1995) criticized the pan-Plains changes that have been made to the traditional Lakota *wacipi* (pow-wow). Although Means himself is a product of urban Indian life, he nonetheless values traditional culture. He describes how in the old days entire clans would turn out for the *wacipi*, and the community as a whole worked hard year round to make it happen. "It was our cotillion ball, our block party—the year's major social event where people did their socializing and made their connections. In the early 1960s when I was a boy, old men carried the U.S. flag around the dance circle. Our people had captured that flag in battle, so we were honoring the courage of our ancestors. Slowly that became perverted. Now, marching the U.S. flag around the circle is to honor military veterans and the U.S. government—to honor our oppressors!" (Means 1995, 116). He goes on to describe the changes that have been made to the drum, dance protocol, and other age-old customs. Means attributes the changes to "the influence of the urban-raised generation, part-time Indians who have taken up the so-called powwow. Ignorant of their traditions, they feel no responsibility to turn away people who aren't qualified to attend religious ceremonies, or to make sure that everyone dresses right, acts right, and is right" (Means 1995, 117).

The pan-Indian concept has some unusual ramifications. For example, in her case study of Aninishinabeg Indian relocatees to an industrial northern city, Jackson (2002, 5–6) recounts a schism that arose in the local Indian community organization between the Pow Wow Committee and other members of the local Indian Center. The Pow Wow Committee was headed by those claiming Indian ancestry, called "wanabees" by their detractors, who were adherents of a pan-Indian identity. On the other hand, those in opposition, although characterized by Jackson as "assimilated Indians," nevertheless were tribally enrolled in their respective tribes. In the heat of a verbal disagreement, the latter held up their enrollment cards to indicate their authenticity as "real Indians" (Jackson 2002).

A concept sometimes applied to explain the mid-twentieth century Indian migration to cities is *reurbanization*. The focus in this chapter on the urban migration to U.S. cities has been viewed as mainly the result of the federal government's termination and relocation programs. While true to a great extent, it is important to note that many tribes have followed a more limited migratory pattern to towns and cities even earlier in the twentieth century. LaGrande (2002) records an earlier influx of Indians moving to Chicago from their poverty-struck reservations, finding work in an industrially expanding city economy. The same phenomenon has occurred for southwestern tribes as well. In a section on economic integration in *Cycles of Conquest* (1962, 550–58), Edward Spicer documented some of the early migratory work patterns of Indians of southwestern United States and northern Mexico. Unable to rely on their pueblo subsistence base, plus an expanding population, the Hopis in the 1930s began taking jobs in railroad yards and small industries in local towns—even before the wartime industrial opportunities of World War II. "By 1950 a colony of several hundred grew up in Winslow, Arizona, the inhabitants of which were linked with families on the reservations and who maintained their social and ceremonial relations in the reservation villages" (Spicer 1962, 554). Earlier in

this chapter we documented the history of the Santa Fe Indian village of Richmond, California, which was settled by Laguna and Acoma Pueblo Indian railroad workers and their families.

The Western Apaches experienced a similar wage labor pattern that frequently took them off the reservations. As early as the 1920s, San Carlos Apache workers were hired in the construction of a railroad across their reservation. They then turned to ranching, road work, and the construction of Roosevelt Dam. They also labored in copper mines bordering the reservation, and as farm laborers for nearby Mormon-owned farms. With the onset of the 1930s Depression, Apache workers retreated to the reservation, where they found good pay in the New Deal Civilian Conservation Corps and the Public Works Administration's shovel-ready jobs, improving reservation infrastructure. Eventually, they developed their own cattle industry, which provided seasonal employment for a segment of the Apache workforce at home on the reservation.

The O'Odham (Pima and Papago) experienced a similar pattern of economic integration, putting them in close proximity to Southwest cities. A permanent colony of Tohono O'Odham miners lived and worked in the border town of Ajo, Arizona. Others had regular seasonal employment with cotton ranches and farms in the eastern part of the state.

The Dineh (Navajos) entered the Southwestern workforce later than the O'Odham or the Apaches. Construction of the Santa Fe Railroad, which ran through their reservation, did not begin until World War II. "The greatest volume of employment annually was with the railroads, which by 1950 employed sixty-five hundred of the eighty thousand Navajos. In addition, large numbers went to work seasonally in the beet fields of Colorado, in the carrot fields of Grants, New Mexico, and Phoenix, Arizona" (Spicer 1962, 556).

Eventually World War II not only resulted in thousands of Indian draftees entering the country's Armed Forces, but it also provided new, off-reservation employment in defense industries and Army bases as far away as California.

We have included in this chapter several examples of *contemporary urban enclaves*, but this is not to infer that the majority of urban Indians live in single clustered neighborhoods. They do not. Susan Lobo has repeatedly countered this erroneous belief in her research publications. "The assumption by some researchers that Indian people in cities must live clustered in urban neighborhoods, ghettos, or enclaves, and that this is synonymous with an Indian community, still continues to persist. . . . Urban Indian communities, because they are dispersed and based on a network of relations, for the most part, may be invisible or misunderstood from the outside and to outsiders, but they are anything but invisible to those who participate in them" (Lobo 2009, 4–5). The false assumption that Indians always live in their own, separate neighborhoods has led U.S. Census "number-crunchers" in their statistical projections to undercount urban Indians.

The U.S. government's termination and relocation programs resulted in a massive migration wave by Native Americans to U.S. cities in the 1950s and 1960s. Paradoxically, it also produced an upsurge in *Indian political activism*, the New Indian or Red Power Movement. The new activism emerged first in the urban Indian communities that had sprung up in the cities, and then returned to Indian Country to mount protests and land occupations. The emergence of the National Indian Youth Council in 1961, the birth of the American Indian Movement a few years later in the Twin Cities of Minnesota, the blockade by the Mohawks of Cornwall Bridge on the U.S.-Canadian border in support of their Jay Treaty, and the occupation of Alcatraz Island led by Indian students in 1969, spawned a new pan-Indian nationalism. In 1972, the Trail of Broken Treaties to Washington, DC, to protest anti-Indian legislation being considered in Congress was followed by the seventy-one-day occupation protest at Wounded Knee on the Pine Ridge Reservation in 1973 and the declaration of an independent Oglala Sioux Nation. This was followed by the Longest Walk in 1978, a spiritual pilgrimage from Alcatraz Island on the west coast to the nation's capital in Washington, DC.

An unexpected consequence of the New Indian Movement was a reverse migration by many activists back to Indian County, to learn (or relearn) Native languages, to engage in the ceremonial cycles, and to benefit from the wisdom of medicine men and tribal elders. At a time when many non-Indian Americans were deserting the rural areas of the United States and moving to the cities, demographers noted a move by many urban Indians back to the reservations and Indian Country.

THEORY

In the introduction to his Indian social history of Chicago, LaGrande (2002) lists four general theoretical schools in *contemporary* urban Indian research. The first group follows the metropolis-satellite model

that is embraced by quantitative anthropologist Joseph Jorgenson. In this paradigm, the metropolis, or world capitalist system, routinely exploits the labor, lands, and resources of Indigenous peoples the world over, including that of the American Indians. Thus, the socioeconomic pressures and government policies leading Native people to move to modern cities in a capitalist political economy are viewed as promoting an exploitative proletarianism. A fully developed thesis of this model as applied to Native American tribes by Jorgensen was published in the *Journal of Ethnic Studies* with the title of "A Century of Political Economic Effects on American Indian Society, 1880–1980." (Jorgensen 1978, 1–82).

Central to this theoretical approach is the concept of *proletarianization*, which has been proposed to explain the vicissitudes of federal Indian policy. Jackson (2002, 84) cites a 1993 article by Alice Littlefield, "Learning to Labor," in which she proposed that proletarianization is a better concept to explain the federal government's boarding school policy than assimilation. "It was rural labor, in particular, that U.S. government policy prepared American Indians for during the period from 1880 to 1930. . . . Federal Indian policy during the New Deal era shifted towards the revival of tribal economies, politics, and cultures that the BIA had earlier tried to destroy . . . the Indians were no longer needed as cheap labor . . . and therefore it was best to get them back onto the reservations where they would not be competing with other Americans for jobs" (quoted in Jackson 2002, 86). The federal government abandoned its New Deal policies designed to strengthen tribal economies when urban industrialization reached its peak in the 1950s. "It now set out to terminate those very tribes, while at the same time relocating individual American Indians to the cities, where job training programs took over the task of proletarianization to prepare their clients for factory work" (Jackson 2002, 86).

"A second group of scholars of the 1960s and 1970s resembled the first group but on a smaller scale. They considered urban Indians as anachronisms who invariably assimilated to the ways of white America. . . . A third group viewed urban Indians primarily through the organizations they formed in cities such as Chicago, Phoenix, and Los Angeles. For this group, urban Indians played an organizational role" (LaGrande 2002, 5). A fourth group of scholars, who studied Indian urbanism in the 1970s, found a stark contrast between traditional Indian life and contemporary industrial life or mainstream culture. Action anthropologist Sol Tax of the University of Chicago is an example of this theoretical school. Tax contrasted "Indians' sharing cultures with urban America's "large, economically oriented, individualized, impersonal, urbanizing society," two opposite ends of the folk-urban continuum (LaGrande 2002, 6).

Anthropological studies for the most part have viewed Indian urbanism as a result of the government's 1950s policies of termination and relocation. But LaGrande contends that the fourth approach fails to consider Indians on their own terms. Urban Indians are like "peaceful conscientious resisters" rather than mere foils to government termination and relocation (2002). Thousands of Indians have lived in cities such as Chicago for decades. We previously noted the existence of earlier migrant patterns for some tribes to cities bordering their reservations. Indeed, LaGrande (2002) documents an early Indian migrant stream to Chicago that was in response to reservation land alienation caused by the 1887 Indian Allotment Act, which exacerbated the lack of employment opportunities and extreme poverty found on reservations. Therefore, "a full understanding of Indian urbanization and migration to Chicago during the latter half of the twentieth century requires an examination of both Chicago and of Indian reservations before this time—especially those in the Upper Midwest and on the Northern Plains" (LaGrande 2002, 19). As recently as 1950, the average yearly Indian reservation wage was only $950, and tribes such as the Yankton Sioux in South Dakota earned an average of only $750 compared to Whites who earned $4,000. Chicago at that time had a far more diversified economy than other major cities and offered service sector job opportunities to Native workers that were better paying.

In short, we may conclude that Indian urban communities and city life is a complex phenomenon.

LAST WORDS

A milestone in Native rights was reached on September 13, 2007, when the United Nations General Assembly adopted the Declaration on the Rights of Indigenous Peoples, which had been slowly working its way through the U.N.'s institutional process for over a decade. "One hundred forty-three member states voted 'yes,' eleven abstained, and four voted against the declaration. Those voting 'no' included the United States, Canada, Australia, and New Zealand—nation-states containing millions of Indigenous peoples. Facing international pressure, the Canadian House of Commons later passed a resolution to endorse the declaration" (Lobo, Talbot, and Morris 2010, 460). Australia and New Zealand subsequently withdrew their opposition, with the United States being the last to reverse its position. President Barack Obama endorsed the Declaration for the United States on December 16, 2010. The Declaration marks the international recognition of the collective rights of the world's 370 million Indigenous peoples. The U.S. approval, however, gave only qualified support to the Declaration when it characterized the document's 46 articles as "aspirations" rather than as international law. "According to the U.S. State Department, the entire Declaration is 'not legally binding or a statement of current international law.' From the standpoint of the United States the Declaration . . . merely expresses 'aspirations'" (Steven Newcomb, quoted in Toensing 2011, 34).

It is important to note that nowhere in the document is the term "Indigenous Peoples" clearly defined, much less a Declaration article dealing with the issues faced by urban Indigenous populations. Nevertheless, implicit in the Declaration is the acknowledgement that unlike ethnic minorities, Indigenous peoples have the "right to self-determination," i.e., the legal right to determine their relationship to the national governments under which they live. As an opinion article in *Indian Country Today* (2010, 4) points out, "Indigenous rights existed prior to and outside the consensual agreements that establish democratic nation states. Indigenous communities are social and cultural formations that are alien to nation state institutions, and therefore need to be addressed on their own grounds and terms. The extension of civil rights, economic and political inclusion, are welcomed by Indigenous peoples, but they also want to retain their own ways of managing local social, cultural and political relations."

This important distinction in international law makes Native Americans fundamentally different from ethnics and U.S. racial minorities, such as African Americans and Latinos. "By this right, an Indigenous people can freely determine its own political status and pursue its economic, social, and cultural development while retaining, if it chooses to do so, the right to participate fully in the political, economic, social and cultural life of the larger nation-state" (Lobo, Talbot, and Morris 2010, 460.) Nation-states, such as Canada and the United

States, need to legally and politically recognize that Indigenous peoples, including urban Indian communities, are neither ethnic nor racial populations historically speaking; nor have they been consenting citizens of the nation states whose territories they have occupied since time immemorial.

CHAPTER REVIEW

DISCUSSION QUESTIONS

1. What were the four main centers of ancient urbanism and cultural development in North and Central America? What were some of their distinguishing features?
2. Who were the Aztecs? How did their social organization and culture contribute to their becoming an urbanized civilization.
3. Explain the government policies that account for the rapid increase of Indian urban migration to U.S. cities in the 1950s and 1960s.
4. What are the main cultural and structural features of Indian urbanism in the United States since the 1950s?

Describe the role of Indian women in the urban Indian community.
5. Give an example of an Indian urban enclave and describe its main characteristics.
6. Describe the scope of American Indian activism in the United States following the 1969 occupation of Alcatraz.
7. What are the four main theoretical schools in contemporary urban Indian research according to LaGrande? In your opinion, based on the evidence in this chapter, which one best explains Indian urbanism?

SUGGESTED READINGS

EDMUNDS, R. DAVID. 2010. "Native Peoples of Mexico." Pages 42–45 in *Native American Voices: A Reader*, edited by Susan Lobo, Steve Talbot, and Traci L. Morris. Upper Saddle River, NJ: Prentice Hall.

FORBES, JACK D. 2010. "The Urban Tradition Among Native Americans." Pages 404–415 in *Native American Voices: A Reader*, edited by Susan Lobo, Steve Talbot, and Traci L. Morris. Upper Saddle River, NJ: Prentice Hall.

JOHNSON, TROY, JOANE NAGEL, and DUANE CHAMPAGNE. 1997. *American Indian Activism: Alcatraz to the Longest Walk*. Urbana: University of Illinois Press.

LAGRANDE, JAMES B. 2002. *Indian Metropolis: Native Americans in Chicago, 1945–75*. Urbana: University of Illinois Press.

LOBO, SUSAN, and KURT PETERS, eds. 2001. *American Indians and the Urban Experience*. Walnut Creek, CA: AltaMira Press.

JACKSON, DEBORAH DAVIS. 2002. *Our Elders Lived It: American Indian Identity in the City*. DeKalb, IL: University of Northern Illinois Press.

KEOUSE, SUSAN APPLEGATE, and HEATHER A. HOWARD, eds. 2009. *Keeping the Campfires Going: Native Women's Activities in Urban Communities*. Lincoln: University of Nebraska Press.

LEON-PORTILLA, MIGUEL. 1962. *The Broken Spears: The Aztec Account of the Conquest of Mexico*, edited and with an introduction by Miguel Leon-Portilla. Boston: Beacon Press.

LOBO, SUSAN. 2002. *Urban Voices: The Bay Area American Indian Community*. Tucson: University of Arizona Press.

TAYAC, GABRIELLE, with photographs by John Harrington. 2002. *Meet Naiche, A Native Boy from the Chesapeake Bay Area*. Tulsa/San Francisco: Smithsonian Institution, National Museum of the American Indian, in association with Council Oak Books.

REFERENCES

ABLON, JOAN. 1972. "Relocated Indians in the San Francisco Bay Area: Social Interaction and Indian Identity." In *Native Americans Today: Sociological Perspectives*, edited by Howard M. Bahr, Bruce A. Chadwick, and Robert C. Day, 412–428. San Francisco: Harper & Row. Original source: 1964. *Human Organization* 23 Winter: 296–304.

BAHR, HOWARD M. 1972. "An End to Invisibility." In *Native Americans Today: Sociological Perspectives,* edited by Bahr, Chadwick, and Day, 404–12. New York: Harper & Row.

BAHR, HOWARD M., BRUCE A. CHADWICK, and ROBERT C. DAY, eds. 1972. *Native Americans Today: Sociological Perspectives* New York: Harper & Row.

BOYER, LANADA. 1997. "Reflections of Alcatraz." In *American Indian Activism: Alcatraz to the Longest Walk,* edited by Troy Johnson, Joane Nagel, and Duane Champagne, 88–103. Urbana: University of Illinois Press.

BURT, LARRY W. 1996. "Termination and Restoration." In *Native America in the Twentieth Century: An Encyclopedia,* edited by Mary B. Davis, 221–23. New York: Garland.

CAHN, EDGAR S., editor. 1969. *Our Brother's Keeper.* New York: New Community Press.

CARDINAL, HAROLD. 1969. *The Unjust Society.* Edmonton, Canada: M.G. Hurtig

CASTILLO, EDWARD D. 1997. "A reminiscence of the Alcatraz Occupation." In *American Indian Activism: Alcatraz to the Longest Walk,* edited by Troy Johnson, Joane Nagel, and Duane Champagne, 119–28. Urbana: University of Illinois Press.

DELORIA, VINE, JR. 1969. *Custer Died for Your Sins.* London: Macmillan.

———. 1995. *Red Earth, White Lies: Native Americans and the Myth of Scientific Fact.* New York: Scribner.

DICKASON, OLIVE PATRICIA, with DAVID T. MCNAB. 2009. *Canada's First Nations: A History of Founding Peoples from Earliest Times.* Toronto, Canada: Oxford University Press.

EDMUNDS, R. DAVID. 2010. "Native Peoples of Mexico." In *Native American Voices: A Reader,* edited by Susan Lobo, Steve Talbot, and Traci L. Morris, 42–45. Upper Saddle River, NJ: Pearson/Prentice Hall.

EITZEN, D. STANLEY, and MAXINE BACA ZINN. 2007. *In Conflict and Order: Understanding Society.* Upper Saddle River, NJ: Pearson Education.

EWEN, ALEXANDER. 2001. "Crisis of Identity." In *Native American Voices: A Reader,* edited by Susan Lobo and Steve Talbot, 113–22. Upper Saddle River, NJ: Prentice Hall.

FAUNTLEROY, GUSSIE. 2012. "Railroad Days for the Pueblo of Laguna." Smithsonian Institution, *National Museum of the America Indian,* Spring: 44–46, 48–49.

FARB, PETER. 1968. *Man's Rise to Civilization as Shown by the Indians of North America From Primeval Times to the Coming of the Industrial State.* New York: E. P. Dutton.

FORBES, JACK D. 2001. "The Urban Tradition Among Native Americans." In *American Indians and the Urban Experience,* edited by Susan Lobo and Kurt Peters, 5–25. Walnut Creek, CA: AltaMira Press.

GARVEY, JOHN, and TROY JOHNSON. 1997. "The Government and the Indians: The American Indian Occupation of Alcatraz Island, 1969–1971." In *American Indian Activism: Alcatraz to the Longest Walk,* edited by Troy Johnson, Joane Nagel, and Duane Champagne, 153–85. Urbana: University of Illinois Press.

GUGLIOTTA, GUY. 2007. "The Maya: Glory and Ruin." *National Geographic* 212 (2): 74–85.

Indian Country Today. 2010. *Opinion:* "21st Century Indian Policy" *Indian Country Today* 3: 4.

Indians of All Tribes. 1970. Feb. "Planning Grant Proposal to Develop and All-Indian University and Cultural Complex On Indian Land, Alcatraz." Published 1973 in *Great Documents in American Indian History,* edited by Wayne Moquin and Charles Lincoln Van Doren. New York: Praeger.

JACKSON, DEBORAH DAVIS. 2002. *Our Elders Lived It: American Indian Identity in the City.* DeKalb, IL: University of Northern Illinois Press.

JOHANSEN, BRUCE E. 2005. Review of *1491: New Revelations of the Americas Before Columbus* by Charles C. Mann. *American Indian Culture and Research Journal* 29 (4): 121–24.

JOHNSON, TROY, DUANE CHAMPAGNE, and JOANE NAGEL. 1997. "American Indian Activism and Transformation: Lessons From Alcatraz." In *American Indian Activism: Alcatraz to the Longest Walk,* edited by Troy Johnson, Joane Nagel, and Duane Champagne, 9–44. Urbana: University of Illinois Press.

JANOVICEK, NANCY. 2009. "Assisting Our Own: Urban Migration, Self-Governance, and Native Women's Organizing in Thunder Bay, Ontario, 1972–1989." In *Keeping the Campfires Going,* edited by Susan Applegate Krouse, and Heather A. Howard, 56–75. Lincoln: University of Nebraska Press.

JORGENSEN, JOSEPH G. 1978. "A Century of Political and Economic Effects On American Indian Society, 1880–1980." *Journal of Ethnic Studies* 6 (3): 1–82.

KATZ, FRIEDRICH. 2000. *The Ancient American Civilizations.* London: Phoenix Press.

KEARNS, RICK. 2007. "Studying pre-Columbian Math and Science." *Indian Country Today* 27 (4): B4.

KROUSE, SUSAN APPLEGATE, and HEATHER A. HOWARD, eds. 2009. *Keeping the Campfires Going: Native Women's Activities in Urban Communities.* Lincoln: University of Nebraska Press.

LADUKE, WINONA. 2005. *Recovering the Sacred: The Power of Naming and Claiming.* Cambridge, MA: South End Press.

LAGRANDE, JAMES B. 2002. *Indian Metropolis: Native Americans in Chicago, 1945–75.* Urbana: University of Illinois Press.

LA VINE, STUART, and NANCY O. LURIE, eds. 1968. *American Indians Today.* Penguin Books.

LOBO, SUSAN. 2001. "Is Urban a Person or a Place? Characteristics of Urban Indian Country." In *American Indians and the Urban Experience,* edited by Susan Lobo and Kurt Peters, 73–84. Walnut Creek, CA: AltaMira Press.

LOBO, SUSAN, COORDINATING ed. 2002. *Urban Voices: The Bay Area American Indian Community.* Tucson: University of Arizona Press.

———. 2009. "Urban Clan Mothers: Key Households in Cities." In *Keeping the Campfires Going: Native Women's Activism in Urban Communities,* edited by Susan Applegate Krouse and Heather A. Howard, 1–21. Lincoln: University of Nebraska Press.

————, and KURT PETERS, eds. 2001. *American Indians and the Urban Experience*. Walnut Creek, CA: AltaMira Press.

————, STEVE TALBOT, and TRACI L. MORRIS, eds. 2010. *Native American Voices: A Reader*. 3rd ed. Upper Saddle River, NJ: Prentice Hall.

LUTZ, LARA. 2008. "Piscataway Park's Role Evolved from Saving a View to Sharing a Point of View." *Chesapeake Bay Journal*, December 1. http://www.bayjournal.comarticle.cfm?article=3476

MACLEOD, WILLIAM CHRISTIE. 1928. *The American Indian Frontier*. New York: Alfred A. Knopf.

MANN, CHARLES C. 2005. *1491: New Revelations of the Americas Before Columbus*. New York: Alfred A. Knopf.

MCDOWELL, BART. 1980. "The Aztecs." *National Geographic* 158 (6): 704–52.

MEANS, RUSSELL, with MARVIN J. WOLF. 1995. *Where White Men Fear to Tread: The Autobiography of Russell Means*. New York: St. Martins Griffin.

National Film Board of Canada. 1969. *You Are on Indian Land*. Directed by Mort Ransen. Produced by George C. Stoney. (Film) 37 minutes. Canada.

NORRIS, TINA, PAULA L. VINES, and ELIZABETH M. HOEFFEL. 2012. *The American Indian and Alaska Native Population: 2010–2010 Census Briefs*. U.S. Census Bureau, Department of Commerce.

PAUKETAT, TIMOTHY R. 2009. *Cahokia: Ancient America's Great City on the Mississippi*. New York: Viking-Penguin. Also, Internet book blurb from Chapter One.

PETERS, KURT M. 2001. "Continuing Identity: Laguna Pueblo Railroaders in Richmond, California." *American Indians and the Urban Experience*, edited by Susan Lobo and Kurt M. Peters, 117–26. Walnut Creek, CA: AltaMira Press.

PEVAR, STEPHEN L. 2004. *The Rights of Indians and Tribes*. New York: New York University Press.

Piscataway Indian Nation. 1999. *The Flickering Flame: The Life and Legacy of Chief Turkey Tayac*. Producers & directors: Janet Cavallo, Jason Corwin (Seneca). (Video) 55 min. United States.

PRICE, JOHN A. 1972. "The Migration and Adaptation of American Indians to Los Angeles." In *Native Americans Today: Sociological Perspectives*, edited by Howard M. Bahr, Bruce A. Chadwick, and Robert C. Day, 428–39. New York: Harper & Row.

SANCHEZ, METECÚHZOMA. 1998. "Xihuitl Tonalamatl Matlactliuanome Tochtli Mexícayotl." (manuscript).

SHERIDAN, THOMAS E., and NANCY J. PAREZO, eds. 1996. *Paths of Life: American Indians of the Southwest and Northern Mexico*. Tucson: University of Arizona Press.

SPICER, EDWARD H. 1962. *Cycles of Conquest*. Tucson: University of Arizona Press.

————. 1980. *The Yaquis: A Cultural History*. Tucson: University of Arizona Press.

STRAUS, TERRY, and DEBRA VALENTINO. 2001. "Retribalilzation in Urban Indian Communities." In *American Indians and the Urban Tradition*, edited by Susan Lobo and Kurt Peters, 85–94. Walnut Creek, CA: AltaMira Press.

TALBOT, STEVE. 1978. "Free Alcatraz: the Culture of Native American Liberation." *Journal of Ethnic Studies* 8 (3): 83–96.

————. 2001. "Pluralistic Religious Beliefs." In *The Native North American Almanac*, edited by Duane Champagne, 718–33. 2nd ed. Farmington Hills, MI: Gale Group.

————. 2010. "First Nations: Indigenous Peoples of Canada." In *Native American Voices: A Reader*, edited by Susan Lobo, Steve Talbot, and Traci L. Morris, 36–41. Upper Saddle River, NJ: Pearson/Prentice Hall.

TAYAC, GABRIELLE, with photographs by John Harrington. 2002. *Meet Naiche: A Native Boy From the Chesapeake Bay Area*. Tulsa/San Francisco: Smithsonian Institution, National Museum of the American Indian, in association with Council Oak Books.

THOMAS, ROBERT K. 1968. "Pan-Indianism." In *The American Indian Today*, edited by Stuart Levine and Nancy O. Lurie, 128–140. Baltimore: Penguin Books.

TOENSING, GALE COUREY. 2011. "Next Step: Implementation." This Week From *Indian Country Today*, January 19, 34–35.

TRUJILLO, OCTAVIANA V. 2001. "Yaqui Cultural and Linguistic Evolution Through a History of Urbanization." In *American Indians and the Urban Experience*, edited by Susan Lobo and Kurt Peters, 49–68. Walnut Creek, CA: AltaMira Press.

WALDMAN, CARL. 2000. *Atlas of the North American Indian*. Rev. ed. New York: Checkmark Books.

WAX, MURRAY L. 1971. *Indian Americans: Unity and Diversity*. Englewood Cliffs, NJ: Prentice-Hall.

WEAVER, HILARY N. 2010. "Indigenous Identity: What Is It, and Who Really Has It?" In *Native American Voices: A Reader*, edited by Susan Lobo, Steve Talbot, and Traci L. Morris. 28–35. Upper Saddle River, NJ: Prentice Hall.

WEIBEL-ORLANDO, JOAN. 2008. "Urban Communities." In *Handbook of North American Indians: vol.2, Indians in Contemporary Society*, edited by Garrick Bailey and William Sturtevant, 308–16. Washington, DC: Smithsonian Institution Press.

WELLS, ROBERT N., JR. 1996. "Ironworkers." In *Native America in the Twentieth Century: An Encyclopedia*, edited by Mary B. Davis, 278. New York: Garland.

WILLOUGHBY, WILLIAM F. 1983. "The President's Rent Check Is Not in the Mail." *Washington Times Magazine*, April 20.

WITT, SHIRLEY HILL. 1968. "Nationalistic Trends Among American Indians." In *The American Indian Today*, edited by Stuart Levine and Nancy O. Lurie, 93–127. Baltimore: Penguin Books.

WOLF, ERIC R. 1982. *Europe and the People Without History*. With a new Preface. Berkeley: University of California Press.

WRIGHT, RONALD. 1992. *Stolen Continents: The "New World" Through Indian Eyes*. New York: Houghton Mifflin.

CREDITS

Photo Credits

FM. **iii:** Photo courtesy of Carolyn Forbes. **xxiv:** Photo courtesy of Susan Lobo.

Chapter 1. **1:** Gerald Dawavendewa/Fourth World Design. **11:** Library of Congress Prints and Photographs Division [LC-DIG-ppmsca-09855].

Chapter 2. **17:** Gerald Dawavendewa/Fourth World Design. **18:** Jean-Claude Deutsch/Paris Match via Getty Images. **31:** John Kahiones Fadden. **44:** Steve Talbot.

Chapter 3. **48:** Gerald Dawavendewa/Fourth World Design. **66:** Library of Congress Prints and Photographs Division. **75:** INTERFOTO/Alamy **79:** AP Photo/Craig A. Young.

Chapter 4. **83:** Gerald Dawavendewa/Fourth World Design. **119:** Cliff Schiappa/AP Images.

Chapter 5. **126:** Gerald Dawavendewa/Fourth World Design. **142:** AP images.

Chapter 6. **166:** Gerald Dawavendewa/Fourth World Design. **180:** Lebrecht Music and Arts Photo Library/Alamy. **195:** Peter Brooker/Rex Features/Alamy.

Chapter 7. **201:** Gerald Dawavendewa/Fourth World Design. **219:** U.S Army Corps of Engineers, Wayne Buchanan/AP Images. **224:** Suzanne Hanover/AP Images.

Chapter 8. **234:** Gerald Dawavendewa/Fourth World Design. **238:** Robyn Waters. **250:** Bettmann/CORBIS. **264:** Ed Greevy.

Chapter 9. **275:** Gerald Dawavendewa/Fourth World Design. **289:** AP Images. **305:** Victor Biro/Alamy.

Chapter 10. **309:** Gerald Dawavendewa/Fourth World Design. **343:** AP Photo/Al Grillo. **346:** AP Photo/Michael Dinneen.

Chapter 11. **353:** Gerald Dawavendewa/Fourth World Design. **376:** Joel Rennich UPI Photo Service/Newscom.

Text Credits

Chapter 1. **8:** *Indian Givers: How the Indians of the Americas Transformed the World.* Columbine, N.Y.: Fawcett. **9:** *Ecocide of Native America: Environment destruction of Indian lands and peoples* by Grinde, Donald; Johansen, Bruce. Reproduced with permission of Clear Light Publishers in the format Republish in a book via Copyright Clearance Center. **9, 10:** Zucker, Jeff, Kay Hummel and Bob Hogfoss. 1983 *Oregon Indians: Culture, History and Current Affairs.* The Oregon Historical Society: Western Imprints. **12:** Talbot (2002) "Academic Indian-ismo: Social Scientific Research in American Indian Studies" Reprinted from the *American Indian Culture and Research Journal*, volume 26, number 4 by permission of the American Indian Studies Center, UCLA. © 2013 Regents of the University of California. **12:** Native American Studies. Lincoln: Neb: University of Nebraska Press. **13:** Gaudry, Adam J. P. 2011 "Insurgent Research," *Wicazo Sa Review*, Vol. 26, No. 1 (Spring): 113–136. **13:** Lobo, Susan, Steve Talbot, and Traci L. Morris 2010 *Native American Voices: A Reader.* Upper Saddle River, N.J.: Pearson Education/Prentice Hall.

Chapter 2. **18:** John Mohawk, "International Principles of Indigenous Rights," *Daybreak*, Vol. 3, No. 1 (Winter): 14–17. **19:** John Mohawk, *A Basic Call to Consciousness.* (Process), 1977. **19:** Mann, Barbara A. and Jerry L. Fields. "A Sign in the Sky: Dating the League of the Haudeno-saunee," *American Indian Culture and Research Journal*, Vol. 21, No. 3: 105–163. **22:** Akweks, Aren, *Migration of the Iroquois*. Illustrations by Kahonhes. 2nd edition. Mohawk Nation at Akwesasne: White Roots of Peace. **22:** John Mohawk, "Origins of Iroquois Political Thought," *Northeast Indian Quarterly*, Summer: 16–20. **23:** Starna, William A., Jack Campisi, and Laurence M. Hauptman, "Iroquois Confederacy," *Native America in the Twentieth Century: An Encyclopedia*: 278–279. Edited by Mary B. Davis. New York: Garland Publishing, Inc. **23:** Murphy, Gerald (preparer), *The Constitution of the Iroquois Nations: The Geat Binding Law*, Gayanashagowa. The Cleveland

Free Net—aa300. Process. **24:** Tooker, Elizabeth, "The League of the Iroquois: Its History, Politics, and Ritual," Vol. 15, *Northwest: Handbook of North American Indians:* 418–441. Bruce G. Trigger, Volume Editor. Washington: Smithsonian Institution. **25:** Smith, Dwight L. "Mutual Dependency and Mutual Trust," The American *Indian Experience: A Profile:* 49–65. Edited by Philip Weeks. Arlington Heights, IL.: Forum Press. **25:** Oswalt, Wendell H., and Sharlotte Neely, *This Land Was Theirs: A Study of Native Americans.* Sixth Edition. Mountain View, CA: Mayfield Publishing Co. **26:** Wallace, Anthony F. C, *The Death and Rebirth of the Seneca.* New York: Random House. **26, 27:** Wright, Ronald, *Stolen Continents: The "New World" Through Indian Eyes.* (Houghton Mifflin Co., 1992). **26:** Fenton, William N. "Northern Iroquoian Cultural Patterns," Volume 15, *Northeast: Handbook of North American Indians:* 296–321. Bruce G. Trigger, Volume Editor. Washington: Smithsonian Institution, 1978. Reprinted with permission. **27:** Graymont, Barbara, *The Iroquois* (New York: Chelsea House, 1988). **29:** Johansen, Bruce E., and Donald A. Grinde, Jr., Commentary: "The Debate Regarding Native American Precedents for Democracy: A Recent Historiography," Reprinted from the *American Indian Culture and Research Journal,* Vol. 14, No. 1 by permission of the American Indian Studies Center, UCLA. © 2013 Regents of California. **32:** "Conclusions: Anthros, Indians, and Planetary Reality," *Indians and Anthropologists: Vine Deloria, Jr., and the Critique of Anthropology:* 209–221. Edited by Thomas Biolsi and Larry J. Zimmerman. Tucson, AZ: The University of Arizona Press. **33:** Lyons, Oren, John Mohawk, et al, *Exiled in the Land of the Free: Democracy, Indian Nations, and the U.S. Constitution.* (Santa Fe, NM: Clear Light Publishers, 1992). **37:** Morgan, Lewis Henry. *League of the Iroquois.* (New York, NY: Corinth Books, 1969). **38:** Donald A. Grinde, Jr. "Iroquois Political Theory and the Roots of American Democracy," *Exiled in the Land of the Free:* 227–280. Edited by Oren Lyons, John Mohawk, et al. (Santa Fee, NM: Clear Light Publishers, 1992). **40:** Donald A. Grinde, Jr. "Native Peoples of the Northeast," *Native America: Portrait of the Peoples:* 55–74. Edited by Duane Champagne. (Detroit: MI.: Visible Ink Press, 1994). **21:** 1988 Congressional Resolution passed by the U.S. House and Senate. **36:** Data created from Morgan n.d. [1877] *Ancient Society.* Chicago: Charles H. Kerr & Co.: 132–133. **30, 31:** Johansen, Bruce E. 1982 *Forgotten Founders: Benjamin Franklin, the Iroquois and the Rationale for the American Revolution.* Ipswich, MA: Gambit Inc. **42:** Troy Johnson, Joane Nagel, and Duane Champagne, *American Indian Activism: Alcatraz to the Longest Walk,* Urbana & Chicago, University of Illinois Press, 1997: 11.

Chapter 3. 49: H. H. Bancroft, *The History of California* (Kessinger Publishing, 2009). **50:** Adapted from Albert Hurtado, *Gold, Mines, and Rancherias: A Socioeconmic History of Indians and Whites in Northern California, 1821–1860.* (University Microfilms International, 1981). **50:** "Historical Demography," Vol. 8, California, *Handbook of North American Indians:* 91–98. Robert F. Heizer, volume editor. Washington: Smithsonian Institution. **51:** Genocide Convention of the United Nations. **51:** Irvin Molotsky, "Senate Votes to Carry Out Treaty Banning Genocide," *New York Times,* October 15, 1988. **51:** David Maybury–Lewis, *Indigenous Peoples, Ethnic Groups, and the State* (Allyn and Bacon, 1977). **55:** Forbes, Jack *Native Americans of California and Nevada.* Happy Camp, CA: Naturegraph Publishers, 1982. **53:** Gabarino and Sasso, *Native American Heritage.,* 3/e (Waveland Press, 1994). **54, 55:** Norton, *Genocide in Northwestern California: When Our Worlds Cried.* San Francisco, CA: The Indian Historian Press. **52:** Margolin, Malcolm, "Traditional California Indian Conservation," *News From Native California,* Vol. 11, No. 2 (Winter): 2-Motorland (etc.). **55:** Kehoe, Alice B. *North American Indians: A Comprehensive Account.* Second Edition. Englewood Cliffs, NJ: Prentice Hall, 1992. **60:** Costo, Rupert, *The Missions of California: A Legacy of Genocide.* San Francisco, CA: The Indian Historian Press. Sherburne Cook, *Expeditions to the Interior of California: Central Valley, 1820–1840.* University of California Anthropological Records 10:5: 151–214. **61:** Hurtado, Albert, *Indian Survival on the California Frontier.* (Yale University Press, 1988). **65:** Alta California, 1852 Letter to the editor, May 21. **65:** *Eureka Humboldt Times.* **65, 66:** Heizer, Robert F. (editor) *The Destruction of California Indians.* University of Nebraska Press, 1974. **66:** Eyewitness account (quoted in Norton, *Genocide in Northwestern California: When Our Worlds Cried,* 1979). **67:** 1982 "Review of *Ishi the Last Yahi: A Documentary History,*" by Robert F. Heizer and Theodora Kroeber, Eds. Berkeley: University of California Press, 1979. *American Indian Culture and Research Journal,* Vol. 6, No. 4: 105–107. **71:** *Marysville Appeal,* December 6, 1861. **74:** Lapena, Frank "Dancing and Singing the Sacredness of the Earth," *News From Native California,* Vol. II, No. 2 (Winter): 17–18. **102:** Eargle, Jr., Dolan H., 1992 *California Indian Country: The Land and the People.* San Francisco, CA: Trees Company Press. From Hurtado, Albert L., *Indian Survival On the California Frontier.* **63:** Copyright © 1988 Yale University Press. Reprinted with permission. **64:** Project Underground 1998 *Gold, Greed, and Genocide.* Research and text by Pratap Chatterjee. Berkeley, CA: Project Underground. **137:** Hurtado, Albert, L. *Indian Survival on the California Frontier.* **69:** Copyright © 1988 Yale University Press. Reprinted with permission. **71:** Heizer, Robert F. and Alan

F. Almqist 1971 *The Other Californians: Prejudice and Discrimination under Spain, Mexico, and the United States to 1920.* Berkeley, CA: University of California Press.

Chapter 4. **84:** Originally translated by James Mooney in 1894. **84:** *Black Elk prayer*, 1931. **87:** Raymond J. DeMallie, *Handbook of North American Indians* (Washington: Smithsonian Institution, 2001). Reprinted with permission. **88:** Raymond J. DeMallie, *Handbook of North American Indians* (Washington: Smithsonian Institution, 2001). **91:** Lame Deer, James (Fire), and Richard Erdoes, *Lame Deer, Seeker of Visions.* New York: Simon and Schuster, 1972. **92:** Brown, Joseph Epes, *The Sacred Pipe: Black Elk's Account of the Seven Rites of the Oglala Sioux.* New York: Penguin Books, 1971. **93:** Means, Russell, with Marvin J. Wolf, *Where White Men Fear to Tread: The Autobiography of Russell Means.* New York: St. Martins Griffin, 1995. **93, 94:** Richard Erdoes, *Crying For a Dream.* Santa Fe: Bear Company, Rochester, VT 05767. Copyright © 1990 by Richard Erdoes, Inner Traditions.com. **98:** Akwesasne Notes, *Voices From Wounded Knee*, Process, 1973. **100:** Utley, Robert M., *The Last Days of the Sioux Nation.* Yale University Press, 1963. **106:** Neihardt, John G., 1979, *Black Elk Speaks: Being the Life Story of a Holy Man of the Oglala Sioux.* Lincoln: University of Nebraska Press. **111:** Christafferson, Dennis M.200, "Sioux, 1930–2000," *Plains: Handbook of North American Indians*, Vol. 13, Pt 2 of 2: 821–839. Edited by Raymond J. DeMallie. Washington: Smithsonian Institution. **113:** From *Voices from Wounded Knee*, 1973. *Akwesasne Notes*, Mohawk Nation at Rooseveltown, NY, 1974, p. 13. **115:** Steve Talbot, *Roots of Oppression: The American Indian Question.* New York: International Publishers, 1981. **117:** Talbot, Steve 1979 "The Meaning of Wounded Knee, 1973: Indian Self-Government and the Role of Anthropology," *The Politics of Anthropology*: 227–258. Edited by Gerrit Huizer and Bruce Mannheim. The Hague: Mouton Publishers. **120:** Peltier, Leonard, *Prison Writings: My Life Is My Sun Dance.* Edited by Harvey Arden. New York: St. Martin's Press, 1999. **87:** Swagerty, William R. 2001 "History of the United States Plains Until 1850," *Plains: Handbook of North American Indians*, Vol. 13, Part 1: 256–279. Edited by Raymond J. DeMallie. Washington: Smithsonian Institution. **91:** 1991 *Lakota Belief and Ritual.* Edited by Raymond J. DeMallie and Elaine A Jahner. Lincoln: University of Nebraska Press. **112:** San Francisco Sunday Examiner and Chronicle 1973 "For Indians It's a Life With Built-in Failure," *San Francisco Sunday Examiner and Chronicle.* March 18. **123:** Schusky, Ernest 1969 *The Right to Be Indian.* Hearings before the Special Subcommittee on Indian Education, Committee on Labor and Public Welfare, 90th Congress. Washington, DC: U.S. Government Printing Office.

Chapter 5. **128:** Bodley, John H. 1990 *Victims of Progress.* Third edition. (Moutain View, CA: Mayfield). **128:** From *Paths of Life: American Indians of the Southwest* by Thomas Sheridan. © 1996 The Arizona Board of Regents. Reprinted by permission of the University of Arizona Press. **129, 130:** Dutton, Bertha P., *American Indians of the Southwest.* (Albuquerque, NM: University of New Mexico Press., 1983). **130:** Francis Paul Prucha, *Atlas of American Indian Affairs*, University of Nebraska Press, 1990, p. 122. **133:** Griffin-Pierce, Trudy, "The Continuous Renewal of Sacred Relations: Navajo Religion," *Native Religions and Cultures of North America: Anthropology of the Sacred*: 121–141. Edited by Lawrence E. Sullivan. (New York: Continuum International.). **136:** Mander, Jerry, "Kit Carson In a Three-Piece Suit," *Bioregions, The Co-Evolution Quarterly* (Winter, 1981): 52–63, © 1981. Reprinted by permission of Jerry Mander, founder and Distinguished Fellow of the International Forum on Globalization. **137:** Rossel, Robert A., Jr., "Navajo History, 1850–1923," Vol. 10, Southwest, *Handbook of North American Indians* (Smithsonian Institution, 1983). Sheridan, Thomas E., and Nancy J. Parezo (editors). **144:** Brew, J. O., "Hopi Prehistory and History to 1850," Vol. 9, Southwest, *Handbook of North American Indians*: 514–523. Alfonso Ortiz, volume editor. (Washington: Smithsonian Institution.). **145:** Hieb, Louis, Hopi, *Native America in the Twentieth Century: An Encyclopedia*: 240–243. Edited by Mary B. Davis. (New York: Garland Publishing, Inc.). **148:** Dockstader, Frederick J. "Hopi History, 1850–1940," Vol. 9, Southwest, *Handbook of North American Indians*: 524–532. Alfonso Ortiz, volume editor. (Washington: Smithsonian Institution.). **152:** Clemmer, Richard O., 1979 "Hopi History, 1940–1974," Vol. 9, Southwest, *Handbook of North American Indians*: 533–538. Alfonso Ortiz, volume editor. (Washington: Smithsonian Institution.). **129:** Howard, Michael C., and Patrick C. McKim 1983 *Contemporary Cultural Anthropology.* (Boston: Little, Brown and Company.). **136:** Griffin-Pierce, in Lawrence Sullivan, ed., *Native Religions and Cultures of North America*, 2000. **134:** Copyright Trudy Griffin-Pierce. **139:** Enders. Gordon W. 1971 "An Historical Analysis of the Hopi-Navajo Land Disputes, 1882–1970" (May). A Thesis Presented to the Department of History, Brigham Young University. In Partial Fulfillment of the Requirements for the Degree Master of Arts. (Duplicate manuscript. Arizona State Historical Museum, Tucson, Arizona)." **141:** Butler, Kristie Lee 1996 "Navajo," *Native America in the Twentieth Century: An Encyclopedia*: 379–384. Edited by Mary B. Davis. (New York: Garland Publishing, Inc.). **142:** Churchill, Ward, and Winona LaDuke 1992 "Native North America: The Political Economy of Radioactive Colonialism," *The State of Native America: Genocide, Colonialism, and Resistance*; 241–160. Edited by

Annette M. James. (Boston, Mass: South End Press.). **144:** Feher-Elston, Catherine 1996 "Navajo-Hopi Land Controversy," *Native America in the Twentieth Century: An Encyclopedia:* 386–589. Edited by Mary B. Davis. (New York: Garland Publishing.). **145:** Hieb, Louis A. 1996 "Hopi," *Native America in the Twentieth Century: An Encyclopedia:* 240–243. Edited by Mary B. Davis. (New York: Garland Publishing, Inc.). **157:** Sills, Marc 1986 Relocation Reconsidered: Competing Explanations of the Navajo-Hopi Land Settlement Act of 1974," *The Journal of Ethnic Studies,* 14: 3 (Fall): 52–83.

Chapter 6. **155:** Paul Prucha, *Atlas of American Indian Affairs,* 1990. **167:** Wilma P. Mankiller, 1993 *Mankiller: A Chief and Her People.* (New York: St. Martin's Press.). **167:** Duane King, "Cherokee in the West: History Since 1776," *Southeast: Handbook of North American Indians,* Vol. 14, Smithsonian Institution, 2004. **168:** Lobo, Susan, and Steve Talbot, *Native American Voices: A Reader.* 2nd edition. Upper Saddle River, NJ: Prentice Hall. **170:** Glen Fleischmann, *The Cherokee Removal,* 1938, NY: Franklin Watts (1971). **169:** Perfue, Theda, and Michael D. Green, editors, *The Cherokee Removal: A Brief History with Documents.* New York: St. Martin's Press, 1995. **178:** Duane Champagne, 1992, *Social Order and Political Change: Constitutional Governments Among the Cherokee, the Choctaw, the Chickasaw, and the Creek.* (Stanford, California: Stanford University Press.). **184, 185:** Mooney, James, *Historical Sketch of the Cherokee.* Chicago, IL: Aldine Publishing Company, 1975. **187:** Duane Champagne, ed., *The Native North American Almanac* (Gale, 1995), p. 208. **186:** Debo, Angie, *And Still the Water Run: The Betrayal of the Five Civilized Tribes.,* Princeton University Press, 1968. **174:** Mankiller, Wilma, and Michael Wallis 1993 *Mankiller: A Chief and Her People.* (New York: St. Martin's Press.).

Chapter 7. **202:** Smohalla (1815–895). **202:** Forder, Simon, "Years of Conflict Upon the Columbia River," term paper submitted to Steve Talbots Native American Studies 70 class in perception, December 13, University of California, Davis. **206:** Zucker, Hummel, and Hogfoss, Western Imprints, The Oregon Historical Society, Oregon Indians, 1983: 43]. **207:** Silverstein, Michael, 1990. "Chinookans of the Lower Columbia," Vol. 7—Northwest Coast, *Handbook of North American Indians:* 533–546. Wayne Suttles, vol. Editor. Washington: Smithsonian Institution. **208:** Marino, Cesare, "History of Western Washington Since 1846," Vol. 7 Northwest Coast, *Handbook of North American Indians:* 169–179. Smithsonian, 1990. **211:** Cohen, Fay, *Treaties On Trial: The Continuing Controversy Over Northwest Indian Fishing Rights.* Seattle: University of Washington Press. **212:** Excerpts from *Empty Nets: Indians, Dams, and the*

Columbia River, second edition, by Robert Ulrich, copyright © 2007. Reprinted with permission of Oregon State University Press. **212:** Pevar, Stephen L., *The Rights of Indians and Tribes.* New York: Bantam Books. **217:** Cohen, Fay, *Treaties On Trial: The Continuing Controversy Over Northwest Indian Fishing Rights.* Seattle: University of Washington Press. **205:** Mankiller, Wilma, and Michael Wallis 1993 *Mankiller: A Chief and Her People.* (New York: St. Martin's Press.). **210:** Grinde, Donald A., and Bruce E. Johansen 1995 *Ecocide of Native America: Environmental Destruction of Indian Land & Peoples.* Santa Fe, NM: Clear Light. (See chapter 6, "Fishing Rights: The Usual and Accustomed Places."). **227:** Lee, Bill 2004 "Consider Indian Viewpoint During Bicentennial," *Yakima Herald-Republic,* June 17, 2004. Copyright © 2004. Reprinted with permission of the *Yakima Herald-Republic.* **230:** Spilde, Katherine A. 2000 "Educating Local Non-Indian Communities About Indian Nation Governmental Gaming: Messages and Methods," *Indian Gaming: Who Wins?:* 83–95. Edited by Angela Mulliis and David Kamper. Los Angeles, CA: UCLA American Indian Studies Center. **226:** "Plant Dumped Tons of Mercury," *The Register-Guard,* June 21, 2004.

Chapter 8. **235:** Trask, Haunani-Kay, *From a Native Daughter: Colonialism & Sovereignty in Hawai'i.* Monroe, ME; Common Courage Press. **238:** Courtesy of Robyn Waters. **237:** Dougherty, Michael, *To Steal a Kingdom: Probing Hawaiian History.* Waimanalo, HI: Island Style Press, 1992. **240:** Dudley, Michael Kioni, and Keana Kealoha Agard 1990 *A Hawaiian Nation II: A Call for Hawaiian Sovereignty.* With an introduction by John Dominis Holt. Honolulu, HI: a Kne O Ka Malo Press. **240:** Teachers guide to the classroom video, *Spirit of the Land,* Hawaii, Continuing Traditions, n.d., page 5. **246:** Laenui, Pk, *American Indian Culture and Research Journal,* Vol. 17, No. 1 (1993): 79–101.). **248:** Takaki, Ronald, *Strangers from a Different Shore: A History of Asian Americans.* New York, NY: Penguin Books, 1989. **260, 261:** Sonoda, Healani, "Settler Racism: Criminalization of the Native Hawaiian," *The Hawaiian News,* Vol. 9, No. 6 (December), 2000. **269:** From Lilikala Kame'eleihiwa, *Native Land and Foreign Desires,* 1992, p. 46. **270:** From Kame'eleihiwa, *Native Land and Foreign Desires,* 1992, p. 155. **271:** From Kame'eleihiwa, *Native Land and Foreign Desires,* 1992, p. 187. **238:** McMurray, David 2002, September "The role of Music and Dance in the Conquest and Rebirth of Native Hawaiian Culture," *Comparative Cultures: Music of Resistance & Cultures of Oppression.* Third Edition (Paper). Written for Anthropology 380, Comparative Cultures, a class offered at Oregon State University. **253:** Zinn, Howard 1999 *A People's History of the United States: 1492—Present.* New York: Perennial Classics/

HarperCollins. **253:** Loewen, James W. 1995 *Lies My Teacher Told Me*. New York, N.Y.: Touchstone. 2001 "Ke One Kani O Mōkua: The Resounding Sands of Mōkua," *Maluhia Me Ka Pono/Peace With Justice*, Vol. 5, No. 1 (March): 1, 12. Published by the American Friends Service Committee—Hawai'i Area Program.

Chapter 9. **280:** McMillan, Alan D. "Canadian Native Distribution, Habitat, and Demograhy." *The Native North American Almanac:*, Gale Research, 1994. **282:** Long, J. Anthony, and Katherine Beaty Chiste. "Aboriginal Peoples in Canada," in *The Native North American Almanac:* 334–354. Edited by Duane Champagne. Detroit: Gale Research, 1994. **283:** Carl Waldman, *Atlas of the North American Indian*, Checkmark Books, 2000), p. 232. **285:** Martin, Ian. "Restoring Linguistic Rights for Aboriginals." *Toronto Star*, June 3, 2005. Copyright © 2005. Reprinted by permission of the author. **286:** Caldwell, Brad. "Fisheries Law: Papers and Articles: *R. v. Marshall*: Supreme court of Canada Recognizes Aboriginal Treaty Rights to Trade Fish." *Westcoast Fisherman* in admiraltylaw. com [http://www.admiraltylaw.com/fisheries/Papers/treatyrights.htm]. **289:** Royal Commission on Aboriginal Peoples. Parliament of Canada, Parliamentary Information and Research Service, 1999. PRB 99-24E. **295:** Winona LaDuke, *All Our Relations*. **299:** "Sustainable Development in the Hudson Bay: James Bay Bio-region" Canadian Arctic Resources Committee. Environmental Committee of Sanikiluaq, Rawson Academy of Aquatic Science. No date. [http://www.carc.org/pubs/v19no3/2.htm]. **300:** Cone, Marla. *Silent Snow: The Slow Poisoning of the Arctic*. New York: Grove Press, 2005. **305:** Nikiforuk, Andrew. "Echoes of the Atomic Age: Cancer Kills Fourteen Aboriginal Uranium Workers." *Calgary Herald*, March 14, 1998, A-1, A-4. [http://www.ccnr.org/deline_deaths.html]. **306:** Gilday, Cindy Kenny. "A Village of Widows." *Arctic Circle*. No date. [http://arcticcircle.uconn.edu/SEEJ/Mining/gilday.html]. **287, 288:** Toughill, Kelly. "Mi'kmaq Own Entire Province, Nova Scotia Court Told." *Toronto Star*, December 9, 2000, n.p. **288:** Lowey, Mark. "Alberta Natives Sue Over Residential Schools." *Calgary Herald*, January 3, 1999, p. A-1. **291:** Hipwell, Bill. "Apology Should Have Been a Thank You." *The Financial Post* [Ottawa, Ontario] February 3, 1998, p. 18. **296:** Sierra Club. Hudson Bay/James Bay Watershed "Eco-region." [http://www.sierraclub.org/ecoregions/hudsonbay.asp]. **298:** Matteo, Enzo di. "Damned Deal: Cree Leaders Call Hydro Pact Signed in Secret a Monstrous Sellout." *Now Magazine* [Toronto], February, 2002. [http://www.nowtoronto.com/issues/2002-02-14/news_story.php]. **302:** Schneider, Howard. "Facing World's Pollution in the North." *Washington Post*, September 21, 1996, A-15. [http://

www.washingtonpost.com/wp-srv/inatl/longterm/canada/stories/pollution092196.htm. Rozell, Ned. "Alaska Science Forum: Dioxins: Another Uninvited Visitor to the North." Geophysical Institute, University of Alaska Fairbanks. November 9, 2000. [http://www.gi.alaska.edu/ScienceForum/ASF15/1515.html]. **304:** Guerette, Deb. "No Clear-cut Answer: Timber Rights Allocation on Lubicon Land a Worrisome Development." *Grande Prairie Daily Herald-Tribune*, March 5, 2001. **290, 291:** Craig, Rachel 1996 "Iñupiat," *Native America in the Twentieth Century: An Encyclopedia*: 274–276. Edited by Mary B. Davis (New York: Garland Publishing.). Stewart, Jane. "Notes for an Address by the Honourable Jane Stewart Minister of Indian Affairs and Northern Development on the Occasion of the Unveiling of Gathering Strength—Canada's Aboriginal Action Plan." Ottawa, Ontario. January 7 1998. Aboriginal Affairs and Northern Development Canada. [https://www.aadnc-aandc.gc.ca/eng/1100100015725/1100100015726]. **298:** "Innu Begin Occupation To Halt Construction At Voisey's Bay." *Drillbits and Tailings*, August 21, 1997, n.p. **299:** "Sustainable Development in the Hudson Bay: James Bay Bio-region" Canadian Arctic Resources Committee. Environmental Committee of Sanikiluaq, Rawson Academy of Aquatic Science. No date. [http://www.carc.org/pubs/v19no3/2.htm]. **300:** Excerpts from *Silent Snow*, copyright © 2005 by Marla Cone. Used by permission of Grove/Atlantic, Inc. Any third party use of this material, outside of this publication, is prohibited.

Chapter 10. **312:** ANCSA P.L. 92–203, Sec. 4b. **312:** Vincent Kvasnikoff, English Bay, Alaska. **313:** Jorgensen, Joseph G. 2003, "Review of *Alaska, an American Colony*," by Stephen Haycox (Seattle: University of Washington Press, 2002), *American Indian Culture and Research Journal* (Vol. 27: No. 3: 95–99). **313:** Kawagley, A. Oscar, *A Yupiaq Worldview: A Pathway to Ecology and Spirit*. Prospect Heights, IL.: Waveland Press. **314:** *Cultural Survival Quarterly*, Fall 1998, p. 32. **316:** Active, John, 1996, "Yupik," *Native America in the Twentieth Century: An Encyclopedia*: 717–718. Edited by Mary B. Davis. New York: Garland Publishing. **321:** Jenness, Diamond, *Eskimo Administration: I. Alaska*. Arctic Institute of North America, Technical Paper No. 10 (July), Montreal, Canada, 1962. **323:** Chance, Norman, *The Eskimo of North Alaska*. New York: Holt, Rhinehart and Winston. **323:** Fainberg, L.A., "The Contemporary Situation of the Eskimos (1940–1960) and the Problem of Their Future in the Works of American and Canadian Ethnographers," *Soviet Anthropology and Archaeology*, Vol. IV, No. 1: 27–45. **328:** Hanrahan, John, and Peter Gruenstein, *The Lost Frontier: The Marketing of Alaska*. (New York: W.W. Norton). **330:** ISEGR (Institute of Social, Economic, and Governmental Research), *Native Land*

Claims. ISEGR, Vol. 4, No. 6 (November). University of Alaska. **332:** From Strong, *The Social Impact of the Trans Alaska Pipeline,* etc., June 1977, Process. **339:** Colt, Stephen, "Alaska Native Regional Corporations," *Native America in the Twentieth Century: An Encyclopedia:* 13–17. Edited by Mary B. Davis. (New York: Garland Publishing.). **341:** NARF (Native American Rights Fund), "Amendments Provide Stop-Gap Protection or Native Land and Corporations," *NARF Legal Review* (Spring): 1–5. **343, 344:** NARF (Native American Rights Fund), 1999, "Alaska Native Subsistence," *Justice Newsletter:* 1–6. **342:** Maas, David C., 2003, "Review of *Take My Land, Take My Life: The Story of Congress's Historic Settlement of Alaska Native Land Claims, 1960–1971,*" by Donald Craig Mitchell (Fairbanks: University of Alaska Press, 2001), in *American Indian Culture and Research Journal,* Vol. 27, No. 1: 167–172. **343:** Flanders, Nicholas E. "The Alaska Native Corporation as Conglomerate: The Problem of Profitability," *Human Organization,* Vol. 48, No. 4: 199–312. **351:** Langdon, Steve J. "Contradictions in Alaska Native Economy and Society," *Contemporary Alaskan Native Economies:* 29–46. Edited by Steve J. Langdon. Lanham, MD: University Press of America. **313:** Swetzof, Paul R. 1996 "Unangan," *Native America in the Twentieth Century: An Encylopedia:* 665–666. Edited by Mary B. Davis (New York: Garland Publishing, Inc.). **317:** Olson, Wallace 1996 "Tlingit," *Native America in the Twentieth Century: An Encyclopedia:* 645–637. Edited by Mary B. Davis (New York: Galand Publishing, Inc.). **330:** Maas, David C. 2003, "Review of *Take My Land, Take My Life: The Story of Congress's Historic Settlement of Alaska Native Land Claims, 1960–1971,*" by Donald Craig Mitchell (Fairbanks: University of Alaska Press, 2001), in *American Indian Culture and Research Journal,* Vol. 27, No. 1: 167–172. **36:** John, Adam, speech reprinted in *Memo,* a quarterly publication of Women Strike for Peace, Fall 1971: **331** Process. **344:** Worl, Rosita 1998 "Competition, Confrontation, and Compromise: The Politics of Fish and Game Allocations," *Cultural Survival Quarterly,* Vol. 22 (Fall 1998), Issue 3: 77–78. Copyright © 1998 Reprinted with permission.

Chapter 11. **356:** Russell Means. **356:** Susan Lobo. **356:** Mann, Charles C. 2005 *1491: New Revelations of the Americas Before Columbus.* New York: Alfred A. Knopf. **356:** Johansen, Bruce E. "Review of *1491: New Revelations of the Americas Before Columbus*" by Charles C. Mann. *American Indian Culture and Research Journal,* 29: 4: 121–124. **357:** Forbes, Jack D. 2001, "The Urban Tradition Among Native Americans," *American Indians and the Urban Experience:* 5–25. Edited by Susan Lobo and Kurt Peters. Walnut Creek, CA.: Altamira Press. **384:** Weaver, Hilary N., 2010, "Indigenous Identity: What Is It, and Who Really Has It?" *Native American Voices: A Reader:*

28–35. Edited by Susan Lobo, Steve Talbot, and Traci L. Morris. (Upper Saddle River, N.J.: Prentice Hall.). **387:** Lobo, Susan "Urban Clan Mothers: Key Households in Cities," *Keeping the Campfires Going: Native Womens Activism in Urban Communities:* 1–21. Edited by Susan Applegate Krouse and Heather A. Howard. Lincoln and London: University of Nebraska Press. **359:** MacLeod, William Christie *The American Indian Frontier.* New York: Alfred A. Knopf. **362:** Wright, Ronald, *Stolen Continents: The New World Through Indian Eyes.* New York: Houghton Mifflin Company. **364:** From Ronald Wright, *Stolen Continents.* New York: Houghton Mifflin, 1992: frontpiece. **369:** Pevar, Stephen L. 2004 *The Rights of Indians and Tribes.* New York University Press. **372:** Lobo, Susan. Coordinating Editor, *Urban Voices: The Bay Area American Indian Community.* Tucson: The University of Arizona Press. **372:** LaGrande, James B. 2002 *Indian Metropolis: Native Americans in Chicago, 1945–75.* Urbana and Chicago: University of Illinois Press. **373:** Jackson, Deborah Davis 2002 *Our Elders Lived It: American Indian Identity in the City.* DeKalb, IL: University of Northern Illinois Press. **375:** Spicer, Edward H., *The Yaquis: A Cultural History.* Tucson, AZ: University of Arizona Press. **375:** E. H. Spicer, *The Yaquis: A Cultural History,* Tucson: The University of Arizona Press, 1980: 159. **376:** Peters, Kurt M. 2001 "Continuing Identity: Laguna Pueblo Railroaders in Richmond, California," *American Indians and the Urban Experience:* 117–126. Edited by Susan Lobo and Kurt M. Peters. Walnut Creek, CA: AltaMira Press. **380:** Poems copyrighted 1972 by J. Hill and Lydia Yellowbird. *Alcatraz Is Not An Island, by Indians of All Tribes.* Edited by Peter blue cloud. (Berkeley: Wingbow Press, 1972) page 16. **380:** Indians of All Tribes Inc. Feb. "Plannlng Grant Proposal to Develop and All-Indian University and Cultural Complex On Indian Land, Alcatraz." (Process). **359:** Weibel-Orlando, Joan 2008 "Urban Communities," *Handbook of North American Indians: Indians in Contemporary Society,* vol. 2: 308–316. Edited by Garrick Bailey and William Sturtevant. Washington, D.C.: Smithsonian Institution. **360:** Wolf, Eric R. 1982 *Europe and the People Without History.* With a new Preface. Berkeley and Los Angeles: University of California Press. **363:** Farb, Peter 1968 *Man's Rise to Civilization as Shown by the Indians of North America From Primeval Times to the Coming of the Industrial State.* New York: E. P. Dutton & Co. **371:** Lobo, Susan 2001 "Is Urban a Person or a Place? Characteristics of Urban Indian Country," *American Indians and the Urban Experience:* 73–84. Edited by Susan Lobo and Kurt Peters. Walnut Creek, CA.: AltaMira Press. **371:** Straus, Terry, and Debra Valentino 2001 "Retribalilzation in Urban Indian Communities," *American Indians and the Urban Tradition:* 85–94. Edited by Susan Lobo and Kurt Peters. Walnut Creek, CA.: Altamira

Press. **373:** Janovicek, Nanvy 2009 "Assisting Our Own: Urban Migration, Self-Governance, and Native Women's Organizing in Thunder Bay, Ontario, 1972–1989," *Keeping the Campfires Going:* 56–75. Edited by Susan Applegate Krouse, and Heather A. Howard. Lincoln and London: University of Nebraska Press. **374:** Trujillo, Octaviana V. 2001 "Yaqui Cultural and Linguistic Evolution Through a History of Urbanization," *American Indians and the Urban Experience:* 49–68. Edited by Susan Lobo and Kurt Peters. Walnut Creek, CA: AltaMira Press. **376:** Sheridan, Thomas E., and Nancy J. Parezo, editors 1996 *Paths of Life: American Indians of the Southwest and Northern Mexico.* Tucson, AZ.: University of Arizona Press. **378:** Tayac, Gabrielle, with photographs by John Harrington 2002 *Meet Naiche: A Native Boy From the Chesapeake Bay Area.* Tulsa/San Francisco: Smithsonian, National Museum of the American Indian, in association with Council Oak Books. **379, 380:** Talbot, Steve 1978 "Free Alcatraz: the Culture of Native American Liberation," *The Journal of Ethnic Studies*, Vol. 8, No. 3 (Fall): 83–96. **383:** Garvey, John, and Troy Johnson 1997 "The Government and the Indians: The American Indian Occupation of Alcatraz Island, 1969–1971," *American Indian Activism: Alcatraz to the Longest Walk:* 153–185. Edited by Troy Johnson, Joane Nagel, and Duane Champagne. Urbana and Chicago: University of Illinois Press. **384:** *Indian Country Today* 2010 Opinion: "21st Century Indian Policy," March 3: 4.

INDEX